T0215692

Maciej Malawski · Krzysztof Rzadca (Eds.)

Euro-Par 2020: Parallel Processing

26th International Conference
on Parallel and Distributed Computing
Warsaw, Poland, August 24–28, 2020
Proceedings

 Springer

Editors
Maciej Malawski 🆔
AGH University of Science and Technology
Krakow, Poland

Krzysztof Rzadca 🆔
University of Warsaw
Warsaw, Poland

ISSN 0302-9743   ISSN 1611-3349 (electronic)
Lecture Notes in Computer Science
ISBN 978-3-030-57674-5   ISBN 978-3-030-57675-2 (eBook)
https://doi.org/10.1007/978-3-030-57675-2

LNCS Sublibrary: SL1 – Theoretical Computer Science and General Issues

This Springer imprint is published by the registered company Springer Nature Switzerland AG
The registered company address is: Gewerbestrasse 11, 6330 Cham, Switzerland

Lecture Notes in Computer Science   12247

Advanced Research in Computing and Software Science
Subline of Lecture Notes in Computer Science

Preface

This volume contains the papers presented at the 26th International European Conference on Parallel and Distributed Computing (Euro-Par 2020), planned for August 24–28, 2020, in Warsaw, Poland. Due to the coronavirus pandemic, Euro-Par was organized this year as a virtual conference.

For over 25 years, Euro-Par has consistently brought together researchers in parallel and distributed computing. Founded by pioneers as a merger of the three thematically related European conference series PARLE and CONPAR-VAPP, Euro-Par started with the aim to create the main annual scientific event on parallel processing in Europe and to be the primary choice of professionals for the presentation of the latest results.

Since its inception, Euro-Par has been covering all aspects of parallel and distributed computing, ranging from theory to practice, from the smallest to the largest parallel and distributed systems and infrastructures, from fundamental computational problems to full-fledged applications, from architecture, compiler, language, and interface design and implementation to tools, support infrastructures, and application performance. Euro-Par's unique organization into topics provides an excellent forum for focused technical discussion as well as interaction with a large, broad, and diverse audience who are researchers in academic institutions, public and private laboratories, or commercial stakeholders. Euro-Par's topics were always oriented towards novel research issues and the current state of the art. Most topics became constant entries, while new themes emerged and were included in the conference. Euro-Par has a tradition of selecting new organizers and chairs for every edition, leading to fresh ideas and variations while staying true to the tradition. Organizers and chairs of previous editions support their successors. In this sense, Euro-Par also promotes networking across national borders, leading to the unique spirit of Euro-Par.

Previous conferences took place in Stockholm, Lyon, Passau, Southampton, Toulouse, Munich, Manchester, Paderborn, Klagenfurt, Pisa, Lisbon, Dresden, Rennes, Las Palmas, Delft, Ischia, Bordeaux, Rhodes, Aachen, Porto, Vienna, Grenoble, Santiago de Compostela, Turin, and Göttingen.

Thus, Euro-Par in Poland followed the well-established format of its predecessors. The 26th edition of Euro-Par was organized with the support of the University of Warsaw, Faculty of Mathematics, Informatics and Mechanics (MIM UW) and AGH University of Science and Technology, Faculty of Computer Science, Electronics and Telecommunications, Department of Computer Science in Krakow. MIM UW is a renowned place for research in mathematics and theoretical computer science, while AGH hosts the largest supercomputer in Poland in its Academic Computer Centre Cyfronet.

The topics of Euro-Par 2020 were organized into 11 tracks, namely:

- Support Tools and Environments
- Performance and Power Modeling, Prediction and Evaluation
- Scheduling and Load Balancing

- High Performance Architectures and Compilers
- Data Management, Analytics and Machine Learning
- Cluster, Cloud and Edge Computing
- Theory and Algorithms for Parallel and Distributed Processing
- Parallel and Distributed Programming, Interfaces, and Languages
- Multicore and Manycore Parallelism
- Parallel Numerical Methods and Applications
- Accelerator Computing

Overall, 158 papers were submitted from 33 countries. The number of submitted papers, the wide topic coverage, and the aim of obtaining high-quality reviews resulted in a difficult selection process involving a large number of experts. As the joint effort of the members of the Program Committee and of the 169 external reviewers, a total of 256 reviewers from 29 countries wrote 632 reviews: 17 papers received three reviews, 129 received four reviews, and 14 received 5 or more, that is, on average, 4 reviews per paper. There were more than 218,000 words in all the reviews. The accepted papers were chosen after offline discussions in our reviewing system followed by a lively discussion during the paper selection meeting which took place via a video conference on April 21, 2020. As a result, 39 papers were selected to be presented at the conference and published in these proceedings, resulting in a 24.6% acceptance rate.

The Technical Program Committee distinguished one best paper: "Maximizing I/O Bandwidth for Reverse Time Migration on Heterogeneous Large-Scale Systems" by Tariq Alturkestani, Hatem Ltaief, and David Keyes.

To increase reproducibility of the research, Euro-Par encourages authors to submit artifacts, such as source code, datasets, and reproducibility instructions. Along with notification of acceptance, authors of accepted papers were encouraged to submit artifacts. Artifacts for 13 papers were submitted (a third of the accepted papers). These artifacts were then evaluated by the Artifact Evaluation Committee (AEC). The committee managed to successfully reproduce results of all the 13 papers. These papers are marked in the proceedings by a special stamp, and the artifacts are available online in the Figshare repository.

In addition to the technical program, we had the pleasure of hosting three keynotes held by:

- Ewa Deelman, University of Southern California, USA
- Geoffrey Fox, Indiana University, USA
- Piotr Sankowski, University of Warsaw, Poland

Euro-Par 2020, though a virtual event this year, encouraged interaction and online discussions, in order to make it a successful and friendly meeting.

The conference program started with two days of workshops on specialized topics. Dora Blanco Heras and Bartosz Baliś ensured coordination and organization of this pre-conference event as workshop co-chairs. After the conference, a selection of the papers presented at the workshops will be published in a separate proceedings volume.

We would like to thank the authors, chairs, Program Committee members, and reviewers for contributing to the success of Euro-Par 2020. Similarly, we would like to extend our appreciation to the Euro-Par Steering Committee for its support. Our mentor, Luc Bougé, devoted countless hours to this edition, making sure we were on time and on track with all the (many) key elements of the conference. Our virtual task force – Emmanuel Jeannot, Paul Kelly, Francisco Rivera, and Denis Trystram – provided invaluable feedback on translating various aspects of a physical conference to the cyberspace. Last but not least, we would like to express our gratitude to the teams and volunteers at UW and AGH, whose relentless enthusiasm and effort made this event possible.

August 2020   Maciej Malawski
                                                               Krzysztof Rzadca

The Euro-Par Steering Committee

Full Members

Luc Bougé (SC Chair)	ENS Rennes, France
Fernando Silva (SC Vice-chair)	University of Porto, Portugal
Dora Blanco Heras (Workshops Chair)	CiTIUS, University of Santiago de Compostela, Spain
Marco Aldinucci	University of Turin, Italy
Emmanuel Jeannot	Inria Bordeaux, France
Christos Kaklamanis	Computer Technology Institute Patras, Greece
Paul Kelly	Imperial College London, UK
Thomas Ludwig	University of Hamburg, Germany
Tomàs Margalef	University Autonoma of Barcelona, Spain
Wolfgang Nagel	Dresden University of Technology, Germany
Francisco Fernández Rivera	CiTIUS, University of Santiago de Compostela, Spain
Krzysztof Rzadca	University of Warsaw, Poland
Rizos Sakellariou	The University of Manchester, UK
Henk Sips (Finance Chair)	Delft University of Technology, The Netherlands
Leonel Sousa	University of Lisbon, Portugal
Domenico Talia	University of Calabria, Italy
Massimo Torquati (Artifacts Chair)	University of Pisa, Italy
Phil Trinder	University of Glasgow, UK
Denis Trystram	Grenoble Institute of Technology, France
Felix Wolf	Technical University of Darmstadt, Germany
Ramin Yahyapour	GWDG, Germany

Honorary Members

Christian Lengauer	University of Passau, Germany
Ron Perrott	Oxford e-Research Centre, UK
Karl Dieter Reinartz	University of Erlangen-Nürnberg, Germany

Organization

General Chairs

Krzysztof Rzadca   University of Warsaw, Poland
Maciej Malawski   AGH University of Science and Technology, Poland

Workshop Chairs

Bartosz Baliś   AGH University of Science and Technology, Poland
Dora Blanco Heras   University of Santiago de Compostela, Spain

PhD Symposium Chairs

Marek Michalewicz   ICM, University of Warsaw, Poland
Ramin Yahyapour   GWDG, Germany

Artifacts Chairs

Maciej Szpindler   ICM, University of Warsaw, Poland
Massimo Torquati   University of Pisa, Italy

Submissions Chair

Paweł Topa   AGH University of Science and Technology, Poland

Publicity

Chair

Michał Zasadziński

Members

Katarzyna Biesialska, Spain
Michael Kuhn, Germany
Adrien Lebre, Fance

Logistics

GlobalCongress

Visual Identity

Alicja Świerczek

Webpage

Paweł Żuk (Webmaster)

Scientific Organization

Topic 1: Support Tools and Environments

Global Chair

Michael Gerndt   Technical University of Munich, Germany

Local Chair

Mariusz Sterzel   AGH University of Science and Technology, Poland

Members

Shajulin Benedict   IIIT Kottayam, India
Thomas Fahringer   University of Innsbruck, Austria
Erwin Laure   Max Planck Computing and Data Facility, Germany
Phil Roth   Oak Ridge National Lab, USA
Robert Mijakovic   Leibniz Supercomputing Centre, Germany

Topic 2: Performance and Power Modeling, Prediction and Evaluation

Global Chair

Arnaud Legrand   Laboratoire d'Informatique de Grenoble, France

Local Chair

Ariel Oleksiak   Poznań Supercomputing and Networking Center,
                                  Poland

Members

Jorge G. Barbosa   University of Porto, Portugal
Vicente Blanco   La Laguna University, Spain
Georges Da Costa   IRIT/Toulouse III, France
Brice Videau   Argonne National Laboratory, USA
Markus Geimer   Juelich Supercomputing Centre, Germany

Topic 3: Scheduling and Load Balancing

Global Chair

Sascha Hunold   Vienna University of Technology, Austria

Local Chair

Joanna Berlinska   Adam Mickiewicz University in Poznań, Poland

Members

Malin Rau   Grenoble INP, France
Fanny Pascual   LIP6, Université Pierre et Marie Curie – Paris 6, France
Lauritz Thamsen   TU Berlin, Germany
Louis-Claude Canon   Université de Franche-Comté, France
Florina M. Ciorba   University of Basel, Switzerland

Topic 4: High Performance Architectures and Compilers

Global Chair

Leonel Sousa   Universidade de Lisboa, Portugal

Local Chair

Paweł Czarnul   Gdańsk University of Technology, Poland

Members

Denis Makoshenko   Intel, Poland
Pedro Diniz   INESC-ID, Portugal
Tomás Burrull   University Autonoma of Barcelona, Spain
Cristina Silvano   Politecnico di Milano, Italy

Topic 5: Data Management, Analytics and Machine Learning

Global Chair

Morris Riedel   Juelich Supercomputing Centre, Germany

Local Chair

Jacek Sroka   University of Warsaw, Poland

Members

Peter Steinbach   Helmholtz-Zentrum Dresden-Rossendorf, Germany
Mihai Capotă   Intel, USA
Steffen Zeuch   DFKI GmbH, Germany
Volodymyr Kindratenko   University of Illinois at Urbana-Champaign, USA
Jorge Amaya   Katholieke Universiteit Leuven, Belgium
Helmut Neukirchen   University of Iceland, Iceland
Markus Goetz   Karlsruhe Institute of Technology, Germany
Gabriele Cavallaro   Jülich Supercomputing Centre, Germany

Topic 6: Cluster, Cloud and Edge Computing

Global Chair

María S. Pérez   Universidad Politecnica de Madrid, Spain

Local Chair

Lukasz Dutka   AGH University of Science and Technology, Poland

Members

Bogdan Nicolae   Argonne National Laboratory, USA
Rafael Mayo   CIEMAT, Spain
Michael Kuhn   University of Hamburg, Germany
Manolis Marazakis   Instutute of Computer Science, FORTH, Greece
Paolo Trunfio   DEIS University of Calabria, Italy
Helene Coullon   Inria Nantes, France
Alberto Sanchez   Universidad Rey Juan Carlos, Spain
Eduardo Huedo   Universidad Complutense de Madrid, Spain
Gabriel Antoniu   Inria Rennes, France
Toni Cortes   Universitat Politècnica de Catalunya, Spain
Pierre Matri   Argonne National Laboratory, USA
Jesus Carretero   University Carlos III of Madrid, Spain

Topic 7: Theory and Algorithms for Parallel and Distributed Processing

Global Chair

Ben Moseley   Carnegie Mellon University, USA

Local Chair

Marek Klonowski   Wroclaw University of Technology, Poland

Members

Peter Kling   University of Hamburg, Germany
Gianluca De Marco   University of Salerno, Italy
Olivier Beaumont   Inria Bordeaux, France
Michele Scquizzato   University of Padova, Italy
Prashant Pandey   Berkeley Lab, USA
Shikha Singh   Williams College, USA
Rezaul Chowdhury   State University of New York at Stony Brook, USA

Topic 8: Parallel and Distributed Programming, Interfaces, and Languages

Global Chair

Phil Trinder   University of Glasgow, UK

Local Chair

Wojciech Turek   AGH University of Science and Technology, Poland

Members

Robert Stewart   Heriot Watt University, UK
Melinda Tóth   Eotvos Lorand University, Budapest, Hungary
Patrick Maier   University of Stirling, UK
Christian Perez   Inria Lyon, France
Cosmin Oancea   University of Copenhagen, Denmark
Dimitrios Nikolopoulos Virginia Tech, USA
Kevin Hammond   University of St Andrews, UK

Topic 9: Multicore and Manycore Parallelism

Global Chair

Arturo Gonzalez   University of Valladolid, Spain

Local Chair

Witold Rudnicki   University of Bialystok, Poland

Members

Bertil Schmidt   University of Mainz, Germany
Agata Janowska   University of Warsaw, Poland
Sven Karlsson   Technical University of Denmark, Denmark
Christoph Kessler   Linköping University, Sweden
Julian Shun   Massachusetts Institute of Technology, USA
Jose Daniel Garcia   University Carlos III of Madrid, Spain

Topic 10: Parallel Numerical Methods and Applications

Global Chair

Hatem Ltaief   King Abdullah University of Science and Technology,
                                      Saudi Arabia

Local Chair

Erin Carson   Charles University, Czech Republic

Members

Hartwig Anzt	Karlsruhe Institute of Technology, Germany
Jakub Šístek	Institute of Mathematics, Czech Academy of Sciences, Czech Republic
Penporn Koanantakool	Google, USA
Sarah Knepper	Intel, USA
Maciej Wozniak	AGH University of Science and Technology, Poland
Edgar Solomonik	University of Illinois at Urbana-Champaign, USA
Piotr Luszczek	University of Tennessee, USA
Ronald Kriemann	Max Planck Institute for Mathematics in the Sciences, Germany
Jed Brown	University of Colorado Boulder, USA
Hussam Al Daas	Max Planck Institute for Dynamics of Complex Technical Systems, Germany
Rio Yokota	Tokyo Institute of Technology, Japan

Topic 11: Accelerator Computing

Global Chair

Alba Cristina Melo	University of Brasilia, Brazil

Local Chair

Lukasz Szustak	Czestochowa University of Technology, Poland

Members

Peter Thoman	University of Innsbruck, Austria
Lin Gan	Tsinghua University, China
Diana Goehringer	TU Dresden, Germany
Antonio J. Peña	Barcelona Supercomputing Center (BSC), Spain

Artifact Evaluation Committee

Maciej Szpindler	ICM, University of Warsaw, Poland
Massimo Torquati	University of Pisa, Italy
Michal Hermanowicz	ICM, University of Warsaw, Poland

Additional Reviewers

Giovanni Agosta	Eric Angel
Ahmad Salim Al-Sibahi	Blair Archibald
Angelines Alberto	Miguel Areias
Muhammad Ali	Rafael Asenjo
Francisco Almeida	Martin Aumüller
Pedram Amini Rad	Mateusz Banaszek

Soeren Becker
Ilja Behnke
Jossekin Beilharz
Naama Ben-David
Julien Bernard
Sebastian Berndt
Julien Bigot
Luc Bougé
Jani Boutellier
Benjamin Brock
Joachim Bruneau-Queyreix
Anna Bukowska
Kyle Burns
Aleksander Byrski
Jerzy Błaszczyński
Marek Błażewicz
Alberto Cabrera
Emile Cadorel
Alexandra Carpen-Amarie
Aurélien Cavelan
Eduardo Cesar
Maverick Chardet
Bogdan Chlebus
Stephen Chou
Jacek Cichon
Johanne Cohen
Alexandru Costan
Paolo D'Arco
Francisco De Sande
David Del Río Astorga
Gabriele Di Stefano
Matthias Diener
Manuel F. Dolz
Maciej Drozdowski
Fanny Dufossé
Kira Duwe
David E. Singh
Pavlos Efraimidis
Ahmed Eleliemy
Marquita Ellis
Ahmet Erdem
Toni Espinosa
Lionel Eyraud-Dubois
Violeta Felea
Javier Fernandez
Pierre Fouilhoux

Daniel Franco
José M. Franco-Valiente
Anna Fuchs
Zhimin Gao
Javier Garcia Blas
Simon Garcia
De Gonzalo
Leszek Gasieniec
Thierry Gautier
Stanislaw Gawiejnowicz
Zoltán Gera
Kain Kordian Gontarska
Paweł Gora
Francisco Gortazar
Philipp Gschwandtner
David Guyon
Levente Hajder
Pierre-Cyrille Heam
Maurice Herlihy
Jan Hidders
Alexander Hirsch
Guillaume Huard
Sascha Hunold
Dejice Jacob
Emmanuel Jeannot
Tomasz Jurdzinski
Lester Kalms
Jannis Klinkenberg
Matthias Korch
Jonas Henrique Korndorfer
András Kovács
Evangelos Kranakis
Bartosz Kryza
Michał Kulczewski
Thomas Lambert
Tian Lan
Alexandra Lassota
Roland Leißa
Felix Lorenz
Giorgio Lucarelli
Bertram Ludäscher
Mikel Lujan
Dániel Lukács
Marcin Łoś
Tobias Maier
Yury Malkov

Georgiana Mania
Loris Marchal
Diogo Marques
Samuel McCauley
Lucas Mello Schnorr
Paolo Missier
Ali Mohammed
Clement Mommessin
Grégory Mounié
Juan Carlos Moure
Jedrzej Musial
André Müller
Maiko Müller
Gonzalo Nicolás
  Barreales
Darin Nikolow
Israt Nisa
Ricardo Nobre
Katzalin Olcoz
John Owens
Dominik Pajak
Gopal Pandurangan
Maciej Pawlik
Elmar Peise
Laurent Philipppe
Mangpo Phothilimthana
Wojciech Piatek
Millian Poquet
Zoltan Porkolab
Bartłomiej Przybylski
Adrian Ramsingh
Anna Reale
Valentin Reis

Daniel Rosendo
Omri Ross
Antonio Juan Rubio-Montero
Philip Salzmann
Helmut A. Sedding
R. Oguz Selvitopi
Jessica Shi
Francesco Silvestri
Bertrand Simon
Victor Sosa
Jannek Squar
Grzegorz Stachowiak
Esteban Stafford
Frederic Suter
Piotr Syga
Samuel Thibault
Leonel Toledo
Massimo Torquati
Yuri Torres de La Sierra
Denis Trystram
Tom Tseng
Grzegorz Waligóra
Michael Willig
Prudence Wong
Yu Xia
Helen Xu
Ke Yi
Shangdi Yu
Artur Zaroda
Steffen Zeuch
Pawel Zielinski
Zachary Zimmerman
Julian Zubek

Euro-Par 2020 Invited Talks

Automating Science Workflows: Challenges and Opportunities

Ewa Deelman

Information Sciences Institute, University of Southern California, USA
deelman@isi.edu

Science workflows help define the processes needed to understand our past, explain our world today, and predict how our planet will evolve tomorrow. They help to logically move from a hypothesis to its testing via appropriate methods, to the generation of findings and their publication. As in other areas of our lives, automation is increasing scientific productivity and is enabling researchers to analyze vast amounts of data (from remote sensors, instruments, etc.) and to conduct large-scale simulations of underlying physical phenomena. These applications comprise thousands of computational tasks and process large, heterogeneous datasets, which are often distributed across the globe. Computational workflows have emerged as a flexible representation to declaratively express the complexity of such applications with data and control dependencies. Automation technologies have enabled the execution of these workflows in an efficient and robust fashion. Up to now automation was based on a variety of algorithms and heuristics that transformed the workflows to optimize their performance and improve their fault tolerance. However, with the recent increased use of AI for automation, new solutions for workflow management systems can be explored. This talk describes some of the unsolved problems in workflow management and considers potential application of AI to address these challenges.

Advancing Science with Deep Learning, HPC, Data Benchmarks and Data Engineering

Geoffrey Fox

Indiana University, USA
gcf@indiana.edu

- We describe how High-Performance Computing (HPC) can be used to enhance Big Data and Machine Learning (ML) systems (HPC for ML) but also how machine learning can be used to enhance system execution (ML for HPC) with promising deep learning surrogates.
- We review the different aspects of data engineering needed to process large scale data and how it is implemented in the Cylon and Twister2 systems to support deep learning and Python notebooks. https://cylondata.github.io/cylon/ and https://twister2.org/.
- We give application examples from COVID-19 daily data, solutions of ordinary differential equations, and earthquakes.
- We show how by working with the industry consortium MLPerf, we may be able to establish a collection of science data benchmarks demonstrating best practices and motivating the next generation cyberinfrastructure.

Breaking the PRAM $O(\log n)$ Complexity Bounds on MPC

Piotr Sankowski

Institute of Informatics, University of Warsaw, Poland
P.Sankowski@mimuw.edu.pl

For over a decade now we have been witnessing the success of *massive parallel computation* (MPC) frameworks, such as MapReduce, Hadoop, Dryad, or Spark. One of the reasons for their success is the fact that these frameworks are able to accurately capture the nature of large-scale computation. In particular, compared to the classic distributed algorithms or PRAM models, these frameworks allow for much more local computation. The fundamental question that arises in this context though is: can we leverage this additional power to obtain even faster parallel algorithms? In particular, graph connectivity seems to require $O(\log n)$ rounds under the 2 Cycle Conjecture. It is thus entirely possible that in this regime, which captures, in particular, the case of sparse graph computations, the best MPC round complexity matches what one can already get in the PRAM model, without the need to take advantage of the extra local computation power.

In this talk, I will summarize our work on refuting that perplexing possibility. In particular, I will introduce the following MPC results that improve upon $O(\log n)$ time algorithms implied by PRAM results:

- an $(2 + \varepsilon)$ – approximation to maximum matching, for any fixed constant $\varepsilon > 0$, in $O\left(\log^2 \log n\right)$ rounds in the case of *slightly sublinear* memory per machine regime [1],
- an $(1 + \varepsilon)$ – approximation to PageRank in $O\left(\log^2 \log n + \log^2 1/\varepsilon\right)$ rounds [2].

Based on joint work with Artur Czumaj, Jakub Lacki, Aleksander Madry, Slobodan Mitrovic, and Krzysztof Onak.

References

1. Czumaj, A., Łącki, J., Madry, A., Mitrović, S., Onak, K., Sankowski, P.: Round compression for parallel matching algorithms. In: Proceedings of the 50th Annual ACM SIGACT Symposium on Theory of Computing, STOC 2018, pp. 471–484. Association for Computing Machinery, New York (2018). https://doi.org/10.1145/3188745.3188764
2. Łącki, J., Mitrović, S., Onak, K., Sankowski, P.: Walking randomly, massively, and efficiently. In: Proceedings of the 52nd Annual ACM SIGACT Symposium on Theory of Computing, STOC 2020, pp. 364–377. Association for Computing Machinery, New York (2020). https://doi.org/10.1145/3357713.3384303

Euro-Par 2020 Topics Overview

Topic 1: Support Tools and Environments

Michael Gerndt and Mariusz Sterzel

Despite an impressive body of research, parallel and distributed programming remains a complex task prone to subtle software issues that can affect both the correctness and the performance of the application. This topic focused on tools and techniques to help tackle that complexity. The topic attracted contributions on tools and environments that address any of the many challenges of parallel and distributed programming related to programmability, portability, correctness, reliability, scalability, efficiency, performance, and energy consumption.

The papers submitted for this track represent the community of tool designers, developers, and users to share their concerns, ideas, solutions, and products for a wide range of parallel platforms. Of particular value were contributions with solid theoretical foundations and with strong experimental validations on production-level parallel and distributed systems that address the expected complexity of exascale.

The track received eight submissions, which were thoroughly reviewed by the members of the track Program Committee. Out of all the submissions and after a careful and detailed discussion among committee members, we finally decided to accept two papers, resulting in a per-topic acceptance ratio of 25%. The paper of Nicolas Morew et al. on "Skipping Non-essential Instructions Makes Data-dependence Profiling Faster" proposes an optimization of dynamic data dependence analysis based on a previous static analysis. Memory references that can be statically evaluated need not be analyzed at runtime thus reducing the analysis overhead. The second paper by Simone Economo et al. on "A toolchain to verify the parallelization of OmpSs-2 applications" discusses a toolchain to detect potential correctness and performance issues in OmpSs applications. This tool chain also combines static and dynamic information to improve the precision and reduce the runtime overhead.

We would like to thank all the authors who submitted papers for their contribution to the success of this track, as well as all the external reviewers for their high-quality reviews and their valuable feedback.

Topic 2: Performance and Power Modeling, Prediction and Evaluation

Arnaud Legrand and Ariel Oleksiak

In recent years, a range of novel methods and tools have been developed for the evaluation, design, and modeling of parallel and distributed systems and applications. At the same time, the term 'performance' has broadened to also include scalability and energy efficiency, and touching reliability and robustness in addition to the classic resource-oriented notions.

The papers submitted to this track represent researchers working on different aspects of performance modeling, evaluation, and prediction, be it for systems or for applications running on the whole range of parallel and distributed systems (multicore and heterogeneous architectures, HPC systems, grid and cloud contexts, etc.). The accepted papers present novel research in all areas of performance modeling, prediction, and evaluation, and to help bring together current theory and practice.

The topic received 17 submissions, which were thoroughly reviewed by the 7 members of the track Program Committee and external reviewers. Out of all the submissions and after a careful and detailed discussion among committee members, we finally decided to accept 5 papers, resulting in a per-topic acceptance ratio of 29%.

We would like to thank the authors for their submissions, the Euro-Par 2020 Organizing Committee for their help throughout all the process, and the Program Committee members and the reviewers for providing timely and detailed reviews as well as for participating in the discussion we carried on after the reviews were received.

Topic 3: Scheduling and Load Balancing

Sascha Hunold and Joanna Berlińska

New computing systems offer the opportunity to reduce the response times and the energy consumption of the applications by exploiting the levels of parallelism. Modern computer architectures are often composed of heterogeneous compute resources and exploiting them efficiently is a complex and challenging task. Scheduling and load balancing techniques are key instruments to achieve higher performance, lower energy consumption, reduced resource usage, and real-time properties of applications.

This topic attracts papers on all aspects related to scheduling and load balancing on parallel and distributed machines, from theoretical foundations for modeling and designing efficient and robust scheduling policies to experimental studies, applications, and practical tools and solutions. It applies to multi-/many-core processors, embedded systems, servers, heterogeneous and accelerated systems, HPC clusters, as well as distributed systems such as clouds and global computing platforms.

A total of 17 submissions were received in this track, each of which received at least 4 reviews. Following a thorough discussion of the reviews among the Seven Program Committee members, four submissions were accepted, giving an acceptance rate of 24%.

The chairs would like to sincerely thank all the authors for their submissions, the Euro-Par 2020 Organizing Committee for all their valuable help, and the reviewers for their excellent work. They all have contributed to making this topic and Euro-Par an excellent forum to discuss scheduling and load balancing challenges.

Topic 4: High Performance Architectures and Compilers

Leonel Sousa and Paweł Czarnul

This topic deals with architecture design, languages, and compilation for parallel high performance systems. The areas of interest range from microprocessors to large-scale parallel machines (including multi/manycore, possibly heterogeneous, architectures); from general-purpose to specialized hardware platforms (e.g., graphic coprocessors, low-power embedded systems); and from architecture to compiler and programming language design.

On the compilation side, topics of interest include programmer productivity issues, concurrent and/or sequential language aspects, vectorization, program analysis, program transformation, automatic discovery and/or management of parallelism at all levels, auto tuning and feedback directed compilation, and the interaction between the compiler and the system at large. On the architecture side, the scope spans system architectures, processor micro-architecture, memory hierarchy, and multi-threading, architectural support for parallelism, and the impact of emerging hardware technologies.

The topic received five submissions, which were thoroughly reviewed by the six members of the track Program Committee and external reviewers. Out of all the submissions and after a careful and detailed discussion among committee members, we finally decided to accept two papers, resulting in a per-topic acceptance ratio of 40%. One of the papers is focused on modeling efficient interconnection networks (considering numbers of servers, routers, and links) applicable to high-end supercomputers and datacenters, while the other optimizes memory movements for heterogeneous computing systems demonstrating benefits for benchmarks implemented with OpenMP offloading constructs.

The chairs express their gratitude to all the authors for their submissions, the Euro-Par 2020 Organizing Committee for all their valuable help, and the reviewers for their excellent work.

Topic 5: Data Management, Analytics and Machine Learning

Morris Riedel and Jacek Sroka

Many areas of science, industry, and commerce are producing extreme-scale data that must be processed – stored, managed, analyzed – in order to extract useful knowledge. This topic seeks papers in all aspects of distributed and parallel data management and data analysis. For example, cloud and grid data-intensive processing, parallel and distributed machine learning, HPC in situ data analytics, parallel storage systems, scalable data processing workflows, and distributed stream processing were all in the scope of this topic.

This year, the topic received 11 submissions, which were thoroughly reviewed by the 10 members of the track Program Committee and external reviewers. Out of all the submissions, and after a careful and detailed discussion among committee members, we finally decided to accept four papers, resulting in a per-topic acceptance ratio of 36%. One paper was nominated for distinction and received the Best Paper Award.

We would like to express our thanks to the authors for their submissions, the Euro-Par 2020 Organizing Committee for their help throughout the process, and the Program Committee members and the reviewers for providing timely and detailed reviews as well as for participating in the discussion we carried on after the reviews were received.

Topic 6: Cluster, Cloud and Edge Computing

María S. Pérez and Lukasz Dutka

While the term Cluster Computing is hardware oriented and determines the organization of large computer systems at one location, the term Cloud Computing usually focuses on the use of these large computer systems. Cluster and Cloud Computing compliment each other; there exist many interdependencies between both fields. In this topic of EuroPar, we particularly address these interdependencies, although also covering issues belonging to only one of these areas.

In both Cluster and Cloud Computing, many relevant research works focus on performance, reliability, and energy efficiency as well as the impact of novel processor architectures. Since Cloud Computing tries to hide hardware and system software details from the users, research issues include various forms of virtualization and their impact on performance, resource management, and business models that address system owner and user interests.

In the last years, and specially due to the increasing number of IoT applications, the combination of local resources together with Cloud Computing, also referred to as "Fog/Edge" Computing, has received growing interest. This concept has led to many research questions, like an appropriate distribution of subtasks to the available systems under the consideration of various constraints.

This year, a total of 22 submissions were submitted to this track, each of which received at least 4 reviews, from the 14 Program Committee members. Following the thorough discussion of the reviews, three submissions were accepted, giving the acceptance rate of 14%. Two of them are related to Edge Computing and the third one is related to virtualization.

The chairs would like to thank the authors for their submissions, the Euro-Par 2020 Organizing Committee for their help throughout all the process, and the Program Committee members and the reviewers for providing timely and detailed reviews as well as and for participating in the discussions.

Topic 7: Theory and Algorithms for Parallel and Distributed Processing

Benjamin Moseley and Marek Klonowski

Distributed and parallel data processing is ubiquitous. Parallel cores are available on smartphones, laptops, servers, and supercomputing nodes. Many devices cooperate in fully distributed and heterogeneous systems to provide even basic services. Despite astonishing progress in recent years, many challenges remain. We urgently need better specific solutions for scalability, load balancing, or efficient communication in increasingly complex systems. Additionally, robust algorithms need to be developed to cope with failures, malicious, or selfish behavior. Such algorithms are needed now in practice, and a theoretical foundation is required to guide the development of improved methods.

This year, a total of 21 submissions were received in this track, each of which received at least four reviews, from the nine Program Committee members. Following the thorough discussion of the reviews, five high-quality, original papers were accepted to this general topic of the theory of parallel and distributed algorithms, with an acceptance rate of 24%.

We would like to thank the authors for their excellent submissions, the Euro-Par 2020 Organizing Committee for their help throughout all the process, and the Program Committee members and the reviewers for providing timely and detailed reviews as well as for participating in the discussions that helped reach the final decision.

Topic 8: Parallel and Distributed Programming, Interfaces, and Languages

Phil Trinder and Wojciech Turek

Parallel and distributed applications require appropriate programming abstractions and models, efficient design tools, and parallelization techniques and practices. This topic attracted papers presenting new results and practical experience in this domain: Efficient and effective parallel languages, interfaces, libraries, and frameworks, as well as solid practical and experimental validation.

The accepted papers emphasize research on high-performance, correct, portable, and scalable parallel programs via appropriate parallel and distributed programming models, interfaces, and language support. Contributions that assess programming abstractions for usability, performance prediction, scalability, self-adaptation, rapid prototypings, or fault-tolerancewere valued. As were abstractions for dynamic or heterogeneous parallel or distributed infrastructures.

This year, the topic received 15 submissions, which were thoroughly reviewed by the 9 members of the track Program Committee and external reviewers. After careful and detailed discussion among committee members, we decided to accept four of the submissions, giving a per-topic acceptance ratio of 27%.

The topic chairs would like to thank all the authors who submitted papers for their contribution to the success of this track, the Euro-Par 2020 Committee for their support, and the external reviewers for their high-quality reviews and valuable feedback.

Topic 9: Multicore and Manycore Parallelism

Arturo Gonzalez-Escribano and Witold Rudnicki

Modern homogeneous and heterogeneous multicore and manycore architectures are now part of the high-end, embedded, and mainstream computing scene and can offer impressive performance for many applications. This architecture trend has been driven by the need to reduce power consumption, increase processor utilization, and deal with the memory-processor speed gap. However, the complexity of these new architectures has created several programming challenges, and achieving performance on these systems is often a difficult task. This topic seeks to explore productive programming of multi- and manycore systems, as well as stand-alone systems with large numbers of cores and various types of accelerators; this can also include hybrid and heterogeneous systems with different types of multicore processors. It focuses on novel research and solutions in the form of programming models, frameworks, and languages; compiler optimizations and techniques; lock-free algorithms and data structures; transactional memory advances; performance and power trade-offs and scalability; libraries and runtime systems; innovative applications and case studies; techniques and tools for discovering, analyzing, understanding, and managing multicore parallelism; and in general, tools and techniques to increase the programmability of multicore, manycore, and heterogeneous systems, in the context of general-purpose, high-performance, and embedded parallel computing.

This year 15 papers covering some of these issues were submitted. Each of them was reviewed by four reviewers. Finally, three regular papers were selected. They discuss topics related to the use of prediction-based policies to optimize resource management in the context of a task-based programming models; the application of parallelism techniques to optimize and improve a graph clustering algorithm with applications in machine learning; and how to combine non-volatile memory with transactional memory when both hardware and software approaches can be chosen.

We would like to express our gratitude to all the authors for submitting their work. We want also thank the all the reviewers for their great job and useful comments. Finally, we would like to thank the Euro-Par Organization and Steering Committees for their continuous help, and for producing a nice working environment to smooth the process.

Topic 10: Parallel Numerical Methods and Applications

Hatem Ltaief and Erin Carson

The need for high-performance computing is driven by the need for large-scale simulation and data analysis in science and engineering, finance, life sciences, etc. This requires the design of highly scalable numerical methods and algorithms that are able to efficiently exploit modern computer architectures. The scalability of these algorithms and methods and their ability to effectively utilize high-performance heterogeneous resources is critical to improving the performance of computational and data science applications.

This conference topic provides a forum for presenting and discussing recent developments in parallel numerical algorithms and their implementation on current parallel architectures, including manycore and hybrid architectures. The submitted papers address algorithmic design, implementation details, performance analysis, as well as integration of parallel numerical methods in large-scale applications.

This year, the topic received 18 submissions, which were thoroughly reviewed by the 13 members of the track Program Committee and external reviewers. Each submission received four reviews. After careful and constructive discussions among committee members, we decided to accept four papers, resulting in a per-topic acceptance ratio of 22%.

We would like to sincerely thank all the authors for their submissions, the Euro-Par 2020 Organizing Committee for all their valuable help, and the reviewers for their excellent work. They all have contributed to making this topic and Euro-Par an excellent forum to discuss parallel numerical methods and applications.

Topic 11: Accelerator Computing

Alba Cristina Melo and Łukasz Szustak

Hardware accelerators of various kinds offer a potential for achieving massive performance in applications that can leverage their high degree of parallelism and customization. Examples include graphics processors (GPUs), manycore co-processors, as well as more customizable devices, such as FPGA-based systems and streaming data-flow architectures.

The research challenge for this topic was to explore new directions for actually realizing this potential. The submitted papers cover the areas related to accelerators: architectures, algorithms, languages, compilers, libraries, runtime systems, coordination of accelerators and CPU, and debugging and profiling tools. We also accepted application-related submissions that contribute new insights into fundamental problems or solution approaches in this domain, including big data, data analytics, machine learning, and computational science/engineering.

The topic received nine submissions, which were thoroughly reviewed by the six members of the track Program Committee and external reviewers. Out of all the submissions and after a careful and detailed discussion among committee members, we finally decided to accept three papers, resulting in a per-topic acceptance ratio of 33%.

The topic chairs would like to thank all the authors who submitted papers for their contribution to the success of this track, the Euro-Par 2020 Committee for their support, as well as all the external reviewers for their high-quality reviews and their valuable feedback.

Contents

Multicore and Manycore Parallelism

Parallel Numerical Methods and Applications

Accelerator Computing

Support Tools and Environments

Skipping Non-essential Instructions Makes Data-Dependence Profiling Faster

Nicolas Morew[1], Mohammad Norouzi[1($\boxtimes$)], Ali Jannesari[2], and Felix Wolf[1]

[1] Technische Universitaet Darmstadt,
Darmstadt, Germany
nicolas.morew@gmail.com,
{norouzi,wolf}@cs.tu-darmstadt.de
[2] Iowa State University, Ames, IA, USA
jannesari@iastate.edu

Abstract. Data-dependence profiling is a dynamic program-analysis technique to discover potential parallelism in sequential programs. Unlike purely static analysis, which may overestimate the number of dependences because it does not know many pointers values and array indices at compile time, profiling has the advantage of recording data dependences that actually occur at runtime. But it has the disadvantage of significantly slowing down program execution, often by a factor of 100. In our earlier work, we lowered the overhead of data-dependence profiling by excluding polyhedral loops, which can be handled statically using certain compilers. However, neither does every program contain polyhedral loops, nor are statically identifiable dependences restricted to such loops. In this paper, we introduce an orthogonal approach, focusing on data dependences between accesses to scalar variables - across the entire program, inside and outside loops. We first analyze the program statically and identify memory-access instructions that create data dependences that would appear in any execution of these instructions. Then, we exclude these instructions from instrumentation, allowing the profiler to skip them at runtime and avoid the associated overhead. We evaluate our approach with 49 benchmarks from three benchmark suites. We improved the profiling time of all programs by at least 38%, with a median reduction of 61% across all the benchmarks.

Keywords: Data dependences · Parallelism discovery · Profiling

1 Introduction

Data-dependence analysis is an essential step in the parallelization of sequential programs. Auto-parallelizing compilers [3,10,16] perform the analysis purely statically. They may overestimate the amount of data dependences because critical information such as the value of pointers and array indices are unknown at compile time. This is why auto-parallelization based on purely static analysis has

© Springer Nature Switzerland AG 2020
M. Malawski and K. Rzadca (Eds.): Euro-Par 2020, LNCS 12247, pp. 3–17, 2020.
https://doi.org/10.1007/978-3-030-57675-2_1

not gained much success beyond the parallelization of loops that satisfy certain constraints.

Another group of tools [5–7,14,18] avoid the limitations of purely static analysis using a dynamic method. They detect parallelization opportunities based on data dependences captured at runtime. Running the program with several representative inputs, they counter the inherent input sensitivity of dynamic data-dependence analysis, also exploiting that data dependences in frequently executed code regions that are subject to parallelization do not change significantly with respect to different inputs [5,6,14]. These tools provide weaker correctness guarantees, although their suggestions more than often reproduce manual parallelization strategies.

Nonetheless, the tools have a high runtime overhead which is caused by profiling every memory access in the program. Many optimizations such as parallelizing the data-dependence profiler itself [6,9] and skipping repeatedly executed memory operations [8] have been proposed to lower the overhead. In addition, taking a fundamentally different route, we recently introduced a hybrid approach [13] to data-dependence analysis. The approach exploited static analysis tools to extract data dependences in loops that follow the constraints of the polyhedral model [2] and profiled only memory accesses outside those loops. This reduced the profiling overhead significantly, but only for programs containing such loops.

However, only few loops are polyhedral. The strict conditions they have to satisfy make it hard for programmers to write a loop in the polyhedral form. More importantly, many data dependences that can be identified statically do not belong to such loops. In this paper, we introduce a method that is orthogonal to our earlier work. Now, we concentrate on static data dependences between accesses to scalar variables—across the entire source code, inside and outside loops. We first identify the memory instructions that belong to these dependences. Then, we run our dependence profiler, but without instrumenting these instructions, allowing the profiler to skip them at runtime and avoid their associated overhead. Eliminating instructions that can belong to all types of loops (e.g., polyhedral, canonical, or non-canonical) or functions (e.g., recursive or non-recursive), our approach is able to reduce the profiling overhead for a wide range of programs. Finally, we merge data dependences extracted statically or dynamically into one output. Here, our goal is to decrease the profiling overhead. Finding parallelization opportunities based on the identified data dependences is described in related work [5–7,14] and outside the scope of this paper. In summary, we make the following specific contributions:

- A hybrid technique to data-dependence analysis that combines the advantages of static and dynamic techniques. Contrary to our earlier work that excluded polyhedral loops from profiling, we now skip instructions that create statically-identifiable data dependences for scalar variables in all types of loops and functions, reducing the profiling overhead for a wider range of programs.

- An implementation as an extension of the data-dependence profiler of DiscoPoP [7], although our approach is generic enough to be implemented in any
  data-dependence profiler.
- An evaluation with 49 programs from three benchmark suites, reducing the
  profiling time by at least 38%, with a median improvement of 61%.

The remainder of the paper is organized as follows. We discuss related work
in Sect. 2. Section 3 presents our approach, followed by an evaluation in Sect. 4.
Finally, we review our achievements in Sect. 5.

2   Related Work

A great deal of research has been made in the field of data-dependence analysis [3,
5–7,10,14,16,18]. Most approaches focus on either static or dynamic analysis
techniques, with only a few attempting to combine them.

autoPar [10] is a static analysis tool which can parallelize array-based
loops [11]. Applying a set of loop transformations such as fusion, fission, inter-
change, unrolling, and blocking, autoPar checks whether or not a data dependence in a loop can be eliminated. If all dependences in the loop are eliminated, it suggests parallelizing the loop. Contrary to autoPar, which finds data
dependences only in specific loops, our method identifies data dependences in
all types of loops and functions. PLUTO [3], is another auto-parallelizing compiler which detects data dependences in polyhedral loops [2]. TaskMiner [16] is
a static analysis tool which translates programs containing recursive functions
into their parallel versions. It exploits LLVM data-dependence analysis to identify dependences. Like TaskMiner, our approach uses LLVM and its features
to identify data dependences involving scalar variables. Contrary to TaskMiner,
which extracts data dependences only in recursive functions, we identify data
dependences in any functions and in loops. In general, static analysis techniques
may overestimate the number of dependences because they lack critical runtime
information at compile time such as the values of pointers and array indices.

Avoiding the limitations of purely static analysis, many tools [5–7,14] capture data dependences during program execution. They profile memory accesses,
which imposes huge runtime overhead. SD3 [6] is a data-dependence profiler
which decreases the overhead by parallelizing the profiler itself. DiscoPoP [7] is
a parallelism discovery tool that contains a data-dependence profiler [9]. The
profiler is based on LLVM and transforms the program into its LLVM-IR representation. It instruments all memory-access instructions with runtime library
calls that track memory accesses at runtime. It skips repeatedly executed memory operations and, like SD3, runs multiple threads to reduce the overhead.
Nonetheless, dependence profiling significantly slows down program execution,
sometimes by more than a factor of 100.

Recently, we introduced a hybrid technique [13] for data-dependence analysis. The technique is called DiscoPoP+ and uses the profiler of DiscoPoP as the
basis of its implementation. It first runs PLUTO to statically identify data dependences in polyhedral loops. Then, it excludes the loops from instrumentation,

profiling only data dependences outside the loops. At the end, it merges static and dynamic dependences. It reduces the profiling overhead significantly, but only for programs containing polyhedral loops. Our approach, however, accelerates the profiling of all types of loops and functions. Based on the control flow graph of the program, it statically identifies data dependences of scalar variables, not including passed-by-reference parameters and pointers. It then identifies memory instructions that create the dependences and excludes them from instrumentation. Skipping such instructions, which may appear inside and outside loops, our method allows the reduction of the profiling overhead for a wide range of programs.

Another hybrid-analysis framework was proposed by Sampaio et al. [17]. Their goal is providing theoretical and practical foundations to apply aggressive loop transformations. They apply static alias and dependence analysis and provide their results to an optimizer. The optimizer, instead of filtering out invalid transformations, performs transformations believed to reduce the execution time. It then generates fast and precise tests to validate at runtime whether the transformations can be taken. In contrast to their work, our contribution happens at a lower level, where we obtain dependences with the aim to accelerate data-dependence profiling.

3   Approach

Below, we explain our hybrid method to the identification of data dependences. Figure 1 shows the basic workflow. Dark boxes highlight our contribution in

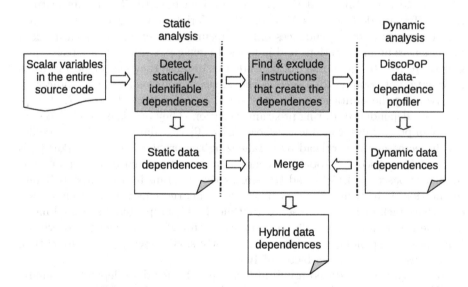

Fig. 1. The workflow of our hybrid data-dependence analysis. Dark boxes show our contributions.

relation to DiscoPoP+, our earlier hybrid approach, PLUTO, a static analyzer, and DiscoPoP, a dynamic data-dependence profiler.

DiscoPoP+ relies on PLUTO to extract data dependences statically. Unlike DiscoPoP+, which statically identifies data dependences only in polyhedral loops, we detect the dependences for scalar variables, excluding aliases, in the entire source code. In addition, we find memory-access instructions that create the dependences and exclude them from instrumentation. Below, in Sect. 3.1, we present the details of our method. The dynamic data-dependence analysis will then skip these instructions during the profiling process. Finally, we merge all dependences we have found—whether of static or dynamic origin—into a single output file. Before we proceed to the evaluation in Sect. 4, we also discuss the relation between the set of dependences extracted by our approach and the purely dynamic technique in Sect. 3.2.

3.1 Data-Dependence Detection and Instruction Identification

We eliminate a memory-access instruction from profiling under certain conditions. They guarantee that the instruction creates only statically-identifiable data dependences and thus, we can safely omit it, without missing any data dependences that a purely dynamic analysis may capture at runtime.

The first condition is that the target address of a memory instruction must be predictable statically. We use Algorithm 1 to detect memory addresses that comply with the condition. Figure 2 serves as an illustrating example.

```
1 void foo(int x){
2 int y = 0;
3 int *p = &y;
4 *p = 4;
5 bar(&x);
6 }
```

Fig. 2. A program containing only aliased variables.

The static analysis we conduct in this paper does not cross function boundaries. This is why we continue profiling memory instructions of variables that create data dependences whose sink and source appear in different functions. Nevertheless, we will investigate the analysis of dependences between functions in the future. According to our algorithm, we first look for memory allocation instructions in a function. We retrieve the symbolic address from an allocation instruction and add it to the set of statically-predictable addresses. In Fig. 2, the set includes initially the address of variables x, y, and p. Then, we look for call and store instructions. We exclude the addresses that are passed by reference to functions; they may create data dependences that cannot be identified statically. In the figure, a reference to variable x is passed to function bar at line 5.

Algorithm 1. Finding memory addresses that are statically predictable.

$staticAddrs = \{\}$
for *each* *instruction* $I \in function\ F$ **do**
  if $I.isAlloca()$ **then**
    $addr = I.getMemAddr()$
    $staticAddrs.insert(addr)$

for *each* *instruction* $I \in function\ F$ **do**
  if $I.isCall()$ **then**
    $params = I.getParams()$
    for *each* *param* $p \in params$ **do**
      if $p.isPassedByReference()$ **then**
        $addr = p.getMemAddr()$
        $staticAddrs.remove(addr)$

  else if $I.isStore()$ **then**
    $var = I.storedVar()$
    if $var.isMemAddr()$ **then**
      $pointeeVar = I.getPointee()$
      $staticAddrs.remove(var)$
      $staticAddrs.remove(pointeeVar)$

It means that we cannot exclude memory-access instructions of variable x from profiling and, thus, we remove the symbolic address of x from the set of static addresses. In addition, pointer variables create data dependences which may not be identified statically. According to Algorithm 1, we detect a pointer variable if a store instruction assigns the address of a variable to another variable. We remove the symbolic address of a pointee from the set of static addresses. In the figure, the address of variable y is assigned to variable p by the implicit store instruction at line 3. All memory instructions of variable y should be profiled and, therefore, we discard them from further analysis.

In Fig. 2, most variables are aliased via pointers or references. In practice, we rarely find programs that contain only aliased variables. Figure 3a shows function fib from BOTS [4]. There, we can skip profiling memory instructions of all variables, namely, i, j, n, and an implicit variable retval, which saves the return value because we can identify data dependences between their accesses statically. Figures 3b to 3d demonstrate the analyses that we perform to extract data dependences statically, using function fib as an example.

First, we convert the program into its LLVM-IR representation and generate the control flow graph (CFG) of the program. The CFG of function fib is shown in Fig. 3b. The CFG contains many instructions that are irrelevant to the data-dependence analysis. We generate a memory-access CFG (MCFG) which has the same structure as the CFG but contains only memory-access instructions.

```
1  int fib(int n) {
2    int i, j;
3    if (n < 2)
4      return n;
5    i = fib(n - 1);
6    j = fib(n - 2);
7    return i + j;
8  }
```

(a) Function fib from BOTS. The memory address of all variables are statically predictable

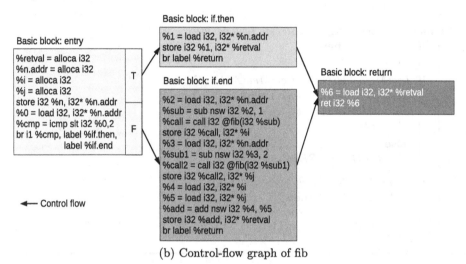

(b) Control-flow graph of fib

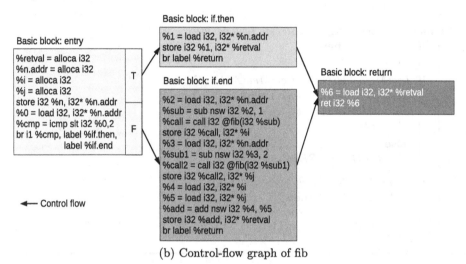

(c) Memory-access graph of fib

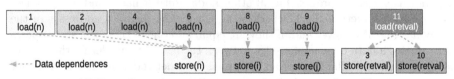

(d) Data dependences that our method extracts from fib

Fig. 3. How we obtain data dependences statically.

Algorithm 2. Traversing the graph of a function to extract data dependences.

Input: I: Return node in the memory-access graph of a function

Function findDepsFor(*node I*):

    if $I.isEntry()||I.isVisited()$ **then**
        $return$;

    for *each* node *J* *directly preceding I* **do**
        checkDepsBetween(I,J);
        findDepsFor(J);

Function checkDepsBetween(*node I, node J*):

    if $J.isEntry()$ **then**
        $return$;

    if $J.getMemAddr() == I.getMemAddr()$ **then**
        if $J.isStore()||I.isStore()$ **then**
            $addDataDeps(I, J)$;
            $return$;

        else
            $checkForRARDep()$;

    for *each* node *K* *directly preceding J* **do**
        if $!K.isVisited()$ **then**
            $K.isVisited = true$
            checkDepsBetween(I,K);

Henceforth, we briefly refer to MCFG as memory-access graph or simply as graph if the context allows it. Figure 3c shows the memory-access graph of function fib.

We traverse the graph to extract data dependences statically. Algorithm 2 shows how. Figure 3d illustrates the dependences that we extract from the memory-access graph of fib. According to the algorithm, we use two recursive functions to traverse the graph of each function in the source code. First, we pass the return node in the graph to function findDepsFor. The function recursively iterates over all nodes preceding the return node and calls function checkDepsBetween to look for dependences between the return node and its preceding nodes. It performs the same process for all other nodes until it has found dependences for all nodes. Function checkDepsBetween checks the memory addresses of the two nodes that it receives and, if they are equal and one of them is a store operation, creates a data dependence edge between the nodes. Considering the control flow, we determine the type of an identified data dependence, that is, whether it must be classified as read-after-write (RAW), write-after-read (WAR), and write-after-write (WAW). In Fig. 3c, the value of variable i is read in node 8. The value was previously stored in node 5. Figure 3d shows the data dependence that our approach adds between the nodes. The type of the dependence is RAW because the value of i is read after it is written.

We do not report read-after-read (RAR) dependences, although we identify them. This dependence type is irrelevant to the parallelization and, strictly speaking, does not even constitute a dependence. Most data-dependence profilers do not report them either. However, instrumenting memory-access instructions relevant to RAR dependences adds to the profiling overhead. If we prove during the static analysis that an instruction is only involved in RAR dependences, we can safely omit the instruction from profiling, without violating the completeness of data dependences captured by purely dynamic analysis. In Algorithm 2, function checkForRARDep determines whether a memory address is only read in a function. In function fib in Fig. 3a, variable n creates only RAR dependences after its memory initialization. We skip profiling all of its memory-access instructions and do not report its RAR data dependences.

We check the dependences between a node and all other nodes preceding it in the memory-access graph of a function. We repeat the process for all functions in a program. The worst-case complexity of our analysis $O(f \cdot n^2)$, where f is the number of functions and n is the maximum number of memory instructions in a function. However, given that during execution many instructions are executed many times, the overhead of the static pre-analysis, which usually takes in the order of minutes, is small in comparison to the profiling overhead the affected instructions would cause. Moreover, our analysis excludes memory-access instructions that can be safely removed during the static analysis. In the worst case, if there are no such instructions in a program, all instructions are instrumented and our approach falls back to the purely dynamic technique. In this case, we cannot reduce the profiling overhead.

In the end, we merge all the data dependences that we have identified using our portfolio of static and dynamic methods into a joint ASCII file. Furthermore, we compact the dependence data, combining all dependences with the same sink into a single line. The result can be used by parallelism discovery tools to find parallelization opportunities.

3.2 Transitive Data Dependences

Transitive data dependences are the only difference that we came across while comparing the sets of dependences extracted by a purely dynamic profiler and our approach. Consider two memory-access instructions S1 and S2 in a program. If S1 precedes S2 in execution and both either read from or write to the same memory location M, we say that S2 is data dependent on S1. Now consider an additional statement S3 that accesses M, too. We say that there is a transitive data dependence between S1 and S3 if S1 depends on S2 and S2 depends on S3. Transitive data dependences can be derived based on other data dependences that we identify. In Fig. 4, the value of variable x is read in node 2. Nodes 1 and 3 store values in variable x. Our approach identifies a RAW dependence between nodes 1 and 2, and a WAR dependence between nodes 3 and 2. There is a transitive data dependence between nodes 3 and 1. The type of the dependence is WAW. We can identify the transitive data dependence and its type by following the chain of the identified dependences, starting from node 3 to node 2 and further to node 1. Note that transitive data dependences only provide additional information and are not important for parallelization, as long as the chain of dependences that create a transitive data dependence are extracted. Since our method identifies the dependences that constitute transitive dependences, we do not generate and report transitive dependences to keep the set of data dependences concise.

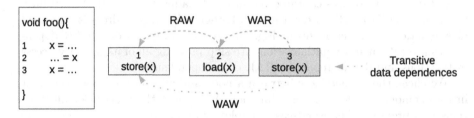

Fig. 4. A transitive data dependence.

4   Evaluation

We performed a range of experiments to evaluate the effectiveness of our approach. We used the following benchmarks: NAS Parallel Benchmarks 3.3.1 [1] (NPB), a collection of programs derived from real-world computational fluid-dynamics applications, Polybench 3.2 [15], a set of benchmarks including polyhedral loops mainly, and the Barcelona OpenMP Task Suite (BOTS) 1.1.2 [4], a suite that all the benchmarks contain recursive functions. Since Polybench has been designed as a test suite for polyhedral compilers, it is well suited for comparison with DiscoPoP+ [13]. Also, the NBP benchmarks contain many polyhedral loops. In addition, we used BOTS to measure the usefulness of our method for recursive functions.

We compiled the benchmarks using clang 8.0.1, which is also used by the data-dependence profiler of DiscoPoP. We ran the benchmarks on an Intel(R) Xeon(R) Gold 6126 CPU @ 2.60 GHz with 64 Gb of main memory, running Ubuntu 14.04 (64-bit edition). We profiled the benchmarks using the inputs packaged with the programs. Our evaluation criteria are the completeness of the data dependences in relation to purely dynamic profiling and the profiling time. We compared the sets of data dependences extracted by the DiscoPoP profiler with and without our technique. Transitive data dependences were the only difference between the two sets. We identified all the dependences that created the transitive data dependences and thus, the set of dependences detected by our method can be used further to parallelize the programs.

To measure the improvements in the profiling time, we executed the benchmarks with the vanilla version of the DiscoPoP profiler. We executed each benchmark five times in isolation, calculated the median of the execution times, and used it as our baseline. Then, we profiled the benchmarks using our method. Again, we ran each benchmark fives times in isolation and recorded its median execution time, which we then compared with the baseline. We repeated the process to obtain the median execution times for DiscoPoP+. We used the same input to execute the benchmarks with each approach. Table 1 shows the relative slowdown of each approach for the three benchmark suites. Figure 5 presents the relative reduction of the profiling overhead for each benchmark.

Whether we can reduce the profiling time of a benchmark depends on its memory access pattern. In theory, the more memory accesses that occur without using pointers and aliases, the more effective our method will be. If the variables in a program are mostly pointers or passed by reference to functions, we fail to reduce the profiling overhead significantly. Notably, our method lowered the profiling time in all test cases.

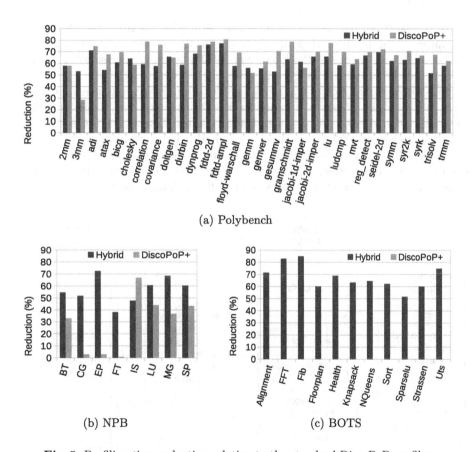

(a) Polybench

(b) NPB

(c) BOTS

Fig. 5. Profiling-time reduction relative to the standard DiscoPoP profiler.

For Polybench, our hybrid technique reduced the profiling overhead to a lesser degree than DiscoPoP+ because these benchmarks contain polyhedral loops.

Table 1. Relative slowdown caused by standard DiscoPoP vs. DiscoPoP+ vs. our hybrid approach.

Benchmark suites	Standard DiscoPoP			DiscoPoP+			Hybrid approach		
	Min	Max	Median	Min	Max	Median	Min	Max	Median
BOTS	29	124	80	29	124	80	6	55	28
Polybench	70	200	121	17	70	37	24	85	43
NPB	25	116	88	22	113	53	7	71	36

DiscoPoP+ eliminates these loops from profiling, whereas our approach skips only a subset of the memory instructions within those loops. This is why the median improvement of the profiling time is 70% with DiscoPoP+, but only 61% with our hybrid method.

BOTS does not contain any polyhedral loops, which is why DiscoPoP+ did not improve the profiling time at all. In contrast, the median improvement of the profiling time by our method across all BOTS benchmarks was 64%. In Fib, we reduced the profiling time even by 84%.

In NPB, we found polyhedral loops in all benchmarks. Nevertheless, because these loops did not consume a major fraction of the execution time, excluding them did not make the profiling significantly better. DiscoPoP+ obtained only a median reduction of 35% for these benchmarks. Our approach, on the other hand, identified many variables in time-consuming loops. It skipped profiling the memory-access instructions related to those variables and improved the profiling time by a median percentage of 57% across all benchmarks in the suite.

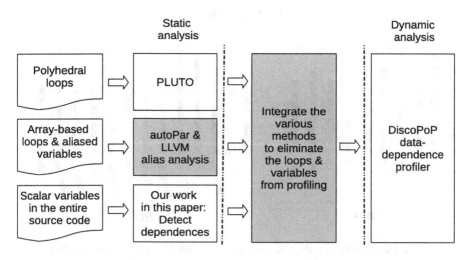

Fig. 6. The workflow of our future hybrid data-dependence analysis. Dark boxes show the contributions of our future work.

Overall, compared to the vanilla version of DiscoPoP, we reduced the profiling time of all programs by at least 38%, with a median reduction of 61% across all the three benchmark suites.

5 Conclusion

Our hybrid approach to data-dependence analysis allows the profiler to skip the memory instructions of scalar variables whose dependences can be extracted statically. However, we still instrument memory operations of aliased variables to capture their data dependences at runtime, avoiding the loss of any data dependence that a purely dynamic method would extract. We implemented our approach as an extension of an advanced data-dependence profiler and decreased the profiling time by at least 38%, with a median reduction of 61% across 49 programs from three benchmark suites, making it far more practical than before. Having a faster profiler, DiscoPoP tool is able to identify parallelism opportunities in larger and longer-running programs. However, our method is generic enough to be implemented in any data-dependence profiler.

Our objective for the future work is to reduce the profiling overhead further and for a wider range of programs. Figure 6 shows the workflow of our future hybrid data-dependence analysis. First, we will aim to exploit LLVM alias analysis to statically detect data dependences for aliased scalar variables and eliminate their memory accesses from profiling. Then, we will investigate the inclusion of other promising tools such as autoPar, which statically identifies data dependences for array variables. Finally, we will combine them with DiscoPoP+ and our approach from this paper, creating a superior tool for hybrid data-dependence analysis.

Acknowledgements and Data Availability Statement. This work was funded by the Hessian LOEWE initiative within the Software- Factory 4.0 project. The datasets and code generated during and/or analysed during the current study are available in the Figshare repository: https://doi.org/10.6084/m9.figshare.12555083 [12].

References

1. Bailey, D.H., et al.: The NAS parallel benchmarks. Int. J. Supercomput. Appl. **5**(3), 63–73 (1991). https://doi.org/10.1177/109434209100500306
2. Benabderrahmane, M.-W., Pouchet, L.-N., Cohen, A., Bastoul, C.: The polyhedral model is more widely applicable than you think. In: Gupta, R. (ed.) CC 2010. LNCS, vol. 6011, pp. 283–303. Springer, Heidelberg (2010). https://doi.org/10.1007/978-3-642-11970-5_16
3. Bondhugula, U.: Pluto - an automatic parallelizer and locality optimizer for affine loop nests (2015). http://pluto-compiler.sourceforge.net/. Accessed 13 June 2019
4. Duran, A., Teruel, X., Ferrer, R., Martorell, X., Ayguade, E.: Barcelona OpenMP tasks suite: a set of benchmarks targeting the exploitation of task parallelism in OpenMP. In: Proceedings of the International Conference on Parallel Processing (ICPP), Vienna, Austria, pp. 124–131, September 2009

5. Ketterlin, A., Clauss, P.: Profiling data-dependence to assist parallelization: framework, scope, and optimization. In: Proceedings of the International Symposium on Microarchitecture (MICRO), Vancouver, B.C., Canada, pp. 437–448, December 2012. https://doi.org/10.1109/MICRO.2012.47

6. Kim, M., Kim, H., Luk, C.K.: SD3: a scalable approach to dynamic data-dependence profiling. In: Proceedings of the International Symposium on Microarchitecture (MICRO), Atlanta, GA, USA, pp. 535–546, December 2010. https://doi.org/10.1109/MICRO.2010.49

7. Li, Z., Atre, R., Huda, Z.U., Jannesari, A., Wolf, F.: Unveiling parallelization opportunities in sequential programs. J. Syst. Softw. **117**(C), 282–295 (2016). https://doi.org/10.1016/j.jss.2016.03.045

8. Li, Z., Beaumont, M., Jannesari, A., Wolf, F.: Fast data-dependence profiling by skipping repeatedly executed memory operations. In: Wang, G., Zomaya, A., Perez, G.M., Li, K. (eds.) ICA3PP 2015. LNCS, vol. 9531, pp. 583–596. Springer, Cham (2015). https://doi.org/10.1007/978-3-319-27140-8_40

9. Li, Z., Jannesari, A., Wolf, F.: An efficient data-dependence profiler for sequential and parallel programs. In: Proceedings of the International Parallel and Distributed Processing Symposium (IPDPS), Hyderabad, India, pp. 484–493, May 2015. https://doi.org/10.1109/IPDPS.2015.41

10. Liao, C., Quinlan, D.J., Willcock, J.J., Panas, T.: Semantic-aware automatic parallelization of modern applications using high-level abstractions. Int. J. Parallel Program. **38**(5), 361–378 (2010). https://doi.org/10.1007/s10766-010-0139-0

11. Liao, C., Quinlan, D.J., Willcock, J.J., Panas, T.: Extending automatic parallelization to optimize high-level abstractions for multicore. In: Müller, M.S., de Supinski, B.R., Chapman, B.M. (eds.) IWOMP 2009. LNCS, vol. 5568, pp. 28–41. Springer, Heidelberg (2009). https://doi.org/10.1007/978-3-642-02303-3_3

12. Morew, N., Norouzi, M., Jannesari, A., Wolf, F.: Artifact and instructions to generate experimental results for Euro-Par proceeding 2020 paper: skipping Non-essential Instructions Makes Data-dependence Profiling Faster, July 2020. https://doi.org/10.6084/m9.figshare.12555083. https://springernature.figshare.com/articles/software/Artifact_and_instructions_to_generate_experimental_results_for_Euro-Par_proceeding_2020_paper_Skipping_Non-essential_Instructions_Makes_Data-dependence_Profiling_Faster/12555083/1

13. Norouzi, M., Ilias, Q., Jannesari, A., Wolf, F.: Accelerating data-dependence profiling with static hints. In: Yahyapour, R. (ed.) Euro-Par 2019. LNCS, vol. 11725, pp. 17–28. Springer, Cham (2019). https://doi.org/10.1007/978-3-030-29400-7_2

14. Norouzi, M., Wolf, F., Jannesari, A.: Automatic construct selection and variable classification in OpenMP. In: Proceedings of the International Conference on Supercomputing (ICS), Phoenix, AZ, USA, pp. 330–342, June 2019. https://doi.org/10.1145/3330345.3330375

15. Pouchet, L.N.: Polyhedral suite (2011). http://www.cs.ucla.edu/~pouchet/software/polybench/. Accessed 31 Jan 2020

16. Ramos, P., Mendonca, G., Soares, D., Araujo, G., Pereira, F.M.Q.: Automatic annotation of tasks in structured code. In: Proceedings of the International Conference on Parallel Architectures and Compilation Techniques (PACT), Limassol, Cyprus, pp. 20–33, May 2018. https://doi.org/10.1145/3243176.3243200
17. Sampaio, D., Ketterlin, A., Pouchet, L., Rastello, F.: Hybrid data dependence analysis for loop transformations. In: Proceedings of the International Conference on Parallel Architecture and Compilation Techniques (PACT), Los Alamitos, CA, USA, pp. 439–440, September 2016. https://doi.org/10.1145/2967938.2974059
18. Wilhelm, A., Cakaric, F., Gerndt, M., Schuele, T.: Tool-based interactive software parallelization: a case study. In: Proceedings of the International Conference on Software Engineering (ICSE), Gothenburg, Sweden, pp. 115–123, June 2018. https://doi.org/10.1145/3183519.3183555

A Toolchain to Verify the Parallelization of OmpSs-2 Applications

Simone Economo[1,2]([✉]) [ID], Sara Royuela[1] [ID], Eduard Ayguadé[1] [ID],
and Vicenç Beltran[1] [ID]

[1] Barcelona Supercomputing Center (BSC),
Barcelona, Spain
{simone.economo,sara.royuela,
eduard.ayguade,vbeltran}@bsc.es
[2] DIAG Antonio Ruberti,
Sapienza Università di Roma, Rome, Italy

Abstract. Programming models for task-based parallelization based on compile-time directives are very effective at uncovering the parallelism available in HPC applications. Despite that, the process of correctly annotating complex applications is error-prone and may hinder the general adoption of these models. In this paper, we target the OmpSs-2 programming model and present a novel toolchain able to detect parallelization errors coming from non-compliant OmpSs-2 applications. Our toolchain verifies the compliance with the OmpSs-2 programming model using local task analysis to deal with each task separately, and structural induction to extend the analysis to the whole program. To improve the effectiveness of our tools, we also introduce some ad-hoc verification annotations, which can be used manually or automatically to disable the analysis of specific code regions. Experiments run on a sample of representative kernels and applications show that our toolchain can be successfully used to verify the parallelization of complex real-world applications.

Keywords: Synchronization · Software testing and debugging · Parallel programming

1 Introduction

In the last twenty years, the conceptual hardware organization of computing systems has changed significantly. Complex multi-core and heterogeneous architectures are ubiquitous nowadays and represent a cost-effective way to support the high degree of parallelism of many High-Performance Computing (HPC) applications. Several new ideas have been put into the software in terms of parallel programming supports to adapt to this paradigm shift [17]. In order to implement parallelization via these supports, applications need to be redesigned or ported to a different programming language with parallelization constructs. In some cases, the user is also responsible for how the parallelism is implemented. A direct consequence of this is that the effort of maintaining the source

© Springer Nature Switzerland AG 2020
M. Malawski and K. Rzadca (Eds.): Euro-Par 2020, LNCS 12247, pp. 18–33, 2020.
https://doi.org/10.1007/978-3-030-57675-2_2

code increases, and tasks like debugging or testing become quite tricky. Parallel programming models based on compiler directives such as OpenMP [2] are an alternative to the approaches mentioned above. These models allow the programmer to disclose parallelism within programs through source-code annotations, which are interpreted by the compiler as commands to perform transformations that parallelize the code. The annotation-based approach is very effective as it allows users to parallelize applications incrementally without sacrificing the programmability and portability of code. Starting from the sequential version of the application, the user can add more and more annotations to specify the parallelism of different parts of the application. Despite the high potential of annotation-based models, the parallelization process remains manual and prone to errors by the user. Incorrect usage of annotations can lead to performance and correctness issues and many hours of bug-hunting, thus forcing developers to debug their programs in conventional (and typically ineffective) ways to try to get to the root cause of the problem.

In this article, we focus on the OmpSs-2 task-based programming model. OmpSs is a shared-memory multiprocessing API developed at the Barcelona Supercomputing Center (BSC) for C, C++, and Fortran programs. OmpSs takes from OpenMP its idea of providing a way to, starting from a sequential program, produce a parallel version through **pragma** annotations in the source code. Parallelization is achieved by annotating certain code regions as tasks that can execute independently on the available threads, and synchronization constraints between them. OmpSs has also been a forerunner for many of the task-based features later introduced in OpenMP. The second version of OmpSs, called OmpSs-2, features a fine-grained data-flow execution model for tasks that has been recently proposed for integration into OpenMP [16]. The OmpSs programming model is interesting because it has clear rules when it comes to specifying tasks and synchronization constraints. For this reason, it is possible to verify that applications comply with it in a programmatic manner. Applications that are compliant to the OmpSs programming model are less likely to be affected by parallelization errors that undermine the performance and correctness of the program. Therefore, proving that an application complies with the rules of OmpSs eliminates some of the errors that can be introduced upon parallelizing the code of an application, thus potentially saving many hours of tedious debugging.

In this work, we illustrate a programmatic approach to checking parallelization errors in OmpSs-2 based on local task analysis to verify task-level compliance, and structural induction to verify application-level compliance. We also propose a novel toolchain that implements this analysis for real-world OmpSs-2 applications. The toolchain is based on a framework that involves three pieces: compile-time analysis to check the compliance of code before execution, run-time analysis to verify code that could not be checked at compile-time, and verification annotations to mark code that should not be explicitly analyzed by our toolchain. Our experiments suggest that our toolchain's hybrid nature is key to making our programmatic approach viable for checking the compliance of real-world applications.

2   Task-Based Parallelization in OmpSs-2

In this section, we describe the parallelization annotations available in the OmpSs-2 task-based programming model, and the rules that must be respected to comply with it. Failing to do so is a *compliance error*, denoted with the 'E' prefix, which may impact both the performance and the correctness of the parallelized application. We describe these errors in detail in the rest of this section.

2.1   Tasks and Dependencies

OmpSs-2 allows expressing parallelism through *tasks*, independent pieces of code that can be executed by the computing resources at runtime. Whenever the program flow reaches a section of code declared as a task, the system creates an instance of that task and delegates its execution to the OmpSs-2 runtime system. Tasks are created via the `task` directive. Any directive that defines a task can also appear within the definition of a task, thus naturally supporting task nesting. Note that, in OmpSs-2, everything is a task. The user program runs in the context of an implicit task region, called the *initial task*. This makes all user-defined tasks to be nested tasks to that initial region.

OmpSs-2 tasks commonly require to access data to do meaningful computation. These data references can be declared via the `in`, `out`, or `inout` clauses[1]. The set of all data references constitutes the *dataset* of a task. Each time a new task is created, its dataset is matched against those of previously-created tasks to produce execution-order constraints between them. We call these constraints *dependencies*. This process creates a *task dependency graph* at runtime that guarantees a *correct* order of execution for the application, i.e., an order which respects the dependencies between tasks. Tasks aren't considered for execution until all their predecessors in the graph, if any, have finished.

Whether the task actually uses data in the declared way is the responsibility of the programmer. In Listing 1.1 it is an error (E1) to access a from inside T1, because a is not in the dataset of T1 and thus doesn't generate any dependency. If there is another task T2 accessing the same variable, the two tasks can't synchronize their accesses. Another error (E2) is declaring an element in the dataset that is not accessed. For example, if T2 declares to access d when the variable is not accessed, there may be undesired synchronization between T2 and another task T3 accessing the same variable.

2.2   Dependency Domains

The OmpSs-2 model states that dependencies between any two tasks can be established if those tasks share the same *dependency domain*. By default, a task t can only have dependencies with its *sibling tasks*, i.e., tasks that share with t

---

[1] For a thorough explanation of the admitted syntax for data references, see the official OmpSs-2 specification: https://pm.bsc.es/ftp/ompss-2/doc/spec/.

```
1  int a, b;
2  long c[N];
3
4  #pragma oss task in(b) out(c[i:j]) label(T1)
5  {
6    a = 5; // Error E1: No matching dependency for 'a'
7  }
8  #pragma oss task inout(a, b, d) label(T2)
9  {
10   a += b; // OK
11   // Error E2: No matching access for 'd'
12 }
13 #pragma oss task in(d) label(T3)
14 {
15   int x = d; // OK
16 }
17
```

Listing 1.1. Definition of tasks and dependencies.

```
1  #pragma oss task in(a) weakout(b) label(T1)
2  {
3    int x = a; // OK
4    #pragma oss task out(b, c) label(T1.1)
5    { ... }
6    // Error E3: No matching 'c' dependency in T1
7  }
8  #pragma oss task in(b) weakout(d) label(T2)
9  {
10   int y = b; // OK
11   // Error E4: No matching 'd' dependency in T2.1
12   #pragma oss task out(b) label(T2.1)
13   { ... }
14 }
15
```

Listing 1.2. Connecting tasks via weak dependencies.

the same parent task. To connect two tasks that are not siblings, the dependency model in OmpSs-2 supports *weak dependencies*. These are created via the weakin, weakout, and weakinout clauses, but are not real dependencies. Their sole purpose is to inform the runtime that some descendant of a task is accessing the data elements specified in the weak variant. To connect the dependency domains of two arbitrary tasks t_1 and t_2, we must propagate the dataset of both t_1 and t_2 upwards, using the weak prefix, until we find a common ancestor t_a (which can coincide with t_1 or t_2). By doing this, the runtime will merge the dependency domain of all tasks from t_1 to t_a, and from t_2 to t_a, thus being able to establish a dependency between t_1 and t_2.

The mechanism of synchronization via weak dependencies can be unintuitive at times. In Listing 1.2, failing to weakly pass the reference to c from T1.1 upwards is an error (E3) because the model states that if dependency domains are not properly connected, accesses to the same object in different domains cannot be synchronized. Another error (E4) is to declare an object in the weak dataset of T2, when no descendant task is accessing it. Even if the runtime doesn't perform any actions on T2 that require the enforcement of those dependencies, it may suggest an error elsewhere, e.g., a missing out reference to d in task T2.1.

```
1  #pragma oss task label(T1)
2  {
3    int x = 0, y = 2;
4    #pragma oss task inout(x) label(T1.1)
5    { ... }
6    #pragma oss task in(x) inout(y) label(T1.2)
7    { ... }
8    #pragma oss taskwait in(x)
9    assert(x == 1); // OK
10   // Error E5: No 'taskwait' or 'taskwait in(x, y)' before the assertion
11   assert(x == y);
12 }
13
```

Listing 1.3. Synchronization via the `taskwait` construct.

2.3   Taskwait Synchronization

By design in OmpSs-2, to synchronize the code of task t with any of its descendants t' we need to use the `taskwait` directive. Taskwait synchronization means that the runtime waits until the previously-created descendant tasks (including the non-direct children tasks) complete their execution. The set of sibling tasks targeted by a taskwait depends on the data references added to the `taskwait` directive. If no data references are specified, the taskwait blocks the task waiting for the completion of all previous descendant tasks.

Appropriately placing taskwaits in task code is a process prone to mistakes in OmpSs-2 applications. In Listing 1.3, failing to place a `taskwait` before the last assert is an error (E5) because the parent task is allowed to execute the statement without waiting for its children (which access both x and y) to finish.

3   Programmatically Checking Compliance

Our programmatic approach verifies application-level compliance through task-level compliance analysis and inductive reasoning on the recursive structure of OmpSs-2 applications. The former is used to verify the absence of errors in each task separately; the second is used to verify increasing portions of the program until we reach the initial entry point. These two techniques rely respectively on two aspects of the OmpSs-2 model: (1) compliance errors in a task t can be verified without having to look at the internal code of other tasks, nor at the datasets of tasks at nesting levels that cannot be directly reached from t; (2) the code of the program can be represented as a hierarchy of tasks, with the initial task wrapping the initial entry point. Any task-based programming model satisfying these properties admits a programmatic approach for checking compliance like the one described in this section.

3.1   Task-Level Compliance

Table 1 provides a compact list of the errors that were discussed in Sect. 2. To check that a task is free of these errors, OmpSs-2 states that we only look at

Table 1. Compliance errors in OmpSs-2

E	Description
$E1$	No matching dependency for an access
$E2$	No matching access for a dependency
$E3$	No matching dependency in the parent task
$E4$	No matching dependency in the child task
$E5$	No taskwait between an access and previous tasks

what happens (i) within the code of the task itself, (ii) in the dataset annotations of its parent (if any), and (iii) in the dataset annotations of its children (if any). This fact is exploited in our tools to analyze each task separately. We call *local task analysis* (LTA) the kind of processing we carry out to check that a single task is compliant with the OmpSs-2 model. It is local because such analysis does not need to reason globally, i.e., at the level of the whole program. To understand how local task analysis works, let's consider a task t in the program. Let t_p be its parent task, and t_c be a child task. Let $d_{(t,i)}$ be the i-th dataset element of t, defined as a tuple $\langle m, clk, r \rangle$, where $m \in \{read, write\}$ is the access mode, clk is the time at which the corresponding task was created, and r is the memory range of that entry. Let $a_{(t,j)}$ be the j-th memory access performed by t, defined as a tuple $\langle m, clk, r \rangle$ with m being once again the access mode, clk being the time at which the access was performed, and r the memory range of the access. Let $\mathcal{D}_t$ be the set of all dependencies of t. Let $\mathcal{A}_t$ be the sequence of all accesses of t (also called the *access-set* of t). Finally, let $\mathcal{W}_t$ be the set of taskwaits dependencies inside task t. Each entry $w_{(t,k)}$ is a tuple $\langle m, clk, r \rangle$, where clk is the time at which the corresponding taskwait was created, and m and r are defined like their counterparts in $d_{(t,i)}$. In the following, we show a conceptual description of LTA, focusing on the errors E1, E3, and E5 for the sake of simplicity. LTA for the remaining cases can be defined likewise.

Condition 1 (E1 detection). *Verify if there is at least one access performed by t that does not have a corresponding dataset entry. Formally speaking, check if, for each $a_{(t,j)} \in \mathcal{A}_t$, there is no $d_{(t,i)} \in \mathcal{D}_t$ for which:*

- $a_{(t,j)}.r \subseteq d_{(t,i)}.r$, *and*
- $d_{(t,i)}.m = a_{(t,j)}.m$

If there is any $a_{(t,j)}$ for which it is true, then t is affected by E1.

Condition 2 (E3 detection). *Verify if there is at least one dataset entry of t (weak or not) that does not have a corresponding dataset entry in its parent (at least weak). Formally speaking, check if, for each $d_{(t,i)} \in \mathcal{D}_t$, there is no $d_{(t_p,i_p)} \in \mathcal{D}_{t_p}$ for which:*

- $d_{(t,i)}.r \subseteq d_{(t_p,i_p)}.r$, *and*
- $d_{(t,i)}.m = d_{(t_p,i_p)}.m$

If there is any $d_{(t,i)}$ for which it is true, then t is affected by E3.

Condition 3 (E5 detection). *Verify if there is at least one access performed by t such that: (i) the access has a corresponding dataset entry in one of the previously-created child tasks; (ii) at least one amongst the access and the dataset entry is a write; (iii) the access is not guarded by a taskwait that blocks until the termination of the conflicting child task. Formally speaking, check if, for each* $a_{(t,j)} \in \mathcal{A}_t$, *there is at least one* $d_{(t_c,i_c)} \in \bigcup_{t_c} \mathcal{D}_{t_c}$ *for which:*

- $a_{(t,j)}.r \subseteq d_{(t_c,i_c)}.r$, *and*
- $a_{(t,j)}.m = write$, *or* $d_{(t_c,i_c)}.m = write$, *or both, and*
- $a_{(t,j)}.clk > d_{(t_c,i_c)}.clk$, *and*
- *there is no* $w_{(t,k)} \in \mathcal{W}_t$ *for which:*
  - $w_{(t,k)}.clk < a_{(t,j)}.clk$, *and*
  - $w_{(t,k)}.clk > d_{(t_c,i_c)}.clk$, *and*
  - $w_{(t,k)}.r \cap d_{(t_c,i_c)}.r \neq \varnothing$, *and*
  - $w_{(t,k)}.m = write$, *or* $d_{(t_c,i_c)}.m = write$, *or both.*

If there is any $a_{(t,j)}$ *for which it is true, then t is affected by E5.*

Conditions 1 to 3 give us a way to detect the errors in Table 1. However, to make these conditions operational, we need to convert them into an algorithm, and the mathematical structures on which such conditions rely must be turned into concrete data structures. Section 4 briefly describes an experimental implementation of LTA based on compile-time and run-time analysis.

3.2 Application-Level Compliance

Local task analysis is used in our approach to check that a task is free of compliance errors. However, we need a way to prove that the entire application is also free of these errors. To do this, we reason inductively on the task-nested structure of OmpSs-2 applications. The OmpSs-2 model represents a program as a hierarchy of tasks. It states that no parts of the program can be executed outside of a task. The recursive nature of tasks can be exploited to prove application-level compliance using *structural induction*, which is a generalization of the inductive proof technique over natural numbers. The property that we wish to prove inductively is *OmpSs-2 compliance*, defined as follows:

Definition (OmpSs-2 compliance). A task t is OmpSs-2 compliant if and only if the following condition holds: (1) the task is not affected by any of the errors in Table 1, and (2) for every task t' that is a child of t, t' is also OmpSs-2 compliant.

By using LTA and structural induction on the nested task structure of an OmpSs-2 application, it is possible to prove its compliance in an incremental manner. According to the definition of OmpSs-2 compliance, if the initial task is OmpSs-2 compliant, then the whole application is compliant.

3.3 Capabilities of the Programmatic Approach

In Sect. 2, we introduced the notion of compliance error and explained that it might affect the parallelization of an application in an undesired way. Generally speaking, we call *parallelization error* any error that was introduced upon parallelizing the original sequential program, and that affects the parallelized program's behavior in an unintended way. In this article, we are concerned with two main types of parallelization errors: performance and correctness errors. *Performance errors* can create additional synchronization constraints that defer the execution of a task unnecessarily. *Correctness errors* are typically caused by an unintended lack of synchronization between tasks that alters the original sequential program' semantics. Parallelization errors can be hard to spot and to debug. Usually, they don't manifest predictably, as it depends on the relative timing between the interfering tasks. Nevertheless, it can be shown that the absence of compliance errors is a sufficient condition for the absence of specific parallelization errors [7], such as those described in this article. However, it is worth observing that not all compliance errors produce parallelization errors. There are cases in which the application doesn't comply with the model, but the synchronization between tasks doesn't produce correctness or performance errors at run-time. Viceversa, not all parallelization errors that may negatively affect the application are compliance errors that can be detected with this approach. Some parallelization errors are *semantics errors*, i.e., errors that require a knowledge of the semantics of the application to be detected programmatically. These errors are out of the scope of this work. Lastly, limitations coming from concrete LTA implementations (such as those mentioned in Sect. 4) may too affect the accuracy of the analysis.

4 An OmpSs-2 Verification Toolchain

This section describes our novel toolchain for checking the compliance of OmpSs-2 applications[2]. It is made of three key elements: (1) a static source-code analyzer that works at compile-time (also called the *compile-time tool*); (2) a dynamic binary-code analyzer that works at run-time (aka the *run-time tool*); (3) a set of `pragma` directives and clauses (also called *verification annotations*) that can be used as an interface between the user, the compile-time tool, and the run-time tool. The reason behind this hybrid architecture is to overcome some limitations of both compile-time and run-time analysis that might undermine the effectiveness of the programmatic approach described in Sect. 3.

---

[2] Compared to the reference description in Sect. 2, our tools support additional OmpSs-2 features: `commutative` and `concurrent` dependencies (treated like `inout`), explicit release of dependencies, `final` and `if` clauses. Primitives for task reductions, atomic operations, and critical regions are currently unsupported. Additional information, included the instructions on how to install and use the toolchain, can be found here: https://github.com/bsc-pm/ompss-2-linter.

4.1 Manual User Pass

Initially, users can annotate portions of code that must be ignored by our toolchain. To this extent, we have introduced support for ad-hoc verification annotations into the Mercurium source-to-source compiler [9]. They instruct the compile-time and run-time tools to pause the analysis inside the wrapped code region. The verification annotations we introduced in OmpSs-2 are: (1) the lint directive, followed by optional in, out, or inout data-references; and (2) the verified clause, optional in the task construct.

The lint directive can be used to ignore code inside tasks. To extend its applicability, users can also declare which accesses to shared-memory (if any) performed within the ignored region are relevant for LTA. For the compile-time tool, the directive is especially useful to mark calls to inaccessible code. In the first example of Listing 1.4, the MPI_Send and MPI_Recv functions are not available for analysis, but their semantics is clear: they respectively read/write N bytes from/to memory. For the run-time tool, marking code is useful to prevent tracing memory accesses that, albeit executed inside tasks, don't relate to the application business logic. This scenario includes, amongst many, accesses performed in libraries to shared-memory variables that are not visible to the application, as well as accesses to shared-memory objects that are synchronized independently of OmpSs-2 (e.g., spinlocks). In the MPI example, the implementation of MPI_Send and MPI_Recv may perform accesses to some internal variables used for synchronization purposes, hence not relevant for LTA.

```
1  #pragma oss lint in(sendbuf[0:size]) out(recvbuf[0:size])
2  {
3    MPI_Send(sendbuf, size, MPI_BYTE, dst, block_id+10, MPI_COMM_WORLD);
4    MPI_Recv(recvbuf, size, MPI_BYTE, src, block_id+10, MPI_COMM_WORLD,
5        MPI_STATUS_IGNORE);
6  }
7
8  double A[N/TS][M/TS][TS][TS];
9  #pragma oss lint out (A[i][j])
10 for (long ii = 0; ii < TS; ii++)
11   for (long jj = 0; jj < TS; jj++)
12     A[i][j][ii][jj] = value ;
13
14 for (int i = 0; i < N; ++i) {
15   #pragma oss task verified(i != 0 && i != N-1 && i % M != 0)
16   { ... }
17 }
18
```

Listing 1.4. Examples of the lint directive and the verified clause.

The verified clause works at the level of whole tasks. It is used to tell both tools that the task is OmpSs-2 compliant, and that no LTA is needed. It accepts an optional boolean expression to decide, at run-time, whether that particular task instance has to be verified. This expression can be used to conditionally evaluate task instances that are more likely to be subject to programming errors (e.g., tasks related to boundary loop iterations). It can also be used to implement task-level sampling and reduce the overall memory tracing overhead of the application (e.g., instrument a fraction of all task instances at run-time). In the third example of Listing 1.4, we only instrument a subset of the tasks that represent distinct loop iterations: the first task, the last task, and one every M of the remaining ones.

4.2 Compile-Time Pass

The compile-time tool aims at two main goals. The first goal is to anticipate errors that are independent of the input of the application and may later appear at run-time. To this extent, we have extended Mercurium and its built-in infrastructure for static analysis with an LTA implementation, evaluating task-level compliance for every task definition in the source code. Notice that compile-time LTA cannot always derive the full program state at every point in the code. Additionally, it cannot analyze code that is unavailable at compile-time (e.g., code coming from other compilation units, or code that is dynamically loaded). When lacking information, it doesn't state anything about OmpSs-2 compliance and leaves task-level analysis to the run-time tool. The run-time tool circumvents these limitations, but only for specific input and while introducing overhead during the execution of the application. For this reason, to ease the burden of the run-time tool, the second goal of the compile-time tool is to mark those sections of code that have been verified by the compiler and therefore do not need to be instrumented at run-time. In the second example of Listing 1.4, a nested loop structure is used to perform a linear array walk. The compile-time tool can detect this scenario and can mark it with a verification annotation. The TS^2 accesses performed within the loop are ignored by the run-time tool, but an equivalent representation of these accesses is placed in the annotation so as to be considered at run-time.

The algorithm to place verification annotations around portions of code, or whole task definitions, performs a bottom-up/inside-out traversal over the *Parallel Control Flow Graph* (PCFG) [18]. It uses induction variables and scalar evolution analysis in an attempt to wrap adjacent statements incrementally until a terminating condition is encountered (e.g., a call to a function whose code is not reachable). The compile-time tool also makes use of the manually-placed verification annotations to try to extend their scopes to more extensive code regions. At the end of this pass, any detected error is reported to the user before execution. The parts of the code that could be verified statically are marked using verification annotations, while the others are left for run-time instrumentation.

4.3 Run-Time Pass

The run-time tool is invoked to complement the compile-time analysis and to provide complete coverage of the code, but only for a given input. Run-time analysis can observe the actual program execution state at any moment in time, so it doesn't need to be conservative. However, it has other limitations. It cannot always distinguish memory accesses that are relevant for LTA (e.g., accesses to shared-memory variables visible to the application) from non-relevant ones (e.g., access to shared-memory variables private to a library and synchronized separately). Additionally, the instrumentation introduced at run-time for the sake of tracing can alter the timing of some events, thus leading to observe artificial and slower application executions.

In order to circumvent such accuracy and overhead issues, run-time analysis exploits verification annotations placed by the user or by the compile-time tool, and only runs LTA for code that lacks such annotations. The tool operates at two different levels of abstraction: (1) the abstraction provided by the OmpSs-2 programming model to deal with tasks and dependencies, as explained in Sect. 2; (2) the abstraction provided by the target Instruction Set Architecture (ISA) to recognize accesses to memory, which in our case is AMD64[3]. Our run-time instrumentation tool is based on Intel Pin [13] and is composed of three main components: the Pin Virtual Machine (VM) to perform dynamic binary instrumentation, and two modules that perform memory access tracing on the binary executable. The *frontend* module (or *trace generator*) is devoted to intercepting the accesses performed by the application at run-time, as well as generating the actual traces. The *backend* module (or *trace processor*) is responsible for the processing of traces and the generation of the final report for the user. At the end of this pass, the tool generates a report of the encountered errors for that specific application execution, thus complementing the report produced at compile-time.

5 Experimental Assessment

In this section we provide an experimental evaluation of the analysis overhead[4] of our toolchain on a set of nine different benchmarks, made of five execution kernels (*matmul, dot-product, multisaxpy, mergesort,* and *cholesky*) and four proxy application (*nqueens, nbody, heat,* and *HPCCG*). These benchmarks are representative of real-world scientific applications and use popular HPC libraries for advanced mathematical operation (such as Intel MKL) as well as well-known APIs for coarse-grained parallelism (i.e., MPI). Our objective is to demonstrate that our toolchain can be effectively used to evaluate the task-based parallelization of these applications.

All the experiments have been conducted on the MareNostrum4 supercomputer. Each compute node is equipped with two 24-core Intel Xeon Platinum 8160 CPUs, totaling 48 cores per node, and 96 GB of main memory. The interconnection network is based on 100 Gbit/s Intel OmniPath HFI technology. The MPI benchmarks (*nbody, heat,* and *HPCCG*) are run on four different nodes, while the other benchmarks are run on a single node. Figure 1 shows the slowdown (y-axis) and the absolute execution time (numbers on top of bars, in seconds) for running the selected benchmarks through the run-time tool. Each bar represents a different benchmark and a different set of experiments. The _lint suffix represents the case of running the benchmark without the aid of the compile-time tool, but using the lint directive to manually annotate calls to third-party libraries. The _autolint suffix represents the case of running the

---

[3] Although our tool targets the AMD64 instruction set, this does not limit the scope of our work as it can be easily ported to other ISA and processor models.

[4] A comprehensive evaluation of the accuracy of our toolchain will be provided in a subsequent study.

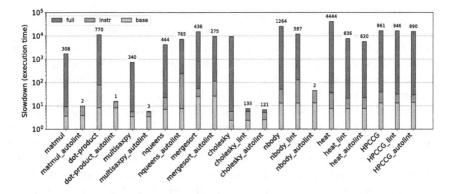

Fig. 1. Slowdown (y-axis) and absolute execution time (numbers on top of bars, in seconds) for the selected benchmarks.

benchmark with the aid of the compile-time tool, which places additional `lint` directives (if possible) around regions of verified code. The absence of a suffix means that the benchmark is run without the aid of the compile-time tool or `lint` directives. For each bar, we also report a breakdown of the slowdown, split into three different contributions: (a) the instrumentation cost to run the application using Pin (the `base` label in the legend); (b) the instrumentation cost to actually instrument memory instructions, without processing them (the `instr` label); (c) the full instrumentation + processing cost (the `full` label in the legend).

As we can see from the figure, the slowdown for the pure runtime instrumentation case (no suffix) can be quite high for some benchmarks (e.g., *dot-product* or *mergesort*). In the case of *cholesky*, the overhead is considerably high due to the heavy use it makes of Intel's MKL library. It is reported with a truncated bar and no number on top because it exceeded the maximum time allocation for a single job (two days). We conducted an extended analysis of these cases and detected the major source of overhead to be the insertion of accesses in an ad-hoc interval tree, used to aggregate contiguous accesses coming from the same instruction over time and compare them with task dependencies. Although we intend to develop a more efficient implementation for this data structure, we are still bound to pay the instrumentation cost depicted in the `base` and `instr` cases. Nevertheless, we think that the observed slowdown doesn't limit the effectiveness of our tools. Except for *cholesky*, we note that the absolute execution time of all the instrumented benchmarks is in the order of minutes, thus not undermining the toolchain's usability. Moreover, using larger input sizes is often unnecessary. In many task-based HPC applications (which are well-represented by the benchmarks we use), a change in the input size typically has a considerable impact on *how many* tasks are executed, rather than *which* types of tasks. Even when it substantially modifies the control flow at run-time (e.g., by activating different tasks, or code paths inside tasks), these variations could have been stimulated already with smaller input sizes.

In all those cases in which it is necessary to test an application with large or production-level inputs, we can exploit the lint and verified annotations to focus the analysis only on the specific code activated by those inputs. This approach makes our toolchain more effective because it allows us to spare the tracing overhead on the parts that could be tested with smaller inputs. In our experiments, the improvements in terms of the slowdown in the lint case were often significant. By appropriately marking calls to external libraries with verification annotations, the run-time instrumentation tool only intercepts a number of accesses that are proportional to the number of data-references specified in the in, out, or inout parameters of the pragma itself. This aspect is critical for the case of *cholesky*, as each task only performs a single call to a function in the MKL library, but those calls internally perform a huge number of accesses to memory that are the main source of overhead. Improvements can also be observed for the case of MPI benchmarks, which use the Intel MPI library, although the impact tends to be smaller than that observed in the previous benchmarks. For example, while *heat* is communication-intensive and so protecting calls to MPI is highly effective, *nbody* and *HPCCG* are computation-intensive. Therefore, the use of pragmas doesn't improve the execution overhead by much.

The autolint case brings the most evident benefits, as it can be seen for *matmul, dot-product,* and *multisaxpy*. In this case, the compile-time tool can automatically wrap whole for-loop cycles into pragmas, or even mark whole tasks within loops as verified. In all these cases, the performance improvements are drastic because the instrumentation tool can disable tracing during most of the application's execution time. We note that these improvements are not uncommon for real-world scenarios, as many kernels have a regular loop structure, which can be easily analyzed using techniques like those mentioned in Sect. 4.2. The case of *nqueens* is peculiar because it internally uses recursion. In this case, the compile-tool is unable to recognize this execution pattern and ends up marking each memory-accessing statement independently. The net effect of this is a deterioration of the run-time overhead, compared to when the compile-time tool is disabled. Similar considerations can be made for the MPI benchmarks and especially for *HPCCG*, where the main kernel performing an MKL-like *dgemm* operation couldn't be annotated at all because a sparse matrix representation is internally used. As for *cholesky*, we observe that each task only performs a single call to an MKL library function. Thus, the compile-time tool can successfully promote the manual lint directives to verified clauses at the level of tasks. However, this brings little additional benefits compared to the lint case.

Overall, our experimental evaluation suggests that the absolute execution cost of running the selected applications against the toolchain is affordable. Furthermore, the synergistic exploitation of compile-time analysis and verification annotations can drastically reduce this cost.

6   Related Work

The strategies for verifying the parallelization of applications can be classified in static tools, which analyze the code at compile-time, and dynamic tools, which analyze the code at run-time. As for the fork-join part of OpenMP, there are static solutions focused on the polyhedral model to detect errors in OpenMP parallel loops [5], or on symbolic analysis and Satisfiability Modulo Theories (SMT) to detect data races and deadlocks [14]. A more general solution is provided by Lin [12], who described a control flow graph and a region tree to statically detect non-concurrent blocks of code and race conditions in OpenMP2.5 programs with the Sun Studio 9 Fortran compiler. Techniques to detect synchronization issues in task-based OpenMP programs also exist and are focused on race conditions that may produce non-deterministic output and run-time failures [18]. In concurrent models based on tasking such as Ada, there have been efforts to introduce model checking techniques at compile-time [1]. However, although these techniques are very mature, their usefulness depends on contracts that are written by programmers, hence are liable to have errors. For the dynamic detection of parallelization errors, most of the literature is focused on tools that check for data and determinacy races, using the Happens-Before (HB) relation to detect if two memory accesses are concurrent [11,19]. Archer [3] adapts ThreadSanitizer, which can detect data races in unstructured parallel programs, to the case of basic OpenMP tasking with no dependencies. It employs a static phase to discard all sequential code, and a dynamic phase to check for data races in the remaining concurrent parts. Sword [4] is a tool that is capable of detecting all and only data races in OpenMP programs comprised of nested fork-join parallelism (i.e., `parallel` constructs). TaskSanitizer [15] is a tool that detects determinacy races in task-parallel OpenMP programs by computing the HB relation on tasks. ROMP is another tool targeting OpenMP with tasking [10]. It uses an approach close to Sword to build the HB relation for nested fork-join parallelism parts, and one similar to TaskSanitizer for the HB relation of tasks with dependencies. StarSscheck [6] is a run-time tool to detect parallelization errors commonly occurring in StarSs applications (task dependencies without nesting).

Our approach significantly differs from the ones adopted by the above works. First of all, we don't explicitly check for correctness errors. Our tools look for compliance errors, which may affect both correctness and performance. The detection of such errors is based on a programmatic approach that is compatible with the OmpSs-2 programming model, but that can be ported to all task-based programming models satisfying the properties in Sect. 3. To this extent, our analysis is also different. Being always local to a task, it only compares accesses and data references of a task with other data references. In comparison, algorithms built around the HB relation directly compare accesses from a task with accesses from another task, thus having to perform a number of comparisons that, in principle, can be quite higher than LTA. Lastly, to improve the overall accuracy and overhead of detection, our toolchain combines the best of static and dynamic techniques with the proposal of verification annotations, which are used as an abstract interface between the user, the compile-time tool, and the run-time tool.

7   Conclusions and Future Work

We have presented a toolchain to detect parallelization errors in applications using OmpSs-2, a task-based parallel programming model. Our toolchain is composed of a compile-time tool that analyzes source code, and a run-time tool that analyzes binary code. The outcome of our toolchain is a report which informs the user about compliance errors of OmpSs-2 applications. Our tools only perform local task analysis of code, i.e., independently for each task. Because of the way the OmpSs-2 programming model is defined, we can evaluate the compliance with the model for each task and then infer it for the whole program. We have also introduced verification annotations to mark specific code regions as verified. Our compile-time and run-time analysis tools can safely ignore the code inside these regions. At the same time, they can also be informed about any relevant access performed within verified code regions. Thanks to these annotations, we can improve both the performance and accuracy of the analysis. Experiments run on a series of benchmarks varying from simple execution kernels to real-world applications suggest that our tools can effectively analyze a wide range of applications with acceptable overhead. Future work is aimed at improving our analysis to detect inefficient parallelization constructs and suggesting the use of more efficient ones.

Acknowledgments and Data Availability Statement. This project is supported by the European Union's Horizon 2021 research and innovation programme under grant agreement No 754304 (DEEP-EST), by the European Union's Horizon 2020 research and innovation programme under grant agreement No 871669 (AMPERE) and the Project HPC-EUROPA3 (INFRAIA-2016-1-730897), by the Ministry of Economy of Spain through the Severo Ochoa Center of Excellence Program (SEV-2015-0493), by the Spanish Ministry of Science and Innovation (contract TIN2015-65316-P), and by the Generalitat de Catalunya (2017-SGR-1481).

The datasets and code generated during and/or analysed during the current study are available in the Figshare repository: https://doi.org/10.6084/m9.figshare. 12605180 [8].

References

1. AdaCore, Altran, Astrium Space Transportation, CEA-LIST, ProVal at INRIA and Thales Communications: Project Hi-Lite: GNATprove (2017). http://www.open-do.org/projects/hi-lite/gnatprove
2. Arb: OpenMP specification v5.0 (2018). https://www.openmp.org/wp-content/uploads/OpenMP-API-Specification-5.0.pdf
3. Atzeni, S., et al.: ARCHER: effectively spotting data races in large OpenMP applications. In: 2016 IEEE International Parallel and Distributed Processing Symposium (IPDPS), pp. 53–62 (2016)
4. Atzeni, S., Gopalakrishnan, G., Rakamaric, Z., Laguna, I., Lee, G.L., Ahn, D.H.: SWORD: a bounded memory-overhead detector of OpenMP data races in production runs. In: 2018 IEEE International Parallel and Distributed Processing Symposium (IPDPS), pp. 845–854 (2018)

5. Basupalli, V., et al.: ompVerify: polyhedral analysis for the OpenMP programmer. In: Chapman, B.M., Gropp, W.D., Kumaran, K., Müller, M.S. (eds.) IWOMP 2011. LNCS, vol. 6665, pp. 37–53. Springer, Heidelberg (2011). https://doi.org/10.1007/978-3-642-21487-5_4
6. Carpenter, P.M., Ramirez, A., Ayguade, E.: Starsscheck: a tool to find errors in task-based parallel programs. In: D'Ambra, P., Guarracino, M., Talia, D. (eds.) Euro-Par 2010. LNCS, vol. 6271, pp. 2–13. Springer, Heidelberg (2010). https://doi.org/10.1007/978-3-642-15277-1_2
7. Economo, S.: Techniques and tools for program tracing and analysis with applications to parallel programming. Ph.D. thesis, Sapienza Università di Roma (2020)
8. Economo, S., Royuela, S., Ayguadé, E., Beltran, V.: Artifact and instructions to generate experimental results for the conference proceeding 2020 paper: a Toolchain to Verify the Parallelization of OmpSs-2 Applications, July 2020. https://doi.org/10.6084/m9.figshare.12605180
9. Ferrer, R., Royuela, S., Caballero, D., Duran, A., Martorell, X., Ayguadé, E.: Mercurium: design decisions for a S2S compiler. In: Cetus Users and Compiler Infrastructure Workshop in Conjunction with PACT (2011)
10. Gu, Y., Mellor-Crummey, J.: Dynamic data race detection for OpenMP programs. In: Proceedings of the International Conference for High Performance Computing, Networking, Storage, and Analysis, SC 2018. IEEE Press (2018)
11. Jannesari, A., Bao, K., Pankratius, V., Tichy, W.F.: Helgrind+: an efficient dynamic race detector. In: 2009 IEEE International Symposium on Parallel Distributed Processing, pp. 1–13, May 2009
12. Lin, Y.: Static nonconcurrency analysis of OpenMP programs. In: Mueller, M.S., Chapman, B.M., de Supinski, B.R., Malony, A.D., Voss, M. (eds.) IWOMP -2005. LNCS, vol. 4315, pp. 36–50. Springer, Heidelberg (2008). https://doi.org/10.1007/978-3-540-68555-5_4
13. Luk, C.K., et al.: Pin: building customized program analysis tools with dynamic instrumentation. In: Proceedings of the 2005 ACM SIGPLAN Conference on Programming Language Design and Implementation, PLDI 2005, pp. 190–200. Association for Computing Machinery (2005)
14. Ma, H., Diersen, S.R., Wang, L., Liao, C., Quinlan, D., Yang, Z.: Symbolic analysis of concurrency errors in OpenMP programs. In: 2013 42nd International Conference on Parallel Processing, pp. 510–516 (2013)
15. Matar, H.S., Unat, D.: Runtime determinacy race detection for OpenMP tasks. In: Aldinucci, M., Padovani, L., Torquati, M. (eds.) Euro-Par 2018. LNCS, vol. 11014, pp. 31–45. Springer, Cham (2018). https://doi.org/10.1007/978-3-319-96983-1_3
16. Perez, J.M., Beltran, V., Labarta, J., Ayguadé, E.: Improving the integration of task nesting and dependencies in OpenMP. In: 2017 IEEE International Parallel and Distributed Processing Symposium (IPDPS), pp. 809–818 (2017)
17. Reinders, J.: Intel Threading Building Blocks - Outfitting C++ for Multi-Core Processor Parallelism. O'Reilly Media (2007)
18. Royuela, S., Ferrer, R., Caballero, D., Martorell, X.: Compiler analysis for OpenMP tasks correctness. In: Computing Frontiers. ACM (2015)
19. Serebryany, K., Iskhodzhanov, T.: ThreadSanitizer: data race detection in practice. In: Proceedings of the Workshop on Binary Instrumentation and Applications, WBIA 2009, pp. 62–71. Association for Computing Machinery (2009)

Performance and Power Modeling, Prediction and Evaluation

Towards a Model to Estimate the Reliability of Large-Scale Hybrid Supercomputers

Elvis Rojas[1,2(✉)], Esteban Meneses[2,3(✉)], Terry Jones[4(✉)],
and Don Maxwell[4(✉)]

[1] National University of Costa Rica, San José, Costa Rica
erojas@una.ac.cr
[2] Costa Rica Institute of Technology, Cartago, Costa Rica
emeneses@cenat.ac.cr
[3] Costa Rica National High Technology Center, San José, Costa Rica
[4] Oak Ridge National Laboratory, Oak Ridge, TN, USA
{trjones,maxwellde}@ornl.gov

Abstract. Supercomputers stand as a fundamental tool for developing our understanding of the universe. State-of-the-art scientific simulations, big data analyses, and machine learning executions require high performance computing platforms. Such infrastructures have been growing lately with the addition of thousands of newly designed components, calling their resiliency into question. It is crucial to solidify our knowledge on the way supercomputers fail. Other recent studies have highlighted the importance of characterizing failures on supercomputers. This paper aims at modelling component failures of a supercomputer based on Mixed Weibull distributions. The model is built using a real-life multiyear failure record from a leadership-class supercomputer. Using several key observations from the data, we designed an analytical model that is robust enough to represent each of the main components of supercomputers, yet it is flexible enough to alter the composition of the machine and be able to predict resilience of future or hypothetical systems.

Keywords: Fault tolerance · Resilience · Failure analysis · Failure modelling

Notice: This manuscript has been authored by UT-Battelle, LLC under Contract No. DE-AC05-00OR22725 with the U.S. Department of Energy. The United States Government retains and the publisher, by accepting the article for publication, acknowledges that the United States Government retains a non-exclusive, paid-up, irrevocable, worldwide license to publish or reproduce the published form of this manuscript, or allow others to do so, for United States Government purposes. The Department of Energy will provide public access to these results of federally sponsored research in accordance with the DOE Public Access Plan (http://energy.gov/downloads/doe-public-access-plan).

© Springer Nature Switzerland AG 2020
M. Malawski and K. Rzadca (Eds.): Euro-Par 2020, LNCS 12247, pp. 37–51, 2020.
https://doi.org/10.1007/978-3-030-57675-2_3

1   Introduction

Large-scale machines provide a valuable tool to push the envelope in many scientific disciplines. From unveiling the mysteries of the universe formation to making sense of the myriad data in the global economy, supercomputers are indispensable. Getting more powerful every year, supercomputers barely keep up with the insatiable need for computing in scientific simulations and data analysis. To maintain the required growth in computing power, hardware engineers have employed increasingly complex and heterogeneous designs. Modern supercomputers assemble an immense amount of processors, accelerators, memory modules, and more parts. The inevitable consequence of such arrangement is a threateningly high failure rate [21, 22]. Therefore, it is mandatory to understand the reliability of supercomputers to sustain the rate of scientific discovery.

The last decade has seen several meetings, studies, and reports about supercomputer reliability [3, 21, 22]. An inter-agency report [21] found that one high priority area was *fault characterization*. As technologies become more complex to provide high scalability, reliability becomes more difficult. Therefore, it is crucial to describe failure types along with their frequency and impact. A meeting on failures at exascale level computing [22] also highlighted the importance of such characterization, but insisted on building strong statistical models for failure analysis and the development of fault tolerant algorithms. Finally, other study [3] recommended exploring future failure characterization paradigms to guide the selection of hardware components for future machines. This paper addresses the concerns of the community by providing a reliability model for supercomputers based on the failure characterization of hardware components.

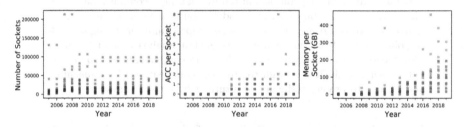

Fig. 1. Features in recent supercomputers. The top 20 supercomputers from the last 15 years show the number of processor sockets has stagnated, but accelerators and memory size per socket continues to increase.

We focus our model on the study of failure rates of three components: processors, accelerators, and memory. Figure 1 shows a historical view of the integration of these components on the top 20 machines of the Top 500 list [25] for the last 15 years. The left part shows the number of processor sockets in each machine. That number increased initially, but stagnated at around 100,000 sockets. However, the number of accelerators per socket has been on the rise, as depicted by the middle figure. The memory size per socket has swelled at a faster pace.

Here then is a list of the contributions of this paper:

- A collection of insights on a five-year failure record of a leadership-class super-computer is provided in Sect. 2. One of these findings include the trends or epochs in the failure data, automatically detected by an algorithm.
- A whole-system failure model using Mixed Weibull distributions in Sect. 3. Our model outperforms the traditional Weibull distribution and allows the representation of different configurations according to the prominence of a component in the machine: processors, accelerators, or memory.
- Failure rate predictions for different hypothetical exascale machine configurations in Sect. 3.2. Such projections are correlated with power consumption of each configuration to understand the trade-offs between performance and energy.

1.1 Related Work

Several studies have analyzed the behavior of failures in large-scale systems [3–5,11,12,16,18,19,29], including studies that analyzed failures of specific super-computer components such as GPU [15,23,24] or memory [1,10,20]. This paper also analyzes large-scale system failures, but with the distinctive focus on building a reliability model to understand and project system behavior.

The literature contains studies of modelling the reliability of large-scale systems. In [9], the authors used modelling to examine the impact of failure distributions on application performance. They used the *flexible checkpoint model* (FCM) to determine the application execution time and the optimal checkpoint interval. In [27], the authors developed performance models to predict the application completion time under system failures. Another modelling study [14] analyzed failure traces from five large multi-site infrastructures to model failures and generate failure scenarios. Other researchers modelled the failure behavior using signal analysis theory [6]. They characterized each signal and proposed corresponding models, merging all the information to offer an overview of the whole system. In [7,28], the failure correlation in time and space was analyzed. The time-varying behavior of failures was modelled focused on peak failure periods. The authors characterized the duration of peaks, the peak inter-arrival time, and the duration of failures during peaks. Regarding the space-correlated failures, the model considered groups of failures that occur within a short time interval. With modelling, they found that space correlated failures are dominant in terms of resource downtime in seven of the analyzed systems.

Similar to this paper, all those previous studies have concentrated on modelling failures in large-scale systems. Modelling was used for the following purposes: analyze correlations, predict execution times, compute optimal checkpoint intervals, and analyze performance optimizations. In this paper, we analyze and classify the system failures by component. Based on that, we model failures based on the Mixed Weibull distribution to finally make reliability projections using different system configurations. This paper differs both in the approach and the purpose of modelling. Almost all studies used small datasets with under 1.5 years or hypothetical extreme-scale systems [9]. We base our results on real-life data from a 5-year failure record from a leadership-class supercomputer.

Another study on modelling failures was described in [8]. They analyzed five years of system logs to model hardware failures of multiple heterogeneous components. They modelled each component and developed integrated failure models given the component usage. They divided the event data into epochs due to missing data in the event log. Before the modelling stage, a statistical analysis of failures was performed. That modelling study differs from our work in multiple dimensions: we analyzed a failure dataset of five consecutive years of a modern hybrid supercomputer, we automatically determined epochs using a time series analysis algorithm, the reliability model was implemented using Mixed Weibull distributions, and we presented a series of failure projections based on different hardware configurations.

In our previous work [13,17], we developed the process to ingest the raw failure data and derive human understandable information from the Titan failure set. In this work, we introduce an analysis that reveals distinctive epochs of failure rates; we delve into these epochs and uncover a number of interesting observations peculiar to each; and, most importantly, we introduce a new mathematical model that is shown to categorize failures more accurately than other proposed models as determined by the Kolmogorov-Smirnov goodness of fit test.

2   Insights from a Real-Life Hybrid Supercomputer

2.1   Failure Dataset

We analyzed failure events from Titan supercomputer. Titan was a Cray XK7 system located at the Oak Ridge Leadership Computing Facility (OLCF) and was one of the earliest supercomputers that used a hybrid architecture (CPU and GPU). It had 18,688 nodes and each node had an AMD 16-core Opteron CPU (299,008 cores in the whole system), an NVIDIA Tesla K20 GPU and 32 GB of main memory. Titan had a peak performance of 17.59 petaFLOPs and by the time it was decommissioned, it was in the ninth position according to the Top500 ranking [25]. Every abnormal incident on Titan was automatically registered into a failure database. The database was automatically constructed by a program designed by the system administrators that used the SEC (simple event correlator) program [26]. Using correlation rules, SEC analyzes output streams from each node and merges multiple reports of the same incident into a single database entry.

In this work, we analyzed five full years of failure events on Titan from 2014 to 2018. In this five-year span, the total number of events in the failure database was 2,663,512. After a filtering stage, the number of events in the failure database was dramatically reduced by 99.78%. The remaining 0.22% of events correspond to what we describe as 5654 *unique failures*, distributed as 565, 649, 1824, 1291, and 1325 events for years 2014–2018, respectively. This massive reduction in the event database is due to the presence of multiple redundant messages and warnings for the same failure.

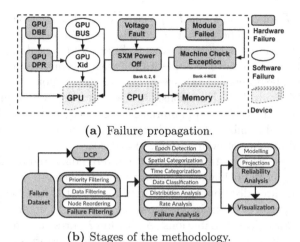

(a) Failure propagation.

(b) Stages of the methodology.

```
Input: data[] // failure data time series
Input: N // epoch granularity
Output: epochs[] // list of meaningful epochs
1 data_ema[] ← Compute_EMA(data[]) // computing exponential moving average
2 data_signals[] ← Compute_B&B(data_ema[], data[]) // computing bull&bear signals
3 fragments[] ← Compute_fragments(data_signals[]) // computing epoch fragments
4 segments[] ← Compute_segments(fragments[],N) // computing epoch segments
  // computing linear trend of each segment
5 foreach s ∈ segments[] do
6     e ← Extract_epoch(data[],s) // extracting original epoch values from data
7     line ← Compute_linear_fit(e) // compute least squares linear fit
8     epochs[] ← epochs[] ∪ {e,line} // adding new epoch
9 end
```

(c) Algorithm to detect trends in time series.

Fig. 2. Data analysis methodology.

Figure 2a shows this redundancy as the cause-effect dependency of events on the database. These are potential dependencies because in some cases an event can occur in isolation without the occurrence of the preceding event in the graph. For instance, a GPU DBE (double bit error) failure may generate a GPU DPR (double page retirement) failure and then a GPU XID failure (a general software GPU error). In that case, the filtering process only considers the failure with the highest priority (i.e. GPU DBE) and discards the other derived failures. Nevertheless, in some cases, the GPU XID or GPU DPR failures can be generated in isolation. Relevant data on discarded failures is attached to the highest priority failure, to avoid losing information. Figure 2a shows three types of hardware components (GPU, CPU, and memory) and how these components might be affected by system failures.

2.2 Methodology

Figure 2b summarizes the stages of the methodology, implemented as a collection of Python scripts and available at https://github.com/elvinrz/FailureAnalysis.

The first stage, *Data cleaning and Preprocessing (DCP)*, prepares all input files in a consistent format. The second stage, *Failure Filtering*, takes the preprocessed data and performs a series of tasks to filter redundant data. The priority filtering task is used to remove redundant data with less priority or that depends on other events. The others two tasks were used to remove non-significant events, such as heartbeat faults, which are considered as warnings by system administrators. This paper focuses on system failures only. Consequently, user failures were discarded. The total number of user failures removed was 816,826, representing 30% of the total number of events from 2014 to 2018.

The third stage, *Failure Analysis*, uses the filtered data and performs a series of analysis to model the behavior of failure events in the system. We performed data fitting with three distributions (Weibull, Exponential and Lognormal) and we used the Kolmogorov-Smirnov Goodness of Fit Test to determine how close the data fits a statistical distributions. Algorithm 2c presents an adjusted procedure to model the time series trends. The algorithm performs an exponential moving average (EMA) and it uses a least squares polynomial fit to calculate the trend segments. The algorithm outputs trends of failures event segments throughout the years. Therefore, we are able to automatically detect epochs in the data.

The *Reliability Analysis* stage is used to describe the background of the statistical model that was used in this study. We implemented the Mixed Weibull distribution to analyze real and synthetic failure data. In addition, Mixed Weibull distributions were used to perform a series of projections when changing the proportion of the system components (CPU, GPU and memory) to determine the reliability and the power consumption of exascale machines. The *Visualization* stage displays the results of the previous analyses. We plot all necessary visualizations to show categorizations, correlations, and probability distributions.

2.3   Insights

Observation #1: *Most system failures in Titan are processor, accelerator, or memory related.* Table 1 shows the failure distribution of hardware components according to failure classification on Fig. 2a. The failures related to processor, accelerator, and memory represent 92.45% of all failures.

Table 1. Failure count by category and epochs.

Category	Type	E1	E2	E3	E4	%
GPU	XID, DBE, BUS, DPR, SXM P. Off	933	834	1291	1508	80.87
CPU	Machine Check Excep. (Bank 0, 2, 6)	33	9	5	14	1.11
Memory	Machine Check Excep. (Bank 4, MCE)	214	80	124	173	10.49
Total						92.45

Observation #2: *GPU failures are dominant, particularly those associated to GPU memory.* Table 1 shows that 80.87% of all failures are related to GPU. The share of GPU memory failures (DBE, DPR) from the total amount is 52.08%.

Observation #3: *The time series of GPU failures can be divided into four distinctive epochs.* Figure 3 shows the result of using Algorithm 2c on the failure time series of three hardware components. The GPU time series presents four epochs: three blue segments representing a trend to increase failure rate and a single orange segment representing the decrease of failure events. This result is a refinement of a previous composition manually made by experts using the same data [17].

Observation #4: *The time series of processor and memory failures have a single epoch.* The result of applying Algorithm 2c to the CPU and memory failure time series reveals only one epoch for each. Figure 3 depicts this result.

Observation #5: *Epochs 2 and 3 on GPU failure time series reflect abnormal behavior of hardware components.* Table 1 reports the number of GPU failures in each epoch. Epochs 2 and 3 together are composed of 63 weeks (24.23% of total weeks) and contain 46.53% of the GPU failures. In contrast, Epoch 1 is composed of 42% of total weeks and only has 20.4% of GPU failures. Epoch 4 has a similar behavior as Epoch 1. According to the system administrators of Titan, epochs 2 and 3 represent abnormal behavior due to a massive failure of GPU components (Epoch 2) and the replacement of those parts (Epoch 3).

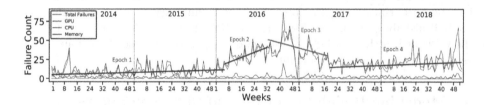

Fig. 3. Failure time series 2014–2018 for the three main hardware components.

Observation #6: *Hardware component failures are statistically independent.* We tested the possible dependence between failures of different hardware components. Figure 2a shows the failure categorization by component. Using a time window of 300 s, we counted if there was a couple of events from different components in the same time window. This analysis was performed before the filtering process to take into account all events of interest (heartbeat faults and user failures were excluded). The results show the total number of correlated failures is 25 out of 5218 total failures. Such a minute portion statistically rules out any correlation and, as a consequence, any dependence.

Observation #7: *Time between failures of processor and memory components follows a Weibull distribution.* We studied the *Cumulative Distribution Function*

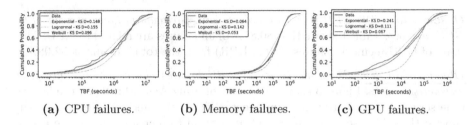

(a) CPU failures.   (b) Memory failures.   (c) GPU failures.

Fig. 4. Cumulative distribution function for CPU, memory, and GPU failures.

(CDF) of the MTBF data. Three different distributions were tested (exponential, lognormal and Weibull). We used the *Kolmogorov-Smirnov Goodness of Fit Test (KST)* to determine which distribution better models the MTBF data. For CPU and memory components, we used the four epochs to perform the distribution analysis because the failures of these two components were significantly less than the GPU failures. Figure 4 shows the CDF of the three components, and we see that the *Weibull* distribution fits better the MTBF data than *LogNormal* and *Exponential* distributions. Low D values resulting from the KST represent a better fit. In all cases the KST of the *Weibull* distribution was the smallest with values of D equals to 0.096 for the CPU, and 0.053 for the memory. We do not reject the null hypothesis (the data comes from a specific distribution) because the computed D values were lower than the critical values.

Observation #8: *Time between GPU failures follows a Weibull distribution.* For the GPU time series, the four epochs were analyzed and in all epochs the Weibull distribution was the best fit. The KST test resulted in $D = 0.067$ for the GPU at Epoch 1. In light of Observation #5, for the rest of the paper, we use only Epoch 1 data for modelling.

3   Modelling Reliability of Hybrid Supercomputers

3.1   Analytical Model

The theory of reliability provides a rich framework to study, analyze, and model failure data from supercomputers. In the literature, the mean-time-between-failures (MTBF) is a popular metric to describe the reliability of large-scale machines [3,21,22]. To find such value, it is necessary to develop a model. The *reliability function* is the most frequently used function to perform life data analysis. It provides the probability of a component functioning with no failure for an amount of time. It is a function of time and a flexible way to derive the MTBF of a system. A key element to build a precise reliability function for a system is to find an appropriate distribution function for life data analysis. For instance, finding a distribution function for the probability of a component failing at time t. Let us call $f(x)$ this distribution function. Using $f(x)$, we compute $U(t) = \int_0^t f(s)ds$ as the probability of a component failing by time t.

Function $U(t)$ is called the *unreliability function* and it is basically the cumulative distribution function of $f(x)$. Finally, the reliability function $R(t)$ can be derived using $U(t) + R(t) = 1$. In the rest of the paper, we concentrate on finding a function $f(x)$ that best fits the data and provides a precise reliability function for the system. The literature shows that Weibull distribution is a good fit for supercomputer reliability data on time between failures [17,19,24]. The Weibull probability distribution function is given by $f(x; \alpha, \beta) = \frac{\alpha x^{\alpha-1}}{\beta^\alpha} e^{-(\frac{x}{\beta})^\alpha}$, where α is the *shape* parameter and β is the *scale* parameter. A value of $\alpha < 1$ points to a decreasing failure rate, $\alpha = 1$ means the failure rate is constant (in which case the Weibull distribution equals an Exponential distribution), and $\alpha > 1$ indicates an increasing failure rate. The scale parameter β represents how spread out the distribution is.

Although a Weibull distribution may adequately capture the failure data of *all components* in a supercomputer, it may fall short for modelling scenarios where the behavior of the components differ from one another. For instance, Sect. 2 presented a case where several components show different failure profiles. For those cases, we may resort to a refined probability function, called a Mixed Weibull (or Mixture Weibull) function and defined as:

$$f(x) = w_1 f_1(x) + w_2 f_2(x) + ... + w_n f_n(x) \tag{1}$$

with $w_i > 0$ and $\sum_{i=1}^{n} w_i = 1$. Each f_i is a Weibull distribution function and represents an independent population. Consequently, Eq. 1 models a system where failures come from different, independent families and it becomes an appropriate framework to represent failures of components in a supercomputer, given Observation #6 from Sect. 2. Mixed Weibull models are a better fit for the failure data of supercomputers. Figure 5 shows a comparison of a single Weibull function versus a Mixed Weibull function in fitting the failure data from Epoch 1 of all components of Titan. Figure 5a presents how well the two alternatives fit the failure data using the KST test. The Mixed Weibull models performs better than the single Weibull function, which can be seen in the probability plot of Fig. 5b. We propose using a Mixed Weibull distribution function to model the failures in a supercomputer:

$$f(x) = w_{GPU} f_{GPU}(x) + w_{CPU} f_{CPU}(x) + w_{MEM} f_{MEM}(x) \tag{2}$$

with $w_{GPU} + w_{CPU} + w_{MEM} = 1$. Values for w_i in Eq. 2 will depend on the actual proportion of failure of each component in the supercomputer. To validate our premises, Table 2 presents the results of an algorithm that automatically finds components of a Mixed Weibull distribution on a collection of data assuming there are 3 independent sources of failures. We can see how closely such results match the real proportions of the components.

Table 2. Mixed Weibull and 2P Weibull.

Distribution	Component	Shape	Scale	MTBF (Hours)	Estimate proportion	Real proportion
3 Mixture Weibull	1	0.871	1208	15.66	0.208	0.181
	2	0.934	59666		0.7544	0.791
	3	2.778	289484		0.0376	0.028
Weibull 2P	cpu, gpu, mem	0.62	40634.57	16.33		

3.2 Extreme-Scale Projections

We use Eq. 2 to estimate MTBF values of exascale systems and contrast those values with their corresponding power consumption. We developed different supercomputer configurations taking into account three components: processor, accelerator, and memory. The proportion of these components was varied to reach exascale performance.

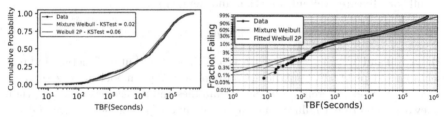

(a) Mixture and 2P Weibull CDF.   (b) Mixture and 2P Weibull probability plot.

Fig. 5. Epoch 1 statistical analysis. We chose Epoch 1 for modelling failures of Titan supercomputer, since Epoch 1 represents an expected failure behavior according to the system administrator. However, the same analysis could have been done using any other epoch.

Assumptions. The previous model analysis of this paper was made with failure data of Titan supercomputer (Epoch 1). The failure data was generated from an AMD 16-core Opteron CPU, an NVIDIA Tesla K20 GPU, and 32 GB of main memory. Nevertheless, to make realistic projections, we updated the CPU and GPU components to the actual time. We used the specifications of the AMD Epyc 7742 and the NVIDIA V100 that have 2.3 TFlops of performance, 225 W TDP and 7.8 TFlops of performance and 250 W TDP respectively. Regarding memory, we only multiply the amount of RAM by a factor depending on the projection.

To project the power consumption of an exascale machine, we considered the power draw of processors and accelerators. These components and the memory determine the maximum power required by a subsystem. Currently, the maximum power consumption of a supercomputer or HPC system is determined by the sum of the power of its subsystems [2]. Nevertheless, we did not take into consideration the memory power in the projections for its relatively low power consumption. Also, cooling, network, and storage power consumption was left out of the power projections.

Size and Failure Data. All the projections were made based on failure data of Epoch 1 (from January 2014 to February 2016) produced by the CPU (32 failures), GPU(930 failures) and memory (213 failures) components. The failure data of Epoch 1 was the result of the execution of 18,688 nodes with a proportion of 1:1:1(1 GPU:1 CPU:32 GB RAM). For that reason, if we wanted to model a different component proportion we needed to generate synthetic data. The synthetic data was randomly generated for each component, but based on the Weibull shape and scale of the real data to ensure the same failure behavior. To determine the total number of failures (ϕ) required to perform the projections we used the following equation $\phi = \sum_{i=1}^{K}(\pi_i * \delta_i * s * \frac{1}{N})$, where K is the total number of hardware components, π_i is the proportion of component i, δ_i is the number of failures of component i and N is the total number of nodes on a real HPC system. Note that inside the equation the number of sockets s of the new projected system is calculated as $\frac{1\ exaflop}{\sum_{j=1}^{K}(\tau_j * \pi_j)}$, where τ_j is the number of teraflops of component j.

Reliability Measure. We used the MTBF as a metric to measure the system reliability. The system MTBF was calculated based on the mean Weibull and the proportion of the total failure data of each component population. The MTBF values were calculated as the mean of performing 100 times each experiment. Systems with low MTBF are less reliable.

Projections. We developed a series of exascale supercomputer projections varying the component proportions. Tables 3 and 4 show two experiments. One experiment only shows the change of the GPU proportion and the other shows the result of changing the proportion of the three components. We see in Table 3 that when increasing the number of GPUs the MTBF decreases. This is a normal behavior considering that we were increasing the component with the highest failure rate. Titan supercomputer in Epoch 1 had an MTBF of 42.3 h with the proportion 1:1:1 and the same proportion of an exascale machine has 9.98 h. Nevertheless, Titan only had 0.027 exaflops relative to the projected exascale machine. Regarding the power consumption, we see that the simplest proportion (1:1:1) has the highest power consumption because to reach exascale performance it is necessary to use 99,010 sockets. Also, note that with the increase of GPUs the power decreases. Comparing the projection (3:1:1) with real life, we can use Summit supercomputer that has the same component proportion (6 GPUs and 2 CPUs). At this time Summit is the fastest supercomputer in the world according to the Top500 list [25], and has a power consumption of 10 KW with 200 petaFLOPs of performance. We can assume that Summit could reach exascale performance with a size five times larger and this could increase the power consumption to 50 KW that is 24% more than the projected power consumption. Finally, it is important to remark that each of the proportions corresponds to real supercomputers: Titan (1:1:1), ABCI (2:1:1), Summit (3:1:1) and Lassen (4:1:1). All those supercomputers are listed on the records of the Top500 list [25].

Table 3. Projections changing the GPU proportion.

Proportion (gpu:cpu:mem)	Sockets	Data proportion (gpu:cpu:mem)	Total failures	MTBF (Hours)	CPU TDP (KW)	GPU TDP (KW)	System TDP (KW)
1:1:1	99010	5.3:5.3:5.3	6228	9.98	22277	24753	47030
2:1:1	55866	6:3:3	6315	9.52	12570	27933	40503
3:1:1	38911	6.3:2.1:2.1	6373	9.36	8755	29183	37938
4:1:1	29851	6.4:1.6:1.6	6344	8.97	6716	29851	36567

Table 4 shows other possible configurations. Although this study was focused on hybrid supercomputers, we also made one projection without GPU with the proportion 0:1:1. This proportion corresponds to Tianhe-2A supercomputer that has only Intel Xeon E5 CPUs. This projection needed 77% more sockets regarding the projection with one GPU (1:1:1), 52% more power consumption and the system reliability decrease with an MTBF of 8.06. This projection can give us an idea of how beneficial could be to implement supercomputers with at least one GPU per CPU. With projections 1:2:1 and 3:1:2 we see how the system can be with more CPUs and memory, respectively. Note that with the proportion with more CPUs the best obtained MTBF value was 12.06. The worst MTBF value was obtained with many GPUs (8:1:1). Such configuration also brings the best power consumption. Also, the memory size increase decreases the system reliability.

As a result of the projections we can conclude that hybrid supercomputers are a good solution to reach exascale performance. Hybrid supercomputers need less hardware and the power consumption is remarkably less than supercomputers without GPUs. Nevertheless, it is necessary to take into consideration that the system reliability could be affected by the increase in the GPU proportion.

Table 4. Projections changing multiple component proportions.

Proportion (gpu:cpu:mem)	Sockets	Data proportion (gpu:cpu:mem)	Total failures	MTBF (Hours)	CPU TDP (KW)	GPU TDP (KW)	System TDP (KW)
0:1:1	434783	0:23.2:23.2	5684	8.06	97826	0	97826
1:2:1	80646	4.3:8.6:4.3	5191	12.06	36291	20162	56452
3:1:2	38911	6.3:2.1:4.2	6821	8.7	8755	29183	37938
8:1:1	15456	6.64:0.83:0.83	6378	7.94	3478	30912	34390

4   Final Remarks

This paper presented the Mixed Weibull distribution function as a more appropriate model for failure characterization and prediction in hybrid exascale supercomputers. Starting from a collection of insights on a five-year failure record of a leadership-class supercomputer, we built a whole-system failure model using Mixed Weibull distributions. These models allow the failure prediction of different configurations according to the prominence of a component in the machine: processor, accelerator, or memory. In the future, we plan on exploring two avenues of research. First, we will evaluate the Mixed Gamma distribution for modelling failures on supercomputers. Second, we will extend the power consumption model to include missing hardware components (storage, network, cooling, memory) and application characteristics during execution.

Acknowledgment. This research was partially supported by a machine allocation on Kabré supercomputer at the Costa Rica National High Technology Center. Early versions of this manuscript received valuable comments from Prof. Marcela Alfaro-Cordoba at University of Costa Rica.

References

1. Bautista-Gomez, L., Zyulkyarov, F., Unsal, O., McIntosh-Smith, S.: Unprotected computing: a large-scale study of dram raw error rate on a supercomputer. In: Proceedings of the International Conference for High Performance Computing, Networking, Storage and Analysis, SC 2016, pp. 645–655, November 2016. https://doi.org/10.1109/SC.2016.54

2. Borghesi, A., Bartolini, A., Lombardi, M., Milano, M., Benini, L.: Predictive modeling for job power consumption in HPC systems. In: Kunkel, J.M., Balaji, P., Dongarra, J. (eds.) ISC High Performance 2016. LNCS, vol. 9697, pp. 181–199. Springer, Cham (2016). https://doi.org/10.1007/978-3-319-41321-1_10

3. Cappello, F., Al, G., Gropp, W., Kale, S., Kramer, B., Snir, M.: Toward exascale resilience: 2014 update. Supercomput. Front. Innov. Int. J. **1**(1), 5–28 (2014). https://doi.org/10.14529/jsfi140101

4. Di, S., Gupta, R., Snir, M., Pershey, E., Cappello, F.: Logaider: a tool for mining potential correlations of HPC log events. In: 2017 17th IEEE/ACM International Symposium on Cluster, Cloud and Grid Computing (CCGRID), pp. 442–451, May 2017. https://doi.org/10.1109/CCGRID.2017.18

5. El-Sayed, N., Schroeder, B.: Reading between the lines of failure logs: understanding how HPC systems fail. In: 2013 43rd Annual IEEE/IFIP International Conference on Dependable Systems and Networks (DSN), pp. 1–12, June 2013. https://doi.org/10.1109/DSN.2013.6575356

6. Gainaru, A., Cappello, F., Kramer, W.: Taming of the shrew: modeling the normal and faulty behaviour of large-scale HPC systems. In: 2012 IEEE 26th International Parallel and Distributed Processing Symposium, pp. 1168–1179, May 2012. https://doi.org/10.1109/IPDPS.2012.107

7. Gallet, M., Yigitbasi, N., Javadi, B., Kondo, D., Iosup, A., Epema, D.: A model for space-correlated failures in large-scale distributed systems. In: D'Ambra, P., Guarracino, M., Talia, D. (eds.) Euro-Par 2010. LNCS, vol. 6271, pp. 88–100. Springer, Heidelberg (2010). https://doi.org/10.1007/978-3-642-15277-1_10

8. Heien, E., LaPine, D., Kondo, D., Kramer, B., Gainaru, A., Cappello, F.: Modeling and tolerating heterogeneous failures in large parallel systems. In: Proceedings of 2011 International Conference for High Performance Computing, Networking, Storage and Analysis, SC 2011, pp. 1–11, November 2011. https://doi.org/10.1145/2063384.2063444

9. Levy, S., Ferreira, K.B.: An examination of the impact of failure distribution on coordinated checkpoint/restart. In: Proceedings of the ACM Workshop on Fault-Tolerance for HPC at Extreme Scale, FTXS 2016, pp. 35–42. ACM, New York (2016). https://doi.org/10.1145/2909428.2909430

10. Li, S., et al.: System implications of memory reliability in exascale computing. In: Proceedings of 2011 International Conference for High Performance Computing, Networking, Storage and Analysis, SC 2011, pp. 46:1–46:12. ACM, New York (2011). https://doi.org/10.1145/2063384.2063445

11. Martino, C.D., Kalbarczyk, Z., Iyer, R.K., Baccanico, F., Fullop, J., Kramer, W.: Lessons learned from the analysis of system failures at petascale: the case of blue waters. In: 2014 44th Annual IEEE/IFIP International Conference on Dependable Systems and Networks, pp. 610–621, June 2014. https://doi.org/10.1109/DSN.2014.62

12. Martino, C.D., Kramer, W., Kalbarczyk, Z., Iyer, R.: Measuring and understanding extreme-scale application resilience: a field study of 5,000,000 HPC application runs. In: 2015 45th Annual IEEE/IFIP International Conference on Dependable Systems and Networks, pp. 25–36, June 2015. https://doi.org/10.1109/DSN.2015.50

13. Meneses, E., Ni, X., Jones, T., Maxwell, D.: Analyzing the interplay of failures and workload on a leadership-class supercomputer. In: Cray User Group (CUG) Conference, May 2015

14. Minh, T.N., Pierre, G.: Failure analysis and modeling in large multi-site infrastructures. In: Dowling, J., Taïani, F. (eds.) DAIS 2013. LNCS, vol. 7891, pp. 127–140. Springer, Heidelberg (2013). https://doi.org/10.1007/978-3-642-38541-4_10

15. Nie, B., Tiwari, D., Gupta, S., Smirni, E., Rogers, J.H.: A large-scale study of soft-errors on GPUs in the field. In: 2016 IEEE International Symposium on High Performance Computer Architecture (HPCA), pp. 519–530. IEEE Xplore Digital Library, Barcelona, March 2016. https://doi.org/10.1109/HPCA.2016.7446091

16. Oliner, A., Stearley, J.: What supercomputers say: a study of five system logs. In: 37th Annual IEEE/IFIP International Conference on Dependable Systems and Networks (DSN 2007), pp. 575–584, June 2007. https://doi.org/10.1109/DSN.2007.103

17. Rojas, E., Meneses, E., Jones, T., Maxwell, D.: Analyzing a five-year failure record of a leadership-class supercomputer. In: International Symposium on Computer Architecture and High Performance Computing (SBAC-PAD), October 2019. https://doi.org/10.1109/SBAC-PAD.2019.00040

18. Schroeder, B., Gibson, G.: A large-scale study of failures in high-performance computing systems. IEEE Trans. Dependable Secure Comput. 7(4), 337–350 (2010). https://doi.org/10.1109/TDSC.2009.4

19. Schroeder, B., Gibson, G.A.: Understanding failures in petascale computers. J. Phys. Conf. Ser. 78 (2007). https://doi.org/10.1088/1742-6596/78/1/012022

20. Schroeder, B., Pinheiro, E., Weber, W.D.: Dram errors in the wild: a large-scale field study. In: Proceedings of the Eleventh International Joint Conference on Measurement and Modeling of Computer Systems, SIGMETRICS 2009, pp. 193–204. ACM, New York (2009). https://doi.org/10.1145/1555349.1555372

21. Schulz, M., Lucas, B., Macaluso, T., Quinlan, D., Wu, J.: Inter-Agency Workshop on HPC Resilience at Extreme Scale National Security Agency Advanced Computing Systems, 21–24 February 2012 Coordinating Representatives John Daly (DOD) Bill Harrod (DOE/SC) Thuc Hoang (DOE/NNSA) (2012)

22. Snir, M., et al.: Addressing failures in exascale computing. Int. J. High Perform. Comput. Appl. 28(2), 129–173 (2014). https://doi.org/10.1177/1094342014522573

23. Tiwari, D., Gupta, S., Gallarno, G., Rogers, J., Maxwell, D.: Reliability lessons learned from GPU experience with the titan supercomputer at oak ridge leadership computing facility. In: Proceedings of the International Conference for High Performance Computing, Networking, Storage and Analysis, SC 2015, pp. 1–12. IEEE Xplore Digital Library, Austin, November 2015. https://doi.org/10.1145/2807591.2807666

24. Tiwari, D., et al.: Understanding GPU errors on large-scale HPC systems and the implications for system design and operation. In: 2015 IEEE 21st International Symposium on High Performance Computer Architecture (HPCA), pp. 331–342. IEEE Xplore Digital Library, Burlingame, February 2015. https://doi.org/10.1109/HPCA.2015.7056044

25. Top500.org: Top500 supercomputing sites (2018). https://www.top500.org/. Accessed 19 Aug 2018

26. Vaarandi, R.: Sec - simple event correlator (2018). https://simple-evcorr.github.io. Accessed 19 Aug 2018

27. Wu, M., Sun, X., Jin, H.: Performance under failures of high-end computing. In: Proceedings of the 2007 ACM/IEEE Conference on Supercomputing, SC 2007, pp. 1–11, November 2007. https://doi.org/10.1145/1362622.1362687

28. Yigitbasi, N., Gallet, M., Kondo, D., Iosup, A., Epema, D.: Analysis and modeling of time-correlated failures in large-scale distributed systems. In: 2010 11th IEEE/ACM International Conference on Grid Computing, pp. 65–72, October 2010. https://doi.org/10.1109/GRID.2010.5697961

29. Zheng, Z., et al.: Co-analysis of RAS log and job log on Blue Gene/P. In: 2011 IEEE International Parallel Distributed Processing Symposium, pp. 840–851, May 2011. https://doi.org/10.1109/IPDPS.2011.83

A Learning-Based Approach for Evaluating the Capacity of Data Processing Pipelines

Maha Alsayasneh$^{(\boxtimes)}$ and Noel De Palma

Univ. Grenoble Alpes, CNRS, LIG, Grenoble, France
{maha.alsayasneh,noel.depalma}@univ-grenoble-alpes.fr

Abstract. Data processing pipelines are made of various software components with complex interactions and a large number of configuration settings. Identifying when a pipeline has reached its maximum performance capacity is generally a non-trivial task. Metrics exported at the software and at the hardware levels can provide insightful information about the current state of the system, but it can be difficult to interpret the value of a metric, or even to know which metrics to focus on. Considering a popular pipeline composed of Kafka, Spark Streaming, and Cassandra, this paper proposes a learning-based approach to automatically infer the state of such a pipeline solely by analyzing metrics. Our results show that we are able to achieve a high prediction accuracy when predicting on new configurations and when the number of data sources changes. Furthermore, our analysis demonstrates that the best prediction results are obtained when metrics of different types are combined.

Keywords: Performance bottleneck · Data processing pipeline · Machine learning

1 Introduction

Applications deployed in distributed environments are composed of a variety of software components. These components provide different functionalities *e.g.,* publish-subscribe messaging, real-time analysis of streaming data, and storage. To achieve scalability, each component can be divided into a number of partitions spread on separate machines for parallel processing. Additionally, for fault tolerance, each component or partition of a component typically has a number of replicas. These components (and their internal replicas and partitions) have many interactions, involving both control messages and data. With such a complex and diverse architecture, it is generally difficult to understand the overall behavior of the system and how its performance can be improved.

Data processing pipelines are an important class of applications that allow running real-time analysis on data streams [12]. Similarly to other ubiquitous applications such as Web stacks [13], such pipelines are typically based on a

M. Malawski and K. Rzadca (Eds.): Euro-Par 2020, LNCS 12247, pp. 52–67, 2020.
https://doi.org/10.1007/978-3-030-57675-2_4

multi-tier architecture, where components are organized in layers. Although simpler to analyze that applications based on a large number of micro-services [14], determining if such an application has reached its maximum capacity in a given configuration can still be challenging [24]. Being able to answer this question is important because it is the first necessary step to take decisions about the reconfiguration of the system, for instance regarding resource provisioning [26]. Answering this question is difficult because the throughput of the system can be impacted by many factors, including the hardware and software configurations, the application logic, and the workload. Also, the system may exhibit a very different bottleneck depending on the situation. Hence, in a given configuration of the system, it can be challenging to determine whether the throughput is limited by the clients (data sources) injecting data in the pipeline or by the components processing the data.

Monitoring data can provide information about the current state of the system. However, analyzing these data to draw accurate conclusions is challenging. Significant opportunities remain to be discovered [25]. Some research efforts focus on analyzing distributed systems logs [6]. However, while detailed logs from realistic systems contain valuable details, they tend to be so huge that they are overwhelming to performance engineers, who as a result can not directly benefit from them. An alternative is to leverage metrics that can transparently be exported at the system and at the application level, to conclude about the state of the application. But analyzing metrics can also be arduous. While there exists a large number of methodologies and tools for analyzing the performance of distributed systems [17], there is no consensus on which technique(s) to use in a given situation. Different saturated configuration typically exhibit different symptoms (e.g., resource saturation versus idle time). Moreover, the number of potential metrics to be considered is often very large.

We posit that to simplify the work of the programmers and users of multi-tier architectures, it would be ideal to identify a small set of key metrics that can provide valuable information about the performance currently achieved by the system. Building a tool that can automatically conclude about the state of the system based on the analysis of these metrics would be very helpful. This paper presents a learning-based approach that allows achieving such goals for the case of data processing pipelines.

Our study consider a data processing pipeline composed of widely used software components, namely Kafka [19], Spark Streaming [29] and Cassandra [20]. This stack is nowadays a de facto standard in production for data analytics [12]. To run our analysis, we export more than 70 metrics at the hardware and at the software levels. Using classic machine learning classification algorithms (Decisions Trees, Random Forests, etc.), we demonstrate that it is possible to build a model that can accurately determine whether the pipeline has reached its maximum capacity based on the analysis of metrics. We show the generalization capabilities of the model by testing with various software configurations (e.g., changing the number of Kafka partition or the number of Spark executors), with different workloads (a simple WordCount, a Twitter sentiment analysis, and a machine-learning-based Flight delay prediction application), and with different numbers of clients. Also, to understand what kinds of metrics provide useful information about the state of the system, our analysis compares the results obtained when using different subsets of metrics. Our results show that we are able to achieve a prediction accuracy close to 80% when predicting whether the data processing pipeline has reached its maximum capacity for a new configuration, for a new number of clients or for a new workload. It also shows that, contrary the approach that is often adopted to solve such a problem [15], it is better to build models that combines information from different kinds of metrics rather than focusing on a single kind of metrics (*e.g.*, resource consumption metrics).

The remainder of the paper is organized as follows. We discuss the state of the art in Sect. 2. The methodology is presented in Sect. 3. We present and study the results in Sect. 4. Concluding remarks are given in Sect. 5.

2 Related Work

Many works have used machine learning techniques to identify performance issues in distributed systems [14,17], and several of these studies focus on multi-tier applications [18,21,22,24]. The results obtained in these works show the efficiency of machine learning techniques to solve such a problem. However, the objective of these works is often different from the one studied in this paper. Related studies mostly focus on achieving a pre-defined service-level objective (SLO) [18,22]. On the other hand, our works aims at determining whether a data processing pipeline has reached its maximum capacity in terms of throughput in a given configuration. Trying to ensure a pre-defined SLO is a different problem for two major reasons. On one hand, it might be easier to relate the value of a metric to a specified SLO, than to try to determine whether the system could achieve a higher throughput if more data were injected, because many factors (software configuration, workload, etc.) can affect the maximum achievable throughput. On the other hand, it might be a more difficult problem because the required SLO might be far below the maximum capacity that the system can achieve which in its turn can influence the analysis of the metrics that are used to build prediction models. The work by Rao et al. [24] is the one that shares the most similarities with ours since it applies machine learning techniques to determine when a multi-tier Web stack has reached its maximum capacity. However, their approach relies on the analysis of hardware performance counters and we will show that hardware metrics are often of little help to conclude about the state of a data processing pipeline. Note that to the best of our knowledge, our study is the first evaluation of learning-based approaches to automatically infer the capacity of a data processing pipeline using metrics.

Different kinds of metrics have been considered to analyze the performance of distributed applications. Resource consumption metrics are often seen as an important source of information on this matter [14,15,21,24]. Metrics related to the response time [22] or to the time spent by requests waiting to be processed [18,30] have also been studied. Our study integrates metrics of these kinds, as well as other kinds of metrics, and shows that combining metrics of different types is often the solution that allows to make the best predictions.

In their work, Malkowski et al. [21] show that an analysis of the general trend of the evolution of metrics (*e.g.*, metric reaching a plateau when a bottleneck appears) can be used to identify metrics that can provide valuable information about the state of the system. We evaluate this approach in our study through a set of metrics called the *recommended* metrics, as described in Sect. 3.3.

3   Description of the Study

This section starts by a general overview of our approach. Then we provide all the details about our study.

3.1   Identifying the Limiting Component in a Multi-tier System

Our work evaluates the use of machine learning approaches for analyzing metrics to determine the status of a data processing pipeline. Here the status refers to whether the pipeline has reached its maximum capacity, or if the throughput could increase if more clients were sending data to be processed. Through our evaluation, we want to assess: i) to which extend predictions can be made with such an approach; ii) what kind of metrics allow making the best predictions.

For this study, we consider a popular data processing pipeline composed of the Apache software Kafka [19], Spark Streaming [29], and Cassandra [20]. To better assess the validity of the results, and to observe the impact of having multiple components interacting in a pipeline, our evaluation also presents results for a simpler case where a Kafka cluster is receiving messages from clients and storing them in partitions[1].

Our study evaluates whether general-enough models can be built to make accurate predictions even in executions that are very different. To this end, we consider various configurations for the components of the pipeline and different workloads as described in the following. These changes imply that the maximum throughput that can be reached by the pipeline is different from one experiment to another (depending on the configuration and the workload, the maximum throughput that can be achieved in our experiments ranges from 677 K msg/s to 3650 K msg/s for the full pipeline) and that the number of clients required to reach this throughput also changes.

To make our prediction, we use metrics that can be transparently exported during the execution of the pipeline. These metrics include system-level metrics that represent hardware resource consumption on the nodes running the pipeline, and software-level metrics that are provided by each component of the pipeline. To build our models out of these metrics, we use classic machine learning classifiers (Decision Tree, Random Forest, etc.). To understand what kind of metrics should be used to make predictions, we compare the results of models built using different subsets of exported metrics.

---

[1] We also studied the case of a 2-tier pipeline composed of Kafka and Spark Streaming but we do not include these results in the paper due to the lack of space. In any case, the results were confirming the main conclusions drawn from the two other cases.

3.2   The Data Processing Pipeline

Description of the Components. In the following, we briefly describe the components of the considered data processing pipeline.

Kafka is a publish/subscribe messaging system. Publish/subscribe messaging is a pattern that is characterized by the sender (publisher) of a piece of data (message) not specifically directing it to receiver. Instead, the publisher classifies the messages somehow, and receivers (subscribers) subscribe to receive certain classes of messages. In addition to the publisher and the subscriber, Kafka has a broker, a central point where messages are published, to facilitate classifying and receiving messages. Apache Kafka uses Zookeeper [16] to store metadata about the Kafka cluster, as well as consumer client details. Essentially, ZooKeeper is a centralized service for maintaining configuration information, naming, and providing distributed synchronization.

Spark is a unified analytics engine for big data processing. Spark has stream-processing capabilities, which makes it able to handle real-time data. Spark uses micro-batching[2] for real-time streaming.

Cassandra is a distributed NoSQL database management system, designed to handle extremely large amounts of data and to provide high availability.

Description of the Configurations. To evaluate the robustness of our predictions with respect to changes in the configurations of the pipeline components, we run evaluations considering the following changes. For Kafka, the changes in settings are about the number of partitions (evaluated cases: 1, 3, 12, and 24 partitions), the size of messages (evaluated cases: 100, 500, 1000, and 10000 bytes), the compression algorithm (evaluated cases: no compression and Snappy compression algorithm[3]), and the acknowledgment policy, that defines the number of replicas that should deliver a message for it to be considered as received (evaluated cases: 1 and all). For Spark, the changes are about the number of executors (evaluated cases: 3 and 12 executors). For Cassandra, the changes are about the consistency level that defines the number of replicas that should be contacted to complete an operation (evaluated cases: 1 and all). In all cases, the replication factor for both Kafka and Cassandra is set to 3.

For the full pipeline, we evaluated 10 different combinations of settings. For the Kafka cluster case, 12 different combinations of settings are evaluated.

The last settings that we make vary during the experiments is the number of clients sending data to the pipeline. For each configuration, we run experiments with different number of clients, starting from 2 clients until reaching 32 clients with a step of 2. For each number of clients, we measure the throughput observed after 15 min of execution and we collect all required metrics as described in Sect. 3.3. As we are interested in determining when the system reaches its maximum capacity, all clients always try to send messages at their maximum rate.

---

[2] Micro-batching allows a process/task to treat a stream of data as a sequence of small batches.

[3] https://cwiki.apache.org/confluence/display/KAFKA/Compression.

The Workloads. Three workloads with different characteristics ranging from simple transformation of data to machine learning algorithms are used:

Wordcount (WC) is a standard micro-benchmark for big data [11]. We use a randomly generated corpus of English words as dataset.

Twitter Sentiments Analysis (TSA) monitors people's opinion on different topics. We use the SentiWordNet [5] dictionary for opinion mining and as a dataset, we use recent tweets in English crawled through the Twitter API[4].

Flight Delays Prediction (FDP) uses machine learning (with a logistic regression classification algorithm) to predict the delays of airline flights. We use input data from the U.S. Department of Transportation's (DOT) Bureau of Transportation Statistics (BTS)[5].

For all workloads, the data are received by Kafka, then transmitted to Spark to be processed, and finally Spark stores the results in Cassandra. In the case of the Kafka cluster, we use the same dataset as with the WC application as workload, and received data are simply saved on disk.

3.3   The Studied Metrics

In the following, we present the metrics collected during the experiments. We also present the subsets that we consider for training models.

Collected Metrics. During each run, we collect the value of some software-level and system-level metrics. At the system level, we collect metrics that represent the CPU utilization on each node, and the bandwidth consumption regarding accesses to memory, to the storage and to the network. At the software level, each component in the pipeline can export an enormous number of metrics. However not all of them related to the performance of the system. We keep only the metrics providing operational information while discarding metrics that reflect the health of the software component with respect to failures. At the end, we obtain 68 different metrics at the software level (36 for Kafka, 10 for Spark, and 22 for Cassandra). Examples of the exported metrics are: `network_threads_usage` exported by Kafka (this metric represents the usage, in percent, of network handler threads which are responsible for reading and writing data to the clients across the network), `processing_time` exported by Spark (this metric represents the time (in sec) spent to complete all the streaming jobs of a batch), and `pending_tasks` exported by Cassandra (this metric represents the total number compaction tasks in queue). Note that no metrics are collected on the client side.

To better describe the collected metrics, we use the classification presented in Table 1 that groups metrics based on the kind of information they provide. For example, we consider that a metric that shows the size of a queue of pending requests belongs to the `Queue Size` type. All categories described in Table 1

---

[4] https://archive.org/details/twitterstream.
[5] http://stat-computing.org/dataexpo/2009/the-data.html.

are represented in the collected metrics. The last column is the table gives the number of metrics included in each group.

As metrics are collected over several instances, partitions and/or replicas of a component, it should be mentioned that the values we use as input for our models are the average values over all instances of a component. We do not lose information by using the average as in general the metrics values do not significantly vary between the instances of a component.

The data related to resource consumption are obtained via `psutil` (python system and process utilities)[6]. The data on the software component level are obtained via Java Management Extensions (JMX)[7].

Table 1. Representative types of exported metrics.

Metric type	Description	Total number
Resource Consumption (RC)	Represents the average percentage of resource utilization. We collect 6 metrics per each component of the pipeline	18
Idle Threads (ITD)	Represents the average percentage of threads that are idle (*i.e.*, threads that wait for an incoming request to process or wait for a reply from other threads)	3
Error Rate (ER)	Represents the average number of messages sent per second that resulted in errors	11
Queue Waiting Time (QWT)	Represents the average request waiting time (in ms) in the queue before it has been served by the server. As an example, in the Kafka cluster use case, requests wait in a queue, after they have been received by Network threads, to be served by Handler threads	6
Queue Size (QS)	Represents the size of a queue in terms of pending requests/responses. Such a queue can be for incoming requests that have been received from the client but not yet served by the server. It can also be for outgoing responses that have not been sent back to the requesting clients	6
Latency (LY)	Represents the average amount of time that a system needs to process a message/request and send back a reply to the client. More generally, latency means the time for any operation to complete	16
Processing Time (PT)	Represents the average amount of time it takes to process a client request. For example, this type includes the processing time that a stream processing engine (*i.e.*, Spark Streaming) needs to process one batch of data within the streaming batch interval	2
In/Out Data (IOD)	Represents the average number of requests/responses received/sent per time unit e.g., the number of requests that a Kafka producer is able to send per second	14
Uncategorized (UC)	Represents the set of metrics that do not fall in any of the previous categories e.g., a metric that represents the rate of closed client connections events is put in this category	10

Selections of Metrics. In the following, we present the different selections of metrics that are given as input to a classification algorithms to build the predictive models. These selections are:

---

[6] https://psutil.readthedocs.io.
[7] https://en.wikipedia.org/wiki/JMX.

All (AL): It includes all metrics exported during our evaluations.

Software-level (SW): It includes all software-level metrics, *i.e.*, resource consumption metrics are excluded.

Hardware-level (HW): It includes only resource consumption metrics.

Response time (RT): It only includes metrics belonging to the *Latency* type, as defined in Table 1. This selection is representative of the kinds of metrics used in some related work [18,28].

Waiting time (WT): It only includes metrics belonging to the *Queue Waiting Time* type, as defined in Table 1. This selection is representative of the kinds of metrics used in some related work [30].

Recommended (RM): This is selection of software metrics that a simple manual analysis allows identifying as useful for determining the status of the system. Resorting to the ideas proposed in [21], two kinds of metrics are excluded from this set compared to SW: (i) Metrics for which the behavior never changes no matter the number of clients (*e.g.*, the value of a metric is always the same or is always proportional to the number of clients); (ii) Misleading metrics where an important change can be observed but which does not correspond to the point where the system reaches its maximum capacity [3]. By excluding these metrics, we obtain a combination of metrics from the following types: ITD, QWT, QS, and PT (see Table 1).

3.4 The Learning Approach

In this last part, we describe the solutions that we use to build classification models, as well as, the methodology to train and evaluate models.

The Classifiers. To build models, we study 5 different classifiers including Decision Tree (DT) [9], Random Forest (RF) [8], Support Vector machines (SVM) [2], Logistic Regression (LR) [7], and Gradient Boosting Tree (GBT)[8]. We consider multiple classifiers to ensure that our conclusions are not simply due to a bad choice of classifier. We decide not to consider classifiers like Neural Networks because these solutions usually required huge amounts of training data and require a dedicated expertise to be properly tuned. We use the classifiers as black boxes *i.e.*, we use the default classification functions without tuning their hyperparameters [27]. We make this choice because our goal is to demonstrate the feasibility of the approach and not to find the most optimal classification algorithm for our problem. Furthermore, using default classification functions show that one can apply our methodology without having a high degree of expertise in machine learning. Before being provided as input to the classifiers, a classical standardization preprocessing step is applied to the data[9].

---

[8] https://scikit-learn.org/stable/modules/generated/sklearn.ensemble.GradientBoos tingClassifier.html.

[9] https://scikit-learn.org/stable/modules/preprocessing.html.

Data Labeling. Data used for our study are labeled into two classes: (i) `server`: this class represents the data points where the system has reached its maximum capacity; (i) `client`: this class represents the data points where adding more clients would improve the throughput of the system.

Defining the border between these two classes is not always simple. There are situations where adding one more client only leads to a small improvement in the throughput. To identify data points that belong to the `server` class, we run, for each configuration, experiments where we allocate more hardware resources to the processing pipeline. If the throughput improves when allocating more resources, we consider that the corresponding data belong to the `server` class.

Training and Testing Models. To deal with the limited number of samples included in our dataset, we use the *Leave-p-out cross-validation schema* [4] to train and test models. This schema involves using p observations as the test set and the remaining observations as the training set. The experiment is repeated until all subsets observations have been considered as part of the p observation in the test set [10]. In all experiments we consider $p = 2^{10}$.

To illustrate the use of this validation scheme, we consider the case of the generalization to new setups of the pipeline. Other evaluations presented in Sect. 4.2 follow the same methodology. For the case of the generalization to new setups, the method involves removing all runs of two configuration setups from the training set, training the model on all setups but the two removed ones (*i.e.,* the training set), and then performing a prediction on the removed setups (*i.e.,* the test set). This training process is repeated for all setups pairs, and the average performance on predictions for all setups is reported.

4 Evaluation

This section presents the results of our evaluation. It studies the ability of models to identify when the data processing pipeline has reached its maximum capacity. Before detailing the results, we describe the experimental setup.

4.1 Experimental Setup

All runs of the data processing pipeline are executed on a cluster of nodes equipped with 2 8-core Intel Xeon E5-2620 v4 CPUs with 2 hyperthreads per core, 64 GB of RAM, a 600 GB HDD, and a 10 Gbps Ethernet interface. We use 9 nodes to deploy the full data processing pipeline: 3 nodes for the Kafka cluster, 3 nodes for the Spark Streaming cluster, and 3 nodes for the Cassandra cluster. Zookeeper instances are deployed on the same nodes as Kafka instances. For the Kafka cluster application, 3 nodes are used. Each client is run on a separate node and 32 threads, one per hyperthread, are used for each client.

---

[10] Using $p = 1$ could lead to erroneous conclusions due to overfitting.

All experiments use Debian 8 with a 3.16.0 Linux kernel, OpenJDK version 1.8.0_131, Scala 2.11, ZooKeeper 3.4.10, Kafka 0.11, Spark Streaming 2.1.0, and Cassandra 3.0.9. To build machine learning models, we use Scikit-learn [23], an open-source machine learning library for the Python programming language.

For each considered configuration and each number of clients, 5 15-min-long runs are executed. Each run is included in the dataset. Thus, the size of the dataset is represented by: *number of setups* × *number of runs* × *run duration* × *number of exported metrics*. Thus, for the full pipeline, the dataset size is: *10* × *5* × *15* × *86* = 64500 rows.

4.2   Results

The study compares the relative performance of models based on the metrics selections described in Sect. 3.3. We check the robustness of these models when generalizing to: new setups, new numbers of clients, and new setups with new numbers of clients. We also evaluate models that predict for a new workload. For each model, the training and testing process is executed 5 times using the leave-p-out scheme described in Sect. 3.4. Presented results are the average accuracy over these 5 runs with the standard deviation presented as error bars. For all experiments, a baseline corresponding to always predicting the majority class (`server` for the Kafka cluster and `client` for the full pipeline) is represented using a dashed line.

Generalizing to New Setups. Figure 1 shows the average accuracy for different metrics selections with different classifiers for the Kafka cluster and the full pipeline use cases when predicating on new setups. The X-axis represents the different metrics selections models with the different classifiers. The Y-axis represents the average model accuracy in predicting whether the system has reached its maximum capacity.

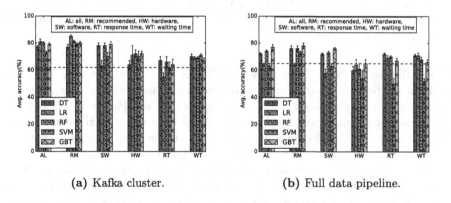

(a) Kafka cluster.   (b) Full data pipeline.

Fig. 1. Average accuracy when predicting on a new setup.

Results show that for both cases, most models manage to improve the predictions compared with the baseline. We also observe that the selections including combination of software-level metrics perform better (*i.e., All, Software,* and *Recommended*) compared to models built with a single type of metrics (*i.e., Hardware, Response time,* and *Waiting time*). Models based on the *Recommended* selection of metrics achieve the best accuracy (up to 85% for the Kafka cluster and 78% for the full pipeline). Models based on *Hardware* metrics achieve low accuracy especially on the full pipeline case.

We analyzed the results to understand why wrong predictions were occurring. We observed that some setups are more prone to wrong predictions, and that these setups correspond to cases where the pipeline reaches its maximum capacity with a very low number of clients. In these cases, we further observed that the value of some metrics were harder to interpret as several of them where having a significant change in their values for numbers of clients that did not correspond to the point where the system reached its maximum capacity.

For the resource consumption metrics, we noticed that in general the evolution of their values when increasing the number of clients was not correlated with the evolution of the throughput. Very often, the values were always remaining low. This explains why models based on these metrics tend to achieve a low accuracy. It illustrates the fact that complex interactions between the components of such processing pipelines make it difficult to identify a clear resource bottleneck in the system.

Generalizing to New Numbers of Clients. Figure 2 presents results for models that try to make predictions for number of clients that never appear in the training set. In this experiment, the tested setups also appear in the training set but with runs involving different numbers of clients. The same observations as in Fig. 1 can be made. Models based on a combination of different types of metrics perform better that models based on a single type. In this case, models based on a single kind of metrics barely manage to be as good as the baseline for predictions on the full pipeline. Best results are still achieved with models based on *recommended* metrics: up to 88% of accuracy for the Kafka cluster and 77% for the full pipeline.

Generalizing to New Numbers of Clients and New Setups. Figure 3 presents predictions results for a hard case where we test with a number of clients and a setup that never appear in the training set. For example, we have executions for a number of clients equals to 10 for a setup Z in the test set and the training set neither contains information about the setup Z nor runs with 10 clients for other setups. The conclusions of the previous experiments still apply in this case. Furthermore, we observe that for the full pipeline, models based on a single kind of metrics achieve an accuracy lower than the baseline. The best accuracy, achieved with models based on *recommended* metrics, is 83% for the Kafka cluster and 75% for the full pipeline.

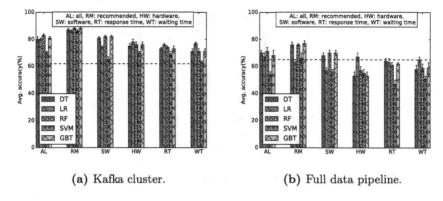

(a) Kafka cluster.   (b) Full data pipeline.

Fig. 2. Average accuracy when predicting on new numbers of clients.

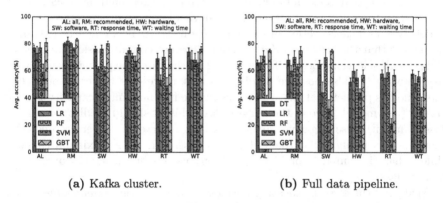

(a) Kafka cluster.   (b) Full data pipeline.

Fig. 3. Average accuracy when predicting on new numbers of clients and new setups.

Generalizing to a New Workload. In this experiment, we check the robustness of the built models when generalizing to new workload application, *i.e.,* WordCount (WC), Twitter Sentiments Analysis (TSA), and Flight Delays Prediction (FDP) for the full pipeline. The test set contains executions of one workload while the training data contains executions of the two left workloads. To avoid clutter, for this test we only present results with the GBT classifier, as this classifier was always a good one in the previous experiments.

Results presented in Fig. 4 show that models are able to predict results for very different workloads. This is especially true with the models based on the *recommended* metrics that achieve the best results in average. A lower accuracy is in general obtained when predicting for the WC application. This can be explained by the fact that this application is very different from the two other ones, as processing the data only involves a few simple operations.

Discussion. The results of our evaluations show that models built based on a combination of software metrics of different kinds are able to make accurate pre-

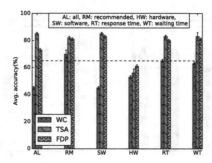

Fig. 4. Average accuracy when predicting on a new workload.

dictions and to generalize in different cases. On the other hand, in general, models based on the selection of *all* metrics achieve a lower accuracy compared with models based on the selection of *recommended* metrics. This might be explained by the fact that the *recommended* selection does not contain misleading metrics while the *all* selection does. Still, depending on the case, the percentage of errors vary between (i) false positive predication that represents the error prediction where models predict that the system has reached its maximum capacity while it has not (i.e., models predict the `server` class while it should predict the `client` class), and (ii) false negative predication that represents the error prediction where models predict that the system has not reached its maximum capacity while it has (i.e., models predict the `client` class while it should predict the `server` class).

Analyzing the error predication for models based on the *recommended* selection for all classifiers, we observe that a significant part of the errors are made for points that correspond to the gray zone (between 30% and 45% of the total number of errors). Part of these errors are explained by the fact that, as we discussed in Sect. 3.4, there are runs where it is not always clear whether the pipeline has actually reached its maximum capacity: provisioning more resources to the pipeline improves the throughput but adding more clients also improves a bit the performance. In our evaluation, we considered the runs in this *gray* zone, as runs where the pipeline had reached its maximum capacity (`server` class), but predicting the `client` class for these runs would not be a major error. Apart from these minor errors, between 25% and 34% of the errors are false positives and between 28% and 39% of the errors are false negatives.

Results also show that in general models achieve a better accuracy for the Kafka use case than for the full pipeline. The reason is that in the case of the full pipeline, the components and their internal replicas have many complex interactions, involving both control messages and data. These various and complex interactions make it difficult to find metrics that provide valuable information about the status of the system in a large number of different configurations and workloads. This also explains why models based on a single kind of metrics are generally bad when making predictions for the full pipeline. Evaluations with a pipeline composed of Kafka and Spark Streaming also show that the obtained models are less accurate than for the simple case of the Kafka cluster.

To understand whether the results presented in this paper are specific to the case of our data processing pipeline or if they are more generally applicable to multi-tier systems, we ran the same analysis using a LAMP Web stack comprising an Apache server that executes PHP code and interacts with a MySQL database. Due to space limitations we do not include these results but the main conclusions of our study also apply in this case: i) models robust to changes in the configuration and the workload can be built based on machine learning classifiers applied to metrics, to determine when the system has reached its maximum capacity; ii) models that achieve the best accuracy rely on a combination of software metrics of different types.

5 Conclusion

This paper studies the use of a learning-based approach to automatically determine whether a data processing pipeline has reached its maximum capacity solely based on metrics. The considered pipeline is composed of the ubiquitous software components Kafka, Spark Streaming, and Cassandra. Our results show that we are able to build models that are robust to changes in the configuration of the components, in the number of connected clients, and in the application logic. For the different tested cases, best models achieve an accuracy in the predictions between 75% and 88%. Furthermore, an important part of the mistakes is done for runs where it is not fully clear that the maximum capacity of the pipeline as actually been reached. Finally, comparing the results obtained when building models based on different selections of metrics shows that a combination of software metrics of different types is necessary to obtain a good prediction accuracy. In the future, we plan to study how to leverage these predictions to apply automatic scaling strategies for such data processing pipelines.

Acknowledgments. This work is supported by the EU AURA FEDER Project Studio Virtuel. Experiments presented in this paper were carried out using the Grid'5000 testbed, supported by a scientific interest group hosted by Inria and including CNRS, RENATER and several Universities as well as other organizations [1].

References

1. Grid'5000. http://www.grid5000.fr. Accessed 19 Jan 2020
2. Aggarwal, C.C.: Data Classification: Algorithms and Applications. Chemical Rubber Company (CRC Press), Boca Raton (2014)
3. Alsayasneh, M.: On the identification of performance bottlenecks in multi-tier distributed systems. Ph.D. thesis, Université Grenoble Alpes (2020)
4. Arlot, S., Celisse, A., et al.: A survey of cross-validation procedures for model selection. Stat. Surv. **4**, 40–79 (2010)
5. Baccianella, S., Esuli, A., Sebastiani, F.: SENTIWORDNET 3.0: an enhanced lexical resource for sentiment analysis and opinion mining. In: International Conference on Language Resources and Evaluation (LREC), vol. 10 (2010)

6. Beschastnikh, I., Wang, P., Brun, Y., Ernst, M.D.: Debugging distributed systems. Queue **14**(2), 91–110 (2016)
7. Bishop, C.M.: Pattern Recognition And Machine Learning. Springer, Heidelberg (2006)
8. Breiman, L.: Random forests. Mach. Learn. **45**(1), 5–32 (2001)
9. Breiman, L., Friedman, J.H., Olshen, R.A., Stone, C.J.: Classification and regression trees. Wiley Interdisc. Rev.: Data Min. Knowl. Discov. **1**(1), 14–23 (1984)
10. Celisse, A., et al.: Optimal cross-validation in density estimation with the l^2-loss. Ann. Stat. **42**(5), 1879–1910 (2014)
11. Dean, J., Ghemawat, S.: Mapreduce: simplified data processing on large clusters. Commun. ACM **51**(1), 107–113 (2008)
12. Estrada, R., Ruiz, I.: Big Data Smack. Apress, Berkeley (2016)
13. Fowler, M.: Patterns of Enterprise Application Architecture. Addison-Wesley Longman Publishing Co., Inc., Boston (2002)
14. Gan, Y., et al.: Seer: leveraging big data to navigate the complexity of performance debugging in cloud microservices. In: Architectural Support for Programming Languages and Operating Systems (ASPLOS), pp. 19–33. ACM (2019)
15. Gregg, B.: Systems Performance: Enterprise and the Cloud. Pearson Education, London (2014)
16. Hunt, P., Konar, M., Junqueira, F.P., Reed, B.: ZooKeeper: wait-free coordination for internet-scale systems. In: USENIX Annual Technical Conference (USENIX ATC), vol. 8 (2010)
17. Ibidunmoye, O., Hernández-Rodriguez, F., Elmroth, E.: Performance anomaly detection and bottleneck identification. ACM Comput. Surv. (CSUR) **48**(1), 1–35 (2015)
18. Jung, G., Swint, G., Parekh, J., Pu, C., Sahai, A.: Detecting bottleneck in n-tier IT applications through analysis. In: State, R., van der Meer, S., O'Sullivan, D., Pfeifer, T. (eds.) DSOM 2006. LNCS, vol. 4269, pp. 149–160. Springer, Heidelberg (2006). https://doi.org/10.1007/11907466_13
19. Kreps, J., Narkhede, N., Rao, J., et al.: Kafka: a distributed messaging system for log processing. In: International Workshop on Networking Meets Databases (NetDB), pp. 1–7 (2011)
20. Lakshman, A., Malik, P.: Cassandra: a decentralized structured storage system. ACM SIGOPS Oper. Syst. Rev. (OSR) **44**(2), 35–40 (2010)
21. Malkowski, S., Hedwig, M., Parekh, J., Pu, C., Sahai, A.: Bottleneck detection using statistical intervention analysis. In: Clemm, A., Granville, L.Z., Stadler, R. (eds.) DSOM 2007. LNCS, vol. 4785, pp. 122–134. Springer, Heidelberg (2007). https://doi.org/10.1007/978-3-540-75694-1_11
22. Parekh, J., Jung, G., Swint, G., Pu, C., Sahai, A.: Issues in bottleneck detection in multi-tier enterprise applications. In: IEEE/ACM International Workshop on Quality of Service (IWQoS), pp. 302–303. IEEE (2006)
23. Pedregosa, F., et al.: Scikit-learn: machine learning in Python. J. Mach. Learn. Res. **12**(Oct), 2825–2830 (2011)
24. Rao, J., Xu, C.Z.: Online measurement of the capacity of multi-tier websites using hardware performance counters. In: International Conference on Distributed Computing Systems (ICDCS), pp. 705–712. IEEE (2008)
25. Sambasivan, R.R., Shafer, I., Mace, J., Sigelman, B.H., Fonseca, R., Ganger, G.R.: Principled workflow-centric tracing of distributed systems. In: ACM Symposium on Cloud Computing (SoCC). ACM (2016)

26. Urgaonkar, B., Shenoy, P., Roscoe, T.: Resource overbooking and application profiling in shared hosting platforms. ACM SIGOPS Oper. Syst. Rev. (OSR) **36**(SI), 239–254 (2002)
27. Wang, B., Gong, N.Z.: Stealing hyperparameters in machine learning. In: IEEE Symposium on Security and Privacy (SP), pp. 36–52. IEEE (2018)
28. Welsh, M., Culler, D.E.: Adaptive overload control for busy internet servers. In: USENIX Symposium on Internet Technologies and Systems (USITS), Seattle, WA, p. 4-4 (2003)
29. Zaharia, M., Das, T., Li, H., Hunter, T., Shenker, S., Stoica, I.: Discretized streams: fault-tolerant streaming computation at scale. In: ACM Symposium on Operating Systems Principles (SOSP), pp. 423–438 (2013)
30. Zhou, H., et al.: Overload control for scaling WeChat microservices. In: ACM Symposium on Cloud Computing (SoCC). ACM (2018)

Operation-Aware Power Capping

Bo Wang[✉], Julian Miller, Christian Terboven, and Matthias Müller

Chair for HPC, RWTH Aachen University, Aachen, Germany
{wang,miller,terboven,mueller}@itc.rwth-aachen.de

Abstract. Once the peak power draw of a large-scale high-performance-computing (HPC) cluster exceeds the capacity of its surrounding infrastructures, the cluster's power consumption needs to be capped to avoid hardware damage. However, power capping often causes a computational performance loss because the underlying processors are clocked down. In this work, we developed an operation-aware management strategy, called *OAPM*, to mitigate the performance loss. *OAPM* manages performance under a power cap dynamically at runtime by modifying the core and uncore clock rate. Using this approach, the limited power budget can be shifted effectively and optimally among components within a processor. The components with high computational activities are powered up while the others are throttled. The overall execution performance is improved. Employing the *OAPM* on diverse HPC benchmarks and real-world applications, we observed that the hardware settings adjusted by *OAPM* have near-optimal results compared to the optimal setting of a static approach. The achieved speedup in our work amounts to up to 6.3%.

Keywords: Power capping · Performance optimization · Dynamic resource management · RAPL · DVFS · UFS · Performance deviation

1 Introduction

The power draw of high-performance computing (HPC) clusters has been increasing consistently. Nowadays, the peak draw of a cluster may exceed the power capacity of surrounding infrastructures. In this case, the power draw needs to be enforced to remain under a certain limitation to avoid hardware damage, which is called power capping.

On the other hand, power capping causes a reduction on computational performance since the underlying hardware has to be clocked down. To mitigate this performance throttling, we develop in this work a fine-grained and dynamic strategy, called operation-aware power management (*OAPM*). *OAPM* improves the system-default power-capping implementation, such as runtime average power limitation (RAPL) of Intel [7], in terms of accelerating computation on mainstream processors.

Instead of a complete reimplementation of the power capping feature, *OAPM* relies on the available RAPL interface which limits the power draw reliably

© Springer Nature Switzerland AG 2020
M. Malawski and K. Rzadca (Eds.): Euro-Par 2020, LNCS 12247, pp. 68–82, 2020.
https://doi.org/10.1007/978-3-030-57675-2_5

and accurately [12,13,15,28,36]. At the same time, *OAPM* utilizes advanced features of main-stream processors to optimize power consumption and execution performance. The advanced features allow to control the power supply separetly of distinct components within a processor, such as cores and uncore [5] where diverse devices are located, including integrated memory controller (IMC), L3 cache boxes, and QPI agent.

Applying *OAPM* on diverse HPC benchmarks and real-world applications, the hardware settings adjusted are having near to the optimal results of a static-setting approach where possible settings are explored one by one. The achieved speedup amounts to up to 6.3%, compared to with the system-default hardware settings.

This paper is organized as follows. Section 2 introduces related work about power capping. Section 3 describes the investigation environment and preliminary observations. Section 4 presents the *OAPM* design and implementation. Section 5 illustrates and discusses results of applying *OAPM* on benchmarks and real-world applications. The last section concludes this work.

2   Related Work

Since the cluster's peak power draw belonged to the first order concerns at constructing a large-scale HPC cluster, enforcement of a power cap challenges all aspects of the cluster. Authors of [3,9,21,24,27,31] proposed approaches to enforce a power cap for a whole cluster where they maximized the cluster's throughput at the same time. Authors of [6,29,30] recognized power-efficiency variations among processors and employed frequency scaling to minimize the execution time of a power-capped application.

A cluster- and job-level power capping require possibilities to enforce a power limitation on each compute node. Lefurgy et al. [23] proposed a closed-loop approach. Isci et al. [19] developed a per-core DVFS power-budgeting approach. Results of the work [7] made RAPL is introduced into product processors.

The exciting power management approaches does not always promise optimal results on state-of-the-art processors, regarding performance and energy consumption, since processors are getting more and more complicated. A modern processor contain components which can be managed individually. Hackenberg et al. [13] explores the possibilities of separate power management, for core and uncore. They figured out the optimal frequency setting through traverse the whole configuration space. Some works [1,18] employed core DVFS to reduce energy consumption of a whole cluster while Sundriyal et al. [29,30] and Bekele et al. [2] rely on UFS management to reduce energy consumption of applications. Instead of energy reduction, Gholkar et al. [10] presents a solution to optimize the compute performance of power-capped processor based on UFS. Similarly, authors of [37] explored and adjusted a wide range of runtime parameters, including the number of active cores and frequency to improve performance under power capping.

OAPM is made based on previous contributions. It optimizes performance of power-capped processors which helps to reduce the execution time of power-capped applications. Instead of a new implementation to enforce a power cap, it relies on the accurate and reliable RAPL. It employs advanced hardware features of modern processors, including core DVFS and UFS to realize effective optimization.

3 Default Hardware Management Under Power Capping

In this section, we introduce briefly the employed hardware and software at first. The hardware is instrumented with several features to manage power draw, including power capping. Sub-sequentially, we explore the behaviors of the power-capped processors and applications.

3.1 Hardware and Applications

The employed hardware platform in following sections is a compute node of the RWTH CLAIX16 cluster.[1] It possesses two Intel Xeon E5-2650 V4 processors. Each processor has 12 cores where hyper-threading is disabled according to the cluster's default setting. The cores can be clocked up to 2.9 GHz in turbo-boost mode. The maximum frequency can be limited either through DVFS or a power limit. The peak power draw of each processor amounts to 105 W while the minimum hardware-specific power cap amounts to 53 W.

In this work, we focus on the performance of a power-capped processor and we employ diverse single-node benchmarks and applications. The simply FLOPS and TRIAD micro-benchmarks are programmed in assembly to represent computing-intensive and memory-intensive workloads respectively.[2] The well-known NASA parallel benchmarks (OpenMP version) are mainly used at preliminary investigations. Two real-world applications, SWIM and BWAVES, are employed for final evaluations. SWIM makes weather prediction through solving finite-difference approximation of the shallow-water equations [17,26]. BWAVES simulates blast waves in three dimensional transonic transient laminar viscous flow [22]. Both are parallelized using OpenMP.

Since most HPC applications perform simulations iteratively until results converge, as the applications and benchmarks mentioned above, and iterations execute similar operations, we explore these features to implement the *OAPM*.

3.2 Power Management Tools

The power draw of main-stream processors can be managed in different ways. The well-explored dynamic voltage and frequency scaling (DVFS) manages the

---

[1] https://doc.itc.rwth-aachen.de/display/CC/Home.

[2] The FLOPS benchmark has a cycles per instructions (CPI) of 0.8 while the CPI of the TRIAD benchmark amounts to 15.3 on our platform with 12 threads.

clock rate of a processor and the power draw indirectly. The uncore frequency scaling (UFS) is an implementation of DVFS for the uncore area since the Haswell micro-architecture [16]. UFS was investigated by [13] for accuracy and employed in works [6, 29, 30] to save energy to solution. Dynamic duty cycle management [4, 35] is another interface which controls in- and active clock cycles and power.

Compared to all the interfaces mentioned above which manage the power draw indirectly, RAPL [7] allows a direct power management where a user can read current power draw and set a power cap. RAPL manages the power of domains individually where a domain is a group of components. For instance, the employed platform E5-2650 V4 has two meaningful domains, the PKG and DRAM domain3. The PKG domain contains the cores and uncore while the DRAM domain covers the memory system.

In this work, we does not change any setting for the DRAM domain like many other works [9, 11, 25] since the memory system has a relatively low peak power draw and a lower performance compared to the PKG domain.

To limit the power draw employing RAPL, a user needs to set the parameters power cap (PC) and time window (TW). TW determines a time interval calculating average power. For instance, setting PC = 100 W and TW = 0.01 s, RAPL ensures that the total power consumption every 0.01 s does not exceed $100 * 0.01 = 1$ joule through DVFS [7, 36]. In the following sections TW is fixed to 0.01 s, since a low TW causes serious performance fluctuation and a high TS may lead to a short but very high peak power draw which may still threaten the cluster-level power cap.

RAPL does not distinguish between power draws of the core and uncore areas. However, they can be clocked independently through core DVFS and UFS. On the introduced platform, the clock rate can be adjusted through manipulating the address 0x620 and 0x199 of the module specific registers (MSRs).

RAPL, DVFS and UFS can be employed independently and simultaneously to manage the power draw. The most restrictive setting determines the hardware state: with a low power limitation, the processor's components are clocked down regardless of the current frequency setting, and vice versa.

3.3   Frequency Scaling Under Power Capping

To meet a power cap, RAPL scales the clock rate of different components dynamically. Figure 1 illustrates measured average frequency under distinct power caps. Setting the cap to 105 W, the clock rate of the core f_c and uncore f_{unc} amounts to 2.5 GHz and 2.7 GHz for both FLOPS and TRIAD benchmarks, since their peak power draw is much lower than 105 W. Decreasing the cap step by step, the clock rates drop. For both benchmarks, the f_{unc} is dropped at first until f_{unc} is equal to f_c. Then f_c and f_{unc} are lowered similarly.

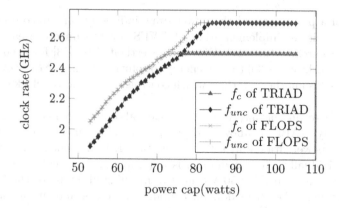

Fig. 1. Average clock rate under distinct power caps (Color figure online)

3.4 Suboptimal Execution Performance of Power-Capped Applications

Power capping causes clock-rate throttling and performance loss when executing applications. Since RAPL scales the f_c and f_{unc} identically as illustrated by Fig. 1, the provoked performance loss can be higher than necessary. Figure 2 illustrates execution-time heatmaps running NPB *BT*, *CG* and *MG* benchmarks capped to 53 W where f_c and f_{unc} are statically fixed at each measurement. The execution time in seconds is color-scaled where red shows higher run-time and blue lower run-time. The system default clock-rate setting is $f_c = 2.9$ GHz and $f_{unc} = 2.7$ GHz. Figure 2 illustrates that the *BT*, *CG*, and *MG* benchmarks have distinct optimal settings. For the *BT* benchmark, an appropriately low f_{unc} shortens the execution time where for the *CG* benchmark a proper higher f_{unc} is preferred. For the *MG* benchmark, a lower f_c with a higher f_{unc} lead to a short execution. The individual optimal settings are determined by the given characters of each benchmark. Table 1 illustrates the measured hardware utilization of the three benchmarks. *BT* has a low *CPI*, a low *L3M* and a low *MB*. Its execution time is sensitive to a low f_c, but robust against a low f_{unc}. *CG* has

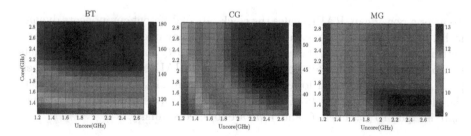

Fig. 2. Execution-time heatmap of NPB benchmarks power-capped to 53 W with distinct clock-rate limitations (Color figure online)

a very high *CPI* and *L3M*, with relatively low memory bandwidth compared to *MG*. *CG* is bound to memory access latency while *MG* is bound to the memory bandwidth. The execution of *CG* is sensitive both to f_c and f_{unc}. The execution of *MG* is robust again a manipulation of f_c.

Table 1. Execution characteristics: CPI for cycles per instruction, L3M for L3 cache misses per 1000 instrunctions, MB for DRAM access bandwidth

	Power(W)	CPI	L3M	MB(GB/s)
BT	87.3	0.47	2.4	17.30
CG	84.1	2.65	229.7	26.80
MG	89.5	0.93	5	58.07

In most cases, the system default setting does not promise the best execution time. Especially, the optimal clock rate setting does not only differ among executions of different applications, but also through a single application's execution time, since the application may perform distinct operations from time to time.

Besides, power capping introduces deviations in terms of execution time. Figure 3 illustrates normalized time of repeatedly-executed regions of the *BT CG*, and *MG* benchmarks. The time deviation under power capping is much stronger than the deviation without a power cap(at 105 W). The lower the power limitation, the higher the deviation. That is because RAPL manages power budget based on average power draw over multiple time slots [37].

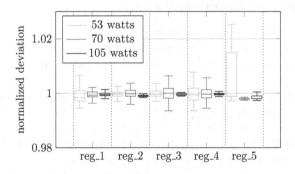

Fig. 3. Performance deviation of five hotspot parallel regions of the *BT*, *CG* and *MG* benchmarks under distinct power caps. Each region was executed in around 200 iterations.

For repeated executions of a same region, the management differs depending on when RAPL starts to work. For instance, the RAPL time window TW is set to 1 s, consisting of 2 time slots each with 0.5 s, and the power cap PC is set to 50 W. For a region consisting of 4 time slots, each with a peak power draw of 40,

60, 60, and 40 W, two possible RAPL managements may occur, as illustrated by Fig. 4a and Fig. 4a. Starting the first TW on the first slot (Fig. 4a), the average power draw of each TW is equal to the set PC. Power capping will not affect the performance. However, starting the first TW on the slot 1 (Fig. 4b), power draw of slot 1 and slot 2 need to be cut where the computation performance will be impaired.

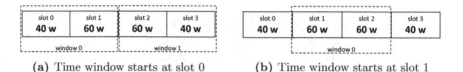

(a) Time window starts at slot 0   (b) Time window starts at slot 1

Fig. 4. Power management of RAPL started on a random slot

4   Operation-Aware Management on Power-Capped Hardware

Assuming HPC applications simulate in iterations and iterations have similar operations, we construct the *OAPM* approach. *OAPM* controls the f_c and f_{unc} dynamically at runtime under a certain power cap, according to executed operations. Therefore, a method is required to recognize the operational pattern.

4.1   Recognition of Operation Patterns

Effective and accurate recognition of operation patterns is vital for a determination of the optimal setting. The pattern recognition of *OAPM* is driven from the top-down analysis from Intel [34], the roofline model [33] as well as the ECM model [14].

Figure 5 illustrates the micro-architecture of typical main-stream processors. Basically, a processor consists of two parts, a front-end and a back-end. The front-end fetches, decodes and schedules instructions while the back-end performs instructions and fetches data if any is missing. In an ideal case, the front-end fetches instructions as much as the back-end can process.

However, the processor can be stalled, i.e. cycle without instruction retired. The causes can be analyzed either on the front-end or on the back-end. If the scheduler (as an instruction depository) is full, the stall occurs due to back-end whose components need to be investigated. If the instructions are waiting for data, the memory control is the performance bottleneck since fetching data from a low-level memory hierarchy is inefficient compared to executing on the computation ports.

Each component in the micro-architecture is instrumented with multiple hardware-performance counters, in order to monitor performance events, like

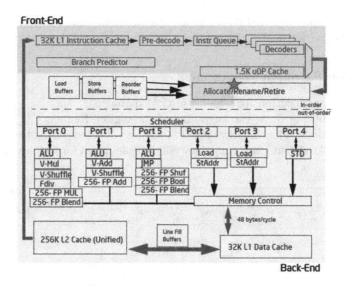

Fig. 5. Micro-architecture of main-stream processors [20].

retired instruction, prefetching etc. In this work, we focus on the state counters which count cycles in certain states, like stalled or unstalled.

Stall cycles can be caused by the front-end or the back-end, especially by data missing in *memory control*. We split the stall cycles into two sub-categories with or without data missing.

In an unstall state, *memory control* can still have data missing, since the instructions are executed by the back-end in an out-of-order fashion. That means an instruction can retire even if data required by other instructions is missing. We split the unstalled state into two sub-categories, pure unstalled state and an unstalled state with pending data.

Considering an execution interval T, it consists of four sub-intervals with

$$T = T_{sm} + T_{sf} + T_{up} + T_{um} \tag{1}$$

where T_{sm} indicates time in a stalled state with data missing, T_{sf} time in a stalled state with other reasons, T_{up} time in an unstalled state without data pending, and T_{um} time in an unstalled state with data missing respectively.

$T_{sm}, T_{sf}, T_{up},$ and T_{um} can be measured and calculated through MSRs. We employ the Linux Perf application programming interface (API) to program the corresponding MSRs as well as read out values. The introduced measurement overheads are in tens of microseconds [32]. The overheads are negligible compared to T whose minimum is set to 0.01 s (see Sect. 4.2).

We define an execution to be memory-bound if $T_{sm} > T_{up}$, i.e. more time spent for waiting data than computation, and otherwise compute-bound. In a memory-bound case, the f_{unc} determines the execution performance where f_c is irrelevant and can be scaled down. In a compute-bound case, the f_c determines the execution performance where f_{unc} is irrelevant and can be scaled down.

4.2 Online Resource Management

For an iterative executions of regions, OAPM manages f_c and f_{unc} at runtime, as illustrated by Fig. 6. At the beginning of the region, frequency is set if there are any indications. Then hardware information is collected during the execution of the region. At the end new frequency will be calculated for the next iteration.

Fig. 6. OAPM process

To reduce the management overheads, *OAPM* switches off the management, after a consistent setting is determined. The region enters a stable state. Besides, a region also enters a stable state, if either minimum f_c or minimum f_{unc} is reached. Same for a short executed region, no frequency management occurs where the overheads exceed potential benefits. In this work, we set the lower bound t_{MIN} of an execution to 0.01 s which is equal to the TW. A higher t_{MIN} excludes most regions of an application for management. The entire management process is illustrated by Fig. 7a.

The collected hardware information is handed over to the calculate frequency function which determines new settings, as illustrated by Fig. 7b. If the measured execution time t_{cur} is shorter than a predefined t_{MIN}, the region is noticed as short. If t_{cur} is longer than a previous execution t_{pre}, the current setting is over-steered. Previous settings need to be rolled back. Otherwise, frequencies are recalculated according to the operational pattern introduced in Sect. 4.1.

In this work, we define a region as the codes surrounded by a OpenMP directive, namely *#pragma omp parallel*. We implement a tool based on OMPT [8] to collect runtime information, including regions' IDs, hardware utilization and execution time. OMPT is an API to support construction of performance tools. It provides a distinct ID for each OpenMP parallel region of the source code. With this kind of IDs we recognize repeated executions of a region.

The implementation available on https://git.rwth-aachen.de/wang/arapl/-/settings/repository.

5 Evaluation

In this section, we firstly investigate the control effectiveness of *OAPM*. Subsequently, we investigate statistic parameters to solve measured deviation issues. Then, we evaluate *OAPM* on real-world applications.

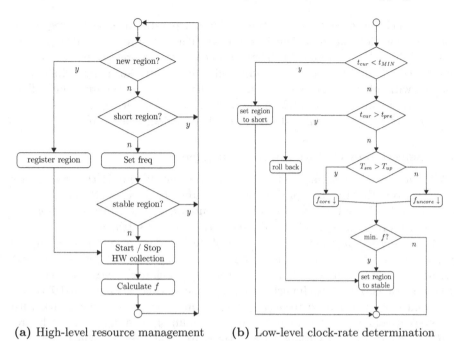

(a) High-level resource management   (b) Low-level clock-rate determination

Fig. 7. Resource management

5.1 Illusion of Frequency Management

Setting the power cap to 53 W, Fig. 8 illustrates the measured power draw and clock rate of the *BT* benchmark with active *OAPM*. The measured power draw exceed rarely the power cap. Most of the time, the measured power draw remains under the power cap, but with 11 exceptions out of 118 samples. The measured maximum power amounts to 53.34 W which is 0.6% over the cap.

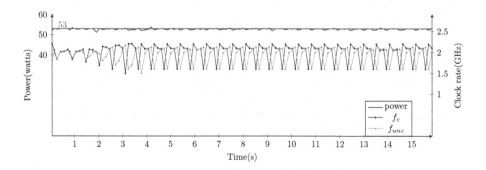

Fig. 8. Measured power draw and clock rate capped to 53 W

The clock rates fluctuate. At the beginning, parallel regions are registered and no limitation on frequency is specified. The measured f_c and f_{unc} have similar values. From around the 1.5th second, previously-registered regions are recognized, f_c and f_{unc} are being adjusted individually. Normally, a high f_c is coupled with a low f_{unc}, or vice versa. After the 4th second, the frequencies fluctuate with a similar pattern. Each parallel region reaches its optimal frequency settings and enters the *stable* state. No further recalculation occurs.

5.2 Selection of OAPM Control Parameters

OAPM achieves a maximal performance improvement only if the frequencies converge to optimal values quickly and accurately. However, performance deviation introduced by Fig. 3 impedes an efficient convergence. In this section, we conducted a robustness study to figure out the optimal settings.

The proposed method collects multiple executions of a region, employs medium or medium values to determine new f_c and f_{unc} setting for the next iteration. Figure 9 illustrates execution time of benchmarks with different statistical settings. Each benchmark with a specific setting was measured 7 times. The values are normalized to average execution time of each benchmark with the system-default setting, namely with maximum f_c and f_{unc}. In the figure, *static_opts* indicates executions with optimal frequency setting which were figured out through repeated measurements each time with fixed f_c and f_{unc}.

The distinct parameter settings, i.e. with different number of iterations and with medium or medium, does not cause a huge difference on execution performance in average. The setting with 3 iterations and medium are robust and provide the overall best execution time.

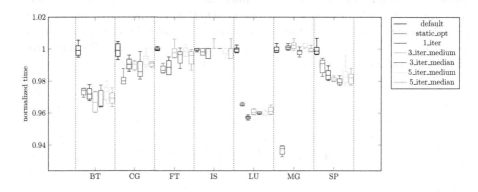

Fig. 9. *OAPM* static parameter tuning. The power cap was set to 53 W.

5.3 Evaluation on Real-World Benchmarks

With the runtime setting "#iterations=3" and medium, we evaluate *OAPM* on two real-world applications, *SWIM* and *BWAVE*.

We power capped the applications each time to 53, 63, 73, 83, 93 and 105 W and measured the execution time. The results are illustrated by Fig. 10.

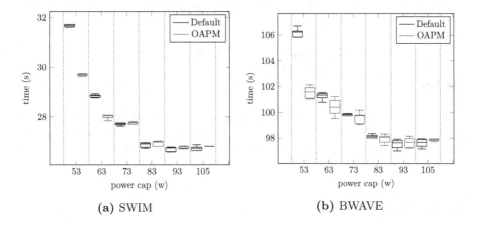

(a) SWIM   (b) BWAVE

Fig. 10. Execution time under power capping

For both applications, *OAPM* succeed in improving their execution speed. At 53 W, the achieved speedup amounts to 6.3% for SWIM and 4.6% for BWAVE compared to *Default* where f_c and f_{unc} are consistently set to their maximum values respectively. With increasing power budget, *OAPM* still provide improvements, however with declining effects, until the power budget exceeds the peak power draw of the applications.

5.4   Discussions

As illustrated by Figs. 9 and 10, OAPM provides performance improvements in most cases, compared to executions with system-default settings. Especially, the achieved run-times is close to the optimal values even better for *LU* benchmark. However, it does not work well for *IS* and *MG*. For *IS* the system-default settings are almost optimal. An improvement potential is invisible. In contrast, *MG* has a high improvement potential. However, its execution cannot be accelerated by *OAPM* since *MG* possesses an increasing executions which is a given property. The execution of a region in current iteration takes longer than the execution in a previous iteration. *OAPM* resets the frequency to system default. No improvement can be made.

6   Conclusion

Large-scale HPC clusters need to be power capped if their power draw exceeds the capacity of the surrounding infrastructures where each computing node needs to be capped.

Under power capping, applications suffer from performance loss, since the hardware is clocked down. The *OAPM* strategy is developed in this work to minimize this performance loss. *OAPM* works for HPC applications with repeating workloads under the assumption that operations through iterations are consistent. *OAPM* scales core and uncore clock rates dynamically to improve computation performance.

OAPM was applied on diverse benchmarks and applications where the execution speed was accelerated up to 6.3% without a power cap exceed. The achieved speedup is near to the optimal values with statically-determined setting, even better.

During measurements, we realized some inconsistent executions among iterations as the *MG* benchmark presented. Besides, an activation of the hyperthreading may effect the improvement of *OAPM*. We will explore such issues in future work.

References

1. Auweter, A., et al.: A case study of energy aware scheduling on superMUC. In: Kunkel, J.M., Ludwig, T., Meuer, H.W. (eds.) ISC 2014. LNCS, vol. 8488, pp. 394–409. Springer, Cham (2014). https://doi.org/10.1007/978-3-319-07518-1_25
2. Bekele, S.A., Balakrishnan, M., Kumar, A.: Ml guided energy-performance trade-off estimation for uncore frequency scaling. In: 2019 Spring Simulation Conference (SpringSim), pp. 1–12. IEEE (2019). https://doi.org/10.23919/SpringSim/2019.8732878
3. Benoit, A., et al.: Shutdown policies with power capping for large scale computing systems. In: Rivera, F.F., Pena, T.F., Cabaleiro, J.C. (eds.) Euro-Par 2017. LNCS, vol. 10417, pp. 134–146. Springer, Cham (2017). https://doi.org/10.1007/978-3-319-64203-1_10
4. Bhalachandra, S., Porterfield, A., Prins, J.F.: Using dynamic duty cycle modulation to improve energy efficiency in high performance computing. In: 2015 IEEE International Parallel and Distributed Processing Symposium Workshop, pp. 911–918. IEEE (2015). https://doi.org/10.1109/IPDPSW.2015.144
5. Burton, E.A., et al.: FIVR—fully integrated voltage regulators on 4th generation intel R coreTM soCs. In: 2014 IEEE Applied Power Electronics Conference and Exposition-APEC 2014, pp. 432–439. IEEE (2014). https://doi.org/10.1109/APEC.2014.6803344
6. Choi, K., Soma, K., Pedram, M.: Fine-grained DVFS for precise energy and performance trade-off based on the ratio of off-chip access to on-chip computation times. In: Proceedings of DATE, pp. 4–9 (2004). https://doi.org/10.1109/TCAD.2004.839485
7. David, H., Gorbatov, E., Hanebutte, U.R., Khanna, R., Le, C.: RAPL: memory power estimation and capping. In: Proceedings of the 16th ACM/IEEE International Symposium on Low power Electronics and Design, pp. 189–194. ACM (2010). https://doi.org/10.1145/1840845.1840883
8. Eichenberger, A.E., et al.: OMPT: an OpenMP tools application programming interface for performance analysis. In: Rendell, A.P., Chapman, B.M., Müller, M.S. (eds.) IWOMP 2013. LNCS, vol. 8122, pp. 171–185. Springer, Heidelberg (2013). https://doi.org/10.1007/978-3-642-40698-0_13

9. Ellsworth, D., et al.: Simulating power scheduling at scale. In: Proceedings of the 5th International Workshop on Energy Efficient Supercomputing, p. 2. ACM (2017). https://doi.org/10.1145/3149412.3149414

10. Gholkar, N., Mueller, F., Rountree, B.: Uncore power scavenger: a runtime for uncore power conservation on HPC systems. In: Proceedings of the International Conference for High Performance Computing, Networking, Storage and Analysis, pp. 1–23 (2019). https://doi.org/10.1145/3295500.3356150

11. Gholkar, N., Mueller, F., Rountree, B., Marathe, A.: PShifter: feedback-based dynamic power shifting within HPC jobs for performance. In: Proceedings of the 27th International Symposium on High-Performance Parallel and Distributed Computing, pp. 106–117. ACM (2018). https://doi.org/10.1145/3208040.3208047

12. Hackenberg, D., et al.: Power measurement techniques on standard compute nodes: a quantitative comparison. In: 2013 IEEE International Symposium on Performance Analysis of Systems and Software (ISPASS), pp. 194–204. IEEE (2013). https://doi.org/10.1109/ISPASS.2013.6557170

13. Hackenberg, D., et al.: An energy efficiency feature survey of the intel Haswell processor. In: 2015 IEEE International Parallel and Distributed Processing Symposium Workshop, pp. 896–904. IEEE (2015). https://doi.org/10.1109/IPDPSW.2015.70

14. Hager, G., Treibig, J., Habich, J., Wellein, G.: Exploring performance and power properties of modern multi-core chips via simple machine models. Concurrency Comput. Prac. Experience **28**(2), 189–210 (2016). https://doi.org/10.1002/cpe.3180

15. Hähnel, M., Döbel, B., Völp, M., Härtig, H.: Measuring energy consumption for short code paths using RAPL. ACM SIGMETRICS Perform. Eval. Rev. **40**(3), 13–17 (2012). https://doi.org/10.1145/2425248.2425252

16. Hill, D.L., et al.: The uncore: a modular approach to feeding the high-performance cores. Intel Technol. J. **14**(3), 30 (2010)

17. Hoffmann, G.R., Swarztrauber, P., Sweet, R.: Aspects of using multiprocessors for meteorological modelling. In: Hoffmann, G.R., Swarztrauber, P., Sweet, R. (eds.) Multiprocessing in Meteorological Models, pp. 125–196. Springer, Berlin (1988). https://doi.org/10.1007/978-3-642-83248-2_10

18. Horvath, T., Abdelzaher, T., Skadron, K., Liu, X.: Dynamic voltage scaling in multitier web servers with end-to-end delay control. IEEE Trans. Comput. **56**(4), 444–458 (2007). https://doi.org/10.1109/TC.2007.1003

19. Isci, C., et al.: An analysis of efficient multi-core global power management policies: maximizing performance for a given power budget. In: 2006 39th Annual IEEE/ACM International Symposium on Microarchitecture (MICRO 2006), pp. 347–358. IEEE (2006). https://doi.org/10.1109/MICRO.2006.8

20. Jackson Marusarz, D.R.: Top-down microarchitecture analysis method. https://software.intel.com/en-us/vtune-cookbook-top-down-microarchitecture-analysis-method. Accessed Jan 2020

21. Kontorinis, V., et al.: Managing distributed ups energy for effective power capping in data centers. In: ACM SIGARCH Computer Architecture News, vol. 40, pp. 488–499, Sept 2012. https://doi.org/10.1109/ISCA.2012.6237042

22. Kremenetsky, M., Raefsky, A., Reinhardt, S.: Poor scalability of parallel shared memory model: myth or reality? In: Sloot, P.M.A., Abramson, D., Bogdanov, A.V., Gorbachev, Y.E., Dongarra, J.J., Zomaya, A.Y. (eds.) ICCS 2003. LNCS, vol. 2660, pp. 657–666. Springer, Heidelberg (2003). https://doi.org/10.1007/3-540-44864-0_68

23. Lefurgy, C., Wang, X., Ware, M.: Power capping: a prelude to power shifting. Cluster Comput. **11**(2), 183–195 (2008). https://doi.org/10.1007/s10586-007-0045-4
24. Patki, T., et al.: Practical resource management in power-constrained, high performance computing. In: Proceedings of the 24th International Symposium on High-Performance Parallel and Distributed Computing, pp. 121–132 (2015). https://doi.org/10.1145/2749246.2749262
25. Rountree, B., et al.: A first look at performance under a hardware-enforced power bound. In: 2012 IEEE 26th International on Parallel and Distributed Processing Symposium Workshops & PhD Forum (IPDPSW), pp. 947–953. IEEE (2012). https://doi.org/10.1109/IPDPSW.2012.116
26. Sadourny, R.: The dynamics of finite-difference models of the shallow-water equations. J. Atmos. Sci. **32**(4), 680–689 (1975). https://doi.org/10.1175/1520-0469(1975)032⟨0680:TDOFDM⟩2.0.CO;2
27. Sarood, O., Langer, A., Gupta, A., Kale, L.: Maximizing throughput of overprovisioned HPC data centers under a strict power budget. In: Proceedings of the International Conference for High Performance Computing, Networking, Storage and Analysis, SC 2014, pp. 807–818. IEEE (2014). https://doi.org/10.1109/SC.2014.71
28. Stantchev, G., Dorland, W., Gumerov, N.: Fast parallel particle-to-grid interpolation for plasma PIC simulations on the GPU. J. Parallel Distribut. Comput. **68**(10), 1339–1349 (2008). https://doi.org/10.1016/j.jpdc.2008.05.009
29. Sundriyal, V., et al.: Comparisons of core and uncore frequency scaling modes in quantum chemistry application GAMESS. In: Proceedings of the High Performance Computing Symposium. Society for Computer Simulation International, p. 13 (2018). https://doi.org/10.13140/RG.2.2.15809.45923
30. Sundriyal, V., Sosonkina, M., Westheimer, B.M., Gordon, M.: Uncore frequency scaling vs dynamic voltage and frequency scaling: a quantitative comparison. Soc. Model. Simul. Int. SpringSim-HPC, Baltimore, MD, USA (2018)
31. Wang, B., et al.: Dynamic application-aware power capping. In: Proceedings of the 5th International Workshop on Energy Efficient Supercomputing, p. 1. ACM (2017). https://doi.org/10.1145/3149412.3149413
32. Weaver, V.M.: Linux perf_event features and overhead. In: The 2nd International Workshop on Performance Analysis of Workload Optimized Systems, FastPath, vol. 13 (2013)
33. Williams, S., Waterman, A., Patterson, D.: Roofline: an insightful visual performance model for multicore architectures. Commun. ACM **52**(4), 65–76 (2009). https://doi.org/10.1145/1498765.1498785
34. Yasin, A.: A top-down method for performance analysis and counters architecture. In: 2014 IEEE International Symposium on Performance Analysis of Systems and Software (ISPASS), pp. 35–44. IEEE (2014). https://doi.org/10.1109/ISPASS.2014.6844459
35. Ye, W., Silva, F., Heidemann, J.: Ultra-low duty cycle mac with scheduled channel polling. In: Proceedings of the 4th International Conference on Embedded Networked Sensor Systems, pp. 321–334 (2006). https://doi.org/10.1145/1182807.1182839
36. Zhang, H., Hoffman, H.: A quantitative evaluation of the RAPL power control system. Feedback Comput. (2015)
37. Zhang, H., Hoffmann, H.: Maximizing performance under a power cap: a comparison of hardware, software, and hybrid techniques. ACM SIGPLAN Not. **51**(4), 545–559 (2016). https://doi.org/10.1145/2872362.2872375

A Comparison of the Scalability
of OpenMP Implementations

Tim Jammer[1,2(✉)], Christian Iwainsky[1], and Christian Bischof[2]

[1] Hessian Competence Center for High Performance Computing
(HKHLR), Technical University Darmstadt,
Darmstadt, Germany
{tim.jammer,christian.iwainsky,
christian.bischof}@tu-darmstadt.de
[2] Department of Scientific Computing,
Technical University Darmstadt, 64283 Darmstadt, Germany

Abstract. OpenMP implementations must exploit current and upcoming hardware for performance. Overhead must be controlled and kept to a minimum to avoid low performance at scale. Previous work has shown that overheads do not scale favourably in commonly used OpenMP implementations. Focusing on synchronization overhead, this work analyses the overhead of core OpenMP runtime library components for GNU and LLVM compilers, reflecting on the implementation's source code and algorithms. In addition, this work investigates the implementation's capability to handle current CPU-internal NUMA structure observed in recent Intel CPUs. Using a custom benchmark designed to expose synchronization overhead of OpenMP regardless of user code, substantial differences between both implementations are observed. In summary, the LLVM implementation can be considered more scalable than the GNU implementation, but the GNU implementation yields lower overhead for lower threadcounts in some occasions. Neither implementation reacts to the system architecture, although the effects of the internal NUMA structure on the overhead can be observed.

Keywords: OpenMp · Scalability · Synchronization · Performance

1 Introduction

OpenMP is currently a de facto standard for intra-node parallelism and frequently used in current HPC codes. Moving towards exascale, new systems offer not only a much higher degree of parallelism in terms of the number of nodes, but also provide more cores per node. Therefore, efficient OpenMP implementations are necessary in order to exploit the intra node parallelism to the best possible extent.

In order to achieve an efficient parallelization, it is important to keep the parallelization overhead as low as possible. For OpenMP runtime implementations, the parallelization overhead occurs in two conceptional ways: On the one hand, overhead occurs from the need for data transfer or data duplication as

© Springer Nature Switzerland AG 2020
M. Malawski and K. Rzadca (Eds.): Euro-Par 2020, LNCS 12247, pp. 83–97, 2020.
https://doi.org/10.1007/978-3-030-57675-2_6

implicitly required by the OpenMP standard or explicitly requested by the user. An example for this is observable, when different threads operate on separate copies of the data without interfering. On the other hand, overhead arises from the need of synchronization, again implicitly and explicitly. An example for this is the coordination effort to ensure that no data races occur and the computed results are identical to a serial version of the program.

In this work, we focus on the synchronization overhead of selected OpenMP runtime libraries and deliberately exclude any effects originating from the user side of the code, such as workload specific load balancing effects. We investigate any synchronization either originating form explicit OpenMP constructs, such as from explicit **barriers**, or implicitly implemented by an OpenMP runtime library, such as a synchronization that is required for task scheduling, or a synchronization to access the internal state of a parallel loop.

Although there are well established OpenMP benchmarks [4,5], most comparisons evaluate an OpenMP parallelized code with an implementation using alternative parallelization methods; examples for such comparisons are works by [13–16]. While this provides a perspective on the ability of OpenMP to deliver performance in a day-to-day usage scenario, this approach relies substantially on the parallelization and programming skills of the implementing person and their knowledge of the different parallelization methods involved. Therefore such approach provides no insight in issues and challenges of an OpenMP implementation itself.

Previous work investigating the performance of the OpenMP implementations is often specialized, i.e. these works analyse the performance in regards to a very specific hardware platform, such as Intel Xeon Phi [24], or target specific features, such as the offloading mechanisms for accelerators [7]. Our work does not focus on any special type of accelerator hardware or construct, as we aim to look at the algorithms used in OpenMP runtime libraries and their performance on standard CPUs used for intra-node parallelism.

For this we draw inspiration on works that investigate different MPI implementations in regards to the effects of different implementation choices [3,18] and [8].

In previous work [11] we discovered that there are scalability issues in the OpenMP runtimes of GNU and LLVM/Intel implementations. A troublesome aspect was, in particular, overheads with a growth-complexity of higher than logarithmic in regards to the number of threads used. However, we did not further investigate the reason for the observered overhead-behaviour. Therefore we will compare and analyse the different implementation choices and algorithms used for implementing an OpenMP runtime library (*RTL*) in this work.

Beyond the algorithmic aspects, we will investigate the additional synchronization overhead originating from the internal structure of modern CPUs, such as the Intel Xeon processor E5-2680 v3 deployed at TU Darmstadt. Here, CPUs come with a number of cores that is not a power of two and exhibit a non-uniform, somewhat "asymetric", internal CPU structure. An example is illustrated in Fig. 1. As one can see, the second ring within the CPU is asymetrically

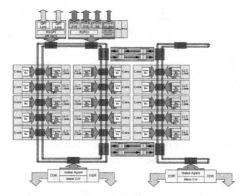

Fig. 1. Schematic of an Intel Xeon E5 v4 series CPU in a medium core count (MCC) (12-14 cores) configuration (src.: https://en.wikichip.org/w/images/f/f6/E5_v4_MCC. png).

populated. This may have an impact on the performance or scalability of a software relying on the lowest latencies to achieve performance.

As both aspects have the potential to severely impact the scalability of OpenMP implementation on current and future systems, this work investigates the overheads from both the software side, comprised of the algorithm and its implementation, as well as the hardware side the RTL is run on. As access to the source-code is mandatory for this endeavour, we consider the two most frequently used open-source compilers and their OpenMP RTL: the *libgomp* [17] used by the GNU compilers and *libomp* [19] used by the LLVM projects compilers. Using the benchmarks previously developed in [11], we evaluate the overall synchronization overhead of the respective OpenMP-RTLs and correlate our findings with the source code and algorithms used, highlighting aspects impacting the scalability and comparing both implementations.

The remainder of this paper is organized as follows: Next, we describe our experimental setup, our evaluation policy, the hardware used and our selection of OpenMP constructs and RTL components. This is followed by the results and analysis of performance and scalability of both OpenMP implementations for each construct/component. Lastly we summarize our results.

2   Experimental Setup

We performed our experiments on the Lichtenberg high performance computer system at TU Darmstadt. The nodes used for our experiments are equipped with two Intel Xeon E5-2680 v3 CPUs running at 2.5 GHz. This leads to four NUMA domains consisting of six cores each. The nodes are each equipped with 64 GB of main memory, although our benchmarks do not directly rely on the amount of memory used. We use the OMP_PROC_BIND environment variable to place threads in either a close or spread configuration and used OMP_PLACES = "threads" in order to control the thread pinning.

To measure the overhead of OpenMP constructs, we decided against using the popular EPCC benchmarks [4,5]: While the EPCC benchmarks are well-designed to capture the overhead of copying data environments, we want to focus on capturing the overhead incurred by individual synchronization constructs. This is, in our oppinion, not possible in the unaltered EPCC benchmarks. To measure the costs of one OpenMP construct in isolation, we used the benchmarks developed in our previous work [11].

These benchmarks create detailed timing measurement for individual RTL operations from an OpenMP implementation with individual timing information for the OpenMP construct calls. Here, before the timing information for a construct is obtained, all threads compute their clock offset with respect to the master thread. This allows accurate measurements, even if the high-precision timer used have slight differences. The clock offsets are calculated in a similar way to the NTP protocol [20], using the cache coherency mechanisms as communication medium. Once the clock differences are known, all the threads synchronize using the mechanism proposed in [11], which is similar to the window based synchronization mechanism for MPI collective operations [10] - i.e. all threads wait until they reached an agreed-upon future point in time.

After the threads have synchronized, each thread takes a time stamp before and after the target OpenMP construct, or within the construct if necessary, as, for example, in a OpenMP parallel clause. With these time stamps, we derive several metrics, such as the minimum cost (first out - last in) or the average cost among all threads (average of end times - last in).

In order to eliminate obvious measurement outliers and to obtain reliable values for the overhead incurred by the different OpenMP constructs, we filter the top 10% of the gathered time measurements, while selecting the sample size such that at least a thousand measurements remain for each case. By discarding the top 10%, we in particular discard those cases, where the process is interrupted for some reason, e.g. by some background task running on the OS[1]. We imply, that we do not have to filter for outliers at the lower bound which is the hardwares performance limit.

3   Results

In this section, we provide an analysis of the scaling behaviour of different OpenMP implementations for the most important OpenMP constructs. As we want to draw attention to the synchronization overhead, we choose those constructs that implicitly or explicitly require synchonization among the threads. Therefore, we consider `barrier` and `critical` as the most important synchronization directives. Furthermore, we consider the `for loop` and `task` constructs for worksharing and we take a look at the fork and join of `parallel` regions, as here it is likely that "costly" thread-management occurs.

On our system, the Intel implementation performed very similar to the LLVM implementation, which is not a surprise considering that the Intel and LLVM

---

[1] For example each node has to respond to the SLURM controller from time to time.

implementations are of the same origin. Therefore and because we want to investigate and correlate our findings with the source code, which is not directly available for the Intel compiler, we omit the Intel implementation for the remainder of this paper and focus on the comparison of GNU with LLVM RTL implementations.

All figures in this section are structured as follows: Each figure shows the overhead of the selected OpenMP construct for both the LLVM and GNU OpenMP runtime implementations. The figures show the distribution of at least a thousand measurements per measurement point with a violin plot. We slightly offset the violins for easier readability. The X axis depicts the number of threads used as input to the measurement. For an easier comparison, most figures share the same X axis scaling with the exception of the figures in Sect. 3.3 and Fig. 12.

The Y axis depicts the resulting time at least one of the threads is not available for execution of the user code, i.e. it is occupied performing the OpenMP runtime operations. A detailed explanation follows in the analysis section below.

3.1 Single

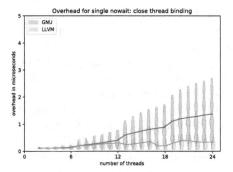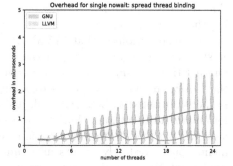

Fig. 2. Overhead of the `single` construct (with `nowait` clause) for all threads that do not execute the single region with close thread binding

Fig. 3. Overhead of the `single` construct (with `nowait` clause) for all threads that do not execute the single region with spread thread binding

An example for OpenMP inducing an implicit synchronization overhead is the `single` construct. Apart from the implicit barrier, some additional synchronization is needed, even if a `nowait` clause is specified, in order to determine which thread should execute the user code in the single region. This overhead is shown in Figs. 2 and 3. We define the overhead as the time that the threads that do not process the `single` region, spend within the `single` region (although a `nowait` clause is specified), as these threads may continue with other useful work. When considering the `single` construct without a `nowait` clause, the overhead consists of the time to enter the `single` region, which is the same time that threads need to skip that region (as shown in Figs. 2 and 3) and the overhead of the implicit barrier, which is discussed later in Sect. 3.2.

Comparing both results (Fig. 2 and 3), we observe that the scaling behaviour is quite the same, regardless whether we choose a close thread configuration (see Fig. 2) or a spread configuration (see Fig. 3). Please note, that influence of the system architecture, i.e. asymetry, can be seen with the close configuration. In particular for the GNU implementation overhead grows when using the next core from another NUMA node (at 6, 12 and 18 threads), be it CPU internal or across sockets. As these subtle details cannot be observed in the spread binding, we will focus on the close binding from now on. We observe, that the LLVM implementation leads to less overhead than GNU's implementation. The overhead and variance grows for the GNU implementation, while staying about the same in the LLVM implementation.

Source analysis shows that GNUs's implementation relies on more atomic *compare and swap* operations being executed, which leads to more blocking between the threads. This explains the increased overhead and variance, as some threads have to wait while others can do the atomic operation without waiting for other threads. In both implementations, a counter is used that counts the number of single regions encountered. At each single region, only one thread is allowed to increment this counter using an atomic *compare and swap* operation. The thread that successfully incremented the counter will continue processing the single region, while other threads will skip it. The general difference of the implementations is that LLVM's implementation first checks with a normal *if* statement (not atomically) if the counter already has been incremented by another thread. Only if a thread sees an opportunity to increment the counter, the LLVM implementation has to apply the more expensive atomic operation properly. Otherwise the thread will just skip the single region without the need for an atomic operation. This leads to less overhead overall, as only a few threads issue an atomic operation that could cause congestion. Altering the GNU implementation accordingly results in a similar overhead comparable to the LLVM implementation that does not grow significantly with the amount of threads.

3.2   Barrier

Figures 4 and 5 show the overhead incurred by performing a barrier. We measure the overhead as the time that passes from the time the last thread arrives at the barrier upto the time the last thread leaves the barrier ("last in last out"). This metric measures the time that at least one thread is performing the barrier construct and not doing other useful work. As the semantic of the barrier forbids that one thread leaves a barrier before all threads have arrived, considering a "first in, last out" rather than a "last in last out" timeframe does not yield much information about the actual overhead incurred, as the time spent waiting for other threads to arrive is not specific to the OpenMP implementation itself. Rather it depends on the application using the barrier.

In Fig. 5, the threads enter the barrier synchronized with only minimal difference in timing. In contrast, Fig. 4 shows the case when the threads enter

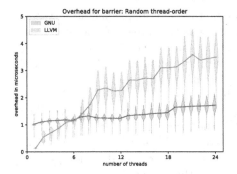
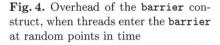
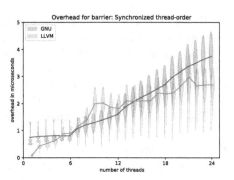

Fig. 4. Overhead of the `barrier` construct, when threads enter the `barrier` at random points in time

Fig. 5. Overhead of the `barrier` construct, when threads enter the `barrier` at the same time

the `barrier` construct at random points in time during a given timeframe. This means that each thread independently considers a timeframe of two times the number of threads microseconds and picks a timepoint uniformly at random at which he enters the `barrier` construct. We think that threads randomly entering a `barrier` should better resemble a real world application, as the `barrier` is a synchronization construct and when all threads enter a barrier synchronous, there is no need to use a `barrier` for synchronization in this case.

Comparing Fig. 4 and Fig. 5 one can, perhaps surprisingly, observe more overhead when the threads enter the `barrier` construct in a synchronous fashion.

This is due to the implementational aspect of the `barrier`. For both GNU and LLVM the `barrier` is implemented in two phases: The first phase gathers which threads have reached the `barrier`. In the second phase all the threads are released from the `barrier`. Some of the work necessary for the gathering is deliberately not represented in our overhead metric, although captured in the raw measurement data. As the semantics of the `barrier` imply, that a thread have to wait for the other threads to arrive, we attribute this overhead to the application domain. Therefore a `barrier` without a workload imbalance may exhibit a higher overhead as the applications work imbalance cannot "shadow" parts of the overhead of this initial synchronization phase.

Comparing the different implementations, the LLVM implementation incurs more overhead when the threads enter the barrier construct in a random order, compared to the GNU implementation. We experimented with different entry patterns, such as random thread order, ascending thread order or descending thread order. As one usually can not predict the order in which the threads will enter a barrier construct in a complex application, we choose to only show our measurements for the random order here. Nevertheless our comparison between LLVM and GNU hold for all tested entry patterns and the important distinction is between a synchronized entry compared to a non-synchronous entry into the `barrier`. The differences between different orderings of a non-synchronous entry are much smaller, although observable in some cases.

Based on our measurements, it seems that the GNU implementation vastly outperforms the LLVM implementation, as long as the threads do not enter the `barrier` in mostly synchronized fashion at the same time. To test the limits, we increased the thread count up to 60 on one of our bigger nodes, a 4 socket system, and observed that the GNU implementation incurs more overhead than the LLVM one when using more than 30 threads.

The reason for this is, that LLVM's implementation utilizes a tree alike scheme to collect which threads have reached the `barrier`. In contrast, the GNU implementation increments a single shared counter. This much simpler implementation of the GNU OpenMP runtime leads to less overhead, as long as the threads do not arrive in a synchronized fasion. It therefore follows, that only the time to increment a counter and signaling all other threads to leave the `barrier` is required for the last thread to release the barrier. In LLVMs implementation of the OpenMP runtime this is more complex. Here the last thread arriving at the barrier has to traverse the full tree in order to validate that all other threads also have arrived at the barrier and to release the barrier. Therefore the cost of GNUs implementation is preferable at a lower thread-count. But with a larger number of threads, the logarithmic complexity of LLVM's implementation results in less overhead than the linear complexity of GNU's implementation, which makes it preferable for large thread counts.

In addition, the performance of the barrier is indeed tightly coupled to the system layout. When looking at the overhead of LLVM's implementation in Fig. 4, one can see that the overhead of the `barrier` increases whenever a new tree layer is introduced at 1, 4, 8, and 16 threads. An additional increase can be observed whenever the next thread is placed on a "new" group of CPU cores, here at 6, 12, and 18 threads in Fig. 4. In the case of the GNU implementation, this characteristic of the system has less of an impact. We can observe that the variance of the overhead grows with the number of threads. This is explained by the fact that the cache line where the shared counter is stored must move between caches. Here the specific thread sequence factors in, as the order the threads are calling the `barrier` influences the locality of the cache line. Timing variance also increases with the number of threads for the LLVM implementation, as the overhead also depends on the exact order the threads enter the `barrier`.

3.3 OpenMP Tasks

OpenMP `tasks` are a popular feature for worksharing. We compare the overhead introduced by the `task` scheduling for two different cases: either a single OpenMP thread creates all tasks, or each OpenMP thread creates an equal share of the tasks (see Figs. 6, 7 and 8, 9 respectively). The total amount of tasks created is the same in both cases. Figures 6 and 8 show the time needed to create one `task`, whereas Figs. 7 and 9 show the time, needed by one thread to change between `tasks`. The scheduling overhead is the time from the end of one `task` until the start of the next one, i.e. the time a thread does not process any `task`. We observe that GNU's implementation results in a much higher overhead. This is a result of GNU's implementation maintaining a more complex priority queue for storing the **tasks** to be scheduled. Dequeuing from this priority queue needs to be protected via a lock to prevent two threads from executing the same **task**. Therefore, this lock induces overhead. This also explains the higher variance with higher thread counts: the probability of the lock being occupied is higher than in low-thread scenarios, leading to more congestion. In contrast, LLVM's implementation maintains multiple queues, one for each thread, with task-stealing when a thread runs out of work. In general this results in less conflicts when dequeueing the next **task** to work on. But this depends on the workload-balance of the application. With an imbalanced workload the additional overhead associated with stealing tasks from another threads queue may outweigh the benefit of using multiple task queues.

We observe less overall overhead, when **tasks** are created by all threads compared to a distributed fashion, where each thread creates some proportion of the **tasks**. When each thread creates a part of the **tasks**, there is a probability for better locality, as each thread can execute the **tasks** created by himself with no need for cache transfers of the administrative data for the **task**[2]. We do not observe a different behavior when one thread creates the **tasks** from within a **single** or a **master** section. This, however, will be most likely offset by data-locality that we factored out in our analysis, as for our benchmark each **task** only consists of time measurement mechanism. As it is a common pattern to create **tasks** within a single or master construct, we think that it might be useful to develop a specialized implementation for this use-case.

3.4   Opening and Closing of Parallel Regions

Looking at the start-up and shut-down of an **parallel** region, we observe another overhead difference between the GNU and LLVM implementation of the OpenMP runtime library.

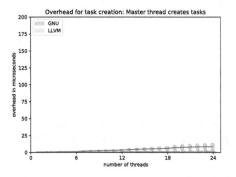
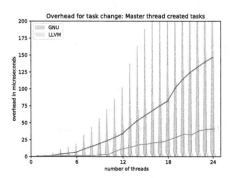

Fig. 6. Overhead of **task** creation, when all tasks are created by the master thread

Fig. 7. Overhead incurred between the processing of two **tasks**, when all tasks are created by the master thread

---

[2] Such as which function this **task** should call or the pointers to the shared variables.

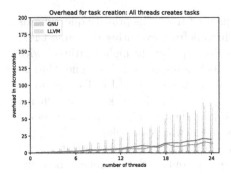

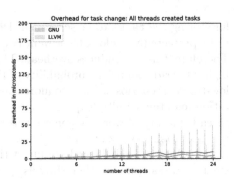

Fig. 8. Overhead of `task` creation, when all threads create some proportion of the tasks

Fig. 9. Overhead incurred between the processing of two `tasks`, when all threads create some proportion of the tasks

We define the start-up overhead as the time-difference from the master thread arriving at the beginning of the `parallel` region until the last thread begins processing the `parallel` region. This measures the time until all threads are up and running the user code. Figure 10 shows the overhead of starting a `parallel` region. One can see that the GNU implementation exhibits a linear scaling behaviour while LLVM's implementation shows a logarithmic growth of the overhead.

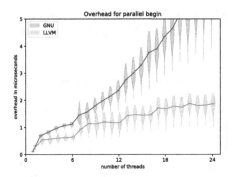

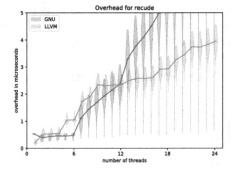

Fig. 10. Overhead of creating a `parallel` region

Fig. 11. Overhead of ending a `parallel` region with the `reduction` clause

In the GNU implementation, the master thread creates all required threads with `pthread_create()`, every time a `parallel` region begins. In contrast, the LLVM implementation utilizes a threadpool, so that no new threads need to be created when a `parallel` region begins. On our machine, the overhead for activating these threads is lower than creating new threads. In case of LLVM, the overhead only consists of a `barrier`, as discussed in Sect. 3.2, where all inactive threads are waiting for a signal by the master thread providing the OpenMP region they should execute next.

The overhead when ending a `parallel` region with a `reduction` clause nis shown in Fig. 11. As with the overhead of opening a `parallel` region, the GNU implementation shows a linear growth, while the LLVM implementation shows a logarithmic growth of the overhead based on the number of threads used. LLVM implements the `reduction` in a tree once the threads arrive at the join barrier. In the GNU implementation all threads write their local values to an array. After the join barrier, the master thread iterates over this array and performs the `reduction`. As one can see in Fig. 11, the `reduction` performed on the master is better for as long as there is no need to transfer a cache line, which is the case up to 6 threads on our system. With more threads the logarithmic complexity of the LLVM implementation is more performant than GNU's linear complexity implementation.

Nevertheless, the LLVM implementation does not seem to be aware of our systems organization into 4 NUMA nodes with 6 cores each. One would expect that an implementation of the `reduction` operation should exploit the system architecture: First reducing the values for each NUMA node, e.g. 6 cores at our system, and then minimizing the inter-thread communication by only exchanging 4 values between the NUMA nodes. But we did not see such an implementation in our study. To strengthen this claim, we simulated the amount of cache misses in such a scenario using valgrind's cachegrind tool [23]. The results are shown in Fig. 12; the Y-axis denotes the amount of cache misses and the X-axis the amount of threads used. Please note that the values for LLVM's and GNU's implementation are not directly comparable in this figure, as the cache misses for the creation of threads and the join barrier are also included. Although our simulation is not ideal, it shows that the number of cache misses increases significantly once more than six threads are used. But there is no significant increase at 12 or 18 threads, as one might expect. At this point we have not been able to identify if a NUMA-aware implementation leads to better performance or not.

This behaviour of the implementations for the `reduction` clause is not different if the `reduction` clause is used from within a `parallel` region, e.g. with a `for` loop worksharing construct.

3.5   For and Critical

For: When investigating the `for` pragma, no significant difference of the scaling behaviour of GNU's and LLVM's OpenMP implementations can be seen. Therefore, we ommited the plots for brevity. When comparing the different scheduling strategies, i.e. static with a dynamic schedule, we observe larger overheads and variance for the dynamic schedule. This higher variance is explained by the algorithm used that, depending on the implementation, has to manage a coordinated todo-list of remaining iterations. For the static schedule, as expected, the

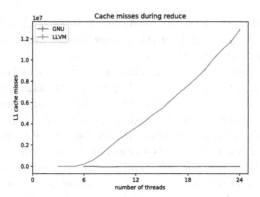

Fig. 12. Cache misses of the `reduction` operation. Note, that the values of LLVM and GNU are not directly comparable, as the cache misses for the creation of threads and the join barrier are also included.

time between two iterations does not depend on the threadcount nor is there a significant variance.

For this experiment, we used the standard chunksize. As the amount of scheduling overhead introduced strongly depends on number of scheduling decisions, it is lower with a larger chunksize. Therefore we often see a tradeoff between the scheduling overhead introduced with lower chunksize and load balancing which is often better with lower chunksizes.

Critical: For the `critical` pragma, we do not find any differences between both implementations as well. As the scaling behaviour also does not show any unexpected behaviour, we omit the visualization here as well. The time needed to perform a `critical` pragma is essentially the time needed to acquire the lock guarding it. Increasing the thread-count directly increases the congestion at the `critical` pragma. Hence, the mean time of acquiring the lock grows as well as the variance, i.e. how long one thread has to wait. With more and more threads, a `critical` section might become more and more congested. Therefore, we advise to use them as sparingly as possible. But as this is an aspect of the application, it cannot be directly addressed inside an OpenMP runtime.

4   Conclusion

In this paper we compared the LLVM and GNU OpenMP runtime libraries in regards to the synchronization overhead incurred for the most important synchronization directives and runtime library components. Using a dedicated benchmark for exposing synchronization overheads regardless of the parallelized workload, we discovered that for higher threadcounts the implementation of the LLVM compiler exhibits overall better performance on our test system. However, for a low number of threads, 6 on our system, the OpenMP implementation of

GNU provides better performance for the `barrier` construct or the `reduction` operation. Our goal is not to provide advise on which compiler to choose to compile an OpenMP application, as this decision will be influenced by many more factors (such as the compilers ability to optimize complex loops). This work rather highlights implementation differences in order to point out room for further improvement.

Especially for the GNU implementation, we observed that a workload balanced application may incur an increased overhead than an imbalanced one at a `barrier`, as none of the `barrier` overhead is "shadowed" by the workload imbalance.

For `task` constructs we observe less overall overhead in our tests, when `tasks` are created by all threads compared to a distributed fashion, where each thread creates some proportion of the `tasks`. Choosing the most efficient task scheduling algorithm and implementation based on the systems NUMA architecture and the application workload is a research area by itself, e. g. covered by [6,21,25]. Our findings confirm that there is still room for improvement in this area, especially for the GNU implementation.

Please note, that, although previous work [1,2,9,22,24] proposed the development of implementations that adopt their behaviour depending on the number of threads and the system layout, this has not yet been implemented in the run-time libraries of current GNU or LLVM compilers. As such, neither the GNU nor the LLVM compilers offer the best possible implementation for all different thread counts. In our opinion a good OpenMP implementation would adapt its behaviour in regards to the number of threads used, e.g. using a combination of GNU's linear behaviour with low overhead for low thread counts and LLVM's logarithmic implementation for higher thread counts. We also did not observe that the GNU nor LLVM implementation adapt their algorithms to systems with multiple different NUMA nodes, although the effects of this organization are observable. Especially for tree-like schemes, as used by LLVM, a better performance may be possible if the tree were to be aligned with the NUMA domains of the system used. We will investigate this and potential solutions in future work.

Acknowledgments and Data Availability Statement. Measurement for this work were conducted on the Lichtenberg high performance computer of the TU Darmstadt. This work was supported by the Hessian Ministry for Higher Education, Research and the Arts through the Hessian Competence Center for High-Performance Computing and the Deutsche Forschungsgemeinschaft (DFG, German Research Foundation) – Project-ID 265191195 – SFB 1194.

The datasets and code generated during and/or analysed during the current study are available in the Figshare repository: https://doi.org/10.6084/m9.figshare.12555263 [12].

References

1. Al-Khalissi, H., Shah, S.A.A., Berekovic, M.: An efficient barrier implementation for OpenMP-like parallelism on the Intel SCC. In: 2014 22nd Euromicro International Conference on Parallel, Distributed, and Network-Based Processing, pp. 76–83. IEEE (2014). https://doi.org/10.1109/pdp.2014.25
2. Bari, M.A.S., et al.: Arcs: adaptive runtime configuration selection for power-constrained OpenMP applications. In: 2016 IEEE International Conference on Cluster Computing (CLUSTER), pp. 461–470. IEEE (2016). https://doi.org/10.1109/cluster.2016.39
3. Brightwell, R.: A comparison of three MPI implementations for red storm. In: Di Martino, B., Kranzlmüller, D., Dongarra, J. (eds.) EuroPVM/MPI 2005. LNCS, vol. 3666, pp. 425–432. Springer, Heidelberg (2005). https://doi.org/10.1007/11557265_54
4. Bull, J.M.: Measuring synchronisation and scheduling overheads in OpenMP. In: Proceedings of First European Workshop on OpenMP. vol. 8, p. 49 (1999)
5. Bull, J.M., O'Neill, D.: A microbenchmark suite for OpenMP 2.0. ACM SIGARCH Comput. Arch. News **29**, 41–48 (2001). https://doi.org/10.1145/563647.563656
6. Clet-Ortega, J., Carribault, P., Pérache, M.: Evaluation of OpenMP task scheduling algorithms for large NUMA architectures. In: Silva, F., Dutra, I., Santos Costa, V. (eds.) Euro-Par 2014. LNCS, vol. 8632, pp. 596–607. Springer, Cham (2014). https://doi.org/10.1007/978-3-319-09873-9_50
7. Diaz, J.M., et al.: Analysis of OpenMP 4.5 offloading in implementations: correctness and overhead. Parallel Comput. **89**, 102546 (2019). https://doi.org/10.1016/j.parco.2019.102546
8. Gabriel, E., et al.: Open MPI: goals, concept, and design of a next generation MPI implementation. In: Kranzlmüller, D., Kacsuk, P., Dongarra, J. (eds.) EuroPVM/MPI 2004. LNCS, vol. 3241, pp. 97–104. Springer, Heidelberg (2004). https://doi.org/10.1007/978-3-540-30218-6_19
9. Gupta, R., Hill, C.R.: A scalable implementation of barrier synchronization using an adaptive combining tree. Int. J. Parallel Program. **18**(3), 161–180 (1989). https://doi.org/10.1007/bf01407897
10. Hoefler, T., Schneider, T., Lumsdaine, A.: Accurately measuring collective operations at massive scale. In: 2008 IEEE International Symposium on Parallel and Distributed Processing, pp. 1–8. IEEE (2008). https://doi.org/10.1109/ipdps.2008.4536494
11. Iwainsky, C., et al.: How many threads will be too many? on the scalability of OpenMP implementations. In: Träff, J.L., Hunold, S., Versaci, F. (eds.) Euro-Par 2015. LNCS, vol. 9233, pp. 451–463. Springer, Heidelberg (2015). https://doi.org/10.1007/978-3-662-48096-0_35
12. Jammer, T., Iwainsky, C., Bischof, C.: Artifact and instructions to generate experimental results for EuroPar 2020 paper: A Comparison of the Scalability of OpenMP Implementations (Jul 2020). https://doi.org/10.6084/m9.figshare.12555263, https://springernature.figshare.com/articles/datasetArtifact_and_instructions_to_generate_experimental_results_for_EuroPar_2020_paper_A_Comparison_of_the_Scalability_of_OpenMP_Implementations_/12555263/1
13. Kang, S.J., Lee, S.Y., Lee, K.M.: Performance comparison of OpenMP, MPI, and MapReduce in practical problems. Adv. Multi. **2015**, (2015). https://doi.org/10.1155/2015/575687

14. Krawezik, G.: Performance comparison of MPI and three OpenMP programming styles on shared memory multiprocessors. In: Proceedings of the Fifteenth Annual ACM Symposium on Parallel Algorithms and Architectures, pp. 118–127 (2003). https://doi.org/10.1145/777412.777433

15. Krawezik, G., Cappello, F.: Performance comparison of MPI and OpenMP on shared memory multiprocessors. Concurrency Comput. Prac. Experience 18(1), 29–61 (2006). https://doi.org/10.1002/cpe.905

16. Kuhn, B., Petersen, P., O'Toole, E.: OpenMP versus threading in C/C++. Concurrency Prac. Experience 12(12), 1165–1176 (2000). https://doi.org/10.1002/1096-9128(200010)12:12⟨1165::aid-cpe529⟩3.0.co;2-1

17. Libgomp: GNU offloading and multi processing runtime library: The GNU OpenMP and OpenACC implementation. Tech. rep., GNU libgomp (2018). https://gcc.gnu.org/onlinedocs/gcc-8.3.0/libgomp.pdf

18. Liu, J., et al.: Performance comparison of MPI implementations over InfiniBand, Myrinet and Quadrics. In: Proceedings of the 2003 ACM/IEEE Conference on Supercomputing, p. 58 (2003). https://doi.org/10.1145/1048935.1050208

19. LLVM: LLVM OpenMP runtime library. Tech. rep., the LLVM Project (2015). http://openmp.llvm.org/Reference.pdf

20. Mills, D.L.: Internet time synchronization: the network time protocol. IEEE Trans. Communi. 39(10), 1482–1493 (1991). https://doi.org/10.1109/26.103043

21. Muddukrishna, A., et al.: Locality-aware task scheduling and data distribution on NUMA systems. In: Rendell, AlP, Chapman, B.M., Müller, M.S. (eds.) IWOMP 2013. LNCS, vol. 8122, pp. 156–170. Springer, Heidelberg (2013). https://doi.org/10.1007/978-3-642-40698-0_12

22. Nanjegowda, R., et al.: Scalability evaluation of barrier algorithms for OpenMP. In: Müller, M.S., de Supinski, B.R., Chapman, B.M. (eds.) IWOMP 2009. LNCS, vol. 5568, pp. 42–52. Springer, Heidelberg (2009). https://doi.org/10.1007/978-3-642-02303-3_4

23. Nethercote, N.: Cachegrind: a cache profiler. Tech. rep., Valgrind Developers (2019). https://valgrind.org/docs/manual/cg-manual.html

24. Rodchenko, A., et al.: Effective barrier synchronization on Intel Xeon Phi coprocessor. In: Träff, J.L., Hunold, S., Versaci, F. (eds.) Euro-Par 2015. LNCS, vol. 9233, pp. 588–600. Springer, Heidelberg (2015). https://doi.org/10.1007/978-3-662-48096-0_45

25. Terboven, C., et al.: Assessing OpenMP tasking implementations on NUMA architectures. In: Chapman, B.M., Massaioli, F., Müller, M.S., Rorro, M. (eds.) IWOMP 2012. LNCS, vol. 7312, pp. 182–195. Springer, Heidelberg (2012). https://doi.org/10.1007/978-3-642-30961-8_14

Evaluating the Effectiveness of a Vector-Length-Agnostic Instruction Set

Andrei Poenaru[✉] and Simon McIntosh-Smith

Department of Computer Science,
University of Bristol, Bristol, UK
{andrei.poenaru,cssnmis}@bristol.ac.uk

Abstract. In this paper we evaluate the efficacy of the Arm Scalable
Vector Extension (SVE) instruction set for HPC workloads using a set
of established mini-apps. Exploiting the vector capabilities of SVE will
be a key factor in achieving high performance on upcoming generations
of Arm-based processors. SVE is a flexible instruction set, but its design
is fundamentally different from other contemporary SIMD extensions,
such as AVX or NEON, which could present a challenge to its adoption.
We use a selection of mini-apps which covers a wide range of scientific
application classes to investigate SVE, using a combination of static and
dynamic analysis. We inspect how SVE capabilities are used in the mini-
apps' kernels, as generated by all SVE compilers available at the time
of writing, for both arithmetic and memory operations. We compare our
findings against similar data gathered on currently available processors.
Although the extent to which vector code is generated varies by mini-app,
all compilers tested successfully utilise SVE to vectorise *more* code than
they are able to when targeting NEON, Arm's previous-generation SIMD
instruction set. For most mini-apps, we expect performance improvements as SVE width is increased.

Keywords: Instruction sets · SVE · Vectorisation · SIMD · Data
parallelism

1 Introduction

Modern processors rely on SIMD hardware to provide high performance for
scientific applications. Vector hardware is not a new concept, with its origins
reaching back to the CRAY-1 in 1975, but taking advantage of such capabilities
has become increasingly important over the past few years.

Current x86-based processors offer SIMD capabilities through the 256-bit
AVX2 and 512-bit AVX-512 instruction sets. Arm-based alternatives, however,
have so far only offered 128-bit vectors through the instruction set previously
known as NEON, which is now part of the ARMv8 Advanced SIMD (ASIMD)
instruction group. The relatively short width of ASIMD vectors, combined with
the reduced flexibility of this instruction set originally designed for media and

© Springer Nature Switzerland AG 2020
M. Malawski and K. Rzadca (Eds.): Euro-Par 2020, LNCS 12247, pp. 98–114, 2020.
https://doi.org/10.1007/978-3-030-57675-2_7

signal processing, has limited the performance of Arm-based processors on a number of scientific applications [13].

The next generations of high-performance Arm processors will use the Scalable Vector Extension (SVE) to provide more powerful vector operations [20]. Unlike current SIMD implementations, SVE is a vector-length-agnostic (VLA) instruction set, allowing each implementation to choose a vector width between 128 and 2048 bits, in increments of 128 bits, with SVE binaries being portable between implementations. The first SVE-capable hardware will become available in 2020 [22], but a number of tools that enable SVE experiments through either emulation or simulation are already available. In this paper, we use these SVE tools to assess the efficacy of the new vector instruction set across a range of common HPC problem classes.

This paper makes several contributions:

- A comparison of the vectorisation efficiency of several HPC mini-apps on contemporary vector platforms from Arm and Intel;
- An analysis of SVE usage on the mini-apps, inspecting executed vector code and memory access patterns and their relation to SVE vector widths;
- An evaluation of the state of currently available SVE compilers and performance analysis tools.

2   Background

Initially vital in many-core devices such as GPUs [3] and the Intel Xeon Phi [16], vector code is now important in *all* high-performance processors. Utilising the wide vector units in the latest generations of x86 processors is the only way to approach peak performance [5].

Vector code is generally produced by optimising compilers, but compiler-backed auto-vectorisation cannot be assumed to be optimal [7,18]. Therefore, it is important to evaluate its effectiveness on new hardware platforms. Furthermore, differences in instruction sets and their implementation in hardware can cause different behaviour on two distinct processors, even when the same benchmark and toolchain are used.

On x86 processors there are many variants of AVX available, and the optimal code for each variant may be significantly different [24], but with the Arm SVE instruction set, the generated machine code does not depend on a fixed vector width. Instead, executables automatically exploit the widest vector size available at run-time, using an approach similar to that of the very first vector computers [21]. This is particularly attractive for benchmarks based on real-world scientific applications, as they tend to steer clear of platform- or vendor-specific optimisations and instead opt for portable code.

Mini-apps are benchmarks built by reducing full-size scientific applications to the smallest implementation that preserves its performance characteristics, while eliminating non-critical features such as input/output [2]. The main computation kernels in mini-apps are closely similar sometimes identical to those in their parent applications. Mini-apps are also lightweight in terms of dependencies, not requiring specialised libraries to run, which often contrasts with large-scale scientific applications. The mini-apps used in this paper have previously been used as part of a comprehensive benchmarking suite for studying the performance of a new supercomputer, Isambard, the first production-ready system based on ARMv8 processors [13,14]; McIntosh-Smith et al. also present an extensive overview of the current status of Arm in HPC.

SVE will be implemented in upcoming generations of Arm-based HPC processors, including the Fujitsu A64FX [23] and the Marvell ThunderX4 [19]. Because SVE supports vector widths between 128 and 2048 bits, chip designers need to select the vector width to be used in their implementation. It is, thus, important to estimate how this choice will affect the performance of applications run on such future processors, and experiments are already being run to determine the impact of SVE width on scientific kernels [6].

3   Methodology

In this paper, we study the efficacy of SVE over a number of mini-apps, each representative of a different class of scientific problems. The applications use only OpenMP or MPI, require no external libraries, and rely on automatic vectorisation by the compiler, i.e. no platform-specific intrinsics are used. The mini-apps studied are: STREAM, the established memory bandwidth benchmark [11]; BUDE, a molecular docking application developed at the University of Bristol [15]; TeaLeaf, a heat-diffusion mini-app [10]; CloverLeaf, a hydrodynamics code that solves Euler's equations of compressible fluid dynamics [8]; MegaSweep, a STREAM-style benchmark that uses the main kernel from SNAP, a deterministic discrete ordinates transport proxy application [4]; Neutral, a Monte-Carlo neutral particle transport mini-app [9]; and MiniFMM, a Fast Multipole Method mini-app that uses OpenMP tasks for parallelisation [1].

We performed the experiments described in this paper using a combination of static and dynamic analysis tools. The compilers used were the latest versions of the three main SVE toolchains available at the time of writing: Arm HPC Compiler 19.2, GCC 8.2, and Cray Compiler (CCE) 9.0; for SVE, a prerelease version of the Cray Compiler, 9.0a, was used. We enabled most compiler optimisation with the flags `-O3 -ffast-math -mcpu=thunderx2t99+sve`; full reproducibility details can be found in Sect. 8. In all experiments, we used a single OpenMP thread and MPI process (where applicable), and the inputs were chosen such that the non-instrumented run time is below 5 seconds on a single core of a ThunderX2 processor. We used compiler optimisation listings and annotated source code to count vectorised loops in each mini-app, and we confirmed that vector instructions are run using hardware counters.

Because no SVE-equipped hardware is available today, we ran the SVE versions of the mini-apps using the Arm Instruction Emulator (ArmIE)[1]. ArmIE

---

[1] https://developer.arm.com/tools-and-software/server-and-hpc/compile/arm-instruction-emulator.

runs base AArch64 instructions natively on the host, and switches to emulation when encountering SVE instructions. It also allows user-defined instrumentation code, known as instrumentation *clients*, to be run over both the native and emulated parts of the application. We used custom instrumentation clients to record data about the instructions executed and the memory accesses performed by the programs. We limited instrumentation to the core computation kernels in the mini-apps, such that data is not collected for the initialisation and shutdown stages of the applications, because these are generally not important when measuring real-world performance. Recording data outside the kernels can skew the results by showing a misleadingly high number of scalar instructions if these sections are not optimised for vectorisation. To define the regions where data was collected, we inserted special instructions to start and stop instrumentation, which are invalid AArch64 instructions but are recognised and honoured by our ArmIE client.

We classified dynamically recorded instructions into several categories: scalar AArch64 (A64), vector AArch64 (i.e. Advanced SIMD/NEON), SVE arithmetic, SVE memory loads, SVE memory stores, SVE moves, and SVE control flow. We used the memory access trace data to describe each operation as ⟨load/store, contiguous/non-contiguous, some/all vector lanes active⟩. The SVE vector width was set by stepping through the powers of two between 128 and 2048.

4 Results

4.1 Compiler Vectorisation Efficiency

We analysed the static vectorisation efficiency of SVE compared to AVX by looking at certain loops in the kernels of each mini-app. We selected loops to cover the majority of the mini-apps' run times, as reported by a profiled run on a real ThunderX2 processor. For targeting Arm, both with SVE and NEON, we used the three main HPC compilers: Arm's HPC compiler, GCC, and the Cray Compiler; for x86, we used the same versions of GCC and Cray, but we used the Intel Compiler 19.0 instead of the Arm HPC Compiler.

Table 1 shows, for each application, the number of loops considered, the percentage of run time that they represent, and the number of loops vectorised by each compiler on each platform. We show TeaLeaf twice once using a CG solver, once using a PPCG solver because the two runs cover very different code paths, and both are representative of real workloads. There are no MiniFMM results with the Cray Compiler because the application's build system does not currently support the Cray Compiler.

Aggregating the results across mini-apps, we observed that the compilers which can generate code for all the instructions sets vectorised the highest number of loops on SVE.

We then studied the factors influencing vectorisation on each mini-app individually. TeaLeaf with the PPCG solver was fully vectorised on all the platforms, by all compilers. TeaLeaf with CG and BUDE achieved 80% or more

Table 1. Number of loops vectorised by each compiler on the top loop-nests, selected by percentage of total run time on a ThunderX2 processor, in the mini-apps studied. The results for AVX2 and AVX-512 were identical; here they share the *AVX* label.

Application	% Time (Total Loops)	SVE			NEON			AVX		
		Arm	Cray	GCC	Arm	Cray	GCC	Intel	Cray	GCC
STREAM	92.4 (4)	4	4	4	4	4	4	4	4	4
BUDE	98.6 (4)	4	3	3	3	4	3	4	4	3
TeaLeaf (cg)	87.2 (8)	5	6	8	5	6	8	8	6	6
TeaLeaf (ppcg)	91.2 (6)	6	6	6	6	6	6	6	6	6
CloverLeaf	62.5 (10)	9	10	6	8	9	6	10	9	8
MegaSweep	70.3 (4)	1	4	0	1	1	0	4	1	0
Neutral	85.8 (2)	0	0	0	0	0	0	0	0	0
MiniFMM	98.1 (8)	7	—	5	3	—	5	7	—	5
Total	(46)	36	32	32	30	30	32	43	28	32

vectorisation with all compilers; it should be possible to achieve full vectorisation, as shown by the Intel compiler on AVX and GCC on Arm. CloverLeaf and MiniFMM showed all loops except one vectorised with Arm, Cray, and Intel, but only about half with GCC; GCC reports that further vectorisation is not beneficial according to its cost model, on all platforms, due to indirect access. MegaSweep was not vectorised by GCC on any platform, but fully vectorised by Cray on SVE and Intel on x86, which suggests vectorisation is possible, but not all compilers understand the loops' structure. Neutral was not vectorised at all, on any platform, due to the deeply nested branching in its algorithm.

When targeting x86, all compilers vectorised the same number of loops on both AVX2, e.g. for Broadwell, and AVX-512, e.g. for Skylake.

4.2 Dynamic Instruction Analysis

After we obtained vectorised code for the mini-apps, we recorded dynamic instruction execution traces at each power-of-two SVE vector length between 128 and 2048 bits. We added a NEON-only and a non-vectorised (scalar) run for each application, to serve as baselines against which to compare the SVE results. The traces allowed us to identify the types of SVE instructions executed and how their dynamic count varies with the chosen vector length.

Figure 1 shows the dynamic instruction count analysis for the **STREAM** benchmark, where instructions are grouped by type: scalar AArch64, NEON (AArch64 ASIMD), and several groups of SVE operations; a lower number of instructions executed is generally better. In the scalar and NEON-only cases, the Arm and Cray Compiler showed similar behaviour, but the GCC version ran more than twice as many instructions because it did not make use of load/store pair instructions, an operation in which two 64-bit values can be read from/written to memory in a single instruction. When targeting SVE, all

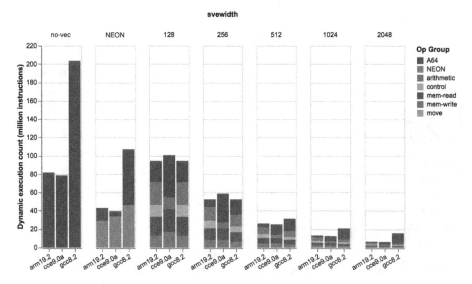

Fig. 1. Dynamic instruction count and grouping for STREAM. Lower is generally better. *A64* refers to scalar instructions; *NEON* refers to base-AArch64 ASIMD vector instructions; the remaining groups are all SVE instructions.

three compilers performed similarly, and we saw a decrease in the total instruction count as we increased vector length, since each instruction had increasingly more active lanes. No compiler generated load/store pairs for SVE, so the instruction count at 128 bits the same vector length that NEON uses is close to that observed for GCC when targeting NEON. The Arm and Cray compilers, but not GCC, chose to use scalar A64 instructions for loop control flow, which resulted in the the scalar instruction count also varying with SVE width.

BUDE, a heavily compute-bound application, ran vector code almost exclusively, which results in a clear inverse relation between the dynamic instruction count and the vector length. All compilers performed very similarly for this application. The results are shown in Fig. 2.

TeaLeaf and **CloverLeaf** exhibited similar behaviour: the code was only partially vectorised, leading to a mixture of SVE and scalar instructions. As the SVE length was increased, the number of executed SVE instructions decreased, but the number of scalar instructions executed stayed constant. The non-SVE part comes largely from outer-loop code, since in these cases only the innermost loop is vectorised by the compilers. Figure 3 shows the CloverLeaf results; TeaLeaf follows an almost-identical profile.

MegaSweep was only vectorised by the Cray Compiler. As with STREAM, CCE performed control flow using scalar instructions, so the instruction counts followed a similar profile here. Because the GCC- and Arm-compiled versions were not vectorised, all instructions run were scalar A64 and their execution count did not change with SVE width.

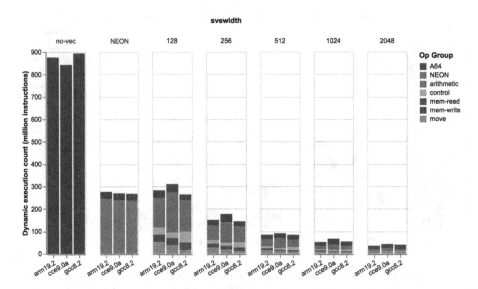

Fig. 2. Dynamic instruction count and grouping for BUDE. Lower is generally better. *A64* refers to scalar instructions; *NEON* refers to base-AArch64 ASIMD vector instructions; the remaining groups are all SVE instructions.

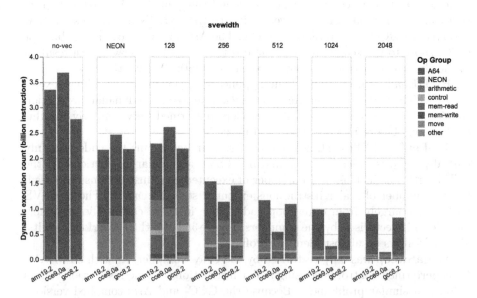

Fig. 3. Dynamic instruction count and grouping for CloverLeaf.

Figure 4 shows the dynamic instruction analysis for **MiniFMM**. This application's build system does not currently support the Cray Compiler, so results are only shown for GCC and Arm. Even though the application was (partially) vectorised, the instruction count did not decrease significantly when increasing the SVE vector width over 512 bits, in contrast to the applications presented previously. Due to an interaction between the way MiniFMM vectorises over particles and the small scale of the problem run, not all the lanes in SVE registers were being utilised at high vector lengths; since the vectors were partially empty, the total instruction count did not decrease linearly.

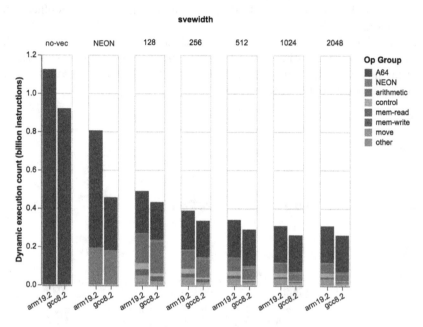

Fig. 4. Dynamic instruction count and grouping for MiniFMM.

Neutral is excluded from this analysis because it was not vectorised at all.

4.3   SVE Vector Lane Utilisation

Because SVE instructions employ per-lane predication, observing that SVE instructions are being *executed* is not enough to conclude that the application is using vector operations efficiently it is possible that a large portion of the elements, potentially all but one, are masked out. This means that vector register can be underpopulated, almost empty. To investigate this, we looked at per-lane utilisation of SVE registers when running the mini-apps.

For applications with a high degree of vectorisation, e. g. BUDE, TeaLeaf, or CloverLeaf, vector operations were performed using all the lanes, i. e. at maximum utilisation. For MiniFMM, however, the number of active lanes varied: at

512-bit-wide SVE and below, most instructions used 80% or more of the lanes available, but when increasing the SVE length further, vector register utilisation peaked between 512 and 768 bits. Vector utilisation was virtually identical across both compilers tested, Arm and GCC.

Figure 5 shows a histogram of the number of active bits in SVE operations, grouped in 128-bit-wide bins. Increasing the SVE width past 512 bits brings little benefit for MiniFMM, as only a minority of the operations performed use more than 512 bits. When the vector width is set to 1024 bits, less than 5% of the instructions use the full available width, and further increasing the width to 2048 bits produces no change in vector utilisation.

In contrast, Fig. 6 shows how BUDE, a mini-app that vectorises efficiently, was able to fully utilise vectors in *all* operations, even at the highest widths allowed by SVE. The other mini-apps investigated in this paper showed the same perfect vector utilisation efficiency as BUDE. These results cover both 32- and 64-bit floating-point data types: BUDE uses 32-bit data (`float`), and the other mini-apps use 64-bit types (`double`).

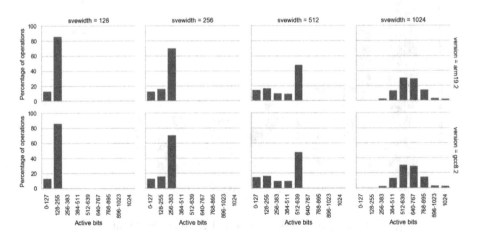

Fig. 5. Histogram showing the number of active bits in the SVE operations performed by MiniFMM. The application cannot saturate the full widths of the vectors when the SVE length is 512 bits or higher.

4.4   SVE Memory Operations

Finally, we looked at how the mini-apps are able to take advantage of SVE for memory operations. Since all SVE instructions are predicated per-lane, including contiguous and strided memory operations, every SVE memory instruction can differ in the number of bytes transferred.

We found that SVE usage for memory operations varied greatly between applications. Mini-apps with lower degrees of vectorisation, such as MegaSweep,

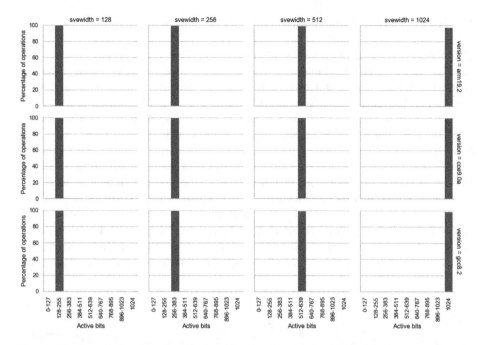

Fig. 6. Histogram showing the number of active bits in the SVE operations performed by BUDE. Vectorisation is perfectly efficient at all SVE widths.

used little SVE for memory accesses, but even applications with a higher degree of vectorisation showed a mixture of SVE and non-SVE memory operations. In BUDE, about three quarters of the memory instructions were SVE instructions; in CloverLeaf, TeaLeaf, and MiniFMM, between a quarter and a third of the memory operations were SVE. In MiniFMM, of the SVE operations, about a third were gathers, while there were no scatters; the other applications utilised contiguous accesses almost exclusively. All applications utilised all the SVE lanes in their memory operations, except for MiniFMM, where about half the SVE memory operations, including all the gathers, were only partially filled.

Figures 7 and 8 show the distributions of memory accesses in BUDE and MiniFMM, respectively. These two mini-apps form the most contrasting pair in the set of mini-apps evaluated. The observations here are consistent with Sects. 4.2 and 4.3: BUDE vectorises very efficiently, and MiniFMM utilises some SVE-specific features but does not always utilise all vector lanes available.

These results are collected from the version of the applications compiled with the Arm Compiler 19.2 and run on 512-bit SVE, which is the vector length utilised in the upcoming Fujitsu A64FX processor. The absolute numbers of vector operations varies between the versions built with different compilers and when adjusting the SVE width, but the same important characteristics can be seen in all cases, and the conclusions drawn are similar.

5   SVE Usage Discussion

The **STREAM** benchmark runs simple, predictable memory operations. All
the compilers tested were able to successfully use SVE at all vector lengths to
vectorise this code, and at run-time the vectors were fully utilised. This is the
expected behaviour for the benchmark.

BUDE is a heavily compute-bound benchmark, and thus complementary
to STREAM. This application shows very efficient utilisation of SVE: the main
kernels all execute vectorised operations, which scale with the chosen SVE length.
At 128 bits, the amount of code run both vector and scalar is almost identical to
the established NEON version, which indicates that good code is generated by
all the compilers. Increasing the vector length by 2× reduces by half the number
of instructions run up to 1024 bits; at 2048 bits, the total number of executed
vector instructions becomes smaller than the number of scalar instructions.

Even though more than half of the main loops in **TeaLeaf** are vectorised
by all the compilers, only relatively few vector instructions are executed at run-

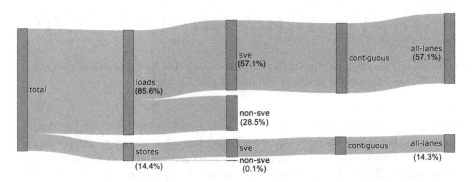

Fig. 7. Relative counts, by number of instructions, of memory operations in BUDE.
All memory accesses are contiguous and most are performed through SVE instructions.

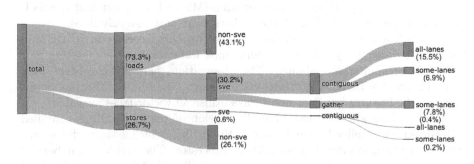

Fig. 8. Relative counts, by number of instructions, of memory operations in MiniFMM.
This applications shows a mixture of SVE and non-SVE operations, and the SVE ones
show a further split between contiguous and non-contiguous accesses. Not all lanes are
always used in SVE operations for MiniFMM.

time: for 128-bit SVE, these represent less than a third of the total instructions run for the Arm and GCC versions. Increasing the vector length decreases the count, but only with around 50% efficiency and up to 1024 bits; there is virtually no change going to 2048 bits. The Arm-compiled executable runs comparatively more instructions than the GCC version, by 35–40%, depending on the chosen vector length. With the Cray executable, less than 10% of the instructions run are vector operations, even though the compiler vectorised the same loops as Arm and GCC; at 1024 and 2048 bits, the vector code run is NEON, and not SVE, which we suspect is due to a compiler bug.

The **CloverLeaf** benchmark shows characteristics similar to TeaLeaf, but with more vector instruction utilisation. In all three versions, vector instructions account for between a third and half of the total instruction count at 128 bits; all three compilers produce a similar total dynamic instruction count. The SVE instruction count scales as expected up to the largest vector width possible, 2048 bits. The Cray-compiled version initially runs the highest number of total instructions, but it decreases sharply at 256 and 512 bits; at 512 bits more than two thirds of the code executed is SVE, and at 2048 bits the total count constitutes 22% of those of the Arm and GCC versions, suggesting that the Cray compiler optimises better for higher vector lengths.

This also hints at the importance of the loop chosen for vectorisation: if a compiler is able to vectorise the outer loop, as CCE is, and perhaps also to collapse the inner loop when doing so, the reduction in instruction count at high vector lengths can be considerable. On the other hand, the same strategy may not be desirable at smaller vector lengths, where vectorising the inner-most loop may be optimal. This would imply that, for optimal code generation, the compiler either needs to know the hardware vector width at compile-time, or it needs to generate several code paths and dynamically choose the optimal one when the vector length information becomes available at run-time.

A related issue is that the compilers tested in the study use a generic cost model for SVE, which may not accurately reflect any real implementation. With access to the cost model of a real SVE processor, the compilers may generate different code to take advantage of the implementation's strengths.

In CloverLeaf, SVE memory accesses represent about half the total memory operations performed, both when reading and writing, and the vast majority of those are contiguous operations.

Of the mini-apps included in this study, **MegaSweep** shows the most notable difference between the three compilers: Cray is the only one that successfully vectorises the code, both on NEON and SVE. The binary it produces runs 2.5× fewer total instructions than Arm and GCC at 128 bits, and the amount of SVE instructions executed scales almost perfectly up to 2048 bits, although the 1024-bit binary highlights a compiler issue where some of the code run is NEON, not SVE, which reduces the scaling efficiency in this particular case. At 2048 bits, the Cray version runs 10.5× fewer instructions than the GCC alternative. The Cray version also successfully utilises SVE for memory access, all of which are contiguous and are able to exploit the full lengths of the vectors.

Neutral does not vectorise with any of the compilers, so no SVE is being run. Due to the nature of the Monte-Carlo algorithm, there is little structure in the access patterns in the kernels. As Martineau and McIntosh-Smith explained, it is possible to force vector code generation, but it will be comprised almost entirely of indirect, variable-stride accesses that do not improve performance [9]; the compilers make the right choice to generate scalar instructions in this case.

In general it is desirable to utilise as much of the available vectors as possible, but partial utilisation does not always signal a problem. The **MiniFMM** result exhibits the flexibility of SVE: even though the parallelisation strategy in the application cannot fill the vectors above 512 bits, the hardware can still efficiently utilise its resources by executing partially masked operations. These operations should not be any more expensive than regular operations with full vectors, and so are more efficient than falling back to scalar code.

6   Relevance of SVE for HPC

The results presented in Sects. 4 and 5 show that SVE is a viable, competitive vector instruction set for HPC applications. For HPC workloads, it represents a noticeable improvement over NEON, bringing high-performance Arm processors in line with current-generation x86 processors, both in terms of the available vector length and the flexibility of the operations.

Even though no SVE hardware is currently available, we have found the SVE toolchains to be mature already. Generating SVE code only required enabling the SVE extension in the target architecture flag, and the compilers were successful in utilising SVE where expected. Compared to NEON, more loops were vectorised with SVE by all compilers, and the Arm and Cray compilers achieved a similar or higher degree of vectorisation on SVE compared to AVX-512.

One of the main advantages of SVE arose from its per-lane predication, which allowed loops with heavy control flow to be vectorised without additional cost. This additional flexibility meant it was sometimes beneficial to vectorise loops on SVE even when it was not on other instructions sets.

In the wider context, these results suggest that many HPC applications should be able to utilise SVE and benefit from doing so. The flexibility of SVE allows a wide range of loops to be turned into vector code, including cases where vectorisation is not possible with NEON or AVX, e. g. with irregular and unpredictable access patterns. Compute-bound applications can exploit high vector widths, bringing the number of instructions required significantly lower than on (128-bit) NEON. Partially filled operations allow vector instructions to be generated and executed even when the application cannot fill whole vector registers, a more efficient alternative than falling back to scalar code.

While in this study we have shown that SVE HPC applications behave well in an *emulated* environment, we cannot make any claims regarding their performance on real hardware. Implementations of SVE are likely to come with caveats and performance characteristics which cannot be determined *a priori*, and so it is impossible to predict which types of operations will be fast and which will bring little improvement over scalar code. There are currently no widely available tools to generate and run SVE code tuned for a specific microarchitecture definition, without which such a study is infeasible.

7 Future Work

The analysis presented in this study covers the three main SVE compilers available at the time of writing. However, Fujitsu A64FX systems are expected to be available in the near future, and Fujitsu will supply a proprietary compiler to accompany their processor. Optimisations applied by this compiler may be key in extracting high performance from the A64FX, so analysing the binaries it produces should prove a valuable research direction.

Further work will be enabled when the compilers are able to generate *tuned* binaries. The early versions used in this study only use a generic model of an SVE processor, because neither the compilers nor ArmIE currently allow the user to specify microarchitectural details, except the SVE width. Once a tuned binary can be generated, running it on its target platform will enable quantifying of the tuning benefit, and an even wider range of experiments is possible if these tuning parameters can be adjusted dynamically. This class of experiments for microarchitectural design-space exploration with arbitrary hypothetical processor configurations is one of the main goals of the upcoming SimEng simulator developed at the University of Bristol [12].

Finally, evaluation of full-size HPC applications on real inputs is intractable with the currently available emulation tools. The overhead incurred by ArmIE increases by several orders of magnitude when the instrumented application needs to use system calls, dynamically linked libraries, and file operations. For such experiments, benchmarking real hardware remains the only viable option.

8 Reproducibility

All mini-apps used in this study are open-source software and can be downloaded from their respective homepages. Detailed build and run instructions for each application, the custom ArmIE instrumentation clients used for this paper, and scripts to aggregate and plot the collected data can be found at https://github.com/UoB-HPC/sve-analysis-tools/tree/euro-par-2020.

9 Conclusion

In this work, we have presented an analysis of SVE usage across a number of mini-apps that span several common HPC problem classes. We have looked at how currently available compilers are able to utilise SVE to automatically vectorise the mini-apps' code, how much of the executed code is SVE, the efficiency of the executed SVE vector instructions, and whether new ways of accessing memory introduced with SVE are utilised in these mini-apps.

We found that SVE was generally well targetted by the compilers: in most cases, compilers were able to utilise SVE at least as well as AVX and NEON, and often better. The available compilers for SVE were only surpassed by the Intel compiler targetting AVX on select few occasions. Most SVE binaries used wide vectors efficiently, with all lanes being active for the vast majority of the run time; MiniFMM was the only exception, where SVE efficiency varied depending on the SVE width utilised. In terms of memory accesses, vectorised mini-apps were able to use SVE instructions to efficiently load and store data, and MiniFMM also made use of gather operations, either fully or only partially filled. We saw little use of SVE scatter instructions, but this is expected given the optimised memory access patterns on the mini-apps studied.

We conclude that SVE is a promising instruction set, and HPC applications and toolchains appear ready to take advantage of it to deliver performant code running on upcoming generation of Arm-based high-performance processors.

Data Availability Statement. The datasets and code generated during and/or analysed during the current study are available in the Figshare repository: https://doi.org/10.6084/m9.figshare.12608042 [17].

References

1. Atkinson, P., McIntosh-Smith, S.: On the performance of parallel tasking runtimes for an irregular fast multipole method application. In: de Supinski, B.R., Olivier, S.L., Terboven, C., Chapman, B.M., Müller, M.S. (eds.) IWOMP 2017. LNCS, vol. 10468, pp. 92–106. Springer, Cham (2017). https://doi.org/10.1007/978-3-319-65578-9_7
2. Crozier, P.S., et al.: Improving performance via mini-applications. Technical report SAND2009-5574 (2009). https://doi.org/10.2172/993908
3. Deakin, T., McIntosh-Smith, S., Gaudin, W.: Expressing parallelism on many-core for deterministic discrete ordinates transport. In: 2015 IEEE International Conference on Cluster Computing, pp. 729–737, September 2015. https://doi.org/10.1109/CLUSTER.2015.127
4. Deakin, T., Gaudin, W., McIntosh-Smith, S.: On the mitigation of cache hostile memory access patterns on many-core CPU architectures. In: Kunkel, J.M., Yokota, R., Taufer, M., Shalf, J. (eds.) ISC High Performance 2017. LNCS, vol. 10524, pp. 348–362. Springer, Cham (2017). https://doi.org/10.1007/978-3-319-67630-2_26
5. Hammond, S., Vaughan, C., Hughes, C.: Evaluating the intel skylake xeon processor for HPC workloads. In: 2018 International Conference on High Performance Computing Simulation (HPCS), pp. 342–349, July 2018. https://doi.org/10.1109/HPCS.2018.00064

6. Kodama, Y., Odajima, T., Matsuda, M., Tsuji, M., Lee, J., Sato, M.: Preliminary performance evaluation of application kernels using arm SVE with multiple vector lengths. In: 2017 IEEE International Conference on Cluster Computing, pp. 677–684. IEEE (2017)

7. Maleki, S., Gao, Y., Garzar'n, M.J., Wong, T., Padua, D.A.: An evaluation of vectorizing compilers. In: 2011 International Conference on Parallel Architectures and Compilation Techniques, pp. 372–382. IEEE (2011). https://doi.org/10.1109/PACT.2011.68

8. Mallinson, A., Beckingsale, D., Gaudin, W., Herdman, J., Levesque, J., Jarvis, S.: Cloverleaf: preparing hydrodynamics codes for exascale. In: Cray User Group, May 2013

9. Martineau, M., McIntosh-Smith, S.: Exploring on-node parallelism with neutral, a Monte Carlo neutral particle transport mini-app. In: 2017 IEEE International Conference on Cluster Computing (CLUSTER), pp. 498–508, September 2017. https://doi.org/10.1109/CLUSTER.2017.83

10. Martineau, M., McIntosh-Smith, S., Gaudin, W.: Assessing the performance portability of modern parallel programming models using TeaLeaf. Concurr. Comput. Pract. Exp. **29**(15), e4117 (2017). https://doi.org/10.1002/cpe.4117

11. McCalpin, J.D.: Memory bandwidth and machine balance in current high performance computers. IEEE Comput. Soc. Tech. Comm. Comput. Archit. (TCCA) Newsl. **2**, 19–25 (1995)

12. McIntosh-Smith, S.: Enabling processor design space exploration with SimEng. In: ModSim: Workshop on Modeling and Simulation of Systems and Applications (2019)

13. McIntosh-Smith, S., Price, J., Deakin, T., Poenaru, A.: A performance analysis of the first generation of HPC-optimized arm processors. Concurr. Comput. Pract. Exp. **31**(16), e5110 (2019). https://doi.org/10.1002/cpe.5110

14. McIntosh-Smith, S., Price, J., Poenaru, A., Deakin, T.: Benchmarking the first generation of production quality arm-based supercomputers. Concurr. Comput. Pract. Exp. p. e5569 (2019). https://doi.org/10.1002/cpe.5569

15. McIntosh-Smith, S., Price, J., Sessions, R.B., Ibarra, A.A.: High performance in silico virtual drug screening on many-core processors. Int. J. High Perform. Comput. Appl. **29**(2), 119–134 (2015). https://doi.org/10.1177/1094342014528252

16. Pennycook, S.J., Hughes, C.J., Smelyanskiy, M., Jarvis, S.A.: Exploring SIMD for molecular dynamics, using intel xeon processors and intel xeon phi coprocessors. In: 2013 IEEE 27th International Symposium on Parallel and Distributed Processing, pp. 1085–1097, May 2013. https://doi.org/10.1109/IPDPS.2013.44

17. Poenaru, A., McIntosh-Smith, S.: Artifact and instructions to reproduce experimental results for Euro-Par 2020 paper. In: Evaluating the Effectiveness of a Vector-Length-Agnostic Instruction Set, July 2020. https://doi.org/10.6084/m9.figshare.12608042, https://springernature.figshare.com/articles/dataset/Artifact_and_instructions_to_reproduce_experimental_results_for_Euro-Par_2020_paper_Evaluating_the_Effectiveness_of_a_Vector-Length-Agnostic_Instruction_Set_/12608042/1

18. Pohl, A., Cosenza, B., Juurlink, B.: Portable cost modeling for auto-vectorizers. In: 2019 IEEE 27th International Symposium on Modeling, Analysis, and Simulation of Computer and Telecommunication Systems (MASCOTS), pp. 359–369. IEEE (2019)

19. Schor, D.: Marvell lays out arm server roadmap. https://fuse.wikichip.org/news/2956/marvell-lays-out-arm-server-roadmap

20. Stephens, N., et al.: The arm scalable vector extension. IEEE Micro **37**(2), 26–39 (2017). https://doi.org/10.1109/MM.2017.35
21. Stringer, L.: Vectors: how the old became new again in supercomputing. https://www.hpcwire.com/2016/09/26/vectors
22. Trader, T.: Cray, Fujitsu both bringing Fujitsu A64fX-based supercomputers to market in 2020. https://www.hpcwire.com/2019/11/12/cray
23. Yoshida, T.: Fujitsu high performance CPU for the post-k computer. In: Hot Chips 30 Symposium (HCS), Series Hot Chips, vol. 18 (2018)
24. Zhao, B., Gao, W., Zhao, R., Han, L., Sun, H., Li, Y.: Performance evaluation of NPB and SPEC CPU2006 on various SIMD extensions. In: Wang, Y., Xiong, H., Argamon, S., Li, X.Y., Li, J.Z. (eds.) BigCom 2015. LNCS, vol. 9196, pp. 257–272. Springer, Cham (2015). https://doi.org/10.1007/978-3-319-22047-5_21

Scheduling and Load Balancing

Parallel Scheduling of Data-Intensive Tasks

Xiao Meng and Lukasz Golab[✉]

University of Waterloo, Waterloo, Canada
{x36meng,lgolab}@uwaterloo.ca

Abstract. Workloads with precedence constraints due to data dependencies are common in various applications. These workloads can be represented as directed acyclic graphs (DAG), and are often data-intensive, meaning that data loading cost is the dominant factor and thus cache misses should be minimized. We address the problem of parallel scheduling of a DAG of data-intensive tasks to minimize makespan. To do so, we propose greedy online scheduling algorithms that take load balancing, data dependencies, and data locality into account. Simulations and an experimental evaluation using an Apache Spark cluster demonstrate the advantages of our solutions.

Keywords: Parallel scheduling · Data-intensive tasks · Caching

1 Introduction

In the era of big data, many computational tasks are data-intensive: their data loading cost is higher than the subsequent computation cost. These tasks usually have precedence constraints due to data dependencies, represented as a directed acyclic graph (DAG). Examples include scientific workflows, *continuous queries* in streaming and publish-subscribe systems, and Extract-Transform-Load (ETL) pipelines in relational databases. Here, the DAG of tasks is periodically executed on a batch of new data. It is critical to finish these tasks as soon as possible (i.e., minimize the *makespan*) to accommodate the next batch of data. Otherwise, we will fall behind or will have to increase the batch size, thus increasing data latency, which is not desirable in real-time analytics. Sequencing data-intensive tasks then becomes a significant problem because some sequences may incur more cache misses than others, leading to a longer makespan[1].

Scheduling algorithms often assume that the execution times (or estimates) of tasks are known. However, the *cold* versus *hot* (with data already in memory/cache) runtimes of data-intensive tasks may be very different, by an order of magnitude or more. Furthermore, predicting the contents of the cache at any

---

[1] We assume a storage hierarchy with significant speed gaps between different levels, and use the term *cache* more generally, referring to SRAM cache memory, RAM memory, or distributed memory in a platform such as Spark, as appropriate.

M. Malawski and K. Rzadca (Eds.): Euro-Par 2020, LNCS 12247, pp. 117–133, 2020.
https://doi.org/10.1007/978-3-030-57675-2_8

point in time is difficult in modern data processing environments with multiple tenants, virtualization, and shared resources.

There has been previous work on a problem we call Serial Data-Intensive Scheduling (SDIS): given a DAG of tasks with data dependencies, SDIS finds an ordering of the tasks that obeys the precedence constraints given by the DAG and aims to minimize the likelihood of cache misses [6]. Knowing the contents of the cache at any time is not required; the only assumption was that the cache uses an LRU-based strategy, where the longer the wait, the slimmer the chance of unused data remaining in the cache.

However, this problem remains unsolved in distributed and parallel settings, such as a Spark [16] cluster or a multi-core database management system. That is the problem we address in this paper – the Multi-Processor Data-Intensive Scheduling (MPDIS) problem to minimize the makespan of a DAG of data-intensive tasks. The additional complexity of MPDIS over SDIS comes from two factors: 1) a larger search space of possible schedules and 2) a load balancing requirement missing from serial scheduling. Thus, a solution to the MPDIS problem must simultaneously ensure load balancing and data locality. We make the following contributions towards solving this problem:

1. We define the MPDIS problem of scheduling a DAG of data-intensive tasks on multiple processors, assuming a shared LRU cache, but without knowing the contents of the cache at any point in time.
2. We propose three greedy online algorithms to solve the MPDIS problem using cache metrics from the Programming Language and Compiler literature.
3. Using simulations and a Spark cluster, we experimentally show the effectiveness of our algorithms against existing techniques on real-world based DAGs.

The remainder of this paper is organized as follows. In Sect. 2, we review related work. We formulate our scheduling problem in Sect. 3 and propose solutions in Sect. 4. We present experimental results in Sect. 5 and we conclude in Sect. 6.

Example 1: Consider the DAG of tasks in Fig. 1, with edges showing data dependencies (e.g, the data output of task zero is the data input to task 3). Assume each task produces an output of unit size. Suppose for each of the six tasks, the computation cost (hot runtime) is one time unit while the loading cost of one data unit is ten time units. Assume the cache can hold up to two data items at the same time. Figure 2 shows two schedules, labelled S1 and S2, for two processing units, labelled PU1 and PU2. The task runtimes are coloured blue and plotted on a time axis. The figure also shows the contents of the cache at various points in time; e.g., "01" indicates that the cache currently holds the outputs of tasks zero and one.

For both schedules, there will be cache misses for items 0 and 1 since the cache is initially empty. This means that tasks 0 and 1 run cold, for a total of 11 time units (10 time units to load the data plus one time unit for the computation). For the first schedule, S1, at time 11, tasks 0 and 1 finish, and

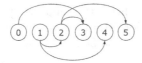

Fig. 1. Example DAG of data-intensive tasks.

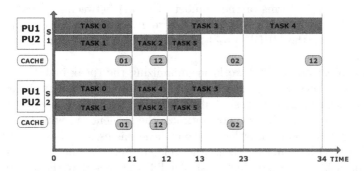

Fig. 2. Two schedules for example DAG from Fig. 1 on two processors.

both of their outputs are in the cache. Task 2 is started on processor 2. Task 3 waits for task 2 to finish because its input is the output of task 2. Task 3 takes one time unit because the data needed for task 2, namely the data output of task 1, is in the cache. At time 12, when task 2 is finished, task 3 and task 5 are started. The output of task 2 is in the cache, evicting the output of task 0 according to the LRU policy. Thus, now the cache holds the outputs of tasks 1 and 2. This means that task 3 causes a cache miss for item 0, and finishes at time 23, while task 5 finishes earlier at time 13 (because its input, which was the output of task 2, was in the cache). At this time, the cache holds the outputs of tasks 0 and 2. Thus, task 4 causes a cache miss for item 1, and therefore finishes at time 34.

In schedule S2, when tasks 0 and 1 terminate, tasks 2 and 4 run hot because their input (the output of task 1) is in the cache. When tasks 2 and 4 are done, the cache now contains the output of task 2 (which evicts the output of 0) and the output of task 1 (note that task 4 does not produce any output for use by subsequent tasks). This means that task 5 runs hot, but task 3 incurs a cache miss because it requires the output of task 0. Note that schedule S2 incurs fewer cache misses and has a shorter makespan, highlighting the need for a scheduling strategy for data-intensive workloads.

2   Related Work

Scheduling DAGs of tasks on multiple processors to minimize makespan is an NP-Complete problem with only a few exceptions [10]. Therefore, many heuristics have been proposed; however, data-intensive tasks were not considered. In particular, [7] compared these heuristics empirically and found that Heterogeneous Earliest Finish Time (or HEFT) is among the best for multiprocessor DAG scheduling. We will use a modified HEFT as a baseline in our experimental comparison (Sect. 5).

In terms of data-intensive scheduling, there has been work on the SDIS problem [6] mentioned earlier. A solution was given that minimizes the distance in a serial schedule (in terms of the number of tasks) between the first and the last access of every data item. Heuristics were given to solve this minimization problem. However, the MPDIS problem, which is the focus of our work, was not considered.

We also point out related work on minimizing the (peak or total) memory footprint of parallel schedules; see, e.g., [5,11]. However, to the best of our knowledge, these methods do not consider data-intensive tasks; they schedule tasks to optimize memory usage but do not optimize the sequence in which data items are inserted into memory in order to avoid cache misses.

Scheduling with setup times is another related topic, in which there are different types of tasks, and scheduling a task of a different type than the previous task requires some setup time; in general, the execution time of a task may include a setup time that is dependent on the tasks that have been executed up to now [4]. However, the MPDIS problem is more complex because the sequence of tasks executed up to now may not be sufficient to determine the contents of the cache.

Since Spark [16] is one target system for our solutions, we briefly discuss data-intensive scheduling in Spark. The work on memory caching in Spark (e.g., [9,14, 15]) does not consider data dependencies among tasks, as we do. Furthermore, in a system such as Spark, there is a shared cache, but also local memory and disk. There has been work on the problem of *reducer placement* to schedule reducers (of a given task) on nodes that have much of the required data already in local memory [12]. MPDIS is an orthogonal problem of sequencing tasks, and reducer placement solutions may be applied independently to assign the reducers of a given task to the available machines, and further improve performance.

3   Problem Definition and Assumptions

We consider data-intensive (as defined earlier), non-preemptible tasks, with precedence constraints corresponding to data dependencies. Precedence constraints are expressed as a directed acyclic graph (DAG) $G = (V, E)$, where each node $v \in V$ represents a task and each directed edge $e = (u, v) \in E$ represents a precedence constraint. An edge in the DAG denotes that the data output of one task is the data input to another. Thus, an edge (u, v) requires that task u has to be completed before task v starts. Optional input may include the size the data output of each task, represented as an edge weight in the DAG. Tasks are scheduled on n *homogeneous* processing units that share a fast storage layer with an LRU-based replacement policy (which, as explained earlier, may be an SRAM cache, RAM memory, or distributed memory). However, we assume that the contents of the fast storage layer cannot be reliably predicted at any point in time, as motivated earlier. This means that we cannot know with certainty whether a task will run cold or hot.

A precedence constraint (u, v) indicates that the output of u is the input to v. The intuition behind our scheduling objective is to schedule v as soon as possible after u. The longer we wait, the more likely it is that other tasks will be scheduled, which may require other data inputs. Thus, the longer we wait, the more likely it is that the output of u will be evicted from an LRU cache, causing a cache miss when v runs. To formalize this intuition, we use the following data locality metrics from prior work (our solutions are independent of the data locality metric, and we will experiment with both of these metrics in Sect. 5):

- *Stack Distance* (SD) [8] is a metric from the programming languages and compiler literature. The stack distance between two accesses of a data item counts the *distinct* number of other data items that were accessed in between. The more data items accessed in between, the more likely it is that the original data item is no longer in the cache when it is accessed again[2]. We compute the stack distance of a schedule as the sum of the stack distances between every pair of consecutive references to the same data item, with "reference" denoting producing the item as output or consuming the item as input. If a task references more than one output, then we sequence these accesses in lexicographic order for computation (e.g., in Fig. 1, task 3 first accesses the output of task 0 and then the output of task 2).
- *Total Maximum Bandwidth* (TMB) was proposed in prior work on the SDIS problem [6]. TMB considers the first and the last access of a data item, and counts the distinct number of other data items that were accessed in between. (SD measures the same quantity, but for each pair of consecutive accesses of a data item.)

Example 2: Consider two data items, A and B. Suppose they are accessed in the following sequence: A, B, A, B, A. The stack distance of this sequence is three: one distinct item (B) is accessed between the first and the second access of A; B is again accessed between the second and the third access of A; plus, one distinct item (A) is accessed between the two accesses of B. The TMB of this sequence is two: one distinct item (B) is accessed between the first and the last access of A (not including A itself); plus, one distinct item (A) is accessed between the first and the last access of B.

Example 3: Recall the DAG in Fig. 1 and assume the following schedule: [0, 1, 2, 3, 4, 5]. That is, the tasks are sequenced as shown in the figure. The output of task 1 becomes the input to tasks 2 and 4. Thus, the output of task 1 is referenced three times: by task 1 at creation time, by task 2, and by task 4. The stack distance between the first and second reference is zero: no other tasks ran

---

[2] *Reference Distance* (RD) is a related metric that counts the total number of data accesses in between, not the distinct data accesses. SD was shown to be more accurate than RD in quantifying data locality [8], so we will not consider RD any further.

in between. The stack distance between the second and the third reference is two: task 3 ran in between and it accessed the outputs of task 0 and 2. Thus, it is more likely that the output of task 1 was evicted from the cache before it is needed by task 4. In total, we have:

- task 0 produces output that is referenced once by task 3. In between, task 1 produced output referenced by task 2, giving a stack distance of one.
- task 1 produces output that is referenced twice (becomes the input to two downstream tasks), giving stack distances of zero and two, respectively.
- task 2 also produces output that is referenced twice, with the corresponding stack distances of zero (nothing runs between tasks 2 and 3), and two (task 3 additionally references the output of task 0 and task 4 requires the output of task 1).

This gives a stack distance of $1 + 0 + 2 + 0 + 2 = 5$ for the entire schedule.

We now reiterate the two data-intensive scheduling problems mentioned earlier.

Problem 1: Serial Data-Intensive Scheduling (SDIS). Given a DAG of tasks with precedence constraints, produce a serial schedule that obeys the precedence constraints with the smallest SD or TMB.

A version of SDIS that minimized TMB was studied in [6]. In this paper, we solve the following problem:

Problem 2: Multi-Processor Data-Intensive Scheduling (MPDIS). Given a DAG of tasks with precedence constraints and n processing units sharing a fast memory layer, produce a parallel schedule across the n processors that obeys the precedence constraints, with the smallest SD or TMB over a serialized representation of the parallel schedule according to task start times (we compute stack distance over this serialized representation since all processing units access the same cache).

Example 4: We compute SD for the complete schedules in Fig. 2 below. S1 [0, 1, 2, 3, 5, 4] costs $1 + 2 + 1 = 4$ and S2 [0, 1, 4, 2, 3, 5] costs $1 + 0 + 1 = 2$. Note that S2 has a smaller stack distance and a shorter completion time.

We remark that there exists a weighted version of Problem 2, where instead of counting the number of other data items accessed between two references of some data item, we count the total size of the other data items accessed. Similarly, TMB can be extended to its weighted version, abbreviated WTMB [6]. Data item sizes can be given as edge weights in the precedence DAG.

4   Solutions

We present three solutions to the MPDIS problem in this section. Our solutions are *online*, meaning that tasks are scheduled on-the-fly rather than being statically assigned to processing units in a pre-defined order. We do not consider offline algorithms that assemble a complete schedule apriori. Given our assumptions, even if we enumerated the possible schedules, we could not compute their makespans since task runtimes may be cold or hot, depending on the contents of the cache, which we cannot predict in advance.

4.1 Parallel SDIS (PS)

The first solution, Parallel SDIS, is an extension of the SDIS solution from [6] that produces a serial schedule to minimize TMB (and can be modified to minimize SD instead). First, we generate a single-threaded schedule S using the existing SDIS solution. Then, whenever a processing unit is available, we schedule the next task from S, call it t, on this processing unit. Note that if t is not schedulable at this time (i.e., all the tasks it depends on have not yet terminated), then the processing unit is idle until t becomes schedulable.

Example 5: Fig. 3 shows an example of Parallel SDIS on two processing units (PU1 and PU2) using the DAG from Fig. 1, assuming the computation and loading times listed in Table 1, and assuming the cache can hold two data items. Assume we use SD as the data locality metric instead of TMB. Here, an optimal SDIS schedule using SD is [0, 1, 4, 2, 3, 5]. Given this SDIS schedule, our Parallel SDIS algorithm proceeds as follows. First, task 0 is scheduled on PU1 and runs cold for 51 time units. At the same time, task 1 is scheduled on PU2 and runs cold for 11 time units. When task 1 terminates, the next task in the SDIS schedule is task 4, which is now scheduled on PU2. Task 4 is now schedulable (because it only relies on task 1, which just terminated), and runs hot until time 12. At this time, the cache holds the outputs of task 1. Next in the SDIS schedule is task 2, which is scheduled on PU2 and runs hot until time 13. At this time, the cache holds the output of tasks 1 and 2. Next, task 3 is scheduled on PU2, but it must wait until task 0 terminates. Thus, task 3 begins running only at time 51 and terminates at time 52. When task 0 terminates at time 51, the last task is task 5, which is now scheduled on PU1. Task 5 runs hot for 10 time units, terminating at time 61. The makespan is thus 61.

Time Complexity: The complexity of PS depends on the complexity of the underlying SDIS solution. For example, the heuristic solution from [6] has a complexity of $O(|E||V|^2 + |V|^3 \log |V|)$, where $|E|$ and $|V|$ is the number of edges and vertices, respectively, in the DAG. After generating such a solution, we insert the serial schedule into a queue and pop the next schedulable task from the queue whenever a processing unit becomes available. Checking whether a task t is schedulable has a complexity of $O(|E|)$ (assume we have a hash map of completed tasks; then it suffices to find the edges incident on t and check if the predecessors of t all exist in the set of completed tasks), and this is done for all $|V|$ tasks.

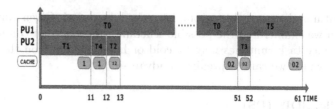

Fig. 3. Schedule for example DAG generated by Algorithm PS.

Table 1. Data loading and computation runtimes of tasks for example DAG from Fig. 1.

Task	Loading (time units)	Computation (time units)
0	50	1
1	10	1
2	10	1
3	60	1
4	10	1
5	10	10

4.2   Online Greedy (OG)

Notice a potential problem with the Parallel SDIS algorithm: since it uses a single-threaded sequencing as a seed, the next task in the schedule may not yet be schedulable in parallel with another task that is currently running. This causes some processing units to be idle (e.g., PU2 in Fig. 3 is idle from time 13 to time 51). To address this problem, we propose an Online Greedy (OG) algorithm. OG does not compute a single-threaded schedule beforehand. Instead, whenever a processor becomes available, OG chooses the next *schedulable* task that yields the smallest SD or TMB when added to the current partial schedule (with ties broken arbitrarily). Thus, OG does not stall as long as there is at least one schedulable task.

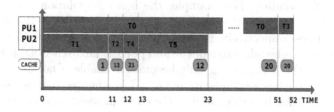

Fig. 4. Schedule for example DAG generated by Algorithm OG.

Example 6: Fig. 4 shows an example of OG on two processing units, again using the DAG from Fig. 1, the parameters listed in Table 1, and assuming the cache can hold two data items. Assume again that we use SD as the data locality metric. At the beginning, the only schedulable tasks are 0 and 1. Breaking ties randomly, we assign task 0 to PU1 and task 1 to PU2, and both tasks run cold. When task 1 finishes at time 11 and PU2 becomes free, there are two schedulable tasks: task 2 and task 4. To decide which task to schedule on PU2, we compute the SD of the following partial schedules and choose the task that gives the partial schedule with the lowest SD: [0, 1, 2] and [0, 1, 4]. Both are zero, so we break ties randomly. Let task 2 run on PU2.

Next, task 2 terminates at time 12 (it ran hot because the output of task 1 is in the cache). At this time, tasks 4 and 5 are schedulable. To decide which one to schedule next, we compute the SD of the following partial schedules and again choose the task that gives the partial schedule with the lowest SD: [0, 1, 2, 4] and [0, 1, 2, 5]. Both are again zero, so we break ties randomly. Let task 4 run on PU2 (it runs hot because the output of task 2 is in the cache), finishing at time 13. Now, task 0 is still running on PU1, so the only schedulable task is task 5. Thus, we run task 5 on PU2. It runs hot because the output of task 2 is in the cache, terminating at time 23. At this time, there are no schedulable tasks, so PU2 is idle. When task 0 terminates at time 51, the only remaining task is task 3, which runs hot until time 52. Note that the OG schedule terminates nine time units earlier than the PS schedule described in Example 6 (52 vs. 61).

Time Complexity: Computing the SD or TMB of a (partial) schedule requires $O(|E|)$ time: we loop over all the outgoing edges of the tasks already in the schedule, which gives $O(|E|)$. When making a scheduling decision, we compute the SD or TMB for $O(|V|)$ tasks that may be scheduled next, giving $O(|V||E|)$. The total number of scheduling decisions is $O(|V|)$, giving a complexity of $O(|V|^2|E|)$.

4.3   Greedy Complete Schedule (GCS)

At any point in time, algorithm OG greedily chooses a task whose addition to the current partial schedule yields the lowest total SD or TMB. We now observe that, in contrast to other on-line scheduling settings, we know the workload in advance: it is given in the form of a DAG. To leverage this observation, we propose a Greedy Complete Schedule (GCS) algorithm. The intuition is as follows: when a processing unit becomes available, we choose a schedulable task that leads to a *complete schedule* with the lowest SD or TMB. When deciding which task to schedule next, we "simulate" a complete schedule by greedily and repeatedly adding the next task that minimizes SD or TMB, until all the remaining tasks have been scheduled.

Example 7: Consider again the DAG from Fig. 1 and the task runtimes from Table 1. Assume again that there are two processing units, PU1 and PU2, and that we want to minimize SD. First, we schedule task 0 on PU1 and task 1 on PU2. At time 11, task 1 finishes and PU2 frees up. There are now two schedulable tasks: 2 and 4. GCS now performs the following steps. If we were to schedule task 2 next, the partial schedule would be $[0, 1, 2]$. To simulate a complete schedule, we greedily keep adding tasks that minimize the SD of the partial schedule. Thus, we first compute the SD of the following schedules: $[0, 1, 2, 3]$ (with $SD = 5$), $[0, 1, 2, 4]$ (with $SD = 1$), and $[0, 1, 2, 5]$ (with $SD = 2$). Since adding task 4 leads to the lowest SD, the simulated schedule now becomes $[0, 1, 2, 4]$. Next, we consider adding tasks 3 and 5 to the simulated schedule, i.e., we compute the SD of $[0, 1, 2, 4, 3]$ and $[0, 1, 2, 4, 5]$. It turns out that $[0, 1, 2, 4, 5]$ has a lower SD. This gives a complete simulated schedule of $[0, 1, 2, 4, 5, 3]$. Similarly, returning to the initial partial schedule of $[0, 1]$, if we were to schedule task 4 next instead of task 2, the partial schedule would be $[0, 1, 4]$, and we simulate a complete schedule starting with this prefix. Finally, to decide between task 2 and task 4, we choose the task whose complete simulated schedule has a lower SD.

There is a potential problem with the above method: when simulating a greedy complete schedule, we need to know the set of schedulable tasks at every step. However, for this, we need to know which tasks have already terminated at any point in time, yet we do not know the task runtimes (because we do not know whether the tasks will run hot or cold). The simplest assumption to make is that tasks terminate in first-in-first-out (FIFO) order. For example, assuming a partial schedule $[0, 1, 2, 4]$ and two processing units, the FIFO assumption means that the next scheduling decision happens when task 0 terminates, and we update the set of schedulable tasks accordingly. However, in practice, task 1, task 2 or even task 4 could terminate before task 0, leading to a different set of schedulable tasks at this point in time. To sum up the challenge that must be addressed in our setting: *while we know the workload in advance, we do not know the order in which tasks will terminate.* As a result, we cannot predict the complete schedule throughout the execution of a workload, even if we assume a deterministic greedy heuristic at every scheduling step.

In algorithm GCS, we mitigate the above problem as follows. Instead of generating only one complete schedule assuming FIFO task termination order, we generate multiple possible complete schedules for each candidate task under consideration. One of these possible complete schedules assumes FIFO order. For the other schedules, we iterate through the partial schedule, and swap the completion order of every pair of consecutive tasks already started but not yet completed. For example, if the current partial schedule is $[0, 1, 2]$ and all three of these tasks are still running, we would consider completing the following swapped partial schedules: $[1, 0, 2]$, $[0, 2, 1]$. For each of these partial schedules, we generate a complete schedule as discussed above, and compute its SD. Finally, for each candidate task to be scheduled next, we record the lowest SD of any of its simulated complete schedules, and we select the task with the lowest SD of the best simulated schedule (we also experimented with choosing the task with the lowest average SD of all of its simulated full schedules, and obtained similar results).

Time Complexity: Algorithm GCS incurs an extra $O(|V|^3)$ factor compared to OG, for a complexity of $O(|V|^5|E|)$. This is because it no longer suffices to compute the SD of the partial schedule of each schedulable task when making a scheduling decision. Instead, it takes $O(|V|^2|E|)$ time to assemble a complete schedule (specifically, $O(|V||E|)$ time to decide on the next task to add to the schedule, and there are $O(|V|)$ remaining tasks). Furthermore, there are $O(|V|)$ complete schedules to test, resulting from swapping the completion order of the tasks in the current partial schedule.

5   Experimental Evaluation

In this section, we present experimental results comparing our solutions (PS, OG, and GCS) with two baselines: B1 and B2. B1 is random scheduling, which chooses a random schedulable task whenever a processor is available. B2 is the HEFT algorithm, where the idea is to prioritize tasks based on the runtimes of the tasks depending on them. Since we do not know the actual runtimes, which can be cold or hot, we use the sum of the sizes of the data inputs of the dependent tasks (effectively assuming cold runtimes). We start with simulation results (Sect. 5.1) and then present results using a Spark cluster (Sect. 5.2).

5.1   Scheduling Simulation

We identified three DAGs used in real applications and concatenated them to create our first workload, referred to as DAG1 and illustrated in Fig. 5. The DAGs correspond to a network monitoring workflow [6], an image stitching workflow called Montage [1], and an earthquake analysis workflow called CyberShake [1]. Note that there are no dependencies across tasks from the three concatenated DAGs. In other words, DAG1 corresponds to a multi-tenant workload with three independent DAGs of tasks.

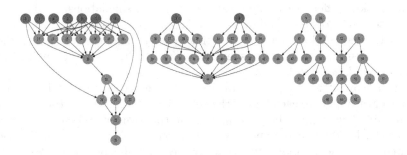

Fig. 5. DAG1 based on three real workloads.

In addition to DAG1, we created several larger versions of it, referred to as DAG1 v2 through DAG1 v6 (illustrations omitted due to space constraints). DAG1 v2 horizontally duplicates DAG1; DAG1 v3 vertically "grows" DAG1 by duplicating each level of tasks; DAG1 is similar to DAG1 v3 but adds more data dependencies among the tasks; DAG1 v5 combines horizontal and vertical duplication; and DAG1 v6 adds more data dependencies to DAG1 v5. The number of tasks and edges in each DAG, as well as the average number of schedulable tasks at any point in the schedule (abbreviated $|SS|$), are presented in Table 2. Increasing the size and the complexity of the DAG correspondingly increases the number of schedulable tasks at any point in time. On the other hand, small DAGs may limit parallelism opportunities.

Table 2. Number of tasks, edges (precedence constraints), and the average size of the schedulable task set ($|SS|$) for each DAG.

DAG	DAG1	v2	v3	v4	v5	v6
$|V|$	63	113	113	113	145	145
$|E|$	96	192	205	240	224	237
$|SS|$	7.2	12.4	11.6	11.2	16.1	15.2

Our simulation environment, implemented in Python, has two components: cache simulation and schedule simulation. For cache simulation, we used PyLRU [2]. By keeping the key of a data item in the LRU cache through a dictionary data structure, we simulate the cache contents at any given time. Schedule simulation uses a scheduler module, in which we implemented various scheduling algorithms for comparison. The input parameters include the DAG, with edge weights corresponding to data sizes (to compute weighted SD and weighted TMB), the cold and hot runtimes (defined as functions of the input data size), the cache size, and the number of cores/processing units. The simulator then schedules the tasks as prescribed by the given scheduling algorithm, and keeps track of statistics such as the simulated I/O, processor idle percentage, and makespan.

We consider different cache pressure points in our simulations. To do so, we set the cache size to 20 GB and we vary the input size to each task. Tasks at the first level of the DAG are set to be ten times slower than other tasks (i.e., they consume ten times more data) to simulate workloads that compute smaller data products over large raw data.

We start by setting the total data size in the simulation to 120 GB, which is the sum of the inputs to each task in the DAG. This gives a data to cache ratio of 6:1. In Table 3, we report the performance gap (in terms of makespan) between B1 and OG for different numbers of threads ranging from one to 8. We used weighted SD as the data locality metric for these initial experiments. We notice that increasing the level of parallelism does not lead to a bigger performance improvement of OG over B1. Therefore, for more cache pressure, we increase the size of the data from 120 GB to 240 GB, 480 GB, 600 GB, and 840 GB. This gives data to cache ratios between 6:1 and 42:1.

Figure 6 shows the results, with makespan on the y-axis (in seconds) and data size on the x-axis. The figure contains five sets of bars, one for each data size, as labelled. Each set contains seven bars, corresponding to the different

Table 3. Performance gap between B1 and OG in terms of makespan (120 GB data size).

Number of threads	1	2	4	8
Performance gap (B1/OG)	*1.95x*	*1.83x*	*1.84x*	*1.72x*

scheduling algorithms and locality metrics we test, from right to left: B1, B2, PS using weighted SD, PS using weighted TMB (WTMB), OG using weighted SD, OG using WTMB, and GCS[3].

Additionally, for the largest, 840 GB, data size, we show I/O volume and the percentage of processing unit idle time for each scheduling algorithm in Table 4. Note that some idle time may be due to the workload: if there are only two tasks that can initially be scheduled, then regardless of the sequencing, only two processing units will initially be busy. Additionally, processing units may be idle if they are assigned a task that is currently not yet schedulable; this may happen in PS, but we designed OG and GCS to avoid these situations.

We make the following observations based on the simulation results:

Table 4. I/O transfer and CPU idle time percentage for DAG1 (840 GB data size).

Method	I/O (GB)	Method	CPU idle %
B1	*1741*	B1	*12.5*
B2	*1597*	B2	*13.7*
PS(SD)	*1207*	PS(SD)	*12.8*
PS(WTMB)	*1210*	PS(WTMB)	*12.9*
OG(SD)	*921*	OG(SD)	*7.9*
OG(WTMB)	*940*	OG(WTMB)	*8.2*
GCS	*930*	GCS	*8.0*

Observation 1: (weighted) SD gave schedules with smaller makespans than (weighted) TMB by up to 15%.

Observation 2: Both baselines, B1 and B2, give schedules with similar makespans.

Observation 3: For DAG1, as cache pressure (data size) increases, the improvement of OG and GCS over the baselines stabilizes at around 2.3x (as shown in Fig. 6). For DAG1-v2, the gap stabilizes at 3.1x; For DAG1-v3, the gap is at 2.9x; for DAG1-v4, the gap stabilizes around 3.2x (similar to v2);

---

[3] We only report GCS results using weighted SD; results using WTMB were worse and are omitted from the figures.

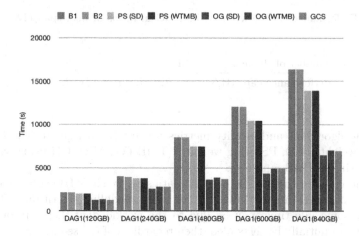

Fig. 6. DAG1 experiments (x-axis: data size; y-axis: makespan).

DAG1-v5 significantly increases the gap to 4.5x; and DAG1-v6 stabilizes at 4.3x (figures omitted due to space constraints). Thus, the more complex the DAG, the more potential for improvement over the baselines. The I/O volumes reported in Table 4 show a similar trend, helping to explain the reason for the improved workload runtimes due to our scheduling methods.

Observation 4: From the reported CPU idle times in Table 4, PS causes more CPU idle times than OG than GCS. This, along with the drop in I/O volumes also reported in Table 4, explains the trend shown in the figures: while PS outperforms the baselines in terms of the makespan of the workload, OG and GCS further outperform PS by a factor of two in many cases (especially for larger data sizes).

Observation 5: GCS rarely outperformed OG on the tested workloads and sometimes produced worse schedules. This suggests that simulating complete schedules without knowing the completion order of the tasks is not an effective strategy, even after allowing for some swaps as we do in GCS. Instead, a simple online greedy heuristic such as OG can work well in practice.

5.2   Data-Intensive Scheduling in Spark

For Spark experiments, we used a private cluster of 8 nodes (and a subset of 4 nodes from this cluster) running Ubuntu Linux 18.10. Each node is equipped with four Intel Xeon E5-2620 2.10 GHz 6-core CPUs, 64 GB of DDR3 RAM and 2.7 TB of local storage. The cluster runs Apache Spark 2.3.1 and Apache Hadoop 2.6 for HDFS.

We use the TPC-DS benchmark as the dataset generator [13], with scale factor 200. We again use the DAG from Fig. 5, with the tasks corresponding to data-intensive queries from the TPC-DS benchmark that were identified as such by [6]. We use Spark standalone mode to simplify the setup and to avoid the impact of cluster managers such as YARN [3].

We use a default Spark configuration, and each executor is given all the cores available on a worker by default. We let Spark control its distributed memory cache using the default LRU strategy. We experimented with two setups. In the 4-node setup, we use four nodes in the cluster and we limit the number of concurrent tasks to 4. In the 8-node setup, we use all 8 nodes and we limit the number of concurrent tasks to 8.

To isolate the impact of task sequencing, we do not perform any dynamic resource allocation (e.g., giving some tasks more resources if some cores are idle). Additionally, since we focus on data-intensive tasks, data I/O is the bottleneck, not processing time. Thus, resource reallocation would be expected to have a limited impact on makespan. We implemented the workload as a packaged application, and included the scheduling algorithms as callable routines in the code.

We compared our algorithms, PS, OG and GCS, with the baselines, and the results are presented in Fig. 7, with makespan on the left and the number of cache misses on the right. We show results for both setups: 4 nodes with up to 4 concurrent tasks and 8 nodes with up to 8 concurrent tasks. We only use weighted SD in this experiment since previous experiments showed that weighted TMB produces worse schedules. We also monitor the total cache misses when running different schedules (we were unable to reliably compute the total I/O volume in Spark). To measure this, we collect the cache misses using Linux tools on each server first, and then we aggregate the statistics for a final total cache misses of the system.

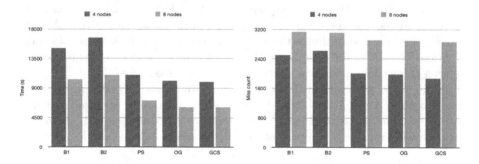

Fig. 7. Spark tests: makespan using 4 and 8 nodes (left figure; x-axis: algorithm; y-axis: runtime), and number of cache misses (right figure; x-axis: algorithm; y-axis: number of misses).

Observation 6: Increasing the available resources while at the same time increasing the maximum parallelism level leads to a decrease in schedule makespans.

Observation 7: In terms of makespan, PS outperforms the baselines by about 30%. OG further outperforms PS by about 20%, and the performance of OG and GCS was nearly identical. Figure 7 shows similar trends in terms of cache misses, suggesting a reason for the improved performance of our solutions compared to the baselines. However, the performance improvement of OG/GCS over PS is not as high as in the simulations, likely because Spark jobs incur some overhead regardless of sequencing.

6 Conclusions

We defined the MPDIS problem of scheduling a DAG of data-intensive tasks (with precedence constraints due to data dependencies) on multiple processing units. To measure data locality, we considered two cache metrics proposed in prior work: stack distance and total maximum bandwidth. We proposed online scheduling algorithms: Parallel SDIS (PS), a straightforward extension of serial scheduling of data-intensive tasks to a parallel setting; Online Greedy (OG), which addresses a problem with PS, namely the fact that it may leave some processing units idle while ensuring data locality; and Greedy Complete Schedule (GCS), which is based on OG but leverages the knowledge of the workload provided in the DAG. Experimental results showed that PS reduces makespan and I/O volume compared to the baselines, and OG further improves upon PS. GCS did not perform better than OG, showing that knowing the workload may not be sufficient in our setting as we do not know the completion order of tasks (and therefore cannot infer the set of schedulable tasks at any particular point in the future).

We assumed an architecture in which multiple processing units share a cache. In future work, we will study new versions of the MPDIS problem for shared-nothing settings. One version is to partition the workload across multiple shared-nothing clusters, and optimize the stack distance of the schedules within each partition. The additional complexity of this new problem is due to the interaction between partitioning and data locality of the partitioned schedules.

In this work, we assumed that once a processor finishes a task and becomes idle, it obtains a single new task. To reduce the scheduling overhead, we can instead schedule a batch of ready tasks at every scheduling round. In future work, we will evaluate the impact of such batch scheduling on data locality.

References

1. Pegasus. https://confluence.pegasus.isi.edu/display/pegasus/WorkflowGenerator
2. Pylru 1.2.0. https://pypi.org/project/pylru/
3. Spark standalone. https://spark.apache.org/docs/latest/spark-standalone.html
4. Allahverdi, A.: The third comprehensive survey on scheduling problems with setup times/costs. Eur. J. Oper. Res. **246**(2), 345–378 (2015)
5. Arras, P.A., Fuin, D., Jeannot, E., Stoutchinin, A., Thibault, S.: List scheduling in embedded systems under memory constraints. Int. J. Parallel Prog. **43**, 1103–1128 (2015)

6. Bär, A., Golab, L., Ruehrup, S., Schiavone, M., Casas, P.: Cache-oblivious scheduling of shared workloads. In: IEEE International Conference on Data Engineering, pp. 855–866 (2015)
7. Canon, L.C., Jeannot, E., Sakellariou, R., Zheng, W.: Comparative evaluation of the robustness of dag scheduling heuristics. In: Grid Computing, pp. 73–84 (2008)
8. Coffman, E.G., Denning, P.J.: Operating Systems Theory. Prentice-Hall, New Jersey (1973)
9. Deslauriers, F., McCormick, P., Amvrosiadis, G., Goel, A., Brown, A.D.: Quartet: harmonizing task scheduling and caching for cluster computing. In: USENIX Workshop on Hot Topics in Storage and File Systems (2016)
10. Kwok, Y.K., Ahmad, I.: Static scheduling algorithms for allocating directed task graphs to multiprocessors. ACM Comput. Surv. (CSUR) 31(4), 406–471 (1999)
11. Marchal, L., Simon, B., Vivien, F.: Limiting the memory footprint when dynamically scheduling dags on shared-memory platforms. J. Parallel Distrib. Comput. 128, 30–42 (2019). https://doi.org/10.1016/j.jpdc.2019.01.009
12. Meng, X., Golab, L.: Optimal reducer placement to minimize data transfer in MapReduce-style processing. In: 2017 IEEE International Conference on Big Data, pp. 339–346 (2017)
13. Nambiar, R.O., Poess, M.: The making of TPC-DS. In: International Conference on Very Large Data Bases, pp. 1049–1058 (2006)
14. Xu, E., Saxena, M., Chiu, L.: Neutrino: revisiting memory caching for iterative data analytics. In: USENIX Workshop on Hot Topics in Storage and File Systems (2016)
15. Yang, Z., Jia, D., Ioannidis, S., Mi, N., Sheng, B.: Intermediate data caching optimization for multi-stage and parallel big data frameworks. In: IEEE International Conference on Cloud Computing, pp. 277–284 (2018)
16. Zaharia, M., et al.: Apache spark: a unified engine for big data processing. Commun. ACM 59(11), 56–65 (2016). https://doi.org/10.1145/2934664

A Makespan Lower Bound for the Tiled Cholesky Factorization Based on ALAP Schedule

Olivier Beaumont[1]([✉])[iD], Julien Langou[2][iD], Willy Quach[3][iD], and Alena Shilova[1][iD]

[1] Inria Bordeaux – Sud-Ouest and Université de Bordeaux, Bordeaux, France
olivier.beaumont@inria.fr
[2] University of Colorado Denver, Denver, USA
[3] Northeastern University, Boston, USA

Abstract. Due to the advent of multicore architectures and massive parallelism, the tiled Cholesky factorization algorithm has recently received plenty of attention and is often referenced by practitioners as a case study. However, we note that a theoretical study of the parallelism of this algorithm is currently lacking. In this paper, we present new theoretical results about the tiled Cholesky factorization in the context of a parallel homogeneous model without communication costs. By a careful analysis on the number of tasks of each type that run simultaneously in the ALAP (As Late As Possible) schedule without resource limitation, we are able to determine precisely an upper bound on the number of busy processors at any time (as degree 2 polynomials). We then use this information to find a closed form formula for a lower bound on the minimum time to schedule a tiled Cholesky factorization of size n on P processors. We show that this lower bound outperforms (is larger than) classical lower bounds from the literature. We also demonstrate that $\text{ALAP}(P)$, an ALAP-based schedule where the number of resources is limited to P, has a makespan extremely close to the lower bound, thus establishing both the effectiveness of $\text{ALAP}(P)$ schedule and of our new lower bound on the makespan.

Keywords: Scheduling · Cholesky factorization · CPU · GPU · Lower bounds

1 Introduction

A large fraction of time-consuming tasks performed on supercomputers are linear algebra operations. With the advent of multicore architectures and massive parallelism, it is therefore of particular interest to optimize and understand their parallel behavior. In this paper, we consider the problem of the dense tiled Cholesky factorization. The algorithm first splits the initial matrix into square

J. Langou—Supported by NSF award #1645514.

M. Malawski and K. Rzadca (Eds.): Euro-Par 2020, LNCS 12247, pp. 134–150, 2020.
https://doi.org/10.1007/978-3-030-57675-2_9

sub-matrices, or *tiles* of the same size. The tile size is chosen so as to achieve a good efficiency on the target architecture.

The tiled Cholesky factorization algorithm has recently received plenty of attention, either as an algorithm in itself [16,19] or as a case study for task-based schedulers [1,2,5,12,20,23]. Examples of task-based schedulers which have considered the scheduling of tiled Cholesky factorization are DAGuE [9], StarPU [4,13], SMPSs [21], and SuperMatrix [22]. Let us also note that OpenMP since 3.1 supports task-based parallelism. The tiled Cholesky factorization algorithm is also used in practice and is implemented in Dense Linear Algebra state of the art libraries, for example DPLASMA [8], FLAME [15], and PLASMA [10]. Recently, the practical design of good static schedule for heterogeneous resources has been considered in [3] and extensions to incomplete factorization [18], sparse matrices [17] have also been proposed.

One of our main goals in this paper is to obtain a tight theoretical lower bound on the parallel time to achieve a Cholesky factorization, based on the individual costs of the different kernels on a homogeneous architecture without communication cost. Trivial lower bounds can be derived from general bounds of the literature on scheduling. Specifically, the time to process Cholesky factorization is trivially bounded both by the length of the critical path (the longest path in the task graph from the source node to the sink node) and by the overall work divided by P, the number of available resources. To our best knowledge, no theoretical study on the execution time of any schedule for the tiled Cholesky factorization have been determined beyond these trivial bounds. Therefore, in many situations, it is impossible to assess the efficiency of a given schedule or implementation, because of the low quality of available lower bounds. This motivates this paper.

In this paper, we assume homogeneous processing units. While the heterogeneous setting is more general, establishing theoretical bounds in the heterogeneous case is much more difficult (see [6] for a recent survey in the case of two types of resources). We also make the assumption that communication cost is zero. We justify this assumption (no communication cost) in two ways. First, if the tile size is large enough, it is possible to overlap communications and computations. Indeed, if the dimension of the tile is $s \times s$, the tile (memory) size is s^2 while all kernels involved in Cholesky factorization have a complexity s^3. It has been shown experimentally using task-based schedulers [1,2,5,12,20] that it is possible to almost completely overlap communications and computations. Secondly, we note that the lower bound on the execution time also holds true in the case when communication costs are taken into account, so that any practical implementations will execute slower than this model. The lower bounds that we exhibit are not trivial and are relevant for practical applications, as demonstrated in Sect. 5. Another technical assumption is that we are assuming that the time to perform the SYRK operation is not larger than the time to perform the GEMM operation. This is a mild assumption. It is very likely to be true. One reason being that, if not, one can replace the SYRK kernels by GEMM kernels.

We can relate our work to the recent work of Agullo et al. [2] where the authors provide lower bound as well. The authors consider a more complicated model (heterogeneous) but rely on the linear programming formulation to find the schedule. We consider a simpler model (homogeneous) but we provide closed-form solutions and a tighter analysis. We are considering comparing both approaches as future work. We can also relate our work to the work of Cosnard, Marrakchi, Robert, and Trystram [14]. In this work, the authors study the scheduling of Gaussian elimination. A minor difference is that they work on LU while we work on Cholesky. The main difference is that they concentrate on an algorithm that works on the columns of the matrix, while our algorithm works on tiles.

In addition, it is of great interest to better understand how to efficiently schedule the parallel execution of the tiled Cholesky factorization algorithm. Indeed, even if a dynamic runtime scheduler is used, its behavior can be guided by priorities corresponding to a good static schedule in order to efficiently perform the parallel factorization, as shown in [3] in the context of StarPU. A contribution of our paper is to advocate the use of the ALAP (As Late As Possible) schedule where tasks are scheduled from the end as opposed from the start. We show that this simple heuristic turns out to provide results that are very close to the lower bound, therefore proving that it can be used in practice, for instance to fix priorities in a task based runtime scheduler.

The rest of the paper is organized as follows. In Sect. 2, tiled Cholesky factorization is presented. More specifically, we consider two different settings that correspond to different relative costs of the different kernels involved in tiled Cholesky factorization. We prove that these two cases are enough to cover all possible settings and typically correspond to the CPU and GPU settings and we provide the analysis of the critical path for each task. Then, in the case of the CPU case (Sect. 3.1) and to the GPU case (Sect. 3.2), we carefully analyze the number of tasks for every kernel at any instant of the factorization, when assuming an infinite number of processing resources. In turn, in Sect. 4, we prove that in the case of P processors, this analysis can be used to design a tight lower bound. In Sect. 5, we show using simulations that the makespan (the length) of the ALAP schedule with P processors is close to the theoretical bound, even for a small number of tiles, this demonstrates that the ALAP schedule is efficient and that the bound is tight. Concluding remarks and perspectives are finally proposed in Sect. 6.

2   Cholesky Factorization

2.1   Cholesky Algorithm

Given a Symmetric Positive Definite (SPD) matrix A, the Cholesky factorization computes a (lower) triangular matrix L such that $A = LL^T$. It is a core operation to solve linear systems in the case of SPD matrices as it allows to solve systems of the form $Ax = b$ by reducing it to computing solutions of $Ly = b$, and then $L^T x = y$. In order to compute the Cholesky factorization when using many processing units, the matrix A is split into $n \times n$ square tiles of size s, where s is chosen so as to perform kernels efficiently (as it improves data locality) and to allow to overlap communications and computations. Algorithm 1 depicts tiled Cholesky factorization.

Algorithm 1. Tiled Cholesky Factorization

---

    for $k = 0$ to $n - 1$ **do**
      $A_{k,k} \leftarrow POTRF(A_{k,k})$ $\{POTRF_k\}$
      for $i = k + 1$ to $n - 1$ **do**
        $A_{i,k} \leftarrow TRSM(A_{k,k}, A_{i,k})$ $\{TRSM_{i,k}\}$
      end for
      for $j = k + 1$ to $n - 1$ **do**
        $A_{j,j} \leftarrow SYRK(A_{j,k}, A_{j,j})$ $\{SYRK_{j,k}\}$
        for $i = j + 1$ to $n - 1$ **do**
          $Ai, j \leftarrow GEMM(A_{i,k}, A_{j,k})$ $\{GEMM_{i,j,k}\}$
        end for
      end for
    end for

In Algorithm 1 and in the remainder of this paper, the tasks corresponding to POTRF kernels will be denoted as $POTRF_i$ with $1 \leq i \leq n$ and correspond themselves to the Cholesky factorization of a real symmetric positive definite block of the matrix. The tasks corresponding to TRSM kernels will be denoted as $TRSM_{i,j}$ with $1 \leq j < i \leq n$ and correspond to the resolution of a triangular linear system of size s. The tasks corresponding to SYRK kernels will be denoted as $SYRK_{i,j}$ with $1 \leq j < i \leq n$ and correspond to a matrix multiplication with symmetric matrices, whereas the tasks corresponding to GEMM kernels, denoted as $GEMM_{i,j,k}$ with $1 \leq k < j < i \leq n$ correspond to general matrix product. Therefore, since we can always replace SYRK by GEMM, we will assume in the rest of the paper that the time to perform SYRK is at most the time to perform GEMM. The dependencies between the tasks are given by

- $POTRF_j \to TRSM_{i,j}$, $j < i \leq n$;
- $TRSM_{i,j} \to SYRK_{i,j}$, $j < i \leq n$; $TRSM_{i,j} \to GEMM_{i,k,j}$, $j < k < i \leq n$;
- $TRSM_{i,j} \to GEMM_{k,i,j}$, $j < i < k \leq n$;
- $SYRK_{i,j} \to SYRK_{i,j+1}$, $j+1 < i \leq n$; $SYRK_{i,i-1} \to POTRF_i$, $1 < i \leq n$;
- $GEMM_{i,j,j-1} \to TRSM_{i,j}$, $1 < j < i \leq n$;
- $GEMM_{i,j,k} \to GEMM_{i,j,k+1}$, $k + 1 < j < i \leq n$.

Table 1. Number of tasks of each type

Type of task	POTRF	SYRK	TRSM	GEMM
Number of tasks	n	$\frac{n(n-1)}{2}$	$\frac{n(n-1)}{2}$	$\frac{n(n-1)(n-2)}{6}$

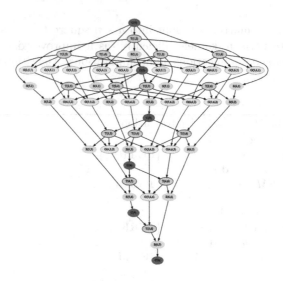

Fig. 1. DAG of a 6 × 6 Cholesky factorization

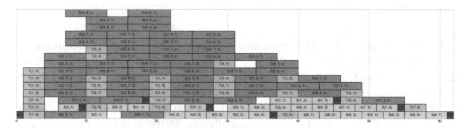

Fig. 2. ALAP schedule without resource limitation on 8 × 8 tiles with 1, 3, 3, 6 weights

Table 2. Kernel Performance (absolute and relative)

	POTRF	SYRK	TRSM	GEMM
GPU	11.55	1.277	3.420	1.733
CPU	11.27	47.76	44.02	87.60

time in ms

	POTRF	SYRK	TRSM	GEMM
GPU	1.00	0.11	0.30	0.15
CPU	1.00	4.24	3.91	7.77

ratio wrt POTRF

Figure 1 depicts the Directed Acyclic Graph (DAG) of the dependencies between the tasks of a 6 × 6 tiled Cholesky Factorization and the number of tasks for each kernel is given in the Table 1.

2.2 Kernel Performance

Table 2 (left part) describes the duration of individual tasks when $s = 960$ on an Intel Xeon E5-2680 (CPU) and an Nvidia GK110BGL GPU unit (GPU). All measurements were performed using CHAMELEON library [11], version 0.9.1.

We can observe that, with respect to CPU, GPUs are typically very fast for GEMM (an improvement of 50 with respect to CPU), fast for SYRK and TRSM (a respective improvement of 37 and 13) but relatively slow for POTRF (a slight slowdown). In Table 2 (right part), we give the relative duration of POTRF, TRSM, SYRK and GEMM with respect to POTRF. Note that throughout the paper, the results are stated in general terms and expressed as C, T, S and G respectively and we stress that our theoretical analysis below is valid for any values of (C, S, T, G). Nevertheless, by analyzing the critical paths as in Sects. 2.3 and 2.4, we can observe (with the additional trivial assumption $S \leq G$ discussed above) that there are only two different situations, depending on the respective values of $S + C$ and G. These two cases will be analyzed separately in the following. For convenience, we will denote them as CPU case (when $S + C \leq G$) and GPU case (when $S + C > G$) because each of these cases is quite emblematic of what can be encountered on a core or on an accelerator. In the same way, for convenience, for numerical illustrations, we will use $(1, 3, 3, 6)$ for (C, T, S, G) as emblematic values for a CPU and $(12, 3, 1, 2)$ for a GPU. These values are close to our experimental values and have also been used in the literature. Typically, $(1, 3, 3, 6)$ corresponds exactly to the ratios of the number of floating point operations for the different cores.

2.3   Critical Paths in the CPU Case, $S + C \leq G$

Based on the above described dependencies, we can compute the critical path for each task involved in the Cholesky factorization, *i.e.* the longest path from this node (itself included) to the end of the last task of the graph, *i.e.* POTRF(n) if $n \times n$ is the size of the matrix (expressed in number of tiles). Let us assume that $S + C \leq G$, this is the CPU case. In this case, in particular $S + C + T \leq G + T$, so that the edges SYRK($i + 1, i$) → POTRF($i + 1$) are not part of the critical paths (except those starting at SYRK($i + 1, i$) nodes). Due to lack of space, we refer the reader to the companion research report [7] for the proofs and only detail the case of POTRF tasks in the CPU case.

- Case of POTRF(i), $1 \leq i \leq n$ node: the critical path from POTRF(i), $i < n$ is given by POTRF(i) → (TRSM(i, n) → GEMM($i + 1, n, i$)) → ... → (TRSM($n - 2, n$) → GEMM($n - 1, n, n - 2$)) → TRSM($n - 1, n$) → SYRK($n, n - 1$) → POTRF(n). Its length is given by $L(C, i) = C + (n - i - 1)(T + G) + T + S + C$. Therefore, the overall Critical Path CP is given by CP $= 2C + T + S + (n - 2)(T + G)$ and $L(C, i) =$ CP $- (i - 1)(T + G)$.
- Case of TRSM(i, j), $1 \leq i < j \leq n$: $L(T, i, j) =$ CP $- C - (i - 1)(T + G)$.
- Case of SYRK(i, j), $1 \leq j < i < n$: $L(S, i, j) =$ CP $- (i - 1)(T + G) + (i - j)S$.
- Case of SYRK(n, j), $1 \leq j < n$: $L(S, n, j) = (n - j)S + C$.
- Case of GEMM(i, j, k), $1 \leq k < i < j \leq n$:
  $L(G, i, j, k) =$ CP $- C + G + T - iT - kG$.

2.4   Critical Paths in the GPU Case, $S + C \geq G$

Let us now consider the case when $C + S \geq G$, which corresponds to GPU situation. In this case, in particular $S + C + T \geq G + T$, so that $\text{SYRK}(i+1, i) \rightarrow \text{POTRF}(i+1)$ are now used in critical paths.

- Case of $\text{POTRF}(i), 1 \leq i < n$:
  $L(C, i) = C + (n-i)(T + S + C)$. In particular, $\text{CP} = C + (n-1)(T + S + C)$.
- Case of $\text{TRSM}(i, j), 1 \leq i < j \leq n$:
  $L(T, i, j) = (j - i - 1)(T + G) + (n - j + 1)(T + S + C)$.
- Case of $\text{SYRK}(i, j), 1 \leq j < i \leq n$:
  $L(S, i, j) = (i - j)S + C + (n - i)(T + S + C)$.
- Case of $\text{GEMM}(i, j, k), 1 \leq k < i < j \leq n$:
  $L(G, i, j, k) = (i - k)G + (j - i - 1)(T + G) + (n - j + 1)(T + S + C)$.

2.5   ALAP Schedule

Let us now define the ALAP schedule for the $n \times n$ tiled Cholesky factorization without resource limitation (the case with resource limitation will be considered in Sect. 5). In the ALAP schedule without resource limitation, we consider the Cholesky graph from the end, *i.e.* we reverse the task graph depicted in Fig. 1 and we schedule tasks in this order as soon as they are available. Therefore, ALAP on the original graph is simply the inverse of the ASAP schedule on the reversed graph. A first observation that can be made is that using the ALAP schedule without resource limitation, then every task starts its execution at a instant that differs from the makespan by exactly its critical path (as defined in Sects. 2.3 and 2.4) to the end of the schedule. We will denote in what follows the difference between the starting time of a task and the makespan as the distance of this task. Therefore, the ALAP schedule is optimal with an infinite number of processing resources and more specifically as soon as the number of processors is larger than a given threshold. Indeed, without resource limitation, the distance of the initial task is by construction the critical path of the Cholesky graph. In Sects. 3.1 (CPU case) and 3.2 (GPU case), we precisely evaluate the number of tasks of each type running at any instant of the ALAP schedule without resource limitation, and then we use these bounds to compute a lower bound on the execution time of any schedule in Sect. 4. Figure 2 depicts the execution of an ALAP schedule (without resource limitation) on a 8×8 tiled Cholesky factorization, with the time on the x-axis.

3   ALAP Schedule Analysis Without Resource Limitation

3.1   Case $S + C \leq G$

In the ALAP Schedule without resource limitation, each task T starts at time $\text{CP} - t_T$, where CP denotes the Critical Path of Cholesky factorization and t_T denotes the critical path from task T. In what follows, given an instant $\text{CP} - d$, our goal is to determine an upper bound on the number of tasks of each type and an upper bound on the work performed by the tasks of each type and whose execution terminates after the instant $CP - d$.

We will denote respectively by

- $\#GEMM(d), \#TRSM(d), \#SYRK(d)$ and $\#POTRF(d)$ as upper bounds on the number of tasks of each type that are being processed at this instant $CP - d$ using the ALAP schedule
- $W_{GEMM}(d), W_{TRSM}(d), W_{SYRK}(d)$ and $W_{POTRF}(d)$ as upper bounds on the work performed by tasks of each type whose execution terminates after the instant $CP - d$

Both the number of tasks and the overall work will be used later in Theorem 1 to prove a lower bound. Due to the length of derivations, we refer the interested reader to [7] for complete formulas (in terms of n, C, S, T, G) and proofs. In the present paper, we provide the detailed analysis for $\#GEMM(d)$. For the other cases, whose proofs are based on the same techniques, we only provide the explicit the explicit formulas.

Case of GEMM Tasks. Let us now establish the result for GEMM tasks. $GEMM(i, j, k)$ runs at all instants such that $CP - C + T - iT - kG \leq d \leq CP - C + T - iT - kG + G$, so that in particular $\frac{CP-d-C+T-iT}{G} \leq k \leq \frac{CP-d-C+T-iT}{G} + 1$ so that at most one value of k is possible, for a fixed pair (i, d), where $k = \lceil \frac{CP-d-C+T}{G} - \frac{iT}{G} \rceil$.

In order to determine how many triplets (i, j, k) correspond to a tasks $GEMM(i, j, k)$ running at time $CP - d$, we need to check to consider the constraints on (i, j, k) valid triplets, *i.e.* $1 \leq k < i < j \leq n$.

- The first constraint states that $k \geq 1$. Using the above defined value for k, we can rewrite the condition

$$k \geq 1 \Leftrightarrow \frac{CP - d - C + T}{G} \geq \frac{iT}{G} \Leftrightarrow i \leq \frac{CP - d - C + T}{T}.$$

This constraint can be rewritten as $i \leq n + \frac{nG+C+S-2G-d}{T}$. Note that in particular, when d is small enough, *i.e.* $d \leq nG + C + S - 2G$, then above constraint becomes trivial and can be replaced by $i \leq n$. Otherwise, if $d \geq nG + C + S - 2G$, then the constraint becomes $i \leq n - \lceil d - (nG + C + S - 2G)/T \rceil$.
- The second constraint states that

$$k < i \Leftrightarrow \frac{CP - d - C + T}{G} - \frac{iT}{G} \leq (i - 1) \Leftrightarrow CP - d - C + T + G \leq i(G + T).$$

This constraint can be rewritten as

$$(n - i - 2)(T + G) \leq d - (C + G + S + 2T) \Leftrightarrow i \geq n - \lceil d - (C + S + T)/T + G \rceil.$$

Due to these constraints, we will obtain different formulas for the number of GEMMs, depending on the value of d.

- If $d \leq (n-2)G + C + S + T = d_G$, then the only constraints are $i \geq n - \lceil \frac{d-(C+S+T)}{T+G} \rceil$ and $i < j \leq n$ so that

$$\#\mathrm{GEMM}(d) = \sum_{l=1}^{\lceil \frac{d-(C+S+T)}{T+G} \rceil} l = (\lceil \frac{d-(C+S+T)}{T+G} \rceil)(\lceil \frac{d-(C+S+T)}{T+G} \rceil + 1)/2,$$

$$\#\mathrm{GEMM}(d) \leq B_1^{\mathrm{GEMM}} d^2 + C_1^{\mathrm{GEMM}} d + D_1^{\mathrm{GEMM}},$$

where $B_1^{\mathrm{GEMM}} = \frac{1}{2(G+T)^2}$, $C_1^{\mathrm{GEMM}} = \frac{(3G+T-2C-2S)}{2(G+T)^2}$ and $D_1^{\mathrm{GEMM}} = \frac{(G-C-S)(2G+T-C-S)}{2(G+T)^2}$.

In order to estimate $W_{\mathrm{GEMM}}(d)$, we rely on the integral of $\#\mathrm{GEMM}(t)$ between 0 and d so that $W_{\mathrm{GEMM}}(d) \leq A_1^{\mathrm{GEMM},W} d^3 + B_1^{\mathrm{GEMM},W} d^2 + C_1^{\mathrm{GEMM},W} d$, where $A_1^{\mathrm{GEMM},W} = \frac{B_1^{\mathrm{GEMM}}}{3}$, $B_1^{\mathrm{GEMM},W} = \frac{C_1^{\mathrm{GEMM}}}{2}$ and $C_1^{\mathrm{GEMM},W} = D_1^{\mathrm{GEMM}}$.

- If $d \geq \mathrm{CP} - C - T$, then there is no GEMM task to perform (only TRSMs and one POTRF remain) and in this case, $\#\mathrm{GEMM}(d) = 0$.
- If $d_G = (n-2)G + C + S + T \leq d \leq \mathrm{CP} - C - T$, then the constraints are $n - \lceil \frac{d-(C+S+T)}{T+G} \rceil \leq i \leq n - \lceil \frac{d-(nG+C+S-2G)}{T} \rceil$ and $i < j \leq n$, so that

$$\#\mathrm{GEMM}(d) \leq (B_2^{\mathrm{GEMM}} d^2 + C_2^{\mathrm{GEMM}} d + D_2^{\mathrm{GEMM}}),$$

where $B_2^{\mathrm{GEMM}} = \frac{1}{2(G+T)^2} - \frac{1}{2T^2}$, $C_2^{\mathrm{GEMM}} = \frac{1}{2(T+G)} + \frac{1}{2T} - \frac{C+S-G}{(T+G)^2} + \frac{(n-2)G+C+S}{T^2}$ and $D_2^{\mathrm{GEMM}} = 1 - \frac{C+S+T}{2(T+G)} - \frac{(n-2)G+C+S}{2T} + \frac{(C+S-G)^2}{2(T+G)^2} - \frac{((n-2)G+C+S)^2}{2T^2}$

In order to estimate $W_{\mathrm{GEMM}}(d)$, we rely on the integral of $\#\mathrm{GEMM}(t)$ between d_G and d plus $W_{\mathrm{GEMM}}(d_G)$ so that

$$W_{\mathrm{GEMM}}(d) \leq A_2^{\mathrm{GEMM},W} d^3 + B_2^{\mathrm{GEMM},W} d^2 + C_2^{\mathrm{GEMM},W} d + D_2^{\mathrm{GEMM},W},$$

where $A_2^{\mathrm{GEMM},W} = \frac{B_2^{\mathrm{GEMM}}}{3}$, $B_2^{\mathrm{GEMM},W} = \frac{C_2^{\mathrm{GEMM}}}{2}$, $C_2^{\mathrm{GEMM},W} = D_2^{\mathrm{GEMM}}$ and $D_2^{\mathrm{GEMM},W} = (A_1^{\mathrm{GEMM},W} - A_2^{\mathrm{GEMM},W})d_G^3 + (B_1^{\mathrm{GEMM},W} - B_2^{\mathrm{GEMM},W})d_G^2 + (C_1^{\mathrm{GEMM},W} - C_2^{\mathrm{GEMM},W})d_G$.

Case of POTRF Tasks. Clearly, at any instant, at most one POTRF task can be running since there is a dependency path $\mathrm{POTRF}(i) \longrightarrow \mathrm{TRSM}(i, i+1) \longrightarrow \mathrm{SYRK}(i+1, i) \longrightarrow \mathrm{POTRF}(i+1)$, therefore $\forall d \geq 0$, $\#\mathrm{POTRF}(d) \leq 1$ and the total amount of work done after $\mathrm{CP} - d$ is defined by $\forall d \geq 0$, $W_{\mathrm{POTRF}}(d) \leq C^{\mathrm{POTRF},W} d + D^{\mathrm{POTRF},W}$, where $C^{\mathrm{POTRF},W} = \frac{C}{T+G}$ and $D^{\mathrm{POTRF},W} = \frac{C(2G+T-S-C)}{T+G}$.

Case of TRSM Tasks. $\mathrm{TRSM}(i, j)$ runs at all instants such that $\mathrm{CP} - C - (i-1)(T+G) - T \leq d \leq \mathrm{CP} - C - (i-1)(T+G)$. From above inequalities, we can prove [7] that the amount of the TRSM tasks running at the time $\mathrm{CP} - d$ is either 0 or $\#\mathrm{TRSM}(d) = \left\lceil \frac{d-S-C+G}{T+G} \right\rceil \leq C^{\mathrm{TRSM}}d + D^{\mathrm{TRSM}}$, where $C^{\mathrm{TRSM}} = \frac{1}{T+G}$ and $D^{\mathrm{TRSM}} = \frac{2G-S-C+T}{T+G}$. and $W_{\mathrm{TRSM}}(d) \leq B^{\mathrm{TRSM},W}d^2 + C^{\mathrm{TRSM},W}d + D^{\mathrm{TRSM},W}$, where $B^{\mathrm{TRSM},W} = \frac{T}{2(T+G)^2}$, $C^{\mathrm{TRSM},W} = \frac{T(3T+3G-2S-2C)}{2(T+G)^2}$ and $D^{\mathrm{TRSM},W} = \frac{T(T+G-S-C)(2T+2G-S-C)}{2(T+G)^2}$.

Case of SYRK Tasks. Clearly, at any instant, at most one $\mathrm{SYRK}(n,j)$ task can be running since there is a dependency path $\mathrm{SYRK}(n,j) \longrightarrow \mathrm{SYRK}(n,j+1)$, so that $\forall d \geq 0$, $\#\mathrm{SYRK}(n,j,d) \leq 1$.

Let us now consider the case of tasks $\mathrm{SYRK}(i,j)$ for $1 \leq j < i < n$. $\mathrm{SYRK}(i,j)$ runs at all instants such that $\mathrm{CP} + (T+G) - i(T+G-S) - jS - S \leq d \leq \mathrm{CP} + (T+G) - i(T+G-S) - jS$ From above inequalities, we can prove [7] that

- If $d \leq (n-1)S + 2C + T = d_S$, then $\#\mathrm{SYRK}(d) \leq C_1^{\mathrm{SYRK}}d + D_1^{\mathrm{SYRK}}$, where $C_1^{\mathrm{SYRK}} = \frac{1}{T+G}$ and $D_1^{\mathrm{SYRK}} = \frac{G-2C-S}{T+G}$. Similarly, we obtain that $W_{\mathrm{SYRK}}(d) \leq B_1^{\mathrm{SYRK},W}d^2 + C_1^{\mathrm{SYRK},W}d + D_1^{\mathrm{SYRK},W}$, where $B_1^{\mathrm{SYRK},W} = \frac{C_1^{\mathrm{SYRK}}}{2}$, $C_1^{\mathrm{SYRK},W} = D_1^{\mathrm{SYRK}} + 1$ and $D_1^{\mathrm{SYRK},W} = -C$.
- If $d > (n-1)S + 2C + T = d_S$, then $\forall d > nS + 2C - G$, $\#\mathrm{SYRK}(d) \leq C_2^{\mathrm{SYRK}}d + D_2^{\mathrm{SYRK}}$, where $C_2^{\mathrm{SYRK}} = \frac{-S}{(T+G)(T+G-S)}$ and $D_2^{\mathrm{SYRK}} = 1 + \frac{S((n-1)(T+G)-G+2C+S)}{(T+G)(T+G-S)}$. Similarly, $W_{\mathrm{SYRK}}(d) \leq B_2^{\mathrm{SYRK},W}d^2 + C_2^{\mathrm{SYRK},W}d + D_2^{\mathrm{SYRK},W}$, where $B_2^{\mathrm{SYRK},W} = \frac{C_2^{\mathrm{SYRK}}}{2}$, $C_2^{\mathrm{SYRK},W} = D_2^{\mathrm{SYRK}}$ and $D_2^{\mathrm{SYRK},W} = (B_1^{\mathrm{SYRK},W} - B_2^{\mathrm{SYRK},W})d_S^2 + (C_1^{\mathrm{SYRK},W} - C_2^{\mathrm{SYRK},W})d_S + (n-1)S$.

3.2 Case $S + C \geq G$

We can establish the same results in the GPU case, using the same type of proof techniques than in the case of GEMM tasks when $S + C \leq G$. We refer the interested reader to [7], where all detailed proofs are presented, and we just summarize results below.

Case of POTRF Tasks. $\forall d \geq 0$, $\#\mathrm{POTRF}(d) \leq 1$. and $\forall d \geq 0$, $W_{\mathrm{POTRF}}(d) \leq C^{\mathrm{POTRF},W}d + D^{\mathrm{POTRF},W}$, where $C^{\mathrm{POTRF},W} = \frac{C}{T+S+C}$ and $D^{\mathrm{POTRF},W} = C$.

Case of TRSM Tasks. Let $d_T \leq (n-1)(T+G) + C + S - G$. Then

- When $d \leq d_T$, then $\#\mathrm{TRSM}(d) = \left\lfloor \frac{d+G-C-S}{C+S+T} \right\rfloor + 1 \leq \frac{d+G+T}{C+S+T} = C_1^{\mathrm{TRSM}}d + D_1^{\mathrm{TRSM}}$ where $C_1^{\mathrm{TRSM}} = \frac{1}{C+S+T}$ and $D_1^{\mathrm{TRSM}} = \frac{G+T}{C+S+T}$ and $W_{\mathrm{TRSM}}(d) \leq \frac{C_1^{\mathrm{TRSM}}}{2}d^2 + D_1^{\mathrm{TRSM}}d$.

– When $d \geq d_T$, then $\#\mathrm{TRSM}(d) = \leq C_2^{\mathrm{TRSM}}d + D_2^{\mathrm{TRSM}}$ where $C_2^{\mathrm{TRSM}} = -\frac{T+G}{(C+S-G)(C+S+T)}$ and $D_2^{\mathrm{TRSM}} = 2 + \frac{(n-1)(T+G)}{C+S-G} - \frac{C+S-G}{C+S+T}$ and $W_{\mathrm{TRSM}}(d) \leq B^{\mathrm{TRSM},W}d^2 + C^{\mathrm{TRSM},W}d + D^{\mathrm{TRSM},W}$ where $B^{\mathrm{TRSM},W} = \frac{C_2^{\mathrm{TRSM}}}{2}$, $C^{\mathrm{TRSM},W} = D_2^{\mathrm{TRSM}}$ and $D^{\mathrm{TRSM},W} = \frac{C_1^{\mathrm{TRSM}} - C_2^{\mathrm{TRSM}}}{2}d_T^2 + (D_1^{\mathrm{TRSM}} - D_2^{\mathrm{TRSM}})d_T$.

Case of SYRK Tasks. $\forall d \geq 0$, $\#\mathrm{SYRK}(d) \leq C^{\mathrm{SYRK}}d + D^{\mathrm{SYRK}}$, where $C^{\mathrm{SYRK}} = \frac{-S}{(C+S+T)(C+T)}$ and $D^{\mathrm{SYRK}} = 1 + \frac{(n-1)S}{(C+T)} + \frac{CS}{(C+S+T)(C+T)}$ and $W_{\mathrm{SYRK}} \leq \frac{C^{\mathrm{SYRK}}}{2}d^2 + C^{\mathrm{SYRK}}d$.

Case of GEMM Tasks. Let $d_G \leq nG + S + C - 2G$. Then

– When $d \geq d_G$, then $\#\mathrm{GEMM}(d) \leq B_1^{\mathrm{GEMM}}d^2 + C_1^{\mathrm{GEMM}} + D_1^{\mathrm{GEMM}}$, and $W_{\mathrm{GEMM}} \leq \frac{B_1^{\mathrm{GEMM}}}{3}d^3 + \frac{C_1^{\mathrm{GEMM}}}{2}d^2 + D_1^{\mathrm{GEMM}}d$, where $B_1^{\mathrm{GEMM}} = \frac{1}{2(G+S+T)(T+G)}$, $C_1^{\mathrm{GEMM}} = \frac{3T+4G+S}{2(G+S+T)(T+G)}$ and $D_1^{\mathrm{GEMM}} = 1$.
– When $d_G \leq d \leq n(G+T) + S + C - 2G$, then $\#\mathrm{GEMM}(d) \leq B_2^{\mathrm{GEMM}}d^2 + C_2^{\mathrm{GEMM}} + D_2^{\mathrm{GEMM}}$, where $B_2^{\mathrm{GEMM}} = \frac{1}{2(G+S+T)(T+G)} - \frac{1}{2(T+S+C-G)(T)}$, $C_2^{\mathrm{GEMM}} = \frac{3T+4G+S}{2(G+S+T)(T+G)} - \frac{nG}{2(T+S+C-G)(T)}$ and $D_2^{\mathrm{GEMM}} = 1 - \frac{n^2G^2}{2(T+S+C-G)(T)}$ and $W_{\mathrm{GEMM}} \leq \frac{B_2^{\mathrm{GEMM}}}{3}(d^3 - d_1^3) + \frac{C_2^{\mathrm{GEMM}}}{2}(d^2 - d_1^2) + D_2^{\mathrm{GEMM}}(d - d_1) + \frac{B_1^{\mathrm{GEMM}}}{3}d_1^3 + \frac{C_1^{\mathrm{GEMM}}}{2}d_1^2 + D_1^{\mathrm{GEMM}}d_1$, where $d_1 = nG + S + C - 2G$.

4   Lower Bound for Cholesky with P Resources

4.1   CPU Case, $S + C \leq G$

Using the above bounds on the number of tasks, we can bound, for any distance d to CP the number of tasks that would be processed simultaneously using the ALAP schedule without resource limitation. The upper bound on the overall number of tasks $f_{\#}(t)$ processed at any instant t, $0 \leq t \leq \mathrm{CP}$ is therefore given as a degree 2 polynomial, whose coefficients depend on whether $t \leq \mathrm{CP} - d_G$, $\mathrm{CP} - d_G < t \leq \mathrm{CP} - d_S$ and $t > \mathrm{CP} - d_S$ (where d_G and d_S are defined in Sect. 3.1). Similarly, let us denote by $f_W(t)$ the upper bound on the work performed by ALAP schedule after instant t. $f_W(t)$ is given as a degree 3 polynomial, whose coefficients depend on whether $t \leq \mathrm{CP} - d_G$, $\mathrm{CP} - d_G < t \leq \mathrm{CP} - d_S$ and $t > \mathrm{CP} - d_S$.

Figure 3 displays the upper bound on the overall number of tasks processed at any instant t, $0 \leq t \leq \mathrm{CP}$, and the same information for each type of task, GEMM, TRSM, SYRK. All plots correspond to the case where $G = 6$, $T = S = 3$ and $C = 1$, that corresponds to our sample model for a CPU node. Due to lack of space, we refer the interested reader to companion research report [7] to find the counterparts of Fig. 3 in the GPU case.

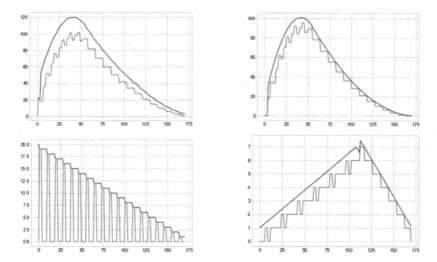

Fig. 3. Evolution of the number of tasks of each type with d, $n = 20$, CPU case, for all instants between 0 and 170 (the length of the critical path). Subfigures depict the overall number of tasks (left, up), GEMM tasks (right, up), TRSM tasks (left, down) and SYRK tasks (right, down)

4.2   Lower Bounds

Let us define t_P as the largest instant such that $f_\#(t) \leq P$ for any $t \geq t_P$, or $t_P = \text{CP}$ if the number of resources is large enough. This instant can be determined easily by studying $f_\#(t)$, which is described as a degree 2 polynomial on several intervals. As we have seen above, both $f_\#(t)$ and the set of intervals to be considered depend only whether $S + C \leq G$ (CPU case) or $S + C \geq G$ (GPU case).

Lemma 1. *Let us denote by $\mathcal{S}$ any valid schedule with P processors. Then, $\mathcal{S}$ cannot perform more work between* MAKESPAN$(\mathcal{S}) - (\text{CP} - t_P)$ *and* MAKESPAN$(\mathcal{S})$ *than* ALAP(P) *and this amount of work is upper bounded by* $f_W(t_P)$.

Proof. Intuitively, no schedule can perform more tasks during the last $\text{CP} - t_P$ instants. Indeed, during these instants, all the tasks whose critical path is less than t_P are processed using ALAP. Moreover, no other task can start as close to the CP in any schedule. $f_\#(t)$ (resp. $f_W(t)$) and is an upper bound on the number of tasks (resp. the overall work) processed simultaneously at time t by ALAP schedule without resource limitation. Moreover $\text{CP} - t_P$ is the largest instant where the ALAP schedule without resource limitation and with at most P processors coincide, so that we can upper bound the work performed by any schedule (by optimality of ALAP after $\text{CP} - t_P$) by $f_W(t_P)$. This finishes the proof of the lemma. $\qquad\square$

Theorem 1. *A makespan lower bound for any schedule is* $(\text{CP} - t_P) + \frac{W - f_W(t_P)}{P}$.

Proof. The overall work W to perform for Cholesky factorization is given by $W = nC + \frac{n(n-1)}{2}(S + T) + \frac{n(n-1)(n-2)}{6}G$. In any schedule $\mathcal{S}$, we have proved in Lemma 1 that an upper bound for the amount of work W_{END} that can be processed during the last $\text{CP} - t_P$ time units is $f_W(t_P)$. Similarly, a trivial upper bound for the amount of work W_{BEGIN} processed during the first $\text{MAKESPAN}(\mathcal{S}) - (\text{CP} - T_p)$ time units is $P(\text{MAKESPAN}(\mathcal{S}) - (\text{CP} - T_p))$, so that $W = nC + n(n-1)/2 * (S + T) + n(n-1)(n-2)/6 * G = W_{\text{BEGIN}} + W_{\text{END}} \leq f_W(t_P) + P(\text{MAKESPAN}(\mathcal{S}) - (\text{CP} - T_p))$ and

$$\text{MAKESPAN}(\mathcal{S}) \leq \frac{W - f_W(t_P)}{P} + (\text{CP} - T_p) \quad \square$$

$\square$

5   Simulation Results

In the above sections, we have established a theoretical lower bound on the time necessary to achieve a Cholesky factorization on an homogeneous platform consisting of P GPUs or P CPUs. This lower bound was established using a detailed analysis of the ALAP schedule and we expect this bound to be close to the makespan achieved by ALAP. Our goal in this section is to establish through simulation our intuition.

We performed simulations with different problem sizes ($n = 30$ or 40 and two different configurations of tasks lengths corresponding either to the CPU case ($G = 6$, $C = 1$, $S = T = 3$) or to the GPU case ($G = 2$, $C = 12$, $S = 1$ and $T = 3$) in Fig. 4. In this simulation, we plot the speedup achieved by the different heuristics against theoretical bounds. The first theoretical (trivial) bound on the achievable speedup on P processors is $\min(P, W/CP)$ (**red**). The second bound is the one established in Sect. 4, based on a detailed analysis of ALAP schedule for Cholesky factorization (**green**).

We consider the following heuristics:

- **ALAP (blue)** is the heuristic that we described in Sect. 2.5 when there is no resource limitation. In the presence of resource limitations, when at a given moment, the number of available tasks is greater than the number of available resources, we define the highest priority task as the one that maximizes the length of the longest path between POTRF(1) and this task.
- **ASAP (yellow)** As Soon As Possible, is the dual heuristic with respect to ALAP. Tasks are processed as soon as they become ready when there is no resource limitation. In the presence of resource limitations, when at a given moment, the number of available tasks is greater than the number of available resources, we define the highest priority task as the one that maximizes the length of the longest path between this task and POTRF(n).

- **LAPACK (purple)** corresponds to the Cholesky factorization implemented in the LAPACK library. It consists in n bulk-synchronized steps. During step i, POTRF(i) is first performed, then all TRSM(i, j) tasks and finally all SYRK(j, i) tasks and all GEMM(j, k, i) tasks can be interleaved and can be executed concurrently if enough resources are available.

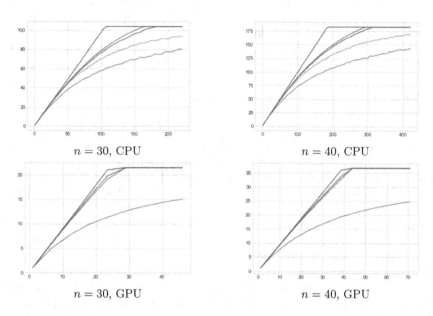

$n = 30$, CPU $n = 40$, CPU

$n = 30$, GPU $n = 40$, GPU

Fig. 4. Evolution of speedup with the number of processors P with CPU weights: ($C = 1$, $S = 3$, $T = 3$, $G = 6$) on the top, and GPU weights: ($C = 12$, $S = 1$, $T = 3$, $G = 2$) on the bottom. (Color figure online)

We note that, since we plot speedup, our lower bounds on the makespan become upper bounds on the speedup. We see that our new upper bound on the speedup (green) is lower than the trivial bound (red). Another observation is that the length of the ALAP schedule (blue) and our new lower bound (green) are always extremely close. This confirms the tightness of our analysis and the excellent performance of the ALAP schedule. In the companion research report [7], the reader will find more results ($n = 20$ in particular) and also an asymptotic analysis which suggests that ALAP is uniformly asymptotically optimal as the problem size becomes larger. In other words, as n increases, the maximum ratio over all P between the ALAP schedule makespan and our lower bound uniformly tends to 1. For example, we can observe that, using either our model GPU weights or our model CPU weights as soon as n gets larger than 40, for any processor count P, ALAP is at least 5% optimal. And, as n increases, ALAP approaches optimality (for any processor count P).

6   Conclusion and Perspectives

In this paper, we have studied in detail the makespan of Cholesky's factorization on a homogeneous platform. For example, this platform can be made of GPUs only, or CPUs only, or anything really. We have obtained a sharp lower bound on the completion time of the factorization, regardless of the scheduling used, which is based on a detailed study of the ALAP schedule. In particular, this bound requires determining the number of simultaneous tasks of each type at any instant in the ALAP schedule.

This lower bound allows us to make several observations. First of all, ALAP scheduling behaves remarkably well in the case of CPUs as in the case of GPUs, always significantly better than the LAPACK schedule and better than ASAP scheduling in the case of CPUs. The proximity between the ALAP completion time and the lower bound, in all the scenarios, allows us to accurately estimate the time required for Cholesky factorization. Indeed, the ALAP completion time provides an upper bound on the time needed whereas the theoretical lower bound provides a lower bound. The proximity between the two thus guarantees both the quality of the approximation of the time needed to perform the factorization, the quality of the theoretical lower bound and the quality of the ALAP scheduling which provides the upper bound.

This work opens many perspectives. From a theoretical point of view, the generalization of the technique used in the case of Cholesky factorization to other types of task graphs, in linear algebra and elsewhere, is open. The techniques used in this paper are highly computational and the results are technically quite complex, but generalization and automation may be envisaged. Another interesting issue is the possibility to extend these results to heterogeneous platforms. Indeed, it has been observed using dynamic runtime schedulers, typically on Cholesky factorization, that heterogeneity allows an "optimal" use of resources, by executing tasks on the most suitable type of resources. Unfortunately, in the heterogeneous case, the known lower bounds are extremely coarse and do not allow to assess the closeness to optimality of a schedule. This raises the question on whether our approach can help.

References

1. Agullo, E., Hadri, B., Ltaief, H., Dongarra, J.: Comparative study of one-sided factorizations with multiple software packages on multi-core hardware. In: ACM/IEEE Conference on Supercomputing, Portland, OR, SC 2009, November 2009. https://doi.org/10.1145/1654059.1654080
2. Agullo, E., et al.: Bridging the gap between performance and bounds of Cholesky factorization on heterogeneous platforms. In: HCW 2015 (2015). https://doi.org/10.1109/IPDPSW.2015.35
3. Agullo, E., Beaumont, O., Eyraud-Dubois, L., Kumar, S.: Are static schedules so bad? A case study on Cholesky factorization. In: 2016 IEEE International Parallel and Distributed Processing Symposium (IPDPS), pp. 1021–1030. IEEE (2016). https://doi.org/10.1109/IPDPS.2016.90

4. Augonnet, C., Thibault, S., Namyst, R., Wacrenier, P.A.: StarPU: a unified platform for task scheduling on heterogeneous multicore architectures. Concurr. Comput. Pract. Exp. **23**, 187–198 (2011). https://doi.org/10.1002/cpe.1631. Special Issue: Euro-Par 2009

5. Badia, R.M., Herrero, J.R., Labarta, J., Pérez, J.M., Quintana-Ortí, E.S., Quintana-Ortí, G.: Parallelizing dense and banded linear algebra libraries using SMPSs. Concurr. Comput. Pract. Exp. **21**(18), 2438–2456 (2009). https://doi.org/10.1002/cpe.1463

6. Beaumont, O., et al.: Scheduling on two types of resources: a survey. arXiv preprint arXiv:1909.11365 (2019)

7. Beaumont, O., Langou, J., Quach, W., Shilova, A.: A Makespan Lower Bound for the Scheduling of the Tiled Cholesky Factorization based on ALAP Schedule, February 2020. https://hal.inria.fr/hal-02487920, working paper or preprint

8. Bosilca, G., et al.: Flexible development of dense linear algebra algorithms on massively parallel architectures with DPLASMA. In: IEEE International Symposium on Parallel and Distributed Processing Workshops, pp. 1432–1441, May 2011. https://doi.org/10.1109/IPDPS.2011.299

9. Bosilca, G., Bouteiller, A., Danalis, A., Herault, T., Lemarinier, P., Dongarra, J.: DAGuE: a generic distributed DAG engine for high performance computing. Parallel Comput. **38**(1–2), 37–51 (2012). https://doi.org/10.1016/j.parco.2011.10.003

10. Buttari, A., Langou, J., Kurzak, J., Dongarra, J.: A class of parallel tiled linear algebra algorithms for multicore architectures. Parallel Comput. **35**(1), 38–53 (2009). https://doi.org/10.1016/j.parco.2008.10.002. http://www.sciencedirect.com/science/article/pii/S0167819108001117

11. Chameleon: a dense linear algebra software for heterogeneous architectures (2014). https://project.inria.fr/chameleon. Accessed June 2020

12. Chan, E., Van Zee, F.G., Bientinesi, P., Quintana-Ortí, E.S., Quintana-Ortí, G., van de Geijn, R.: SuperMatrix: a multithreaded runtime scheduling system for algorithms-by-blocks. In: PPoPP 2008, pp. 123–132. ACM (2008). https://doi.org/10.1145/1345206.1345227

13. Cojean, T., Guermouche, A., Hugo, A., Namyst, R., Wacrenier, P.A.: Resource aggregation for task-based Cholesky factorization on top of modern architectures. Parallel Comput. **83**, 73–92 (2019). https://doi.org/10.1016/j.parco.2018.10.007

14. Cosnard, M., Marrakchi, M., Robert, Y., Trystram, D.: Parallel Gaussian elimination on an MIMD computer. Parallel Comput. **6**(3), 275–296 (1988). https://doi.org/10.1016/0167-8191(88)90070-1

15. Gunnels, J.A., Gustavson, F.G., Henry, G.M., van de Geijn, R.A.: Flame: formal linear algebra methods environment. ACM Trans. Math. Softw. **27**(4), 422–455 (2001). https://doi.org/10.1145/504210.504213

16. Gustavson, F., Karlsson, L., Kågström, B.: Distributed SBP Cholesky factorization algorithms with near-optimal scheduling. ACM Trans. Math. Softw. **36**(2), 1–25 (2009). https://doi.org/10.1145/1499096.1499100

17. Jacquelin, M., Zheng, Y., Ng, E., Yelick, K.: An asynchronous task-based fan-both sparse Cholesky solver. SIAM J. Sci. and Stat. Comput. **9**(2), 327–340 (2016). https://doi.org/10.1137/1.9781611975215.8

18. Kim, K., Rajamanickam, S., Stelle, G., Edwards, H.C., Olivier, S.L.: Task parallel incomplete Cholesky factorization using 2D partitioned-block layout. arXiv preprint arXiv:1601.05871 (2016)

19. Kurzak, J., Buttari, A., Dongarra, J.: Solving systems of linear equations on the CELL processor using Cholesky factorization. IEEE Trans. Parallel Distrib. Syst. **19**(9), 1175–1186 (2008). https://doi.org/10.1109/TPDS.2007.70813
20. Kurzak, J., Ltaief, H., Dongarra, J., Badia, R.M.: Scheduling dense linear algebra operations on multicore processors. Concurr. Comput. Pract. Exp. **22**(1), 15–44 (2010). https://doi.org/10.1002/cpe.1467
21. Pérez, J.M., Badia, R.M., Labarta, J.: A flexible and portable programming model for SMP and multi-cores. Technical report, Barcelona Supercomputing Center - Centro Nacional de Supercomputación, June 2007
22. Quintana-Ortí, E.S., Quintana-Ortí, G., van de Geijn, R.A., Van Zee, F.G., Chan, E.: Programming matrix algorithms-by-blocks for thread-level parallelism. ACM Trans. Math. Softw. **36**(3) (2009). https://doi.org/10.1145/1527286.1527288
23. Song, F., YarKhan, A., Dongarra, J.: Dynamic task scheduling for linear algebra algorithms on distributed-memory multicore systems. In: SC 2009 (2009). https://doi.org/10.1145/1654059.1654079

Optimal GPU-CPU Offloading Strategies for Deep Neural Network Training

Olivier Beaumont[1,2](✉) ⓘ, Lionel Eyraud-Dubois[1,2] ⓘ, and Alena Shilova[1,2] ⓘ

[1] Inria Bordeaux – Sud-Ouest, Bordeaux, France
{olivier.beaumont,lionel.eyraud-dubois,alena.shilova}@inria.fr
[2] University of Bordeaux, Bordeaux, France

Abstract. Training Deep Neural Networks is known to be an expensive operation, both in terms of computational cost and memory load. Indeed, during training, all intermediate layer outputs (called activations) computed during the forward phase must be stored until the corresponding gradient has been computed in the backward phase. These memory requirements sometimes prevent to consider larger batch sizes and deeper networks, so that they can limit both convergence speed and accuracy. Recent works have proposed to offload some of the computed forward activations from the device memory to the main memory and requires to determine which activations should be offloaded and when these transfers should take place. We prove that this problem is NP-complete in the strong sense, and propose two heuristics based on relaxations of the problem. We then conduct a thorough experimental evaluation of standard deep neural networks.

Keywords: Memory management · Deep Neural Network · Dynamic programming · Scheduling

1 Introduction

Training for Deep Learning Networks (DNNs) has become a major compute intensive application [9,10], typically performed on GPU clusters. The training phase involves two traversals of the graph representing the DNN, one in direct order which is called forward propagation and one in reverse order called backward propagation. This incurs high memory usage: the tensors computed during the forward phase, called forward activations, must be kept in memory until the associated backward operation is performed, since they are required to compute the gradients and to update the weights. Therefore, memory issues become crucial when performing training in DNNs, and the memory limitation of current hardware often prevents data scientists from considering larger models, larger image sizes or larger batch sizes [15,18].

For instance, when using ResNet101 with relatively small images of size 224×224 and a batch size of 32, the resulting size during training is around 5GB. For applications which require to detect small objects in the images [4], the image

© Springer Nature Switzerland AG 2020
M. Malawski and K. Rzadca (Eds.): Euro-Par 2020, LNCS 12247, pp. 151–166, 2020.
https://doi.org/10.1007/978-3-030-57675-2_10

resolution must be increased, and the memory required for storing activations increases quadratically with the image resolution. The situation is even worse when moving to 3D object recognition [6] or video based DNNs such as 3D-Resnet [8] or CDC [19].

Many approaches have been proposed in the literature in order to circumvent this memory issue. In this paper, we focus on an *offloading* approach (also called *memory swapping*), which consists in reducing memory usage on the GPU (device memory) by transferring some activations to the CPU (main memory), which is expected to be at least one order of magnitude larger. The corresponding algorithmic question is to determine which activations should be offloaded and when, and also when offloaded activations should be brought back (prefetched) from the main memory to the device memory. This approach has been recently considered in [1,13,14,16,20,21], where the authors advocate the general idea and propose several static heuristics to decide which activations should be offloaded. In this paper, we provide a deeper analysis of this problem. More specifically, we prove that the general problem, even for sequential models, is strongly NP-complete where only fully integral data transfers are possible and we analyze two relaxations of the problem for which we can derive optimal algorithms. These algorithms can then be used as heuristics for the general problem.

The rest of the paper is organized as follows. In Sect. 2, we discuss previous works regarding offloading, as well as other techniques to reduce memory usage during the training phase. In Sect. 3, we present the model and notations used throughout the paper, and assess the complexity of the problem. In Sect. 4, we propose a first relaxation where activations can be partially or completely offloaded into the main memory, and derive an optimal strategy. In Sect. 5, we consider the case where partial offloading is not possible, but where communications can be interrupted, and we present a dynamic programming algorithm to find the optimal schedule. In Sect. 6, we provide experimental results and we assess the efficiency of our heuristics against the previous approach [1,13,21], before presenting conclusions and perspectives in Sect. 7.

2   Related Work

In order to reduce the memory usage of storing the forward activations on a processing device, we can identify two kinds of approaches: checkpointing or offloading.

Checkpointing techniques consist selecting only a few activations that are kept in memory, and then to dynamically recompute the others at runtime. This allows to explore a tradeoff between memory usage and computational cost. The use of checkpointing strategies has recently been advocated for DNN in several papers [5,7,11], where it is referred as gradient checkpointing or rematerialization.

Offloading is a potentially complementary approach first proposed in [16]. In [16], the authors propose a simple and effective mechanism of memory virtualization, that nevertheless introduces unnecessary idle time by enforcing some synchronization between data transfers and computations of later forward activations. This approach has been later improved in [1]. Nevertheless, in both papers, the algorithmic strategies to decide which activations to offload into the main memory are relatively straightforward. Proposed strategies consist in trying to offload either all activations or only those that correspond to convolutional layers (either all convolutions or every second one). Indeed, convolutional layers are known to induce a large computational time with respect to their input size, which make them good candidates to overlap offloading and processing.

Several follow-up works offer improvements over this first attempt. In order to reduce the overhead incurred by the communications, some authors [17] recommend to add compression to decrease the communication time, while others [12] design a memory-centric architecture to help with data transfers. In [13,14], the authors implement memory virtualization by manipulating the computational graphs and inserting special operations called *swap in* and *swap out* that send the activations in and out of the device memory. Such an approach can be applied to any arbitrary Computation Graph that represent neural network training graphs. The authors of [13] improve the candidate selection and prefetching mechanisms by introducing thresholds to filter out different possibilities. Moreover, some works try to combine offloading with other memory optimizing techniques. Memory swapping and memory pooling are implemented together in [21], where candidates for swapping are found by assigning priority scores to all activations. Finally, gradient checkpointing is combined with the simple offloading approach from [16] in [20].

As a complement to these practical approaches, in this paper we perform the first theoretical analysis of the underlying optimization problem and present both a complexity proof and optimal solutions to two of its relaxations.

3   Model and Complexity

3.1   Computation Model

We consider the training phase of sequential DNNs, as depicted on Fig. 1. This training phase consists of two types of computations: forward propagations $(F_i)_{1 \leq i \leq L}$ and backward propagations $(B_i)_{1 \leq i \leq L}$. The forward step F_i requires x_i as input, and computes x_{i+1}. The backward step B_i requires x_{i+1}, x_i and y_{i+1} as inputs, and computes y_i. The objective of the elementary training phase

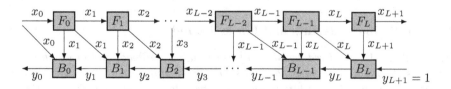

Fig. 1. Data dependencies induced the training phase of Sequential Deep Neural Networks.

is to perform the whole computation and to obtain y_0 in the smallest possible time. This computation is performed on a processing device (typically a GPU or TPU) with limited memory M_{GPU}. We denote u_{F_i} the time to process F_i, and u_{B_i} the time to process B_i. As mentioned before, the training phase is very memory intensive: since they will be needed for the backward phase, all x_i values must be stored during the forward phase, and they can only be freed once their corresponding B_i operation has been performed.

We will use the following memory model. Each data (x_i and y_i) has a given memory usage, denoted respectively by $|x_i|$ and $|y_i|$. To perform an operation (either F_i or B_i), it is necessary to have all inputs stored into memory, to reserve the memory space to store the output, and to reserve space for the temporary memory usage of the operation, denoted with ex_i^F for F_i and ex_i^B for B_i. For example, running the F_i operation requires to have at least $|x_i| + |x_{i+1}| + \mathrm{ex}_i^F$ memory available.

In order to decrease memory usage, we assume that it is possible to *offload* some of the forward data to another memory storage (typically the main memory of the machine). The size of this memory is assumed to be large enough to store all the results and thus is not a constraint; but the speed of data transfers is limited by bandwidth β. The offloaded data can then be *prefetched* during the backward phase, so that it is available when needed to perform the corresponding backward operation. Such memory hierarchy has been considered by [1,16] as well, *i.e.* there are one GPU with limited memory and one CPU with large enough memory to store all activations of some arbitrary neural network and both are connected with the network with the bandwidth β, which we assume is fully used for any communications. More complicated cases such as multiple GPU and one CPU are out of scope of this paper and they will be left for the future work. Additionally, we assume that transfers and computations could be overlapped while only one transfer at a time is possible. Let us point out that generally x_i needs to be stored in memory in its entirety throughout the transfer: during the offloading, the memory is only released after the complete transfer, and during the prefetching, the memory is reserved as soon as the transfer begins.

We can state the decision problem associated to offloading.

Problem 1 (Offloading). Consider a training phase with L operations, with processing times u_{F_i} and u_{B_i}, data sizes $|x_i|$ and $|y_i|$, temporary memory usage ex_i^F and ex_i^B, where $0 \leq i \leq L$. Is it possible to perform this computation on a processing device with memory M_{GPU} and bandwidth β between processing device and main memory, with an execution time at most T?

3.2 Preliminary Results and Lower Bound

Proposition 1. *For fixed decisions of which data to offload, and in which order transfers should be performed, the best schedule is obtained with a* no-wait *policy, where each action (computation and data transfers) is performed as early as possible, as soon as data is available and there is enough memory.*

Given the activation sizes and the temporary memory usage, it is easy to compute the total amount of used memory (both on the computing device and in the additional memory) during the execution of each operation. We denote by m_{F_i} or m_{B_i} the amount of data required to be stored on both devices to perform F_i or B_i respectively. Let us additionally denote as M_{peak} the maximum of these values: $m_{F_i} = \mathrm{ex}_i^F + \sum_{j \leq i+1} |x_j|$, $m_{B_i} = \mathrm{ex}_i^B + |y_i| + |y_{i+1}| + \sum_{j \leq i+1} |x_j|$, i.e. $M_{peak} = \max\left(\max_{0 \leq i \leq L} m_{B_i}, \max_{0 \leq i \leq L} m_{F_i}\right)$.

Since any valid schedule must process the operation which achieves the memory peak while using at most M_{GPU} memory on the computing device, the following result holds.

Proposition 2. *The amount of data offloaded by any valid schedule is at least* $M_{peak} - M_{GPU}$.

Since any valid schedule must perform all computations, and must transfer at least this amount of data twice (for offloading and prefetching), the following lower bound on the optimal makespan holds true.

Proposition 3. *The value* $LB = \max(\sum_i u_{F_i} + u_{B_i}, 2\frac{M_{peak} - M_{GPU}}{\beta})$ *is a lower bound on the optimal makespan.*

3.3   Complexity Results

Theorem 1. *Problem 1 is strongly NP-complete.*

Proof. Problem 1 clearly belongs to NP: given the start time of all forward and backward operations, and the set of offloaded data with the corresponding start time of transfers, checking that the schedule satisfies all constraints can be done in linear time.

We prove that this problem is strongly NP-hard and therefore strongly NP-complete by a reduction from the 3-partition problem: given a set of integers $\{u_0, u_2, \ldots, u_{3m-1}\}$ such that $\sum_i u_i = mV$, is it possible to partition it into m parts $\{S_1, \ldots, S_m\}$ so that for any $j \leq m$, $|S_j| = 3$ and $\sum_{i \in S_j} u_i = V$. This problem is known to be NP-complete in the strong sense. Given an instance of 3-partition, we consider the following instance of Problem 1, depicted on the Figure below:

- $L = 5m$, $\beta = V$, $M_{\mathrm{GPU}} = mV$, $T = 2m$;
- $u_{F_i} = 0$ and $|x_i| = u_i$ for $1 \leq i < 3m$;
- $u_{F_i} = 1$ and $|x_i| = 0$ for $i = 3m + 2k, 0 \leq k < m$;
- $u_{F_i} = 0$ and $|x_i| = V$ for $i = 3m + 2k + 1, 0 \leq k < m$;
- $u_{B_i} = 0$ and $|y_i| = 0$ for all i, except $u_{B_{3m}} = m$.

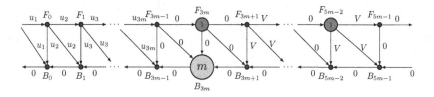

We claim that this instance can be scheduled in time $T = 2m$ if and only if the 3-partition instance is positive.

Let us first assume that there exists a solution to the 3-partition instance, *i.e.* sets $(S_j)_{1 \le j \le m}$ such that $\sum_{i \in S_j} u_i = V$. We can build a schedule which starts F_{3m+2k} at time k for $0 \le k < m$, and executes B_{3m} from time m to time $2m$. At time 0, before the execution of F_{3m}, the memory usage is exactly $mV = \sum_i u_i$. During the execution of F_{3m+2k}, activations x_i for $i \in S_k$ are transferred. Since $\beta = V$, this takes time exactly 1. The memory used at the end of F_{3m+2k} is thus $(m - 1)V$, which allows to immediately start $F_{3m+2k+1}$. At the end of the forward phase, the memory is filled with m activations of size V. At the beginning of B_{3m}, the memory is empty: all activations of size u_i can be prefetched during the execution of B_{3m}, allowing to finish the backward phase. This schedule induces no idle time, and finishes in time exactly $T = 2m$.

Let us now assume that there exists a valid schedule of duration $T = 2m$, *i.e.* without any idle time on the processing device. For $j < m$, let us define the set S_j as the indices of the activations whose transfers are included in the execution of F_{3m+2j}. Since F_{3m+1} starts immediately after the end of F_{3m}, and since memory is only released once the transfer has been completed, the amount of data sent during F_{3m} is at least V. Since $\beta = V$ and $u_{F_{3m}} = 1$, the amount of data is exactly V, thus $\sum_{i \in S_0} u_i = V$. The same argument applies for all $j < m$, which shows that the sets S_j are a valid solution for the 3-partition instance, and completes the proof.   □

From the proof of Theorem 1 follows that even when we know which activations should be offloaded, it is difficult to decide the order in which the transfers should be done. Indeed, it is clear in the instances used in the proof that the first $3m$ activations need to be offloaded, but finding the optimal ordering is hard. Because of this negative complexity result, we study two different relaxations of Problem 1 in the next sections, by relaxing the constraints stating that activations must be sent in entirety before the corresponding memory can be released. In such scenarios, all activations can be sent as soon as they are computed, *i.e.* in increasing order of their indices. This allows to compute optimal solutions in reasonable time, and the resulting algorithms can then be used as heuristic solutions for Problem 1.

4   Fractional Relaxation

In a first relaxation, let us consider that it is possible to perform partial offloading: any communication can be stopped at any time, and the data that has been transferred up to that time can be released from memory, even if the rest of the activation is still present on the computing device. With this model, it is possible to compute an optimal solution with a greedy algorithm. Let us first prove results about the structure of optimal solutions, and then use that structure to design an optimal greedy algorithm.

Structure of Optimal Solutions. In this section, let us analyze special *eager* schedules. A schedule is said *eager* if it offloads the first k activations $x_0, x_1, \ldots, x_k$ (where the last one can be partially offloaded). A schedule is said *ordered* if the data is offloaded in order of increasing indices, and prefetched in order of decreasing indices.

Lemma 1. *Any valid solution $\mathcal{S}$ can be transformed into a eager and ordered solution $\mathcal{S}'$ with the same makespan.*

Proof. Let us denote by M_{off} the amount of activation data offloaded by the schedule $\mathcal{S}$, and let us consider in $\mathcal{S}$ the time intervals $\mathcal{I}_{\text{off}}$ spent offloading data, and the time intervals $\mathcal{I}_{\text{fetch}}$ spent prefetching data. Let us consider the schedule $\mathcal{S}'$ in which all operations and data transfers are performed at the same instants as in $\mathcal{S}$, only changing which data is transferred. The first intervals of $\mathcal{I}_{\text{off}}$ are used to transfer x_0 (since it is possible to stop any communication at any time, using several intervals to transfer x_0 is not a problem), the next ones are used to offload x_1, and so on, until the amount M_{off} is reached, and similarly for the prefetched data, in reverse order. Clearly $\mathcal{S}'$ is eager and ordered.

Since the x_i values become available in the forward phase by order of increasing indices, and are consumed in the backward phase by order of decreasing indices, it is clear that transfers in $\mathcal{S}'$ are valid: an activation is offloaded only after having been produced, and in the backward phase an activation is prefetched before being used. Furthermore, since transfers occur at the same instants and at the same speed as in $\mathcal{S}$, the memory usage of $\mathcal{S}'$ is exactly the same as the memory usage of $\mathcal{S}$ at any instant. The modified $\mathcal{S}'$ schedule is thus valid. □

Greedy Algorithm. According to this result, we consider only eager and ordered schedules. It is thus sufficient to find the amount of offloaded data which results in the smallest makespan. The next result shows that it is best to offload the least possible amount of data. The complete proof of this result can be found in the companion paper [3].

Lemma 2. *Let $\mathcal{S}$ and $\mathcal{S}'$ be no-wait, ordered and eager schedules which offload a quantity of data Q and Q' respectively, with $Q < Q'$. Then the makespan of $\mathcal{S}$ is not larger than the makespan of $\mathcal{S}'$.*

With Lemma 1 and 2, since $M_{peak} - M_{\text{GPU}}$ is a lower bound on the amount of data that any schedule has to offload, we can characterize an optimal schedule for this relaxed problem.

Theorem 2. *For a given instance, the no-wait, eager, ordered schedule which offloads a quantity $M_{peak} - M_{GPU}$ of data is optimal.*

By rounding up the number of offloaded activations, this result provides a heuristic for the original integral problem, that we call GREEDY. The GREEDY heuristic returns the no-wait, eager, ordered schedule which offloads (entirely) the first k activations, where k is the smallest index such that $\sum_{i \le k} |x_i| \ge M_{peak} - M_{\text{GPU}}$.

However, it may happen that this GREEDY schedule offloads too much data because of the rounding procedure. In the next section, we thus analyze a more sophisticated relaxation in order to obtain a more precise algorithm.

5   Fractional Communications

Let now consider another formulation of Problem 1, in which an activation must be either entirely offloaded or not offloaded at all. However, it is still allowed to stop a communication at any time and resume it later. In this section, we first prove that this problem is NP-complete in the weak sense, and then propose a pseudo-polynomial optimal algorithm based on Dynamic Programming.

5.1   Complexity

Problem 2 (Offloading with interruptions).   Consider a training phase with L operations, with processing times u_{F_i} and u_{B_i}, data sizes $|x_i|$ and $|y_i|$, temporary memory usage ex_i^F and ex_i^B, where $0 \le i \le L$. Is it possible to perform this computation on a processing device with memory M_{GPU} and bandwidth β between the processing device and the main memory, with an execution time at most T, if communications can be interrupted and partial?

Let us first note that Proposition 1 also holds for this problem (it is always better to schedule with a no-wait policy). We can also state a result similar to the one of the fully fractional case.

Lemma 3.   *Any valid solution $\mathcal{S}$ can be transformed into an ordered solution $\mathcal{S}'$ with the same makespan.*

The proof is the same as the one of Lemma 1: transforming $\mathcal{S}$ using the correct order provides a valid schedule. The result is weaker, because an eager schedule which offloads the same data might not be valid for Problem 2 (the last activation might not be fully offloaded).

The next theorem shows that Problem 2 is less difficult than Problem 1. Its proof is omitted here and can be found in the companion report [3].

Theorem 3.   *Problem 2 is NP-complete in the weak sense.*

5.2   Structure of Optimal Solutions

According to Lemma 3, our objective is now to find the best ordered schedule. In this section, we derive properties of all ordered and no-wait schedules, which will allow to obtain a dynamic programming algorithm in the next section.

Forward and Backward Phases. Let us consider any ordered, no-wait schedule $\mathcal{S}$. Let M_{F_i} denote the device memory occupied at the end of F_{i-1} (it should contain all data not offloaded at this instant, plus x_i which is the output of F_{i-1}). Let Δ_{F_i} denote the amount of data from $x_0, \ldots, x_{i-1}$ that $\mathcal{S}$ offloads after the end of F_{i-1}. If this amount is zero, let us denote by Av_F the time between the end of the last offload and the end of F_{i-1}, and let $\Delta_{F_i} = -Av_F \cdot \beta$. Moreover, let us set $\Delta_{F_i}^+ = \max\{0, \Delta_{F_i}\}$. We aim to characterize the delay ϵ_i^F between the end of F_{i-1} and the start of F_i.

Let us first remark that since $\mathcal{S}$ is a valid schedule, there is enough memory to process F_i at some point, which means that $\Delta_{F_i}^+$ needs to be large enough,
$$M_{F_i} - \Delta_{F_i}^+ + \mathrm{ex}_i^F + |x_{i+1}| \leq M_{\mathrm{GPU}}$$

If $M_{F_i} + \mathrm{ex}_i^F + |x_{i+1}| \leq M_{\mathrm{GPU}}$, then F_i can start immediately after the end of F_{i-1}, and since $\mathcal{S}$ is no-wait, then $\epsilon_i^F = 0$. Otherwise, processing F_i can start as soon as enough memory has been released by offloading data at rate β. This yields $\epsilon_i^F = \frac{M_{F_i} + \mathrm{ex}_i^F + |x_{i+1}| - M_{\mathrm{GPU}}}{\beta}$. In summary,

$$\epsilon_i^F = \max\left(0, \frac{M_{F_i} + \mathrm{ex}_i^F + |x_{i+1}| - M_{\mathrm{GPU}}}{\beta}\right) \tag{1}$$

Let us now derive recursive equations to obtain $M_{F_{i+1}}$ and $\Delta_{F_{i+1}}$ from M_{F_i} and Δ_{F_i}. These equations depend on whether x_i is offloaded in $\mathcal{S}$.

If x_i is offloaded, then the amount of data ready to be offloaded at the end of F_{i-1} is $\Delta_{F_i}^+ + |x_i|$. Until the end of F_i, the amount of data that can be offloaded is at most $(\epsilon_i^F + u_{F_i})\beta$. Hence we obtain

$$\Delta_{F_{i+1}} = \Delta_{F_i}^+ + |x_i| - (\epsilon_i^F + u_{F_i})\beta \tag{2}$$

$$M_{F_{i+1}} = M_{F_i} + |x_{i+1}| - \min\left(\Delta_{F_i}^+ + |x_i|, (\epsilon_i^F + u_{F_i})\beta\right). \tag{3}$$

If x_i is not offloaded, we can write similar equations, except that $|x_i|$ is not added to the amount of data to be offloaded. This yields

$$\Delta_{F_{i+1}} = \Delta_{F_i} - (\epsilon_i^F + u_{F_i})\beta \tag{4}$$

$$M_{F_{i+1}} = M_{F_i} + |x_{i+1}| - \min\left(\Delta_{F_i}^+, (\epsilon_i^F + u_{F_i})\beta\right) \tag{5}$$

Let us now derive similar results about the backward phase. We first modify $\mathcal{S}$ to process all backward operations and perform all prefetching operations as *late* as possible without changing the makespan of the schedule. We then define M_{B_i} as the device memory occupied right before processing B_{i-1} (thus it does not take into account the output of B_{i-1}, which is y_{i-1}). Let us also define Δ_{B_i} as the amount of data from $x_L, x_{L-1}, \ldots, x_i$) that $\mathcal{S}$ prefetches before starting B_{i-1}, and if this amount is zero, then $\Delta_{B_i} = -Av_B \cdot \beta$, where Av_B is the time between the start of B_{i-1} and the start of the first prefetch operation. Finally, let ϵ_i^B denote the delay between the end of B_i and the start of B_{i-1}.

With the same reasoning as above, we obtain

$$\epsilon_i^B = \max\left(0, \frac{M_{B_i} + \text{ex}_i^F + |x_{i+1}| + |y_{i+1}| - M_{\text{GPU}}}{\beta}\right) \tag{6}$$

$$\Delta_{B_{i+1}} = |x_i| + \max\left(0, \Delta_{B_i} - (\epsilon_i^B + u_{B_i})\beta\right) \qquad \text{if } x_i \text{ is offloaded} \tag{7}$$

$$\Delta_{B_{i+1}} = \Delta_{B_i} - (\epsilon_i^B + u_{B_i})\beta \qquad \text{otherwise} \tag{8}$$

Computing $M_{B_{i+1}}$ is not necessary, as one can notice that for all i, $M_{B_i} - \Delta_{B_i}^+ = |y_i| + |x_i| + \sum_{j<i,j \text{ not offloaded}} |x_j|$, and $M_{F_i} - \Delta_{F_i}^+ = |x_i| + \sum_{j<i,j \text{ not offloaded}} |x_j|$. Thus, $M_{B_i} - \Delta_{B_i}^+ = |y_i| + M_{F_i} - \Delta_{F_i}^+$, which allows to compute M_{B_i} once all three other values are known.

Idle Time Between Phases. The connection between forward phase and backward phase is defined through Lemma 4 that shows how to compute the idle time between them. The proof of this result is provided in [3].

Lemma 4. *The idle time between phases are given in Eq. (9):*

$$\epsilon_G = \max \begin{cases} 0, \\ \frac{\Delta_{F_{L+1}} + \Delta_{B_{L+1}}}{\beta}, \\ \max_{\{j \leq L| \sum_{i=j+1}^{L} \beta u_{B_i} < -\Delta_{B_{L+1}}\}} \frac{R_j^B + M_{F_{L+1}} - M_{GPU}}{\beta} - \sum_{i=j+1}^{L} u_{B_i}, \\ \max_{\{j \leq L| \sum_{i=j+1}^{L} \beta u_{F_i} < -\Delta_{F_{L+1}}\}} \frac{R_j^F + M_{B_{L+1}} - M_{GPU}}{\beta} - \sum_{i=j+1}^{L} u_{F_i}, \end{cases} \tag{9}$$

where $R_j^B = \text{ex}_j^B + |y_j| + |y_{j-1}| - \sum_{i>j+1} |x_i|$ *and* $R_j^F = \text{ex}_j^F - \sum_{i>j+1} |x_i|$.

5.3   Resulting Algorithm

To formalize the dynamic programming algorithm, let us define $\text{IDLE}(i, m, d_F, d_B)$ as the smallest possible sum of idle times between (i) the start of the schedule and the end of F_{i-1} and (ii) the start of B_{i-1} and the end of the schedule, for all schedules S such that $M_{F_i} = m$, $\Delta_{F_i} = d_F$, $\Delta_{B_i} = d_B$.

Any schedule starts with a memory occupation of $|x_0|$, and no idle time, so we can define $\text{IDLE}(0, |x_0|, 0, 0) = 0$, and $\text{IDLE}(0, m, d_F, d_B) = \infty$ for all other values of m, d_F, d_B. In order to compute $\text{IDLE}(i, m, d_F, d_B)$ for all i and all relevant values of m, d_F, d_B, we use hash tables IDLE_i indexed with (m, d_F, d_B), with the understanding that if (m, d_F, d_B) is not stored in IDLE_i, then $\text{IDLE}(i, m, d_F, d_B) = \infty$. This leads to Algorithm 1, where IDLE_i values are used to update IDLE_{i+1} values, with two possible cases, either with a schedule that offloads x_i, or with a schedule that does not.

Algorithm 1. Dynamic Programming Algorithm for Fractional Communications

---

IDLE$_i \leftarrow$ HashTable() for $0 \le i \le L$
IDLE$_0(|x_0|, 0, 0) = 0$
for $i \in \{0, \dots, L\}$ **do**
    for $M_{F_i}, \Delta_{F_i}, \Delta_{B_i} \in$ IDLE$_i$ **do**
        $M_{B_i} \leftarrow |y_i| + \Delta_{B_i}^+ + M_{F_i} - \Delta_{F_i}^+$
        if $|x_{i+1}| + \max(M_{F_i} + \text{ex}_i^F - \Delta_{F_i}, M_{B_i} + \text{ex}_i^B + |y_{i+1}| - \Delta_{B_i}) \le M_{\text{GPU}}$ **then**
            Compute $\epsilon_i^F, \epsilon_i^B$ from equations (1) and (6)
            Compute M_F, Δ_F, Δ_B if x_i is offloaded (equations (2), (3) and (7))
            IDLE$_{i+1}(M_F, \Delta_F, \Delta_B) \leftarrow \min\left(\text{IDLE}_{i+1}(M_F, \Delta_F, \Delta_B), \text{IDLE}_i(M_{F_i}, \Delta_{F_i}, \Delta_{B_i}) + \epsilon_i^F + \epsilon_i^B\right)$
            Compute $M_F', \Delta_F', \Delta_B'$ if x_i is not offloaded (equations (4), (5) and (8))
            IDLE$_{i+1}(M_F', \Delta_F', \Delta_B') \leftarrow \min\left(\text{IDLE}_{i+1}(M_F', \Delta_F', \Delta_B'), \text{IDLE}_i(M_{F_i}, \Delta_{F_i}, \Delta_{B_i}) + \epsilon_i^F + \epsilon_i^B\right)$
for $M_F, \Delta_F, \Delta_B \in$ IDLE$_{L+1}$ **do**
    Compute ϵ_G according to equation (9)
    TOTALIDLE$(M_F, \Delta_F, \Delta_B) \leftarrow$ IDLE$_{L+1}(M_F, \Delta_F, \Delta_B) + \epsilon_G$
Get $M_F^*, \Delta_F^*, \Delta_B^*$ which minimizes TOTALIDLE$(M_F, \Delta_F, \Delta_B)$
Backtrack in IDLE$_{L+1}, \dots,$ IDLE$_0$ to obtain optimal offload decisions

---

Once IDLE$_{L+1}$ is computed, TOTALIDLE can be found by adding the corresponding idle time ϵ_G between the forward and backward phases. Then, the smallest value in TOTALIDLE is the smallest possible idle time for any ordered, no-wait schedule. Finally, we can identify which offload decisions have led to this idle time, and then obtain the description of the corresponding schedule.

The number of values kept in the hash table can be bounded in the following way: M_F is between 0 and M_{GPU}, Δ_F and Δ_B are between $-\sum_i(u_{F_i})\beta$ and M_{GPU}. The number of possible values is thus $O(M_{\text{GPU}}(M_{\text{GPU}} + u_{F_i}\beta)^2)$, and the complexity of Algorithm 1 is $O(LM_{\text{GPU}}(M_{\text{GPU}} + u_{F_i}\beta)^2)$, which is indeed pseudo-polynomial.

This optimal algorithm for the fractional communications model can be turned into heuristic DYNPROG for the original problem. DYNPROG computes the optimal set of activations for the relaxed model with Algorithm 1, and outputs the no-wait, ordered schedule which offloads exactly these activations.

Practical Considerations. The integration of offloading in Deep Learning frameworks is generally not completely trivial. A first solution is the one adopted by VDNN[1] and consists in implementing an ad-hoc system to do the training by directly managing computation operations and data transfer operations between the main memory and the device memory. It is possible to use a solution of this type, by directly integrating our algorithms in addition to the heuristics proposed in [1]. This solution allows great flexibility and low-level management of all data movements and allocations, but it limits the possible adoption by not relying on classical Deep Learning frameworks. TFLMS [13] is directly built on top of TensorFlow. The principle consists in modifying the task graph by explicitly integrating swap tasks (between the device memory and the main memory). This approach is very interesting because it has a high level of integration with

---

[1] https://github.com/shriramsb/vdnn-plus-plus/.

TensorFlow, but on the other hand, it is only possible to specify the relative order of the transfer tasks with respect to the computation tasks and not to perform them at specific dates. As the scheduling of tasks is controlled by TensorFlow itself, it is therefore not possible a priori to make just-in-time communications and allow for a perfect overlap of computations and communications. The situation with PyTorch is also complex, because implementing an offloading solution requires to transfer not only easily accessible tensors, but also the complete data structure that are necessary for executing backward operations. Manipulating this requires operating on PyTorch internals and is out of the scope of this paper. Therefore, we rely on simulations to compare algorithms and scheduling, and we postpone their implementation in Deep Learning frameworks until there is an easier and more explicit support of data exchange.

As mentioned above, the dynamic program algorithm has a pseudo-polynomial complexity, and its running time can get large for deep networks. To keep the running time reasonable, we implement a rounding procedure (the details are given in the research report [3]). This allows to keep all running times below 25 s. Since this computation is performed only once for the whole training phase, such an execution time is completely acceptable.

6   Experimental Analysis

Experimental Setting. This section presents experimental results obtained on three different kinds of networks: ResNet, DenseNet, and Inception v3. We have slightly modified these networks to represent them as linear chains, by grouping each non-linear part of the graph in a virtual layer. We have obtained the values of u_F, u_B, ex^F, ex^B, and the sizes of x_i and y_i by performing measures on sample data on a node equipped with a Nvidia Tesla V100-PCIE GPU card with 15.75 GB of memory. We also measured the bandwidth β to transfer data using PyTorch from the GPU to the RAM, and obtained around 12.5 GB/s.

We use all available depths for ResNet (18, 34, 50, 101, 152) and DenseNet (121, 161, 169 and 201). We use three different image sizes: small images of shape 224×224, medium images of shape 500×500, and large images of shape 1000×1000. During the training phase, for higher efficiency, it is classical to process images in *batches*, where several images are processed independently. For each model and image size, we consider different batch sizes that are powers of 2, starting from the smallest batch size that ensures a reasonable throughput. For each case, we compute schedules with five different algorithms: GREEDY (Sect. 4), DYNPROG (based on Algorithm 1, see Sect. 5.3), AUTOSWAP, TFLMS and VDNN, where the last three approaches are based on the state-of-the-art methods used in the previous works. AUTOSWAP [21] is a score-based heuristic which uses a weighted average of 4 priority scores to decide which activations should be offloaded in priority. The best weight combination is obtained with Bayesian Optimization. TFLMS [13] is a heuristic designed for general graphs (not necessarily sequential) in high bandwidth settings, but it does not use any profiling information and thus cannot adapt to the available memory. TFLMS

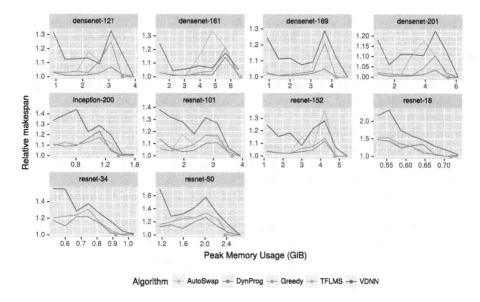

Fig. 2. Experimental results for image size 224 and batch size 32.

is parameterized with the number of tensors to be offloaded and how many layers in advance the data should be prefetched, and we present the performance achieved by the best configurations. In VDNN++ [1], the authors identify convolutional layers as having a much longer computation latency. Their approach is to offload the input of either all convolutional layers, or of half of them. In our implementation of VDNN, we identify as candidates the layers for which the ratio $\frac{u_{F_i}}{|x_i|}$ is above a given threshold. For all possible thresholds, we compute the no-wait, ordered schedule which offloads all these candidates, and the one which offloads half of them. VDNN outputs the best schedule out of all these choices.

Representative Results. A representative selection of achieved results is depicted in Fig. 2, where different types of network of different length are considered with a given image and batch size. For each network, we run all algorithms with a memory limit varying from the minimum amount of memory required to run the network, to M_{peak} which allows to process the network with no offloading. In each case, we also compute the lower bound LB (Proposition 3), and the plots show the ratio of the makespan achieved by each algorithm to the lower bound, thus points where the ratio is 1 correspond to optimal solutions. We observe that both GREEDY and DYNPROG outperform the VDNN heuristic in all cases, especially in low memory scenarios. Once correctly parameterized, TFLMS is able to obtain optimal makespan for the highest memory limit values. But it is unable to delay forward computations until enough memory is available, and thus can not adapt to low memory settings when bandwidth is scarce. AUTOSWAP often produces the same solution as the GREEDY algorithm (for a much higher computational cost), but its performance depends on the random procedure of

Bayesian Optimization and is thus very inconsistent. The DYNPROG approach obtains significantly better performance than GREEDY. The difference is small in many cases, except for the DenseNet networks where DYNPROG is able to consistently obtain almost optimal solutions. The spike that can be observed on these graphs for GREEDY and VDNN correspond to the memory limit M_{GPU} for which both terms of the lower bound LB are almost equal (*i.e.*, the total execution time is very close to the time to transfer $M_{peak} - M_{\text{GPU}}$). Such cases are more difficult to solve because both criteria need to be optimized carefully.

Overall, DYNPROG obtains much more stable performance than VDNN and AUTOSWAP, and produces solutions over a much wider range than TFLMS. Furthermore, DYNPROG is able to consistently achieve a ratio below 1.2, which means that its throughput is at least 83% of the highest possible throughput.

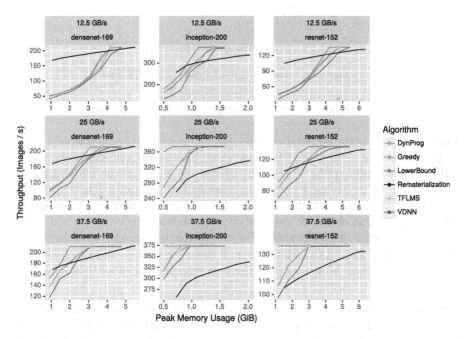

Fig. 3. Comparison to rematerialization for image size 224 and batch size 32, for various bandwidth values.

Comparison to Rematerialization. An alternative to offloading is rematerialization [7], in which memory savings are achieved by discarding activations and recomputing them later. In Fig. 3, we compare the throughput (in terms of processed images per second) obtained by the offloading algorithms and by an optimal rematerialization strategy [2]. We observe that for the bandwidth measured on our hardware, the rematerialization is significantly more interesting, except for the higher memory limits. However, if the bandwidth is two or three times larger, the interest of offloading becomes significant, allowing to perform at optimal throughput over a wide range of memory limits.

More results are available in the companion paper [3].

7 Conclusions

In this paper, we address the problem of memory usage during the training phase of Deep Neural Networks. Previous works [1,13,14,16,20,21] advocated to offload some of the data onto the main memory, and to prefetch them back when needed. We propose a formal algorithmic model of the corresponding scheduling problem, where the goal is to identify which activations should be offloaded so as to minimize the total execution time. We prove that this problem is NP-Complete in the strong sense, and we propose two heuristics based on relaxations of the problem. The GREEDY heuristic always offloads the first activations in the network. This very simple technique nevertheless achieves good results in our experimental evaluation. The DYNPROG algorithm is a more sophisticated approach which takes into account the fact that activations cannot be partially transferred which allowed to obtain mostly better solutions. In any case, both algorithms provide significant improvements over the previous approaches.

A promising research direction is the validation through real experiments, that would allow to confirm the relevance of the assumptions made in the model. Since our theoretical analysis shows that being able to offload activations partially makes the problem much easier, it could be very interesting to assess in which cases this could be technically feasible. Finally, this offloading technique is complementary of the checkpointing approach: some activations can be transferred to the main memory while others can be recomputed. Solving the mixed checkpointing and offloading corresponding algorithmic problem might be challenging, but would certainly yield a significant improvement for training large and deep models.

References

1. Shriram, S.B., Garg, A., Kulkarni, P.: Dynamic memory management for GPU-based training of deep neural networks. In: IEEE International Parallel and Distributed Processing Symposium (IPDPS). IEEE Press (2019). https://doi.org/10.1109/IPDPS.2019.00030
2. Beaumont, O., Eyraud-Dubois, L., Herrmann, J., Joly, A., Shilova, A.: Optimal checkpointing for heterogeneous chains: how to train deep neural networks with limited memory. Research Report RR-9302, Inria Bordeaux Sud-Ouest, November 2019. https://hal.inria.fr/hal-02352969
3. Beaumont, O., Eyraud-Dubois, L., Shilova, A.: Optimal GPU-CPU Offloading Strategies for Deep Neural Network Training, October 2019. https://hal.inria.fr/hal-02316266, working paper or preprint
4. Carranza-Rojas, J., Goeau, H., Bonnet, P., Mata-Montero, E., Joly, A.: Going deeper in the automated identification of herbarium specimens. BMC Evol. Biol. 17(1), 181 (2017). https://doi.org/10.1186/s12862-017-1014-z
5. Chen, T., Xu, B., Zhang, C., Guestrin, C.: Training deep nets with sublinear memory cost. arXiv preprint arXiv:1604.06174 (2016)
6. Feng, Y., Zhang, Z., Zhao, X., Ji, R., Gao, Y.: GVCNN: group-view convolutional neural networks for 3D shape recognition. In: IEEE CVPR, pp. 264–272. IEEE (2018). https://doi.org/10.1109/CVPR.2018.00035

7. Gruslys, A., Munos, R., Danihelka, I., Lanctot, M., Graves, A.: Memory-efficient backpropagation through time. In: Advances in Neural Information Processing Systems, pp. 4125–4133 (2016). https://doi.org/10.5555/3157382.3157559
8. Hara, K., Kataoka, H., Satoh, Y.: Can spatiotemporal 3D CNNs retrace the history of 2D CNNs and imagenet? In: IEEE CVPR, pp. 6546–6555. IEEE (2018). https://doi.org/10.1109/CVPR.2018.00685
9. He, K., Zhang, X., Ren, S., Sun, J.: Deep residual learning for image recognition. In: IEEE CVPR. IEEE (2016). https://doi.org/10.1109/cvpr.2016.90
10. Huang, G., Liu, Z., van der Maaten, L., Weinberger, K.Q.: Densely connected convolutional networks. In: IEEE CVPR. IEEE (2017). https://doi.org/10.1109/CVPR.2017.243
11. Kumar, R., Purohit, M., Svitkina, Z., Vee, E., Wang, J.: Efficient rematerialization for deep networks. In: Advances in Neural Information Processing Systems, pp. 15146–15155 (2019)
12. Kwon, Y., Rhu, M.: Beyond the memory wall: a case for memory-centric HPC system for deep learning. In: 2018 51st Annual IEEE/ACM International Symposium on Microarchitecture (MICRO), pp. 148–161. IEEE (2018). https://doi.org/10.1109/MICRO.2018.00021
13. Le, T.D., Imai, H., Negishi, Y., Kawachiya, K.: TFLMS: large model support in tensorflow by graph rewriting. arXiv preprint arXiv:1807.02037 (2018)
14. Meng, C., Sun, M., Yang, J., Qiu, M., Gu, Y.: Training deeper models by GPU memory optimization on tensorflow. In: Proceedings of ML Systems Workshop in NIPS (2017)
15. Pleiss, G., Chen, D., Huang, G., Li, T., van der Maaten, L., Weinberger, K.Q.: Memory-efficient implementation of densenets. arXiv preprint arXiv:1707.06990 (2017)
16. Rhu, M., Gimelshein, N., Clemons, J., Zulfiqar, A., Keckler, S.W.: vDNN: virtualized deep neural networks for scalable, memory-efficient neural network design. In: The 49th Annual IEEE/ACM International Symposium on Microarchitecture, p. 18. IEEE Press (2016). https://doi.org/10.1109/MICRO.2016.7783721
17. Rhu, M., O'Connor, M., Chatterjee, N., Pool, J., Kwon, Y., Keckler, S.W.: Compressing DMA engine: leveraging activation sparsity for training deep neural networks. In: 2018 IEEE International Symposium on High Performance Computer Architecture (HPCA), pp. 78–91. IEEE (2018). https://doi.org/10.1109/HPCA.2018.00017
18. Rota Bulò, S., Porzi, L., Kontschieder, P.: In-place activated batchnorm for memory-optimized training of DNNs. In: IEEE CVPR, pp. 5639–5647. IEEE (2018). https://doi.org/10.1109/cvpr.2018.00591
19. Shou, Z., Chan, J., Zareian, A., Miyazawa, K., Chang, S.F.: CDC: convolutional-de-convolutional networks for precise temporal action localization in untrimmed videos. In: IEEE CVPR, pp. 5734–5743. IEEE (2017). https://doi.org/10.1109/CVPR.2017.155
20. Wang, L., et al.: SuperNeurons: dynamic GPU memory management for training deep neural networks. SIGPLAN Not. **53**(1), 41–53 (2018). https://doi.org/10.1145/3200691.3178491
21. Zhang, J., Yeung, S.H., Shu, Y., He, B., Wang, W.: Efficient memory management for GPU-based deep learning systems. arXiv preprint arXiv:1903.06631 (2019)

Improving Mapping for Sparse Direct Solvers
A Trade-Off Between Data Locality and Load Balancing

Changjiang Gou[1,2], Ali Al Zoobi[3], Anne Benoit[1], Mathieu Faverge[4(✉)],
Loris Marchal[1], Grégoire Pichon[1], and Pierre Ramet[4]

[1] Univ Lyon, EnsL, UCBL, CNRS, Inria, LIP,
Lyon, France
[2] East China Normal University, Shanghai, China
[3] Inria Sophia-Antipolis, Valbonne, France
[4] Bordeaux INP, CNRS, Univ. Bordeaux, Inria,
Talence, France
`mathieu.faverge@inria.fr`

Abstract. In order to express parallelism, parallel sparse direct solvers take advantage of the elimination tree to exhibit tree-shaped task graphs, where nodes represent computational tasks and edges represent data dependencies. One of the pre-processing stages of sparse direct solvers consists of mapping computational resources (processors) to these tasks. The objective is to minimize the factorization time by exhibiting good data locality and load balancing. The proportional mapping technique is a widely used approach to solve this resource-allocation problem. It achieves good data locality by assigning the same processors to large parts of the elimination tree. However, it may limit load balancing in some cases. In this paper, we propose a dynamic mapping algorithm based on proportional mapping. This new approach, named STEAL, relaxes the data locality criterion to improve load balancing. In order to validate the newly introduced method, we perform extensive experiments on the PASTIX sparse direct solver. It demonstrates that our algorithm enables better static scheduling of the numerical factorization while keeping good data locality.

Keywords: Processor mapping · Load balancing · Data locality · Sparse direct solvers

1 Introduction

For the solution of large sparse linear systems, we design numerical schemes and software packages for direct parallel solvers. Sparse direct solvers are mandatory when the linear system is very ill-conditioned for example [5]. Therefore, to obtain an industrial software tool that must be robust and versatile, high-performance sparse direct solvers are mandatory, and parallelism is then necessary for reasons of memory capability and acceptable solution time. Moreover, in order to solve efficiently 3D problems with several million unknowns, which is

© Springer Nature Switzerland AG 2020
M. Malawski and K. Rzadca (Eds.): Euro-Par 2020, LNCS 12247, pp. 167–182, 2020.
https://doi.org/10.1007/978-3-030-57675-2_11

now a reachable challenge with modern supercomputers, we must achieve good scalability in time and control memory overhead. Solving a sparse linear system by a direct method is generally a highly irregular problem that provides some challenging algorithmic problems and requires a sophisticated implementation scheme in order to fully exploit the capabilities of modern supercomputers.

There are two main approaches in direct solvers: the multifrontal approach [2,7], and the supernodal one [11,18]. Both can be described by a computational tree whose nodes represent computations and whose edges represent transfer of data. In the case of the multifrontal method, at each node, some steps of Gaussian elimination are performed on a dense frontal matrix and the remaining Schur complement, or contribution block, is passed to the parent node for assembly. In the case of the supernodal method, the distributed memory version uses a right-looking formulation which, having computed the factorization of a supernode corresponding to a node of the tree, then immediately sends the data to update the supernodes corresponding to ancestors in the tree. In a parallel context, we can locally aggregate contributions to the same block before sending the contributions. This can significantly reduce the number of messages. Independently of these different methods, a static or dynamic scheduling of block computations can be used. For homogeneous parallel architectures, it is useful to find an efficient static scheduling.

In order to achieve efficient parallel sparse factorization, we perform the three sequential preprocessing phases:

1. The ordering step, which computes a symmetric permutation of the initial matrix such that the factorization process will exhibit as much concurrency as possible while incurring low fill-in.
2. The block symbolic factorization step, which determines the block data structure of the factorized matrix associated with the partition resulting from the ordering phase. From this block structure, one can deduce the weighted elimination quotient graph that describes all dependencies between column-blocks, as well as the supernodal elimination tree.
3. The block scheduling/mapping step, which consists in mapping the resulting blocks onto the processors. During this mapping phase, a static optimized scheduling of the computational and communication tasks, according to models calibrated for the target machine, can be computed.

When these preprocessing phases are done, the computation on the actual data, that is the numerical factorization, can start.

The optimization problem that needs to be solved at the scheduling/mapping stage is known to be NP-hard, and is usually solved using a proportional mapping heuristic [16]. This mono-constraint heuristic induces idle times during the numerical factorization. In this paper, we extend the proportional mapping and scheduling heuristic to reduce these idle times. We first detail in Sect. 2 proportional mapping heuristic with its issues and related work, before describing the original application in the context of the PASTIX solver [12] in Sect. 3. Then, in Sect. 4, we explain the introduced solution before studying its impact on a large set of test cases in Sect. 5. Conclusion and future work directions are presented in Sect. 6.

2 Problem Statement and Related Work

Among different mapping strategies that are used by both supernodal and multifrontal sparse direct solvers, the subtree to subcube mapping [8] and the proportional mapping [16] are the most popular. These approaches consist of tree partitioning techniques, where the set of resources mapped on a node of the tree are split among disjoint subsets, each mapped to a child subtree.

The proportional mapping method performs a top-down traversal of the elimination tree, during which each node is assigned a set of computational resources. All the resources are assigned to the root node, which performs the last task. Then, the resources are split recursively following a balancing criterion. The set of resources dedicated to a node are split among its children, proportionally to their weight or any other balancing criterion. This recursive process ends at the leaves of the tree, or when entire subtrees are mapped onto a single resource.

The original version of the proportional mapping [16] computes the splitting of resources depending on the workload of each subtree, but more sophisticated metrics can also be used. In [17], a scheduling strategy was proposed for tree-shaped task graphs. The time for computing a parallel task (for instance at the root node of the elimination tree) is considered as proportional to the length of the task and to a given parallel efficiency. This method was proven efficient in [3] for a multifrontal solver. The proportional mapping technique is widely used because it helps reducing the volume of data transfers due to its data locality. In addition, it allows us to exhibit both tree and node parallelism.

Note that alternative solutions to the proportional mapping have been proposed, such as the 2D block-cyclic distribution of SUPERLU [14], or the 1D cyclic distribution of SYMPACK [13]. In the latter, the non load-balanced solution is compensated by a complex and advanced communication scheme that balances the computations in the nodes to get good performance results out of this mapping strategy.

As stated earlier, sparse direct solvers commonly use the proportional mapping heuristic to distribute supernodes (a full set of columns, i.e., 1D distribution that share the same row pattern) onto the processors. Note that each supernode can be split into smaller nodes to increase the level of parallelism, which modifies the original supernodes tree structure as shown in Fig. 2. This heuristic provides a set of candidate processors for each supernode, which is then refined dynamically when going up the tree, as in MUMPS [1] or PASTIX [12], with a simulation stage that affects a single processor among the candidates, while providing a static optimized scheduling. The proportional mapping stage, by its construction, may however introduce idle time in the scheduling. This is illustrated on Fig. 1. The ten candidate processors of the root supernode are distributed among the two sons of weight respectively 4 and 6. The Gantt diagram points out the issue of considering a single criterion heuristic to set the mapping: no work is given to processor p_9 due to the low level of parallelism of the right supernode, whereas it could benefit to the left supernode.

A naive way to handle this issue is to avoid the proportional mapping stage, and consider only the scheduling stage with all processors as candidates for each

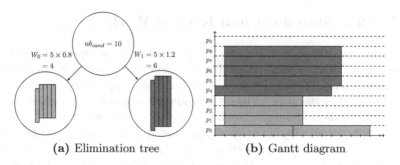

(a) Elimination tree   (b) Gantt diagram

Fig. 1. Illustration of proportional mapping: elimination tree on the left, and Gantt diagram on the right.

node of the tree. The drawback of this method is that 1) it does not preserve the data locality, and 2) it drastically increases the complexity of the scheduling step. This solution has been implemented in the PASTIX solver for comparison, and it is referred to as ALL2ALL, since all processors are candidates to all nodes.

3 Description of the Application

At a coarse-grain level, the computation can be viewed as a tree T whose nodes (or vertices) represent supernodes of the matrix, and where the dependencies are directed towards the root of the tree. Because sparse matrices usually represent physical constraints and thanks to the nested dissection used to order the matrix, supernodes at the bottom of the tree are usually small and supernodes at the top are much larger. Each supernode is itself a small DAG (Directed Acyclic Graph) of tasks as illustrated on Fig. 2. A more refined view shows that the dependencies between two supernodes consist of dependencies between tasks of these supernodes. Another way to put it is that the computation is described as a DAG of tasks, tasks are partitioned into supernodes, and the quotient graph of supernodes is the tree T (with some transitivity edges). Note that with 1D distribution, as targetted here, the DAG within can also be seen as a tree with dependencies toward the roots. Thus, in this paper, we will use either nodes or supernodes to denote the vertices of the tree T as they can be used interchangeably.

This structure in two levels allows us to both reduce the cost of the analysis stage by considering only the first level (supernodes), while increasing the parallelism level (nodes) during the numerical factorization with finer grain computations.

We denote by $root(T)$ the node at the root of tree T, and by w_i the computational weight of the node i, for $1 \leq i \leq n$: this is the total number of operations of all tasks within node i. Also, $parent(i)$ is the parent of node i in the tree (except for the root), and $child(i)$ are the children nodes of i in the tree. Given a subtree T_i of T (rooted in $root(T_i)$), $W_i = \sum_{j \in T_i} w_j$ is the computational weight of this subtree.

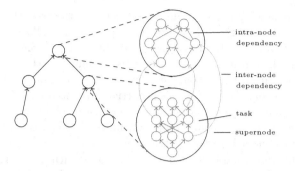

Fig. 2. Structure of the computation: tree of supernodes, each supernodes being made of several tasks.

As stated above, each node i of the tree is itself made of $n_i \geq 1$ tasks $i_1, \ldots, i_{n_i}$, whose dependencies follow a directed acyclic graph (DAG). Each of these tasks is a linear algebra kernel (such as matrix factorization, triangular solve or matrix product) on block matrices. Hence, given a node i and its parent $j = parent(i)$ in the tree, only some of the tasks of i need to be completed before j is started, which allows some pipelining in the processing of the tree.

When running on a parallel platform with a set P of p processors, nodes and tasks are distributed among available processing resources (processors) in order to ensure a good load-balancing. If node i is executed on $alloc[i] = k$ processors, its execution time is $f_i(k)$; this time depends on w_i and on the structure of the DAG of tasks.

Following the structure of the application, the mapping is done in two phases: the first phase, detailed in Sect. 3.1, consists in using the Proportional Mapping algorithm [16] to compute a mapping of nodes to subsets of processors. The second phase, detailed in Sect. 3.2, refines this mapping by allocating each task of a node i to a single processor of the subset allocated to i in the first step.

3.1 Coarse-Grain Load Balancing Using Proportional Mapping

The proportional mapping process follows the sketch of Algorithm 1. First, all processors are allocated to the root of the tree. Then, we compute the total weight of its subtrees (i.e., the sum of the weight of their nodes), and allocate processors to subtrees so that the load is balanced. Then, we recursively apply the same procedure on each subtree.

Algorithm 1. Proportional mapping with integer number of processors

---

function *PropMapInt*(tree T, set P of processors):
Allocate all processors in P to the root of tree T
For each subtree T_i of T, compute its total weight W_i
Find subsets of processors P_i such that $\max(W_i/|P_i|)$ is minimal and $\sum |P_i| = |P|$
For each subtree T_i of T, call *PropMapInt*(T_i, P_i)

Apart from balancing the load among branches of the tree, the proportional mapping is known for its good data locality: a processor is allocated to nodes of a single path from a leaf to the root node, and only to nodes on this path. Thus, the data produced by a node and used by its parents mostly stay on a single processor, and no data transfer is made except for the necessary redistribution of data in the upper levels of the tree. This is particularly interesting in a distributed context, where communications among processors are costly.

We can wonder if Algorithm 1 really optimizes load-balancing, as subtrees with similar total weight W_i may exhibit different levels of parallelism, and thus end up with a different completion time, as illustrated with the example of Fig. 1. The formula $W_i/|P_i|$ correctly computes the duration of the subtree processing only for perfect parallelism. We propose here another mapping algorithm that optimizes the total computation time, under the constraint of perfect data locality. It iteratively adds processors to the root, and recursively to the subtree with the largest completion time (see Algorithm 2). In this mapping algorithm, $alloc[i]$ represents the number of processors allocated to node i, and $endTime[i]$ represents the completion time of task i. We assume that the function $f_i(k)$, that gives the duration of node i on k processors, is non-increasing with k and is known to the algorithm.

Algorithm 2. Greedy mapping with integer number of processors

---

function $GreedyMappingInt$(tree T, number of processors p):
$alloc[1, 2, ..., n] = [0, ..., 0]$
$endTime[1, 2, ..., n] = [\infty, ..., \infty]$
for $k = 1, \ldots, p$ **do**
  Call $AddOneProcessor(root(T))$
end for

function $AddOneProcessor$(task i):
$alloc[i] \leftarrow alloc[i] + 1$
if i is a leaf **then**
  $endTime[i] \leftarrow f_i(alloc[i])$ (duration of node i on $alloc[i]$ processors)
else
  Let j be the child of i with largest $endTime[j]$
  $AddOneProcessor(j)$
  $endTime[i] \leftarrow \max_{j \in child(i)}(endTime[j]) + f_i(alloc[i])$
end if

Theorem 1. *The GreedyMappingInt algorithm (Algorithm 2) computes an allocation with minimum total completion time under the constraint that each processor is only allocated to nodes on a path from a leaf to the root.*

Note that this result, proven in the companion research report [9], does not require a particular speed function for tasks: it is valid when the processing time of a task does not increase with the number of processors allocated to the task.

Algorithm 3. Proportional mapping with shared processors among subtrees

---

function *ProportionalMappingShared*(tree T, number of processors p):
for each processor $k = 1, \ldots, p$ **do**
    $avail\_time[k] = \sum_{i \in T} w_i/p$
end for
Call *PropMapSharedRec*($T, 1, p$)

function *PropMapSharedRec*(subtree T, indices *first_proc*, *last_proc*):
if *last_proc* = *first_proc* **then**
    Map all nodes in subtree T to processor *first_proc*
    $avail\_time[first\_proc] = avail\_time[first\_proc] - \sum_{i \in T} w_i$
else
    Map node $r = root(T)$ to all processors in *first_proc*, ..., *last_proc*
    for each $k = first\_proc, \ldots, last\_proc$ **do**
        $avail\_time[k] = avail\_time[k] - w_r/(last\_proc - first\_proc)$
    end for
    $next\_proc \leftarrow first\_proc$
    Sort the subtrees of T by non-increasing total weight
    for each subtree T_i in this order **do**
        $cumul\_time \leftarrow 0$
        $w_{subtree} \leftarrow \sum_{j \in T_i} w_j$
        $first\_proc\_for\_subtree \leftarrow next\_proc$
        while $cumul\_time < w_{subtree}$ **do**
            $new\_time\_share \leftarrow min(w_{subtree} - cumul\_time, avail\_time[next\_proc])$
            $cumul\_time \leftarrow cumul\_time + new\_time\_share$
            $avail\_time[next\_proc] \leftarrow avail\_time[next\_proc] - new\_time\_share$
            if $avail\_time[next\_proc] = 0$ **then** $next\_proc \leftarrow next\_proc + 1$
        end while
        PropMapSharedRec(T_i, *first_proc_for_subtree*, *next_proc*)
    end for
end if

However, both previous mapping algorithms suffer a major problem when used in a practical context, because they forbid allocating processors to more than one child of a node. First, some nodes, especially leaves, have very small weight and several of them should be mapped on the same processor. Second, allocating integer numbers of processors to nodes creates unbalanced workloads, for example, when three processors have to be allocated to two identical subtrees. All implementations of the proportional mapping tackle this problem (including the first one in [16]). For example, the actual implementation in PASTIX, as sketched in Algorithm 3, allows "border processors" to be shared among branches, and keeps track of the occupation of each processor to ensure load-balancing. It first computes the total time needed to process the whole tree, and sets the initial availability time of each processor to an equal share of this total time. Whenever some (fraction of a) node is allocated to a processor, its availability time is reduced. Hence, if a processor is shared on two subtrees T_1, T_2, the work allocated by T_1 is taken into account when allocating resources for T_2.

Note also that during the recursive allocation process, the subtrees are sorted by non-increasing total weights before being mapped to processors. This allows us to group small subtrees together in order to map them on a single processor, and to avoid unnecessary splitting of processors.

3.2   Refined Mapping

After allocating nodes of the tree to subsets of processors, a precise mapping of each task to a processor has to be computed. In PASTIX, this is done by simulating the actual factorization, based on the prediction of both the running times of tasks and of the time needed for data transfers. The refined mapping process is detailed in Algorithm 4. Thanks to the previous phase, we know that each task can run on a subset of processors (the subset associated to the node it belongs to), called *candidate processors* for this task. We associate to each processor a ready queue, containing tasks whose predecessors have already completed, and a waiting queue, with tasks that still have some unfinished predecessor. At the beginning of the simulation, each task is put in the waiting queue of all its candidate processors (except tasks without predecessors, which are put in the ready task queue of their candidate processors). Queues are sorted by decreasing depth of the tasks in the graph (tasks without predecessors are ordered first). The depth considered here is an estimation of the critical path length from the task to the root of the tree T.

A ready time is associated both to tasks and processors:

- The ready time $RP[k]$ of processor k is the completion time of the current task being processed by k (initialized with 0).
- The ready time $RT[i]$ of task i is the earliest time when i can be started, given its input dependencies. This is at least equal to the completion time of each of its predecessors, but also takes into account the time needed for data movement, in case a predecessor of i is not mapped on the same processor as i. The ready time of tasks with non-started predecessor is set to $+\infty$.

4   Proposed Mapping Refinement

Our objective is to correct the potential load imbalance (and thus idle times) created by the proportional mapping, as outlined in Sect. 2, but without impacting too much the data locality. We propose a heuristic based on work stealing [4] that extends the refined mapping phase (see Algorithm 4) using simulation (see Algorithm 5). Intuitively, we propose that if the simulation predicts that a processor will be idle, this processor tries to steal some tasks from its neighbors.

Algorithm 4. Precise scheduling and mapping using simulation

---

for all task i **do**

    If i is a leaf, put i in the ready queue of every processor in $candidate(i)$, otherwise put it in the waiting queue.

end for

while all tasks have not been mapped **do**

    For each processor k, consider the triplet $\langle i, k, t \rangle$ where i is the first task in the ready queue of processor k and t is the starting time of i on k ($t = \max(RT[i], RP[k])$)

    Consider F, the set of all such triplets

    Select the triplet $\langle i, k, t \rangle$ in F with the smallest t (if ties, choose the one with largest depth)

    Schedule task i on processor k at time t

    Update the ready times of processor k and of the successors of i on all their candidate processors

    Update the ready queue and waiting queue of processor k, as well as of candidates processors of successors of i

end while

In the proposed refinement, we replace the update of the ready and waiting queues of the last line in Algorithm 4 by a call to *UpdateQueuesWithStealing* (Algorithm 5). For each processor k, we first detect if k will have some idle time, and we compute the duration d of this idle slot. This happens in particular when the ready time of the first task in its waiting queue is strictly larger than the ready time of the processor ($RT[i] > RP[k]$) and ready queue is empty. Whenever both queues are empty, the processor will be idle forever, and thus d is set to a large value. Then, if an idle time is detected (the ready queue is empty and d is a positive value), a task is stolen from a neighbor processor using function *StealTask*. Otherwise, the ready and waiting queues are updated as previously: the tasks of the waiting queue that will be freed before the processor becomes available are moved to the ready queue.

When stealing tasks, we distinguish between two cases, depending whether we use shared or distributed memory. In shared memory, the two possible victims of the task stealing operation are the two neighbors of processor k, considering that processors are arranged in a ring. In the case of distributed memory, we first try to steal from two neighbor processors *within the same cluster*, that is, within the set of processors that share the same memory. Stealing to a distant processor is considered only when clusters are reduced to a single element. Once steal victims are identified (set S), we consider the first task of their ready queues and select the one that can start as soon as possible. If the task is able to start during the idle slot of processor k (and thus reduce its idle time), it is then copied into its ready queue.

Algorithm 5. Update ready and waiting queues with task stealing

function *UpdateQueuesWithStealing*(nb. of proc. p, switch *IsSharedMem*):
for $k = 1$ **to** p **do**
  if $waiting\_queue_k \neq \emptyset$ **then**
    Let i be the first task in $waiting\_queue_k$
    $d \leftarrow RT[i] - RP[k]$
  else
    $d \leftarrow +\infty$
  end if
  if $ready\_queue_k = \emptyset$ and $d > 0$ **then**
    $StealTask(k, p, d, IsSharedMem)$
  else
    Let i be the first task in $waiting\_queue_k$
    while $RT[i] \leq RP[k]$ **do**
      Move task i from $waiting\_queue_k$ to $ready\_queue_k$
      Let i be the first task in $waiting\_queue_k$
    end while
  end if
end for

function *StealTask*(proc. k, proc. nb. p, idle time d, switch *IsSharedMem*):
set $S \leftarrow \emptyset$
if *IsSharedMem* = *false* **then**
  set $S_k \leftarrow \{k-1, k+1, k-2, k+2\}$
  for $j = 1$ **to** 4 **do**
    if $S_k[j] \geq 0$, $S_k[j] < p$, $S_k[j]$ is in the same cluster as k and $|S| < 3$ **then**
      add $S_k[j]$ to S
    end if
  end for
end if
if *IsSharedMem* = *true* or S is empty **then**
  set $S \leftarrow \{k-1 \pmod p, k+1 \pmod p\}$
end if
Build the set O with the first element of each ready queue of processors in S
Let o be the task of O with minimum $RT[o]$
if $RT[o] < RP[k] + d$, **then** insert o into $ready\_queue_k$

5 Experimental Results

Experiments were conducted on the *Plafrim*[1] supercomputer, and more precisely on the miriel cluster. Each node is equipped with two INTEL XEON E5-2680v3 12-cores running at 2.50 GHz and 128 GB of memory. The INTEL MKL 2019 library is used for sequential BLAS kernels. Another shared memory experiment was performed on the crunch cluster from the LIP[2], where a node is equipped with four INTEL XEON E5-4620 8-cores running at 2.20 GHz and 378 GB of

---

[1] https://www.plafrim.fr.
[2] http://www.ens-lyon.fr/LIP/.

memory. On this platform, the INTEL MKL 2018 library is used for sequential BLAS kernels. The PASTIX version used for our experiments is based on the public git repository[3] version at the tag 6.1.0.

In the following, the different methods used to compute the mapping are compared. All to All, referred to as ALL2ALL, and Proportional mapping, referred to as PROPMAP, are available in the PASTIX library, and the newly introduced method is referred to as STEAL. When the option to limit stealing tasks into the same MPI is enabled, we refer to it as STEALLOCAL. In all the following experiments, we compare these versions with respect to the ALL2ALL strategy, which provides the most flexibility to the scheduling algorithm to perform load balance, but does not consider data locality. The multi-threaded variant is referred to as SharedMem, while for the distributed settings, pMt stands for p MPI nodes with t threads each. All distributed settings fit within a single node.

In order to make a fair comparison between the methods, we use a set of 34 matrices issued from the SuiteSparse Matrix collection [6]. The matrix sizes range from $72K$ to $3M$ of unknowns. The number of floating point operations required to perform the LL^t, LDL^t, or LU factorization ranges from 111 GFlops to 356 TFlops, and the problems are issued from various application fields.

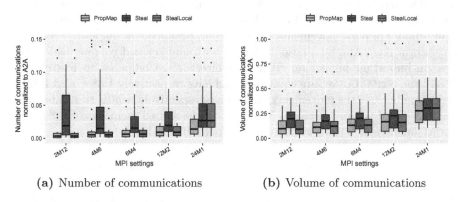

(a) Number of communications   (b) Volume of communications

Fig. 3. MPI communication number (*left*) and volume (*right*) for the three methods: PROPMAP, STEAL, and STEALLOCAL, with respect to ALL2ALL.

Communications. We first report the relative results in terms of communications among processors in different clusters (MPI nodes), which are of great importance for the distributed memory version. The number and the volume of communications normalized to ALL2ALL are depicted in Fig. 3a and Fig. 3b respectively. One can observe that all three strategies largely outperform the ALL2ALL heuristic, which does not take communications into account. The number of communications especially explodes with ALL2ALL as it mainly moves around leaves of the elimination tree. This creates many more communications with a small volume. This confirms the need for a proportional-mapping-based strategy to minimize the number of communications. Both numbers and volumes

---

[3] https://gitlab.inria.fr/solverstack/pastix.

of communications also confirm the need for the local stealing algorithm to keep it as low as possible. Indeed, STEAL generates 6.19 times more communications on average than PROPMAP, while STEALLOCAL is as good as PROPMAP. Note the exception of the 24M1 case where STEAL and STEALLOCAL are identical. No local task can be stolen. These conclusions are similar when looking at the volume of communication with a ratio reduced to 1.92 between STEAL and PROPMAP.

The distribution of the results is shown by boxplot. It shows five summary statistics (median, two hinges and two whiskers), and all "outlying" points individually. The lower and upper hinges correspond to the first and third quartiles. The upper whisker extends from the hinge to the largest value no further than $1.5 \times IQR$ from the hinge (where IQR is the inter-quartile range, or distance between the first and third quartiles). The lower whisker extends from the hinge to the smallest value at most $1.5 \times IQR$ of the hinge. Data beyond the end of the whiskers are called "outlying" points and are plotted individually [15].

Data Movements. Figure 4 depicts the number and volume of data movements normalized to ALL2ALL and summed over all the MPI nodes with different MPI settings. The data movements are defined as a write operation on the remote memory region of other cores of the same MPI node. Note that accumulations in local buffers before send, also called fan-in in sparse direct solvers, are always considered as remote write. This explains why all MPI configurations have equivalent number of data movements. As expected, proportional mapping heuristics outperform ALL2ALL by a large factor on both number and volume, which can have an important impact on NUMA architectures. Compared to PROPMAP, STEAL and STEALLOCAL are equivalent and have respectively $1.38\times$, and $1.32\times$, larger number of data movements on average respectively, which translates into 9%, and 8% of volume increase. Note that in the shared memory case, STEAL-LOCAL behaves as STEAL as there is only one MPI node.

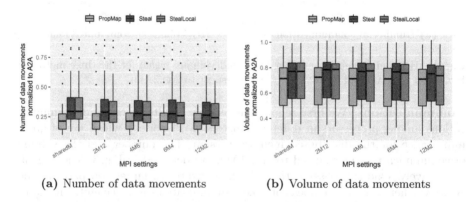

(a) Number of data movements   (b) Volume of data movements

Fig. 4. Shared memory data movements number (*left*) and volume (*right*) within MPI nodes for PROPMAP, STEAL, and STEALLOCAL, with respect to ALL2ALL.

Simulation Cost. Figure 5 shows the simulation cost in seconds (duration of the refined mapping via simulation) on the left, and that of PROPMAP, STEAL and

STEALLOCAL with respect to ALL2ALL on the right. Figure 6 shows the original simulated factorization time obtained with these heuristics and a normalized version. Note that, for the sake of clarity, some large outliers are removed from Fig. 6a. As stated in Sect. 2, the ALL2ALL strategy allows for more flexibility in the scheduling, hence it results in a better simulated time for the factorization in average. However, its cost is already 4x larger for this relatively small number of cores. Figure 5a shows that the proposed heuristics have similar simulation cost to the original PROPMAP, while Fig. 6 shows that the simulated factorization time gets closer to ALL2ALL, and can even outperform it in extreme cases. Indeed, in the 24M1 case, STEAL outperforms ALL2ALL due to bad decisions taken by the latter at the beginning of the scheduling. The bad mapping of the leaves is then never recovered and induces extra communications that explain this difference. In conclusion, the proposed heuristic, STEALLOCAL, manages to generate better schedules with a better load-balance than the original PROPMAP heuristic, while

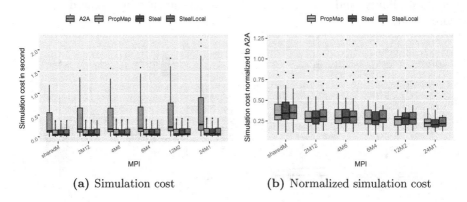

(a) Simulation cost   (b) Normalized simulation cost

Fig. 5. Final simulation cost in second (*left*) and simulation cost of PROPMAP, STEAL and STEALLOCAL, normalized to ALL2ALL (*right*).

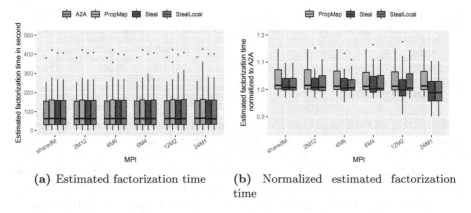

(a) Estimated factorization time   (b) Normalized estimated factorization time

Fig. 6. Estimated factorization time (*left*), and that of PROPMAP, STEAL, and STEALLOCAL, normalized to ALL2ALL (*right*).

generating small or no overhead on the mapping algorithm. This strategy is also able to limit the volume of communications and data movements as expected.

Factorization Time for Shared Memory. Figure 7 presents factorization time and its normalized version in a shared memory environment, on both `miriel` and `crunch` machines. Note that we present only the results for STEAL, as STEALLOCAL and STEAL behave similarly in shared memory environment. For the sake of clarity, some large outliers are removed from Fig. 7a. On `miriel`, with a smaller number of cores and less NUMA effects, all these algorithms have almost similar factorization time, and present variations of a few tens of GFlop/s over 500GFlop/s in average. STEAL slightly outperforms PROPMAP, and both are slower than ALL2ALL respectively by 1% and 2% in average. On `crunch`, with more cores and more NUMA effects, the difference between STEAL and PROPMAP increases in favor of STEAL. Both remain slightly behind ALL2ALL, respectively by 2% and 4%; indeed, ALL2ALL outperforms them since it has the greatest flexibility, and communications have less impact in a shared memory environment.

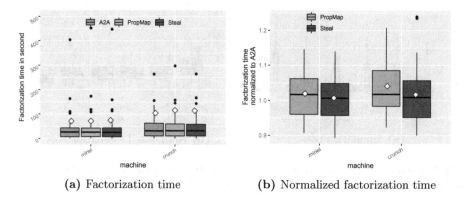

(a) Factorization time   (b) Normalized factorization time

Fig. 7. Factorization time (*left*), and that of PROPMAP and STEAL, normalized to ALL2ALL (*right*), on `miriel` and `crunch`. White diamonds represent mean values.

6   Conclusion

In this paper, we revisit the classical mapping and scheduling strategies for sparse direct solvers. The goal is to efficiently schedule the task graph corresponding to an elimination tree, so that the factorization time can be minimized. Thus, we aim at finding a trade-off between data locality (focus of the traditional PROPMAP strategy) and load balancing (focus of the ALL2ALL strategy). First, we improve upon PROPMAP by proposing a refined (and optimal) mapping strategy with an integer number of processors. Next, we design a new heuristic, STEAL, together with a variant STEALLOCAL, which predicts processor idle times in PROPMAP and assigns tasks to idle processors. This leads to a limited loss of locality, but improves the load balance of PROPMAP.

Extensive experimental and simulation results, both on shared memory and distributed memory settings, demonstrate that the STEAL approach generates almost the same number of data movements than PROPMAP, hence the loss in locality is not significant, while it leads to better simulated factorization times, very close to that of ALL2ALL, hence improving the load balance of the schedule.

PASTIX has only recently been extended to work on distributed settings, and hence we plan to perform further experiments on distributed platforms, in order to assess the performance of STEAL on the numerical factorization in distributed environments. Future working directions may also include the design of novel strategies to further improve performance of sparse direct solvers.

Acknowledgments and Data Availability Statement. This work is supported by the Agence Nationale de la Recherche, under grant ANR-19-CE46-0009. Experiments presented in this paper were carried out using the PlaFRIM experimental testbed, supported by Inria, CNRS (LABRI and IMB), Université de Bordeaux, Bordeaux INP and Conseil Régional d'Aquitaine (https://www.plafrim.fr/).

The datasets and code generated during and/or analysed during the current study are available in the Figshare repository: https://doi.org/10.6084/m9.figshare.12562682 [10].

References

1. Amestoy, P.R., Buttari, A., Duff, I.S., Guermouche, A., L'Excellent, J.Y., Uçar, B.: MUMPS. In: Padua, D. (ed.) Encyclopedia of Parallel Computing, pp. 1232–1238. Springer, Heidelberg (2011). https://doi.org/10.1007/978-0-387-09766-4_204
2. Amestoy, P.R., Duff, I.S., L'Excellent, J.Y.: Multifrontal parallel distributed symmetric and unsymmetric solvers. Comput. Methods Appl. Mech. Eng. **184**(2), 501–520 (2000)
3. Beaumont, O., Guermouche, A.: Task scheduling for parallel multifrontal methods. In: Kermarrec, A.-M., Bougé, L., Priol, T. (eds.) Euro-Par 2007. LNCS, vol. 4641, pp. 758–766. Springer, Heidelberg (2007). https://doi.org/10.1007/978-3-540-74466-5_80
4. Blumofe, R.D., Leiserson, C.E.: Scheduling multithreaded computations by work stealing. J. ACM **46**(5), 720–748 (1999)
5. Davis, T.A.: Direct Methods for Sparse Linear Systems. Society for Industrial and Applied Mathematics (2006). https://doi.org/10.1137/1.9780898718881
6. Davis, T.A., Hu, Y.: The University of Florida sparse matrix collection. ACM Trans. Math. Softw. **38**(1) (2011). https://doi.org/10.1145/2049662.2049663
7. Duff, I.S., Reid, J.K.: The multifrontal solution of indefinite sparse symmetric linear. ACM Trans. Math. Softw. **9**(3), 302–325 (1983)
8. George, A., Liu, J.W., Ng, E.: Communication results for parallel sparse Cholesky factorization on a hypercube. Parallel Comput. **10**(3), 287–298 (1989)
9. Gou, C., et al.: Improving mapping for sparse direct solvers: a trade-off between data locality and load balancing. Research report RR-9328, Inria (2020). hal.inria.fr

10. Gou, C., et al.: Artifact for Euro-Par2020 Paper - Improving mapping for sparse direct solvers: a trade-off between data locality and load balancing, July 2020. https://doi.org/10.6084/m9.figshare.12562682.   https://springernature.figshare. com/articles/dataset/Artifact_for_Euro-Par2020_Paper_--_Improving_mapping_ for_sparse_direct_solvers_A_trade-off_between_data_locality_and_load_balancing/ 12562682/1

11. Heath, M.T., Ng, E., Peyton, B.W.: Parallel algorithms for sparse linear systems. SIAM Rev. **33**(3), 420–460 (1991). https://doi.org/10.1137/1033099

12. Hénon, P., Ramet, P., Roman, J.: PaStiX: a high-performance parallel direct solver for sparse symmetric definite systems. Parallel Comput. **28**(2), 301–321 (2002)

13. Jacquelin, M., Zheng, Y., Ng, E., Yelick, K.A.: An asynchronous task-based fanboth sparse cholesky solver. CoRR (2016). http://arxiv.org/abs/1608.00044

14. Li, X.S., Demmel, J.W.: SuperLU_DIST: a scalable distributed-memory sparse direct solver for unsymmetric linear systems. ACM Trans. Math. Softw. **29**(2), 110–140 (2003). https://doi.org/10.1145/779359.779361

15. McGill, R., Tukey, J.W., Larsen, W.A.: Variations of box plots. Am. Stat. **32**(1), 12–16 (1978). http://www.jstor.org/stable/2683468

16. Pothen, A., Sun, C.: A mapping algorithm for parallel sparse Cholesky factorization. SIAM J. Sci. Comput. **14**(5), 1253–1257 (1993)

17. Prasanna, G.S., Musicus, B.R.: Generalized multiprocessor scheduling and applications to matrix computations. IEEE Trans. Parallel Distrib. Syst. **7**(6), 650–664 (1996)

18. Rothburg, E., Gupta, A.: An efficient block-oriented approach to parallel sparse Cholesky factorization. In: Proceedings of the 1993 ACM/IEEE Conference on Supercomputing, pp. 503–512 (1993). https://doi.org/10.1145/169627.169791

High Performance Architectures and Compilers

Modelling Standard and Randomized Slimmed Folded Clos Networks

Cristóbal Camarero[1(✉)], Javier Corral[1], Carmen Martínez[1], and Ramón Beivide[1,2]

[1] Computer Science and Electronics Department, University of Cantabria, Avenida de los Castros, 39005 Santander, Spain
cristobal.camarero@unican.es
[2] Barcelona Supercomputing Center, Carrer de Jordi Girona, 29, 31, 08034 Barcelona, Spain
ramon.beivide@bsc.es

Abstract. Fat-trees (FTs) are widely known topologies that, among other advantages, provide full bisection bandwidth. However, many implementations of FTs are made slimmed to cheapen the infrastructure, since most applications do not make use of this full bisection bandwidth. In this paper Extended Generalized Random Folded Clos (XGRFC) interconnection networks are introduced as cost-efficient alternatives to Extended Generalized Fat Trees (XGFT), which is a widely used topological description for slimmed FTs. This is proved both by obtaining a theoretical model of the performance and evaluating it using simulation. Among the results, it is shown that a XGRFC is able to connect 20k servers with 27% less routers than the corresponding XGFT and still providing the same performance under uniform traffic.

Keywords: Folded Clos · Extended Generalized Fat-Tree · Random topologies

1 Introduction

Nowadays, high-end supercomputers and datacenters are becoming extremely big, connecting hundreds of thousands servers. In consequence, the interconnection networks employed in these systems are becoming more costly and important. With such large sizes, the network cost can be a significant fraction of the total system cost. Deployment network cost includes NICs, routers and wires. The cost of large networks tends to be dominated by the cost of the required wires, but for raw comparisons, the number of network routers can be employed, as the number of wires linearly depends on it.

Fat-trees [1] (FTs), a popular instance of the folded Clos network [5], have been utilized in many high-end systems. The use of FTs entails important benefits. In theory, they can manage any admissible traffic at full rate; they are equipped with a very simple deadlock free routing; they are robust; and, their

© Springer Nature Switzerland AG 2020
M. Malawski and K. Rzadca (Eds.): Euro-Par 2020, LNCS 12247, pp. 185–199, 2020.
https://doi.org/10.1007/978-3-030-57675-2_12

partitioning is easier than in other networks. Nevertheless, the high cost of FTs becomes prohibitive in very large deployments. In addition, depending of the application, the nature of its communications can be quite different. There is an important class of classic number-crunching applications showing a high degree of communication locality for which FTs reveal overprovisioned [8,9]. Having in mind these applications, and in order to reduce the high cost of FTs, many deployed big systems have used different slimmed versions of them. Most of slimmed fat-trees can be studied under the model of Extended Generalized Fat Trees (XGFT) introduced in [11]. But nowadays, there is another important set of applications as those coming from big data and analytics that employ global communications and really require the capacity and redundancy of a FT; many of them require all-to-all (uniform) traffic. Moreover, other HPC applications, such as spectral codes perform a 3D Fast Fourier Transform, utilizing large all-to-all communications [12].

In [3] and [2] randomized versions of folded Clos networks were introduced. These topologies are more scalable, allow for easy upgrades of the system and entail less cost. Therefore, it has sense to consider the slimmed variants of such topologies, which are introduced in this paper and denoted as Extended Generalized Random Folded Clos (XGRFC). We compare XGRFCs and XGFTs both in their topological merits and performance. We will show that XGRFCs inherit the scalability among other properties of random folded Clos, thus providing cost gains respect to slimmed fat-trees. Corresponding performance, we will firstly make a theoretical model that relates the communication pattern of the application, the fitness ratio of the slimmed topology and the performance. For illustrating it, we select a synthetic traffic pattern as to resemble applications needing global communications. This approach is validated using experimental simulation. As it will be shown, just randomizing the stages of slimmed FTs provides similar performance (throughput and fairness) but at smaller cost. In fact, there are outstanding cases such as uniform traffic, in which XGRFCs provide 38% more throughput than its XGFT counterpart.

This paper is organized as follows. In Sect. 2 folded Clos interconnection networks are summarized and Extended Generalized Fat-trees are revisited. In Sect. 3 Extended Generalized Random Folded Clos are introduced. In Sect. 4 a wide experimentation is presented to prove our results. Finally, in Sect. 5 the main achievements of the paper are summarized.

2   Folded Clos Networks

Folded Clos interconnection networks are widely considered for datacenters [5]. These interconnection networks are indirect, since there are two different kind of routers: those which are connected to servers, and the ones that are only connected to other routers. The routers are arranged into *levels* such that the links that join two different levels constitute a *stage*. Typically, the first level or Level 1 is the one that contains the routers directly connected to servers, known as *leaf routers*. We will consider that in the last level the *spine routers* have all their links in the last stage, that is, the network is *folded*. If an indirect network has l levels of routers it is said to have *height* $h = l - 1$. A common example of folded Clos networks are FTs [1]. In Table 1 the notation used along the paper is summarized and a example illustrating it is graphically represented in Fig. 1.

Table 1. Notation

Symbol	Meaning
R	Router radix
M	Servers per leaf router
S	Total number of servers
γ	Average injection rate per server
n_i	Number of routers at level i
m_i	Number of links from level $i + 1$ to i in each router
w_i	Number of links from level i to $i + 1$ in each router
e_i	Total number of links connecting routers of levels i and $i + 1$

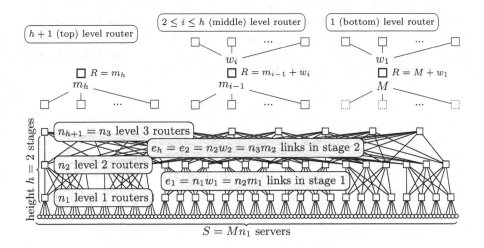

Fig. 1. Graphical representation of the notation using XGFT$(2; 4, 7; 3, 3)$.

Folded Clos networks are typically considered being *up/down connected* that is, for every pair of leaves, there is a path beginning with some up-links followed by the same number of down-links. Then, a simple deadlock-free routing can be made following these paths, which is one of the main advantages of Clos networks over other kind of networks. All networks considered in the paper are up/down connected (with very high probability when probabilistic).

Let us denote by w_i the number of links from each router in level i to routers in level $i+1$ and m_i the number of links from each router in level $i+1$ to routers in level i. Let us denote by n_i the number of routers in level i. Then, the number of links e_i that constitute stage i can be calculated as

$$e_i = n_i w_i = n_{i+1} m_i, 1 \leq i \leq h. \tag{1}$$

It follows that any n_i can be calculated from n_1:

$$\frac{n_{i+1}}{n_1} = \prod_{k=1}^{i} \frac{w_k}{m_k}. \tag{2}$$

Our study will be restricted to those networks that are built with identical routers, that is, the following *Regularity Eq.* 3 are fulfilled:

$$R = m_i + w_{i+1}, \ 1 \leq i \leq h-1,$$
$$R = m_h, \tag{3}$$
$$R = w_1 + M,$$

where M denotes the number of servers per leaf router.

A further assumption that can be made is to have, in all non-top levels, the same ratio of up-links. Note that the top level does not have up-links, so it cannot be included. Although from a theoretical point of view this *Constant Radix Ratio Property* seems very natural, it is not necessarily the best choice. In fact, later we consider some examples that fulfill it and others that do not. This assumption is formally stated as

$$\frac{m_i}{w_{i+1}} = \frac{M}{w_1}, \ 1 \leq i \leq h-1. \tag{4}$$

This ratio is called *fitness ratio* in [8] and *contention factor* in [7], making both references the constant ratio assumption. Another notation for the same concept is *blocking ratio* in [13]. This assumption can be rewritten using the Regularity Eq. 3 as

$$m_i = M, \qquad 1 \leq i \leq h-1,$$
$$w_i = R - M, \quad 1 \leq i \leq h. \tag{5}$$

Additionally, since $\frac{S}{e_h} = \frac{M}{w_1} \prod_{i=1}^{h-1} \frac{m_i}{w_{i+1}}$, for topologies with constant radix ratio the amount gmr $= \sqrt[h]{S/e_h}$ is the fitness ratio. And for all topologies, regardless of fulfilling the constant ratio property, gmr is the geometric mean of those ratios.

Remark 1. Note that for our convenience, n_1 denotes the number of leaf routers and $S = Mn_1$ is the total number of servers, although in [11] the authors directly use n_1 as the number of servers.

Most of the folded Clos in the industry roughly fit into the Extended General-ized Fat Tree (XGFT) network topology [11]. This definition allows to consider alternative topologies based on fat-tres but with less cost, what in some publi-cations are named as *slimmed fat-trees* [7], *fit-trees* [8], *tapered fat-trees* [9] and other variations. The original definition in [11] was recursive. Next, in Defini-tion 1 a new definition avoiding recursion is given, which simplifies the analysis of the topology.

Definition 1. *The Extended Generalized Fat Tree* $\mathrm{XGFT}(h; m_1, \ldots, m_h; w_1, \ldots, w_h)$ *topology of height h consists on n_k routers in level k, with k ranging from 1 to $h+1$, where n_k is computed as*

$$n_k = \prod_{i=1}^{k-1} w_i \prod_{i=k}^{h} m_i, \ 1 \le k \le h+1. \tag{6}$$

Routers are connected to contiguous levels such that, the router at position x of level k, $1 \le k \le h$ is connected with the routers at position y of level $k+1$ if and only if there are integer numbers q, r, t, and u satisfying

$$x = (qm_k + r)g + u, \quad 0 \le r < m_k, \quad 0 \le u < g,$$

$$y = (qg + u)w_k + t, \quad 0 \le t < w_k, \quad 0 \le q < \prod_{i=k+1}^{h} m_i, \tag{7}$$

where $g = \prod_{i=1}^{k-1} w_i$.

Note that both Eq. 1 and Eq. 6 are not independent. If the system of equa-tions is reduced, then it is obtained that it is equivalent to Eq. 1 with the restrictions corresponding to Level 1:

$$n_1 = \prod_{i=1}^{h} m_i.$$

Example 1. Let us consider router radix $R = 36$, very commonly used by indus-try, which will be used henceforward in the paper. Then, $\mathrm{XGFT}(2; 18, 36; 18, 18)$ is the FT for this router radix and 3 levels. In the remainder of the paper $\mathrm{XGFT}(2; 22, 36; 14, 14)$ and $\mathrm{XGFT}(2; 26, 36; 10, 10)$ will be also considered. Note that these topologies are slimmed variants of the FT, with respective fitness ratios $\frac{22}{14} = 1.57$ and $\frac{26}{10} = 2.6$, which will imply different performance. Their topological properties, together other topologies that will later introduced in the paper, are summarized in Table 2.

The high cost of a non-blocking FT interconnection network is better exploited when the application packets reach the routers in the $h + 1$ level. However, scientific applications constitute particular communication patterns. In fact, by means a thorough study, in [8] the authors demonstrated that a sig-nificant percentage of scientific applications send most traffic to near neighbours.

Table 2. Topologies evaluated and their topological parameters.

Scenario	Topology	Servers	Routers	e_1	e_2	gmr
A	XGFT(2; 18, 36; 18, 18)	11664	1620	11664	11664	1
B	XGFT(2; 22, 36; 14, 14)	17424	1492	11088	7056	1.57
B	XGRFC(2; 22, 36; 14, 14; 792, 504, 196)	17424	1492	11088	7056	1.57
B	XGRFC(2; 18, 36; 11, 18; 684, 418, 209)	17100	1311	7524	7524	1.51
C	XGFT(2; 26, 36; 10, 10)	24336	1396	9360	3600	2.60
C	XGRFC(2; 26, 36; 10, 10; 936, 360, 100)	24336	1396	9360	3600	2.60
C	XGRFC(2; 18, 36; 5, 18; 720, 200, 100)	22320	1020	3600	3600	2.51

Thus, it may be worth to dimension the topology for these applications, which would allow to reduce costs. In the following it is established a relation between links in the different stages and the injection rate per server.

Let γ be the average injection rate per server. Thus, there is a total of γS phits (packet units) that are being created on each cycle. Let p_i be the fraction of packets which reach some router at level i, potentially going further up. Clearly, it is hold that, $1 = p_1 \geq p_2 \geq \cdots \geq p_{h+1} \geq 0$. Then $\gamma S p_i$ is the total rate of packets reaching the routers in level i, giving the following immediate bound on the injection rate

$$\gamma S p_{i+1} \leq e_i. \tag{8}$$

In the case of using the constant ratio in Eq. 5, we have the following nice expression:

$$\gamma p_{i+1} \leq \left(\frac{R - M}{M}\right)^i, \ 1 \leq i \leq h. \tag{9}$$

Example 2. As an example of the previous bound we consider an extreme scenario in which all packets reach level 3, that is, $p_3 = 1$. Then, the maximum throughput is $(w/M)^2$, which is represented in Fig. 2 for router radix $R = 36$. In this figure, it can be seen that the throughput is maximum when half of the ports go upward ($R = 2w$) and it decreases acutely (in fact hyperbolically) with reductions on w. Thus, it is clear that reducing the cost of a folded Clos by reducing the w_i terms has great impact on performance; at least for applications that have relatively many global communications. Note that the three points A, B and C in the figure correspond to the interconnection networks summarized in Table 2.

In an XGFT, for any given leaf router, there are exactly $m_1 \cdots m_t$ leaf routers at distance at most $2t$, including itself. From this, it follows that, in a uniform traffic pattern the probability that a packet reaches level i is, in the XGFT, $p_i = 1 - \prod_{k=i-1}^{h} m_k^{-1}$. For the particular case of radix $R = 36$ we get that $p_{h+1} = 35/36 = 0.972$, which is very close to 1. This means that the traffic pattern considered in Example 2 in fact closely resembles the uniform traffic pattern in the XGFT, but this does not hold for an arbitrary folded Clos. In the general case, assuming that there are not multiple links between any pair of routers we get $1 - \frac{m_1 w_1}{n_1} \leq p_3 \leq 1 - \frac{m_1}{n_1}$ for uniform traffic. If $m_1 = 22$, $w_1 = 14$ and $n_1 = 792$, then we obtain $0.611 \leq p_3 \leq 0.972$.

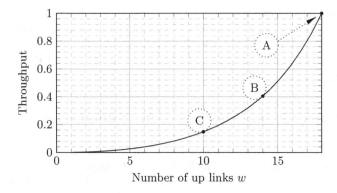

Fig. 2. Theoretical maximum throughput with constant ratio of w up-links from the 36 total links when all packets reach level 3. Labels A, B, and C denote topologies in Table 2.

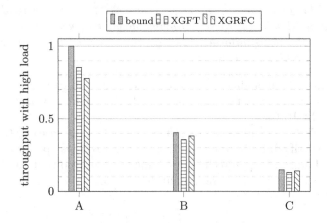

Fig. 3. Achieved throughput under heavy load and global communication pattern. Labels A, B, and C denote topologies in Table 2.

The formulas in Eq. 9 can be validated by experimental simulation. We use parameters as in Example 1 and Example 2, and the predicted throughput is shown in Fig. 2. For each of the points A, B, and C we compare the bound with the simulation values of the corresponding XGFT and the simulation values of a random analogue topology. These random topologies, called XGRFCs, are folded Clos with the links in each stage wired randomly; they are detailed in the next section. We have performed the simulations with a synthetic traffic pattern designed to reproduce the $p_3 = 1$ assumption. Therefore, all the packets reach the last level routers, so links in the last stage are widely used. Specifically, each time a packet is generated, a server at maximum distance is selected in a random uniform way as the destination of the packet. As it can be seen in Fig. 3, where both the simulation results and the values predicted are represented, the theoretical model accurately estimates the achieved throughput. In a more deep analysis, it has to be noticed that XGFT is always at the same relative distance to the upper bound provided by the theoretical model. However, the greater the fitness ratio, the tighter the difference between the simulated throughput and its theoretical bound in XGRFCs.

3   Extended Generalized Random Folded Clos

Random Folded Clos (RFC) networks were introduced in [3] as an alternative to FTs that increases scalability, facilitates graceful expansion and reduces cost. These interconnection networks can be roughly described as folded Clos networks in which each level is randomly interconnected. Next, a generalization of these networks, in the same flavour that XGFTs, is presented.

Definition 2. *Let us define a Extended Generalized Random Folded Clos, and denote it by* $\text{XGRFC}(h; m_1, \ldots, m_h; w_1, \ldots, w_h; n_1, \ldots, n_{h+1})$, *a random multistage interconnection network selected among all the possible with the given parameters chosen near-uniformly. The parameters need to satisfy Eqs. 1 and 3 like any other multistage network.*

An implementation of almost uniform random bipartite graphs was presented in [3]. This algorithm was used to construct RFCs, and equivalently it can be used to build XGRFCs.

Although XGFTs are always up/down connected, in the case of XGRFCs this fact has to be verified. In [3], the conditions under a RFC is up/down connected were proved. Using the same techniques it might be proved that XGRFCs tend to be up/down connected with probability $e^{-e^{-x}}$ for

$$x = n_{h+1}^{-1} \prod_{i=1}^{h} w_i^2 - \ln \binom{n_1}{2}.$$

Proving this result is out of the scope of this paper, both because its mathematical complexity and because it is possible to compute the up/down condition directly. The up/down distances can be quickly computed with a slight modification of the Breadth First Search, which shows if the network is actually up/down connected. Although in the networks used in our examples such probability is so close to 1 that the check is not necessary, the computation is going to be performed anyway to populate the routing tables. In cases closer to the threshold, i.e., with the x in the probabilistic formulae close to 0, checking the up/down connectivity would be necessary. If the check fails, then we have just to generate again a different network with another seed for the random number regenerator.

Example 3. Let us consider $R = 36$ and the topologies XGRFC(2; 18, 36; 11, 18;) 684,418,209 and XGRFC(2; 18, 36; 5, 18; 720, 200, 100). Their topological properties are summarized in Table 2. As it can be seen, XGRFC(2; 18, 36; 11, 18;)

684,418,209 connects 2% less servers but with 12% less routers of the corresponding XGFT. In the case of XGRFC(2; 18, 36; 5, 18; 720, 200, 100), cost gain is more important, since 27% less routers are needed to connect 8% less servers. When applying the probabilistic formulae we get values $x \geq 80$, which means that the probability of being up/down-connected is greater than $1 - 10^{-x/\ln(10)} \geq 1 - 10^{-34}$, which is almost 1. Therefore, it is practically impossible to generate a XGRFC up/down disconnected with these parameters. However, once the XGRFC is generated, its up/down connectivity is verified, and in the case it is not fulfilled, it is just a matter of generating another one.

Example 4. For large networks, sometimes it is possible to find an up/down XGRFC connecting the same amount of servers than a XGFT with the same radix and fitness ratio, but having one less level. The size of the network for which this is possible grows with the fitness ratio. The topologies and their properties in this example are summarized in Table 3. To illustrate a 4 to 3 level reduction, we can consider the XGFT(3; 54, 54, 92; 38, 38, 38) of radix 92 that connects 1.4M servers. Then, the XGRFC(2; 54, 92; 38, 38; 268272, 188784, 77976) is a random analogue with one less level that is up/down connected with a probability around 0.92. As an example of a 5 to 4 level reduction, we can consider the XGFT(4; 10, 10, 10, 16; 6, 6, 6, 6) of radix 16 that connects 160 K servers. Then, the XGRFC(3; 10, 10, 16; 6, 6, 6; 16000, 9600, 5760, 2160) is a random analogue with one less level that is up/down connected with a probability around 0.95. These cases suppose an improvement in latency from the lesser height in addition to the cost reduction by having less routers and cables.

Table 3. Topological Parameters of Topologies in Example 4.

Levels	Topology	Radix	Servers	Routers	*links*	gmr
4	XGFT(3; 54, 54, 92; 38, 38, 38)	92	1.45M	644K	22.4M	1.42
3	XGRFC(2; 54, 92; 38, 38; 268272, 188784, 77976)	92	1.45M	535K	17.4M	1.42
5	XGFT(4; 10, 10, 10, 16; 6, 6, 6, 6)	16	160K	36.1K	208K	1.67
4	XGRFC(3; 10, 10, 16; 6, 6, 6; 16000, 9600, 5760, 2160)	16	160K	33.5K	188K	1.67

Another property that XGRFCs inherit from the RFCs is the expandability. In a fully populated XGFT, that is with all the Mn_1 servers, expanding the system implies making drastic changes, such as increasing the height, changing the fitness ratio or replacing the routers with others with greater radix. On the contrary, in a XGRFC this is possible by just adding some routers in each level and randomly rewiring some of the links in each stage. Note that the number of routers added in the first level must be a multiple of $\prod_{k=1}^{h} \frac{m_k}{\gcd(w_k, m_k)}$ in accordance with Eq. 1. Otherwise, some routers would have unwired ports. This provides a simple way to gradually increment the capacities of a system based on a XGRFC.

4 Evaluation

To conclude the study, this section is devoted to the experimental evaluation. In Subsect. 4.1 the experimental set up is described, including topologies evaluated, simulator, traffic patterns, etc. In Subsect. 4.2 experimental results for the simulated topologies are shown.

4.1 Experimental Set Up

Next, different topologies are evaluated by simulation. The experiments have been done using the functional simulator in [10]. The simulations have been performed considering a router with 4 virtual channels, input buffers of length 4 packets and virtual cut-through as flow control. Every packet has 16 phits. Both link latency and router arbitration take 1 cycle.

For the experiments, we use the topologies summarized in Table 2. As asserted before, most of the folded Clos in the industry are XGFTs, thus we compare XGRFCs and XGFTs. Firstly, we evaluate the family B with smallest fitness ratio (other than 1). Later, we compare the results with the ones denoted by C. In both cases, one XGFT and two different XGRFCs are compared. The first XGRFC is always done using the same resources as the XGFT, that is, the same number of servers, routers and cables. On the contrary, the second one has been selected to provide lower cost and the same performance under global traffic patterns. This has been done by enforcing the same number of links in the last level and reducing the ones in the first level to the minimum possible.

All these topologies are compared in terms throughput, average latency and Jain's fairness index [6]. The throughput and average latency are common measures, with throughput being the injection rate from the servers and the average latency being the average number of cycles required to consume the packet. Jain's fairness index is a function of the coefficient of variation on the injection across the servers. A value of this index of $\frac{k}{S}$ is compatible with having k servers generating the same amount of traffic and the $S-k$ remaining servers generating no traffic at all. Some compatible scenarios with a $\frac{8}{10}$ index would be to have $S = 130$ servers from which either only 104 are working or 81 are working with rate 16 and the remaining 49 with the lower rate 9. Thus, a bad Jain index may mean that a few servers have important issues or that many servers have a poor performance, both being inadmissible.

The experiments have been done using three synthetic traffic patterns, that have been slightly adapted from [4]. These traffic patterns have been selected to represent typical application behaviour, which are:

- *Uniform:* each generated packet has as destination a random compute node selected uniformly.
- *Random-pairing:* the set of switches is initially divided into pairs in a random uniform way. Each compute node generates packets with destination any of the compute nodes in the switch paired to its switch. This traffics pattern is a case of a random permutation of the switches, which is more adversarial than a permutation of the compute nodes.

– *Fixed-random:* at the beginning, each switch selects a different switch in a random uniform way. During the simulation each node generate packets towards the selected compute node. It is not a permutation since some compute nodes in different switches can have selected the same destination.

An up/down route is constructed as follows: first taking up links till a common ancestor is reached, and then going down. Only up/down routes are considered, and when various routes exist, one is selected randomly. Unlike what happens in XGFTs, in XGRFCs for some pairs of leaf routers, there are up/down routes of different lengths, as illustrated in Fig. 4. In this schematic example, we have tried to show a situation that it is common in XGRFCs. Two routers (in the leaf level) can communicate using different routes. The one in solid red is minimum, that is, it provides distance 2. However, at least two more routes are possible in this example, those depicted in dashed blue and dotted green, but in this case with longer length, providing distance 4. Thus, in these topologies it is possible to use two different routing algorithms: *minimal_routing*, in which only minimum up/down routes are considered, and *all_paths_routing*, using all possible up/down routes. In the next sections, when illustrative, both routings are used for XGRFCs.

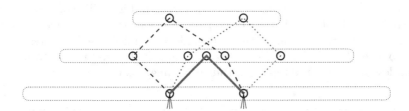

Fig. 4. Up/down paths of different lengths: one of length 2 and two of length 4 (Color figure online).

4.2   Experimental Results

First, let us consider the results of the simulations for the topologies with a smaller fitness ratio, that is, scenario B. In Fig. 5, the results for both throughput and latency of the different interconnection networks under uniform traffic pattern are shown. In these graphs, random topologies have been evaluated using minimal_routing and all_paths_routing. As it can be seen, random networks benefit from minimal routing under uniform traffic pattern. In this case, the XGRFC with the same resources as the XGFT provides 38% more throughput. However, as it will be seen later, in XGRFCs all the up/down routes should be used under other non-uniform traffic patterns. With all_paths_routing, all the topologies provide almost the same throughput. Note that the latency graph perfectly corresponds with the one being expected from the observed throughput. Since this happens across all experiments, latency graphs are no longer shown in favour of showing Jain's fairness results.

Concerning the random pairing traffic pattern, the results of the experiments can be seen in Fig. 6. As mentioned before, in random topologies, restricting to minimal routes not only constitutes a disadvantage for throughput but also has harmful consequences on fairness. Considering the throughput results for all_paths_routing, the XGFT provides the best performance. For the corresponding XGRFC with the same resources, this performance falls a 5%. The cheaper XGRFC with 12% less routers provides 27% less throughput.

Finally, the results for the fixed random traffic pattern are shown in Fig. 7. In this case only the evaluation with all the routes is shown, since restricting only to minimal routes has the same problems that has already been observed in random pairing traffic. It can be seen that XGRFC provides 20% more throughput than XGFT when it uses the same resources. However, the cheaper version provides 7% less performance than XGFT. Nevertheless, when analyzing fairness, it can be observed that both random topologies have an excellent behaviour, and XGFT exhibits an important problem.

Now, let us analyze what happens for a greater fitness ratio, that is, scenario C. In this case, only the results for uniform traffic are shown in Fig. 8, since the other traffic patterns provide similar outcomes. As it can be observed, the behaviour is almost the same as the one shown in Fig. 5. The only difference that can be highlighted is that the discrepancy between throughput measured for both minimal_routing and all_paths_routing, has been decreased with respect to the topologies denoted by B. Note that this happens because more fitness ratio implies less routers in the top level, thus providing less path diversity.

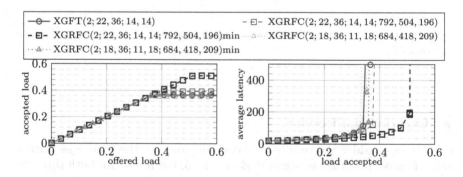

Fig. 5. Uniform traffic: average accepted load and average latency. Scenario B.

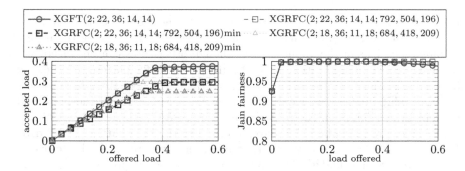

Fig. 6. Randompairing traffic: average accepted load and Jain fairness index. Scenario B.

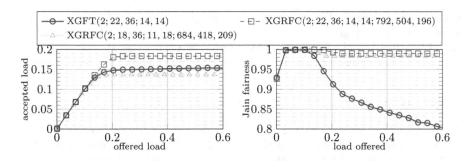

Fig. 7. Fixedrandom traffic: average accepted load and Jain fairness index. Scenario B.

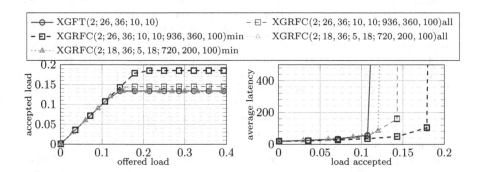

Fig. 8. Uniform traffic: average accepted load and average latency. Scenario C.

5 Conclusions

It has been proved that the performance of a slimmed folded Clos, both standard or with random interconnection, can be estimated in terms of the nature of communications of the application. Although other cases can be considered, we have selected an application with a totally global traffic pattern, in which all its communications use the links at the last stage. This global traffic is almost uniform traffic in the considered topologies. We have measured the impact of different fitness ratios on the performance, both with a theoretical model and corroborated by simulation. We have shown that the information provided by the model would be of great interest for systems designers to make a better usage of their procurement budget. Moreover, random topologies provide greater cost savings, since it is possible to build them with fewer resources, in exchange for an assumable degradation of the performance and an improvement in fairness. Furthermore, extended random folded Clos topologies provide higher scalability, great expansion and better fault tolerances than the extended fat trees counterparts do.

Acknowledgements. This work has been supported by the Spanish Ministry of Science, Innovation and Universities under contract TIN2016-76635-C2-2-R (AEI/FEDER, UE). The first author is supported by the Spanish Minister of Science and Innovation programme Juan del Cierva Formación reference FJCI-2017-31643.

References

1. Al-Fares, M., Loukissas, A., Vahdat, A.: A scalable, commodity data center network architecture. In: Proceedings of the ACM SIGCOMM 2008 Conference on Data Communication, SIGCOMM 2008, pp. 63–74. ACM, New York (2008)
2. Camarero, C., Martínez, C., Beivide, R.: On random wiring in practicable folded clos networks for modern datacenters. IEEE Trans. Parallel Distrib. Syst. **29**(8), 1780–1793 (2018). https://doi.org/10.1109/TPDS.2018.2805344
3. Camarero, C., Martínez, C., Beivide, R.: Random folded Clos topologies for datacenter networks. In: Proceedings of the 23rd IEEE Symposium on High Performance Computer Architecture, HPCA 2017, pp. 193–204 (2017)
4. Chen, D., Eisley, N., Heidelberger, P., et al.: Looking under the hood of the IBM Blue Gene/Q network. In: Proceedings of the International Conference on High Performance Computing, Networking, Storage and Analysis, SC 2012, pp. 69:1–69:12. IEEE Computer Society Press, Los Alamitos (2012)
5. Clos, C.: A study of non-blocking switching networks. Bell Syst. Tech. J. **32**(2), 406–424 (1953)
6. Jain, R., Chiu, D., Hawe, W.: A quantitative measure of fairness and discrimination for resource allocation in shared computer systems. In: DEC Research Report TR-301, pp. 598–607, June 1984
7. Jokanovic, A., Sancho, J.C., Labarta, J., Rodriguez, G., Minkenberg, C.: Effective quality-of-service policy for capacity high-performance computing systems. In: 2012 IEEE 14th International Conference on High Performance Computing and Communication, 2012 IEEE 9th International Conference on Embedded Software and Systems, pp. 598–607, June 2012

8. Kamil, S., Oliker, L., Pinar, A., Shalf, J.: Communication requirements and interconnect optimization for high-end scientific applications. IEEE Trans. Parallel Distrib. Syst. **21**(2), 188–202 (2010)
9. León, E.A., Karlin, I., Bhatele, A., et al.: Characterizing parallel scientific applications on commodity clusters: an empirical study of a tapered fat-tree. In: Proceedings of the International Conference for High Performance Computing, Networking, Storage and Analysis, pp. 909–920, November 2016
10. Navaridas, J., Miguel-Alonso, J., Pascual, J.A., Ridruejo, F.J.: Simulating and evaluating interconnection networks with INSEE. Simul. Model. Pract. Theor. **19**(1), 494–515 (2011)
11. Ohring, S.R., Ibel, M., Das, S.K., Kumar, M.J.: On generalized fat trees. In: Proceedings of 9th International Parallel Processing Symposium, pp. 37–44, April 1995
12. Rodríguez, G.: Understanding and reducing contention in generalized fat tree networks for high performance computing. Ph.D. thesis, Facultad de Informática, U. Politécnica de Cataluña (2011)
13. Shpiner, A., Haramaty, Z., Eliad, S., Zdornov, V., Gafni, B., Zahavi, E.: Dragonfly+: low cost topology for scaling datacenters. In: 2017 IEEE 3rd International Workshop on High-Performance Interconnection Networks in the Exascale and Big-Data Era (HiPINEB), pp. 1–8 (2017)

OmpMemOpt: Optimized Memory Movement for Heterogeneous Computing

Prithayan Barua[✉], Jisheng Zhao, and Vivek Sarkar

Georgia Institute of Technology, Atlanta, GA, USA
{prithayan,jzhao367,vsarkar}@gatech.edu

Abstract. The fast development of acceleration architectures and applications has made heterogeneous computing the norm for high-performance computing. The cost of high volume data movement to the accelerators is an important bottleneck both in terms of application performance and developer productivity. Memory management is still a manual task performed tediously by expert programmers. In this paper, we develop a compiler analysis to automate memory management for heterogeneous computing. We propose an optimization framework that casts the problem of detection and removal of redundant data movements into a partial redundancy elimination (PRE) problem and applies the lazy code motion technique to optimize these data movements. We chose OpenMP as the underlying parallel programming model and implemented our optimization framework in the LLVM toolchain. We evaluated it with ten benchmarks and obtained a geometric speedup of $2.3\times$, and reduced on average 50% of the total bytes transferred between the host and GPU.

Keywords: Compiler optimization · GPUs · OpenMP · Memory management

1 Introduction

As high-performance computing enters an era of extreme heterogeneity, there is an increasing proliferation of general and special purpose accelerators as well as a concerted effort by higher-level parallel programming models to support heterogeneous computing, e.g., OpenMP, OpenACC, X10, Chapel, Julia. Data movement between the host and accelerators is a fundamental operation in heterogeneous computing, and parallel programming models vary in supporting data movement either explicitly or implicitly. Data movement is also a significant source of overhead, both in execution time and energy. Thus, minimizing data movement while maintaining the correctness of a program is one of the most important optimizations that compilers and application developers focus on [1,6,7,11,17].

We propose a program analysis framework to enable the compiler to automatically detect and remove redundant memory copies. We use OpenMP 4.5[1] as

---

[1] www.openmp.org/wp-content/uploads/openmp-4.5.pdf.

© Springer Nature Switzerland AG 2020
M. Malawski and K. Rzadca (Eds.): Euro-Par 2020, LNCS 12247, pp. 200–216, 2020.
https://doi.org/10.1007/978-3-030-57675-2_13

an example parallel programming model to demonstrate our optimization framework. We can offload a region of code to accelerators like GPUs using OpenMP. An application developer can specify several different kinds and combinations of OpenMP directives to extract optimal performance from specific hardware. But the developer also needs to ensure the correctness and absence of data races while manually optimizing the application. Given the complexity of OpenMP specifications, this is a nontrivial task and requires time-consuming efforts from expert programmers. Tools like OmpSan [4] help developers debug incorrect usage of OpenMP memory mapping directives. Our objective is to investigate how the compiler can optimize the memory management operations, while the user only needs to specify synchronization operations needed for correctness.

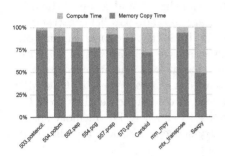

Fig. 1. Compute time vs memory copy

Figure 1 shows the significance of the data movement overhead for 10 OpenMP GPU applications discussed later in Sect. 5. In this experiment, the kernels don't use any explicit memory mapping and rely on the default behavior, which is to copy data from a host to the GPU before launching the kernel and back to the host after it executes. It compares the % time spent on computing vs. data transfer operations. The experiment illustrates the inefficiency of the default mapping since except for the compute-intensive *mm_mpy* and *saxpy* kernels, over 70% of the time is spent on memory transfer operations in the remaining benchmarks. In this paper, we formalize the data movement optimization problem and define an intermediate representation suitable for the analysis of memory accesses and data movements in heterogeneous computing. Then, we introduce our optimization framework hat uses the intermediate representation to perform lazy code motion and partial redundancy elimination on data movement operations.

The main contributions of this paper include:

1. We introduce a general optimization framework to apply partial redundancy elimination, that uses dataflow analysis to identify redundancies in data movement, and a code transformation to eliminate such redundancies.
2. We extend past work on Heap SSA [9] to a new Location-Aware heap SSA (LASSA) to consider heterogeneous memory spaces. We implement construction of LASSA, and its associated optimizations, in the LLVM tool chain.
3. We evaluate our approach using real-world heterogeneous computing applications.

2   Background

2.1   OpenMP Execution Model

In this section, we briefly discuss the OpenMP programming model. We use the term device to refer to a computing resource. The host device is the CPU that begins executing the program. There are optional accelerators like a GPU that are called target devices. An OpenMP program begins as a single thread of sequential execution, called the master thread, which runs on the host device. The OpenMP target directive specifies a block of code to offload to the device. One or more target devices can be available to the host for offloading code and data. The target directive generates a new target task, which may execute on a target device. The target task starts with an initial thread, and teams of threads can be optionally created depending on the usage of team/parallel constructs.

An important aspect of the memory model[2] [10] is that the tasks running on the host and tasks running on the target devices have separate states that are not shared. Each host device and target device has at least one attached storage resource(s) that is private to them. This is called a *memory space* in OpenMP terminology. When the host and target task need to communicate, they do so by explicitly copying data from one memory space to another. The memory space is a persistent resource, e.g., the target memory space retains all data allocated in its space unless it is explicitly deleted.

2.2   Heap SSA Form

Heap SSA [9] is an intermediate representation that extends Array SSA form [14] to capture reads and writes to heap-allocated data. Heap SSA models each access of a disjoint memory space as a distinct logical "heap array". Heap SSA employs use:$u\phi$ and definition:$d\phi$ operators to chain memory load and store operations, respectively. It was designed for strongly typed languages like Java, but it is also applicable to weakly typed languages by introducing a uniform heap array that captures element-level dataflow information for heap data structures [21].

3   Motivation

Figure 2 shows some typical cases of redundant memory copies that programmers need to detect and optimize manually. Here, *memcpy_host2device* copies an array from host to device, while *memcpy_device2host* copies it back from the device to host. It shows a dummy CFG in which the dotted line represents an arbitrary sequence of code, which respects the condition mentioned alongside it.

Redundancy Pattern 1. Figure 2a is the simplest use case; if a kernel launched on the device does not update an array, then there is no need to copy the array back to the host. The default behavior of OpenMP target constructs is to copy in and out every array.

---

[2] www.openmp.org/wp-content/uploads/openmp-4.5.pdf.

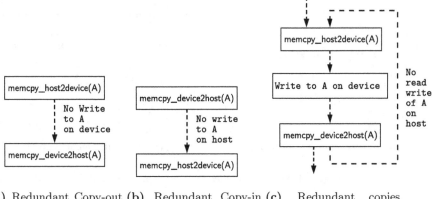

(a) Redundant Copy-out from device   (b) Redundant Copy-in to device   (c) Redundant copies within loop

Fig. 2. Common patterns of redundancy

```
1   int A[10];
2   #pragma omp target map(A)
3   {
4      for (i = 0 ; i < 10; i++)
5         A[i] = i;
6   }
7   print(A)
8   #pragma omp target map(A)
9   {
10     for (i = 0 ; i < 10; i++)
11        A[i] + = i;
12  }
13  print(A)
```

```
1   int A[10];
2   #pragma omp target data map(tofrom:A)
3   {
4      #pragma omp target map(alloc:A)
5      {
6         for (i = 0 ; i < 10; i++)
7            A[i] = i;
8      }
9      #prargma omp target update from(A)
10     print(A)
11     #pragma omp target map(alloc:A)
12     {
13        for (i = 0 ; i < 10; i++)
14           A[i] + = i;
15     }
16  }
17  print(A)
```

(a) Default memory map   (b) Explicitly specify data copies

Fig. 3. Redundancy Pattern 2

Redundancy Pattern 2. Figure 2b shows the second pattern, when a host-to-device copy is redundant since the array is already the latest version on the device because of the persistent device storage. After executing a kernel on the device, we copy the array back from device-to-host. Figure 3a shows this coding pattern using OpenMP target offloading constructs. Line 2 launches a kernel on the device that updates the array A. Then the kernel launched on line 8 reads and updates the array A in the device memory. The print statement on line 7 is executed on the host. It only reads the array, and it is not updated on the host before launching the second kernel. The device already has the latest version of the array on line 8, and thus the copy is redundant. Figure 3b shows the usage of *target data map* clause on line 2 to handle such redundancies. We explicitly leave the array on the device's persistent memory for later use.

```
1  int A[10];
2  for (t = 0 ; t < 100; t++) {
3    #pragma omp target map(A)
4    {
5      for (i = 0 ; i < 10; i++)
6        A[i] += i;
7    }
8  }
9  print(A)
```

```
1   int A[10];
2   #pragma omp target data map(tofrom:A)
3   {
4     for (t = 0 ; t < 100; t++) {
5       #pragma omp target map(alloc:A)
6       {
7         for (i = 0 ; i < 10; i++)
8           A[i] += i;
9       }
10    }
11  }
12  print(A)
```

(a) Kernel Launch within loop   (b) Explicit memory copies

Fig. 4. Redundant copies within loop, Pattern 3

This example motivates our claim that optimizing even simple memory copy redundancies requires nontrivial understanding of OpenMP spec and the knowledge of all the available directives and their possible usage.

Redundancy Pattern 3. Figure 2c shows another pattern where a host loop launches a kernel on the device iteratively. This host loop does a host-to-device copy before launching the kernel and again device-to-host copy after it finishes. Both these copies are redundant since the host does not access the copied memory inside the loop. Figure 4a shows the OpenMP example for the third case, the target construct on line 3 executes host-to-device copy before launching the kernel on the device and then device-to-host copy after the kernel returns. But, since the outer loop of line 2, executing on the host does not access the array, both the copies are loop-invariant. In this case, it is legal to move the host-to-device memory copy before the loop, and the device-to-host memory copy after the outer loop. Figure 4b shows the usage of memory map environments to remove the redundancy.

In this section, we presented three simple examples of redundant memory copies to motivate our work. But these patterns can be generalized to complex real-world use cases. The dotted line of the CFG can denote arbitrarily complex source code. Hence the redundant memory copies can even occur across different function calls and source files. This makes manual detection of redundant memory copies and its optimization much more complicated and error-prone. Several OpenMP application developers have provided similar feedback regarding these issues related to manual optimization of memory management. The common uses cases are usually scientific applications with large legacy codebases, that are being ported to GPUs using the OpenMP *target offloading* feature launched in version *4.5*. The nontrivial effort required for manual memory management is our motivation to develop a compiler optimization to automate removal of such redundant memory copies.

3.1 Challenges

To address the problem introduced above, we need to address the following challenges:

- Representation of concurrent memory accesses to the same array elements;
- Reasoning about the definition-use (def-use) relationships among array accesses across different memory spaces;
- Whole program analysis that infers optimal program points for inserting memory copy operations, and detects redundant data movements.

4 Our Approach

Problem Statement. Based on the programming-model, first, the compiler needs to identify where to insert the memory copy operations to ensure correctness. Then an analysis is required to determine partially and fully redundant memory copies. Finally, a code transformation is needed to remove all the redundancies.

Proposed Solution. We design an intermediate representation to express the memory model of the programming paradigm and develop an analysis based on that representation, to optimize redundant memory copies between different memory spaces. We make the following basic assumptions

- We assume that pointer analysis can disambiguate named arrays. If the alias analysis fails to identify each array uniquely, our optimization fails.
- To keep the analysis simple, any element-level access is conservatively assumed to access the entire array. This constraint can be removed by performing an index range analysis for each array access.

4.1 Location Aware Heap SSA

The heterogeneous computing patterns mainly deal with array-based data structures over one or more memory spaces of different devices. In this section, we introduce the Location-Aware Heap SSA (LASSA) IR, which extends Heap SSA [9] to take into account the memory space in which each array resides. To uniquely identify each array access in a LASSA program, we create a new version of the array for every corresponding access to it. We define LASSA operators that map an array version in one memory space to another array version in the same or different memory space. We call these array versions as a definition. We use the notation, D_i^r, to denote the ith definition in memory space r.

Definition 1. *We define the following operators in LASSA for an array A:*

1. $A_i^r = d\phi(A_j^r)$ *creates a new definition. such that, A_j^r is the prevailing definition of A just prior to A_i^r in the memory space r.*
2. $A_k^r = c\phi(A_i^r, A_j^r)$, *creates a control merge of the definitions $\{A_i^r, A_j^r\}$.*
3. $A_i^r = u\phi(A_j^r)$, *denotes the read of A.*

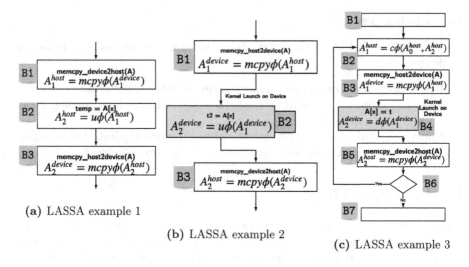

Fig. 5. Example LASSA operators, shaded blocks are executed on device

4. $A_i^r = mcpy\phi(A_j^p)$, *creates a new definition of A, due to a copy from memory space p to memory space r, this is a new operator that was not present in Heap SSA.*

The semantics of the $d\phi$ and $u\phi$ operators are associated with the respective memory write and read operations. The $u\phi$ operator also generates a dummy definition, for array reads. The main purpose of the $u\phi$ operator is to remove redundant copy statements. The control merge operator $c\phi$ merges the reaching definitions from two incoming paths and creates a new definition. The $u\phi$, $d\phi$ and $c\phi$ are the same operators as in Heap SSA [9]. A $mcpy\phi$ is associated with a program point where the memory from source memory space data is flushed/written out to the destination memory space. This guarantees the copied data is visible to any subsequent memory operations. We can use $mcpy\phi$ for both synchronous or asynchronous memory copy. But, the placement of the operator depends only on when the actual write is visible, as defined by the memory concurrency model. For an array A and device memories $dev1, dev2$, We use the notation $A_{dev1,dev2}$ to denote that both the memory spaces $dev1$ and $dev2$ have exactly the same copy of array A. We now discuss some example LASSA representations.

Case 1. Figure 5a shows an example LASSA IR for case 1. Basic Block $B1$ copies data back from the device to the host, assuming there is some preceding kernel that executes on the device not shown here. Assuming A_1^{device} is the most recent version of the array on the device, the copy creates A_1^{host}, a new version of the array on the host represented by $A_1^{host} = mcpy\phi(A_1^{device})$. Next, $B2$ reads a location of the array on the host, represented by the $u\phi$ operator. Finally, $B3$ uses the $mcpy\phi$ operator to denote the host-to-device memory copy.

Case 2. Figure 5b shows the LASSA IR for case 2. $B2$ is a kernel executed on device, denoted by the shaded block in the figure. $B1$ denotes the host-to-device memory copy with the $mcpy\phi$ operator, and it updates the version of the array on device to A_2^{device}. After the copy, A_1^{device} is the updated version of the array on the device read by the $u\phi$ operator of $B2$. $B3$ copies the array back to the host after $B2$ finishes execution on the device.

Case 3. In Figure 5c, $B4$ is a kernel launched on device, which is executed inside a loop. This represents the loop invariant case. $B3$ copies the array from the host-to-device, and $B5$ copies the array back from the device-to-host. $B2$ is the entry block of the loop, it merges the control from the back edge. Assuming A_0^{host} is the last version of array on the host before entry to loop, the $A_1^{host} = c\phi(A_0^{host}, A_2^{host})$ merges the A_2^{host} from loop body to create a new version A_1^{host}. $B4$ updates the array on device, denoted by the $d\phi$ operator which creates the version A_2^{device}, that is copied back to the host at $B5$.

4.2 Redundancy

We will use the data flow analysis defined in Chapter 10 of the compiler textbook [20] for partial redundancy elimination [8,15] of memory copies across different memory spaces. In this section, we define the data flow properties in terms of the $mcpy\phi$ LASSA operator.

Definition 2 *Availability:* *An $mcpy\phi$ of A is said to be available between two memory spaces* m *and* p, *at a basic block* B, *if any memory copy of A between* m *and* p *is redundant at* B *since both memory spaces have the same version of the array after the last copy. This is a forward analysis.*

Availability implies, after the last copy: $D_i^m = mcpy\phi(A, D_j^p)$, D_i^m is still the most recent version of the array A on memory space m, and D_j^p is the most recent version of array A on memory space p. It is computed using a forward analysis. Given a basic block B, $AvailOut(B)$ denotes the availability at the exit of B. $DEExpr(B)$ and $UEExpr(B)$ is the set of downward and upward exposed $mcpy\phi$ operators respectively. They are defined in Table 1. $ExprKill(B)$ denotes the memory copies that are killed due to an update. We use the same definition of $AvailOut$ from [20],

$$AvailOut(n) = \bigcap_{m \in preds(n)} (DEExpr(m) \cup (AvailOut(m) \cap \overline{ExprKill(m)}))$$

$AvailOut(inputBlock) = \phi$, and for all other blocks $AvailOut(B) = All\ Copies,$

Definition 3 *Anticipability:* *An $mcpy\phi$ of* A *is anticipable (very busy) between memory spaces* m *and* p, *on exit of a basic block* B, *if every path that leaves* B, *executes a memory copy of* A *between* m *and* p, *and it is legal to hoist it to the end of* B.

Table 1. Transfer functions for the basic block local properties

LASSA operators	Downward exposed	Upward exposed	Killed copy
Explanation	if $A_{\{p,q\}} \in DEExpr(B)$ then, the version of A on p and q are same at the end of B	if $A_{\{p,q\}} \in UEExpr(B)$ then, copy from p to q can be hoisted up at the head of B	Killed Copy
Initialization	$DEExpr(B) = \{\}$	$UEExpr(B) = \{\}$	$ExprKill(B) = \{\}$
Analysis direction	Forward	Backward	Forward
$D_i^r = d\phi(A, D_i^r)$	$DEExpr(B) \setminus A_{\{r,x\}} \forall x$	$UEExpr(B) \setminus A_{\{r,x\}} \forall x$	$ExprKill(B) \cup A_{\{r,x\}} \forall x$
$D_i^r = u\phi(A, D_j^r)$	$DEExpr(B)$	$UEExpr(B)$	$ExprKill(B)$
$D_i^r = mcpy\phi(A, D_j^q)$	$DEExpr(B) \cup A_{\{q,r\}}$	$UEExpr(B) \cup A_{\{q,r\}}$	$ExprKill(B)$

Table 2. Computing availability and anticipability

	Available out
Figure 5a $B1$	$A_{\{host,device\}}$
Figure 5a $B2$	$A_{\{host,device\}}$
Figure 5b $B1$	$A_{\{host,device\}}$
Figure 5b $B2$	$A_{\{host,device\}}$

(a) Redundancy

	Available out	Anticipable in
$B1$	ϕ	$A_{\{host,device\}}$
$B2$	ϕ	$A_{\{host,device\}}$
$B3$	$A_{\{host,device\}}$	$A_{\{host,device\}}$
$B4$	ϕ	ϕ
$B5$	$A_{\{host,device\}}$	$A_{\{host,device\}}$
$B6$	$A_{\{host,device\}}$	ϕ
$B7$	$A_{\{host,device\}}$	ϕ

(b) Partial redundancy

Anticipability is computed by a backward analysis using the following equations,

$$AntIn(m) = UEExpr(m) \cup (AntOut(m) \cap \overline{ExprKill(m)})$$

$$AntOut(n) = \bigcap_{m \in succ(n)} AntIn(m), \quad m \neq Exit\ Block$$

$AntOut(Exit\ Block) = \phi$, and for all other blocks $AntOut(n) = All\ Copies$

To compute the availability and anticipability, we define a lattice over the $mcpy\phi$ of array variables. We use $A_{\{src,dst\}}$ to denote that the memory copy of A between src and dst is redundant, that is both memory spaces have exactly the same copy of A. Our analysis is based on the "lazy code motion" data-flow-equations from [8]. Table 1 defines the local properties used to compute the availability and anticipability.

Definition 4 *Redundancy*: *A copy statement between memory spaces* m *and* p *for a particular array* A *is redundant, if both the memory spaces already have the same version of* A.

A memory copy, $D_i^p = mcpy\phi(A, D_j^m)$ is redundant if $A_{\{m,p\}} \in AvailOut(D_j^m)$

Example of Redundancy. Consider Fig. 5a and Fig. 5b, in both these cases $B1$ and $B3$ have an $mcpy\phi$ operator, and there is no write to the array between this pair of $mcpy\phi$ statements. Thus, as Table 2a shows, $A_{\{host,device\}}$ is available at the entry to basic block $B3$ which means the host and device memory space have the same copy of the array and any further copy is redundant. Thus we can remove the memory copy from the $B3$ in the first two cases.

Definition 5 *Partial Redundancy*: *A copy statement between memory spaces* m *and* p *for a particular array* A, *constitutes a partial redundancy, if both the memory spaces already have an updated copy on some but not all paths reaching the copy statement.*

Example of Partial Redundancy. Consider the loop invariant case in Fig. 5c. As Table 2b shows, The memory copy of $B3$ is anticipable at the entry of both $B1$ and $B2$, that is to the entry block of the loop. But the device definition in $B4$ makes sure that the $B5$ copy is not redundant. Now, the copy of $B5$ is available at the exit of $B5$ and also till the loop exit block $B7$. Consider the two edges of $B1 - B2$ and $B6 - B2$, $A_{\{host,device\}}$ is available only on the back edge $B6 - B2$, but not on the entry to the loop. Hence it is partially redundant at $B2$.

4.3 Lazy Code Motion

Partial redundancy elimination (PRE) [15] eliminates redundant computation of expressions in programs by moving invariant computations out of loops and also eliminating identical computations that are performed more than once on any execution path. In this paper, we use the formulation from [20] and [8]. Our customized PRE algorithm for data movements has the following steps:

1. *Basic block local properties*: compute the local properties of upward-exposed and downward-exposed $mcpy\phi$ operators using the transfer functions defined over LASSA operators in Table 1.
2. *Solve the data flow equations*: compute available and anticipable copy operations according to Definition 2 and Definition 3.

210   P. Barua et al.

3. *Determine Earliest and Latest placement*: given the solutions of availability
   and anticipability, we can determine the earliest point in the program at
   which it is safe to hoist the copy statement. It is profitable to insert a copy
   statement at a basic block B, if it makes other copy statements redundant.
   Again we use the original data flow equations [20], to solve for earliest and
   later placement.
4. *Redundant copies*: this translates to identifying redundant memory copy
   statements according to Definition 4.
5. *Code rewrite*: identify the program point to insert the memory copy, and the
   set of redundant memory copies that can be deleted.

Note that dataflow analysis on the LASSA IR ensures that the transformed
program produces the same output as the original output. The semantics of the
$mcpy\phi$ IR ensures the legality of the optimization.

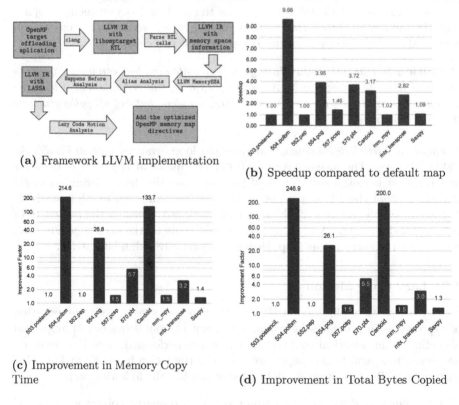

(a) Framework LLVM implementation

(b) Speedup compared to default map

(c) Improvement in Memory Copy
Time

(d) Improvement in Total Bytes Copied

Fig. 6. Experimental framework and results

5   Evaluation

Implementation. We implemented our analysis in the LLVM 9.0.1 compiler framework[3]. Figure 6a shows an overview of our analysis and the optimization framework. We used *Clang* to emit LLVM IR using the target-independent "libomptarget" OpenMP offloading library. The analysis pass then analyzes the API calls and their arguments to infer the offload pragmas specified by the user. We implemented an Andersen like flow-insensitive alias analysis, and also used two LLVM built-in analyses: scalar evolution for array index analysis and memory SSA[4] for chaining memory access and data copy operations.

For optimal memory copy insertion, we developed our analysis pass *OmpMemOpt*. It performs an inter-procedural analysis to detect redundant memory copies. Based on the analysis results, we infer the optimal places to insert the OpenMP memory copy constructs. Finally, we developed a Perl script to insert the appropriate memory mapping directives into the input source files. Thus, given an OpenMP target offloading application with no explicit memory management, our tool analyzes the program and finally generates the modified source files after adding the optimal set of OpenMP memory map directives.

Experimental Setup. We use the OpenMP benchmarks from SPEC ACCEL v1.2 to evaluate our analysis and optimizations. We exclude Fortran applications from our evaluation, since they are not supported by our current tool chain; we also exclude benchmarks that do not use target offloading. We show results for the 6 SPEC benchmarks, and also include 4 other applications: *saxpy, Cardoid ,Matrix Multiply* and *Matrix Transpose*.

Our experimental results were obtained from a Linux (Ubuntu 18.04.3) workstation, Intel Core i5-7600 CPU (3.50GHz), 16GB memory and an Nvidia "TITAN Xp" GPU with 12GB memory and CUDA 10.1.

Experimental Result and Discussion. We removed all the explicit memory mapping constructs specified in the benchmarks to obtain our baseline. The host performs host-to-device copy in the baseline version before launching every kernel on the device and device-to-host copy after the kernel finishes execution.

After running our optimization on the benchmark, we have three versions of each application: the baseline, *OmpMemOpt* optimized version, and the original hand-optimized benchmark. We compare the performance of these three versions to evaluate our framework. We measure the efficiency on such metrics: the improvement of execution time, the reducing of data volumes and time consumed on data movement.

---

[3] http://llvm.org/.
[4] https://llvm.org/docs/MemorySSA.html.

We did the following study for the comparison with baseline code. Figure 6b shows the overall speedup obtained by our approach compared to the naive data mapping baseline. As we can see except *503* and *552*, all the benchmarks show a speedup ranging from 1.02× to almost 10×. The 503 and 552 bench-

Table 3. Comparison of our achieved speedup with manually optimized speedup

Benchmark	In put	Memory copy time	Total time	Manual speedup	Our speedup
503.postencil	ref	954491.4	983668.3	33.5	1.0
503.postencil	test	3108.6	3205.2	25.6	1.0
503.postencil	train	3116.8	3211.5	25.5	1.0
504.polbm	ref	497859.3	553697.4	9.5	9.5
504.polbm	test	2014.5	2243.0	7.0	7.0
504.polbm	train	30222.4	33615.8	9.4	9.3
552.pep	ref	563182.7	671546.9	5.7	1.0
552.pep	test	469.8	653.9	3.6	1.0
552.pep	train	35889.8	42726.6	5.8	1.0
554.pcg	ref	807757.1	1040824.3	4.5	3.9
554.pcg	test	24129.3	31056.1	4.4	4.0
554.pcg	train	88261.0	113651.9	4.5	4.0
557.pcsp	ref	1204141.9	1308006.4	2.0	1.5
557.pcsp	test	20098.1	20229.1	1.5	1.5
557.pcsp	train	464849.7	475782.2	2.0	1.5
570.pbt	ref	3750608.5	4221773.7	3.7	3.7
570.pbt	test	1321807.1	1339861.0	2.6	2.6
570.pbt	train	2563893.7	2728456.2	3.6	3.6
Cardoid		838.5	1163.8	3.17	3.17
mm_mpy		750.8	54555	1.02	1.02
mtx_transpose		16.66	17.7	2.8	2.8
Saxpy		154.7	315.9	1.09	1.09

marks did not get a chance to be optimized due to limitations in the precision of the alias analysis used—flow-insensitive pointer analysis could not disambiguate the array references in those two benchmarks.

Figure 6c explains the reason for the speedup, by showing the improvement factor of memory copy time, compared to the baseline. A significant point to note here is that the performance gain is mostly dependent on the problem size (i.e., input data size). This also implies that the efficiency depends on the data volume reduced for transfer.

Finally, Fig. 6d gives a quantization study of the data volume transferred between the host and the device. It shows the reduction in total bytes copied. As is evident, there is a correlation between the factor by which total bytes are reduced and the obtained speedup. The speedup also depends on the pattern of computation. As the *Matrix Multiplication* example shows, even though there is a 1.5× reduction of memory-copy-time, it does not result in a speedup since the application is compute-intensive. In the benchmark *Cardoid*, there is an outer loop which iterates for 100 iterations, and launches an inner loop on the target device. The default semantics of the **target** construct would perform host-to-device and device-to-host copy in each iteration. But, since there is no host access, there is no need to copy the data back and forth every time. This is why almost 100% of the memory copies are eliminated after our optimization. Benchmark *Saxpy* is similar to *Cardoid*, there is an outer loop that launches the target task every iteration, and redundantly copies the data in every iteration.

Table 3 shows the comparison of speedup obtained from our approach with the manually optimized version. The manually optimized version is the original source released as the SPEC ACCEL benchmarks. The 3rd and 4th columns give the memory copy time and total execution time for baseline code (i.e. naive memory mapping version). The 5th column shows the speedup obtained by comparing user manually optimized code against baseline. And the last column shows the speedup got from our approach. In general, the user manually optimized version gives the better improvement by comparing the last two columns, and our approach (i.e. compiler optimization) got similar performance on *504.polbm* and *570.pbt*. As mentioned above, there is no improvement from *503.postencil* and 552.pep due to the precision issues from pointer alias analysis. This study shows the compiler's potential to automatically generate as efficient code as a programmer's manually optimized version.

6   Related Work

The problem of code generation and communication optimization for distributed memory machines is a classical problem, studied for a long time. Amarasinghe and Lam [1] introduced a data flow analysis framework to generate remote message read/write code, and then detect and remove redundancies in homogeneous distributed computing. Chavarria and Mellor-Crummey [6] proposed a communication coalescing optimization to reduce redundant data transfer for high-performance Fortran applications. Dathathri et al. [7] introduced a polyhedral model to enable static analysis and automatically generate efficient data movement code for non-shared address spaces.

Load elimination and partial code motion are the classic optimizations for eliminating redundant memory loads in a sequential program. In [5], Bodik et al. phrased the load-reuse problem as a path-sensitive analysis problem on the dataflow graph. Their algorithm can detect the reuse pattern for both scalar variable and pointer-based memory load operations. Recently, GPU based heterogeneous computing is becoming the mainstream configuration of high-performance computing. Several compiler optimizations and runtime techniques have been developed for reducing the communication overhead. In [12], Jablin et al. introduced a CPU-GPU Communication Manager (CGCM), which employs a static analysis with a runtime library to optimize CPU-GPU communication. Ramashekar and Bondhugula introduced BBMM [19] for communication optimizations on a multi-GPU system. They applied communication optimization for the tiled loop nest and generated the OpenCL code that uses BBMM runtime API to perform buffer management and data communication.

Ashcraft et al. built a compilation technique [3] that performs whole-program analysis to make the optimal placement of data transfer operations. Their approach is based on a liveness analysis to identify the preliminary scheduling locations for the data transfer and then use the dominator tree to optimize the locations. In [16], Mendonca et al. developed an automatic annotation mechanism for enabling GPU based data parallelism from the source code and eliminate the redundant CPU-GPU data copies.

There are also several runtime based communication optimization techniques for eliminating the CPU-GPU redundant memory copies. Asai et al. [2] discussed a runtime based approach using data dependence analysis for reducing the memory copy operations in a GPU-enabled version of the Apache Spark framework. Kim et al. developed a runtime communication optimization: Unnecessary Data Transfer Elimination (UDTE) [13], which uses a page-fault mechanism to avoid redundant CPU-GPU memory copies.

Compared with past work, our approach introduced a general compiler optimization framework that optimizes data movement across different memory spaces in heterogeneous computing. The related work mentioned above addressed this problem using runtime based mechanisms. Our framework reduces data movement overheads, and is applicable to parallel programming models that support heterogeneous computation.

7   Conclusion

In this work, we addressed the problem of optimizing data movement across different computation devices in a heterogeneous computing application. Given that many parallel programming language models (e.g., OpenMP, OpenACC) support offloading of computations and data to different accelerators, automatic elimination of redundant memory copies to improve performance, while still ensuring correctness, is an important challenge for compilers. To address this problem, we developed an optimization framework to identify redundant data movements and perform code transformations to eliminate those redundancies. We first extended Heap SSA to a Location-Aware heap SSA form (LASSA), an intermediate representation that can track host-to-device memory copies across multiple devices. Then, we performed a partial redundancy elimination dataflow analysis on LASSA to address the problem of removing redundant data transfers. We evaluated our technique on 10 benchmarks written in OpenMP 4.5 with target offloading constructs. Our approach demonstrated a geometric mean speedup of $2.3\times$ and saved a geometric mean of $3.48\,\text{GB}$ in redundant data transfers. For one of our future work directions, we plan to explore the use of immutability information [18] to further reduce the data transfers performed.

References

1. Amarasinghe, S.P., Lam, M.S.: Communication optimization and code generation for distributed memory machines. In: Proceedings of the ACM SIGPLAN 1993 Conference on Programming Language Design and Implementation, PLDI 1993, pp. 126–138. Association for Computing Machinery, New York (1993). https://doi.org/10.1145/155090.155102
2. Asai, R., Okita, M., Ino, F., Hagihara, K.: Transparent avoidance of redundant data transfer on GPU-enabled apache spark. In: Kaeli, D.R., Cavazos, J. (eds.) 11th Workshop on General Purpose Processing using GPUs, GPGPU@PPoPP 2018, Vosendorf (Vienna), Austria, 25 February 2018, pp. 22–30. ACM (2018). https://doi.org/10.1145/3180270.3180276

3. Ashcraft, M.B., Lemon, A., Penry, D.A., Snell, Q.: Compiler optimization of accelerator data transfers. Int. J. Parallel Program. **47**(1), 39–58 (2017). https://doi.org/10.1007/s10766-017-0549-3

4. Barua, P., Shirako, J., Tsang, W., Paudel, J., Chen, W., Sarkar, V.: OMPSan: static verification of openmp's data mapping constructs. In: IWOMP (2019). https://doi.org/10.1007/978-3-030-28596-8_1

5. Bodík, R., Gupta, R., Soffa, M.L.: Load-reuse analysis: design and evaluation. In: Proceedings of the ACM SIGPLAN 1999 Conference on Programming Language Design and Implementation, PLDI 1999, pp. 64–76, Association for Computing Machinery, New York (1999). https://doi.org/10.1145/301618.301643

6. Chavarría-Miranda, D., Mellor-Crummey, J.: Effective communication coalescing for data-parallel applications. In: Proceedings of the Tenth ACM SIGPLAN Symposium on Principles and Practice of Parallel Programming, PPoPP 2005, pp. 14–25. Association for Computing Machinery, New York (2005). https://doi.org/10.1145/1065944.1065948

7. Dathathri, R., Reddy, C., Ramashekar, T., Bondhugula, U.: Generating efficient data movement code for heterogeneous architectures with distributed-memory. In: Proceedings of the 22nd International Conference on Parallel Architectures and Compilation Techniques, PACT 2013, pp. 375–386. IEEE Press (2013)

8. Drechsler, K.H., Stadel, M.P.: A variation of knoop, rüthing, and steffen's lazy code motion. SIGPLAN Not. **28**(5), 29–38 (1993). https://doi.org/10.1145/152819.152823

9. Fink, S., Knobe, K., Sarkar, V.: Unified analysis of array and object references in strongly typed languages. In: Palsberg, J. (ed.) SAS 2000. LNCS, vol. 1824, pp. 155–174. Springer, Heidelberg (2000). https://doi.org/10.1007/978-3-540-45099-3_9

10. Hoeflinger, J.P., de Supinski, B.R.: The OpenMP memory model. In: Mueller, M.S., Chapman, B.M., de Supinski, B.R., Malony, A.D., Voss, M. (eds.) IWOMP -2005. LNCS, vol. 4315, pp. 167–177. Springer, Heidelberg (2008). https://doi.org/10.1007/978-3-540-68555-5_14

11. Jablin, T.B., Jablin, J.A., Prabhu, P., Liu, F., August, D.I.: Dynamically managed data for CPU-GPU architectures. In: Proceedings of the Tenth International Symposium on Code Generation and Optimization, pp. 165–174. CGO 2012, Association for Computing Machinery, New York (2012). https://doi.org/10.1145/2259016.2259038

12. Jablin, T.B., Prabhu, P., Jablin, J.A., Johnson, N.P., Beard, S.R., August, D.I.: Automatic CPU-GPU communication management and optimization. In: Hall, M.W., Padua, D.A. (eds.) Proceedings of the 32nd ACM SIGPLAN Conference on Programming Language Design and Implementation, PLDI 2011, San Jose, CA, USA, 4–8 June 2011, pp. 142–151. ACM (2011). https://doi.org/10.1145/1993498.1993516

13. Kim, J., Lee, Y., Park, J., Lee, J.: Translating openMP device constructs to openCL using unnecessary data transfer elimination. In: West, J., Pancake, C.M. (eds.) Proceedings of the International Conference for High Performance Computing, Networking, Storage and Analysis, SC 2016, Salt Lake City, UT, USA, 13–18 November 2016, pp. 597–608. IEEE Computer Society (2016). https://doi.org/10.1109/SC.2016.50

14. Knobe, K., Sarkar, V.: Array SSA form and its use in parallelization. In: Proceedings of the 25th ACM SIGPLAN-SIGACT Symposium on Principles of Programming Languages, POPL 1998, pp. 107–120. Association for Computing Machinery, New York (1998). https://doi.org/10.1145/268946.268956

15. Knoop, J., Rüthing, O., Steffen, B.: Lazy code motion. In: Proceedings of the ACM SIGPLAN 1992 Conference on Programming Language Design and Implementation, PLDI 1992, pp. 224–234. Association for Computing Machinery, New York (1992). https://doi.org/10.1145/143095.143136
16. Mendonca, G.S.D., Guimarães, B.C.F., Alves, P., Pereira, M.M., Araujo, G., Pereira, F.M.Q.: DawnCC: automatic annotation for data parallelism and offloading. TACO **14**(2), 13:1–13:25 (2017). https://doi.org/10.1145/3084540
17. Pai, S., Govindarajan, R., Thazhuthaveetil, M.J.: Fast and efficient automatic memory management for GPUs using compiler-assisted runtime coherence scheme. In: Proceedings of the 21st International Conference on Parallel Architectures and Compilation Techniques. PACT 2012, pp. 33–42. Association for Computing Machinery, New York (2012). https://doi.org/10.1145/2370816.2370824
18. Pechtchanski, I., Sarkar, V.: Immutability specification and its applications. Concurr. Comput.: Pract. Experience **17**(5–6), 639–662 (2005)
19. Ramashekar, T., Bondhugula, U.: Automatic data allocation and buffer management for multi-GPU machines. ACM Trans. Archit. Code Optim. **10**(4), 1–26 (2013). https://doi.org/10.1145/2544100
20. Torczon, L., Cooper, K.: Engineering A Compiler, 2nd edn. Morgan Kaufmann Publishers Inc., San Francisco (2007)
21. Zhao, J., Burke, M.G., Sarkar, V.: Parallel sparse flow-sensitive points-to analysis. In: Proceedings of the 27th International Conference on Compiler Construction, CC 2018, Vienna, Austria, 24–25 February 2018, pp. 59–70. ACM (2018)

Data Management, Analytics and Machine Learning

Accelerating Deep Learning Inference with Cross-Layer Data Reuse on GPUs

Xueying Wang[1,2], Guangli Li[1,2], Xiao Dong[1,2], Jiansong Li[1,2], Lei Liu[1(✉)], and Xiaobing Feng[1,2]

[1] State Key Laboratory of Computer Architecture,
Institute of Computing Technology,
Chinese Academy of Sciences,
Beijing, China
[2] School of Computer Science and Technology,
University of Chinese Academy of Sciences,
Beijing, China
{wangxueying,liguangli,dongxiao,
lijiansong,liulei,fxb}@ict.ac.cn

Abstract. Accelerating the deep learning inference is very important for real-time applications. In this paper, we propose a novel method to fuse the layers of convolutional neural networks (CNNs) on Graphics Processing Units (GPUs), which applies data reuse analysis and access optimization in different levels of the memory hierarchy. To achieve the balance between computation and memory access, we explore the fusion opportunities in the CNN computation graph and propose three fusion modes of convolutional neural networks: straight, merge and split. Then, an approach for generating efficient fused code is designed, which goes deeper in multi-level memory usage for cross-layer data reuse. The effectiveness of our method is evaluated with the network layers from state-of-the-art CNNs on two different GPU platforms, NVIDIA TITAN Xp and Tesla P4. The experiments show that the average speedup is 2.02 × on representative structures of CNNs, and 1.57× on end-to-end inference of SqueezeNet.

Keywords: Deep learning · Layer fusion · Performance optimization

1 Introduction

Convolutional neural networks (CNNs) have become more and more popular in deep learning applications, including image classification and video recognition. For modern heterogeneous parallel computing platforms such as Graphics Processing Units (GPUs), there has been a rising interest in efficient implementation of deep learning systems. There are several kinds of operators in deep neural networks, such as convolution, batch normalization, and activation. Generally, GPU-based deep learning systems launch kernels for a single operation many times, which may cause extra data transmission overheads. Complex computation tasks are usually bounded by arithmetic bandwidth and large-scale data

© Springer Nature Switzerland AG 2020
M. Malawski and K. Rzadca (Eds.): Euro-Par 2020, LNCS 12247, pp. 219–233, 2020.
https://doi.org/10.1007/978-3-030-57675-2_14

transmission are bounded with memory bandwidth. The bottleneck of executing kernel varies depending on the applications and GPU devices. For pooling, activation and some kind of convolution operations with small size, the workloads are limited by the transmission speed of memory access.

CNN architectures are going deeper and have become too complicated to infer in real-time systems. The increasing size of deep CNNs demands more on computing systems and GPUs provide the primary computation for CNN applications. However, the performance of CNN inference is subject to computation and memory bandwidth constraints. There is an increasing gap between memory bandwidth and computing performance on emerging GPUs.

Meanwhile, CNNs are tending to be very deep, such as GoogLeNet [16], and usually consist of dozens or hundreds of layers. Some novel architectures, such as inception and residual connections, resulting in deeper and wider neural networks. For accelerating the inference, some light-weight and efficient CNNs are proposed, such as SqueezeNet [9] and MobileNet [8].

The inference systems are usually parallel and have hierarchical memory and the memory access bandwidth is the potential bottleneck for accelerating neural networks. In the architectural design of the GPU, the latency of global memory is much higher than shared memory. New GPU architectures are emerging, Volta, Turing and Ampere. However, the new hardware architectures are focused on the single layer execution time rather than the data reuse across layers in different memory level.

As such, reusing shared memory data can achieve much more performance improvement besides the benefits of hardware upgrades. Inspired by kernel fusion [6,14,17,19], we propose a cross-layer data reuse approach by fusing kernels to increase the data locality and reuse efficiency cross the layers.

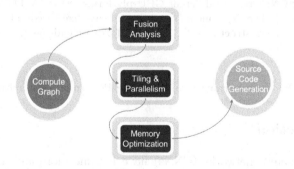

Fig. 1. Workflow of our cross-layer data reuse method

Unfortunately, few works have addressed the issue of how to formally describe and fuse deep CNNs across layers in detail. In particular, the performance of our method can catch up with the existing acceleration library. Our goal is to develop a strategy for generating high performance code of deep CNN applications by exploring the cross-layer data reuse. We design a cross-layer data reuse optimization method, which inputs the compute graph of CNN layers and generates the source code for GPUs (Fig. 1). The fusion strategies include analyzing the input graph for fusion, tiling the data and parallelism on devices and optimizing the memory usage on multi-level memory hierarchy.

The main contributions of this paper are:

- To find more optimization opportunities for subsequent fusing, we characterize the computational procedure in CNNs and summarized three fusion modes (straight, merge and split) formally.
- We propose a fusion method that can reuse on-chip memory by making full use of multi-layer memory on GPUs. Based on the method, we build a code generator, which can automatically generate a high-performance fused kernel according to determined fusion mode.
- We conduct experiments on representative networks and analyze the results. The experimental results show that the performance of our method outperforms the GPU-accelerated deep neural network library, cuDNN [4].

2   Hierarchy of Modern GPUs

In this section, we first introduce the memory hierarchy for modern GPU architectures, which is the basis for CNN application optimization. Then, we give a motivating example and describe the data reuse methodology in convolution applications.

2.1   Hierarchy of GPUs and CUDA

Compute Unified Device Architecture (CUDA) is a parallel computing platform and programming model for GPUs [13], which exposes programmers to the concepts of memory hierarchy and threads hierarchy [3]. Accelerating deep learning performance on complex memory hierarchy needs to make full use of memory units and compute units.

As shown in Fig. 2, there are many programmable memories at different levels of GPU devices. GPU memory units vary from access pattern to management. Modern GPUs contain a lot of Stream Multiprocessors (SMs) which are parallel executed on the board. Each SM has its shared memory, which can be accessed by threads in the same block. Multiple blocks can be launched on the SM, but each block can only access its private shared memory. Registers and local memory can only be visited by a single thread. If the size of the required resisters is larger than the size each thread allocated, local memory will be used. Constant memory, texture memory, and global memory can be visited by all threads. Constant memory is a kind of read-only memory, which needs to be transferred to GPU device memory from CPU memory before launching the kernel. Texture memory is read-only and optimized for 2D access. Generally, data will be prepared by copying memory data from host memory to global memory before the kernel launched.

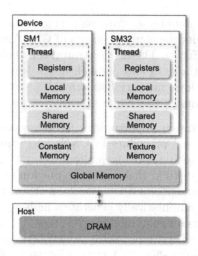

Fig. 2. GPU memory hierarchy

On-chip memory is fast and close to chips while off-chip memory is slow and far away from chips. Different types of memory have different access patterns. Registers and local memory are both private to each thread. But registers are on-chip and have low latency and local memory is off-chip and has high latency. Shared memory is organized by equal-sized banks. Accessing data in the same bank simultaneously will cause shared memory bank conflict and get higher latency. The global memory is off-chip and large memory capacity, but also has high access latency. The average latency is about 7000× higher than register latency and 5× higher than shared memory latency [5].

GPUs have become the most popular accelerator with high computational throughput. Large and deep neural networks require substantial computing and memory throughput and existing methods do not make good use of this multi-level memory hierarchy for the complex architecture of GPUs.

2.2 Motivating Example

Convolution operation is the most time-consuming part of the whole neural network. Convolution, pooling, activation, element-wise concatenation and addition are basic operations and layers in recent neural networks. Although the deep convolutional operations are compute-bound, the pooling, activation, element-wise operation and convolution layers with small input channels are memory-bound. This requires a mechanism to achieve a balance between computation and memory access.

The benefit of cross-layer data reuse on two CNN layers is the difference in latency and throughput between shared memory and global memory. The original and fused main kernel structures are shown in Fig. 3. LD.G and ST.G illustrate global memory data load and store instructions. LD.S and ST.S are

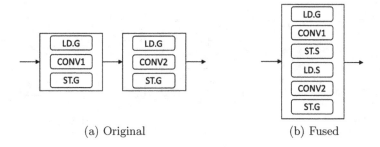

(a) Original   (b) Fused

Fig. 3. CNN motivating example

the load and store instructions, which read and write on shared memory. `CONV1` and `CONV2` are the computation of the first and the second convolution layers. Figure 3a depicts the original kernels, which individually compute two convolutional operators. Each kernel loads the input data from global memory and stores the result to global memory, which implies twice execution of `LD.G` and `ST.G`. As shown in the Fig. 3b, one fused convolutional kernel only contain once `LD.G` and `ST.G`, and use the `ST.S` and `LD.S` to buffer the intermediate data.

Each layer may fetch data from off-chip memory, compute in on-chip memory and store to off-chip memory. But fused convolution layers can reduce the off-chip global memory read/store transactions between two layers. We load data from shared memory and store data in shared memory, which means converts the global memory load/store to the shared memory load/store.

3   Method

In this section, the method of fusing convolutional layers on GPUs is depicted in detail. First, we analyze the fusion optimization opportunities of diverse convolution neural networks and sum up three typical fusion modes. In the second step, we use the data dependency to determines the size of the redundant data on each SM and the size of the tile, which takes the relationship between the input CNN layer and the sequence layer into consideration. Finally, the use of multi-level memory on the device is optimized during the parallel code generation phase.

3.1   Fusion Mode Formulation

The neural network architecture is constantly changing and it is necessary to formalize some common architectures for neural network fusion, similar to the hierarchical representations [11] in Neural Architectural Search.

Subject to the capacity of shared memory and high latency caused by bank conflict, the cross-layer data can not be stored in on-chip memory and reused on more than two layers. Using too much shared memory resources will cause the high access latency for shared memory bank conflict, which may cause performance decrease.

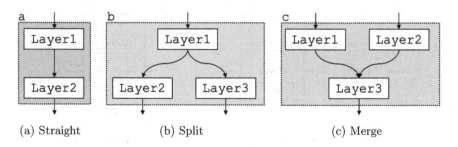

(a) Straight   (b) Split   (c) Merge

Fig. 4. Different fusion mode

To conclude the common layer architectures in the convolutional neural networks, we propose three basic fusion modes. As described in Fig. 4, the cross-layer relationships are summarized to three fusion modes. Figure 4a describes the straight fusion mode, which makes the output data of Layer1 reuse for Layer2. Figure 4b gives a split mode, which Layer1 can be the input of both Layer2 and Layer3. Figure 4c is a merge mode that has two layers as the input of the third layer, which suggests that Layer3 needs the correct computation results of Layer1 and Layer2.

These three basic modes can be widely found in most deep neural networks. For example, neural networks with sequential layers (rather than residual and inception structures) are ubiquitous, which can be divide into mode (a) Straight. Residual module and inception connection make the network wider, deeper and more complicated. There are a variety of mixed fusion modes in such neural network architectures, which brings challenge to cross-layer data reuse analysis.

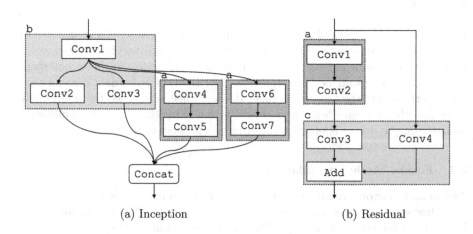

(a) Inception   (b) Residual

Fig. 5. Fusion example for inception and residual neural networks

Figure 5 abstracts the convolution layers in the network (some other operations, such as ReLU and pool, are omitted). In this figure, the boxes represent layers, arrows represent the dataflow dependency, dotted boxes represent fusion blocks and the letter upon the dotted box represents fusion mode.

In Fig. 5a, the inception module for fusion strategy is depicted, which includes two modes, mode a and mode b. In the mode b block, the output data of Conv1 can reuse and input the Conv2 and Conv3. As shown in Fig. 5b, the residual connection is divided into three fusion blocks. The block who belongs to mode a contains Conv1 and Conv2, that the result of Conv1 will be reuse. The block which is mode c means the Add operations can reuse the results of Conv3 and Conv4 on-chip.

3.2   Tiling and Parallelism

Unifying CNN layers into a single kernel is a challenge for layer fusion because of the different data size and filter shape diversity. Tiling is an important parallel strategy on GPU programming. The fundamental problem for layer fusion is how to tile the data on the parallel system with multi-level memory hierarchy, which called hierarchy overlapped tiling [20].

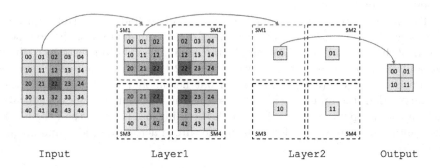

Fig. 6. Tiling and parallelism example

Our tiling strategy is to tile each output images and feature maps into small tiles on the dimension height and width, and implement implicit General Matrix Multiplication (GEMM) convolution algorithm. Each single output pixel depends on all input pixels through all channels within the window of filter, and the convolution operations whose filter height and width are larger than 1×1 need redundant computation and data storage. There is no need to pay additional attention to element-wise operations because of data independency.

Considering data reuse across layers, the parallel model for the fused layers is restricted by the CNN layer parameters. The filter with large size, which is larger than 1, will cause redundant computing for data dependence. Figure 6 shows a tiling example for two fused neural network layers computation on 4 SMs. The SMs are parallel on GPUs, and shared memory of each block is isolate and private, which means that redundant data storage is necessary for on-chip data reuse. The center data replicates in each SM and the border data around the center in `Layer1` are redundant in adjacent SM, which makes it be available for the subsequent `Layer2`. The tiling size will greatly affect the performance, too large or too small will cause performance degradation. The small tiling size will result in too much data redundant computation and reduce the earning of data reuse. As shown in Fig. 6, tiling size of 3×3 will make 36 elements stored on the GPUs while the input size is 25 if the convolution filter size is 3. The tiling size of one will not cause any redundant data, which also means that the convolutional filter size will influence the tiling strategy.

However, the larger tiling size is not always better. There is a tradeoff between choosing large size and small size. The large tiling size will occupy more computing resources, which reduces the degree of parallelism of the computation. As the intermediate data storage location, shared memory is an important bottleneck resource for the cross-layer data reuse. More shared memory are allocated by each thread block, fewer thread blocks can be processed simultaneously by an SM. If shared memory or register is unavailable to process at least one block on each SM, the kernel will fail for resource limitation. In the worst case, the number of parallel blocks on an SM is reduced to 1 and the latency cannot be hidden. Therefore, it is recommended to use less than 1/3 shared memory to achieve high performance [3].

To this end, we design a simple tunning tool to find a relatively optimal tiling size. The tunning tool only searches for the combination of the common factors of the output layer. For example, the combination (4,3) means 4×4 tiling size and (3,3) grid size. For the output size (12,12), the tunning search space will be $\{(4,3), (2,6), (3,4), (6,2)\}$. If output height and width are prime, the size larger than the number will be chosen as the basis for tuning. We allocate each thread one point computation, and if the tiling size is larger than the block size limitation, there will be for loops inside thread across the width and height dimension.

3.3 Memory Optimization

Memory bandwidth, compute resources, instruction and memory latency are three common limiters to performance for a kernel. For CPU programming, it can be safe to ignore the cache line size or the number of registers. But for GPUs, a runtime error occurs when the size of the programmable memory requested exceeds the computing resources. Improper memory usage will cause drastic performance degradation. For this, the memory strategy needs to be carefully considered while programming on GPUs.

Shared Memory Usage. For the optimization of shared memory, reduce bank conflict with memory padding and use synchronization statements to guarantee the correctness of data in memory.

When a warp accessing different words with the address in the same bank, a 32-way bank conflict will occur. To avoid the shared memory bank conflict, our method generates code with memory padding. Extra unused shared memory is paid to allocate a redundant column and row for padding, which is effective in reducing bank conflict. Memory padding strategy will work after only padding on either row or column in most situation, which will not cause too much resource waste than padding both row and column.

To guarantee the correctness of the data in shared memory, explicit barrier and memory fences are necessary. __syncthreads() is intra-block synchronization in CUDA, which is used in each thread block to ensure that all threads writing partial results to shared memory have completed before any threads read the final results. Threads in a block will wait for all threads to execute this instruction, which maintains correctness of data in memory with less performance loss.

Read-only Data Optimization. Constant memory and read-only cache are optimized for read-only data accessing, which can speed up the data load efficiently. Constant memory has restricted size, which usually is 64 KB, and read-only cache is 48KB. The unified L1/texture cache is read-only cache, which is an alternative to L2 cache when accessing read-only data in global memory.

The input data of the first layer and the filter weight of the convolution layers are read-only and do not need to write back during computation. The strategy for our layer fusion cases are using global memory with read-only cache for input data and using constant memory for filter and bias data. If the size of filter and bias data exceeds the constant memory restriction, global memory with read only cache will be used.

Padding Strategy. Obviously, these convolution layers are not aligned, especially when padding and stride operations exist. There are two alternatives for padding operations, using branch statement or fill in extra data to the margin. Because there are no branch prediction mechanisms on GPUs, flow control constructs, such as if and else clause, will cause great penalty performance. Extra data movement will lead to memory bandwidth bottleneck.

Padding operation widely exists in CNNs, for keeping the output size consistent with the input size. For layer fusion, we need to conduct padding operation on shared memory within a kernel execution. After the first layer computation, we preprocess the data with padding so that there is no padding operation in next layer.

4 Experiments

In this section, experimental setup and performance results are given. The caffe prototxt files are used as the input in the experiments, and the neural network structures are extracted from the deep neural network compute graph.

4.1 Experimental Setup

When developing applications on the GPU, the correctness needs to be paid attention to first, and then the performance of the code is improved. To verify the correctness and compare the performance, we use cuDNN [4], one of the most popular deep learning accelerator libraries on GPUs, as a baseline. The cuDNN is a deep learning library, which is closed-source and NVIDIA hardware limited. Most of the deep learning frameworks use cuDNN as computational back-ends. To eliminate the effect of the algorithm, we use the latest and best-performing version, cuDNNv7, as the baseline and a tool to check the correctness of results. The routine `cudnnConvolutionBiasActivationForward()` applies a bias and then an activation to the convolutions, which combines these operations into one kernel. For a fair comparison, we choose the same convolutional algorithm to compare the performance between cuDNN library and our method. We set `IMPLICIT_GEMM` as a convolution algorithm instead of other specially optimized algorithms, which implicitly performs GEMM without actually form the matrix that holds the data.

Three basic modes for fusing convolution layers are shown in Fig. 4, which is concluded from the mainstream neural networks. Compute graphs extracted from different neural networks are used to perform our fusion optimization method. We extract 4 different convolution neural network layers from state-of-the-art networks, GoogleNet [16], MobileNet [8], SqueezeNet [9] and ResNet [7]. As shown in Table 1, the ID represents the fusion mode and the test case number. Input and output are clarified with the size information, each with shape [Channel, Height, Width]. The batch size of input data is set to 1. Filter size is depicted by [Output Channel, Input Channel, Filter Height, Filter Width]/padding, stride, group.

Table 1. Convolutional neural network layers in the fusion experiment

ID	Input	Filter1 Size	Filter2 Size	Filter3 Size	Output
a.1	[192,28,28]	[16,192,1,1]/0,1,1	[32,16,5,5]/2,1,1	-	[32,28,28]
a.2	[16,80,80]	[16,1,3,3]/1,1,16	[16,1,1,1]/0,1,1	-	[16,80,80]
b.1	[64,56,56]	[16,64,1,1]/0,1,1	[64,16,1,1]/0,1,1	[64,16,3,3]/1,1,1	[128,56,56]
c.1	[64,56,56]	[256,64,1,1]/0,1,1	[256,64,1,1]/0,1,1	[64,256,1,1]/0,1,1	[64,56,56]

We evaluate the experimental results on two different GPU devices, NVIDIA TITAN Xp and Tesla P4. TITAN Xp GPU achieves a peak throughput of 12.15 TeraFLOPS, 6074 GB/s shared memory bandwidth and 547.7 GB/s global memory bandwidth with 30 SMs. P4 GPU is Pascal architecture and has a 5.5 TeraFLOPS single-precision peak performance, 2721 GB/s shared memory bandwidth, 192 GB/s global memory bandwidth with 20 SMs.

The code was compiled using the NVIDIA CUDA compiler (version 10) with flags '-O3'. We execute each kernel over 5 times for run-to-run variation counting and report the average time. GPU timers are used to collect the time information of the applications.

4.2   Performance Results and Analysis

The performance of different applications is often strongly influenced by parallel strategies and memory access performance. We implement our layer fusion method with four different neural network architectures and demonstrate the performance on two different GPU devices. To clarify the effectiveness of the whole neural network with our method, we conduct the fusion method on the SqueezeNet [9]. The profiling analysis is conducted on the kernels to find out the relationship between our method and cuDNN on memory and computation.

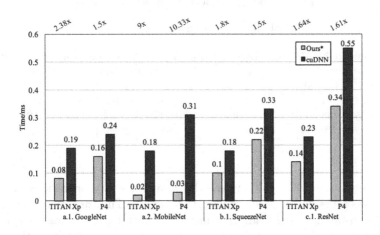

Fig. 7. The Experiment result of convolutional neural network fusion

In Fig. 7, we show the speedup of four test cases on TITAN Xp and P4 GPUs. The left bar of each group is the execution time of fused layers and the right bar is the sum of the execution time of each cuDNN kernels. The fusion test cases achieve 1.8×, 9.8×, 1.6× and 1.62× speedup. The average speedup on TITAN Xp is 2.29× and P4 is 1.91×. The experiment a.2 comes from MobileNets and contains depth-wise convolution operations, which called 'group convolution' in cuDNN library. It calls corresponding grouped convolutional kernels multiple times, which causes performance degradation and 10.33× speedup on P4 GPU.

We also evaluate our fusion method on the light-weight convolutional neural network, SqueezeNet [9]. There are 8 mode b blocks that we can apply our fusion method in this neural networks. In Fig. 8, we show the execution time of our fused kernels and cuDNN kernels. The speedup of the whole SqueezeNet on TITAN Xp is 1.57×, and the speedup of the fused blocks to original layers is 1.34×. The last convolutional layer in the neural network consumes too much more time than the smaller size layers, which is an unusual situation. For this, we conduct the tiling and parallel strategy of our method on this layers and achieves 4.64× speedup on this single layer.

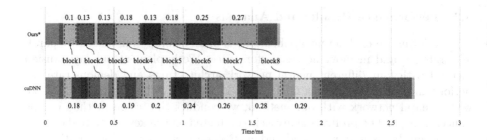

Fig. 8. The Experiment result of SqueezeNet

Table 2. Profiling metrics on memory

| | Executed Load/Store Instructions | | | Global Memory Store Transactions | | |
	Ours*	cuDNN	Ratio	Ours*	cuDNN	Ratio
a.1	927472	129690	7.14:1	6272	18816	1:3
a.2	129600	514998	1:3.97	25600	102400	1:4
b.1	1903552	433542	4.39:1	100352	225792	1:2.25
c.1	2654720	1588384	1.67:1	34008	91296	1:2.68

In Table 2, the GPU profiling metrics about memory operations are compared between the fused kernels and cuDNN kernels. The `ldst_executed` metric counts the total executed load/store instructions and `gst_transactions` gains additional insight into the number of the global memory store transactions. The global memory store transactions metric reports the number of coalesced global memory store transactions, which implies the quantity of global memory access and evaluates the global write operations saved by our methods. The reason why we use the global memory store metric rather than the global memory store metric is that texture memory is utilized as data storage, which will be not counted in the global memory load metrics. All data need be stored in global memory finally and global memory store transactions metric is much more objective to describe the quantity of global memory transactions.

Our method will introduce redundant computation and also increase the number of load/store instructions but still get an acceleration ratio. The test case a.2 is group convolution from MobileNet, which is abnormal for executing the same kernel 17 times. In addition to this structure, we catch 4.4x more load-/store instructions execution on devices. The global memory store transactions ratio between our layer fusion method and the baseline is 1:2.98 on average, while we have much more load/store instructions. Our method will introduce redundant computation and also load/store instruction but still get a satisfactory acceleration ratio.

5   Related Work

To the best of our knowledge, our work is the first about how to generate high performance code by fusing two or more convolutional layers on GPUs, which can achieve competitive performance with the cuDNN library.

Much effort has been made to optimize CNN applications. Li et al. [10] transpose the data and apply different data layouts on different operations to explore the impact of data layouts on the performance of convolutional layers and memory-bound pooling layers. Data reuse has been explored on fusing CNN layers. Alwani et al. [1] proposed pyramid-shaped multi-layer sliding window to handle the input feature maps and verified on FPGA.

Besides the direct code optimization strategy and algorithm, inference framework and DSL are the two main code optimization ways for different parallel devices. CNN inference framework [12] generates Vulkan code and achieve reasonable performance on different platforms. Halide [15] is a domain specific language for image processing applications, which introduces the principle of increasing the producer-consumer locality and adopts the loop fusion optimization strategy. TVM [2] is a compiler to generate portable code for deep learning applications across diverse hardware platforms. The source code generated by our method is easy to understand and modify, which is also portable among different GPU platforms.

Kernel fusion is also a hot research point in GPU kernel optimization. Wu et.al [19] introduce the benefits of kernel fusion in data warehousing applications. Wahib et.al [17] optimize the code with kernel fusion and utilize a heuristic search algorithm for choosing a near-optimal fusion configuration. The source-to-source compiler [6] explores the automatic kernel fusion algorithm for basic linear algebra subprograms routines on GPUs. Recently, the work of Qiao, B et.al [14] depicts kernel fusion problem as finding some cut set of kernels to fuse in DAG-graph. Vertices in the graph represent kernels and edges represent the relationship between kernels. They provide an algorithm about how to choose kernels while our method provides a method about how to fuse kernels better.

6   Conclusion

Considering the characteristics of deep convolution neural networks and underlying GPU architectures, we proposed a cross-layer data reuse method. The experiments of real-world CNNs show that our method achieves competitive performance and supports the possibility to generate inference code for deep learning applications.

The effectiveness of layer fusion method is evaluated on different test cases and the end-to-end neural network and we get 2.02x and 1.57x speedup on GPUs even with more instructions executed. We hope that the result of our method will support future research and application about the layer fusion and our method will be widely used and accelerate inference stage for deep learning applications on GPUs.

Acknowledgements and Data Availability Statement. The authors thank Zhen Zhang for helpful discussion. This work is supported by the National Key R&D Program of China under Grant No.2017YFB1003103, and the Science Fund for Creative Research Groups of the National Natural Science Foundation of China under Grant No.61521092.

The datasets and code generated during and/or analysed during the current study are available in the Figshare repository: https://doi.org/10.6084/m9.figshare.12571928 [18].

References

1. Alwani, M., Chen, H., Ferdman, M., Milder, P.: Fused-layer CNN accelerators. In: 2016 49th Annual IEEE/ACM International Symposium on Microarchitecture (MICRO). IEEE, October 2016. https://doi.org/10.1109/micro.2016.7783725
2. Chen, T., et al.: Tvm: an automated end-to-end optimizing compiler for deep learning. In: Proceedings of the 12th USENIX conference on Operating Systems Design and Implementation, pp. 579–594. USENIX Association (2018)
3. Cheng, J., Grossman, M., McKercher, T.: Professional Cuda C Programming. Wiley, Hoboken (2014)
4. Chetlur, S., et al.: cuDNN: efficient primitives for deep learning. arXiv preprint arXiv:1410.0759 (2014)
5. Fang, M., Fang, J., Zhang, W., Zhou, H., Liao, J., Wang, Y.: Benchmarking the gpu memory at the warp level. Parallel Comput. **71**, 23–41 (2018). https://doi.org/10.1016/j.parco.2017.11.003
6. Filipovič, J., Madzin, M., Fousek, J., Matyska, L.: Optimizing CUDA code by kernel fusion: application on BLAS. J. Supercomputing **71**(10), 3934–3957 (2015). https://doi.org/10.1007/s11227-015-1483-z
7. He, K., Zhang, X., Ren, S., Sun, J.: Deep residual learning for image recognition. In: 2016 IEEE Conference on Computer Vision and Pattern Recognition (CVPR). IEEE, June 2016. https://doi.org/10.1109/cvpr.2016.90
8. Howard, A.G., et al.: Mobilenets: Efficient convolutional neural networks for mobile vision applications. arXiv preprint arXiv:1704.04861 (2017)
9. Iandola, F.N., Han, S., Moskewicz, M.W., Ashraf, K., Dally, W.J., Keutzer, K.: Squeezenet: Alexnet-level accuracy with 50x fewer parameters and< 0.5 mb model size. arXiv preprint arXiv:1602.07360 (2016)
10. Li, C., Yang, Y., Feng, M., Chakradhar, S., Zhou, H.: Optimizing memory efficiency for deep convolutional neural networks on GPUs. In: SC16: International Conference for High Performance Computing, Networking, Storage and Analysis. IEEE, November 2016. https://doi.org/10.1109/sc.2016.53
11. Liu, H., Simonyan, K., Vinyals, O., Fernando, C., Kavukcuoglu, K.: Hierarchical representations for efficient architecture search. arXiv preprint arXiv:1711.00436 (2017)
12. Mazaheri, A., Schulte, J., Moskewicz, M.W., Wolf, F., Jannesari, A.: Enhancing the programmability and performance portability of GPU tensor operations. In: Yahyapour, R. (ed.) Euro-Par 2019. LNCS, vol. 11725, pp. 213–226. Springer, Cham (2019). https://doi.org/10.1007/978-3-030-29400-7_16
13. Nvidia CUDA: Compute unified device architecture programming guide (2007)
14. Qiao, B., Reiche, O., Hannig, F., Teich, J.: From loop fusion to kernel fusion: a domain-specific approach to locality optimization. In: 2019 IEEE/ACM International Symposium on Code Generation and Optimization (CGO). IEEE, February 2019. https://doi.org/10.1109/cgo.2019.8661176

15. Ragan-Kelley, J., Barnes, C., Adams, A., Paris, S., Durand, F., Amarasinghe, S.: Halide. ACM SIGPLAN Not. **48**(6), 519–530 (2013). https://doi.org/10.1145/2499370.2462176
16. Szegedy, C., et al.: Going deeper with convolutions. In: 2015 IEEE Conference on Computer Vision and Pattern Recognition (CVPR). IEEE, June 2015. https://doi.org/10.1109/cvpr.2015.7298594
17. Wahib, M., Maruyama, N.: Scalable kernel fusion for memory-bound GPU applications. In: SC14: International Conference for High Performance Computing, Networking, Storage and Analysis. IEEE, November 2014. https://doi.org/10.1109/sc.2014.21
18. Wang, X.: Artifact and instructions to generate experimental results for conference proceeding 2020 paper: accelerating deep learning inference with cross-layer data reuse on GPUs, July 2020. https://doi.org/10.6084/m9.figshare.12571928. https://springernature.figshare.com/articles/software/Artifact_and_instructions_to_generate_experimental_results_for_conference_proceeding_2020_paper_Accelerating_Deep_Learning_Inference_with_Cross-Layer_Data_Reuse_on_GPUs/12571928/1
19. Wu, H., Diamos, G., Wang, J., Cadambi, S., Yalamanchili, S., Chakradhar, S.: Optimizing data warehousing applications for GPUs using kernel fusion/fission. In: 2012 IEEE 26th International Parallel and Distributed Processing Symposium Workshops & PhD Forum. IEEE, May 2012. https://doi.org/10.1109/ipdpsw.2012.300
20. Zhou, X., Giacalone, J.P., Garzarán, M.J., Kuhn, R.H., Ni, Y., Padua, D.: Hierarchical overlapped tiling. In: Proceedings of the Tenth International Symposium on Code Generation and Optimization. ACM Press (2012). https://doi.org/10.1145/2259016.2259044

Distributed Fine-Grained Traffic Speed Prediction for Large-Scale Transportation Networks Based on Automatic LSTM Customization and Sharing

Ming-Chang Lee[1]([✉]), Jia-Chun Lin[1], and Ernst Gunnar Gran[1,2]

[1] Department of Information Security and Communication Technology, Norwegian University of Science and Technology, 2815 Gjøvik, Norway
{ming-chang.lee,jia-chun.lin,ernst.g.gran}@ntnu.no
[2] Simula Research Laboratory, 1364 Fornebu, Norway

Abstract. Short-term traffic speed prediction has been an important research topic in the past decade, and many approaches have been introduced. However, providing fine-grained, accurate, and efficient traffic-speed prediction for large-scale transportation networks where numerous traffic detectors are deployed has not been well studied. In this paper, we propose DistPre, which is a distributed fine-grained traffic speed prediction scheme for large-scale transportation networks. To achieve fine-grained and accurate traffic-speed prediction, DistPre customizes a Long Short-Term Memory (LSTM) model with an appropriate hyperparameter configuration for a detector. To make such a customization process efficient and applicable for large-scale transportation networks, DistPre conducts LSTM customization on a cluster of computation nodes and allows any trained LSTM model to be shared between different detectors. If a detector observes a similar traffic pattern to another one, DistPre directly shares the existing LSTM model between the two detectors rather than customizing an LSTM model per detector. Experiments based on traffic data collected from freeway I5-N in California are conducted to evaluate the performance of DistPre. The results demonstrate that DistPre provides time-efficient LSTM customization and accurate fine-grained traffic-speed prediction for large-scale transportation networks.

Keywords: Hyperparameter tuning · Lightweight LSTM · Large-scale transportation networks · Traffic speed prediction · Distributed and parallel processing · The Nelder-Mead method

1 Introduction

Accurate traffic-speed prediction is crucial to achieve efficient proactive traffic management and control for large-scale transportation networks. During the past

© Springer Nature Switzerland AG 2020
M. Malawski and K. Rzadca (Eds.): Euro-Par 2020, LNCS 12247, pp. 234–247, 2020.
https://doi.org/10.1007/978-3-030-57675-2_15

decade, many approaches and methods have been introduced for short-term traffic speed prediction. They can be classified into two main categories: parametric
approaches and nonparametric approaches. The former category of approaches
simplifies the mapping function to a known form, i.e., these approaches require
a pre-defined model. A typical example is the autoregressive integrated moving average approach (ARIMA) [1]. On the other hand, the nonparametric
approaches make no assumptions about the form of the mapping function,
i.e., they require no pre-defined model structure. The k-nearest neighbors (k-
NN) method [3,6], artificial neural network (ANN) [5], recurrent neural network
(RNN) [15], etc., all belong to this category. As a special type of RNN, long short-
term memory [8], abbreviated as LSTM, is superior in time series prediction with
long temporal dependencies. Prior studies such as [17,26,27] have shown that
LSTM provides better prediction accuracy than many other approaches and
neural networks. Therefore, LSTM is chosen as a building block for traffic speed
prediction in this paper.

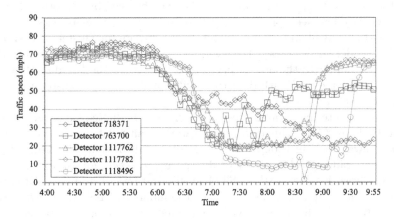

Fig. 1. The traffic speed collected by five randomly-chosen detectors on freeway I5-N
in California between 4 a.m. and 10 a.m. in a typical weekday.

However, several issues still need to be addressed to achieve fine-grained,
accurate, and efficient traffic speed prediction for large-scale transportation networks. For example, in large-scale transportation networks, numerous detectors,
such as loop detectors or traffic cameras, are deployed in different places to collect
traffic data. Depending on the density of nearby population and other factors,
the traffic observed/collected by detectors at different locations may have diverse
patterns. For instance, Fig. 1 shows that five detectors deployed on freeway I5-N
in California [23] observe completely different traffic patterns between 6 a.m. and
10 a.m. in a typical weekday. In order to provide fine-grained traffic-speed prediction for achieving better transportation services and management, we suggest
that each detector should have its own LSTM model to predict the traffic speed
of its coverage. However, such an approach would be expensive, time consuming,

and impractical because we might need to manually configure LSTM hyperparameters and train the corresponding LSTM model for each individual detector several times before we find an LSTM model that is able to accurately make predictions. Note that LSTM hyperparameters are parameters whose values are set before the training process of an LSTM starts.

To address the above issue, we propose DistPre, which is a distributed fine-grained traffic speed prediction scheme for large-scale transportation networks. DistPre customizes an LSTM model for a detector by automatically determining LSTM hyperparameter values and training the corresponding LSTM model based on the Nelder-Mead method [19], which is a commonly applied method used to find the minimum or maximum of an objective function in a multi-dimensional space. To make the above customization process time-efficient for large-scale transportation networks, we propose that detectors should share the same LSTM model if they observe similar traffic patterns. More specifically, DistPre works in an incremental, distributed, and parallel manner. Whenever DistPre encounters an unprocessed detector i, it checks if the traffic-speed pattern observed by detector i is similar to the one observed by any other detector that previously has been processed by DistPre. If the answer is negative, DistPre requests an available compute node from a computer cluster to customize an LSTM model for detector i. However, if the traffic-speed pattern observed by detector i is similar to the one observed by a detector j, DistPre directly shares the LSTM of detector j with detector i without requiring to customize a new LSTM model for detector i.

To demonstrate the performance of DistPre, we conducted experiments on an Apache Hadoop YARN cluster using real-world traffic data collected by detectors on freeway I5-N in California. The results confirm that DistPre is able to provide fine-grained and accurate traffic speed prediction for large-scale transportation networks due to the LSTM customization. In addition, DistPre is scalable, efficient, and cost-effective since the number of LSTM models needed does not proportionally increase with the number of detectors, due to the LSTM sharing feature of DistPre.

The rest of the paper is organized as follows: Sect. 2 briefly introduce LSTM, LSTM hyperparameters, and the Nelder-Mead method. Section 3 presents related work, while Sect. 4 introduces the details of DistPre. In Sect. 5, we evaluate the performance of DistPre. Section 6 concludes this paper and outlines future work.

2   LSTM, LSTM Hyperparameters, and the Nelder-Mead Method

In this section, we introduce LSTM, LSTM hyperparameters, and the Nelder-Mead method.

LSTM and LSTM Hyperparameters: LSTM [8] is designed to learn long-term dependencies and model temporal sequences. The architecture of LSTM is similar to that of RNN except that the nonlinear units in the hidden layers are memory blocks. Each block contains memory cells, an input gate, an output gate, and a forget gate. The input gate decides whether the input should be stored in the memory cells or not. The output gate determines if current memory contents should be output. The forget gate decides if current memory contents should be erased. These features enable LSTM to preserve information over long time lags, thus addressing the vanishing gradient problem [7].

It is well-known that the prediction performance of LSTM highly depends on choosing appropriate values for the following hyperparameters:

- Learning rate (denoted by R_{Learn})
- The number of hidden layers (denoted by N_{Layer})
- The number of hidden units (denoted by N_{Unit})
- Epochs (denoted by ep)

The **learning rate** controls how much the weights of LSTM are adjusted with respect to the loss gradient. The lower the value, the less is the chance to miss any local minima, but it prolongs the training process. A **hidden layer** is a layer between the input layer of LSTM and the output layer of LSTM. The more complex the training dataset is, the more hidden layers are required to learn the training dataset. A **hidden unit** is a neuron in a hidden layer. It is responsible for taking in a set of weighted inputs and produce an output through an activation function. Too many hidden units may result in overfitting, while too few hidden units might cause underfitting. An **epoch** is defined as one forward pass and one backward pass of all the training data. Too many epochs might overfit the training data, whereas too few epochs may underfit the training data.

Due to the importance of the above-mentioned hyperparameters to the learning performance and computational efficiency of LSTM, this paper takes all of them into consideration. One of this paper's goals is to automatically determine appropriate values for these hyperparameters such that the resulting LSTM model is able to achieve high prediction accuracy and that human effort can be greatly reduced.

The Nelder-Mead Method (NMM): NMM [19] is a popular optimization method for non-linear functions. In this paper, we use it to automatically find appropriate values for the above-mentioned LSTM hyperparameters. NMM minimizes the target objective function by generating an initial simplex based on a predefined vertex and then performing a function evaluation at each vertex of the simplex. Note that a simplex has $n+1$ vertices in $\mathbb{R}^n$ where n is the number of dimensions of the parameter space. A sequence of transformations is then performed iteratively on the simplex, aiming to decrease the function values at its vertices. Possible transformations include reflection, expansion, contraction, and shrinking. We refer readers to the original paper [21] for more details about these transformations. The above process terminates when the sample standard deviation of the function values of the current simplex fall below a predefined threshold.

In our context, the initial simplex has five vertices. Each vertex consists of four values assigned to the four LSTM hyperparameters. One of the five vertices is the so called predefined vertex, and it consists of four default values separately assigned to the four LSTM hyperparameters. The remaining four vertices are automatically determined by NMM in a deterministic way. In other words, NMM always produces the same four vertices given a predefined vertex. Note that the terms *vertex* and *hyperparameter setting* are interchangeable. In this paper, the function evaluation is to derive the prediction error introduced by an LSTM model trained with a certain dataset under a specific hyperparameter setting. If the prediction error of an LSTM model is no larger than a predefined threshold, NMM terminates the search.

3   Related Work

Traffic prediction approaches introduced in the past two decades can be classi-fied into two categories: parametric approaches and nonparametric approaches. In parametric approaches, a model structure needs to be determined before-hand based on some theoretical assumptions. The ARIMA model is a typi-cal and widely used parametric approach [2]. ARIMA is designed to fit time series data so as to predict future data points in the time series. Many ARIMA-based approaches were also introduced to improve prediction accuracy, includ-ing [13,24,25].

Different from parametric approaches, nonparametric approaches do not require a predefined model structure. There is no need to make assumptions about the mapping function. Typical examples include k-NN, ANN, RNN, hybrid approaches, etc. Le et al. [10] addressed traffic speed prediction using big traffic data obtained from static sensors and proposed local Gaussian Processes to learn and make predictions for correlated subsets of data. Jiang and Fei [9] introduced a data-driven vehicle speed prediction method based on Hidden Markov mod-els. However, these two approaches focus on predicting traffic on a road section or a small region. They might be difficult to use in large-scale transportation networks.

Ma et al. [18] used deep learning theory to predict traffic congestion evolution in large-scale transportation networks. Furthermore, Ma et al. [16] predicted traf-fic speed in large-scale transportation networks by representing traffic as images and employing convolutional neural networks to make prediction. However, both of these methods require the scale of the target transportation network to be fixed and specified in advance. Lee et al. introduced DALC [11] to predict traffic speed at each individual detector in large-scale transportation networks based on LSTM. However, DALC only focuses on auto-tuning two LSTM hyperparam-eters, i.e., the number of hidden layers and epochs for each detector of the target transportation network.

Different from these methods, DistPre proposed in this paper is designed in an incremental manner. DistPre can handle an increasing number of detectors on the fly without pre-fixing the scale of the target transportation network, and it is able to automatically tune more LSTM hyperparameters for each detector if needed. These practical features make DistPre a much better solution for providing fine-grained traffic speed prediction for large-scale and growing transportation networks.

4   The Details of DistPre

The architecture of DistPre consists of a master node and a set of worker nodes. The master node decides when it is necessary to customize an LSTM model for each detector in the target transportation networks. Each worker node waits for an instruction from the master node and conducts the required LSTM customization process for a given detector upon request.

Figure 2 illustrates the algorithm of DistPre running on the master node. Let $G = \{D_1, D_2, ..., D_x\}$ be a list of detectors that already have their own LSTMs customized by DistPre. It is clear that G is empty before DistPre is employed and launched. Whenever DistPre encounters an unprocessed detector (denoted by U_i) in the target transportation network, the master node first normalizes L_i, which is a list of traffic-speed values previously observed by U_i. Note that $L_i = \{v_{i,1}, v_{i,2}, ..., v_{i,T}\}$ where $v_{i,t}$ is the traffic-speed value observed by U_i at time point t, $t = 1, 2, ..., T$. The normalization is to divide $v_{i,t}$ by f where f is a predefined fixed value (e.g., 70 to represent the speed limit in mph). The normalized L_i, denoted by N_i, will be $\{n_{i,1}, n_{i,2}, ..., n_{i,T}\}$ where $n_{i,t} = v_{i,t}/f$.

Input: An unprocessed detector U_i
Output: A decision to customize an LSTM model for U_i or to share an LSTM model with U_i
Procedure:

1	Let M be a boolean variable and let M be false;
2	Let $G = \{D_1, D_2, ..., D_x\}$ be a list of detectors having their own LSTMs customized by DistPre;
3	Let $L_i = \{v_{i,1}, v_{i,2}, ..., v_{i,T}\}$ be a list of traffic-speed values previously observed by U_i;
4	Normalize L_i into N_i by dividing each value in L_i by f;
5	**for** $j = 1$ to $x\{$ // x is the total number of detectors in G;
6	Calculate AARD$_{i,j}$ based on Equation 1;
7	**if** AARD$_{i,j} < thd_{AARD}\{$
8	Share the LSTM model of D_j with U_i;
9	Let M be true;
10	break;$\}\}$
11	**if** M==false $\{$
12	Request an available worker node to customize an LSTM model for U_i;
13	Append U_i to the end of G;$\}$

Fig. 2. The LSTM auto-tuning and sharing algorithm performed by the master node.

The master node decides whether to customize an LSTM model for U_i or not by sequentially comparing U_i with every detector (denoted by $D_j, j=1, 2, ..., x$) in G in terms of their normalized traffic-speed pattern based on the following equation:

$$AARD_{i.j} = \frac{1}{T} \sum_{i=1}^{T} \frac{|n_{i,t} - n_{j,t}|}{n_{i,t}} \qquad (1)$$

where $AARD_{i.j}$ is the average absolute relative difference between the traffic-speed patterns collected by U_i and D_j, and $n_{j,t}$ is the normalized traffic-speed value collected by D_j at time point t, implying that $n_{j,t} = v_{j,t}/f$. If $AARD_{i,j}$ is less than a predefined threshold thd_{AARD} (implying that U_i and D_j observe a similar traffic-speed pattern), the master node directly shares the LSTM of D_j with U_i (see lines 7 to 10 of Fig. 2).

However, if the master node is unable to find any detector that has observed a similar traffic-speed pattern with U_i (i.e., line 11 holds), the master node requests an available worker node from the cluster to customize an LSTM model for U_i, and then appends U_i to the end of G to indicate that U_i will have its own LSTM model customized by DistPre. Based on how each detector is appended to G, it is clear that every detector in G must have observed a distinct traffic-speed pattern.

On the other hand, whenever a worker node receives an LSTM customization request for U_i from the master node, it utilizes NMM to automatically find appropriate values for the four abovementioned hyperparameters by using the following initial hyperparameter setting as the predefined vertex:

$$R_{Learn} = 0.01, N_{Layer} = 1, N_{Unit} = 2, ep = 100$$

Note that the predefined vertex consists of four low hyperparameter values. The goal is to enable NMM to start with a simple LSTM model since such a model introduces less computational cost than a more complex LSTM model.

When the worker node finds a hyperparameter setting which enables the corresponding LSTM to reach the required prediction accuracy for U_i (i.e., the corresponding AARE value calculated based on Eq. 2 is lower than or equal to a predefined threshold thd_{AARE}, the worker node terminates the customization process and outputs the LSTM model to be the LSTM model of U_i.

$$AARE = \frac{1}{W} \sum_{w=1}^{W} \frac{|s_w - \widehat{s_w}|}{s_w} \qquad (2)$$

Note that, in Eq. 2, W is the total number of data points considered for comparison, w is the index of a data point, s_w is the actual traffic-speed value at w, and $\hat{s}_w$ is the forecast traffic-speed value at w.

5   Performance Evaluation

To evaluate DistPre, we chose freeway I5-N as our target transportation network. I5-N is a major route from the Mexico-United States border to Oregon with a total length of 796.432 miles. In our experiments, DistPre incrementally provides its LSTM customization and sharing service until the 110 detectors that are

Table 1. Four LSTM hyperparameters and their domains used by DistPre.

Hyperparameter	Domain	Description
R_{Learn}	[0.01, 0.2]	Discrete with step = 0.01
N_{Layer}	[1, 10]	Discrete with step = 1
N_{Unit}	[2, 40]	Discrete with step = 2
ep	[100, 1000]	Discrete with step = 20

deployed on I5-N are completely covered. Note that the distance between two consecutive detectors is around 5 miles. We crawled the traffic data collected by each of these 110 detectors for six continuous working days from the Caltrans performance measurement system [4], which is a database of traffic data collected by detectors placed on state highways throughout California. The traffic data of each detector was then split into a training dataset (the first 5 days) and a testing dataset (the last day). Due to the fact that all the traffic data is aggregated at 5-min intervals, DistPre follows the same interval for prediction.

In this experiment, DistPre was deployed on a cluster running Apache Hadoop YARN 2.2.0 [22]. The cluster consists of one master node and 30 worker nodes. Each node runs Ubuntu 12.04.1 LTS with 2 CPU cores, 2 GB of RAM, and 100 GB of storage. As mentioned earlier, four LSTM hyperparameters were considered to be auto-tuned by DistPre. Table 1 lists the domain of these LSTM hyperparameters. For each hyperparameter, we chose a range of values for NMM to conduct its search process. Note that the maximum value for each hyperparameter was determined according to our previous experience [11].

The goal of this experiment is to study the impact of the LSTM sharing function and the number of worker nodes on the performance of DistPre. To this aim, the four cases listed in Table 2 were designed. In Case 1, we allowed only one worker node of the cluster to support the operation of DistPre. In addition, we disabled the LSTM sharing function of DistPre. In other words, each detector always gets its own LSTM model, and all the LSTM customizations are sequentially performed by a single worker node. In Case 2, we still limited a single worker node to support DistPre, but we enabled the LSTM sharing function. Therefore, detectors were able to share an LSTM model if they observed similar traffic patterns. In Case 3 and Case 4, we increased the number of worker nodes

Table 2. The details of the four cases.

Case No	Number of worker nodes involved	The LSTM sharing function
1	1	Disabled
2	1	Enabled
3	30	Disabled
4	30	Enabled

to 30, while we disabled and enabled the LSTM sharing function in Case 3 and Case 4, respectively.

Note that $thd_{AARD} = 0.1$ and $thd_{AARE} = 0.05$ in all the cases. If two detectors have 90% similarity in their monitored traffic-speed patterns, we consider that they have similar patterns. This is why we set thd_{AARD} to be 0.1. The same reason for thd_{AARE}: We consider that it is satisfactory if a detector is able to provide 95% prediction accuracy. This is why we set thd_{AARE} to be 0.05. Note that these two thresholds are configurable if one wants to change the degree of similarity or achieve a different level of prediction accuracy. The following five performance metrics are chosen in this experiment:

1. Total LSTM customization duration (TLCD). This is the time period starting when DistPre is launched and ending when all the 110 detectors have obtained their LSTM models. Apparently, if TLCD is short, it means that DistPre is time efficient.
2. The total number of LSTMs generated by DistPre over time.
3. Average AARE, calculated as below:

$$Average\ \text{AARE} = \frac{\sum_{r=1}^{Z} \text{AARE}_r}{Z} \tag{3}$$

where AARE_r is the AARE value associated with the LSTM model of detector r, where $r=1,2, ...,Z$, and Z is the total number of the detectors in the target transportation network. Note that AARE_r is calculated based on Eq. 2, and that Z equals 110 in this experiment.
4. Average AAE, calculated as below:

$$Average\ \text{AAE} = \frac{\sum_{r=1}^{Z} \text{AAE}_r}{Z} \tag{4}$$

where AAE_r is the average absolute error (AAE) value associated with the LSTM model of detector r, and AAE_r is defined as

$$\frac{1}{W} \sum_{w=1}^{W} |s_{r,w} - \widehat{s_{r,w}}| \tag{5}$$

A low AAE value implies that the forecast values are close to the actual values.
5. Average RMSE, calculated as below:

$$Average\ \text{RMSE} = \frac{\sum_{r=1}^{Z} \text{RMSE}_r}{Z} \tag{6}$$

where RMSE_r is the root mean square error associated with the LSTM model of detector r, and RMSE_r is defined as

$$\sqrt{\frac{1}{W} \sum_{w=1}^{W} (s_{r,w} - \widehat{s_{r,w}})^2} \tag{7}$$

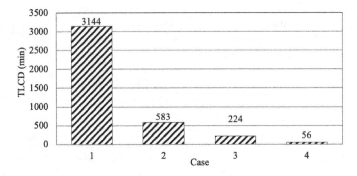

Fig. 3. The number of LSTM models customized by DistPre versus with the number of detectors processed by DistPre.

A low RMSE value suggests that the forecast values are close to the actual values.

Figure 3 shows the TLCD results of DistPre in the four cases. Case 1 leads to the longest TLCD, which is around 3144 min. This is because only one worker node was employed to customize an LSTM model for each individual detector in Case 1, and there is no sharing of LSTM models among detectors. We can see that TLCD is significantly reduced in Case 2. The required TLCD is reduced by 81.46% (=(3144-583)/3144) from Case 1 to Case 2, implying that enabling detectors to share their LSTM models greatly reduces the number of times LSTM models need to be customized, even though there is only one worker node supporting the operation of DistPre.

When 30 worker nodes are used by DistPre and the sharing function is disabled, i.e., Case 3, the required TLCD is reduced to 224 min, meaning that the distributed and parallel processing further improves the performance of DistPre, even when compared to Case 2 (single worker node, LSTM model sharing enabled). By further enabling the sharing function, i.e., Case 4, the total time duration drops to only 56 min. The reduction is around 75% (=(224−56)/224) compared with Case 3, and 98% (=(3144−56)/3144) compared with Case 1. This great performance improvement is mainly due to two factors. Firstly, by means of DistPre, only 31 out of the 110 detectors require a customized LSTM. Secondly, the work of LSTM customization is distributed to 30 worker nodes.

Altogether, the above results demonstrate that DistPre is able to provide the LSTM customization service in a time-efficient and scalable way for detectors in large-scale transportation networks. This feature is very important since large-scale transportation networks usually contain numerous detectors and the amount may keep increasing. Furthermore, note that the number of worker nodes could be increased even further to handle even larger transportation networks when needed.

Figure 4 illustrates the number of LSTM models customized by DistPre over time, i.e., as new detectors are processed. We can see that Case 1 and Case 3

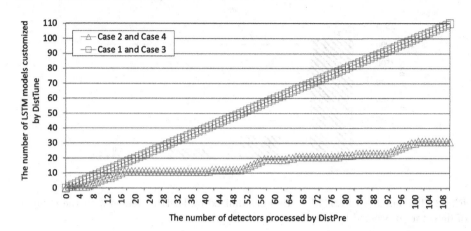

Fig. 4. The number of LSTM models customized by DistPre versus with the number of detectors processed by DistPre.

have identical results: Whenever DistPre processed a new unknown detector, one more LSTM model is customized. The reason is that the LSTM sharing function is disabled in both cases, so every detector always gets its own customized LSTM model from DistPre. On the other hand, in Case 2 and Case 4, there is no one-to-one relationship between the number of LSTM models customized and the number of detectors processed by DistPre. When DistPre processed a new unknown detector, the number of customized LSTM models did not always increase due to the LSTM sharing function. In fact, when all the 110 detectors were processed by DistPre, only 31 LSTM models were generated and customized by DistPre. This also explains why DistPre in Case 2 and Case 4 have shorter TLCD than DistPre in Case 1 and Case 3, respectively.

From the perspective of prediction performance, both Case 1 and Case 3 have the same results when it comes to average AARE, average AAE, and average RMSE as shown in Fig. 5, 6, and 7, respectively.

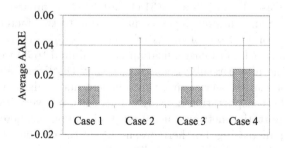

Fig. 5. The average AARE results in four cases

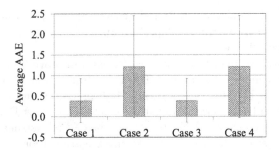

Fig. 6. The average AAE results in four cases

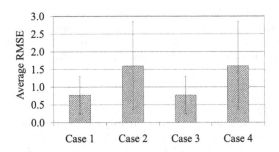

Fig. 7. The average RMSE results in four cases

The main reason is that the algorithm of NMM is deterministic. No matter which worker node executes NMM for a given detector, the result is always the same. Due to the same reason, the prediction accuracy results in Case 2 and Case 4 are identical, but they are both lower than those in Case 1 and Case 3. This is because not all the detectors in Case 2 and Case 4 have customized LSTMs that perfectly fit their training data. Nevertheless, the average AARE values in Case 2 and Case 4 still satisfy our requirement since they are both lower than the predefined thd_{AARE} (i.e., 0.05).

6   Conclusion and Future Work

In this paper, we have introduced DistPre, a distributed scheme to achieve fine-grained, accurate, and efficient traffic speed prediction for a large amount of detectors deployed in large-scale transportation networks. DistPre automatically customizes an LSTM models with an appropriate hyperparameter setting for a detector based on NMM. By enabling any trained LSTM model to be shared between different detectors that all observe similar traffic-speed patterns, DistPre enables fine-grained and time-efficient traffic speed prediction in large-scale transportation networks. The required LSTM customization time does not proportionally increase when the number of detectors handled by DistPre increases. Our experiments based on real traffic data, collected by the Caltrans performance measurement system, demonstrate the great performance of DistPre in both prediction accuracy and time efficiency.

As future work, we plan to extend DistPre and improve its performance by taking continuous monitoring and LSTM re-customization into account such that any detector is able to keep providing high prediction accuracy under any circumstances. In addition, we would like to investigate how DistPre can take advantage of a heterogeneous HPC cluster like the eX^3 infrastructure [20] to further improve the performance of DistPre by investigating appropriate scheduling approaches such as [12,14].

Acknowledgments. This work was supported by the project eX^3, *Experimental Infrastructure for Exploration of Exascale Computing*, funded by the Research Council of Norway under contract 270053 and the scholarship under project number 80430060 supported by Norwegian University of Science and Technology.

References

1. Ahmed, M.S., Cook, A.R.: Analysis of freeway traffic time-series data by using Box-Jenkins techniques. Transp. Res. Rec. **722**(1), 1–9 (1979)
2. Box, G.E., Jenkins, G.M., Reinsel, G.C., Ljung, G.M.: Time Series Analysis: Forecasting and control, 5th edn. Wiley, Hoboken (2015)
3. Bustillos, B., Chiu, Y.C.: Real-time freeway-experienced travel time prediction using N-curve and k nearest neighbor methods. Transp. Res. Rec. **2243**(1), 127–137 (2011). https://doi.org/10.3141/2243-15
4. California Department of Transportation: PeMS. http://pems.dot.ca.gov/. Accessed 5 July 2020
5. Chan, K.Y., Dillon, T.S., Singh, J., Chang, E.: Neural-network-based models for short-term traffic flow forecasting using a hybrid exponential smoothing and Levenberg-Marquardt algorithm. IEEE Trans. Intell. Transp. Syst. **13**(2), 644–654 (2012). https://doi.org/10.1109/TITS.2011.2174051
6. Davis, G.A., Nihan, N.L.: Nonparametric regression and short-term freeway traffic forecasting. J. Transp. Eng. **117**(2), 178–188 (1991). https://doi.org/10.1061/(ASCE)0733-947X(1991)117:2(178)
7. Hochreiter, S.: The vanishing gradient problem during learning recurrent neural nets and problem solutions. Int. J. Uncertainty Fuzziness Knowl.-Based Syst. **6**(2), 107–116 (1998). https://doi.org/10.1142/S0218488598000094
8. Hochreiter, S., Schmidhuber, J.: Long short-term memory. Neural Comput. **9**(8), 1735–1780 (1997). https://doi.org/10.1162/neco.1997.9.8.1735
9. Jiang, B., Fei, Y.: Vehicle speed prediction by two-level data driven models in vehicular networks. IEEE Trans. Intell. Transp. Syst. **18**(7), 1793–1801 (2017). https://doi.org/10.1109/TITS.2016.2620498
10. Le, T.V., Oentaryo, R., Liu, S., Lau, H.C.: Local Gaussian processes for efficient fine-grained traffic speed prediction. IEEE Trans. Big Data **3**(2), 194–207 (2017). https://doi.org/10.1109/TBDATA.2016.2620488
11. Lee, M.C., Lin, J.C.: DALC: distributed automatic LSTM customization for fine-grained traffic speed prediction. In: Proceedings of the 34th International Conference on Advanced Information Networking and Applications, pp. 164–175 (2020). https://doi.org/10.1007/978-3-030-44041-1_15, https://arxiv.org/abs/2001.09821

12. Lee, M.C., Lin, J.C., Yahyapour, R.: Hybrid job-driven scheduling for virtual MapReduce clusters. IEEE Trans. Parallel Distrib. Syst. **27**(6), 1687–1699 (2016). https://doi.org/10.1109/TPDS.2015.2463817

13. Lee, S., Fambro, D.B.: Application of subset autoregressive integrated moving average model for short-term freeway traffic volume forecasting. Transp. Res. Rec. **1678**(1), 179–188 (1999). https://doi.org/10.3141/1678-22

14. Lin, J.C., Lee, M.C.: Performance evaluation of job schedulers under Hadoop YARN. Concurr. Comput.: Pract. Exp. **28**(9), 2711–2728 (2016). https://doi.org/10.1002/cpe.3736

15. van Lint, J.W.C., Hoogendoorn, S.P., van Zuylen, H.J.: Freeway travel time prediction with state-space neural networks: modeling state-space dynamics with recurrent neural networks. Transp. Res. Rec. **1811**(1), 30–39 (2002). https://doi.org/10.3141/1811-04

16. Ma, X., Dai, Z., He, Z., Ma, J., Wang, Y., Wang, Y.: Learning traffic as images: a deep convolutional neural network for large-scale transportation network speed prediction. Sensors **17**(4), 818 (2017). https://doi.org/10.3390/s17040818

17. Ma, X., Tao, Z., Wang, Y., Yu, H., Wang, Y.: Long short-term memory neural network for traffic speed prediction using remote microwave sensor data. Transp. Res. Part C: Emerg. Technol. **54**, 187–197 (2015). https://doi.org/10.1016/j.trc.2015.03.014

18. Ma, X., Yu, H., Wang, Y., Wang, Y.: Large-scale transportation network congestion evolution prediction using deep learning theory. PLOS One **10**(3), (2015). https://doi.org/10.1371/journal.pone.0119044

19. Nelder, J.A., Mead, R.: A simplex method for function minimization. Comput. J. **7**(4), 308–313 (1965). https://doi.org/10.1093/comjnl/7.4.308

20. Simula Research Laboratory: The eX^3 Research Infrastructure. https://www.ex3.simula.no. Accessed 5 July 2020

21. Singer, S., Nelder, J.: Nelder-mead algorithm. Scholarpedia **4**, 7 (2009). https://doi.org/10.4249/scholarpedia.2928

22. The Apache Software Foundation: Apache Hadoop YARN, Version 3.2.1 (2019). https://hadoop.apache.org/docs/current/hadoop-yarn/hadoop-yarn-site/YARN.html. Accessed 5 July 2020

23. Wikipedia contributors: Interstate 5 in California – Wikipedia, the free encyclopedia (2020). https://en.wikipedia.org/wiki/Interstate_5_in_California. Accessed 5 July 2020

24. Williams, B.: Multivariate vehicular traffic flow prediction: evaluation of ARIMAX modeling. Transp. Res. Rec. **1776**(1), 194–200 (2001). https://doi.org/10.3141/1776-25

25. Williams, B.M., Hoel, L.A.: Modeling and forecasting vehicular traffic flow as a seasonal ARIMA process: theoretical basis and empirical results. J. Transp. Eng. **129**(6), 664–672 (2003). https://doi.org/10.1061/(ASCE)0733-947X(2003)129:6(664)

26. Yu, R., Li, Y., Shahabi, C., Demiryurek, U., Liu, Y.: Deep learning: a generic approach for extreme condition traffic forecasting. In: Proceedings of the 2017 SIAM International Conference on Data Mining. Society for Industrial and Applied Mathematics, pp. 777–785 (2017). https://doi.org/10.1137/1.9781611974973

27. Zhao, Z., Chen, W., Wu, X., Chen, P.C., Liu, J.: LSTM network: a deep learning approach for short-term traffic forecast. IET Intell. Transp. Syst. **11**(2), 68–75 (2017). https://doi.org/10.1049/iet-its.2016.0208

Optimizing FFT-Based Convolution on ARMv8 Multi-core CPUs

Qinglin Wang[1,2]([✉]) [iD], Dongsheng Li[1,2], Xiandong Huang[1,2], Siqi Shen[1,2], Songzhu Mei[1,2], and Jie Liu[1,2]

[1] Science and Technology on Parallel and Distributed Processing Laboratory, National University of Defense Technology, Changsha 410073, China
wangqinglin.thu@gmail.com
[2] College of Computer, National University of Defense Technology, Changsha 410073, China

Abstract. Convolutional Neural Networks (CNNs) are widely applied in various machine learning applications and very time-consuming. Most of CNNs' execution time is consumed by convolutional layers. A common approach to implementing convolutions is the FFT-based one, which can reduce the arithmetic complexity of convolutions without losing too much precision. As the performance of ARMv8 multi-core CPUs improves, they can also be utilized to perform CNNs like Intel X86 CPUs. In this paper, we present a new parallel FFT-based convolution implementation on ARMv8 multi-core CPUs. The implementation makes efficient use of ARMv8 multi-core CPUs through a series of computation and memory optimizations. The experiment results on two ARMv8 multi-core CPUs demonstrate that our new implementation gives much better performance than two existing approaches in most cases.

Keywords: CNNs · Convolution · FFT · ARMv8 · Parallel algorithm.

1 Introduction

Convolutional Neural Networks (CNNs) are widely found in various machine learning applications such as computer vision [4,10]. In some specific tasks, such as image classification [6], their performance even exceeds human capabilities. The main reason is the application of large-scale training data sets and deep convolutional neural network structures. As a result, they are often very time-consuming. There are usually convolutional, pooling, activation, and fully-connected layers in CNNs. Most of CNNs' execution time is spent on the convolutional layers. Therefore, it is particularly important to improve the performance of the convolutional layers.

Granted by the National Key Research and Development Program of China (No. 2018YFB0204301), and the National Natural Science Foundation of China under grant nos. 61602500, 91530324 and 91430218.

M. Malawski and K. Rzadca (Eds.): Euro-Par 2020, LNCS 12247, pp. 248–262, 2020.
https://doi.org/10.1007/978-3-030-57675-2_16

Some of the most common approaches to performing convolutions include matrix multiplication-based, Winograd-based and Fast Fourier Transform (FFT)-based approaches [7,9,16–18]. The matrix multiplication-based approach directly transforms a convolution into matrix multiplications, which are carried out via general matrix multiplication routines (GEMM) in the Basic Linear Algebra Subprograms (BLAS) library, and then is also labeled as a GEMM-based approach. Its main disadvantage is the explosion of memory requirements and the suboptimal performance of BLAS library on the produced matrices. The Winograd-based approach can reduce the arithmetic complexity of convolutions by means of Winograd minimial filtering algorithms. However, it maybe introduces non-negligible loss of accuracy and is mainly applicable to convolutional layers with small filters. The FFT-based approach converts convolutions in the time domain into multiplications in the frequency domain, so the computation requirement of convolutions is also reduced and its accuracy loss is negligible. In the performance, the FFT-based implementations generally outperform the Winograd-based ones [19]. Thus, the FFT-based approach is suitable for more convolutional layers than the Wingorad-based one. To further improve performance of convolutions, it is very interesting to study efficient parallelization of the FFT-based approach on parallel hardware resources.

Currently, many efforts have focused on efficient implementations of FFT-based convolutions on various hardware platforms. Mathieu and Vasilache et al. [11,15] first examined the performance of different implementations of FFT-based convolutions on GPUs. Zlateski et al. [19–21] mainly studied high performance implementations of FFT-based convolutions on Intel many-core CPUs. However, there is relatively little work about the optimization of FFT-based convolutions on ARMv8 multi-core CPUs.

Along with the performance enhancement of ARMv8 multi-core CPUs [12,13], they can also be utilized to perform deep neural networks like Intel X86 CPUs. However, there is absence of high-performance convolution primitives for the ARMv8 architecture. In this paper, we propose a parallel FFT-based convolution implementation on ARMv8 multi-core CPUs. Our implementation consists of four stages: FFT transforms of input feature maps and filters, complex matrix multiplications, and IFFT transforms of output feature maps. All four stages are vectorized and thread-level parallelized. The transformed data of input feature maps and filters is stored back to memory according to the access order in the optimized implementation of complex matrix multiplications, so that the unnecessary data movement is avoided. The custom data layouts for internal tensors are proposed to support the optimization above efficiently. Our implementation is tested on Phytium FT-1500A [12] and FT-2000plus [13]. The convolutional layers from Alexnet and VGG are used to test the performance of an existing FFT-based implementation in NNAPCK, a GEMM-based one used in Caffe and our new one. Compared with the GEMM-based implementation, our implementation gets speedups of 1.48–16.19 and 3.86–78.08 times on two CPUs above, respectively. Our optimization is better than the FFT-based implementation of NNPACK in most cases on FT-1500A, and superior to the latter in all test cases on FT-2000plus. The corresponding maximum speedups are 2.16 and 7.04 times, respectively.

The structure of this paper is as follows. Section 2 introduces the detailed definition and one naive FFT-based implementation of convolutions. Section 3 describes our algorithm and optimizations on ARMv8 multi-core CPUs. The performance results are analyzed in Sect. 4. Finally, Sect. 5 concludes this paper and gives our future work.

2   Background

2.1   Convolution

A convolution takes input feature maps I and filters F as input and produces output feature maps O. In C code style, input and output feature maps with BCHW (batch, channel, height, width) layout are written as $I[B][C][H_i][W_i]$ and $O[B][C'][H_o][W_o]$, and the corresponding filters are $F[C'][C][H_f][W_f]$. The convolution in deep learning networks is expressed as

$$O_{b,c',h',w'} = \sum_{c=0}^{C-1} \sum_{hf=0}^{H_f-1} \sum_{wf=0}^{W_f-1} (I_{b,c,h' \times s+hf,w' \times s+wf} \times F_{c',c,hf,wf}), \tag{1}$$

where $b \in [0, B)$, $c' \in [0, C')$, $h' \in [0, H_o)$, $w' \in [0, W_o)$, $c \in [0, C)$, B is the mini-batch size, C and C' denote the number of input and output channels, $H_{i/o/f}$ and $W_{i/o/f}$ represent spatial dimensions of different tensors, and s is the stride size. In the following, we only consider the case where the stride size is 1.

2.2   FFT-Based Convolution

The convolution theorem shows that a convolution in the time domain can be transformed into element-wise multiplications in the frequency domain. Applied to the field of deep learning, it makes the Eq. 1 become:

$$O_{b,c'} = \sum_{c=0}^{C-1} IFFT(FFT(I_{b,c}) \odot FFT^*(F_{c',c})), \tag{2}$$

where FFT and $IFFT$ are 2D Fast Fourier Transforms and Inverse Fast Fourier Transforms respectively, $\odot$ denotes element-wise complex multiplication, and $*$ represents complex conjugation.

In FFT and IFFT, the discrete Fourier basis is chosen to be the largest among the spatial dimensions of three tensors [15]. When the spatial dimensions of some tensors are smaller than the Fourier basis, they are zero-padded to be the same size. However, the spatial dimensions of F are often much smaller than those of the feature maps tensors, so that the overhead of padding is non-trivial. Thus, the tile-based approach is often used to reduce the overhead. At the same time, the linearity of the Fourier transforms allows that the sum in Eq. 2 is performed before IFFT. So, the Eq. 2 is transformed to:

$$O_{b,c',\alpha,\beta} = IFFT(\sum_{c=0}^{C-1}(FFT(I_{b,c,\alpha,\beta}) \odot FFT^*(F_{c',c}))), \qquad (3)$$

where α and β denote the spatial coordinates of each tile.

Each component of the element-wise complex multiplication is labeled as (φ, γ). The sum and the element-wise complex multiplication can be merged into complex matrix multiplications as follows:

$$Z^{(\varphi,\gamma)} = G^{(\varphi,\gamma)}D^{(\varphi,\gamma)}, \qquad (4)$$

where $D^{(\varphi,\gamma)}_{c,b,\alpha,\beta} = FFT(I_{b,c',\alpha,\beta})^{(\varphi,\gamma)}$ and $G^{(\varphi,\gamma)}_{c',c} = FFT^*(F_{c',c})^{(\varphi,\gamma)}$. Thus, the original implementation of a FFT-based convolution is listed in Algorithm 1. It mainly consists of four procedures: FFT transforms of input feature maps and filters, complex matrix multiplications, and IFFT transforms of output feature maps.

Algorithm 1: Native FFT-based Convolution Algorithm.

---
   input: I, F

   output: O

1 $\delta \times \delta$ is the tile size.

2 $X \times \Delta$ is the number of tiles in each feature map.

3 **for** $c' = 0: 1: C'$ **do**

4   **for** $c = 0: 1: C$ **do**

5        $g = FFT^*(F_{c',c}) \in \mathbb{C}^{\delta \times \delta}$

6   Scatter g to matrices G: $G^{(\varphi,\gamma)}_{c',c} = g_{\varphi,\gamma}$

7 **for** $b = 0: 1: B$ **do**

8   **for** $c = 0: 1: C$ **do**

9   **for** $\alpha = 0: 1: X$ **do**

10   **for** $\beta = 0: 1: \Delta$ **do**

11            $d = FFT(I_{b,c,\alpha,\beta}) \in \mathbb{C}^{\delta \times \delta}$

12   Scatter d to matrices D: $D^{(\varphi,\gamma)}_{c,b,\alpha,\beta} = d_{\varphi,\gamma}$

13 **for** $\varphi = 0: 1: \delta$ **do**

14   **for** $\gamma = 0: 1: \delta$ **do**

15        $Z^{(\varphi,\gamma)} = G^{(\varphi,\gamma)}D^{(\varphi,\gamma)}$

16 **for** $b = 0: 1: B$ **do**

17   **for** $c' = 0: 1: C'$ **do**

18   **for** $\alpha = 0: 1: X$ **do**

19   **for** $\beta = 0: 1: \Delta$ **do**

20   Gather z from matrices Z: $z_{\varphi,\gamma} = Z^{(\varphi,\gamma)}_{c',b,\alpha,\beta}$

21            $F_{b,c',\alpha,\beta} = IFFT(z)$

---

3   Algorithm and Optimizations

This section gives an overview of our FFT-based convolution algorithm, and presents our optimizations.

3.1   Algorithm Overview

FFT and IFFT operations in FFT-based convolution only involve the Fourier transformation between real and complex numbers. For the Fourier transformation of real numbers, the Hermitian symmetry shows that only half of the complex numbers need to be stored and the remaining can be acquired by complex conjugation [15]. Thus, we can apply the symmetry to reduce the memory space requirement and computation of complex matrix multiplications.

In order to call the complex general matrix multiplication (CGEMM) routines, elements of the FFT results should be scattered to non-adjacent storage locations. There are packing operations in the CGEMM routines, which reorganize the data in the order of access. Both the scattering and packing operations are often expensive. Thus, we can combine these two data movement operations above to further reduce memory overhead. In other words, the results of FFT can be directly scattered in the order of access in complex matrix multiplication implementations.

Algorithm 2 shows the overview of our parallel FFT-based convolution implementation, which still consists of four stages: FFT transforms of input feature maps and filters, complex matrix multiplications, and IFFT transforms of output feature maps. All four stages are vectorized and parallelized by multiple threads. The FFT results of input feature maps and filters are carefully stored in accordance with the order of access in complex matrix multiplications, so that the efficiency of memory access is greatly improved.

3.2   Data Layout

In this paper, we mainly focus on BCHW data layout. Therefore, the input and output data layout in our implementation is consistent with that in Algorithm 1, and we only need to consider how internal tensors in our implementation are stored in memory. There are mainly three internal tensors for storing the results of two Fourier transformations and one complex matrix multiplication, marked as transformed inputs D, transformed filters G, and transformed outputs Z. The data layout is influenced by two primary factors. The one is the loading order of elements in the complex matrix multiplications. The other is that the space range of memory access should be minimized to get better space locality. Under the two constraints above, we store three internal tensors as $D[\delta^2/S][C/C_{l1}][B/B_r][X \times \Delta][C_{l1}][B_r][S]$, $G[\delta^2/S][C/C_{l1}][C'/C_r'][C_{l1}][C_r'][S]$, and $Z[C'/C_r'][B/B_r][X \times \Delta][\delta^2/S][B_r][C_r'][S]$, where S is the granularity of scattering and gathering operations, and C_{l1}, C_r' and B_r are the block sizes in the complex matrix multiplications, which will be explained in Sect. 3.4.

Algorithm 2: Parallel FFT-based Convolution Algorithm.

---

    input: I, F

    output: O

1 $\delta \times \delta$ is the tile size.

2 $X \times \Delta$ is the number of tiles in each feature map.

3 S is the granularity of scattering and gathering operations.

4 L is the vector register width, given a specific datatype.

5 B_r, C'_r, C_{l1} and C'_{l2} are the block sizes in complex matrix multiplications.

6 z', g' and d' are the sub-tensors of the tensors Z, G and D.

7 **for** $cs' = 0$: C'_r: C' **do in parallel**

8   **for** $cs = 0$: L: C **do in parallel**

9   **for** $cofs = 0$: 1: L **do**

10   **for** $cofs' = 0$: 1: C'_r **do**

11          $c' = cs' + cofs'$, $c = cs + cofs$

12          $g = FFT^*(F_{c',c})$

13   Scatter g to matrices G;

14 **for** $bs = 0$: B_r: B **do in parallel**

15   **for** $cs = 0$: L: C **do in parallel**

16   **for** $\mu = 0$: 1: $X \times \Delta$ **do**

17   **for** $cofs = 0$: 1: L **do**

18   **for** $bofs = 0$: 1: B_r **do**

19            $b = bs + bofs$, $c = cs + cofs$

20            $d = FFT(I_{b,c,\mu})$

21   Scatter d to matrices D

22 **for** $\varphi = 0$: 1: δ^2/S **do**

23   **for** $cs = 0$: C_{l1}: C **do**

24   **for** $cs' = 0$: C'_{l2}: C' **do in parallel**

25   **for** $bs = 0$: B_r: B **do in parallel**

26   **for** $\mu = 0$: 1: $X \times \Delta$ **do in parallel**

27   **for** $cofs' = 0$: C'_r: C'_{l2} **do**

                // Micro-kernel

28              $z'[B_r][C'_r][S] += \sum_{c=cs}^{cs+C_{l1}} g'_c[C'_r][S] \times d'_c[B_r][S]$

29   store z' back to matrices Z

30 **for** $cs' = 0$: C'_r: C' **do in parallel**

31   **for** $bs = 0$: B_r: B **do in parallel**

32   **for** $\alpha = 0$: 1: X **do**

33   **for** $\beta = 0$: 1: Δ **do**

34   **for** $bofs = 0$: 1: B_r **do**

35   **for** $cofs' = 0$: 1: C'_r **do**

36              $c' = cs' + cofs'$, $b = bs + bofs$

37   Gather z from matrices Z

38              $O_{b,c',\alpha,\beta} = IFFT(z)$

3.3 Fourier Transformations

In FFT transforms, D and G are calculated from input feature maps I and filters F. The spatial dimensions of input feature maps are subdivided into 2D tiles of size $\delta \times \delta$, each of which has δ^2 elements. There are a total of $X \times \Delta$ tiles per feature map. The discrete Fourier basis is set to be δ. The Radix-2 Cooley-Tukey algorithm [2] is applied to implement FFT transform of each 2D tile, and δ is chosen to be a power of 2. When the width and height of some tiles are not powers of 2, zeros are padded to their boundaries. As the padding and transformation overhead increase with the size of zero padding [9], δ can not be set much larger than the spatial dimensions H_f and W_f of F, which are often small. As a result, FFT transform of each tile cannot provide sufficient parallelism for thread-level parallelism. In Algorithm 2, we deal with FFT transform of each tile by vectorization and apply multiple threads to perform FFT transform of different tiles in parallel. For the transformation of I, the thread-level parallelization is performed on the dimensions of the mini-batch size and input channels. For the transformation of F, the thread-level parallelization is carried out on the dimensions of the input and output channels.

Given a specific datatype, the vector register width in ARMv8 CPUs is labeled as L. In the detailed implementation of 2D FFTs, δ-point 1D FFTs of every L columns are first carried out in parallel by means of vector units in ARMv8 CPUs. Due to the Hermitian symmetry, only $\delta/2 - 1$ complex numbers and 2 real numbers need to be saved for the δ-point 1D FFT of each column, and then δ-point 1D FFTs of only $\delta/2$ rows need to be done. In order to avoid matrix transpose operation, the vectorization is directly applied to δ-point 1D FFT of each row. Finally, only $\delta^2/2 - 2$ complex numbers and 4 real numbers are required to be stored. As δ is small, the number of twiddle factors is also small, and their values are encoded into the implementation.

In IFFT transforms, output feature maps O are computed from the result Z of complex matrix multiplications. 2D IFFTs are applied to the tiles, each of which is gathered from Z and includes $\delta^2/2 - 2$ complex numbers and 4 real numbers, and produce the tiles of $\delta \times \delta$ real numbers, which are stored back to the corresponding locations of O. For the data layout of Z, the purpose of setting the dimension δ^2/S to be the inner dimension of $X \times \Delta$, rather than the outer dimension of C'/C'_r, is to reduce the overhead of gather operations above. Like the implementations of FFTs, we only exploit vector-level parallelism in 2D IFFT of each tile, and enforce thread-level task parallelization on the dimensions of the mini-batch size and output channels.

3.4   Complex Matrix Multiplications

As the transforms of input feature maps and filters have stored their outputs in the order of access in complex matrix multiplications, there is no packing in this implementation. The mini-batch size and the number of output channels are often small, so vector units are used to compute multiple complex matrix multiplications and the blocking in δ^2 is used to provide vector-level parallelism. In this way, the scattering and gathering overhead in the transforms can be reduced by a factor of the block size $S/2$.

The ARMv8 architecture often has the on-chip memory hierarchy of at least three levels: register, level-1 (L1) cache and level-2 (L2) cache. It is essential to improve data reuse in every level by means of blocking techniques [5]. The matrices G, D and Z are subdivided into sub-matrices of size $C_{l1} \times C'_r \times S$, $C_{l1} \times B_r \times S$ and $B_r \times C'_r \times S$, respectively. In one case, S elements of the innermost dimension include four real numbers and $S/2 - 2$ complex numbers. In all the left cases, they only consist of $S/2$ complex numbers. Each sub-matrix z' is computed as follows:

$$z'_{i,j}[S] + = \sum_{c=cs'}^{cs'+C_{l1}} g'_{c,j}[S] \times d'_{c,i}[S] \tag{5}$$

where $i \in [0, B_r)$ and $j \in [0, C'_r)$. In register level, the sub-matrix z' can be reused C_{l1} times. There are $C'_r \times S/L$ registers for g', $B'_r \times S/L$ registers for d' and $B'_r \times C'_r \times S/L$ registers for z', so that the block sizes C'_r, B_r and S are dependent on the number of available vector registers Υ in the ARMv8 architecture as follows:

$$\frac{C'_r \times S}{L} + \frac{B_r \times S}{L} + \frac{B_r \times C'_r \times S}{L} \leq \Upsilon \tag{6}$$

At the same time, all the three sub-matrices above should be filled into L1 cache so that the block size C_{l1} is restricted by the size of L1 cache. In most cases, the ratio Ψ between computation and memory access [5] can be obtained via

$$\Psi = \frac{4 \times C'_r \times C_{l1} \times B_r}{C'_r \times C_{l1} + (2 \times C'_r + C_{l1}) \times B_r}. \tag{7}$$

Then, the ratio should be as high as possible, under the constraints above. The computation of each sub-matrix z' is called a micro-kernel of the complex matrix multiplications. The outer loops of the micro-kernels are arranged in an order that maximizes data reuse in L1 and L2 Cache. As shown at lines 22–29 in Algorithm 2, we choose to reuse G and D in L1 and L2 cache, respectively. The block size C_{l2} determines how many times sub-matrices g' are reused in L1 Cache and is also limited by the size of L2 Cache. The time locality of D in L2 Cache is dependent on the size of $B/B_r \times X \times \Delta$.

There are thirty-two vector registers in the ARMv8 architecture. Each vector register can keep four single-precision floating-point numbers. For the micro-kernels, we set S, B_r, and C'_r to be 8, 2 and 4, respectively. All the micro-kernels are implemented in assembly. When the sub-matrices g' and d' includes real numbers, the data movement operations among vector registers are minimized via zeroing some registers in advance. Cache prefetch instructions are interleaved with FMA instructions to request data ahead of time. The thread-level parallelism is extracted from the three loops at lines 24–26 in Algorithm 2, which usually can provide sufficient parallelism.

4 Experimental Results

This section describes the experimental comparisons between our FFT-based convolution implementation and two existing implementations on two ARMv8-based multi-core CPUs.

4.1   Experimental Setup

The experiments are carried out on Phytium FT-1500A [1,12] and FT-2000plus [13] processors. The detailed parameters of these two CPUs are listed in Table 1.

Our FFT-based convolution implementation is compared with two existing implementations. The one is a GEMM-based approach used in Caffe [7], which converts convolution operation of B samples in the mini-batch iteration into B matrix multiplications. Therefore, the approach calls the GEMM routine B times, which is provided by the OpenBLAS library optimized for Phytium FT-1500A and FT-2000plus in the experiment. The other is one FFT-based convolution implementation provided by NNPACK [3]. In the following, our implementation and these two existing implementations are labeled as PFFT-conv, Caffe-conv and NNPACK, respectively. Two tile sizes, 8 × 8 and 16 × 16, are involved in PFFT-conv and NNPACK.

Table 1. Specifications of the experiment platforms

	Phytium FT-1500 A	Phytium FT-2000plus
Architecture	ARMv8	ARMv8
Frequency	1.5 GHz	2.3 GHz
Cores	16	8 Panels, 8 cores/Panel
L1 Data Cache	32 KB/core	32 KB/core
L2 Cache	2 MB/4 cores	2 MB/4 cores
L3 Cache	8 MB/16 cores	

We adopt 13 unique convolutional layers with unit stride from Alexnet [8] and VGG [14] in the tests. The configurations of all convolutional layers are listed in Table 2. The convolutional layers from Alexnet start with the letter A, while the ones from VGG are labeled with the letter V. The mini-batch size for all convolutional layers is 128. In addition, all the tests are iterated ten times and the median run-time is token as the performance of a test.

4.2   Results on FT-1500A

The relative performance of our parallel FFT-based convolution implementation based on Caffe-conv and NNPACK implementations on Phytium FT-1500A is shown in Fig. 1 and Fig. 2. In the comparison, all three implementations are parallelized on all 16 cores of FT-1500A. The column bars at different horizontal coordinates represent speedups on different convolutional layers from Alexnet and VGG.

Compared with Caffe-conv, our approach with the tiles of sizes 16 × 16 and 8 × 8 achieves the speedups of 1.87–16.19 and 1.48–13.34 times, respectively. The

Table 2. Specifications of tested convolutonal layers

Conv layers	B	C	C'	$H_i \times W_i$	$H_f \times W_f$
Aconv2	128	48	128	27×27	5×5
Aconv3	128	256	384	13×13	3×3
Aconv4	128	192	192	13×13	3×3
Aconv5	128	192	128	13×13	3×3
Vconv1.1	128	3	64	224×224	3×3
Vconv1.2	128	64	64	224×224	3×3
Vconv2.1	128	64	128	112×112	3×3
Vconv2.2	128	128	128	112×112	3×3
Vconv3.1	128	128	256	56×56	3×3
Vconv3.2	128	256	256	56×56	3×3
Vconv4.1	128	256	512	28×28	3×3
Vconv4.1	128	512	512	28×28	3×3
Vconv5.1	128	512	512	14×14	3×3

minimum speedups of both two tile sizes are observed on the first convolutional layer of VGG (Vconv1.1) owing to the smallest number of input channels. Except for Vconv1.1, our approach gets the speedup of at least 2.78 times. For all the tested convolutional layers, our implementation with 16×16 tile exceeds the one with 8×8 tile.

Based on the FFT-based implementation with the 16×16 and 8×8 tiles in NNPACK, our implementation with the tiles of the same sizes obtains the speedups of 1.36–1.95 and 1.00–2.16 times, respectively. For the same 16×16 tile, our implementation surpasses the FFT-based one in NNPACK on all the layers. Except for the second convolutional layer of Alexnet, our approach with the tile of size 8×8 gets higher performance than the implementation with the same tile size in NNPACK.

4.3 Results on FT-2000plus

The performance comparison between our parallel FFT-based implementation and two existing implementations (Caffe-conv and NNPACK) on Phytium FT-2000plus is shown in Fig. 3 and 4, respectively. FT-2000plus is a Non-Uniform Memory Access (NUMA) system, and includes eight panels, each of which has eight cores. In the comparison, all the tests are parallelized on all 64 cores of FT-2000plus, and the linux tool *numactl* is applied to interleave memory allocation on all eight panels automatically.

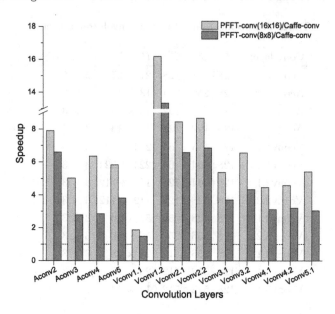

Fig. 1. Speedup of our parallel FFT-based convolution implementation (PFFT-conv) based on GEMM-based implementation (Caffe-conv) on all 16 cores of Phytium FT-1500A.

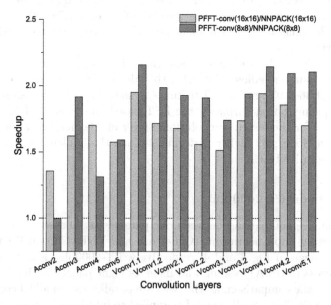

Fig. 2. Speedup of our parallel FFT-based convolution algorithm (PFFT-conv) based on FFT-based implementation in NNPACK (NNAPCK) on all 16 cores of Phytium FT-1500A.

For all the convolutional layers, our implementation is much better than Caffe-conv, as shown in Fig. 3. Against Caffe-conv, our implementation with two tile sizes gets the speedups of 5.35–50.88 and 3.86–78.08 times, which are caused by two main factors. The one is that the matrices produced by Caffe-conv are too small to provide sufficient parallelism for all 64 cores of FT-2000plus and the GEMM routines are not optimized for those matrices. The other is that the memory access of Caffe-conv is not efficient enough [17] and its efficiency further deteriorates on the NUMA structure of FT-2000plus. Due to the influence of the NUMA structure, our implementation with 16×16 tile works worse than the one with 8×8 tile on most convolutional layers.

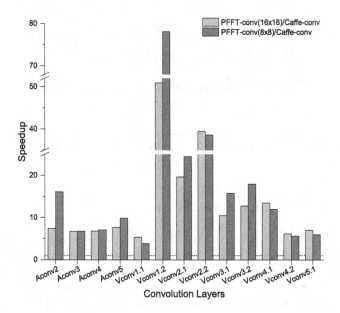

Fig. 3. Speedup of our parallel FFT-based convolution implementation (PFFT-conv) based on SGEMM-based implementation (Caffe-conv) on all 64 cores of Phytium FT-2000plus.

As shown in Fig. 3, our implementation with two tile sizes gets the maximum speedups of 5.91 and 7.04 times based on NNPACK with the same tile sizes, respectively. In addition, our approach is better than NNPACK on all the tested convolutional layers.

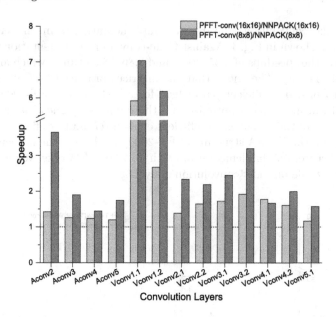

Fig. 4. Speedup of our parallel FFT-based convolution algorithm (PFFT-conv) based on FFT-based implementation in NNPACK (NNAPCK) on all 64 cores of Phytium FT-2000plus.

5 Conclusion and Future Work

In this paper, we have presented a parallel FFT-based convolution implementation on ARMv8 multi-core CPUs, which targets unit-stride convolutional layers with BCHW data layout. Our implementation does not rely on any external computing libraries and consists of four stages: FFT transforms of input feature maps and filters, complex matrix multiplications, and IFFT transforms of output feature maps. Each of all four stages above is vectorized and partitioned to multiple cores in ARMv8 multi-core CPUs. A part of data movement operations in four stages are merged so that the efficiency of memory access is greatly improved. Our implementation now supports two tiles of sizes 16×16 and 8×8, and is verified on Phytium FT-1500A and FT-2000plus processors. For all the tested convolutional layers on two processors, our approach is much better than the GEMM-based one used in Caffe. On FT-1500A, our implementation surpasses the FFT-based one of NNPACK in most cases. On FT-2000plus, our approach is much better than the FFT-based one of NNPACK in all test cases.

In the future, we will focus on the implementation that supports more tile sizes and can automatically determine the optimal tile size.

References

1. Chen, X., Xie, P., Chi, L., Liu, J., Gong, C.: An efficient simd compression format for sparse matrix-vector multiplication. Concurr. Comput.: Pract. Experience **30**(23), e4800 (2018)
2. Cooley, J.W., Tukey, J.W.: An algorithm for the machine calculation of complex fourier series. Math. Comput. **19**(90), 297–301 (1965)
3. Dukhan, M.: NNPACK (2019). https://github.com/Maratyszcza/NNPACK. Accessed 3 Jan 2019
4. Goodfellow, I., Bengio, Y., Courville, A.: Deep Learning. MIT Press, Cambridge (2016)
5. Goto, K., Geijn, R.A.V.D.: Anatomy of high-performance matrix multiplication. ACM Trans. Math. Softw. (TOMS) **34**(3), 12 (2008)
6. He, K., Zhang, X., Ren, S., Sun, J.: Delving deep into rectifiers: surpassing human-level performance on imagenet classification. In: Proceedings of the IEEE International Conference on Computer Vision, pp. 1026–1034 (2015)
7. Jia, Y., et al.: Caffe: convolutional architecture for fast feature embedding. In: Proceedings of the 22nd ACM International Conference on Multimedia, pp. 675–678. ACM (2014)
8. Krizhevsky, A., Sutskever, I., Hinton, G.E.: Imagenet classification with deep convolutional neural networks. In: Advances in Neural Information Processing Systems, pp. 1097–1105 (2012)
9. Lavin, A., Gray, S.: Fast algorithms for convolutional neural networks. In: Proceedings of the IEEE Conference on Computer Vision and Pattern Recognition, pp. 4013–4021 (2016)
10. Li, S., Dou, Y., Niu, X., Lv, Q., Wang, Q.: A fast and memory saved gpu acceleration algorithm of convolutional neural networks for target detection. Neurocomputing **230**, 48–59 (2017)
11. Mathieu, M., Henaff, M., Lecun, Y.: Fast training of convolutional networks through FFTS. In: International Conference on Learning Representations (ICLR2014), CBLS, April 2014 (2014)
12. Phytium: FT-1500A/16 (2020). http://www.phytium.com.cn/Product/detail?language=1&product_id=9. Accessed 3 Jan 2020
13. Phytium: FT-2000plus/64 (2020). http://www.phytium.com.cn/Product/detail?language=1&product_id=7. Accessed 3 Jan 2020
14. Simonyan, K., Zisserman, A.: Very deep convolutional networks for large-scale image recognition. arXiv preprint arXiv:1409.1556 (2014)
15. Vasilache, N., Johnson, J., Mathieu, M., Chintala, S., Piantino, S., LeCun, Y.: Fast convolutional nets with FBFFT: a GPU performance evaluation. In: 3rd International Conference on Learning Representations, ICLR 2015, Conference Track Proceedings, San Diego, CA, USA, 7–9 May 2015 (2015)
16. Wang, Q., Li, D., Mei, S., Lai, Z., Dou, Y.: Optimizing winograd-based fast convolution algorithm on phytium multi-core CPUs (in Chinese). J. Comput. Res. Dev. **57**(6), 1140–1151 (2020). https://doi.org/10.7544/issn1000-1239.2020.20200107
17. Wang, Q., Songzhu, M., Liu, J., Gong, C.: Parallel convolution algorithm using implicit matrix multiplication on multi-core CPUs. In: 2019 International Joint Conference on Neural Networks (IJCNN), pp. 1–7, July 2019. https://doi.org/10.1109/IJCNN.2019.8852012
18. Zhang, J., Franchetti, F., Low, T.M.: High performance zero-memory overhead direct convolutions. In: International Conference on Machine Learning, pp. 5771–5780 (2018)

19. Zlateski, A., Jia, Z., Li, K., Durand, F.: FFT convolutions are faster than winograd on modern CPUs, here is why. arXiv preprint arXiv:1809.07851 (2018)
20. Zlateski, A., Lee, K., Seung, H.S.: ZNN-a fast and scalable algorithm for training 3D convolutional networks on multi-core and many-core shared memory machines. In: 2016 IEEE International Parallel and Distributed Processing Symposium (IPDPS), pp. 801–811. IEEE (2016)
21. Zlateski, A., Lee, K., Seung, H.S.: ZNN i: maximizing the inference throughput of 3d convolutional networks on CPUs and GPUs. In: Proceedings of the International Conference for High Performance Computing, Networking, Storage and Analysis, p. 73. IEEE Press (2016)

Maximizing I/O Bandwidth for Reverse Time Migration on Heterogeneous Large-Scale Systems

Tariq Alturkestani$^{(\boxtimes)}$, Hatem Ltaief, and David Keyes

Extreme Computing Research Center,
King Abdullah University of Science and Technology, Thuwal, Saudi Arabia
{tariq.alturkestani,hatem.ltaief,david.keyes}@kaust.edu.sa

Abstract. Reverse Time Migration (RTM) is an important scientific application for oil and gas exploration. The 3D RTM simulation generates terabytes of intermediate data that does not fit in main memory. In particular, RTM has two successive computational phases, i.e., the forward modeling and the backward propagation, that necessitate to write and then to read the state of the computed solution grid at specific time steps of the time integration. Advances in memory architecture have made it feasible and affordable to integrate hierarchical storage media on large-scale systems, starting from the traditional Parallel File Systems (PFS) to intermediate fast disk technologies (e.g., node-local and remote-shared Burst Buffer) and up to CPU main memory. To address the trend of heterogeneous HPC systems deployment, we introduce an extension to our Multilayer Buffer System (MLBS) framework to further maximize RTM I/O bandwidth in presence of GPU hardware accelerators. The main idea is to leverage the GPU's High Bandwidth Memory (HBM) as an additional storage media layer. The objective of MLBS is ultimately to hide the application's I/O overhead by enabling a buffering mechanism operating across all the hierarchical storage media layers. MLBS is therefore able to sustain the I/O bandwidth at each storage media layer. By asynchronously performing expensive I/O operations and creating opportunities for overlapping data motion with computations, MLBS may transform the original I/O bound behavior of the RTM application into a compute-bound regime. In fact, the prefetching strategy of MLBS allows the RTM application to believe that it has access to a larger memory capacity on the GPU, while transparently performing the necessary housekeeping across the storage layers. We demonstrate the effectiveness of MLBS on the *Summit* supercomputer using 2048 compute nodes equipped with a total of 12288 GPUs by achieving up to 1.4X performance speedup compared to the reference PFS-based RTM implementation for large 3D solution grid.

Keywords: Multilayer Buffer System · Reverse Time Migration · Asynchronous I/O operations · Hierarchical storage media · Heterogeneous systems

© Springer Nature Switzerland AG 2020
M. Malawski and K. Rzadca (Eds.): Euro-Par 2020, LNCS 12247, pp. 263–278, 2020.
https://doi.org/10.1007/978-3-030-57675-2_17

1   Introduction

The execution rate of floating-point operations has typically increased by an order of magnitude every 4 years during the last 30 years of modern computing [4]. This exponential growth in terms of computational power has benefited from processor technology scaling. However, memory and storage systems have not maintained the same rate of technology scaling. Scientific applications that are traditionally compute-bound have undergone a paradigm shift toward an I/O-bound regime. This has been further exacerbated by the limited on-node memory capacity, where I/O operations become a major bottleneck for scaling up critical simulations.

Performing I/O operations is usually necessary for post-processing tasks (e.g., visualization [12]) or for checkpointing the entire application's state (e.g., resilience [16]). For seismic depth imaging simulations in the context of oil and gas exploration, I/O operations play a pivotal role and one that is increasing with the technology scaling gap. The challenge with Reverse Time Migration (RTM), the *de facto* method for subsurface imaging, resides in continuously intertwining computational phases with I/O operations during the time integration.

Based on an adjoint-state formulation, the RTM relies on a finite difference stencil time integration explicit solver to simulate the forward and backward 3D wave propagations. RTM requires combining at regular time steps a forward-propagated source wavefield with a backward-propagated receiver wavefield. This process involves thus a first phase where the 3D domain solutions, or snapshots, of the source wavefield are computed and stored at predetermined imaging time steps. Then, in a second phase, the field data are injected at the receiver locations to compute the receiver wavefield. At each imaging time step, the source snapshots are retrieved from storage, brought in to main memory, and correlated with the receiver snapshots. The combination of the correlated snapshots results in the final image. RTM runs typically for thousands of time steps in production and thus requires out-of-core computations [27] since not all subsequent snapshots can be kept in main memory. To give the proper perspective, we profile representative test cases from a seismic imaging campaign: the I/O time spent during the two aforementioned phases account for about 70% of the entire execution time. The overall RTM performance may therefore be mostly driven by I/O storage subsystem bandwidth. Nor is this I/O dominance special to RTM. As described in [21], in monitoring over 17,000 executions of an earth science code on a DOE petascale system, more than half of the wall-clock time was spent on I/O.

Previously deployed large-scale systems include several layers of hardware storage media, from Dynamic Random Access Memory (DRAM) to node-local /remote-shared Burst Buffer [11,19] to traditional Parallel File Systems (PFS), and all the way down to storage disks. More recently, especially with the advent of AI workloads, GPU-based supercomputers have been considered as one of the main sources of horsepower for the Exascale quest. In this paper, we propose to extend the Multilayered Buffer Storage (MLBS) software library [6] to support I/O operations involved in GPU application workloads. The objective of Multi-layer Buffer System (MLBS) is to maximize the bandwidth utilization of multiple hardware storage media layers, while prefetching the I/O operations for possible overlap with computations. The main idea herein consists of including the High Bandwidth Memories (HBMs) as an additional storage media layer to MLBS. In the context of the RTM application, this means the write (i.e., modeling phase) and read (i.e., propagation phase) operations may potentially be overlapped with the stencil computation kernels running on the GPU devices. In fact, the ultimate goal of the MLBS approach is to ensure that the data is always GPU-resident whenever the RTM needs it in order to mitigate the overhead of out-of-core computations. Our lightweight, non-intrusive MLBS framework provides simple APIs that enable the RTM application to decouple these I/O operations from its critical path, while eagerly pursuing its forward and backward time integration.

We demonstrate the performance superiority of the RTM application with MLBS using 2048 compute nodes, i.e., a total of 12288 NVIDIA V100 GPUs, on the *Summit* supercomputer. By using the GPU's HMBs as an additional storage media layer, we report up to 1.4X performance speedup compared to the reference Parallel File System (PFS)-based RTM implementation for large 3D solution grid, respectively. Last but not least, we provide an online autotuner for MLBS to select at runtime the optimal storage media layers to maximize the overall I/O throughput.

The remainder of the paper is as follows. Section 2 discusses background on high performance storage media and related work. Section 3 states our main contributions. Section 4 gives details on the RTM application. Section 5 highlights the design and implementation of the MLBS GPU support. Section 6 analyzes the performance results of the MLBS-enabled RTM application on homogeneous and heterogeneous systems, i.e., *Shaheen-2* and *Summit* systems, respectively. Section 7 summarizes the paper and describes future work.

2   Background and Related Work

Burst Buffers and High Bandwidth Memory. Due to the importance of closing the gap between I/O and compute throughput, several production supercomputers are currently equipped with high bandwidth intermediate memory and storage subsystems, e.g., High Bandwidth Memory (HBM), DRAM and Burst Buffer (BB) [20]. In particular, many supercomputers are now composed of heterogeneous compute nodes that host multiple Central Processing Units (CPUs) equipped with General Processor Units (GPUs), as seen in Fig. 1. While most of the parallel storage systems in supercomputers are built with cost-effective, low-bandwidth, high-capacity spinning Hard Disk Drives (HDDs), Burst Buffers are built with more expensive but high-bandwidth, low-capacity Solid State Drive (SSD) or Non-Volatile Memory (NVMe) [2]. The two most common types of Burst Buffers are node-local and remote-shared. In the design of the former, as shown in Fig. 1(a), each node is equipped with a local SSDs or NVMe with limited capacity. In the design of the latter, as pictured in Fig. 1(b), arrays of SSDs or NVMe are grouped in separate Burst Buffer nodes. These

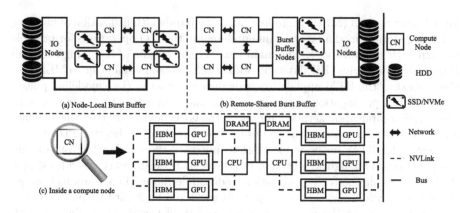

Fig. 1. Designs of (a) Remote-Shared and (b) Node-Local Burst Buffer (c) Heterogeneous compute node similar to *Summit* system.

Burst Buffer nodes are located on the interconnect fabric and compute nodes can access them through the network. For instance, on *Summit* supercomputer, each compute node has 6 NVIDIA V100 GPUs with a local 1.6 TiB NVMe, as highlighted in Fig. 1(c). On *Shaheen-2* supercomputer, all compute nodes share 1.5 PiT of distributed high bandwidth SSDs located on the remote Burst Buffer nodes.

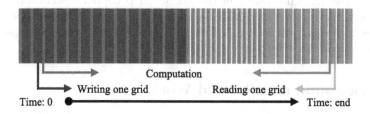

Fig. 2. Observed compute and I/O traces for a master iteration of RTM using *Shaheen-2* supercomputer with Lustre Parallel file system. Red and pink are forward and backward computation, respectively. Blue and green show the write and read I/O operations, respectively. (Color figure onlie)

Runtime Opportunities for Compute and I/O Overlap. In Fig. 2, we provide a typical execution trace of the RTM application, which alternates each compute and I/O phase. In the forward phase, the application computes several iterations before triggering the I/O library to dump the grid solution. The library then conducts the actual writes to the closest storage media (e.g., HBM) before falling back to the next closest storage media (e.g., DRAM) in case the current storage media is full. Once the forward phase is over, in the backward simulation and imaging phase, the application reads back previously written grids in Last In, First Out (LIFO) order and computes the so-called imaging condition at the same time step during the forward phase. Red and pink colored bars represent compute times for forward and backward phases, and blue and green represent write and read, respectively. We can clearly observe how the backward phase reads may be faster in the beginning since the latest snapshots may already be cached. But then, they eventually become slower due to snapshot cache misses. The objective is to overlap the red and pink bars with the blue and green bars to speed up the overall time to solution.

Current Solutions. There are many system-level and hardware-level solutions to reduce the widening performance gap between I/O and compute operations. Many HPC centers have adopted multiple storage layers in their systems. Ranging from HBM to node-local and remote-shared NVMes and SSDs, these layers are helping to reduce the performance gap between I/O and compute operations. Systems such as BurstFS and BurstMem [33,34] propose to redirect I/O calls from PFS to local NVMes and SSDs. Burst Buffer caching systems such as DDN IME [1], DataWarp [15], and Data Elevator [13] accelerate applications writes by redirecting writes from PFS to remote-shared Burst Buffers. GPUDirect Storage [29] is a recently proposed system that moves data between GPUs and a specific local or remote storage without involving the CPU's memory, thereby removing the need for extra data copies. Other systems such as SSDalloc, NVMalloc [9,31] extend the virtual memory space from DRAM only to a wider range of fast memory such as fast SSD and NVMe. Systems in [17,25] have been proposed to show the benefit providing hints for read prefetchers in I/O libraries. GPUfs [28] is a file system that extends traditional file systems and enables asynchronous date swaps between GPUs memory and their internal I/O buffers. More recent works such as Hermes [18], UniviStor [32] and ARCHIE [14] provide buffering solution across all stages of storage layers. They use dedicated processes to perform the caching and prefetching. TB-RTM [5] is an approach that relies on StarPU [8] to taskify and overlap all routines of RTM applications, including I/O operations. Since it is application-oblivious, it does not take advantage of the First In, First Out (FIFO) and LIFO patterns seen in the RTM application.

In contrast to previous work, MLBS is a software-level library solution that consists in overlapping I/O and compute for out-of-core simulations. MLBS provide a holistic solution to enhance the time-to-solution of real multi-threaded distributed-memory GPU-based scientific applications such as RTM using both write behind [7] and prefetching mechanisms. These optimizations permit to stream data across several stacked memory/storage layers (i.e., HBM/DRAM /Burst Buffer (BB)/PFS), while maximizing the throughput at each encountered hardware layer. MLBS is able to properly balance the I/O and compute loads, with minimal and controlled impact on the application computation phases.

3   Contributions

The main contributions of this paper are as follows:

- We introduce the GPU support in MLBS for caching and prefetching I/O operations, in the context of the RTM application.
- We add support for HMBs as a new storage media layer, in addition to the CPU main memory and various BB layers, i.e., node-local and remote-shared, and evaluate its performance impact.
- We evaluate the MLBS scalability on homogeneous *Shaheen-2* and heterogeneous *Summit* systems using up to 2048 compute nodes.
- We deploy an online autotuner into MLBS that monitors and reorders the different storage layers based on their sustained I/O bandwidth.

4   Seismic Depth Imaging Application

High resolution depth images of the subsurface are critical for successful oil and gas exploration. Wave equation-based depth seismic migration techniques such as Reverse Time Migration (RTM) are often employed to meet the oil industry imaging objectives, particularly in complex geological environments such as subsalt exploration. Given a model of the subsurface and seismic data recorded at known receiver locations, an image of the subsurface is formed by combining with an imaging condition, a forward propagated source wavefield with a backward propagated receiver wavefield. Reviews of seismic migration techniques and imaging conditions can be found in [10, 26]. The source and receiver wavefields are computed by solving the wave equation using time or frequency domain solvers. Time domain finite differences solvers are commonly used due to their simplicity and computational efficiency. Second to fourth order stencils are usually considered to compute time derivatives and spatial derivatives are computed using up to sixteenth order stencils. The RTM image is formed by cross-correlating the forward simulated source wavefield with an adjoint (i.e., reverse-time) simulation from receivers. In a first phase, the source wavefield is reversed in time by storing at predetermined imaging time steps (snapshots) the propagation history. Due to the huge volume represented by the snapshots, they are usually offloaded to disks. In a second phase, when the backward receiver propagation reaches one of the imaging time steps, the corresponding source snapshots are read back from disk, and correlated with the receiver snapshots to incrementally calculate the image condition, until the final image is eventually obtained. RTM usually suffers from I/O performance bottlenecks due to unnecessary system synchronizations, which prevent overlapping with computations. The main idea then consists in creating two swim lanes by decoupling the I/O operations from the computational kernels. The final image is formed by combining the image contribution from several seismic gathers which are simultaneously simulated in an embarrassingly parallel fashion.

5   Design and Implementation of a Multilayered Buffer System

MLBS handles all I/O requests for the RTM application while maintaining the following goals: 1) lightweight Application Program Interface (API), 2) overlapping I/O and compute phases using asynchronous executions, 3) prefetching across multi storage layers with minimal impact on the computation kernels. The design of MLBS relies on two components: an API, memory and storage interfaces, and a helper thread engine. MLBS is written in C++ and CUDA and is deployed as a light-wight library.

Application Interface. The main objectives of the MLBS APIs are ease-of-use, non-intrusiveness and high throughput copy from application space to the fastest layer allocation in MLBS space. MLBS uses a simple API that mimics C/C++'s **write()** and **read()** interfaces. Therefore, with minimal code changes, application developers can easily integrate MLBS into their codes. The API requires two inputs from the application at the initialization stage: 1) the size of each data file, and 2) the number of write and read requests, Once the parameters are set, the helper engines are spawned and start their tasks, as detailed in Algorithm 2. Higher throughput for **write()** requests is achieved with a parallel copy of the targeted data using all hardware threads whether the data were located on a CPU or a GPU (see **write** method for GPU based kernel in Algorithm 1). On the other hand, **read()** requests depend heavily on the prefetching strategy employed by the helper engines, the MLBS first layer allocation and the rate of consumption (compute kernel speed) of prefetched data. Ideally, from the application's point of view, a **read()** operation is as fast as a memory pointer swap (see **read** method in Algorithm 1).

Algorithm 1: MLBS API functions: Init, Write and Read

1   **Function** Init(*datasize, ioOps*)
2   SPAWNENGINE(*MLBSEngine, datasize, ioOps*))

3   **Function** inGPUParallelCopy(*src, dest, len*)
4   idx = threadIdx.x + blockIdx.x * blockDim.x;
5   **if** *idx* < *len* **then**
6   dest[i] = src[i]

7   **Function** Write(*filename, data, datasize*):
8   *dest* ← FINDEMPTYSLOTINHBM()   // blocking call
            // GPU based parallel memory to memory copy. Similar method is used on CPUs
9   INGPUCOPY<<<DIMGRID,DIMBLOCK>>>(data, dest, datasize)

10 **Function** Read(*filename, data, datasize*):
11   **while** *file is not yet loaded in MLBS HBM*   // blocking busy loop
12   **do**
13   WAIT( )

14   *src* ← GETFILEPOINTER(*filename*)
15   SWAP(*src, data*)

Helper Threads. The objective of the helpers is to handle all I/O operations: 1) moving the data between the application space and MLBS space, 2) conducting the actual push and pull operations on all available memory and storage layers, 3) moving data across storage layers such as HBM, DRAM and PFS from fastest to slowest, and 4) caching in and out data based on RTM grids (i.e. snapshots) access pattern. Algorithm 2 details how MLBS overlaps compute and I/O with

---

Algorithm 2: MLBS Helper Engine for RTM on *Summit* System

   Data: Size of grids, number of I/O writes and reads
1 **begin**
2   *layers* ⟵ MLBSAuto()   // At run time, survey all available memory and storage
                              // layers and create a list ranked from fastest to slowest
3   *GridsInLayers* ⟵ ...   // calculate the number of grids to keep in each layer
                              // based on grid size and available space
4   **while** *numPushedGrids* < *numGridsToPush* **do**
5   push grid to first layer
6   **if** *HBM layer (1st layer) is full* **then**
7   select oldest grid in HBM layer and push to DRAM layer
8   **if** *DRAM layer (2nd layer) is full* **then**
9   select oldest grid in DRAM layer and push to node-local BB layer
10   **if** *node-local BB layer (3rd layer) is full* **then**
11   select oldest grid in node-local BB layer and push to IBM Spectrum
                    Scale (4th) layer   // Depending on MLBS Auto survey 3rd
                              // and 4th layers could in the opposite order

12   *numPushedGrids* ⟵ *numPushedGrids* + 1

        // Switching to read mode
13   *numPulledGrids* ⟵ 0
14   **while** *numPulledGrids* ≠ *numPushedGrids* **do**
15   **if** *first layer is not full*   // Read operation in the application space frees up
        first layer buffers
16   **then**
17   **for** *i* ⟵ 1; *i* < *numOfLeyers* **do**
18   pull newest grid from $(i+1)th$ layer to *ith* layer
19   *numPulledGrids* ⟵ *numPulledGrids* + 1

LIFO data access pattern, which matches the I/O pattern of the RTM application. From the application developer's inputs, such as the total number of grids and the size of each grid, the number of write and read operations, MLBS helper can then manage the data traffic in the background, while the application carries on its computation. In particular, MLBS helper engine consists of three phases. In the first phase, the engine surveys all available memory and storage layers and creates a list of layers ranked from fastest to slowest (line 2). For example, on *Summit* system the order of BB and PFS (line 11) could be exchanged depending of the runtime sustained throughput as seen in the evaluation in Sect. 6. In the 2nd phase, the engine loops over the 1st layer of MLBS, and evicts oldest data to the next layer of MLBS, e.g., BB or PFS (line 7). It may further push down the oldest files from 2nd layer to the 3rd layer, and repeat to the last layer. In the 3rd phase, i.e., the read phase, the helper engine wait for the application to consume the data that are still in the MLBS 1st layer. As soon as a buffer slot is empty in the 1st layer, the engine fills up the buffer slot with the newest data file from the 2nd layer (line 16). It will also pop up the newest data file from the 3rd layer to the 2nd layer and repeat the same routine for all layers. MLBS maintains a full pipeline across storage layers, while maximizing I/O bandwidth and occupancy.

MLBS Integration. The RTM application presented in this work has two computation kernel engines, GPU and CPU based kernels that rely on CUDA

Algorithm 3: Integrating MLBS into RTM Code on *Summit*

Data: size of grids, number of I/O ops
1 **Function** main()
2   MLBSHandler ← MLBSINIT(*datasize*, *ioOps*)
    // setup all RTM related parameterscopy necessary RTM initial data to GPU memory
    // start forward modeling
3   **for** *i = 0 → numOfSnaps* **do**
4   INGPUCOMPUTEFWD<<<DIMGRID,DIMBLOCK>>>(data, datasize)
5   **if** *(i mod snapRatio)== 0* **then**
6   MLBSHandler.WRITE(i, data, datasize)

    // start backward propagation
7   finalImage ← EMPTYDATAARRAY(datasize)
8   **for** *i = numOfSnaps → 0* **do**
9   INGPUCOMPUTEBKW<<<DIMGRID,DIMBLOCK>>>(data, datasize)
10   **if** *(i mod snapRatio) == 0* **then**
11   MLBSHandler.READ(i, datafwd, datasize)
12   finalImage ← CORRELATE(finalImage, data, datafwd)

---

cores and OpenMP programming models for the parallel computational kernel implementation, i.e., the stencil computation kernel. MLBS uses a Pthread-based implementation for flexibility purposes. To ensure the CPU based kernel OpenMP threads and MLBS Pthreads properly coexist, the total number of threads should match the number of physical cores, which prevents oversubscription overheads. Only the single-threaded MLBS implementation is demonstrated in this paper to avoid performance slowdown on the compute kernel side, since it is part of the critical path. However, the MLBS Pthread-based implementation can support more threads. Ultimately, the makespan of the RTM should be minimized by balancing compute and I/O workloads accordingly through MLBS. Algorithm 3 presents the pseudo-code of the RTM application with MLBS API integration. This pseudo-code assumes a single shot simulation performed on a shared-memory node, without loss of generality, since multiple shots are processed in an embarrassingly parallel fashion. One observes the possible overlapping between lines 4 and 6 as well as between lines 9 and 11 during the forward and the backward integration, respectively. The final image is then generated thanks to the image condition, as shown in line 12.

Given these generic components, MLBS components may be further extended to support various applications, beyond the herein studied RTM application. Thanks to the helper threads, its API permits application developers to instrument the I/O accesses with the flexible memory interface, while customizing the helper engine to match the I/O patterns.

6   Performance Results

6.1   Hardware Settings

We have used the homogeneous Cray XC40 *Shaheen-2* and the heterogeneous IBM-built *Summit* supercomputers as our experimental platforms.

Shaheen-2 is a 6174-node system, each with a dual-socket 16-core Intel Haswell E5-2698 V3 CPU and 128 GB DRAM. *Shaheen-2* operates two PFSs, a 1.5 PiB remote-shared SSD-based DataWarp BB and a 17.6 PiB Hard Disk Drive (HDD)-based Lustre [22] . The sustained bandwidth of DRAM based on the Stream benchmark [24] is 105.9 GiB/s. The I/O bandwidth measured with the IOR benchmark [3] is 1.5 TiB/s and 500 GiB/s, for the DataWarp and Lustre, respectively.

Summit is a 4356-node system, each with a dual-socket 22-core IBM Power 9 CPU, 6 NIVIDA Volta V100 GPUs, and 512 GB DRAM. *Summit* operates two, parallel file systems, a 7.4 PiB node-local SSD-based BB and a 250 PiB HDD-based IBM Spectrum Scale file system. The sustained bandwidth of DRAM is reported to be 272.9 GiB/s [30]. The I/O bandwidth is 9.7 TiB/s and 2.5 TiB/s, for the BB and IBM Spectrum Scale, respectively.

6.2   RTM Application Setup

We evaluate MLBS performance impact on a realistic RTM code that we have developed. The code is written in C++/CUDA and uses MPI to assign each shot to a rank. The computation kernels in this research code use single-precision arithmetic and run on CPUs and/or GPUs. In this evaluation, we set the number of time steps to 2000 and we performed I/O write (in the forward phase) or read (in the backward phase) operations at every 10 time steps. We report only the I/O throughput, since the CPU and GPU kernels are not touched. Each measurement is repeated three times and the average is reported.

On *Shaheen-2*, each node works on one shot and we set the grid size of each shot to 800 × 800 × 800. We then increase the number of nodes from 1 to 2048. With a total of 200 snapshots per shot, each node writes to storage 368 GiB of intermediate data in order to produce the desired seismic image. When 2048 shots are dispatched a total of 772.52 TiB is written to storage.

On *Summit*, each node works on 6 shots simultaneously and we set the grid size of each shot to 700 × 700 × 700. We then increase the number of node from 1 to 2048. With a total of 200 snapshots per shot, each node writes to storage 2.3 TiB of intermediate data in order to produce the desired seismic image. When 12, 288 shots are dispatched a total of 2.6 PiB is written to storage.

Additionally on *Summit* system, using one compute node and one GPU, we evaluate the performance of caching and prefetching using the HBM layer with two small grids, 256 × 256 × 64 and 512 × 512 × 128. This configuration is particularly of interest for domain decomposition when running in strong scaling mode of operation. The number of times steps is increased to 3, 500 and we perform I/O at every 10 time steps. The former grid generates 10 GiB of intermediate snapshots, which can fit entirely on the HBM, while the latter generates 87 GiB, that need to be caching in and out through the different layers of MLBS (i.e., DRAM and PFS). We report the corresponding I/O throughput and the compute times.

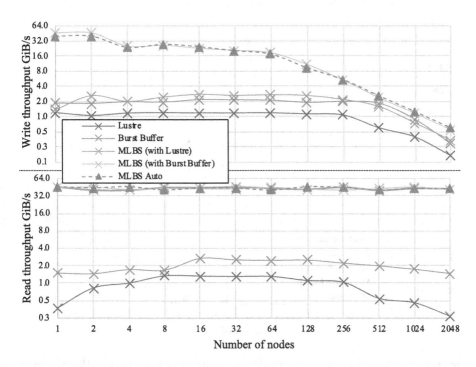

Fig. 3. Per-node **write** (top) and **read** (bottom) throughput in GiB/s for the RTM app on *Shaheen-2*. Every node executes one shot with grid size 800 × 800 × 800 and I/O at every 10th iteration. Burst Buffer is remote-shared.

6.3   RTM on Shaheen-2 and Summit

We measure the aggregate and per-node I/O throughput of the RTM application on *Shaheen-2*'s PFSs, i.e., Lustre and DataWarp. All solution grids are written or read directly to/from the file system. We run the RTM application on *Summit* and collect I/O throughput as well. We then integrate the Pthread-based MLBS implementation into each rank of the RTM application on *Shaheen-2* and *Summit*. We remove one thread from the RTM pool of OpenMP threads and give it to MLBS engine as a helper thread. This does not affect the performance of the computational kernel on *Shaheen-2*, since the stencil kernel is memory-bound, while fully utilizing the vector units for SIMD. On *Summit*, the CPU is only in charge of launching the CUDA stencil kernel. MLBS can therefore use all IBM Power9 CPUs available in the hosts to improve the performance of the memory copies. We test the I/O throughput impact when we allocate 70% of the physical DRAM capacity for MLBS. In our benchmark campaign, we present the HDD-based PFS as the main storage. Then we repeat the experiments with SSD-based BB. Finally, we let MLBS helper engine select the storage media at runtime using its internal autotuner, based on the per-node I/O throughput.

Figure 3 (top) shows per-node **write** throughput of the RTM application on *Shaheen-2*. We observe that the throughput, as seen by the application, is

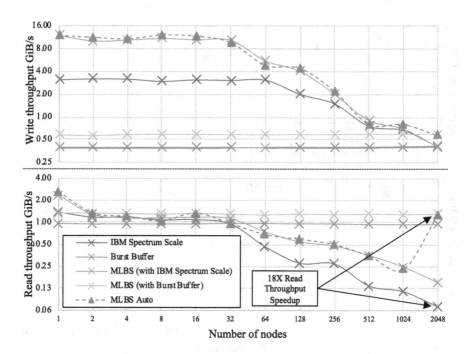

Fig. 4. Per-node `write` (top) and `read` (bottom) throughput in GiB/s for the RTM app on *Summit*. Every node executes six shots, one shot/GPU with grid size 700 × 700 × 700 and I/O at every 10th iteration. Burst Buffer is node-local. MLBS uses HMB and DRAM as the first two layers.

higher when MLBS uses the BB instead of Lustre. We also observe that the performance of `write` using MLBS with Lustre is almost identical to using the BB without MLBS. On the backward phase, as seen in Fig. 3 (bottom), MLBS helper engines succeed in prefetching the snapshots into memory all the times. The RTM in the backward phase shifts truly from IO-bound application to memory-bound (i.e., the kernel speed). Figure 4 (top) and (bottom) show the aggregate and per-node `write` and `read` throughput of the RTM application on *Summit*. Unlike on *Shaheen-2*, the PFS brings a higher throughput to the application. However, as we increase the number of nodes to 2048, the node-local BB performs better. MLBS autotuner configuration is able to switch, at runtime, for the write I/O operations between the SSD-based and the HDD-based file systems at 2048 nodes. The similar switch happens for the read I/O operations during the backward phase. However, the switch for read I/O operations would better benefit if the switch would have happened starting from 64 nodes. The MLBS autotuner eventually reveals that the RTM application should use different hierarchical storage media layers during the forward (i.e., write I/O) and backward (i.e., read I/O) wave propagation. As it is shown in Fig. 4 (bottom), when the number of nodes is 2048, MLBS autotuner read throughput outperforms the reference IBM Spectrum Scale based PFS by 18 times. Since the storage media for

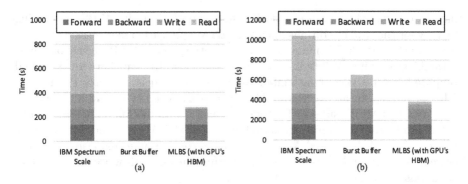

Fig. 5. Computation and I/O time breakdown of (a) small grid of size 256 × 256 × 64 where all intermediate snapshot fit in HMB and (b) a larger 512 × 512 × 128 grid where intermediate snapshots are cached and prefetched on HBM, DRAM and PFS

the write and the read I/O operations are currently coupled, MLBS autotuner is not able to change the storage media layer at runtime. We believe this is a reasonable extension to support online storage media switch in a future work, which would further maximize the obtained overall performance.

Figure 5 (a) and (b) show the forward and backward computation times in addition to `write` and `read` times in seconds. In Fig. 5(a), we use a small grid with 350 snapshots that can fit entirely in the HBM while in Fig. 5(b), only 64 snapshots can be held at one instance. Therefore, continuous caching and prefetching has to take place which is translated into 20% of time to solution. MLBS can achieve up to 3X and 2.5X performance speedup compared to the reference PFS-based RTM implementation for the small and large 3D solution grids, respectively. Although this experiment is done on a single node, since RTM is embarrassingly parallel, one can attain similar improvement factors when running on several *Summit* nodes.

7 Summary and Future Work

We have introduced a GPU extension to our Multilayered Buffer System (MLBS) that further create opportunities to overlap expensive I/O operations with GPU computations in the context of the Reverse Time Migration (RTM) for seismic imaging. MLBS leverages the RTM I/O access patterns and asynchronously pushes and pulls solution grids across hardware stacked storage layers, such as GPU high bandwidth memory/CPU main memory/Burst Buffer/Parallel File Systems. The resulting up and down pipelining of grids between storage layers overlaps with the main RTM computational kernel. It permits the application to carry on as if it does not require out-of-core computations, while achieving up to 2.5X and 1.4X throughput increase, on *Shaheen-2* and *Summit*, respectively. In cases where all intermediate data can fit in a GPU's HBM, which is a realistic case for domain decomposition and strong scaling mode of operations, we show that the computation can proceed as if there is no I/O at all. MLBS prefetching strategy for the read operations makes the RTM application behave as if the data resides in the CPU/GPU main memory, on both systems. MLBS has shown how hierarchical caching of intermediate data can close the gap between I/O and compute for iterative and data intensive applications such as Vector Particle-In-Cell (VPIC), Hardware Accelerated Cosmology Code (HACC) and RTM [6]. We plan to extend MLBS support for topology-aware data motion on heterogeneous systems to further maximize on-node bandwidth [23]. We also intend to further extend our newly proposed MLBS autotuner routine and enable it to switch between memory and storage layers at runtime during both write and read I/O operations.

Acknowledgments. For computer time, this research used the resources of the Supercomputing Laboratory at King Abdullah University of Science & Technology (KAUST) in Thuwal, Saudi Arabia and the Oak Ridge Leadership Computing Facility, which is a DOE Office of Science User Facility supported under Contract DE-AC05-00OR22725. We would like to thank Rached Abdelkhalak from NVIDIA for the insightful discussions and the anonymous reviewers for their constructive comments to improve this paper. This research was partially supported by Saudi Aramco through KAUST OSR contract #3226.

References

1. DDN IME. https://www.ddn.com/products/ime-flash-native-data-cache/
2. High-Performance Storage list. https://www.vi4io.org/. Accessed Feb 2020
3. HPC IO Benchmark Repository. https://github.com/hpc/ior. Accessed Dec 2019
4. TOP500 Supercomputer Lists. https://www.top500.org/lists/top500/. Accessed Feb 2020
5. AlOnazi, A., Ltaief, H., Keyes, D., Said, I., Thibault, S.: Asynchronous task-based execution of the reverse time migration for the oil and gas industry. In: 2019 IEEE International Conference on Cluster Computing (CLUSTER), pp. 1–11. IEEE (2019). https://doi.org/10.1109/cluster.2019.8891054
6. Alturkestani, T., Tonellot, T., Ltaief, H., Abdelkhalak, R., Etienne, V., Keyes, D.: MLBS: transparent data caching in hierarchical storage for out-of-core HPC applications. In: Proceedings of the 26th International Conference on High Performance Computing (HiPC), pp. 312–322. IEEE (2019). https://doi.org/10.1109/hipc.2019.00046
7. Arulraj, J., Perron, M., Pavlo, A.: Write-behind logging. Proc. VLDB Endowment **10**(4), 337–348 (2016). https://doi.org/10.14778/3025111.3025116
8. Augonnet, C., Thibault, S., Namyst, R., Wacrenier, P.A.: StarPU: a unified platform for task scheduling on heterogeneous multicore architectures. Concurr. Comput.: Pract. Experience **23**(2), 187–198 (2011). https://doi.org/10.1002/cpe.1631
9. Badam, A., Pai, V.S.: SSDAlloc: hybrid SSD/RAM memory management made easy. In: Proceedings of the 8th USENIX Conference on Networked Systems Design and Implementation, NSDI 2011, pp. 211–224. USENIX Association, USA (2011)
10. Baysal, E., Kosloff, D.D., Sherwood, J.W.: Reverse time migration. Geophysics **48**(11), 1514–1524 (1983)

11. Bhimji, W., et al.: Accelerating Science With the NERSC Burst Buffer Early User Program. Proceedings of the Cray Users' Group (2016)
12. Byna, S., et al.: Parallel I/O, analysis, and visualization of a trillion particle simulation. In: 2012 International Conference for High Performance Computing, Networking, Storage and Analysis. IEEE, November 2012. https://doi.org/10.1109/sc.2012.92
13. Dong, B., Byna, S., Wu, K., Johansen, H., Johnson, J.N., Keen, N., et al.: Data elevator: low-contention data movement in hierarchical storage system. In: 2016 IEEE 23rd International Conference on High Performance Computing (HiPC), pp. 152–161. IEEE (2016). https://doi.org/10.1109/hipc.2016.026
14. Dong, B., Wang, T., Tang, H., Koziol, Q., Wu, K., Byna, S.: ARCHIE: data analysis acceleration with array caching in hierarchical storage. In: 2018 IEEE International Conference on Big Data (Big Data), pp. 211–220. IEEE (2018). https://doi.org/10.1109/bigdata.2018.8622616
15. Henseler, D., Landsteiner, B., Petesch, D., Wright, C., Wright, N.J.: Architecture and Design of Cray Datawarp. Cray User Group CUG (2016)
16. Ibtesham, D., Arnold, D., Bridges, P.G., Ferreira, K.B., Brightwell, R.: On the viability of compression for reducing the overheads of checkpoint/restart-based fault tolerance. In: 2012 41st International Conference on Parallel Processing, pp. 148–157. IEEE (2012). https://doi.org/10.1109/icpp.2012.45
17. Kim, S., et al.: Enlightening the I/O path: a holistic approach for application performance. In: 15th USENIX Conference on File and Storage Technologies (FAST 17) (2017)
18. Kougkas, A., Devarajan, H., Sun, X.H.: Hermes: a heterogeneous-aware multi-tiered distributed I/O buffering system. In: Proceedings of the 27th International Symposium on High-Performance Parallel and Distributed Computing, pp. 219–230. ACM (2018). https://doi.org/10.1145/3208040.3208059
19. Lee, K., Sullivan, M.B., Hari, S.K.S., Tsai, T., Keckler, S.W., Erez, M.: GPU snapshot: checkpoint offloading for GPU-dense systems. In: Proceedings of the ACM International Conference on Supercomputing, ICS 2019, pp. 171–183 (2019). https://doi.org/10.1145/3330345.3330361
20. Liu, N., et al.: On the role of burst buffers in leadership-class storage systems. In: Proceedings of the 28th Symposium on Mass Storage Systems and Technologies, pp. 1–11. IEEE (2012). https://doi.org/10.1109/msst.2012.6232369
21. Luu, H., et al.: A multiplatform study of I/O behavior on petascale supercomputers. In: Proceedings of the 24th International Symposium on High-Performance Parallel and Distributed Computing. pp. 33–44 (2015). https://doi.org/10.1145/2749246.2749269
22. Markomanolis, G.S., Hadri, B., Khurram, R., Feki, S.: Scientific applications performance evaluation on burst buffer. In: Kunkel, J.M., Yokota, R., Taufer, M., Shalf, J. (eds.) ISC High Performance 2017. LNCS, vol. 10524, pp. 701–711. Springer, Cham (2017). https://doi.org/10.1007/978-3-319-67630-2_50
23. Martinasso, M., Kwasniewski, G., Alam, S.R., Schulthess, T.C., Hoefler, T.: A PCIe Congestion-aware performance model for densely populated accelerator servers. In: SC 2016: Proceedings of the International Conference for High Performance Computing, Networking, Storage and Analysis, pp. 739–749. IEEE (2016). https://doi.org/10.1109/sc.2016.62
24. McCalpin, J.: Memory bandwidth and machine balance in high performance computers. Technical Committee on Computer Architecture Newsletter, pp. 19–25 (1995)

25. Patrick, C.M., Kandemir, M., Karaköy, M., Son, S.W., Choudhary, A.: Cashing in on hints for better prefetching and caching in PVFS and MPI-IO. In: Proceedings of the 19th ACM International Symposium on High Performance Distributed Computing, HPDC 2010, pp. 191–202. ACM (2010). https://doi.org/10.1145/1851476. 1851499

26. Sava, P., Hill, S.: Overview and classification of wavefield seismic imaging methods. Lead. Edge **28**(2), 170–183 (2009). https://doi.org/10.1190/1.3086052

27. Scott, D.S.: Parallel I/O and solving out of core systems of linear equations. In: Proceedings of the 1993 DAGS/PC Symposium, pp. 123–130 (1993)

28. Silberstein, M., Ford, B., Keidar, I., Witchel, E.: GPUfs: Integrating a file system with GPUs. In: Proceedings of the Eighteenth International Conference on Architectural Support for Programming Languages and Operating Systems, ASPLOS 2013, pp. 485–498. Association for Computing Machinery (2013). https://doi.org/ 10.1145/2451116.2451169

29. Thompson, A., Newburn, C.: GPUDirect Storage: A Direct Path Between Storage and GPU Memory, August 2019. https://devblogs.nvidia.com/gpudirect-storage/. Accessed May 2020

30. Vazhkudai, S., et al.: The design, deployment, and evaluation of the CORAL pre-exascale systems. In: Proceedings of the International Conference for High Performance Computing, Networking, Storage, and Analysis, pp. 52:1–52:12. IEEE (2018). https://doi.org/10.1109/SC.2018.00055

31. Wang, C., Vazhkudai, S.S., Ma, X., Meng, F., Kim, Y., Engelmann, C.: NVMalloc: exposing an aggregate SSD store as a memory partition in extreme-scale machines. In: Proceedings of the 26th International Parallel and Distributed Processing Symposium. IEEE (2012). https://doi.org/10.1109/ipdps.2012.90

32. Wang, T., Byna, S., Dong, B., Tang, H.: UniviStor: integrated hierarchical and distributed storage for HPC. In: 2018 IEEE International Conference on Cluster Computing (CLUSTER), pp. 134–144. IEEE (2018). https://doi.org/10.1109/ cluster.2018.00025

33. Wang, T., Mohror, K., Moody, A., Sato, K., Yu, W.: An ephemeral burst-buffer file system for scientific applications. In: SC16: International Conference for High Performance Computing, Networking, Storage and Analysis. IEEE, November 2016. https://doi.org/10.1109/sc.2016.68

34. Wang, T., Oral, S., Wang, Y., Settlemyer, B., Atchley, S., Yu, W.: BurstMem: a high-performance burst buffer system for scientific applications. In: 2014 IEEE International Conference on Big Data (Big Data), IEEE, October 2014. https:// doi.org/10.1109/bigdata.2014.7004215

Cluster, Cloud and Edge Computing

TorqueDB: Distributed Querying of Time-Series Data from Edge-local Storage

Dhruv Garg[1], Prathik Shirolkar[2], Anshu Shukla[1], and Yogesh Simmhan[2(✉)] (iD)

[1] Ericsson Research, Bangalore, India
[2] Indian Institute of Science, Bangalore, India
simmhan@iisc.ac.in

Abstract. The rapid growth in edge computing devices as part of Internet of Things (IoT) allows real-time access to time-series data from 1000's of sensors. Such observations are often queried to optimize the health of the infrastructure. Recently, edge storage systems allow us to retain data on the edge rather than moving them centrally to the cloud. However, such systems do not support flexible querying over the data spread across 10–100's of devices. There is also a lack of distributed time-series databases that can run on the edge devices. Here, we propose *TorqueDB*, a distributed query engine over time-series data that operates on edge and fog resources. TorqueDB leverages our prior work on ElfStore, a distributed edge-local file store, and InfluxDB, a time-series database, to enable temporal queries to be decomposed and executed across multiple fog and edge devices. Interestingly, we move data into InfluxDB on-demand while retaining the durable data within ElfStore for use by other applications. We also design a cost model that maximizes parallel movement and execution of the queries across resources, and utilizes caching. Our experiments on a real edge, fog and cloud deployment show that TorqueDB performs comparable to InfluxDB on a cloud VM for a smart city query workload, but without the associated monetary costs.

Keywords: Edge storage · Time-series database · Distributed querying · Internet of Things · Cloud computing

1 Introduction

Internet of Things (IoT) domains leverage the availability of affordable sensing and computing devices, along with pervasive communications and advances in analytics, to observe and manage cyber-physical systems to enhance their efficiency and resiliency. IoT domains span physical infrastructure such as Smart Cities, Smart Transportation and Industrial IoT, to consumer devices such as smart watches and smart appliances. A key characteristic of IoT applications is

Supported by the DST ICPS Program, Government of India.

M. Malawski and K. Rzadca (Eds.): Euro-Par 2020, LNCS 12247, pp. 281–295, 2020.
https://doi.org/10.1007/978-3-030-57675-2_18

their closed-loop cycle where data about the system is analyzed and decisions are made, typically within seconds, to control the system [11,15]. E.g., in a manufacturing facility, sensors may monitor the temperature and pollution levels to ensure it is safe for the workers, and if not initiate cooling, scrubbing or other safety measures.

Edge devices comparable to Raspberry Pi and Arduino are widely deployed as part of such IoT applications to help gather and transmit observations from the sensors, and also to enact control decision onto their co-located actuators [14]. Traditionally, data collected from the field are sent to the Cloud for storage and analytics, and the control signals are sent back to the field. This introduces high network round-trip latency from the edge to the cloud, and additional network, compute and storage costs at the cloud data center.

Edge computing has gained prominence to make use of the captive computing and storage on edge devices, as well as to reduce the network latency between the edge and the cloud for decision making. Besides running tasks and analytics on such devices [2,3,11], recent works also propose their use for distributed data storage by offering file and block-based semantics for data update and access [5,9,10]. They also use workstation-class *fog resources* located near the edge devices, which help with management and as a gateway to the Internet [13].

Motivation. IoT data tends to be time-series in nature since sensors continuously generate timestamped data. As a result, time-series querying and analytics is a key requirement for IoT applications [8,15]. These operate on data collected over time to check if recent observations exceed historic averages, identify minimum and maximum outliers within time-windows, and to query and visualize data from specific sensor types and time ranges. This complements and is more flexible than Complex Event Processing (CEP) and publish-subscribe systems that operate on streaming data and limit the queries possible [3,7,12]. *Time-series databases (TSDB)* like InfluxDB and Apache Druid are popular for hosting of such IoT data and performing temporal queries, centrally on the cloud [8].

However, both the sensor data producers and the consuming applications for such TSDBs tend to reside on edge devices. Edge applications require *subsecond* query latency when responding to dynamic situations. Moving data from the edge to a TSDB on the cloud, and querying it back from the edge causes *unreliable performance* due to WAN variability. It also introduces additional *network and VM costs*, and *privacy concerns* when data is moved out of the private network to public clouds. There is also a lost *opportunity cost* in not utilizing the captive compute, storage and network capacity available on edge and fog resources.

Requirements and Gaps. A natural progression is to host such time-series databases on edge and fog devices, co-locating the query clients near the data storage and also leveraging the available local compute and storage capacity on them [1]. However, individual edge or fog resources may not have the capacity to scale to workloads from many edge clients. This requires the use of a *distributed*

TSDB operating across multiple edge and fog devices. However, existing systems are either proprietary, do not support distributed execution, or are not light enough to be hosted on edge and fog resources. Further, not all time-series data collected over time will be actively used all the time. Given the overheads of managing distributed databases, only recent or actively used data should be stored in such TSDBs. Lastly, data stored in the TSDB will need to complement storing the data durably as files on the edge. This may required to support time-series analytics or machine learning models that operate outside the database and directly on files hosted on the edge devices [15]. We address these gaps.

Contributions. We propose *TorqueDB (Temporal querying from edge storage Database)* which leverages the *ElfStore* distributed edge-local storage [9] along with *InfluxDB* TSDB to offer a distributed execution model for time-series queries over edge and fog devices. Here, ElfStore retains the persistent time-series data generated by sensors on the edge devices while InfluxDB instances running on the fog are used to host subsets of this data, on-demand, to support user queries. TorqueDB accepts queries defined using the *Flux* language used by InfluxDB, uses the basic search capabilities of ElfStore to identify blocks of interest, inserts and caches them into one or more local InfluxDB instances on the fog, executes subsets of the user query on each fog in parallel, and aggregates the results for returning to the user. This effectively offers a distributed TSDB with an edge-local backing store, and is the *first of its kind system* to offer distributed time-series querying on edge and fog devices.

Next, in Sect. 2 we discuss background on ElfStore and InfluxDB, and related work on edge computing and querying; we introduce the TorqueDB design and query execution model in Sect. 3; we present detailed performance results on a real-world edge and fog deployment in Sect. 4; and lastly offer our conclusions in Sect. 5.

2   Background and Related Work

2.1   ElfStore Distributed Edge-Local Federated Storage

ElfStore [9] is a block-centric distributed storage system on edge and fog resources, for files that grow over time. Edges are connected to a *parent fog* that is present in their local network, and together form a *fog partition*. Many such fog partitions can exist, with fogs being able to talk directly to each other. These all form a peer-to-peer (P2P) network overlay, with edges serving as peers and fogs as super-peers, and its associated scaling characteristics to 1000's of devices.

Edges host data and metadata for a block. Fogs maintain a *mapping* from the block ID to the edge(s), and *indexes* over the block metadata, for blocks in their local partition. This allows fogs to perform basic value-based *searching* for blocks based on their metadata properties, and *lookups* of block replica locations using their block ID. Fogs also use Bloom Filters to maintain *approximate indexes* about contents in other fogs partitions to allow forwarding of metadata search and block retrieval requests across the overlay, within no more than 3 hops.

Since edge devices can have asymmetric reliability, ElfStore uses a block-specific replication level based on the required block reliability and the reliability of the edges chosen for placement. Statistics exchanged between the fogs about the reliability levels and storage capacities of edges in their partitions are used by the replication logic to guarantee a minimum resilience and load balancing of storage. It also recovers from failures by re-replicating blocks from failed edges.

2.2   Influx DB Time-Series Database

InfluxDB is an open-source TSDB optimized for high read and write throughput. It stores data in *buckets* (databases) that contain *measurements* (tables). Each row in a table has a *timestamp* and columns that are either *tags*, which are indefaxed, or *fields*, which can be aggregated on. It has a native *Flux* query language that allows SQL-like queries over time-series data, with support for Select, Project, Aggregate, Window-aggregates and Joins. Besides network APIs provided for data insertion and querying, data can also be bulk-loaded into an InfluxDB table using a *line-protocol* CSV format.

2.3   Querying over Edge Devices

There have been recent works that examine the use of edge computing for *query processing over event streams*, though they do not support distributed time-series queries over a database or use an external edge-storage as the backend.

StreamSight [2] provides a declarative query model for matching complex patterns on data streams. The system compiles these queries into stream processing jobs for continuous execution on engines running on edge devices. The query plan is dynamically updated so that intermediate results are reused and not recomputed. It also supports approximate answers with error-bounds for latency-sensitive execution.

Periodic querying is essential in Industrial IoT. Here, contiguous queries can have overlapping input regions, and the sensor data retrieved by recent queries may be reused for answering the upcoming queries. Zhou et al. [16] proposed a popularity-based caching strategy to leverage these patterns. They show significant reduction in the communication cost, when the number of queries is relatively large. Such caching strategies can also be incorporated into TorqueDB.

HERMES [7] enables query evaluation over data streams across cloud and fog nodes. They use reservoir sampling of incoming observational streams to reduce communication and memory consumption on fog nodes in resource-constrained environments. Similarly, our prior work [3] examines distributed analytics over event streams on edge and cloud using a CEP engine, rather than query over past data that we address in TorqueDB. Their key objective is to schedule a dataflow graph of dependent CEP queries on edge and cloud resources while minimizing the latency and conserving energy. Individual queries are not decomposed unlike TorqueDB does, and we use only edge and fog rather than the cloud.

Others have examined *query rewriting* in other contexts. Schultz et al. [12] design a CEP system with operator placement decisions based on cost functions, and greedily selects a distributed deployment plan over machines in a cluster. They use query rewriting to increase the efficiency of operations by reusing common operators. TorqueDB's execution model operates on queries independently as these are one-off rather than standing CEP queries.

Grunert et al. [4] use query rewriting and containment techniques from databases for efficient and privacy-aware processing of queries in an edge-cloud setup. The input query is split into "fragment" and "remainder" queries. Fragment queries operates on resource constrained edge devices to filter and pre-aggregate data, while remainder queries execute the complex part of the query on fog devices. We do similar rewriting across different levels on fog devices.

There are other edge and fog storage systems that have been proposed as well, besides ElfStore. *DataFog* [5] is a data management platform at the edge on top of Apache Cassandra, for a geo-distributed and heterogeneous edge computing environment. They provided a locality aware distributed indexing mechanism and a replica placement approach to provide spatial proximity. Finally, they employed a TTL based data eviction policy to accommodate the constrained storage capacity at the edge. These can serve as alternative backends for TorqueDB.

3 TorqueDB Architecture

The architecture for TorqueDB is shown in Fig. 1. The *system model* contains edge and fog resources. Each edge is associated with one *parent fog*, which serves as a network gateway to other fogs and the Internet. All edges with the same parent fog form a *fog partition*, and devices in a partition are part of the same private network, with high bandwidth and low latency connectivity. All fogs can communicate with each other directly, either on the same private network or through the Internet. The network link between fogs may be slower than with the edge devices in their partition. We expect edge devices to have resources comparable to a Raspberry Pi with a 4-core low-power CPU, 1–2 GB RAM and 128 GB SD card storage, while the fog resources are comparable to a workstation or low-end server with 4–8-core CPU, 8–16 GB RAM and 500 GB–4 TB HDD.

Edge devices host the input data accumulated from sensors in *blocks* managed by ElfStore. Each block contains rows of time-series data, typically from one or more sensors and for a specific time range. New blocks are added over time. Each block is identified by a unique *block ID*. ElfStore allows application-specific *metadata properties* to be stored for these blocks and searched upon. These contain details such as the table name, sensor ID, sensor types, units, time range, location, etc. A subset of these properties match specific columns present in the time-series data, e.g., the location and the sensor ID column values may be common to all rows in the block, which are surfaced as a property for that block, while the minimum and maximum timestamps for the rows in the block will form the time-range property for that block. As an additional optimization, we also compute *aggregates* over the content in these blocks, such as the number

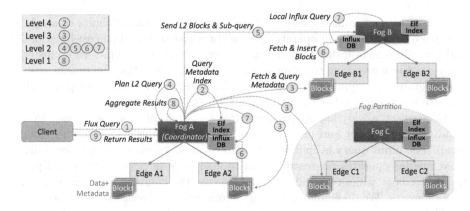

Fig. 1. Architecture and query execution sequence of TorqueDB

of rows, minimum and maximum values for specific columns like temperature and humidity, etc. and store them as metadata properties for the block. ElfStore natively creates *replicas* of a block data and metadata, identified using the same block ID, on multiple edge devices to meet the reliability requirements specified.

Fog resources run ElfStore services to manage the edge devices, replication and block placement, as well as maintain indexes on the metadata for blocks stored in their partition. For TorqueDB, we also host an InfluxDB instance on each fog resource to execute Flux queries. The InfluxDB instance is primarily used as a *query engine* rather than for data management. It is a transient store (and optionally cache) for the time-series data on which complex Flux queries are executed, with the durable storage being the blocks in ElfStore.

This layered design, reusing ElfStore and InfluxDB, has several benefits over designing a distributed TSDB from the ground up. It avoids the complexity of distributed management and resilience of different instances of a TSDB, while leveraging the data reliability guarantees offered by ElfStore. It also allows edge applications that directly operate on the data blocks to be supported by ElfStore [15] while the queries are offloaded to TorqueDB. Lastly, it eliminates the need for redundant copies of data on both the edge-local file storage and the TSDB, instead using the TSDB just as a transient cache.

At this time, we limit our design to executing the Flux queries on InfluxDB instances running on the fog resources. This leverages their higher resource capacity relative to constrained edge devices and limits the coordination overheads. As future work, we propose to examine designs where the InfluxDB is hosted directly on the edge devices themselves to enhance the parallelism and limit data movement.

3.1   Query Lifecycle and Distributed Execution

TorqueDB supports a subset of the *Flux query language*, as illustrated in Fig. 2. Specifically, we support *range queries* over time-stamps (e.g., *time* BETWEEN

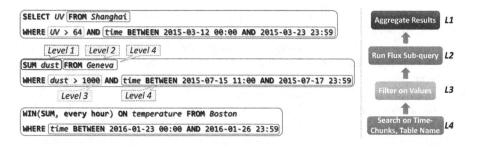

Fig. 2. Sample flux queries and execution levels in TorqueDB

start AND end), *filter queries* over column values (e.g., *dust* > 1000), *aggregation* functions such as sum, average, minimum and maximum over columns values (e.g., SUM *dust*), *aggregation windows* over time (e.g., WIN(SUM, *every hour*)), and *projection* of columns (e.g., SELECT *UV*) to the output. Support for join queries and complex nested queries is planned for future.

Users submit their Flux query to a TorqueDB service, which run on all fog resources. The fog receiving the query is called the *coordinator* for this query (Fig. 1 ①). The distributed execution plan for the query is decomposed into a query tree, with execution happening at *four levels* (Fig. 2). At *level 4 (L4)*, the coordinator attempts to identify the ElfStore blocks that contain the time-series data on which the query depends. For this, it extracts those parts of the query predicates that can be pushed down as a native ElfStore search over the block metadata index (②). Specifically, ElfStore can search for blocks with a given property value, and compose Boolean predicates using AND and OR. These include matching properties such as the table name, location, sensor ID, etc. which require a direct value comparison in the input query.

But ElfStore does not support range queries which are important for time-series data. To address this, we discretize the time-range for rows in a block into granular *time-chunk numbers* relative to an *epoch*, e.g., in *12-hour* increments starting from *2020-01-01 00:00*, and include the chunks numbers that the rows of a block overlap with in its metadata property. A similar discretization is done on the input time-range query into one or more chunk numbers, and composed as an OR on the time-chunk metadata matching any of these chunks numbers. E.g., if the user query has a time-range predicate from *2020-02-14 07:35* to *2020-02-14 20:15*, these overlap with the time-chunks 89 and 90. We search ElfStore for blocks that have time-chunk property with values of 89 or 90. Likewise, when storing blocks, we calculate the chunk numbers for their time-ranges, and store these as a multi-valued property for the time-chunk metadata.

The output of the L4 query is a filtered set of block IDs having the minimal data necessary for further query processing. These are passed as input to *level 3 (L3)*, where the coordinator optionally fetches the actual block metadata to further refine the search space (Fig. 1 ③). In particular, when we have value comparisons over non-timestamp columns present in the data, like "dust" and

"UV", we use the minimum and maximum aggregate metadata values for these columns to decide if the block contains the relevant data or not for further querying. E.g., if the input query has a predicate that only retains rows with $dust \geq 1000$ ppm, then we fetch and use the block metadata to eliminate those whose *maximum dust* is less than 1000. L3 is done only if value comparison predicates are present in the input query.

The output of L3 is again a set of block IDs that are a subset of the block IDs from L4. Now, the coordinator assigns these blocks to the available fog resources to load the block contents into their local InfluxDB instance and execute the Flux query on it. The mapping of blocks to fogs is done by the *Query Planner* discussed in Sect. 3.2 (Fig. 1 ④). The coordinator decomposes and rewrites the input query into *sub-queries* relevant to the blocks assigned to each fog, and sends them these block IDs and sub-query for execution in *level 2 (L2)* (⑤).

In L2, each fog receiving a sub-query and a list of blocks *fetches* the block contents from ElfStore, and *inserts* them into the local InfluxDB instance. We use a thread-pool for the fetch and insert of each block in parallel (Fig. 1 ⑥). All blocks are inserted into a single table, even across queries. This helps with caching, as we discuss later. During insertion, we add the block ID as a column in each row inserted into InfluxDB. These block IDs are also included as a value predicate in the sub-queries. This ensures that a sub-query only targets blocks relevant to the current query being executed on the fog and not other blocks inserted by previous or concurrent queries. This avoids duplicates results. E.g., if L3 returns block IDs $\langle 3, 5, 9 \rangle$ for processing at L2, and $\langle 3, 5 \rangle$ are assigned to *Fog A* and $\langle 9 \rangle$ to *Fog B*. Say *Fog B* already had a copy of block 5 present in it. If we run the two sub-queries on *Fog A* and *Fog B*, we should not get duplicates for matching rows for the block 5 present both in *Fog A* and B. So the sub-query for *Fog A* will have a filter to limit the rows to those with the Block ID field as 3 or 5, while the sub-query for *Fog B* filters in only rows with Block ID 9.

Once all blocks assigned to a fog are inserted into the local InfluxDB, the sub-query is executed on the TSDB and the results returned to the coordinator (Fig. 1 ⑦). Multiple fogs having block assignments will operate in parallel. When the coordinator receives the L2 results from all fogs, in the absence of an aggregation operator, it just *appends* all the results and returns them to the client in *level 1 (L1)* (⑧, ⑨). However, if an *aggregation function* over a column is present, then the L2 query result from each fog will have the aggregation over the subset of rows in that fog. Here, we further aggregate across all these results to return a single result to the user. This aggregation is done inside the coordinator by code specific to each aggregation function. For functions like *mean*, L2 returns the *sum* and the *count*, which are used to compute the global mean.

3.2   Query Planning

In L2, we perform block fetch from ElfStore, insertion into the local InfluxDB and query execution, on one or more fogs. This is the most time-consuming level since it involves fetching the block from SD card on the edge and a network data transfer. The time taken to ingest data into InfluxDB is also significant. So we ensure the parallelism offered by multiple fog and edge devices is fully exploited. Given a set of blocks from L3, the edges (and parent fogs) that their replicas are present in and the available fogs, the goal of query planning is to partition these blocks to the fogs to reduce the execution time for L2. We propose two query planning strategies, *partition-local (QP1)* and *load-balancing (QP2)*.

The block transfer time is constrained by the I/O speed of the edge device ($\approx$100 Mbps seen for a Class 1 SD card), the network bandwidth from the edge to parent fog and from fog to fog ($\approx$100 Mbps–1 Gbps), and the cumulative bandwidth into a fog ($\approx$1 Gbps). In both strategies, we first try and maximize the cumulative disk and network bandwidth from different edge devices in parallel. From the available set of blocks, we maintain a *load count* for each edge, which is the number of blocks selected for reading from this edge and set to 0 at the start. We then sort the blocks in ascending order of the number of edges they are present on (replica count). For each block, in this order, we select one of its edge replicas such that this edge has the least load count among the replica edges, and increment the load count for that edge. This achieves *load balancing of the block-reads* from among the edges hosting the block replicas.

Next, in the *partition-local strategy (QP1)*, we simply assign a block replica to the parent fog for its edge. The intuition is that the bandwidth from the edge to its parent fog is high and one-hop, and the block is kept within this partition.

In the *load-balancing strategy (QP2)*, we prioritize balancing the number of blocks assigned to each fog. This maximizes the parallelism for the data inserts into InfluxDB and the query execution on the fogs. Here, we maintain a count of blocks assigned to a fog, initialized to 0. For each block replica, if the parent fog for the edge is the least loaded among all fogs, the block is assigned to this fog; if not, the block is assigned to the least loaded fog. The fog's load count is incremented, and this repeats for the next block replica.

3.3 Block Caching

Much time in L2 is spent in fetching and inserting the blocks. We propose a caching mechanism where the coordinator maintains a local mapping from block IDs to the fog that has inserted that block into its local InfluxDB. This mapping is updated after the L2 of each query, and lazily propagated across all fogs. The query planner uses this knowledge to assign a block to the fog that it is cached in, and only triggers the QP2 mapping algorithm for blocks that are not cached.

The caching strategy will retain all blocks used in any query within the local InfluxDB of one of the fog resources. This ensures that blocks that are used once are available immediately on a fog for future queries, but unused blocks are not copied from ElfStore. In future, this can be combined with a cache replacement like least recently used (LRU) to more efficiently utilize the disk space, and may also load-balance the cached-block distribution across fogs.

4   Experiment Results

4.1   Setup

Our experiments use a 15-node IoT cluster with 12 Raspberry Pi 4B edge devices (ARMv8 4-core@1.5 GHz, 2 GB RAM, 64 GB UHS-1 SD card) and 3 fog resources (Intel Core i5 6-cores@2.1 GHz 8 GB RAM and 500 GB HDD). These 15-nodes form 3 fog partitions with 1 fog and 4 edges each, connected over hierarchical 1 Gbps switches with an average latency of 0.6 ms. As a baseline, we use a Microsoft Azure Standard D4 v3 VM (Central India) running Intel Xeon E5 4-cores@2.3 GHz, 16 GB RAM and 500 GB HDD. Its performance is comparable to the fog resource based on query benchmarks.

ElfStore runs on the 15-node cluster with uniform replication factor of 3 and no edge failures. TorqueDB is implemented in Java v1.8 and runs on the fogs alongside InfluxDB v1.7.9[1], which is hosted in container. By default, caching is disabled on TorqueDB and we use QP2.

We use data from *Sense your City* in our workload[2], which has ambient monitoring devices from 84 locations in 7 cities worldwide that sense dust, temperature, humidity, UV, etc. The devices report an observation every 3 mins over a 16 month period, to give ≈19.35 *million rows of time-series data*. Each 1 MB block in ElfStore holds 1 day of data per city with 5760 rows of data.

We use a query workload with 6 *predicate patterns*: Project+1 Value Filter (PF); Project+2 Value Filters (PFF); Filter+Simple Aggregate like sum/count/min/max (FSA); Filter+Complex (mean) Aggregate (FCA); 2 Value Filters+Simple Aggregate (FFSA); and 1 Value Filter+Window Aggregate (FW). These queries are inspired by a prior IoT query benchmarking work [6]. They are also designed to cover the common query operators such as projection of specific columns from a tuple into the result set, filters defined on field values, simple and complex aggregation over field values, and moving windows over the time-series tuples. There is also a time-range filter in all cases, with a *small range* being over 3 days and *large range* being 12 days. We permute different values and time ranges to generate 30 instances of each pattern and range for a total of 360 queries. All queries are run from a client that is in the same local network as the fogs.

4.2   Analysis

Figures 3a and 3b show the stack bar plots for the different components of the total execution times for one median query from each type for TorqueDB and for centralized InfluxDB on a cloud VM, for small and large time-range queries.

Performance of TorqueDB. All query types, except PF with a large time-range, complete in under 600 ms, with smaller queries running under 400 ms.

---

[1] https://www.influxdata.com/products/influxdb-overview/.

[2] http://datacanvas.org/sense-your-city/.

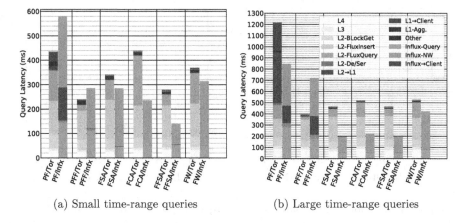

(a) Small time-range queries   (b) Large time-range queries

Fig. 3. Stacked bar plot for median query on TorqueDB (QP2) vs. Cloud InfluxDB

For the small time-range queries, the major fractions of the total execution time spent by TorqueDB are: 39% in inserting data into the InfluxDB in L2, 28% in the query execution at L2, and 14% in data transfer from ElfStore to L2. For the larger queries, the largest fractions are: 36% in inserting rows into InfluxDB in L2, 16% in query execution in L2, and ≈14% in L4 for locating matching blocks in ElfStore and the same in transferring results from L2 to L1. These L2 costs are due to on-demand copying and insertion of the relevant blocks from the edge to the InfluxDB on the fog, and these dominate the overall execution time. As we see later, it can be mitigated by caching.

We also see that the block search, data transfer and insertion times are uniform 170–190 ms for all small time-range queries since the number of blocks transfered and rows inserted are the same at 3 blocks; and likewise the large time-range with 12 blocks inserted take 265–285 ms. The only exception is query type PFF where some blocks are filtered out at L3 and hence the data transfer and insertion costs are smaller.

The variability in the execution times across different query types arise from the actual query execution in L2. Among the query types, PF is the second slowest due to the large result set size returned by the query, though the query itself is not complex. The time spent in transferring data from L2 and L1, and returning the results to the user is higher. PFF is the fastest as its additional filter reduces this result set size substantially. FSA and FFSA perform an extra simple aggregation at L1, besides one and two filters. They are the fourth or third fastest depending on the small or large query range, though their aggregated result set size is only 1 row. FCA performs a complex aggregation for finding the mean by running two aggregation queries for sum and count, and hence is twice as slow as FSA; it is the slowest among all queries. Lastly, FW does a window aggregation within InfluxDB to return 10's of results and is the third slowest.

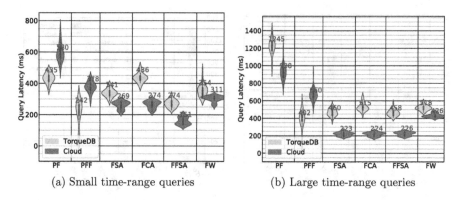

(a) Small time-range queries   (b) Large time-range queries

Fig. 4. Violin plot of query latencies on TorqueDB (QP2) and Cloud InfluxDB

TorqueDB vs. Centralized InfluxDB on the Cloud. Figures 4a and 4b further show the violin plots for the total execution times for different query types and time-ranges, for TorqueDB and centralized InfluxDB on the cloud.

For the small time-range queries, the performance of TorqueDB and InfluxDB on the Cloud are similar, while for the larger time-range, the latter is mostly faster. These differences can be attributed to the query execution times, and to the other overheads. TorqueDB leverages parallel query execution across local InfluxDBs on the fog, and this causes it to have a lower query execution time than the cloud for PF and PPF. But the cloud VM's CPU is faster in performing the aggregation operations, by 19%–147%, for FSA, FCA, FFSA and FW.

Besides this query execution, differences arise from the other components. Specifically, the network latency between the edge client and the cloud dominates for the small time-range queries on InfluxDB cloud, which have smaller query execution times. These overheads of ≈211 ms take 64% of the total query time. But this absolute latency is about the same at ≈255 ms but relatively smaller, at 57% of the total time, for the large time-range queries having longer query execution times. In addition, PF returns a large result set and this incurs costs to return the results to the client. However, for TorqueDB, the larger queries require more block fetches and insertions, and this increases its overall time.

In addition to these, the InfluxDB on the cloud took ≈18 mins to transfer 3.28 GB of data for the 7 cities from the edge to the cloud. This is amortized over a period of time in a real-world scenario. The WAN link between the edge and the cloud also shows more variability, ranging from 27.1–1048 ms latency and 21.2–536 Mbps bandwidth, over a 24 h period. In summary, while TorqueDB is slightly slower than queries on the cloud, the latter will have less deterministic execution times, and also incur additional VM and network costs.

Benefits of Query Planning. The QP1 and QP2 query planning strategies in L2 pick the same set of edges to get the block replicas from, but select different fogs to assign them to; the former reduces cross-partition data transfers and the latter balances the load per fog. In our experiments, we report that QP2 is 0.2–7.6% faster than QP1, on average for the different query types. This is

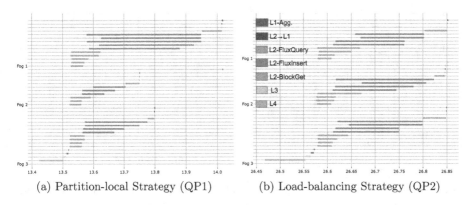

(a) Partition-local Strategy (QP1)   (b) Load-balancing Strategy (QP2)

Fig. 5. Gantt plot of latency for a FFSA large query on TorqueDB using QP1 vs QP2

because the edge–fog and fog–fog bandwidths are comparable in our IoT cluster and hence the benefits of QP1 are not apparent.

However, the load balancing in QP2 does have benefits, in particular where many blocks are fetched and inserted in L2. Figures 5 show the Gantt time-line plot for different time components of a FFSA query with large time-range, running on different fogs, when using QP1 and QP2. The Y axis indicates threads in the 3 fogs and X axis is a relative time-line, in seconds. This fetches 12 blocks in L2. QP1 assigns 5 blocks to Fog 1, 3 blocks to Fog 2 and 4 blocks to Fog 3, since these are the parent fogs for the block replicas chosen. QP2 instead load-balances and assigns 4 blocks to each fog, even though they may cross partition boundaries and cause 2-hops for block transfer. As a result, QP2 achieves an ≈200 ms reduction in the L2 block fetch and InfluxDB insert.

Benefits of Caching. Finally, we evaluate the benefits of caching in TorqueDB. Here, we use query workloads having a mix of 20 queries from each of the 6 types, to give 120 queries for the small and 120 queries for the large time-ranges. This has no (0%) overlaps in the query mix, i.e., all queries are unique. We use these to create two more workloads where 20% of the queries overlap, i.e., are duplicated, and 50% overlap. These 6 query workloads are run on TorqueDB, with and without caching enabled. Figure 6 shows the total execution time for these workloads, and the total numbers of blocks fetched and inserted in L2. These are averaged over 3 runs.

For 0% overlap workload with small time-range, the total number of blocks fetched is the same at 359, both with and without caching. On the other hand, in the large time-range 0% workload, caching results in 17% fewer block fetches than without caching. This is because cached blocks can be reused across queries even without an exact duplication of the queries. Further, the number of blocks fetched proportionally reduces as the number of explicit query overlaps increase to 20% and 50%. However, the impact on the total latency is muted. Since we use four parallel threads per fog in L2, even having one block transfered in L2 can reduce the benefits of caching as that becomes the critical path.

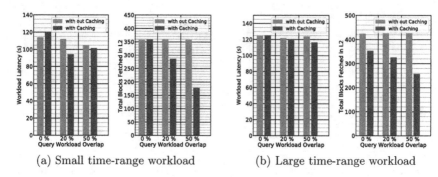

(a) Small time-range workload   (b) Large time-range workload

Fig. 6. Total workload latency and # of L2 blocks transfered, on TorqueDB with and without caching

5   Conclusions

In this paper, we have proposed TorqueDB, a novel platform for distributed execution of time-series queries on edge and fog devices, avoiding the need to keep a central TSDB in the cloud. This reduces monetary costs, keeps the data within the private network if needed, and also avoids the latency variability across a WAN to the cloud for edge applications. TorqueDB also leverages the persistence capabilities of ElfStore which allows non-query applications to use the same master data without creating duplicates within a TSDB. We also use the native TSDB querying of InfluxDB with its Flux query language, that is popular in IoT domains. Our optimizations on the query planning and caching show benefits, and mitigate the costs of on-demand block transfers in TorqueDB to give performance comparable to a central cloud VM.

As future work, we plan to extend the InfluxDB instances to run on the edge, besides the fog. This will avoid the data transfer penalty in L2, and also expose more parallelism for query execution. Support for joins and nested Flux queries is planned as well. It is also worthwhile to examine integrating TorqueDB with other distributed edge storage platforms, besides ElfStore, that may emerge over time. This is conceptually possible as we are only loosely-coupled with ElfStore, using just its public storage and lookup APIs which are likely to be offered by other systems as well. Larger scale experiments on 100's of devices with more heterogeneous compute and network capabilities will validate the scalability and performance further. Examining the impact of device unreliability on the query performance will also be examined, and contrasted against cloud TSDB.

Acknowledgment. The authors thank members of the DREAM:Lab, IISc, including Aakash Khochare, Shriram Ramesh and Sheshadri KR, for their assistance with the design, development and experiments of TorqueDB. This research was supported by grants from the DST ICPS program.

References

1. Abadi, D., et al.: The seattle report on database research. SIGMOD Rec. **48**(4), 44–53 (2020). https://doi.org/10.1145/3385658.3385668
2. Georgiou, Z., Symeonides, M., Trihinas, D., Pallis, G., Dikaiakos, M.D.: Stream-sight: a query-driven framework for streaming analytics in edge computing. In: IEEE International Conference on Utility and Cloud Computing (UCC) (2018). https://doi.org/10.1109/UCC.2018.00023
3. Ghosh, R., Simmhan, Y.: Distributed scheduling of event analytics across edge and cloud. ACM Trans. Cyber-Phys. Syst. **2**(4), 1–28 (2018). https://doi.org/10.1145/3140256
4. Grunert, H., Heuer, A.: Rewriting complex queries from cloud to fog under capability constraints to protect the users' privacy. Open J. Internet Things (OJIOT) **3**(1), 31–45 (2017)
5. Gupta, H., Xu, Z., Ramachandran, U.: Datafog: towards a holistic data management platform for the IoT age at the network edge. In: USENIX HotEdge (2018)
6. Liu, R., Yuan, J.: Benchmarking time series databases with IoTDB-benchmark for IoT scenarios. Technical Report. arXiv:1901.08304, arXiv (2019)
7. Malensek, M., Pallickara, S.L., Pallickara, S.: Hermes: federating fog and cloud domains to support query evaluations in continuous sensing environments. IEEE Cloud Comput. **4**(2), 54–62 (2017). https://doi.org/10.1109/MCC.2017.26
8. Martinviita, M.: Time series database in Industrial IoT and its testing tool. Master's thesis, University of Oulu (2018)
9. Monga, S.K., Ramachandra, S.K., Simmhan, Y.: Elfstore: a resilient data storage service for federated edge and fog resources. In: IEEE International Conference on Web Services (ICWS) (2019). https://doi.org/10.1109/ICWS.2019.00062
10. Nagato, T., Tsutano, T., Kamada, T., Takaki, Y., Ohta, C.: Distributed key-value storage for edge computing and its explicit data distribution method. IEICE Trans. Commun. (2019). https://doi.org/10.1587/transcom.2019CPP0007
11. Patel, P., Ali, M.I., Sheth, A.: On using the intelligent edge for IoT analytics. IEEE Intell. Syst. **32**(5), 64–69 (2017). https://doi.org/10.1109/MIS.2017.3711653
12. Schultz-Moller, N.P., Migliavacca, M., Pietzuch, P.: Distributed complex event processing with query rewriting. In: ACM International Conference on Distributed Event-Based Systems (DEBS) (2009). https://doi.org/10.1145/1619258.1619264
13. Simmhan, Y.: Big data and fog computing. In: Sakr, S., Zomaya, A.Y. (eds.) Encyclopedia of Big Data Technologies. Springer (2019). https://doi.org/10.1007/978-3-319-63962-8_41-1
14. Varshney, P., Simmhan, Y.: Characterizing application scheduling on edge, fog, and cloud computing resources. Softw.: Pract. Experience **50**(5), 558–595 (2019). https://doi.org/10.1002/spe.2699
15. Zhang, W., et al.: LSTM-based analysis of industrial IoT equipment. IEEE Access **6**, 23551–23560 (2018). https://doi.org/10.1109/ACCESS.2018.2825538
16. Zhou, Z.B., Zhao, D., Xu, X., Du, C., Sun, H.: Periodic query optimization leveraging popularity-based caching in wireless sensor networks for industrial IoT Applications. Mob. Netw. Appl. **20**(2), 124–136 (2014). https://doi.org/10.1007/s11036-014-0545-4

Data-Centric Distributed Computing on Networks of Mobile Devices

Pedro Sanches[1], João A. Silva[1], António Teófilo[1,2],
and Hervé Paulino[1(✉)]

[1] NOVA Laboratory for Computer Science and Informatics, Depart. de Informática,
Faculdade de Ciências e Tecnologia, Universidade NOVA de Lisboa,
Caparica, Portugal
{p.sanches,jaa.silva}@campus.fct.unl.pt, ateofilo@deetc.isel.ipl.pt,
herve.paulino@fct.unl.pt
[2] ADEETC, ISEL, Instituto Politécnico de Lisboa, Lisbon, Portugal

Abstract. In the last few years, we have seen a significant increase both in the number and capabilities of mobile devices, as well as in the number of applications that need more and more computing and storage resources. Currently, in order to deal with this growing need for resources, applications make use of cloud services. This raises some problems, namely high latency, considerable use of energy and bandwidth, and the unavailability of connectivity infrastructures. Given this context, for some applications it makes sense to do part, or all, of the computations *locally* on the mobile devices themselves. In this paper we present OREGANO, a framework for distributed computing on mobile devices, capable of processing batches or streams of data generated on mobile device networks, without requiring centralized services. Contrary to current state-of-the-art, where computations and data are sent to *worker* mobile devices, OREGANO performs computations where the data is located, significantly reducing the amount of exchanged data.

Keywords: Mobile devices · Distributed computing · Edge computing

1 Introduction

Smart mobile devices, such as smartphones and tablets, are ubiquitous in our society [1]. Nowadays, people increasingly use these devices for performing the most diverse tasks in their daily lives, from work to leisure. Due to this trend, the volume of data generated by these devices is growing rapidly, and new applications appear that are more and more resource-demanding (e.g., augmented reality apps). Accompanying this increasing demand for performance and better user experience, devices' capabilities have also been improving year after year [5].

Traditionally, in order to meet these needs, mobile applications resort to cloud services [8]. Data generated by the mobile devices is transferred to the cloud,

This work was supported by FCT-MCTES via project DeDuCe (PTDC/CCI-COM/32166/2017) and NOVA LINCS (UID/CEC/04516/2019).

M. Malawski and K. Rzadca (Eds.): Euro-Par 2020, LNCS 12247, pp. 296–311, 2020.
https://doi.org/10.1007/978-3-030-57675-2_19

where it is processed, and the output is replied back. However, in some situations and for some classes of applications [3], this approach may raise some problems. It requires (stable) network connectivity, yet network infrastructures may not exist, may be overloaded, or even destroyed. Furthermore, even assuming infrastructure availability, transferring large amounts of data to and from the cloud can lead to network congestion, increased latency, devices' battery depletion, and possible monetary costs. Also, mobile devices are known to often experience poor or intermittent connectivity, leading to availability issues if applications' logic and data are fully delegated to a remote infrastructure. Additionally, there are the non-negligible costs associated with the service setup and maintenance.

All these problems, along with the ever increasing devices' capabilities, make it pertinent to use the resources available at the network edge, i.e., in the mobile devices, and (partially or fully) process data closer to where it is generated and consumed. This alternative approach appears with the concept of edge computing [12] and has the potential to lessen many of the problems mentioned before. The edge computing paradigm pushed computations and storage beyond the data center, closer to end-user devices, enabling the execution of certain components of edge-enabled systems directly and cooperatively on edge devices. By processing data near its source, applications can be more responsive, while relieving some of the load from both cloud and network infrastructures.

In this paper we present OREGANO, a framework for data-centric distributed computing for networks formed exclusively by co-located mobile devices, without needing cloud services, and even being able to work without access to network infrastructures. OREGANO is capable of processing batches and streams of data generated, and stored, on the devices themselves. It presents a programming and execution model based on the manipulation of sets of data called Mobile Dynamic Datasets (MDDs) (see Sect. 3.2), following the proposal in [9]. MDDs are logical entities that comprise data items of a given type, characterized by a topic (such as a *hash tag* used on social networks). They are stored in a reactive storage and dissemination system with topic-based publish/subscribe functionalities, called THYME [13], and processed by a data-centric batch/stream computing model.

A possible use case for our proposal is a children birthday party, where participants take photos and share them, so that others may collect the ones they have interest on. Initially all photos may be shared with a single tag, #PartyEmily, hence defining one MDD. As the party evolves, participants may ask for the photos of a specific child, by supplying a photo of the child as a query. The resulting set of photos will define a new MDD that may be downloadable and made accessible to all through a new tag, e.g. #EmilyResult.

The current state-of-the-art proposals allow mobile devices to distribute computations and data among a set of mobile devices, as if they were nodes in a computing cluster. Thus, data needs to be moved to where it is needed, i.e., where the computations are being executed. On the contrary, OREGANO is conceptually different from these, as it allows computations to be executed where the data is located, thus reducing data transfers.

The main contributions of this paper are: i) OREGANO, a framework for data-centric distributed computing on networks of mobile devices, capable of processing batches and streams of data generated by the devices, without requiring access to network or cloud infrastructures (Sect. 3); and ii) OREGANO's evaluation in both real world and simulation experiments (Sect. 4).

2   Related Work

Serendipity [11] is a system that enables mobile devices to use computational resources from other mobile devices in the neighborhood. This system is tailored to work in scenarios of intermittent connectivity between mobile devices.

Service-Oriented Heterogeneous Resource Sharing (SOHRS) [7] describes an architecture and a mathematical framework for heterogeneous resource sharing between mobile devices, through service-oriented utility functions.

FemtoClouds [4] allows mobile devices to form computational clouds. It is based on the idea of Cloudlets [10], but all computing/processing is performed by the mobile devices that form the cloud. Task distribution is ensured by a fixed device and the system relies on infrastructure for control and coordination.

MClouds [6] is a system where mobile devices can send computations to neighboring mobile devices or to a fixed cloud, when a given task cannot be completed on the source device due to lack of resources. This system follows a master/slave architecture.

Honeybee [2] is a system where interconnected mobile devices cooperate to execute computations. It uses a master node with a job queue, from which several *worker* nodes take work following the *work stealing* scheduling strategy.

P3-Mobile [14] is a parallel computing system, based on another P3 point-to-point parallel system, which has been adapted to work in a mobile environment. It is a system that allows the dynamic division of tasks.

Compared to OREGANO, only SOHRS and P3-Mobile support different types of communication protocols. Our framework still shares several similarities with some of the other solutions with respect to computing distribution approaches, in that it follows an approach of assigning work, instead of looking for work, something that is made on P3-Mobile and Honeybee. Also, the ability to handle the entry and exit of devices on the network, is a common aspect to all solutions, including ours. Yet, there are aspects that distinguish our solution from the others. Our framework follows a peer-to-peer architecture, rather than master/slave. The programming model followed by our solution also differs from the others, in that it is a data-centric model, in contrast to task-based models—programmers apply processing functions over data sets rather creating computing tasks. Similarly to the other solutions, OREGANO supports the processing of bounded data sets, i.e., batches. However, OREGANO also supports the processing of unbounded data sets, i.e., streams, something that none of the other solutions do.

3 Oregano

OREGANO is a framework for distributed computing on a network of mobile devices. It provides for the processing of bounded and unbounded data sets generated by, and residing on, those same devices. A data set contains all items published under the same topic/tag, being the items themselves stored in the publishing device's memory (and possibly replicated by others). The distributed nature of the data sets is abstracted by the concept of Mobile Dynamic Dataset (MDD), the system's unit of work.

Besides generating data, an OREGANO device may also offer computational *services*. These services are announced, but, in general, they should be an integral part of the application. Meaning that an application that allows users to publish photos and find photos with a given face, should incorporate both the client and server counterparts of the interaction.

Building from the concepts of MDD and Service, OREGANO offers APIs to: a) develop and make available services to process MDDs; and b) publish data and submit queries through a Publish/Subscribe (P/S) mechanism that grows from THYME [13]—a reactive storage system that combines a storage interface with a P/S abstraction (which we will briefly present in Sect. 3.1).

Concerning its architecture, OREGANO is a symmetric distributed system sustained by a set of interconnected mobile devices, which communicate through wireless technologies, such as Wi-Fi, Bluetooth or WiFi-Direct [15]. All devices run the same software stack and have no specific functions permanently assigned. However, at a given instant a device may play one, or more, of the three following roles (which will be detailed in Sect. 3.4): **client** – that emits computational service requests upon an MDD; **scheduler** – that receives service requests and distributes the required computational tasks among the devices hosting the MDD's data; and **computing node** – that executes computational tasks over one or more of the MDD's elements residing in its memory. Lastly, OREGANO does not impose any mobility restrictions on the devices, meaning that these may enter or leave the system at any time.

3.1 THYME in a Nutshell

THYME is a time-aware data storage and dissemination system that follows a data-centric approach, and uses a key-value substrate built on top of a cell-based Distributed Hash Table (DHT). Nodes are clustered into cells, being that messages addressed to a cell are delivered to all nodes within that cell. The use of the cell-based DHT is two-fold: 1) cells are used to store all system data; and 2) cells are exploited to match subscriptions against published content, i.e., cells act as virtual P/S brokers. The work reported in [13] addresses *ad-hoc* networks, being cells defined by the geographic location of the devices. In infrastructure-based solutions, the distribution of the devices across cells is merely logical, bound to the amount of devices and data being published.

In THYME, a data item has some associated metadata, provided at publish time. Among others, it includes a small description and a set of tags related with

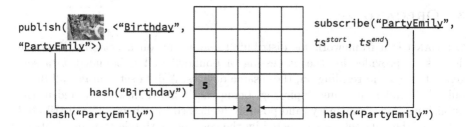

Fig. 1. Publish and subscribe operations in THYME. The tags' hashing determines the cells responsible for managing the metadata (cells 2 and 5) and the subscription (cell 2). Photo taken from Pexels.com (Author: Samaraagenstvo Feeria).

the content (and the system adds the publication time). Metadata is indexed by all its tags, i.e., the cells resultant from hashing each tag replicate the metadata (as in Fig. 1). If desired, the actual content may be replicated in the nodes of the publisher's cell (at the moment of the publication). Figure 1 illustrates the publish and subscribe operations of a photo with tags "Birthday" and "PartyEmily". A subscription comprises, among others, the query defining which tags are relevant, and timestamps defining when the subscription's time frame starts and expires. Regarding this feature, we consider *bounded data sets* to be the ones whose expiration time is in the past, i.e., all data is known in advance, and *unbounded data sets*, the ones that have expiration time in the future.

Hashing each of the query's literal (i.e., tags) determines the cells where to send that part of the query. These cells become (virtual) brokers for the subscription, and are responsible for checking if published content matches the subscription, notifying the subscribers, if needed be. By inspecting the item's description (e.g., a photo thumbnail), a notified subscriber may then decide to download the item from the list of received locations, or not.

Additionally, THYME supports multiple tag namespaces across applications or even within a single application, e.g., to support multiple data sets (like photo galleries, or shared folders). Lastly, it assumes that the nodes' clocks are synchronized (with a negligible skew).

3.2 Mobile Dynamic Dataset (MDD)

An MDD is an abstraction for a data set distributed among several devices. The concept is similar to the Resilient Distributed Data Sets presented in [16], but applied to the reality of mobile distributed computing. As previously stated, an MDD is identified by a tag (a THYME tag in our case). So, every data item published with a given tag becomes part of the same MDD.

The data resides in the devices, and hence MDDs are likely to be partitioned into multiple partitions, that we refer to as MDD partitions (MDDps). Moreover, given that THYME supports replication—both active and passive—there might be multiple locations for each MDD element. Thus, the number of partitions of an MDD also depends on the locations selected for each element. This allows to balance the load of the computational tasks, as we will discuss in Sect. 3.6. Figure 2 illustrates an MDD with three partitions.

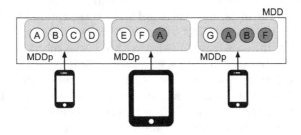

Fig. 2. MDD partitioned across three devices. Red dots depict replicas of the items.

3.3   Oregano Service

In OREGANO, a service processes an input MDD and generates a new one. The output may be simply transient, just to provide a way for the client to obtain the result, or be persisted for future computations. To process an MDD, a service must implement the **process** operation:

    MDDStream<Output> process(MMDStream<PPInput>, [List<Args>])

that defines the computation to be applied to an MDDp. The input partition is received as a Java stream, whose processing produces a new stream of results that will become a partition of the new MDD. There is no obligatory 1-to-1 relationship between the number of items received and produced. The **process** operation may also receive a list of arguments that are part of the service's request. An example is the data representing the face to search in a photo MDD.

A service may also implement the **preProcess** operation to extract from the data items the information needed by the **process** operation:

    PPInput preProcess(Input, [List<Args>])

This mechanism allows for **process** to execute over data that is not explicitly contained in the input MDD. Once again, using the photo application example: the **process** operation may work upon features extracted from the photos, rather than on the photos themselves. The extraction of the features is then defined as a pre-processing function—computed by the **preProcess** operation—that is mapped to all the elements of the input MDDp. The output is a new MDDp of elements of type **PPInput** that becomes the input of the **process** operation.

The pre-processing operation is a 1-to-1 mapping function that may be *eagerly* or *lazily* applied. In the first case, it is applied when the data item is published, whilst, in the second case, it is only applied the first time the data item is to be processed by the service. As will be discussed in Sect. 4.1, this choice entails a trade-off between latency and energy consumption.

Service Request. In OREGANO, services are requested via a novel kind of subscription, called Subscription with Computation (SubC), which adds (to THYME's subscription) the identifier of the computational service to be triggered when a match to the query is found. A SubC is thus defined by a tuple $\langle sid, q, ts^s, ts^e, nid, cid, \overline{args}, hdl \rangle$ where sid is the subscription identifier; q is the query that defines the target MDD; ts^s and ts^e are the timestamps defining the time interval when the subscription is active; nid is the subscriber's node identifier; cid is the computational service identifier; $\overline{args}$ is the list of arguments to be passed to the service (including the tag for the result MDD); and hdl is a result handler. To provide control over service requests that target big MDDs, the contents of the latter are processed in batches of configurable size. The hdl handler is triggered whenever a notification of new results arrive or a failure is detected. Upon the notification of new results, the requester is informed of how many items are yet to be processed, and may ask for the execution of the next batch.

3.4   Execution Model

The OREGANO design is centered on the premise that, in almost every scenario, the computation must be restricted to data residing on the devices' memory. This approach ensures that the computational services do not place a heavy burden of communications in the network. A service request is a control operation that triggers the execution of computational tasks on one, or more, devices, which subsequently notify the requester of data that matches the query. If the result is small enough (with a configurable threshold) it may replace the item's description in the notification message. Otherwise, the notification messages only carry the result's description, and the locations from which it may be subsequently downloaded (via THYME).

Figure 3 depicts a coarse-grained representation of the steps involved in the processing of a service request. SubCs are emitted by OREGANO *clients* to the *schedulers* (step ①), which schedule the necessary computational *tasks* among the devices (*computing nodes*) that host a partition of the target MDD (step ②). Then, these *computing nodes* process their partition. Once concluded and when results are produced, the *computing nodes* notify the *client* that issued the request: either by publishing the results in THYME (step ③), or by sending the notification directly to the client. At the same time, they inform the *scheduler* that their task is completed (step ④). Next, we further detail the roles each OREGANO node may assume.

Client. OREGANO *clients* are able to manage the availability of the services they offer to the system, publish data items (with eager pre-processing, if desired), and issue and manage the execution of SubCs. A SubC triggers two THYME subscriptions: one on the tags specified on the request, and another on a *result* tag that identifies the result MDD. This result tag may be explicitly supplied by the application, when the result is to be persisted (with such tag), or be internally

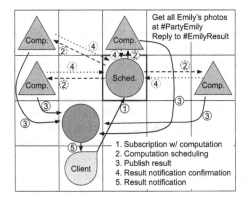

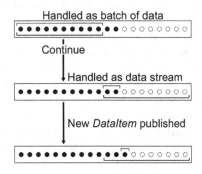

Fig. 3. General execution model.

Fig. 4. Scheduling a *computation request*: in blue, a batch; in red, items in a scheduled task. (Color figure online)

generated by the framework, when it is simply to be used as a mechanism to deliver the results to the requester.

As mentioned in Sect. 3.3, SubCs are processed in batches. The triggering of the execution of a new batch is of the requester's responsibility, and may only be done after receiving the notification that the previous batch has been processed. This iterative mechanism avoids processing items that the client may not want to receive, due to lack of memory, time, or interest, among others. When asking for a new batch, clients must send the desired batch number, as the scheduler is stateless with regards to client requests.

Scheduler. A *scheduler* is responsible for scheduling and managing a SubC. Virtually, it is the THYME cell responsible for managing the MDD's tag. In practice, a random device is chosen from the ones that compose such cell. THYME guarantees (through active replication) that all the devices in a cell replicate the metadata regarding a given tag/MDD.

From this metadata, the *scheduler* is able to select the next batch of items to process, and from the multiple replicas of each item, select the devices on which to execute the desired service. If the MDD is bounded and there are no more items to process, the corresponding reply is sent back to the requesting client, and the procedure is concluded. Conversely, if the MDD is unbounded and the batch is not complete, the data is treated like a stream, and new tasks will be scheduled as new data items are published to the MDD (Fig. 4).

The execution of a scheduled *task* may fail, for instance, if the device responsible for the work leaves the network. Such event is detected by the *scheduler*, via a *heartbeat* mechanism, causing the task to be rescheduled to another device from the ones that replicate the data items to process.

Computing Node. Upon the reception of a task execution request, a device assumes the *computing node* role and executes the following workflow: 1) create an MDDp from the data items to process (locally stored in THYME); 2) for services that require pre-processing, check if every MDD item has already been pre-processed and, if not, pre-process it by calling the `pre-process` operation on the target service; 3) obtain a stream for the MDDp and pass it as argument to a call of `process` on the requested service; and 4) deliver the results according to a *pluggable* strategy. For infrastructure-based scenarios, the default strategy is: if a tag for the new MDD was explicitly supplied, then publish every element of the result MDDp with such tag. Otherwise, contact the service requester directly. If the latter cannot be found, the contact is postponed a given number of times until it is dropped.

3.5 Handling Churn

Churn may interfere with OREGANO at different levels. We have already addressed the issue of *computing nodes* gone missing, but the same may happen with *schedulers* and *clients*. If, in a *computing-scheduler* interaction, a particular *scheduler* cannot be reached, a new one is randomly selected from the same cell. In order for the new node to have the necessary data, scheduling information is also actively replicated within cells. This solution also provides the framework for handling churn in *client-scheduler* interactions.

Lastly, we have the case of missing *clients* on the *computing-client* interaction. The result *delivery strategy* described in the previous section, discards result notifications to absent clients. A more conservative approach can, always, publish the results, even if these were directed to a particular client, i.e., the result tag was automatically generated. Naturally, every publish operation generates metadata and, hence, there is a trade-off between persisting all the results on THYME and, the storage space and network communication required to provide such availability.

3.6 Load Balancing

In OREGANO, devices that publish more data items are likely to be the ones that execute more computational tasks. However, this can be mitigated by activating THYME's active replication, and making all nodes of the publisher's cell to contribute on this enterprise. The load then becomes managed at cell- rather that node-level. Nonetheless, there may still be cells that have more load than others. To overcome this load imbalance, we resort to THYME's passive replication.

As devices that download a data item become replicas of such item, several replicas will pop on the network. Moreover, the more popular items are, the more replicas they will have. The *scheduler* leverages this property and uses an uniform distribution to spread the service requests among all replicas (of a given data item) it knows.

Although the scheduling process is not computation-intensive, the *scheduler* cells can also create sources of load imbalance, since some tags may be more popular than others (and in THYME each tag is managed by a single cell). These cannot be solved via passive replication, because there is no passive replication of metadata. In infrastructure-based scenarios, this imbalance can be mitigated by a dynamic management of the cells' membership, which is ongoing work.

4 Evaluation

Here, we present an evaluation of our framework, both through real world and simulation experiments. With this, we intend to address the following aspects: 1) what is the framework's behavior regarding latency and scalability; 2) which are the energy costs of the operations offered by the framework; and 3) what is the impact of churn in the framework.

4.1 Real World Experiments

For the experiments with real devices, we used OREGANO in a facial recognition Android application. The *app* allows users to publish photos with associated tags, and subscribe with computation to specific tags. We defined an OREGANO service capable of applying facial recognition to images by using the Java interface for OpenCV. As arguments, the service receives a similarity threshold, and the (features of the) faces to search for. The prePprocess operation performs face detection and feature extraction over a published photo. The process operation goes through the input stream (of pre-processed data items) and applies the facial recognition algorithm to every element, returning an output stream with all the photos having faces matching the ones given in the service arguments.

We tested our application using a network composed by six mobile devices (three Motorola Moto G 2nd gen. and three Motorola Nexus 6), connected through a Wi-Fi hot-spot offered by a laptop.

Latency and Scalability. First, we study the impact of the number of available computing devices in the latency of the SubC operation. In the experiment, a single device issues a SubC operation to a specific tag, bound to an MDD containing 30 photos (of equal size), published with pre-processing. Figures 5 and 6 report the operation's latency when varying the number of devices storing the MDD. In both figures, we divide the total latency in two: the *request latency* corresponds to the time taken to manage the operation itself, and the *service latency* corresponds to the time taken by the (facial recognition) service to process the photos.

In Fig. 5, we can observe the request latency is independent of the number of devices, being around six seconds. However, the error bar displaying the standard deviation, reveals a slight variation in the results. This is justified by the heterogeneous device hardware and by the roles each device plays in the experiments. Different devices playing different roles will provide different overall performances, thus affecting the measured latency. To this variation also contributes the fact that the whole process of submitting a service request and scheduling

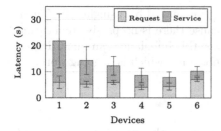

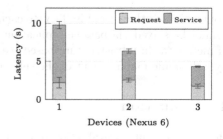

Fig. 5. SubC latency, hetero-hardware.   **Fig. 6.** SubC latency, homo-hardware.

tasks is communication-, rather than, computation-bound. Hence, the additional interactions required to conclude a service request, as the number of computing nodes increases, have a clear impact on the measured latency—noticeable for the six device setup.

Concerning the service latency, it is directly proportional to the number of devices, since the workload is equally divided among all of them. Additionally, the error bar shows a high variability in the results, also due to the heterogeneous hardware. The facial recognition service is computationally intensive, and so, the processing time is highly dependent on the devices' hardware. In our setting, Nexus 6 devices perform the same work more than three times faster than Moto Gs. To remove this entropy factor from our results, hereafter, all reported experiments only make use of Nexus 6 devices.

Figure 6 reports the SubC latency when using this homogeneous setup. The depicted standard deviation confirms the *low variability of the results* claim. We may also observe that the service latency decreases with the number of devices, showing an almost linear behavior. With three devices, the latency of the whole operation is less than half than when using a single device.

Eager Versus Lazy Pre-processing. Figure 7 depicts the impact of the pre-processing mechanism on SubC's latency. The experiment measures service latency when varying the pre-processing strategy (*lazy* or *eager*) and the number of photos that each computing node has to process (10, 15 or 30).

In the *lazy* setting, the `pre-process` operation is deferred to when the local MDDps are processed for the first time, and thus, the service latency values accumulate both the pre-processing and the processing time. Conversely, in the *eager* setting, the service latency only accounts for the MDD's processing time, as all the items were already pre-processed.

In our *app* case-study, the pre-processing stage takes longer than the processing itself, by a factor of roughly three. As a result, the choice between lazy or eager pre-processing has a considerable impact. By ensuring that only items that are effectively processed by a given node are pre-processed in that node, the lazy approach is more energy friendly, hence allowing for devices to participle in the system for longer periods of time. On the other hand, the eager approach can be an alternative if faster response times are desired from the start. This denotes

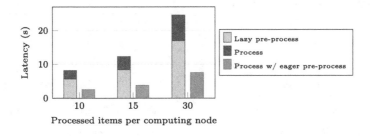

Fig. 7. Service latency: eager and lazy pre-processing.

a trade-off between service latency and wasted resources/energy consumption. Recall that the lazy alternative only impacts on the first time the items are processed by a given service (on a given node). For instance, in our birthday party scenario, photos that are lazily pre-processed for matching against a face, e.g., Emily's, will not have to be pre-processed again to handle a subsequent query for another face, e.g., George's.

Energy Consumption. OREGANO executes on mobile devices, which have known energy limitations. Thus, it is important to measure the impact of the systems' execution on a device's battery. To that end, we measured the consumed energy (in the Nexus 6 devices) by reading the instantaneous current and voltage every second, from the devices' Android API.

Figure 8 displays the amount of energy spent to execute the entire workflow of operations *publication with eager pre-process* (Pub pp) and SubC, when executed individually. The measurements include the energy spent by the device issuing the operation (the client), as well as the energy implicitly spent by the remainder devices involved in the workflows, denoted by M Pub, and M Sub.

Pub pp is the operation that consumes more energy, around 6.64 J. This is mostly due to computationally intensive pre-processing operation for extracting the faces of an image. The management of the publication is delegated on THYME, and it is only displayed here to present a complete view of Pub pp's energy cost (M Pub on the chart).

Regarding the SubC operation and its management, as expected, most of the energy consumption is not at the *client*, but in the scheduling of the tasks and on the execution of the service.

To provide more insightful information, we analyze how much energy is spent when a device executes the following operations continuously over one minute: publication (Pub), publication with pre-process (Pub pp), subscription with computation (SubC), scheduling tasks (Sched), and processing MDDps (Proc). We began by measuring the amount of energy spent by a Nexus 6 when in *stand by*, only connected to a WiFi hot-spot for one minute, which yielded roughly 40 J. Next, we launched our *application* and left it in stand by (exchanging only the messages required by THYME to maintain the network), with spent approximately 20 J more: totaling ≈ 60 J. The additional energy required by the operations under analysis is reported in Fig. 9.

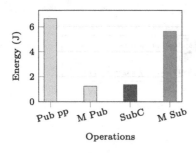
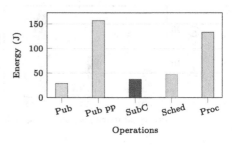

Fig. 8. Energy for a single operation.   **Fig. 9.** Energy for one minute of operations.

SubCs operations spent around 38 J (totaling 98 J), which we consider to be a reasonable amount of energy spent, given that we submitted 15 SubCs and that 98 J correspond to about 0.22% of a Nexus 6's battery. Sched required 47 J, totaling 107 J that corresponds to 0.24% of the battery. Proc yielded the second highest total battery cost, 194 J, to apply the facial recognition algorithm to 75 photos. This corresponds to approximately 0.44% of the Nexus 6's battery, which is also a rather good energy-to-result ratio. Pub pp spent 157 J to publish 40 photos, totaling 220 J that corresponds to about 0.5% of the battery. When the operation is expensive, as in this case study, it must be used wisely.

On OREGANO, a mobile device can play three different roles. Although we presented each of the three battery costs separately, executing the entire workflow of a SubC, on three different devices, spent a total of 400 J. In a scenario on which a mobile device is used for two and a half hours, constantly being used as a client, scheduler or computing node, an average of 133 J (0.3% of a Nexus 6's battery) is potentially spent per minute, which, after 150 min, corresponds to approximately 45% of a Nexus 6's battery. This value is quite reasonable, considering the type and duration of this intensive usage.

4.2   Simulation Experiments

For the simulated environment we implemented a less computationally intensive OREGANO service. It is a text pattern matching service that returns texts that contain a specified textual pattern, such as a word. To simulate the mobile devices, we used the simulator available for THYME that simulates a large number of devices running a THYME-based Android software stack. The simulator handles all inter-device communication, allowing for the insertion of delays and faults, and also provides functionalities for nodes to leave and enter the network at any time. The behavior of each node is defined in a trace file.

Impact of Churn When Scheduling Tasks. To evaluate the impact of churn in the scheduling of tasks, we devised a test where nodes from an MDD's scheduling cell, leave such cell. The nodes' absence may make it impossible to continue (asking for the next batch of) a previous computation request, hence

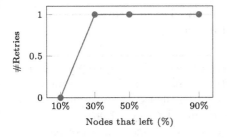

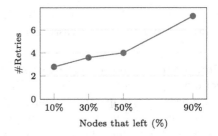

Fig. 10. Scheduler cell churn.   **Fig. 11.** Computing cell churn.

disrupting the operation. The experiment consisted of trying to perform 20 continue operations on a SubC, while observing the number of retries done before the operations executed successfully. A retry occurs whenever the *scheduler* fails to acknowledge a request, leading the client to resend it—if the previously contacted node has left, THYME should detect it, remove it from the cell's membership and, thus, direct the new request to a new node. We used four cells and a total of 16 nodes: one cell with one *client*, another with a node for handling the result tag, a *scheduler* cell with 10 nodes, and a *computing* cell with four nodes.

Figure 10 depicts the results. No retries were necessary when 10% of the nodes left the cell, and only one retry was needed to perform 20 continue operations in up to 90% of absent nodes. This shows that OREGANO is able to mitigate churn in *client-scheduler* interactions, with low impact.

Impact of Churn When Executing Tasks. Additionally, we removed devices performing computing tasks, in order to asses OREGANO's tolerance to churn in *scheduler-computing* interactions. The experiment consisted in performing 50 SubCs operations and observing the number of retries performed by *scheduler* nodes, while scheduling tasks. A total of 16 nodes were divided in four cells: one cell with one *client*, another with one node for handling the result tag, the *scheduler* cell with four nodes, and the *computing* cell with 10 nodes.

Figure 11 shows that an average of 2.8 retries were performed when 10% of the computing nodes were missing, having increased as more nodes were removed from the network, to around of 7.2 retries for 90% of absent nodes. Although THYME is able to detect which nodes left the network, it does not proactively updates the metadata of the items that were published and replicated by such nodes. This means that when OREGANO, specifically the *scheduler*, retrieves metadata of schedule tasks, the contained replica list may be outdated. To avoid rescheduling tasks to devices that were not available, every *scheduler* continuously updates this information. However, the mechanism is purely local and not shared with the remainder members of the cell. Nonetheless, all operations completed with success, assessing OREGANO's ability to deal with churn in *scheduler-computing* interactions. Also, observing that going from 10 to 90% of churn only increased the number of retires in four operations, we may conclude that

OREGANO is not highly affected by churn, being able to recover from failures without exchanging an excessive amount of messages.

Limitations. In both churn experiments, the values observed were positive and met our expectations. It is, however, important to point out that our framework is still negatively impacted by churn, specifically in the experienced latency and in the number of messages exchanged. Regarding latency, OREGANO detects failures whenever an expected acknowledge or heartbeat message is not received in a given time window. This is naturally only detected after pre-defined timeouts have expired, significantly increasing the latency of a computation request. We allow for the dynamic configuration of these timeouts, providing the foundations for the implementation of dynamic adaptive policies dependent on the execution environment.

5   Conclusion

We presented OREGANO, a peer-to-peer framework for data-centric distributed computing on networks of mobile devices. OREGANO offers a novel data-centric mobile-computing-aware way of processing batches or streams of data that are generated by co-located mobile devices, without requiring cloud infrastructures.

Our experiments allowed us to conclude that OREGANO is able to adequately schedule tasks among many devices and that the increase of simultaneous SubC operations does not necessarily means an increase in the latency of individual service requests. Lastly, we showed that the energy consumption of OREGANO is suitable for usage in mobile devices, and that OREGANO is able to tolerate churn of scheduling and computing nodes, and thus is suitable for use in mobile computing networks.

As future work we plan to improve the load balance of computational work between cells, taking the devices battery and CPU power in consideration; and make system timeouts adaptive.

References

1. Cisco: Cisco Annual Internet Report (2018–2023) (2018). https://www.cisco.com/c/en/us/solutions/collateral/executive-perspectives/annual-internet-report/white-paper-c11-741490.html. Accessed June 2020
2. Fernando, N., Loke, S.W., Rahayu, W.: Computing with nearby mobile devices: a work sharing algorithm for mobile edge-clouds. IEEE Trans. Cloud Comput. **7**(2), 329–343 (2019). https://doi.org/10.1109/TCC.2016.2560163
3. Georgakopoulos, D., Jayaraman, P.P., Fazia, M., Villari, M., Ranjan, R.: Internet of things and edge cloud computing roadmap for manufacturing. IEEE Cloud Comput. **3**(4), 66–73 (2016). https://doi.org/10.1109/MCC.2016.91
4. Habak, K., Ammar, M.H., Harras, K.A., Zegura, E.W.: Femto clouds: leveraging mobile devices to provide cloud service at the edge. In: 8th IEEE International Conference on Cloud Computing. CLOUD, pp. 9–16 (2015). https://doi.org/10.1109/CLOUD.2015.12

5. Halpern, M., Zhu, Y., Reddi, V.J.: Mobile CPU's rise to power: quantifying the impact of generational mobile CPU design trends on performance, energy, and user satisfaction. In: IEEE International Symposium on High Performance Computer Architecture. HPCA, pp. 64–76 (2016). https://doi.org/10.1109/HPCA.2016.7446054

6. Miluzzo, E., Cáceres, R., Chen, Y.F.: Vision: mClouds - computing on clouds of mobile devices. In: 3rd ACM Workshop on Mobile Cloud Computing and Services. MCS, pp. 9–14 (2012). https://doi.org/10.1145/2307849.2307854

7. Nishio, T., Shinkuma, R., Takahashi, T., Mandayam, N.B.: Service-oriented heterogeneous resource sharing for optimizing service latency in mobile cloud. In: 1st International Workshop on Mobile Cloud Computing & Networking. MobileCloud, pp. pp. 19–26. ACM (2013). https://doi.org/10.1145/2492348.2492354

8. Pal, S.: Extending mobile cloud platforms using opportunistic networks: survey, classification and open issues. J. Univ. Comput. Sci. **21**(12), 1594–1634 (2015). https://doi.org/10.3217/jucs-021-12-1594

9. Remédios, D., Teófilo, A., Paulino, H., Lourenço, J.: Mobile device-to-device distributed computing using data sets. In: 12th EAI International Conference on Mobile and Ubiquitous Systems: Computing, Networking and Services. MobiQuitous, pp. pp. 297–298. ACM (2015). https://doi.org/10.4108/eai.22-7-2015.2260273

10. Satyanarayanan, M., Bahl, P., Cáceres, R., Davies, N.: The case for VM-based cloudlets in mobile computing. IEEE Pervasive Comput. **8**(4), 14–23 (2009). https://doi.org/10.1109/MPRV.2009.64

11. Shi, C., Lakafosis, V., Ammar, M.H., Zegura, E.W.: Serendipity: enabling remote computing among intermittently connected mobile devices. In: 13th ACM International Symposium on Mobile Ad Hoc Networking and Computing. MobiHoc, pp. pp. 145–154 (2012). https://doi.org/10.1145/2248371.2248394

12. Shi, W., Cao, J., Zhang, Q., Li, Y., Xu, L.: Edge computing: vision and challenges. IEEE Internet Things J. **3**(5), 637–646 (2016). https://doi.org/10.1109/JIOT.2016.2579198

13. Silva, J.A., Paulino, H., Lourenço, J.M., Leitão, J., Preguiça, N.M.: Time-aware reactive storage in wireless edge environments. In: 16th EAI International Conference on Mobile and Ubiquitous Systems: Computing, Networking and Services. MobiQuitous, pp. 238–247. ACM (2019). https://doi.org/10.1145/3360774.3360828

14. Silva, J., Silva, D., Marques, E.R.B., Lopes, L., Silva, F.: P3-mobile: parallel computing for mobile edge-clouds. In: 4th Workshop on CrossCloud Infrastructures & Platforms. CrossCloud@EuroSys, pp. pp. 5:1–5:7. ACM (2017). https://doi.org/10.1145/3069383.3069388

15. Teófilo, A., Remédios, D., Lourenço, J.M., Paulino, H.: GOCRGO and GOGO: two minimal communication topologies for WiFi-direct multi-group networking. In: 14th EAI International Conference on Mobile and Ubiquitous Systems: Computing, Networking and Services. MobiQuitous, pp. 232–241. ACM (2017). https://doi.org/10.1145/3144457.3144481

16. Zaharia, M., et al.: Resilient distributed datasets: a fault-tolerant abstraction for in-memory cluster computing. In: 9th USENIX Symposium on Networked Systems Design and Implementation. NSDI, pp. 15–28 (2012). https://doi.org/10.5555/2228298.2228301

WPSP: A Multi-correlated Weighted Policy for VM Selection and Migration for Cloud Computing

Sergi Vila[1]([⊠])(iD), Josep L. Lérida[1]([⊠])(iD), Fernando Cores[1]([⊠])(iD), Fernando Guirado[1]([⊠])(iD), and Fabio L. Verdi[2]([⊠])(iD)

[1] INSPIRES, Universitat de Lleida, Lleida, Spain
{svila,jlerida,fcores,f.guirado}@diei.udl.cat
[2] Department of Computer Science, Federal University of São Carlos, Sorocaba, Brazil
verdi@ufscar.br

Abstract. Using virtualization, cloud environments satisfy dynamically the computational resource necessities of the user. The dynamic use of the resources determines the demand for working hosts. Through virtual machine (VM) migrations, datacenters perform load balancing to optimize the resource usage and solve saturation. In this work, a policy, named WPSP (Weighted Pearson Selection Policy), is implemented to choose which virtual machines are more suitable to be migrated. For each VM, the policy evaluates both the CPU load and the Network traffic influence on the assigned host. The corresponding Pearson correlation coefficients are calculated for each of the VMs and then weighted in order to provide a relationship between the values and the host behavior. The main goal is to clearly identify and then migrate the VMs that are responsible of the Host saturation but also considering their communications. Using the CloudSim simulator, the policy is compared with the rest of heuristic techniques in the literature, resulting in a reduction of 89% in the number of migrations, and thus reducing the use of bandwidth (5%), network saturation (20%) and over-saturated hosts (51%). Additionally, an improved VM allocation technique to reduce the distance the VMs must travel in order to be migrated is presented, obtaining an average reduction of 87% in the quantity of migrated data.

Keywords: Cloud Computing · Planning · Virtual machines · Migrations · Pearson correlation coefficient · Load balancing · CloudSim

1 Introduction

Cloud Computing has become an effective alternative to local servers for many users, whether to allocate the resources of companies or to compute scientific

This work has been possible thanks to MEIyC-Spain TIN2017-84553-C2-2-R and São Paulo Research Foundation (FAPESP) under the grant #15/19766-9.

© Springer Nature Switzerland AG 2020
M. Malawski and K. Rzadca (Eds.): Euro-Par 2020, LNCS 12247, pp. 312–326, 2020.
https://doi.org/10.1007/978-3-030-57675-2_20

programs in research centers. It provides dynamic and scalable virtualization resources through a network service and forms a virtual computing resource pool allocated to a classic data center. Thus, it is possible to combine the hosts' capacity on an on-demand pay-per-cycle basis, guaranteeing the defined Service Level Agreement (SLA) to the users.

However, variability in the request-rate from the cloud service consumers at any given time can seriously affect not only the Quality of Service (QoS) but also the SLA. The applications, and particularly the network-intensive ones, often need to communicate frequently, and the network I/O performance would affect the overall VM performance notably. In this situation, hosts become overloaded and unable to resolve all the requests, negatively impacting the SLA.

In the literature, there are many methods to avoid overloading hosts in data centers. Some of these are based on load balancing strategies that facilitate the distribution of the workload equally over the available resources [8]. Other proposals apply VM migration to provide the required resources to the VMs responsible for the host overload. However, the migration process can produce unexpected network latency or congestion that becomes critical for achieving and maintaining the performance of the application. That is why the migration process requires correctly identifying a candidate migratable VM that ensures not only the host load reduction but also keeps use of the inter-VMs communication links contained, thus avoiding an SLA violation.

In the present paper, we propose the use of the Pearson correlation factor to correctly identify those VMs that are seriously affecting the host overload, taking into account both the computational and communication resource usage. The proposed method not only tackles the current host state, but also evaluates the previous states captured during the host execution timeline. When the VM is identified, the migration process moves it to another host, releasing the corresponding resources and effectively reducing the host overload. Moreover, our proposal incorporates a weighting factor that provides a much closer relationship between VM correlation and Host behaviour. To avoid unnecessary VM migrations, our proposal attempts to find the balance between the quantity of CPU released by a VM and the communication affinity with the rest of the VMs within the host.

The experimental results have been compared with the most well-known heuristic methods from the literature, and demonstrate that our proposal improves the host usage avoiding the overload and also reducing the global number of VM migrations.

The rest of the work is organized as follows: in Sect. 2, the state of the art used for the present work is described. Section 3 presents the VM selection policy. Section 4 contains the experimental study, and finally, the conclusions and future work are discussed in Sect. 5.

2   State of the Art

In the literature, there are many works related to the virtual machine migration process. Raja et al. in [2] present a survey of VM migration and server consolidation. They evaluated multiple migration schemes and they took into account different parameters to compare them. Their conclusions pointed to the fact that unnecessary and uncontrolled migrations are the main reason for SLA violation. Most of the proposed solutions to initiate the migration process were based on processing discrete data-captures to evaluate the QoS while others were based on applying machine learning-based adaptive thresholds. In the present paper, we propose an effective correlation-based method with data obtained from tracking the host execution time-line taking snapshots periodically.

The correlation between two sets of data is a statistical measure that calculates the strength of the relationship between the relative values of two variables. There are many studies in the literature applied to different fields of knowledge that demonstrate the importance of correlation between multiple parameters for taking correct decisions. Douglas et al. in [4] and Winter et al. in [15] compared some correlation factors and their quality. In the current paper, given the continuous nature of the variables (CPU and network load values) and the sensitivity to variations in the differences between the sample values, we decided to focus on the well-known Pearson correlation coefficient.

There are different works using correlation coefficients applied to Cloud Computing. Choudhary et al. in [6] was based on Spearman's Rank Correlation Coefficient to select the optimal VM according to the present workload and datacenter resources availability to reduce the energy consumption. The results obtained, compared with the VM Random Selection, demonstrated lower energy consumption while maintained the required SLA. Moghaddam et al. in [9] proposed a VM selection algorithm focused on energy reduction and also considering the SLA parameter. The algorithm was based on the Pearson correlation coefficient and was used to determine both VMs' CPU utilization and the correlation with their co-hosted VM. Their proposal was evaluated through simulation in the CloudSim environment, using two different real Cloud data sets by the CoMon project (PlanetLab) and Google. The results show that the correlation improves the VM identification as migratable and reduces the energy consumption. Sun et al. in [13] addressed the problem of online migration of multiple correlated VMs among multiple datacenters. This work was focused on the optimization of migration performance. The authors treated both bandwidth and routing required for the VM migration process and use the correlation to determine those VMs that must be migrated all together. The results reduced the remapping cost and the average migration time and downtime of the VMs.

Our proposal differs mainly from previous works in the fact that we use the correlation coefficients to determine the influence of the VM on the resource usage of the allocated host. We evaluate periodically both computing and communication load for each allocated VM. When an overloaded host has been identified, our method determines the VM candidate to be migrated. Applying our proposal, the overall migrations were reduced, thus reducing the network saturation, increasing the host utilization and without compromising the SLA.

In [1], Abdelsamea et al. presented a host saturation algorithm based on multiple regressions (CPU, RAM and Bandwidth), decreasing the energy consumption and SLA. Additionally, they combined Local Regression (LR) with Loess' method to develop a hybrid version of their algorithm. The results show that the implemented algorithms have better results for energy but obtains worse SLA violation results due to being inversely correlated to energy. Ali [7] et al. presented a Weighted Linear Regression algorithm for resource prediction, CPU, RAM and network bandwidth. The algorithm was compared with other detection techniques in the literature. It shows a decrease in the energy consumption while providing a high level of commitment to the SLA, maintaining a similar level of migrations.

In the present paper, we evaluated not only the similarity in behavior between VMs and Hosts, represented by the correlation factor, but also the influence that these VMs had on generating this behavior. Thus, we propose the use of a weighting factor applied to the correlation factors that allows to identify the most suitable VM to be migrated. Our proposal is also combined with a new assignment method with the main aim of decreasing the distance to be crossed in the migration process and then reducing the network utilization.

3   Problem Statement

The policy presented in this paper, hereinafter referred to as Weighted Pearson Selection Policy (WPSP), is based on three main ideas: (1) evaluating the host execution in the time-line to determine the resource usage behavior of each one and detect the overload situations, (2) evaluating the use of both computing (in terms of CPU usage) and communication (in terms of data transfer volume within the host) VM resource usage to correctly identify the VMs closely related to the host overload, and (3), applying a weighting process to the volume of CPU and network used by the VMs in relation of their host to adjust the obtained correlations, finally defining which VMs are provoking host saturations. Our first goal is to obtain knowledge of the host load during their execution. This information is acquired from snapshots taken of the system periodically. These snapshots contain information about the resources required by VMs and the resources really assigned by the hosts.

The second core element of our proposal is to determine the VM that has the greatest influence on the overloaded hosts' resource usage. Each host allocates multiple VMs and each with different resource requirements. It must be taken into account that some of these VMs can be related to the same service so that migrating any VM does not ensure the reduction of overload as the external host communication can increase due to the new VM allocation. For this, we propose to consider both computation and communication resource usage to identify their influence on the host overload and determine the relationship between the VMs inside the host.

The idea behind the use of the Pearson correlation is to determine the similarities of the CPU and network resources usage between the host and each VM, with the aim of identifying the VMs with a wider impact on the host resource usage. Knowing which VMs are the most influential, we can migrate those causing the biggest impact on the release of resources but triggering a smaller number of migration. The correlation coefficients assume n samples of two variables, x (host) and y (VM). The Pearson correlation coefficient is calculated by Eq. 1, where $\bar{x}$ and $\bar{y}$ represent the arithmetic mean of x and y, respectively. In addition, each pair of values corresponding to the same point in time cannot be altered so as to maintain the consistency of the coefficient obtained.

$$r = \frac{\sum_{i=1}^{n}(x_i - \bar{x})(y_i - \bar{y})}{\sqrt{\sum_{i=1}^{n}(x_i - \bar{x})^2 \sum_{i=1}^{n}(y_i - \bar{y})^2}} \tag{1}$$

The correlation coefficient between two ordered sets of values measures the strength of the relationship between the relative movements of the two variables. The values range is [-1, 1]. A positive correlation means that if one variable increases, the other variable also tends to increase. A negative correlation means that if one variable increases, the other variable tends to diminish. The weakest linear relationship is indicated by a correlation coefficient equal to 0.

In this paper, $rcpu$ measures the relationship between the Host CPU usage (x) and a VM's CPU usage (y), in the same way $rnet$ measures the relationship between the Host internal communications (x) and a VM's data transfers to other VMs inside the same Host (y), both calculated by Eq. 1. The main aim of the WPSP Policy is to identify the candidate VMs to be migrated to eliminate the host saturation with the minimum VM migrations. In order to meet these objectives, we consider that the VM with the highest positive $rcpu$ is the best candidate to be migrated with the aim of reducing host saturation. However, in the case that this VM also has a high positive $rnet$, the migration of the VM will produce an increase in data transfers through the external communication channels, thus fostering the saturation of these channels and producing a negative impact on global performance. To prevent this occurring, we should consider the migration of VMs with a high positive CPU correlation $rcpu \simeq 1$, but with a weak network correlation $rnet$. While there is the possibility of migrating a group of VMs highly correlated with internal communications, this option substantially increases the number of migrations and their cost.

Normalization is the process through which a set of values V, ranging from [$\min(V)$, $\max(V)$] are scaled to [0, 1]. In our policy, the CPU and BW usage of each VM is normalized in this sense. These are essential values ($ncpu$ and $nnet$) for evaluating the role of each VM inside the host, and in collaboration with the correlation value, we can figure which VMs are the most influential in terms of volume and oscillations over time. Equation 2 shows how the $ncpu$ and $nnet$ values are calculated, where x is the value (CPU or network) of the VM, x_{max} the highest value among the VMs of the same host and x_{min}, the minimum.

$$n = \frac{x - x_{min}}{x_{max} - x_{min}} \tag{2}$$

With the aim of considering the VMs' consumption of both CPU and communication resources, we propose a heuristic function computed by Eq. 3. This provides each VM with a value based on the magnitude of both the $rcpu$ and $rnet$ correlation coefficients and the $ncpu$ and $nnet$ ponderation values.

$$hval = \frac{1 - (w * rcpu * ncpu)}{(1 + (w * rcpu * ncpu) - (w * rnet * nnet))} \tag{3}$$

The heuristic function allows the relationship between both correlation coefficients and weighted values to be modelled providing a mechanism to compare the VMs within a Host. The resulting value $hval$ defines the migration priority for each VM, the lowest value being the best option. Additionally, after a specific threshold, $hval\_th$, the VMs are not allowed to be migrated, as can be seen in Fig. 1. The w variable defines the slope of the $hval$ function, and thus controls the $hval$ value scale. With a value of $w = 1$, the $hval$ function tends to 0 irrespective of the values used. On the contrary, with $w = 0$ the resulting values tend to 1. The tuning of the w variable can be useful in exceptional cases with the values located in a bunch. However, with $w = 0.5$, the resulting values are bounded in a smooth curve that allows diversity.

By way of example, Table 1 shows the corresponding $hval$ value for a set of VMs with different combinations of $rcpu$, $rnet$, $ncpu$ and $nnet$ values. Figure 1 shows the $hval$ value for each VM and their location on the plane. It shows the contour lines projected by the $hval$ function on the plane formed by $rcpu$, $rnet$, $ncpu$ and $nnet$ values. We established the premise about which are good candidates VMs to be migrated. Firstly, the VMs that are directly related to the CPU usage of its host, and secondly, the ones that have a high weight, provided that they are also weakly correlated to the internal network communication.

Table 1. Example. $hval$ results for $rcpu$ and $rnet$ correlation classes

Label	$rcpu$	$rnet$	$ncpu$	$nnet$	$hval$
VM0	0.9	0.9	0.9	0.8	0.57
VM1	−0.9	−0.6	0.2	0.3	1.09
VM2	−0.3	0.9	0.0	1.0	1.82
VM3	0.5	0.5	0.8	0.5	0.74
VM4	0.7	0.2	1.0	0.0	0.48

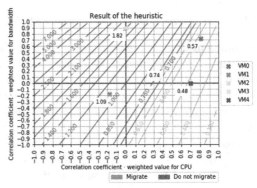

Fig. 1. $hval$ function representation and example results

We can observe this is the case for VM4, obtaining the minimum $hval$ value. It has notable CPU values, with a CPU correlation of 0.7 and big CPU usage with a weight of 1, on the contrary, the network usage is small. VM0 has more CPU correlation than VM4, but also presents higher network load, so it obtains a bigger $hval$ value. By counterpart, VMs 1, 2 and 3 have no chances to be migrated. The reason for VM1 is that it shows low weights. About VM2, its network usage is too much valuable than the CPU load, that is too low. Finally,

VM3 is near the threshold, however CPU usage should be higher. These results show that the *hval* function is suitable to prioritise the candidate VMs to be migrated.

3.1   Weighted Pearson Selection Policy

The WPSP policy proposed in this paper is represented by Algorithm 1. The WPSP policy is executed when the saturation of one of the hosts is detected. The algorithm is executed until the saturation is solved or until no more VMs are selected for migration. First, the VMs able to be migrated are obtained (line 2). Then, the Pearson correlation coefficients are obtained for each VM, in relation to the CPU (*rcpu*) and network (*rnet*) usage in the host $\mathcal{H}$ (lines 4–5). In the case of the *rnet* correlation coefficient, only communications between virtual machines within the same host are taken into account. In lines 6–7, the weighting values *ncpu* and *nnet* are obtained. Next, we obtain the heuristic value *hval* for each VM (line 8). Finally, the VMs with the minimum *hval* are selected for migration until the saturation problem is solved or no more VMs are eligible (*hval* values exceed the WPSP decision threshold *hval_th*). When no VMs meet this criterion, a null value is returned. Algorithm 1 is executed for each over-saturated host in increasing order by their number id. The complexity of Algorithm 1 is $\mathcal{O}(MVM)$, where MVM is the number of migratable VMs in the host.

3.2   Minimum Distance Group VM Allocation Policy

To complement our selection policy, WPSP, being focused on the reduction of migrations, we are interested in an allocation policy that helps it to succeed on this task. We propose an improvement based on the distance the VMs must travel across the network. The "CloudSim most efficient host" allocation technique is improved by applying the Minimum Distance Group, MDG, that is, instead of selecting the most efficient suitable host from the whole datacenter, the hosts are grouped and ordered by number of jumps inside the network, trying to migrate the VM to the nearest group. If this is not possible, the next nearest group is tested each time until it can be allocated, as can be observed in Algorithm 2. If the VM does not fit any host, that is, trying to allocate it at the current CPU usage, the migration is not performed. In general, any criteria for the selection function can be implemented. For this experimentation, the *getPowerAfterAllocation* function provided by CloudSim was selected. This returns the host with the lowest increment in its energy consumption after the VM is located.

4   Experimentation and Results

This section describes the configuration of the experimental environment, mainly based on the CloudSim simulator [5] and the results obtained.

Algorithm 1. Weighted Pearson Selection Policy - VM selection algorithm

---

Require: $\mathcal{H}$: Overloaded host, $VM_{\mathcal{H}}$: set of VMs $\in \mathcal{H}$
Ensure: $\mathcal{SVM}$: Selected migratable VMs
1: declare $\mathcal{MVM}$: migratable VMs, $rcpu$: current cpu correlation values, $rnet$: current network correlation values, $ncpu$: current cpu weighted value, $nnet$: current network weighted value, $\mathcal{H}val$: heuristic values for each $vm \in \mathcal{MVM}$, $hval\_th$: WPSP decision threshold
2: $\mathcal{MVM} \leftarrow$ getMigratableVMs($VM_{\mathcal{H}}$)
3: **for each** $vm \in \mathcal{MVM}$ **calculate**
4:     $rcpu \leftarrow calculate\_cpu\_correlation(\mathcal{H}, vm)$
5:     $rnet \leftarrow calculate\_net\_correlation(\mathcal{H}, vm)$
6:     $ncpu \leftarrow calculate\_cpu\_weight(\mathcal{MVM}, vm)$
7:     $nnet \leftarrow calculate\_net\_weight(\mathcal{MVM}, vm)$
8:     $\mathcal{H}val^{vm} \leftarrow calculate\_hval(rcpu, rnet, ncpu, nnet)$
9: **end for**
10: **while** $isSaturated(\mathcal{H})$ **do**
11:     $vm \leftarrow$ Select $vm \in \mathcal{MVM}$ with min($\mathcal{H}val$) | $\mathcal{H}val \leq hval\_th$
12:     **if** vm is $NULL$ **then**
13:         break
14:     **end if**
15:     $\mathcal{MVM} \leftarrow \mathcal{MVM} - vm$
16:     $\mathcal{SVM} \leftarrow \mathcal{SVM} \cup vm$
17: **end while**
18: **return** $\mathcal{SVM}$

Algorithm 2. MDG - VM allocation algorithm

Require: $\mathcal{H}$: Overloaded host, $\mathcal{VM}$: VM to be migrated, $\mathcal{SH}$: Set of Hosts - $\{\mathcal{H}\}$
1: $bestHost = h_i \in \mathcal{SH}$ min($distance(\mathcal{H}, h_i)$) $\cap$ min($getPowerAfterAlloc(\mathcal{VM}, h_i)$)
2: **return** $bestHost$

4.1   Experimental Setup

The CPU load traces used are part of the PlanetLab environment. They are obtained with the CoMon monitoring system [11]. There is a set of traces corresponding to 10 days of execution with around 1000 virtual machines. The first 400 files of the trace 20110303 are the ones used for the experimental study. Each contains 288 values corresponding to a day of performing. The PlanetLab traces are updated every 5 min. This determines the snapshots ratio in which VMs and Hosts data is obtained in order to evaluate the correlation coefficients.

Table 2 shows the virtual machine configuration. Each VM contains one cloudlet acting as endless tasks, whose percentage of CPU load being defined by the PlanetLab traces. Table 3 shows the main characteristics of the hosts used based on those present by default in CloudSim. The interconnection topology, where central nodes are switches, the leaf nodes being hosts, is shown in Fig. 2.

An interaction is defined as the communication between two VMs throughout the simulation. The network traces, which represent the VM interactions,

Table 2. Virtual machine characteristics

Type	# CPUs	MIPS	BW (Mbps)	RAM (MB)	Quantity
Tiny	1	750	100	870	100
Small	1	1500	100	1740	100
Medium	1	3000	100	1740	100
Large	1	3750	100	613	100

Table 3. Host characteristics

Type	Model	# CPUs	MIPS	BW (Mbps)	Quantity
Small	HP ML110 G4	2	1860	1000	21
Large	HP ML110 G5	2	2660	1000	15

were generated using the FNSS tool [12], obtaining sin cyclo-stationary traffic ($\sigma = 0.8$, $log\psi = -0.33$) according to [10]. This traffic has an equivalent behaviour to the Sprint Europe network [14]. We assume a limit of 3 Mbps for the bandwidth use for each one. Throughout the simulation, the values of the interactions are updated using the network traces. We defined three different types of interaction: low, with an occurrence of 50% and ranged between 0 and 0.6 Mbps; medium, 30% of occurrences, ranged between 0.6 and 1.8 Mbps; and high, with an occurrence of 20%, ranged between 1.8 and 2.85 Mbps.

When the VMs are located to the hosts, the interactions between them are configured. From all the possible interactions inside a host, they are created the 15% of them. Then, from the total interactions between a VM and the rest of VMs from other hosts, the 0,05% of them become real interactions. In order to test the VM preservation capabilities of our policy, and after balancing CPU and network resources, we determined that an initial 15% of internal communications offers enough traffic to maintain the VMs in the same hosts but with opportunities to leave them depending on the CPU load. During the simulation, and

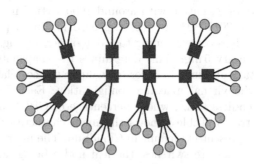

Fig. 2. Topology

Table 4. Configuration parameters of CloudSim

Parameter	Value	Parameter	Value
CPU trace	PL 20110303	BW between Host-VM	100 Mbps
% Internal interactions	15%	BW between Host-Switch	1000 Mbps
% External interactions	0.05%	CPU Saturation limit	70%
# of switches	16	Simulation time	86400 s
# of hosts	36	# of experiments per technique	30
# of virtual machines	400	Host saturation detection technique	CloudSim IQR
Window size	6	VM allocation technique	MDG
Max. BW of the interactions	3 Mbps	Underutilised host shutdowns	Disabled

due to migrations, these percentages varied, increasing the number of external communications and reducing the internal ones.

Table 4 shows a summary of the most important CloudSim configuration parameters used during the experimentation. For each technique, 30 experiments were carried out varying the initial placement of VMs in the hosts, which affected the number and typology of the interactions among the VMs. The metrics analysed in the present work are presented in Table 5.

The WPSP threshold, $hval\_th$, was set at 0.65 after analysing which value obtains the lowest ratio of unsatisfied/satisfied MIPS. Due to space reasons, this analysis is not presented.

4.2   Virtual Machine Selection Policies

The selection policy selects the VM candidate to be migrated. CloudSim's default techniques were used with the aim of compare them with the policy proposed in the present work. The techniques [3] used in the comparison are the following:

- Random Search (RS): Among the candidate VMs to be migrated, one is chosen randomly.
- Minimum Migration Time (MMT): Chooses the VM that requires the least RAM memory.
- Minimum Utilisation (MU): Chooses the VM which requested fewest MIPS during the simulation.
- Maximum Correlation (MC): A linear regression is generated transposing a matrix with the percentage of use of the last 12 instants for each VM, choosing the VM with the highest CPU usage correlation in relation to the rest of the VMs.

4.3   Default Allocation Vs. MDG

In order to investigate the effects of applying the improved version of the Default VM Allocation Algorithm implemented by CloudSim, a comparison with the

Table 5. Metrics for experimentation

Metric	Description
Traffic	Sum of the topology links traffic (MB)
Unsatisfied Traffic	Traffic (MB) that surpassed the available BW
Migration distances	Average number of jumps that a VM must do to be migrated
Number Migrations	Sum of all the migrations done at each snapshot
Unsatisfied VMs	VMs not providing the required MIPS due host over-saturation
Saturated hosts	Hosts that exceed 70% of CPU but can meet the CPU demand
Unsatisfied hosts	Hosts exceeding 100% of CPU, unsatisfying the CPU demand
% Unsatisfied MIPS	Percentage of MIPS not executed due to host over-saturation
Migrated RAM	Sum of all the sizes (MB) of the migrated VMs
RAM in BW (MB)	RAM moved across the network
Time Migrating	Sum of the time (s) the migrated VMs spent moving

different tested VM selection policies is presented, all of them using the VM allocation policy IQR. The metrics analyzed in the present work are shown in Table 5. The median and standard deviation for all of these metrics are shown in Table 6, which summarizes the complete experimentation. Bold values show the best values in DA vs. MDG comparison.

The main objective of the policy is to improve the BW used and the distance the migrated VMs must travel across the network, reducing the distance between the origin and destination hosts. Observing *RAM in BW* values (Table 6-10) is it clear the objective is achieved, reducing the quantity of MB moved across the network by an average of 40%. In a similar way, the number of jumps (Table 6-3) done by migrated VMs is reduced by 25% for WPSP and an average of 45.24% for the rest of the techniques. Moreover, the fact the VMs are migrated to nearby hosts does not affect the rest of the metrics negatively. On the contrary, except for the average ratio of unsatisfied MIPS (Table 6-4), which shows dispersed values from -7% (WPSP) to 3.3% (MC), the rest of the metrics are improved. There is a reason for the improvement in migration jumps being higher in the other metrics. WPSP starts migrating influential VMs, and, hence, VMs with higher CPU demand, which means that not all the VMs fit other hosts, thus limiting the migrations to a few hosts that could be distant. On the contrary, the other techniques migrate all kinds of VM, facilitating nearby hosts for VMs with low CPU demands. The number of *Unsatisfied Hosts* (Table 6-8) is especially reduced, with an average improvement of 12.76% being obtained. Other metrics like *Number of Migrations* (Table 6-5) or *Unsatisfied Traffic* (Table 6-2) obtain little upturns, around 5% on average, but the policy is almost guaranteed not to harm these.

4.4   VM Selection Policies Comparison

The next experiment was conducted to know the degree of improvement in both WPSP and MDG policies against the VM selection policies and the default VM allocation policy provided by CloudSim. Table 6 shows the obtained results. Underline values reveal which is the best value in the entire comparison for each metric.

A high number of saturated hosts produces a huge number of migrations. Nevertheless, the effects of some of those migrations can be negligible on the *Unsatisfied Hosts* metric. Thus, the correct migratable VM selection is crucial for reducing all these metrics and obtaining better performance. To this end, it is vitally important to identify those VMs which are really responsible for the saturation.

The results for both the *Saturated* and *Unsatisfied Hosts* metrics show great differences with regard to the policies tested in the literature. Observing host saturation, there is an average improvement of 10%, with a 9.56% improvement compared to the second best policy, MMT. Regarding Fig. 5, the *Unsatisfied Hosts*, there is a big average improvement of 51% on average, with a 52% improvement over the next technique, RS. Not only is it important to observe how many times the hosts were working over their capacities, but all the MIPS that did not perform during these periods. It can be perceived in Table 6-4, *% of UnsatisfiedMIPS*, that WPSP achieves an improvement of 10% for RS and MC, and a big upturn of 32% for MU. These results are even more impressive considering that our proposal achieves them while performing considerably fewer migrations than the other policies, 86.3% reduction in migrations compared with the policy with fewer migrations (MC) (188.5 vs 1300.5).

Observing the *Number of Migrations*, in Fig. 3, all other methods show a huge number of VM migrations. Our proposal is able to reduce the overall number of migrations by an average of up to 89%. The lower number of migrations provides greater availability of the communication links and this is obtained without any prejudice on the host loads.

Furthermore, analyzing the interconnection links, from the point of view of the used *Traffic*, Table 6-1, and the *Unsatisfied Traffic*, Fig. 4, shows values of up to −5% and −20% respectively. The VMs that were migrated were those that do not interfere in the network links, thus maintaining locally the VMs with inner communications. During the migration process, the VMs must cross

Table 6. DA-MDG VM allocation policies comparison showing median values and standard deviation

Index	Metric	WPSP		MC		MMT		MU		RS	
		DA	MDG	DA	MDG	DA	MDG	DA	MDG	DA	MDG
1	Traffic	1560913	1561781	1646162	1610919	1637468	1602595	1646674	1616205	1652648	1611330
		±18853	±18858	±10219	±20517	±13270	±18263	±10818	±19536	±18118	±20487
2	Unsat. Traffic	229150	228607	277088	263239	273139	261452	317057	300819	281150	264989
		±7341	±6894	±7658	±8779	±7179	±8371	±8992	±10526	±7786	±8888
3	Migration Distances	5.18	4.10	5.17	2.90	5.17	2.76	5.18	2.77	5.18	2.90
		±0.1	±0.2	±0.0	±0.1	±0.0	±0.1	±0.0	±0.1	±0.0	±0.1
4	Unsat. MIPS	2.41	2.24	2.48	2.57	2.12	2.15	3.29	3.14	2.49	2.51
		±0.6	±0.6	±0.6	±0.5	±0.5	±0.5	±0.7	±0.7	±0.5	±0.6
5	# of Migrations	200.0	188.5	1373.0	1300.5	1637.5	1571.0	4455.0	4144.5	1407.0	1409.0
		±17.6	±16.8	±165.7	±144.3	±163.2	±187.6	±606.3	±573.4	±157.8	±159.8
6	Unsat. VMs	7444.5	7039.5	8281.5	7933.0	7624.5	7202.0	15712.5	14022.0	8525.5	8183.5
		±1299	±1161	±1215	±1146	±967	±1034	±2446	±2121	±1082	±1193
7	Overloaded Hosts	3739	3618.5	3979	3882	4001	3872.5	4105.50	3992	3979.5	3819.5
		±281	±309	±310	±315	±249	±295	±280	±309	±310	±320
8	Unsat. Hosts	1441	1382	2799	2382.5	2293	1956	3565	3014	2904.5	2478.5
		±233	±210	±287	±322	±236	±273	±256	±344	±237	±310
9	Migrated RAM	254040	241346	1679898	1630029	1163570	1129352	5547126	5185030	1763130	1757446
		±25818	±23223	±202785	±182689	±118837	±135084	±736097	±700099	±193847	±195479
10	RAM in BW	1304229	987856	8735037	4705944	6027358	3210863	28758469	14255744	9133906	5092168
		±136889	±98238	±1042251	±661415	±618632	±433983	±3820960	±2621023	±1009010	±777004
11	Time migrating	4065	3862	26878	26080	18617	18070	88754	82960	28210	28119
		±413	±372	±3245	±2923	±1901	±2161	±11778	±11202	±3102	±3128

the network to reach their host destination. The traffic generated by these VMs could significantly exceed the data interchanged by default. Even if a method (MDG) is implemented to reduce this issue, the *Number of Migrations* is a determining factor. In Fig. 6, *RAM in BW*, and Table 6-11, *Time Migrating*, our technique has an average improvement of 89.5% and 86.7% over the other techniques. The results are consistent with the average improvement in the *Number of Migrations* (89%).

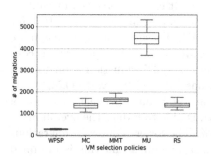

Fig. 3. Number of migrations

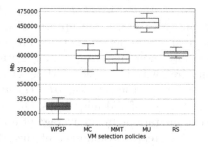

Fig. 4. Unsatisfied Traffic

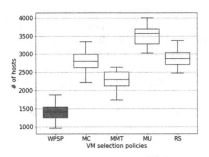

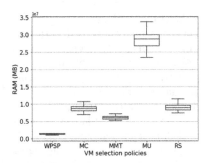

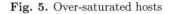

Fig. 5. Over-saturated hosts   **Fig. 6.** RAM across network

5 Conclusions

In this paper, the authors defined a VM selection policy that applies the Pearson correlation coefficient with weighting values to evaluate the influence of the VM CPU and Network utilization on the Host. This allows the correct migratable VMs to be determined that are able to reduce the Hosts overload by up to 10% compared with other methods from the literature, with an improvement of 51% in the number of unsatisfied hosts. The use of our proposal also results in a reduction of up to 5% in the bandwidth used and reduced the data traffic by up to 20%.

Additionally, an improvement, MDG, in the default VM allocation policy provided by CloudSim is implemented. This reduces the distance the migrated VMs must travel across the network. The technique is able to reduce the quantity of data moved by the migrated VMs by 89.5%.

Furthermore, the number of migrations was reduced by up to 89%, which provides better resource usage and load balance. The results show the importance of taking network traffic into consideration in the migration decision process.

In the future, the authors are interested in taking into account the way in which migratable VMs can affect the possible assigned Hosts prior to the migration process. Thus, the assignment process would be much more consistent in the future Host behavior, reducing the final number of migrations and the network utilization. Finally, it could be interesting to discover the limits of WPSP policy in terms of the CPU and network VM stability and ranges.

References

1. Abdelsamea, A., El-Moursy, A.A., Hemayed, E.E., Eldeeb, H.: Virtual machine consolidation enhancement using hybrid regression algorithms. Egypt. Inform. J. **18**(3), 161–170 (2017). https://doi.org/10.1016/j.eij.2016.12.002
2. Ahmad, R.W., Gani, A., Hamid, S.H.A., Shiraz, M., Yousafzai, A., Xia, F.: A survey on virtual machine migration and server consolidation frameworks for cloud data centers. J. Netw. Comput. Appl. **52**, 11–25 (2015). https://doi.org/10.1016/j.jnca.2015.02.002, http://www.sciencedirect.com/science/article/pii/S1084804515000284

3. Beloglazov, A., Buyya, R.: Optimal online deterministic algorithms and adaptive heuristics for energy and performance efficient dynamic consolidation of virtual machines in cloud data centers. Concurr. Comput.: Pract. Exp. **24**(13), 1397–1420 (2012). https://onlinelibrary.wiley.com/doi/abs/10.1002/cpe.1867

4. Bonett, D.G., Wright, T.A.: Sample size requirements for estimating Pearson, Kendall and Spearman correlations. Psychometrika **65**(1), 23–28 (2000). https://doi.org/10.1007/BF02294183

5. Calheiros, R.N., Ranjan, R., Beloglazov, A., De Rose, C.A., Buyya, R.: CloudSim: a toolkit for modeling and simulation of cloud computing environments and evaluation of resource provisioning algorithms. Softw.: Pract. Exp. **41**(1), 23–50 (2011). https://onlinelibrary.wiley.com/doi/abs/10.1002/spe.995

6. Choudhary, S., Kothari, A.: Green data center using Spearmans ranking algorithm. Int. J. Comput. Sci. Inf. Technol. **6**(2), 1672–1676 (2015)

7. Khoshkholghi, M.A.: Resource usage prediction algorithm using weighted linear regression for virtual machine live migration in cloud data centers (2017)

8. Kumar, P., Kumar, R.: Issues and challenges of load balancing techniques in cloud computing: a survey. ACM Comput. Surv. **51**(6), 120:1–120:35 (2019). https://doi.org/10.1145/3281010

9. Moghaddam, S.M., Piraghaj, S.F., O'Sullivan, M., Walker, C., Unsworth, C.: Energy-efficient and SLA-aware virtual machine selection algorithm for dynamic resource allocation in cloud data centers. In: 2018 IEEE/ACM 11th International Conference on Utility and Cloud Computing (UCC), pp. 103–113. IEEE (2018). https://doi.org/10.1109/UCC.2018.00019

10. Nucci, A., Sridharan, A., Taft, N.: The problem of synthetically generating IP traffic matrices: initial recommendations. ACM SIGCOMM Comput. Commun. Rev. **35**(3), 19–32 (2005). https://dl.acm.org/doi/10.1145/1070873.1070876

11. Park, K., Pai, V.S.: CoMon: a mostly-scalable monitoring system for PlanetLab. ACM SIGOPS Oper. Syst. Rev. **40**(1), 65–74 (2006), https://dl.acm.org/doi/10.1145/1113361.1113374

12. Saino, L., Cocora, C., Pavlou, G.: A toolchain for simplifying network simulation setup. SimuTools **13**, 82–91 (2013). https://eudl.eu/doi/10.4108/icst.simutools.2013.251735

13. Sun, G., Liao, D., Zhao, D., Xu, Z., Yu, H.: Live migration for multiple correlated virtual machines in cloud-based data centers. IEEE Trans. Serv. Comput. **11**(2), 279–291 (2018). https://doi.org/10.1109/TSC.2015.2477825

14. Vu, H.T., Hwang, S.: A traffic and power-aware algorithm for virtual machine placement in cloud data center. Int. J. Grid Distrib. Comput. **7**(1), 350–355 (2014). https://doi.org/10.14257/ijgdc.2014.7.1.03

15. de Winter, J.C., Gosling, S.D., Potter, J.: Comparing the Pearson and Spearman correlation coefficients across distributions and sample sizes: a tutorial using simulations and empirical data. Psychol. Methods **21**(3), 273 (2016). https://doi.org/10.1037/met0000079

Theory and Algorithms for Parallel and Distributed Processing

LCP-Aware Parallel String Sorting

Jonas Ellert[1]([✉])[ⓘ], Johannes Fischer[1], and Nodari Sitchinava[2]

[1] Technical University of Dortmund, Dortmund, Germany
jonas.ellert@tu-dortmund.de, johannes.fischer@cs.tu-dortmund.de
[2] University of Hawaii at Manoa, Honolulu, HI, USA
nodari@hawaii.edu

Abstract. When lexicographically sorting strings, it is not always necessary to inspect all symbols. For example, the lexicographical rank of europar amongst the strings eureka, eurasia, and excells only depends on its so called *relevant prefix* euro. The *distinguishing prefix size* D of a set of strings is the number of symbols that actually need to be inspected to establish the lexicographical ordering of all strings. Efficient string sorters should be D-aware, i.e. their complexity should depend on D rather than on the total number N of all symbols in all strings. While there are many D-aware sorters in the sequential setting, there appear to be no such results in the PRAM model. We propose a framework yielding a D-aware modification of any existing PRAM string sorter. The derived algorithms are work-optimal with respect to their original counterpart: If the original algorithm requires $\mathcal{O}(w(N))$ work, the derived one requires $\mathcal{O}(w(D))$ work. The execution time increases only by a small factor that is logarithmic in the length of the longest relevant prefix. Our framework universally works for deterministic and randomized algorithms in all variations of the PRAM model, such that future improvements in (D-unaware) parallel string sorting will directly result in improvements in D-aware parallel string sorting.

Keywords: String sorting · Lexicographical sorting · Parallel · PRAM · Distinguishing prefix · Longest common prefix · LCP · Karp-Rabin fingerprints

1 Introduction

The problem of string sorting is defined as follows: Given k strings $s_1, \ldots, s_k$ of total length $N = \sum |s_i|$ stored in RAM, and an array S of k pointers to the strings ($S[i]$ points to the memory location of s_i), compute a permutation S' of S such that S' lists the strings in lexicographical order ($S'[i]$ points to the lexicographically i-th smallest string). It is commonly known that establishing the lexicographical order on the strings does not necessarily require inspecting all N symbols. In fact, the rank of a string s_i only depends on its shortest

N. Sitchinava—Supported by the National Science Foundation under Grants CCF-1533823 and CCF-1911245.

© Springer Nature Switzerland AG 2020
M. Malawski and K. Rzadca (Eds.): Euro-Par 2020, LNCS 12247, pp. 329–342, 2020.
https://doi.org/10.1007/978-3-030-57675-2_21

prefix $s_i[1..\ell_i]$ that is not a prefix of any another string. The *distinguishing prefix size* of the k strings is defined as $D = \sum_{i=1}^{k} \ell_i$. In simple words, an algorithm that sorts the strings only needs to *inspect* the D symbols that are part of the distinguishing prefix, while all other symbols are irrelevant for the lexicographical ordering. In this paper, we present parallel D-aware string sorting solutions. That is, the time and work complexity of the algorithms depends only on k, D, and possibly σ, but not on N. We present algorithms in the PRAM model and consider the following variations of the model (ordered from the weakest to the strongest): EREW, CREW, Common-CRCW, and Arbitrary-CRCW. Observe that algorithms designed for the weaker models can run on the stronger models within the same complexity measures.

1.1   Related Work

There is a variety of algorithms that aim to efficiently solve the problem of string sorting, most of which belong to one of two classes: The ones that are based on comparison sorting and generally allow arbitrary alphabets, and the ones that use (ideas from) integer sorting and are usually limited to alphabets of polynomial size $\sigma = N^{\mathcal{O}(1)}$.

If comparison sorting is the underlying technique, the well-known information-theoretical lower bound of $\Omega(k \lg k)$ comparisons applies, such that the fastest possible sequential algorithm cannot take fewer than $\Omega(k \lg k + D)$ operations. Ternary quicksort [2] runs in $\mathcal{O}(k \lg k + D)$ time, and thus matches this lower bound. In the Common-CRCW model, JáJá et al. [14] achieve $\mathcal{O}(k \lg k + N)$ work and $\mathcal{O}(\lg^2 k / \lg \lg k)$ time, and also provide a randomized algorithm that requires the same amount of work and $\mathcal{O}(\lg k)$ time with high probability. However, a D-aware modification of the algorithm cannot easily be derived.

In terms of alphabet-dependent sequential algorithms, we can use radix-sort-like approaches to achieve either $\mathcal{O}(N + \sigma)$ time [1, Algorithm 3.2], or even $\mathcal{O}(D + \sigma)$ time [16], where σ is the number of different characters. Hagerup [11] presents an Arbitrary-CRCW algorithm that achieves $\mathcal{O}(N \lg \lg N)$ work and $\mathcal{O}(\lg N / \lg \lg N)$ time, assuming that the alphabet is polynomial in N. Alternatively, it can be implemented to run in $\mathcal{O}(N\sqrt{\lg N})$ work and $\mathcal{O}(\lg^{3/2} N\sqrt{\lg \lg N})$ time in the CREW model, or $\mathcal{O}(N\sqrt{\lg N \lg \lg N})$ work and the same time in the EREW model. Note that Hagerup's algorithm is based on an algorithm by Vaidyanathan et al. [17] that reduces each string to a single integer by repeatedly merging adjacent symbols. Due to the nature of the reduction technique, it always inspects all N symbols, and a D-aware modification cannot easily be derived.

There are practical parallel algorithms that exploit the distinguishing prefix and are fast in practice [4–6]; however, we are not aware of any algorithms with D-aware complexity bounds in the PRAM model.

1.2   Our Contributions

We present a theoretical framework that yields a D-aware version of any existing string sorting algorithm. Particularly, we derive D-aware versions of the algorithms by JáJá et al. and Hagerup that are work optimal with respect to their original counterparts: If the original algorithm requires $w(k, N, \sigma)$ work, then our modification requires $\mathcal{O}(w(k, D, \sigma))$ work. Additionally, in case of Hagerup's algorithm, we are no longer limited to polynomial alphabets. Generally, the new algorithms are only by a $(\lg d)$-factor slower than the original ones, where $d = \max\{\ell_i \mid 1 \le i \le k\}$ denotes the length of the longest relevant prefix.

Our framework is based on the idea of approximating the distinguishing prefix. It yields a 2-approximation of the relevant prefix lengths: For each string s_i, we determine a value $L[i] \in [\ell_i, 2\ell_i)$. In the Arbitrary-CRCW model, this takes expected optimal $\mathcal{O}(D)$ work and $\mathcal{O}(\lg d \cdot (\lg d + \lg k))$ time with high probability

In the weaker EREW model, we achieve $\mathcal{O}(k\sqrt{\lg k} \lg \lg k + D)$ work and $\mathcal{O}(\lg d \cdot (\lg d + \lg k) + \lg^{3/2} k \cdot \lg \lg k)$ time with high probability. An overview of our results is provided in Table 1.

The rest of the paper is structured as follows: In Sect. 2 we introduce the basic notation and definitions regarding the PRAM model and string processing. In Sect. 3 we explain our approximation scheme for the distinguishing prefix, which we use in Sect. 4 to derive deterministic D-aware string sorters. By using Karp-Rabin fingerprinting, we can also derive randomized string sorters, and achieve better complexity bounds for our approximation scheme (Sect. 5). We summarize our results in Sect. 6.

2   Preliminaries

Throughout this paper, we write $\lg x$ to denote the binary logarithm $\log_2 x$, and $[x, y]$ to denote the discrete interval $\{x, x + 1, \ldots, y\}$. Our research is situated in the PRAM model of computation, where multiple processors work on a shared memory. In each processing cycle, each processor may read from a memory cell, write to a memory cell, or perform a simple local operation (logical shifts, basic arithmetic operations etc). We consider the following variations of the PRAM model: EREW (each memory location can be read and written by at most one processor in each time step), CREW (each memory location can be read by multiple processors in each time step, and written by a single processor in each time step), and CRCW (each memory location can be read and written by multiple processors in each time step). For the CRCW model, we consider two variants: In the Common-CRCW model, multiple processors are allowed to write to the same memory location in the same time step only if all of them write the same value. In the Arbitrary-CRCW model, multiple processors are allowed to write different values to the same memory location in the same time step, and an arbitrary processor succeeds. However, the designer of an algorithm for this model may not make any assumptions as to which one it is. The time required

Table 1. New results on D-aware parallel string sorting. The original (D-unaware) results are written in gray. Whenever the model is annotated with *w.h.p.*, the respective algorithms are successful with high probability $1 - \mathcal{O}(k^{-c})$ for an arbitrarily large constant c. We write $\hat{\mathcal{O}}(x)$ to denote *expected* complexity bounds.

a.) Results based on the sorter by Hagerup [11]:			
Model	Work	Time	Theorem
Arbitrary CRCW	$\mathcal{O}(D \lg \lg \max(D, \sigma)))$ $\mathcal{O}(N \lg \lg N)$	$\lg d \cdot \mathcal{O}(\lg D / \lg \lg D + \lg \lg \sigma)$ $\mathcal{O}(\lg N / \lg \lg N)$	Theorem 2 [11] Theorem 4.4
CREW	$\mathcal{O}(D \sqrt{\lg D})$ $\mathcal{O}(N \sqrt{\lg N})$	$\lg d \cdot \mathcal{O}(\lg^{3/2} D \sqrt{\lg \lg D})$ $\mathcal{O}(\lg^{3/2} N \sqrt{\lg \lg N})$	Theorem 2 [11] Theorem 4.5
EREW	$\mathcal{O}(D \sqrt{\lg D \lg \lg D})$ $\mathcal{O}(N \sqrt{\lg N \lg \lg N})$	$\lg d \cdot \mathcal{O}(\lg^{3/2} D \sqrt{\lg \lg D})$ $\mathcal{O}(\lg^{3/2} N \sqrt{\lg \lg N})$	Theorem 2 [11] Theorem 4.5

b.) Results based on the sorter by JáJá et al. [14]:			
Model	Work	Time	Theorem
Common CRCW	$\mathcal{O}(k \lg k + D)$ $\mathcal{O}(k \lg k + N)$	$\lg d \cdot \mathcal{O}(\lg^2 k / \lg \lg k)$ $\mathcal{O}(\lg^2 k / \lg \lg k)$	Theorem 3 [14] Theorem 3.1
Common CRCW w.h.p.	$\mathcal{O}(k \lg k + D)$ $\mathcal{O}(k \lg k + N)$	$\lg d \cdot \mathcal{O}(\lg k + \lg d)$ $\mathcal{O}(\lg k)$	Theorem 4 [14] Theorem 5.1

c.) General results that hold for any parallel string sorter:			
Model	Work	Time	Lemma
Arbitrary CRCW w.h.p.	$\hat{\mathcal{O}}(D) + w(k, 2D, \sigma)$ $w(k, N, \sigma)$	$\lg d \cdot \mathcal{O}(\lg k + \lg d) + t(k, 2D, \sigma)$ $t(k, N, \sigma)$	Lemma 6 –
EREW w.h.p.	$\mathcal{O}(k \sqrt{\lg k} \lg \lg k + D)$ $+ w(k, 2D, \sigma)$ $w(k, N, \sigma)$	$\lg d \cdot \mathcal{O}(\lg k + \lg d) + \mathcal{O}(\lg^{3/2} k \cdot \lg \lg k)$ $+ t(k, 2D, \sigma)$ $t(k, N, \sigma)$	Lemma 7 –

by a PRAM algorithm is the total number of processing cycles. The *work* of a PRAM algorithm is defined as the total number of primitive operations that are performed by all processors, or (equivalently) as the running time of the algorithm when using only a single processor. One of the most fundamental operations in the PRAM model is the *all-prefix-operation*, and its specialization, the *all-prefix-sums-operation*:

Lemma 1 (All-Prefix-Operation, e.g. [7]). *Let $a_1, \ldots, a_n$ be n integers, and let $\oplus$ be a binary associative operator that can be evaluated in constant time. The sequence $a_1, (a_1 \oplus a_2), (a_1 \oplus a_2 \oplus a_3), \ldots, (a_1 \oplus \cdots \oplus a_n)$ can be computed in the EREW model in $\mathcal{O}(n)$ work, $\mathcal{O}(n)$ space and $\mathcal{O}(\lg n)$ time.*

Lemma 2 (All-Prefix-Sums, [9]). *The all-prefix-operation with addition as associative operator can be computed in the Common-CRCW model in $\mathcal{O}(n)$ work, $\mathcal{O}(n)$ space and $\mathcal{O}(\lg n / \lg \lg n)$ time.*

Next, we introduce basic string processing notations. A *string* over the *alphabet* Σ is a finite sequence of *symbols* from the set $\Sigma = \{1, \ldots, \sigma\}$. We write $|s|$ to denote the length of a string s. The x-th symbol of a string is $s[x]$, while the *substring* from the x-th to the y-th symbol is denoted as $s[x..y] = s[x]s[x+1]\ldots s[y]$. The substring $s[1..y]$ is called length-y prefix of s.

Given k strings $s_1, \ldots, s_k$, the length of the *longest common prefix* of two strings s_i, s_j is defined as $lcp(s_i, s_j) = \max\{ \ell \mid s_i[1..\ell] = s_j[1..\ell] \}$. Let $\ell = lcp(s_i, s_j)$. We say that s_i is *lexicographically not larger* than s_j and write $s_i \preceq s_j$, iff either $\ell = |s_i|$, or $\ell < \min(|s_i|, |s_j|)$ and $s_i[\ell + 1] < s_j[\ell + 1]$. The strings are in *lexicographical order* iff we have $s_1 \preceq s_2 \preceq \ldots \preceq s_k$. The *relevant prefix length* of s_i is $\ell_i = \min(|s_i|, 1 + \max\{ lcp(s_i, s_j) \mid 1 \le j \le k \wedge j \ne i \})$. The maximum number of characters that need to be inspected for a single string-to-string comparison is $d = \max\{ \ell_i \mid 1 \le i \le k \}$. Finally, the *distinguishing prefix size* of the strings is defined as $D = \sum_{i=1}^{k} \ell_i$, which is the minimum number of characters that need to be inspected in order to lexicographically sort the strings.

Given k strings of total length N over the alphabet $[1, \sigma]$, let $f(k, N, \sigma)$ be a function indicating the resources (e.g. the time or space) needed by an algorithm to perform some task on the strings. We say that f is *resilient in N* iff multiplying N by a constant factor increases f by at most a constant factor, i.e.,

$$\forall c_1 : \exists c_2 : \forall k, N, \sigma : f(k, c_1 \cdot N, \sigma) \le c_2 \cdot f(k, N, \sigma) \tag{1}$$

(where all variables are from $\mathbb{N}^+$). This property will be useful when determining the worst-case complexity bounds of our algorithms. Note that the equation holds in the practical case where f is composed of a constant number of polynomial and polylogarithmic terms.

3 Approximating the Distinguishing Prefix

In this section, we introduce our framework for D-aware parallel string sorting. The general approach is to approximate the distinguishing prefix, resulting in an array L of size k with $L[i] \in [\ell_i, 2\ell_i)$, i.e. we obtain a 2-approximation of the relevant prefix lengths. Afterwards, we can safely prune each string s_i to its prefix $s_i' = s_i[1..L[i]]$. Clearly, the total length of the strings $s_1', \ldots s_k'$ is less than $2D$, and for any two strings we have $s_i \prec s_j \Leftrightarrow s_i' \prec s_j'$. Therefore, we can then use any (not D-aware) string sorting algorithm to sort the strings in time and work depending solely on k, D, and σ.

Broadly speaking, the approximation scheme performs $\lceil \lg d \rceil + 1$ rounds, where in round r we identify and discard the strings s_i with $\ell_i \in (2^{r-1}, 2^r]$ (starting with round $r = 0$). More precisely, amongst all not yet discarded strings, we determine the ones whose length-2^r prefix is unique. Since any such string has not been discarded in the previous rounds, we have $\ell_i > 2^{r-1}$, while the uniqueness of the length-2^r prefix guarantees $\ell_i \leq 2^r$. By assigning $L[i] \leftarrow \min(|s_i|, 2^r)$, we obtain the desired 2-approximation of ℓ_i. The algorithm terminates as soon as all strings have been discarded (and thus all relevant prefix approximations have been found).

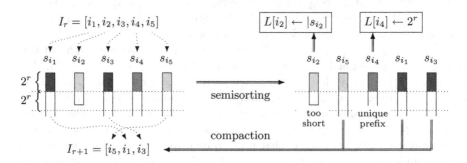

Fig. 1. Round r of our approximation scheme. Equal colors identify equal prefixes (best viewed in color).

Let us look at a single round in technical detail. Let I_r be the set of strings (or more precisely their indices) that survived until round r, and whose length is at least 2^r, i.e. $I_r = \{i \in [1, k] \mid \ell_i > 2^{r-1} \wedge |s_i| \geq 2^r\}$. Initially, before round $r = 0$, we have $I_0 = \{1, \ldots, k\}$. From now on, let $k_r = |I_r|$ denote the number of strings that survived until round r. Before starting the round, we assume that I_r is given as a compact array of k_r words. Each round consists of two phases, which we explain in the following. The description is supported by Fig. 1.

Semisorting Phase. We semisort I_r using the length-2^r prefixes of the corresponding strings as keys (i.e. entry $I_r[j] = i$ is represented by the key $s_i[1..2^r]$). Semisorting is a relaxation of sorting that reorders the entries such that equal keys are contiguous, but different keys do not necessarily have to appear in correct order. In the upcoming sections, we propose different approaches for this phase.

Compaction Phase. Let I_r be semisorted as described above, and let $i = I_r[j]$ be any entry. Furthermore, let $i^- = I_r[j-1]$ and $i^+ = I_r[j+1]$ be the neighboring entries of $I_r[j]$. Due to the semisorting, the length-2^r prefix of s_i is unique iff $s_{i^-}[1..2^r] \neq s_i[1..2^r] \neq s_{i^+}[1..2^r]$. We trivially check this condition for all entries simultaneously in $\mathcal{O}(k_r \cdot 2^r)$ work and $\mathcal{O}(1)$ time in the Common-CRCW model, or in the same work and $\mathcal{O}(\lg 2^r) = \mathcal{O}(r)$ time in the EREW model (which can be easily achieved using Lemma 1). If the prefix of s_i is unique, we assign $L[i] \leftarrow 2^r$ and $I_r[j] \leftarrow 0$ (where $I_r[j] = 0$ indicates that we no longer need to consider s_i in upcoming rounds). Otherwise, we check if s_i is too short to be considered in the next round: If $|s_i| \leq 2^{r+1}$ holds, we assign $L[i] \leftarrow |s_i|$ and $I_r[j] \leftarrow 0$. Finally, we obtain I_{r+1} by moving the non-zero entries of I_r to the front of the array. This requires a single all-prefix-sums-operation [18, Section 3.1], and thus $\mathcal{O}(k_r)$ work and $\mathcal{O}(\lg k_r)$ time in the EREW model, or the same work and $\mathcal{O}(\lg k_r / \lg \lg k_r)$ time in the Common-CRCW model ((Lemmas 1 and 2).

Complexity. Before discussing different approaches for the semisorting phase, we already give general bounds for the work and time complexity of our approximation scheme. For this purpose we only consider the compaction phase, which takes $\mathcal{O}(k_r \cdot 2^r)$ work in round r (regardless of the PRAM model) and thus $\mathcal{O}(\sum_{r=0}^{\infty} k_r \cdot 2^r)$ work in total. This is asymptotically optimal:

$$\sum_{r=0}^{\lceil \lg d \rceil} k_r \cdot 2^r = \sum_{r=0}^{\lceil \lg d \rceil} \sum_{i \in I_r} 2^r \leq \sum_{i=1}^{k} \sum_{r=0}^{\lceil \lg \ell_i \rceil} 2^r < \sum_{i=1}^{k} 2^{\lceil \lg \ell_i \rceil + 1} \leq \sum_{i=1}^{k} 4\ell_i = 4D \quad (2)$$

Next, we focus on the execution time in the EREW model. The compaction phase of round r takes $\mathcal{O}(r + \lg k_r) \subseteq \mathcal{O}(\lg d + \lg k)$ time, resulting in $\mathcal{O}(\lg d \cdot (\lg d + \lg k))$ time for all rounds. In the Common-CRCW model, we have $\mathcal{O}(\lg k_r / \lg \lg k_r) \subseteq \mathcal{O}(\lg k / \lg \lg k)$ time for round r, and thus $\mathcal{O}(\lg d \cdot \lg k / \lg \lg k)$ time in total.

4 Deriving Deterministic D-aware String Sorters

The perhaps easiest solution for the semisorting phase is to use an existing string sorter as a subroutine, e.g. one of the algorithms that we discussed in Sect. 1.1. Then, after finishing the last round of our approximation scheme, we reduce the strings to their length-$L[i]$ prefixes and sort them with the same algorithm that we already used during the semisorting phase. This naturally results in a new D-aware string sorter, as visualized in Fig. 2.

We obtain a general result for an important class of sorters: The ones that do not rely on comparison sorting and typically require $N \cdot w(k, N, \sigma)$ work and $t(k, N, \sigma)$ time for some functions w and t that are resilient in N and non-decreasing in k and N (e.g. Hagerup's algorithm [11]). Using such an algorithm, the semisorting phase of round r takes $(k_r \cdot 2^r) \cdot w(k_r, k_r \cdot 2^r, \sigma)$ work. Summing up all rounds, the total work for semisorting is $\mathcal{O}(D \cdot w(k, D, \sigma))$:

$$\sum_{r=0}^{\lceil \lg d \rceil} (k_r \cdot 2^r) \cdot w(k_r, k_r \cdot 2^r, \sigma) \leq \sum_{r=0}^{\lceil \lg d \rceil} (k_r \cdot 2^r) \cdot w(k, 2D, \sigma) < 4D \cdot w(k, 2D, \sigma) \quad (3)$$

The first inequality holds because w is non-decreasing in k and N, while the second one holds due to Eq. (2). We have $w(k, 2D, \sigma) = \mathcal{O}(w(k, D, \sigma))$ because w is resilient in N. For the same reason, the time for the semisorting phase of round r is $t(k_r, k_r \cdot 2^r, \sigma) \leq t(k, 2D, \sigma) = \mathcal{O}(t(k, D, \sigma))$. Combined with the bounds from Sect. 3 we have:

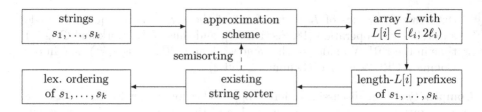

Fig. 2. Deriving D-aware string sorters from existing D-unaware solutions.

Theorem 1. *Let $N \cdot w(k, N, \sigma)$ and $t(k, N, \sigma)$ be the work and time needed by some algorithm to sort k strings of total length N over the alphabet $[1, \sigma]$ (for arbitrarily large σ), with w and t resilient in N and non-decreasing in k and N. Let D be the distinguishing prefix size. Then we can sort the strings in $\mathcal{O}(D \cdot w(k, D, \sigma))$ work and $\mathcal{O}(\lg d \cdot (\lg d + \lg k + t(k, D, \sigma)))$ time. The PRAM model matches the one of the string sorter. If the model is at least as strong as the Common-CRCW model, the time decreases to $\mathcal{O}(\lg d \cdot (\lg k / \lg \lg k + t(k, D, \sigma)))$.*

Note that the theorem requires a string sorter that allows *arbitrary* alphabets. This is due to the fact that (even after the first round) the number k_r of remaining strings can become arbitrarily small. Consequently, the alphabet size might become arbitrarily large compared to the total length $k_r \cdot 2^r$ of the strings that we have to semisort in round r.

Dealing with Large Alphabets. In theory, Theorem 1 directly implies new D-aware string sorters. However, while the theorem applies to sorters for arbitrary alphabets, many of the existing string sorting algorithms are restricted to polynomial alphabets (i.e. $\sigma = N^{\mathcal{O}(1)}$). In the remainder of this section, we show that even such alphabet restricted sorters work with Theorem 1, if we equip them with an additional preprocessing routine. We demonstrate the technique using Hagerup's algorithm [11] as an example. It will be easy to see that it would just as well work with any other string sorter. Recall Hagerup's original result:

Lemma 3 (Hagerup [11], Theorems 4.4 and 4.5). *A set of strings of total length N over the alphabet $[1, N^{\mathcal{O}(1)}]$ can be sorted in $\mathcal{O}(\lg N / \lg \lg N)$ time and $\mathcal{O}(N \lg \lg N)$ work in the CRCW model, or in $\mathcal{O}(N\sqrt{\lg N})$ work and $\mathcal{O}(\lg^{3/2} N \sqrt{\lg \lg N})$ time in the CREW model, or in $\mathcal{O}(N\sqrt{\lg N \lg \lg N})$ work and $\mathcal{O}(\lg^{3/2} N \sqrt{\lg \lg N})$ time in the EREW model.*

Remark: Hagerup does not explicitly state which variant of the CRCW model is used. However, the algorithm relies on a padded integer sorting subroutine that requires the Arbitrary-CRCW model [12]. It appears that all other operations performed by the algorithm require at most the Arbitrary-CRCW model as well.

In order to generalize Lemma 3 to arbitrary alphabets $[1, \sigma]$ with $\sigma \notin N^{\mathcal{O}(1)}$, we perform a preprocessing that reduces the alphabet to $[1, N]$ in an order preserving manner. The general idea is to use an integer sorter to sort the symbols that actually occur in any of the strings. Then, we can simply replace each symbol with its rank amongst the sorted symbols. A similar reduction technique has previously been used by Hagerup [11, p. 389] (but for a different purpose). For now, we only consider the Arbitrary-CRCW model.

First, we create N tuples of the form $\langle i, j, c \rangle$, where c is the j-th symbol of s_i. Initially, the tuples are ordered by their first and second component, i.e. $\langle 1, 1, \cdot \rangle \ldots \langle 1, |s_1|, \cdot \rangle \langle 2, 1, \cdot \rangle \ldots \langle 2, |s_2|, \cdot \rangle \ldots \langle k, 1, \cdot \rangle \ldots \langle k, |s_k|, \cdot \rangle$. In order to store this sequence in a consecutive memory area, we have to determine the position of each tuple within the sequence. Using the all-prefix-sums-operation, we can trivially realize this step in $\mathcal{O}(N)$ work and $\mathcal{O}(\lg N / \lg \lg N)$ time due to Lemma 2. Then, we use the integer sorting algorithm by Bhatt et al. [3] to sort the tuples by their third component, which takes $\mathcal{O}(N \lg \lg \sigma)$ work and $\mathcal{O}(\lg N / \lg \lg N + \lg \lg \sigma)$ time. Let $\langle i_1, j_1, c_1 \rangle \ldots \langle i_N, j_N, c_N \rangle$ be the sorted sequence of tuples. In an array $A \in \{0, 1\}^N$, we mark the (in terms of the sequence) leftmost occurrence of each character, i.e. $\forall h \in [2, N] : c_{h-1} \neq c_h \Leftrightarrow A[h] = 1$. Next, we replace A with its prefix-sums, once again taking $\mathcal{O}(N)$ work and $\mathcal{O}(\lg N / \lg \lg N)$ time due to Lemma 2. Now each entry $A[h]$ contains exactly the rank of the symbol c_h amongst all symbols. Finally, for each $h \in [1, N]$, we replace the j_h-th symbol of the i_h-th string with $A[h] + 1$. Since this reduces the alphabet to (a subset of) $[1, N]$ in an order preserving manner, we can sort the strings using Lemma 3.

In the weaker CREW and EREW models we use the same technique, but replace the algorithm by Bhatt et al. with Han and Shen's integer sorter in the EREW model [13, Theorem 4.1], which sorts the N tuples in $\mathcal{O}(N\sqrt{\lg N})$ work and $\mathcal{O}(\lg^{3/2} N)$ time. We have shown:

Corollary 1. *A set of strings of total length N over the alphabet $[1, \sigma]$ can be sorted in $\mathcal{O}(\lg N / \lg \lg N + \lg \lg \sigma)$ time and $\mathcal{O}(N \lg \lg N + N \lg \lg \sigma)$ work in the Arbitrary-CRCW model, or in $\mathcal{O}(N\sqrt{\lg N})$ work and $\mathcal{O}(\lg^{3/2} N\sqrt{\lg \lg N})$ time in the CREW model, or in $\mathcal{O}(N\sqrt{\lg N \lg \lg N})$ work and $\mathcal{O}(\lg^{3/2} N\sqrt{\lg \lg N})$ time in the EREW model.*

Theorem 2. *A set of k strings over the alphabet $[1, \sigma]$ with distinguishing prefix size D and longest relevant prefix of length d can be sorted in the work and time stated in Table 1(a).*

The theorem follows from Corollary 1 and Theorem 1. Note that the work and time in the Arbitrary-CRCW model are $\mathcal{O}(D \lg \lg D)$ and $\mathcal{O}(\lg d \cdot \lg D / \lg \lg D)$, respectively, if the alphabet is quasipolynomial in the distinguishing prefix size, i.e. $\sigma = D^{(\lg^{\mathcal{O}(1)} D)}$.

4.1   Deriving Comparison-Based Sorters

As mentioned earlier, any comparison-based string sorter requires $\Omega(k \lg k + D)$ work. In this section, we take the $\mathcal{O}(k \lg k + N)$ work algorithm by JáJá et al. [14], and derive an $\mathcal{O}(k \lg k + D)$ work modification, thus matching the lower bound. Assuming that we use the $\mathcal{O}(k \lg k + N)$ work algorithm to realize the semisorting phase of our approximation scheme, the work for semisorting in round r becomes $\mathcal{O}(k_r \lg k_r + k_r \cdot 2^r)$. After the $\lceil \lg \lg k \rceil$-th round, the $k_r \cdot 2^r$ term dominates the $k_r \lg k_r$ term. Therefore, the total work for semisorting is:

$$\mathcal{O}\left(\sum_{r=0}^{\lceil \lg d \rceil} k_r \lg k_r + k_r \cdot 2^r\right) = \mathcal{O}\left(\sum_{r=0}^{\lceil \lg \lg k \rceil - 1} k_r \lg k_r + \sum_{r=0}^{\lceil \lg d \rceil} k_r \cdot 2^r\right) \quad (4)$$

Following Eq. (2), the second sum on the right-hand side of the equation is bounded by $\mathcal{O}(D)$. Unfortunately, there appears to be no such upper bound for the first sum. Therefore, we relax our approximation scheme by simply skipping the initial $\lceil \lg \lg k \rceil$ rounds. This way, the first round that we actually perform is round $r = \lceil \lg \lg k \rceil$, during which we consider prefixes of length $2^{\lceil \lg \lg k \rceil} < 2 \lg k$. Note that consequently we may overestimate the length of relevant prefixes by $2 \lg k$ additional symbols, i.e. we obtain $L'[i] \in [\ell_i, 2 \cdot \max(\lg k, \ell_i))$. Thus, when truncating each string to its prefix $s_i[1..L'[i]]$, the total length of the strings is

$$D' := \sum_{i=1}^{k} L'[i] < 2 \sum_{i=1}^{k} (\lg k + \ell_i) = 2k \lg k + 2D. \quad (5)$$

Therefore, after computing L', we can use the algorithm by JáJá et al. once more to sort the truncated strings in optimal $\mathcal{O}(k \lg k + D') \subseteq \mathcal{O}(k \lg k + D)$ work. The semisorting in round r takes $\mathcal{O}(\lg^2 k_r / \lg \lg k_r) \subseteq \mathcal{O}(\lg^2 k / \lg \lg k)$ time, and there are $\lceil \lg d \rceil - \lceil \lg \lg k \rceil = \mathcal{O}(\lg d)$ rounds. Together with the bounds from Sect. 3 we have:

Theorem 3. *A set of k strings with distinguishing prefix size D and longest relevant prefix of length d can be sorted in the Common-CRCW model in $\mathcal{O}(k \lg k + D)$ work and $\mathcal{O}(\lg d \cdot \lg^2 k / \lg \lg k)$ time.*

Note that we cannot trivially use our approximation scheme to derive a D-aware modification of the randomized string sorter by JáJá et al. [14], which sorts k strings of total length N in $\mathcal{O}(k \lg k + N)$ work and $\mathcal{O}(\lg k)$ time with high probability, i.e. with probability $1 - (1/k)^c$ for any constant $c > 0$. If we were using this algorithm for the semisorting phase, then the probability of successfully sorting the remaining strings in round r would be $1 - (1/k_r)^c$. However, even after the first round, k_r can become arbitrarily small, resulting in a low probability of success. The randomized string semisorters from the next section will allow us to circumvent this problem.

5   Randomized String Semisorting

In this section, we equip our approximation scheme with randomized string semisorters that are based on Karp-Rabin fingerprints [15]. The goal of these fingerprints is to hash substrings to small integers, which allows fast equality testing. Consider the semisorting phase of round r, during which we have to semisort k_r string prefixes of length 2^r each. Instead of directly semisorting the prefixes, we first compute a fingerprint as a representative for each prefix, and then semisort the fingerprints. This way, we can use less complex integer sorting algorithms as a subroutine. Before going into detail, we show how to efficiently compute fingerprints in the EREW model.

In order to define Karp-Rabin fingerprints, we use a prime number $q = \Theta(N^c)$ for some constant $c > 1$, and a value $b \in [q, 2q)$ chosen uniformly at random. The Karp-Rabin fingerprint $\phi_i(x, y)$ of the substring $s_i[x..y]$ is defined as follows:

$$\phi_i(x, y) = \sum_{z=x}^{y} s_i[z] \cdot b^{y-z} \mod q \tag{6}$$

Observe that equal substrings have equal fingerprints, i.e. for every integer $n \geq 0$ it holds $s_i[x..x+n] = s_j[y..y+n] \implies \phi_i(x, x+n) = \phi_j(y, y+n)$. On the other hand, if two substrings are not equal, their fingerprints will be different with high probability. In particular, if $s_i[x..x+n] \neq s_j[y..y+n]$ then $\mathsf{Prob}[\phi_i(x, x+n) = \phi_j(y, y+n)] \leq \frac{n+1}{q} = \mathcal{O}(N^{1-c})$. Thus, by choosing a large enough constant $c > 1$, we can control the probability of false positives when comparing fingerprints instead of substrings. Using the all-prefix-operation, Karp-Rabin fingerprints can be computed efficiently in parallel:

Lemma 4. *For every ℓ-character substring $s_i[x..x+\ell-1]$, the Karp-Rabin fingerprint $\phi_i(x, x+\ell-1)$ can be computed in $\mathcal{O}(\ell)$ work, $O(\ell)$ space, and $\mathcal{O}(\lg \ell)$ time in the EREW model.*

Proof. First, we compute the sequence of exponents $b^0, b^1, \ldots, b^{\ell-1} \pmod{q}$ using the all-prefix-operation with multiplication over $\mathbb{Z}_q$ as the associative operator. Then, we simultaneously compute all values $f_0, \ldots, f_{\ell-1}$ with $f_j = s_i[x+j] \cdot b^{\ell-j-1} \pmod{q}$ in constant time. Finally, the Karp-Rabin fingerprint $\phi_i(x, x+\ell-1)$ is the sum of all the f_j over $\mathbb{Z}_q$, which can be computed via another all-prefix-operation. The stated complexity bounds follow from Lemma 1. $\square$

During round r of our approximation scheme, we can simultaneously compute the fingerprints of all length-2^r prefixes, which takes $\mathcal{O}(k_r \cdot 2^r)$ work and $\mathcal{O}(r) \subseteq \mathcal{O}(\lg d)$ time. It remains to be shown how to semisort the fingerprints. For now, similarly to Sect. 4.1, we skip the first $\lceil \lg \lg k \rceil$ rounds. In the remaining rounds, we use Cole's parallel merge sort [8], which sorts the k_r fingerprints in round r in $\mathcal{O}(k_r \lg k_r) \subseteq \mathcal{O}(k_r \cdot 2^r)$ work and $\mathcal{O}(\lg k_r)$ time. This results in the following complexity bounds:

Lemma 5. *For any constant $c > 0$, the array L' with $L'[i] \in [\ell_i, 2 \cdot \max(\lg k, \ell_i))$ can be computed in the EREW model in $\mathcal{O}(D)$ work and $\mathcal{O}(\lg d \cdot (\lg d + \lg k))$ time w.h.p. $1 - (1/N)^c$.*

Now we can already derive a D-aware modification of the randomized string sorter by JáJá et al. [14]. Just as in Sect. 4.1, we simply compute L' (using Lemma 5), and then run the original string sorter. It follows:

Theorem 4. *For any constant $c > 0$, a set of k strings with distinguishing prefix size D and longest relevant prefix of length d can be sorted in the Common-CRCW model in $\mathcal{O}(k \lg k + D)$ work and $\mathcal{O}(\lg d \cdot (\lg d + \lg k))$ time w.h.p. $1 - (1/k)^c$.*

5.1   Handling the Initial $\lceil \lg \lg k \rceil$ Rounds

Finally, we show how to (semi-)sort the fingerprints in the first $\lceil \lg \lg k \rceil$ rounds. Ideally, we would like to use the randomized semisorter by Gu et al. [10], which sorts k_r fingerprints in the Arbitrary-CRCW model in expected optimal $\mathcal{O}(k_r)$ work and $\mathcal{O}(\lg k_r)$ time with high probability $1 - (1/k_r)^c$. However, as in the previous section, k_r and thus the probability of success can become arbitrarily small. Therefore, we only use the semisorter by Gu et al. in rounds when $k_r > k/\lg^2 k$ (resulting in $\mathcal{O}(k_r)$ work), and Cole's mergesort, otherwise (resulting in $\mathcal{O}(k/\lg k)$ work). This way, in every round the expected work for semisorting fingerprints is $\mathcal{O}(k_r + k/\lg k)$, the time is $\mathcal{O}(\lg k)$, and the probability of success is at least $1 - (\lg^2 k/k)^c > 1 - (1/k)^{(c/2)}$. Summing up the expected work for semisorting during the first $\lceil \lg \lg k \rceil$ rounds, we have:

$$\sum_{r=1}^{\lceil \lg \lg k \rceil} k_r + \sum_{r=1}^{\lceil \lg \lg k \rceil} k/\lg k = \sum_{r=1}^{\lceil \lg \lg k \rceil} k_r + o(k) = \mathcal{O}(D).$$

Together with the bounds for computing fingerprints (see Sect. 5) and for the compaction phase (see Sect. 3), we get:

Lemma 6. *For any constant $c > 0$, the array L with $L[i] \in [\ell_i, 2\ell_i)$ can be computed in the Arbitrary-CRCW model in expected optimal $\mathcal{O}(D)$ work and $\mathcal{O}(\lg d \cdot (\lg d + \lg k))$ time w.h.p. $1 - (1/k)^c$.*

In the weaker EREW model, we can replace the semisorter by Gu et al. with the deterministic integer sorter by Han and Shen [13] that we already used in the proof of Corollary 1. This results in the following bounds:

Lemma 7. *For any constant $c > 0$, the array L with $L[i] \in [\ell_i, 2\ell_i)$ can be computed in the EREW model in $\mathcal{O}(k\sqrt{\lg k} \lg \lg k + D)$ work and $\mathcal{O}(\lg d \cdot (\lg d + \lg k) + \lg^{3/2} k \cdot \lg \lg k)$ time w.h.p. $1 - (1/N)^c$.*

Note that the probability of success is $1 - (1/N)^c$ (rather than $1 - (1/k)^c$ as in Lemma 6) because we no longer use a probabilistic semisorter, and errors can only occur due to fingerprint collisions.

Lemmas 6 and 7 directly imply the results stated in Table 1(c).

6   Conclusion and Open Questions

We presented a theoretical framework that approximates the distinguishing prefix, resulting in the first D-aware string sorters in the PRAM model. It remains an open question, if the $\lg d$ time factor can be avoided without increasing the work. Generally, it is unknown if a constant approximation of the distinguishing prefix can be computed *deterministically* in optimal $\mathcal{O}(D)$ work and reasonable time.

References

1. Aho, A.V., Hopcroft, J.E., Ullman, J.D.: The Design and Analysis of Computer Algorithms, 1st edn. Addison-Wesley, Boston (1974)
2. Bentley, J.L., Sedgewick, R.: Fast algorithms for sorting and searching strings. In: Proceedings of the 8th Annual Symposium on Discrete Algorithms, SODA 1997, New Orleans, LA, USA, January 1997, pp. 360–369 (1997)
3. Bhatt, P., Diks, K., Hagerup, T., Prasad, V., Radzik, T., Saxena, S.: Improved deterministic parallel integer sorting. Inf. Comput. **94**(1), 29–47 (1991). https://doi.org/10.1016/0890-5401(91)90031-V
4. Bingmann, T., Eberle, A., Sanders, P.: Engineering parallel string sorting. Algorithmica **77**(1), 235–286 (2015). https://doi.org/10.1007/s00453-015-0071-1
5. Bingmann, T., Sanders, P.: Parallel string sample sort. In: Proceedings of the 21st Annual European Symposium on Algorithms, ESA 2013, Sophia Antipolis, France, September 2013, pp. 169–180 (2013). https://doi.org/10.1007/978-3-642-40450-4_15
6. Bingmann, T., Sanders, P., Schimek, M.: Communication-efficient string sorting. In: Proceedings of the 34th International Parallel and Distributed Processing Symposium (IPDPS 2020), New Orleans, LA, USA, May 2020, pp. 137–147 (2020). https://doi.org/10.1109/IPDPS47924.2020.00024
7. Blelloch, G.E.: Prefix sums and their applications. In: Reif, J.H. (ed.) Synthesis of Parallel Algorithms, 1st edn. Chapter 1, pp. 35–60. Morgan Kaufmann Publishers Inc. (1993)
8. Cole, R.: Parallel merge sort. SIAM J. Comput. **17**(4), 770–785 (1988). https://doi.org/10.1137/0217049
9. Cole, R., Vishkin, U.: Faster optimal parallel prefix sums and list ranking. Inf. Comput. **81**(3), 334–352 (1989). https://doi.org/10.1016/0890-5401(89)90036-9
10. Gu, Y., Shun, J., Sun, Y., Blelloch, G.E.: A top-down parallel semisort. In: Proceedings of the 27th Symposium on Parallelism in Algorithms and Architectures, pp. 24–34. SPAA 2015, Portland, OR, USA, June 2015 (2015). https://doi.org/10.1145/2755573.2755597
11. Hagerup, T.: Optimal parallel string algorithms: sorting, merging and computing the minimum. In: Proceedings of the 26th Annual Symposium on Theory of Computing, STOC 1994, Montréal, Canada, May 1994, pp. 382–391 (1994). https://doi.org/10.1145/195058.195202
12. Hagerup, T., Raman, R.: Fast deterministic approximate and exact parallel sorting. In: Proceedings of the 5th Annual Symposium on Parallel Algorithms and Architectures, SPAA 1993, Velen, Germany, June 1993, pp. 346–355 (1993). https://doi.org/10.1145/165231.157380
13. Han, Y., Shen, X.: Parallel integer sorting is more efficient than parallel comparison sorting on exclusive write PRAMs. SIAM J. Comput. **31**(6), 1852–1878 (2002). https://doi.org/10.1137/S0097539799352449
14. JáJá, J., Ryu, K.W., Vishkin, U.: Sorting strings and constructing digital search trees in parallel. Theor. Comput. Sci. **154**(2), 225–245 (1996). https://doi.org/10.1016/0304-3975(94)00263-0

15. Karp, R.M., Rabin, M.O.: Efficient randomized pattern-matching algorithms. IBM J. Res. Dev. **31**(2), 249–260 (1987). https://doi.org/10.1147/rd.312.0249
16. Paige, R., Tarjan, R.E.: Three partition refinement algorithms. SIAM J. Comput. **16**(6), 973–989 (1987). https://doi.org/10.1137/0216062
17. Vaidyanathan, R., Hartmann, C.R., Varshney, P.: Optimal parallel lexicographic sorting using a fine-grained decomposition. Technical report. 127, Electrical Engineering and Computer Science, Syracuse University, NY, USA (1991). https://surface.syr.edu/eecs_techreports/127
18. Vishkin, U.: Thinking in parallel: some basic data-parallel algorithms and techniques. Lecture notes at the University of Maryland Institute for Advanced Computer Studies (UMIACS), October 2010. http://users.umiacs.umd.edu/~vishkin/PUBLICATIONS/classnotes.pdf

Mobile RAM and Shape Formation by Programmable Particles

Giuseppe Antonio Di Luna[1], Paola Flocchini[2], Nicola Santoro[3], Giovanni Viglietta[4(✉)], and Yukiko Yamauchi[5]

[1] Sapienza University of Rome, Rome, Italy
diluna@diag.uniroma1.it
[2] University of Ottawa, Ottawa, Canada
paola.flocchini@uottawa.ca
[3] Carleton University, Ottawa, Canada
santoro@cs.carleton.ca
[4] JAIST, Nomi city, Japan
johnny@jaist.ac.jp
[5] Kyushu University, Fukuoka, Japan
yamauchi@inf.kyushu-u.ac.jp

Abstract. In the distributed model *Amoebot* of programmable matter, the computational entities, called particles, are anonymous finite-state machines that operate and move on a hexagonal tessellation of the plane. In this paper we show how a constant number of such weak particles can simulate a powerful Turing-complete entity that is able to move on the plane while computing. We then show an application of our tool to the classical Shape-Formation problem, providing a new and much more general distributed solution. Indeed, while the existing algorithms allow to form only shapes made of arrangements of segments and triangles, our algorithm allows the particles to form also more abstract and general connected shapes, including circles and spirals, as well as fractal objects of non-integer dimension. In lieu of the existing impossibility results based on the symmetry of the initial configuration of the particles, our result provides a complete characterization of the connected shapes that can be formed by an initially simply connected set of particles. Furthermore, in the case of non-connected target shapes, we give almost-matching necessary and sufficient conditions for their formability.

Keywords: Distributed algorithms · Programmable matter · Amoebot · Shape formation · Turing-computable shapes · RAM simulation

1 Introduction

Several parallel and distributed computing models have been devoted to formalizing computations within the interdisciplinary field of Programmable Matter (PM): see [8,10,11,13]. The PM field envisions a myriad of very small

© Springer Nature Switzerland AG 2020
M. Malawski and K. Rzadca (Eds.): Euro-Par 2020, LNCS 12247, pp. 343–358, 2020.
https://doi.org/10.1007/978-3-030-57675-2_22

(micro/nano-sized) entities that are nevertheless able to move and coordinate themselves with the final purpose of solving a specific tasks [15]. Prototypes that will lead to future hardware platforms for PM are being designed and engineered. Examples are the M-blocks: cubes that are able to rearrange themselves by rotations [12], and the Kilobots: small robots that move by vibrations [14]. At the same time, the algorithmic community is formalizing abstract and general models, enabling the development of provably correct algorithms and the feasibility analysis of problems.

In this paper, we consider the popular geometric *Amoebot* model, introduced in [5]. In the Amoebot model, a set of computationally limited identical entities, called *particles*, operate and move on a hexagonal tessellation of the plane (i.e., a triangular grid). Each particle has constant-size memory (i.e., constant with respect to the total number of particles), is anonymous (i.e., it has no ID), is able to communicate only with its direct neighbors on the grid, and it moves by repeating an *expansion action* (in which the particle expands to occupy two neighboring nodes of the grid) and a *contraction action* (in which an expanded particle contracts to a single node of the grid). Research using this model is being carried out within the parallel, distributed, and natural computing fields [2–7]; for a recent survey, see [1]. The main goal of these research efforts is to gain an understanding of the nature and limits of this distributed computational universe.

In this paper, we move one step forward in this quest by providing a construction that simulates a *moving Random-Access Machine* (mRAM) using four particles. Such a construction transforms a set of these weak particles into a powerful Turing-complete entity, able to move on the grid while computing.

We prove the usefulness of our construction by applying it to the well-studied *Shape-Formation* (or Pattern-Formation) problem. In this problem, the particles, initially arranged in an arbitrary connected shape, have to form a given target shape. More precisely, each particle starts with a representation of the target shape in its memory, and coordinates with the other particles to form a suitably scaled-up copy of the shape that includes all particles in the system (this could mean that some particles have to be in the expanded state in the final shape). Usually, the total number of particles n is unknown: as a matter of fact, n cannot be stored in the constant-size memory of a single particle.

Increasingly refined and complex techniques and algorithms have been designed [2,3,5,6], each enlarging the class of shapes that can be formed starting from a simply connected configuration. To date, however, this class includes only target shapes defined as an arrangement of segments and triangles.

Our second contribution is the development, using our mRAM simulation, of a general and universal solution for the Shape-Formation problem: starting from a simply connected shape (i.e., a shape without holes), our algorithm allows the particles to form any feasible *connected* shape for which a "drawing algorithm" exists (i.e., the shape is Turing-computable), including circles and spirals, or more complex fractal objects of non-integer dimension, such as the Sierpinski triangle or the Koch snowflake (see Fig. 1).

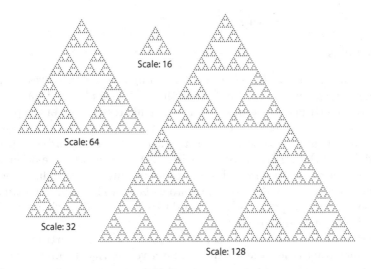

Fig. 1. Sierpinski triangle at various scales, approximated by a system of particles

The aforementioned drawing algorithm is a RAM algorithm that takes as input the number of particles n, and outputs (a representation of) the shape that has to be formed by the n particles. Note that, since the number of instructions of such a drawing algorithm is obviously constant with respect to n,[1] the algorithm itself can fit in the constant-size memory of a single particle, regardless of the number of particles in the system. (By comparison, previous works assumed that each particle has in memory a representation of the target shape expressed as a constant number of segments and triangles [2,3,6].)

With our technique, we can form almost all "feasible" *non-connected* target shapes, and are excluded from our result only very sparse pathological shapes. With regards to the *feasibility* (or not) of a shape, it is known that, depending on the symmetry of the initial configuration, some shapes are not formable regardless of the amount of memory [6]. The negative result of [6] and the positive results of our paper give an almost complete characterization of shapes that are formable starting from a simply connected configuration. Interestingly, in the case of *connected* shapes, the characterization is complete.

Our distributed algorithm is deterministic, and it works even if the schedule of activations is fair but adversarial. More precisely, in each stage, upon activation, a particle exchanges messages with its neighbors, executes some computation, and possibly moves; there is however no restriction on the number of particles that can be concurrently active in the same stage. Moreover, our algorithm works also when the particles do not have *chirality* (i.e., there is no common notion of a clockwise direction on the plane among the particles).

For space reasons, some details have been omitted; the full version is available at https://arxiv.org/abs/2002.03384.

---

[1] By contrast, the *running time* of the drawing algorithm may be any function of n.

2   Model and Problem

2.1   Particles

In the Amoebot model, a *particle* is a computational entity that lives in an infinite regular triangular grid G embedded in the Euclidean plane $\mathbb{R}^2$ (observe that a regular triangular grid corresponds to a hexagonal tessellation of the plane). A particle may occupy either one vertex of G or two adjacent vertices: in the first case, the particle is said to be *contracted*; otherwise, it is *expanded*. When it is expanded, one of the vertices it occupies is called its *head*, and the other vertex is its *tail*. A particle may move through G by repeatedly expanding toward a neighboring vertex of G and contracting into its head. (The traditional Amoebot model also includes a special type of coordinated move called "handover", but we will not need it in this paper.)

No vertex of G can ever be occupied by more than one particle at a time. So, a contracted particle cannot expand into a vertex that is already occupied by another particle. Also, if two or more particles attempt to expand toward the same (unoccupied) vertex at the same time, only one of them succeeds, chosen arbitrarily by an adversary.

At each *stage*, some particles in the system are *active*, and they perform a *look-compute-move cycle*, and the other particles are *inactive*. An adversarial *scheduler* arbitrarily and unpredictably decides which particles are active at each stage. The only restriction on the scheduler is that it cannot keep a particle inactive forever, but it must activate every particle infinitely often. When a particle is activated for a certain stage, it "looks" at the vertices of G adjacent to its head, discovering if they are currently unoccupied, or if they are head or tail vertices of some particle. All particles are *anonymous* (i.e., they are indistinguishable). Each active particle may then decide to expand, contract, or stay still for that stage. When the next stage starts, a new set of active particles is selected, which observe their surroundings and move, and so on.

Each particle has an *internal state* that it can modify every time it is activated. The internal state of any particle is from a finite set: particles have an amount of "memory" whose size is constant with respect to the size of the system, n.

Two particles can also *communicate* by sending *messages* to one another. Each message is taken from a finite set of predefined messages. An active particle can send a message to another particle provided that their heads are adjacent vertices of G. A particle reads the incoming messages from all its neighbors as soon as it is activated.

Each particle labels its six incident edges with *port numbers*, going from 0 to 5. Each particle uses a consistent numbering that is invariant under translation on G. However, different particles may disagree on which of the edges has port number 0 and whether the numbering should follow the clockwise or counterclockwise order: this is called the particles' *handedness*. So, the handedness of a particle does not change as the particle moves, but different particles may have different handedness.

At each stage, each active particle determines which neighboring vertices are occupied, and it reads the incoming messages. Based on these and on its internal state, the particle executes a *deterministic algorithm* that computes a new internal state, the messages to be sent to the neighbors, and whether the particle should expand to some adjacent vertex, contract, or stay still.

2.2 Shapes

A set S of nodes of G is *formable by n particles* if there exists a configuration of exactly n particles (contracted or expanded) that collectively occupy exactly the nodes in S.

A *shape* is a function mapping a positive integer n to a set S_n of nodes of G that is formable by n particles: this set S_n is called the nth *level* of the shape. If such a function is Turing-computable, then the shape is said to be *computable*. If every level of a shape is a connected set, the shape is said to be *connected*.

A shape is *formable* (under condition $\mathcal{C}$) if there exists a distributed algorithm that, for every n, makes any system of n particles (whose initial configuration satisfies condition $\mathcal{C}$) eventually form a copy of the nth level of the shape, possibly translated, rotated by a multiple of 60°, and reflected. The algorithm should succeed regardless of the port numbers of each particle and the choices of the adversarial scheduler, and guarantee that the system remains still after forming the shape.

2.3 Unbreakable Symmetries

A configuration of particles is said to be *unbreakably k-symmetric*, for some integer $k > 1$, if it has a center of k-fold rotational symmetry that does not coincide with any node of G [6]. Observe that unbreakably k-symmetric configurations exist only for $k = 2$ and $k = 3$.

We can extend this notion to a level of a shape in a natural way: the nth level of a shape is k unbreakably symmetric if it is formable by an unbreakably k-symmetric configuration of n particles. Intuitively, the absence of a central node (and therefore of a central particle) and the fact that the configuration is initially symmetric makes it impossible to break the symmetry. Hence, we have a *necessary* condition $\mathcal{C}$ for the formability of a shape:

Proposition 1. *[6] A shape is formable only under the condition that, if its nth level is not unbreakably k-symmetric, then the initial configuration of a system of n particles seeking to form the shape should not be unbreakably k-symmetric, either.*

Note that, when $k = 1$ the shape is not *unbreakably k-symmetric* in such a case, as we will show in next sections, the symmetry of the target shape is irrelevant. In Sect. 5 we will give a strong *sufficient* condition for the formability of a shape, which, together with Proposition 1, almost characterizes the set of computable shapes that can be formed from a simply connected initial configuration of particles (in the case of *connected* computable shapes, it yields a full characterization).

3   Simulating Random-Access Machines

3.1   Random-Access Machines: Definition

A *Random-Access Machine* (RAM) is a model of computation consisting of a finite set of *registers*, each of which can store a non-negative integer, and a *program* consisting of a finite ordered sequence of *instructions*. Each instruction is of one of two types:

- $\mathrm{Inc}(r)$: increment by 1 the value stored in the register r. Then, proceed to the next instruction of the program.
- $\mathrm{TestDec}(r, i)$: if the register r is holding the value 0, jump to the ith instruction of the program. Otherwise, decrement r by 1 and proceed to the next instruction.

The registers initially contain the *input* of the RAM, and then the program is executed starting from the first instruction. We can reserve a register r_t to represent a "termination flag", whose value is initially 0. When r_t is incremented, the value of the other registers is taken as the RAM's *output*. Hence, a RAM is a device that can compute integer functions.

3.2   Simulating Turing Machines by RAMs

In [9, Chapter 11], Minsky shows how RAMs can simulate Turing Machines. Specifically, there is a (small) constant c such that, given any Turing Machine T that computes a function f_T, there exists a RAM Q_T with exactly c registers that computes f_T.

Then, in [9, Chapter 14], he shows that any RAM R can be simulated by a RAM Q'_R having only two registers. This is done by encoding the set of values stored in R's registers as a single integer, which is stored in the first register of Q'_R (the second register of Q'_R is only used for intermediate computations). The code is based on Gödel numbers: for instance, the sequence $(a_1, a_2, a_3, a_4, a_5)$ is encoded as the single integer $2^{a_1} \cdot 3^{a_2} \cdot 5^{a_3} \cdot 7^{a_4} \cdot 11^{a_5}$. In general, the ith integer in the sequence becomes the exponent of the ith prime factor of the code. By the unique-factorization theorem, this encoding is injective and thus non-ambiguous.

The program of Q'_R can be constructed by locally replacing each instruction of R with a small program that simulates it. For instance, it is possible to increment the ith register of R by multiplying the first register of Q'_R by the ith prime number, which in turn can be done in Q'_R by using the two standard instructions and the auxiliary register. Testing if the ith register of R is non-0 amounts to testing if the first register of Q'_R holds a multiple of the ith prime number, etc. In this paradigm, we can stipulate that Q'_R terminates when its second register holds a 0 and the value of its first register is a multiple of the prime number corresponding to the termination flag of R.

As an immediate consequence of the above, we have that the RAMs with only two registers can simulate all Turing Machines, and can therefore compute any computable function.

3.3   Simulating RAMs by Particles

Our goal in this section is to simulate a RAM with two registers by a set of four particles. The layout of our simulator is shown in Fig. 2: the four particles always remain collinear throughout the simulation, and they always maintain their order along the line: first the *pivot P*, then the *marker of the second register M_2*, then the *leader L*, and finally the *marker or the first register M_1*. The number of empty locations between P and M_2 (i.e., their distance minus 1) represents the value stored in the second register of the RAM, and the number of empty locations between M_2 and M_1 (i.e., their distance minus 2) represents the value stored in the first register of the RAM.

At all times during the simulation of the RAM's program, L will remember the index of the instruction that is currently being simulated: since the program of a RAM is constant L only needs a constant amount of memory to do so. Now we have to show that such a system can simulate every possible instruction of the RAM. This is done by letting L move between M_2 and M_1: we assume that L knows in which direction it has to move to find each of these two particles, and for convenience we call these directions "left" and "right", respectively, to match Fig. 2.

Fig. 2. A RAM simulator with the first register holding the value 7 and the second register holding the value 3

When L reaches the relevant particle, it communicates with it and causes it to move according to the current instruction of the program. P, on the other hand, always remains still. Each instruction is simulated as follows:

- Inc(Register 1): L moves toward M_1 until it finds it. Then it gives M_1 the order to move one step to the right, and waits until M_1 has moved.
- TestDec(Register 1, i): if L neighbors both M_2 and M_1, it does nothing (and updates the index of the current instruction to i). Otherwise, it reaches M_1 and orders it to move one step to the left. Then L itself moves one step to the left and waits until M_1 has moved.
- Inc(Register 2): L reaches M_1 and orders it to move one step to the right. When M_1 has moved, L reaches M_2 and orders it to move one step to the right. Then L itself moves one step to the right and waits for M_2.
- TestDec(Register 2, i): L reaches M_2 and asks it if it has a neighbor on the opposite side (i.e., P). If M_2 answers affirmatively, L does nothing (and updates the index of the current instruction to i). Otherwise, it orders M_2 to move one step to the left and waits until it has moved; then it reaches M_1 and orders it to move one step to the left; finally, L itself moves one step to the left and waits until M_1 has moved.

3.4   Adding Control Registers for Mobility

In our Shape-Formation algorithm, we need the RAM simulator to be able to move and to perform actions depending on the shape to be formed. In this section we outline the mechanism that our RAM we will use to move, and the specific actions needed for the Shape-Formation algorithm.

Recall that, in order to simulate a generic Turing Machine T, the RAM Q_T needs only a constant number c of registers. We can augment Q_T by adding a fixed number c' of "flag registers", which are set to 1 when the system has to perform certain special operations. Specifically, assume that T is an algorithmic description of a shape, whose output is a sequence of *plotting operations* of the form "move forward", "move right", "draw a point", etc. Our mobile RAM (mRAM) U_T simulates T exactly like Q_T, with one exception: whenever T outputs a plotting operation, U_T sets and then immediately resets the flag register corresponding to that type of operation (the reason will be explained shortly).

Now, we let the mRAM Q'_{U_T} simulate U_T using only two registers. In Q'_{U_T}, the state of each of the c' flag registers of U_T can be checked by verifying, at the end of a simulated instruction, if the value stored in the first register is a multiple of the prime number associated with the flag register.

As our four-particle system simulates Q'_{U_T}, it can also test the c' flag registers of U_T at the end of every simulated instruction. Indeed, the leader particle L can test if the value stored in the first register is a multiple of a given prime p. It can do so by first moving next to M_1, and then counting modulo p the number of steps it takes to move all the way to M_2 (counting modulo p requires only p states). Since $c + c'$ is a finite constant, L only ever needs to test a constant set of primes to determine the states of all the flag registers, which in turn takes a finite amount of memory and time.

When L determines that one of the c' flags is set, it executes the corresponding plotting operation of T. This translates into a "movement operation", which moves the whole system in some direction or orders a specific particle to remain still forever, marking a point of the shape. The exact nature of these movement operations and the details of their implementation will be described in next sections.

4   Basic Shape-Formation Algorithm

The first part of our Shape-Formation algorithm is taken from the "basic algorithm" of [6], while the second part is entirely different, and will be described in Sect. 5.

An assumption of the basic algorithm, is that the initial configuration of the particles is *simply connected*; another assumption is that the initial configuration and the shape to be formed satisfy the necessary condition of Proposition 1.

As we pointed out in Sect. 2, the basic algorithm only deals with shapes that are made of full triangles and segments, but this assumption is not used in the parts of the basic algorithm that we are going to borrow here. The relevant "phases" of the basic algorithm are as follows:

– *Handedness agreement*: all the particles assume the same handedness (by simply setting an internal flag whose meaning is either "my original handedness is correct" or "my original handedness is incorrect").
– *Leader election*: the particles attempt to elect a single leader. If the initial configuration is unbreakably k-symmetric, they may fail to do so, and elect exactly k leaders instead.
– *Straightening*: the particles arrange themselves in k straight line segments, each with a leader located at an endpoint. If $k > 1$, all the leaders are pairwise adjacent (recall that the only possibilities are $k = 2$ and $k = 3$), and the configuration is unbreakably k-symmetric (hence the k line segments have the same length and form angles of $2\pi/k$).

In the next section we are going to show how to proceed from here: we have a configuration consisting of k straight lines and k leaders, where all particles have the same handedness, and we want to reach an arbitrary configuration (i.e., a level of a computable shape) that is unbreakably k-symmetric if $k > 1$.

5 Forming Turing-Computable Shapes

5.1 Starting Configuration

Recall from Sect. 4 that, starting from a simply connected configuration, all the particles in the system can agree on a common handedness and rearrange themselves to form a configuration C_0 consisting of k equal line segments (with $k \in \{1, 2, 3\}$) each containing a leader particle. Moreover, if $k > 1$, then C_0 is unbreakably k-symmetric, and we may assume that also the shape's level to be formed is unbreakably k-symmetric. In this case, each leader is assigned an equal portion of the shape, corresponding to a sector of plane spanned by an angle of $2\pi/k$. These k sectors are called *principal sectors* of the plane, and the k rays separating them are the *principal rays*: Fig. 3 shows an example for $k = 3$.

As a preliminary move, each leader will reach the far end of the line segment on which it is located. This is done by repeatedly "transferring the leadership" to a neighboring particle. In turn, this amounts to sending a special message to that neighbor, whose meaning is "you are now the leader, and I am a regular particle". So, no particle will actually move in this phase.

When a leader has reached the far end of the segment, it starts the next phase, which consists in building and initializing a mRAM simulator that will eventually form the portion of shape that falls into that principal sector. From this time on, the k leaders will act independently of each other, never meeting again and never interacting.

5.2 From a Shape-Generation Algorithm to a Tracing mRAM

As stated in Sect. 2, we assume that the shape to be formed is computable, i.e., there exists an algorithm A that generates its nth level S_n given the number n as input. By this we mean that A outputs the coordinates of all the points

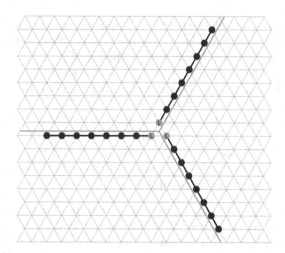

Fig. 3. The final configuration of the basic algorithm, which is the starting point C_0 of our new algorithm. Each leader is assigned a trail of followers, and will guide them in the formation of the part of shape that falls into its principal sector.

of S_n, in an arbitrary order and in some arbitrary coordinate system, and then terminates. Recall that, by definition of shape, there exists a configuration C_f of n particles, expanded or contracted, which collectively form S_n. Additionally, due to Proposition 1, if $k > 1$, then S_n must be unbreakably k-symmetric, and therefore we may take C_f to be an unbreakably k-symmetric configuration of particles. As such, C_f can be translated and rearranged so that its center coincides with the center of C_0. Also, C_f can be decomposed into k equal subsets, called *principal subsets*, each of which entirely lies in a principal sector of C_0, with one exception: some expanded particles of C_f may be crossing a principal ray, and therefore have the head in a principal sector and the tail in another. These will be called *trespassing particles*. Now, from A we can easily produce a modified algorithm A' that only outputs the points that are occupied by one of the principal subsets of C_f, say, C_f'.

Furthermore, given A', we can construct another algorithm A'' that "traces" C_f'. That is, A'' output the points of C_f' in a specific order: it starts generating the points of C_f' that lie next to a principal ray, from the closest to the principal ray's endpoint to the farthest, and then proceeds to the next ray parallel to the principal ray, and so on (each of these rays is called a *scanline*). This is done by taking every point p on every scanline, in order, and executing A'. If A' generates p, then p is generated by A''. If A' generates points that appear on the same scanline but after p, then A'' proceeds along the scanline by one step and executes A' again, etc. Otherwise, A'' moves to the first point of the next scanline, etc. As soon as A' generates only points that lie on already-visited scanlines, A'' terminates. Hence, A'' is a procedure that terminates in a finite amount of time.

As A'' executes A', it can also detect if each location p it generates should be occupied by a single particle or by an expanded particle (indeed, this information is part of the description of C'_f). If it is an expanded particle, and the other location p' occupied by the same particle is on the next scanline, A'' does not generate p: it will generate only p' as soon as it scans it. Along with p', A'' will also generate a "direction of expansion", which goes from p' to p. This is called the *delayed-deployment rule*, and its purpose will be explained later.

An improvement we can make on A'' is that it not only generates the locations of the particles of C'_f, but it also generates the "movements" it makes through the plane to generate them (we introduced these *movement operations* in Sect. 3). Specifically, the possible movement operations are: (1) advance by one step along the current scanline; (2) move to the next scanline; (3) go back by one step along the current scanline; (4) deploy a contracted particle; (5) deploy a particle that will expand in direction d; (6) terminate.

The third type of operation is repeatedly used right after moving to the next scanline, in order to reach its endpoint e and then resume scanning. The only caveat is that, if e should be occupied by a trespassing particle belonging to $C_f \setminus C'_f$, it is skipped by A'', and the scan will not be resumed from e but from the location right before it. This type of behavior is called *trespasser-avoidance rule*, and is illustrated in Fig. 4.

Since we have an algorithm A'', there exists a Turing Machine T that computes the same function: it takes an integer n as input, and it outputs a sequence of movement operations that trace (a sector of) S_n. From Sect. 3 we know that there is a RAM Q_T with c registers that produces the same output when the number n is initially stored in its first register. We can then construct the mobile mRAM U_T, with $c' = 6$ flag registers, each of which corresponds to one of the movement operations above, and is set and reset whenever the corresponding operation has to be performed.

Finally, we can construct the mRAM Q'_{U_T}, which simulates U_T using only two registers, provided that the value 2^n is initially stored in its first register. This mRAM will be simulated by each leader in the system and its trail of particles. In the rest of this section we will show how the RAM simulator of Sect. 3 can be expanded to implement the movement operations above and therefore yield a Shape-Formation algorithm.

5.3   Initializing the Machine

Let us focus on a single leader particle L and its trail of n/k particles. Recall that the leader L is now located at the endpoint of its trail of particles that is farthest from the center of C_0. We want the last four particles on the trail, including L, to start executing the simulator of Q'_{U_T} as described in Sect. 3. First, however, it is necessary to initialize the simulator by storing the value 2^n in its first register, which amounts to placing particle M_1 at a distance of $2^n + 2$ steps away from particle M_2 (refer to Fig. 2).

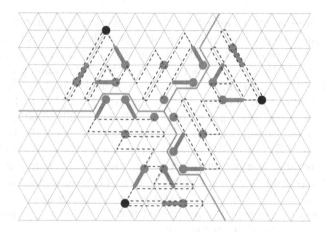

Fig. 4. A configuration forming the nth level of a shape, subdivided into its three principal subsets, each having two trespassing particles. The dashed lines represent the order in which the principal subsets are traced by the algorithm A''. The dark particles represent the last dots of their respective principal subsets.

At first L switches states with its only neighbor, which now becomes the new leader L. The two neighbors of L become M_1 and M_2, and then M_2 sends a message to its other neighbor, which becomes the pivot P.

Then, L has to "push" M_1 exactly 2^n times in order to create the input to the simulator. By "push" we mean that L reaches M_1, orders it to move forward by one step, and waits until M_1 has expanded and then contracted again.

In order to repeat this action the right number of times, the entire trail counts in binary from 0 to $2^n - 1$: this is done by letting each particle hold k binary digits, initially all set to 0. After each push, M_1 adds 1 to the binary number formed by its k digits. L reaches M_1 and takes the carry bit of the addition from M_1. If the carry bit is 1, L adds 1 to its own k digits. If the carry bit of this addition is 1, L moves all the way to M_2 and orders it to increment its k bits by 1, etc. As soon as a carry bit is 0, a message is sent back to L and forwarded by the trail's particles. When the message reaches L, it proceeds with the next push operation, etc.

When the last particle in the trail gets a carry bit of 1, it knows that M_1 has been pushed exactly 2^n times, and it forwards this information to L, which therefore stops pushing and proceeds with the simulation.

5.4   Tracing the Shape

Let the last particle in the trail be called the *rear particle*. The leader will coordinate the simulation of the mRAM that traces the shape pretending that the "pen" is held by the rear particle. That is, the simulator will go on with the computation until a movement operation is reached. If such operation is of type 4 or 5 (i.e., the deployment of a particle), then the rear particle is "dropped", which corresponds to drawing a point of the shape. As explained in Sect. 3, L knows if a movement operation has to be performed by checking, at the end of every simulated instruction of the mRAM, if the value of the first register is a multiple of some prime number and the value of the second register is 0. This implies, in particular, that when a movement operation is executed, the particles P and M_2 are next to each other.

In the following we will explain in greater detail how the system behaves to implement the six possible movement operations.

1. Advancing by one step means that the four-particle mRAM simulator, as well as the whole trail of particles up to the rear particle, has to move by one step along the current scanline. First, L moves next to M_1 and orders it to advance by one step, waiting until it has moved. Then it goes next to M_2 and gives it the same order. L then moves away from M_2 by one step and waits for it. In the meantime, M_2 gives the same order to P and then advances toward L. P does the same as M_2, and so on. When the rear particle is reached by the message, it advances and sends an "all done" message to its predecessor, which forwards it to L. Then, L knows that it may proceed with the simulation.

2. Moving to the next scanline means that the entire trail and four-particle mRAM simulator must move "sideways" by one step, in order to relocate themselves on the next scanline s. The structure of this operation is similar to the previous one. L moves to M_1 and orders it to move sideways onto s. There can be no misunderstanding on the direction of movement, since we are assuming that all particles have already reached an agreement on a common handedness. L waits until M_1 has moved, and then goes to M_2 and gives it the same order. M_2 forwards the order to P, which forwards it to the next particles, etc. When the message reaches the rear particle, it forwards an "all done" message to L, and then moves onto s. When any particle receives the "all done" message, it waits until its predecessor has moved onto s, then it forwards it to its successor and moves onto s. When L has finally moved onto s, the procedure is over.

3. To go back along the current scanline, the operations of item 1 are executed in reverse order. That is, L moves to M_2 and forwards a message to the rear particle, which then moves backwards, and all other particles up to L follow one by one. Then L goes to M_1 and orders it to move backwards.

4. Deploying a contracted particle means that the rear particle has to stop where it is and remain there forever. This is simple to accomplish: L goes to M_2 and forwards a message to the rear particle. When the rear particle gets the message, it orders its predecessor to become the new rear particle and forward an "all done" message to L. From this point on, the old rear particle will stop following the trail, and no other particle will ever communicate with it again.

5. The deployment of a particle that will expand in direction d is similar to the previous item. The only difference is that, after the rear particle has transferred its role to its predecessor, it also expands in direction d. The direction is encoded by taking the forward direction of the trail as 0 and

numbering all other directions from 1 to 5 in clockwise order. There can be no misunderstanding, since we are assuming that all particles have already reached an agreement on a common handedness.

6. When the termination operation is reached, the simulation is over, and a *dismantling procedure* has to be executed, which will be described next.

5.5   Dismantling the Machine

There is one last problem to solve: when the pivot P has been deployed, only three particles are left to deploy: L, M_1, and M_2. Since three particles are too few to simulate a tracing RAM, they have no way to reach their final locations without "losing the way". It is impossible to adapt our algorithm without making an extra assumption on the shape to be formed.

Recall that the algorithm A'' generates all the movement operations that are necessary to draw the principal subset C'_f of the configuration C_f, by tracing it one scanline at a time. The last point plotted by A'' on the last scanline visited is said to be the *last dot* of C'_f (see Fig. 4). A subset of the grid graph G is called a *neighborhood* of point p with radius r if it contains precisely all the vertices of G that have distance at most r from p.

Assumption 1. *For each level S_n of the shape, there exists a configuration C_f of n particles that forms S_n (such that C_f is unbreakably k-symmetric if S_n has to be formed from an unbreakably k-symmetric initial configuration, cf. Proposition 1) and, for each principal subset C'_f, there exists a neighborhood of the last dot, with radius independent of n, that contains at least four particles of C'_f.*

If we make Assumption 1 on the shape to be formed, we can complete our algorithm with a dismantling procedure, which makes L, M_1, M_2, and P reach their final positions without getting lost in the attempt. To this end, we must first modify the tracing algorithm A'' that we previously designed, and produce a new tracing algorithm A'''. Let p_1 be the particle occupying the last dot of C'_f, and let p_2, p_3, p_4 be the three particles of C'_f closest to p_1 (other than p_1 itself). Ties are broken arbitrarily. The new algorithm A''' proceeds exactly like A'', except that it skips the deployment operations (i.e., the operations of type 4 or 5) for p_1, p_2, p_3, p_4, and terminates when the "pen" reaches p_1.

Then we construct another algorithm F that, with input n, generates the paths that three particles have to take from p_1 to reach the locations of p_2, p_3, p_4, making sure to avoid the locations of the other particles of C_f (this is possible because we chose p_2, p_3, p_4 to be closest to p_1). Additionally, if some of the p_is are expanded, F outputs this information, as well as the direction of expansion. It is clear that F is computable and terminates in a finite amount of time.

As before, we observe that there is a Turing machine T that executes A''', and a RAM Q_T that simulates T. However, this time we add an extra register to Q_T, which will store the input value n and will never erase it: this value will be passed as input to F. Again, the mobile mRAM U_T is constructed, which is simulated by a 2-register RAM Q'_{U_T}, which in turn is simulated by particles L,

M_1, M_2, and P. When these four particles are done executing A''', they erase all registers except the one containing n, and execute a simulation of F (again, by simulating a 2-register RAM that executes F). Whenever F outputs a step in a path from p_1 to p_2, p_3, or p_4, this step is memorized by the leader L. At the end of the simulation, L has the three complete paths stored in its memory. Note that this is possible even if the memory of L is of constant size: by Assumption 1, the three paths are contained in a neighborhood of p_1 with radius independent of n, and therefore their length is bounded by a constant.

When the simulation of F is terminated, L starts moving toward P, and orders M_1 and M_2 to do the same. When M_1, L, M_2, and P are in four consecutive locations, L communicates the three paths to the others. At this point, each of the four particles knows what to do to reach its final position, and they all do so in an orderly fashion.

5.6 Conclusion

Our Shape-Formation algorithm demonstrates the following:

Theorem 2. *Under Assumption 1, any computable shape is formable from any simply connected initial configuration.*

The proof of correctness is straightforward, and it relies on two basic facts:

- A four-particle simulator and its trail of particles will never get in the way of other four-particle simulators. This is because each of them stays in its own principal sector; the only exceptions are the trespassers, which are actually not an obstacle due to the trespasser-avoidance rule.
- The particles that have already been deployed will not get in the way of the four-particle simulator that deployed them. This is because the movement operations always make the simulator travel through locations where no particle has been deployed, yet. In particular, the delayed-deployment rule serves this purpose: a deployed particle will always expand toward a location that will never be traversed by the simulator again.

Note that Assumption 1 only excludes shapes whose levels are very sparse around the last dots of their principal subsets. In particular, connected shapes abundantly satisfy the assumption, which in this case reduces to the necessary condition of Proposition 1. Therefore, we have the following characterization of formable connected computable shapes:

Corollary 1. *A necessary and sufficient condition for a connected computable shape to be formable from a simply connected initial configuration is that, if the initial configuration is unbreakably k-symmetric, then also the corresponding level of the shape is unbreakably k-symmetric.*

Our results open several interesting questions. In particular: what happens when the starting configuration is not simply connected? To what other problems can our mobile RAM be applied?

References

1. Daymude, J., Hinnenthal, K., Richa, A., Scheideler, C.: Computing by programmable particles. In: Flocchini, P., Prencipe, G., Santoro, N. (eds.) Distributed Computing by Mobile Entities. Lecture Notes in Computer Science, vol. 11340, pp. 615–681. Springer, Cham (2019). https://doi.org/10.1007/978-3-030-11072-7_22
2. Derakhshandeh, Z., Gmyr, R., Richa, A., Scheideler, C., Strothmann, T.: An algorithmic framework for shape formation problems in self-organizing particle systems. In: Proceedings of NanoCom, pp. 21:1–21:2 (2015)
3. Derakhshandeh, Z., Gmyr, R., Richa, A., Scheideler, C., Strothmann, T.: Universal shape formation for programmable matter. In: Proceedings of the 28th ACM Symposium on Parallelism in Algorithms and Architectures (SPAA), pp. 289–299 (2016)
4. Derakhshandeh, Z., Gmyr, R., Richa, A., Scheideler, C., Strothmann, T.: Universal coating for programmable matter. Theor. Comput. Sci. **671**, 56–68 (2017)
5. Derakhshandeh, Z., Gmyr, R., Strothmann, T., Bazzi, R., Richa, A., Scheideler, C.: Leader election and shape formation with self-organizing programmable matter. In: Proceedings of the International Conference on DNA Computing and Molecular Programming, pp. 117–132 (2015)
6. Di Luna, G.A., Flocchini, P., Santoro, N., Viglietta, G., Yamauchi, Y.: Shape formation by programmable particles. Distrib. Comput. **33**(1), 69–101 (2019). https://doi.org/10.1007/s00446-019-00350-6
7. Luna, G.D., Flocchini, P., Prencipe, G., Santoro, N., Viglietta, G.: Line recovery by programmable particles. In: Proceedings of the International Conference on Distributed Computing and Networking (2018)
8. Michail, O., Skretas, G., Spirakis, P.: On the transformation capability of feasible mechanisms for programmable matter. In: Proceedings of the International Colloquium on Automata, Languages and Programming (ICALP), pp. 136:1–136:15 (2017)
9. Minsky, M.: Computation: Finite and Infinite Machines. Prentice-Hall Inc., Upper Saddle River (1967)
10. Naz, A., Piranda, B., Bourgeois, J., Goldstein, S.: A distributed self-reconfiguration algorithm for cylindrical lattice-based modular robots. In: Proceedings of the IEEE International Symposium on Network Computing and Applications, pp. 254–263 (2016)
11. Patitz, M.J.: An introduction to tile-based self-assembly and a survey of recent results. Nat. Comput. **13**(2), 195–224 (2013). https://doi.org/10.1007/s11047-013-9379-4
12. Romanishin, J.W., Gilpin, K., Rus, D.: M-blocks: Momentum-driven, magnetic modular robots. In: Proceedings of the International Conference on Intelligent Robots and Systems, pp. 253–263 (2013)
13. Rothemund, P.: Folding DNA to create nanoscale shapes and patterns. Nature **440**(7082), 297–302 (2006)
14. Rubenstein, M., Ahler, C., Nagpal, R.: Kilobot: a low cost scalable robot system for collective behaviors. In: Proceedings of the International Conference on Robotics and Automation, pp. 3293–3298 (2012)
15. Toffoli, T., Margolus, N.: Programmable matter: concepts and realization. Phys. D **47**(1), 263–272 (1991)

Approximation Algorithm for Estimating Distances in Distributed Virtual Environments

Olivier Beaumont[1,2], Tobias Castanet[1,2(✉)], Nicolas Hanusse[1], and Corentin Travers[1]

[1] Bordeaux INP, CNRS, LaBRI, UMR5800,
Univ. Bordeaux, 33400 Talence, France
tobias.castanet@labri.fr

[2] Inria Bordeaux - Sud-Ouest, 200, Avenue de la Vieille Tour, 33405
Talence cedex, France

Abstract. This article deals with the issue of guaranteeing properties in Distributed Virtual Environments (DVEs) without a server. This issue is particularly relevant in the case of online games, that operate in a fully distributed framework and for which network resources such as bandwidth are the critical resources. Players typically need to know the distance between their character and other characters, at least approximately. They all share the same position estimation algorithm but, in general, do not know the current positions of others. We provide a synchronized distributed algorithm $\mathcal{A}_{lc}$ to guarantee, at any time, that the estimated distance d_{est} between any pair of characters A and B is always a $1 + \varepsilon$ approximation of the current distance d_{act}, regardless of movement pattern, and then prove that if characters move randomly on a d-dimensional grid, or follow a random continuous movement on up to three dimensions, the number of messages of $\mathcal{A}_{lc}$ is optimal up to a constant factor. In a more practical setting, we also show that the number of messages of $\mathcal{A}_{lc}$ for actual game traces is much less than the standard algorithm sending actual positions at a given frequency.

Keywords: Distributed virtual environments · Online games · Random walks · Distributed approximation algorithms · Peer-to-peer algorithms

1 Introduction

1.1 Context

The term *Distributed Virtual Environment* (DVE) refers to systems where geographically distant users, or players, participate in a highly interactive virtual

Supported by the French ANR project ANR-16-CE40-0023 (DESCARTES).

M. Malawski and K. Rzadca (Eds.): Euro-Par 2020, LNCS 12247, pp. 359–375, 2020.
https://doi.org/10.1007/978-3-030-57675-2_23

world. The main examples of DVEs are online games, where players control characters that interact with each other, and may modify the shared environment. Usually, interactions between characters and/or objects of the environment are enabled when they are sufficiently close in the virtual world. For simplicity, in the rest of the paper, we will use *player* to denote both the player and the character.

The main difference between a DVE and a classical distributed system like a database, is that the states of objects in the virtual environment evolve even without changes issued by the users [14] since non-player characters go about their programmed activities, and objects must respect the physics of the game. Moreover, the amount of inputs per time unit is generally high, as players interact a lot with the environment.

DVE participants need to know the state of the virtual world, in order to display it correctly and to be able to interact with it. The two central aspects that need to be optimized in a DVE are consistency and responsiveness. Inconsistencies arise when two users see different versions of the virtual world. On the other hand, responsiveness, the time interval between when a user executes an action and when the effects of this action is perceived by the player is unsatisfactory when this time delay is noticeable.

One difficulty is related to the number of exchanged messages. In general, increasing the number of communications between players contributes both to responsiveness (changes are transmitted earlier) and consistency (more messages allow a more accurate knowledge of the game's state). On the other hand, it has been shown in [13] that too many messages degrade network performance, leading to inconsistencies.

In practice, many games rely on a simple strategy, where players send updates at a regular rate to other players. The main flaw of this technique is a poor scalability in terms of bandwidth, as the number of messages increases quadratically with the number of players. Scalability is a concern for DVEs: some games are intended to be played by a large number of participants at the same time (e.g. MMORPGs). In addition, many online games are based on a client-server architecture. This has many disadvantages, as maintaining a server is often expensive, and exposes a single point of failure [16]. This leads to the incentive to study peer-to-peer solutions, where players share the role of the server among themselves, but in this context, bandwidth becomes crucial, as the network capacities of peers are usually lower than those of powerful servers. This article focuses on reducing bandwidth usage by limiting the number of exchanged messages. Several versatile techniques have been proposed to achieve this goal.

Data compression regroups techniques that can reduce bandwidth usage, but that are dependent on the application. For example Delta encoding [16], is an implementation trick where only differences between states are sent.

Dead-reckoning is a widely used tool, standardized in the Appendix E of [3]. Each player predicts the positions of the other players, extrapolating their movements after each update, typically based on their speed and acceleration.

Error induced by dead-reckoning can be measured by different means [4,17], but Dead-reckoning aims at bounding *the additive error* on the players positions.

The players know their own actual positions at any time, and for the other players, they only know estimated positions. Since all the players share the same estimation algorithm, each player is able to detect if the error on his/her own position as seen by another player is above a given threshold. When this happens, *the player sends a message to this player to correct the outdated estimated position.* Research on dead-reckoning improved bandwidth usage mainly in two ways : get the best prediction possible [10], or improve the update policies (a survey on different update policies is given in [15]).

Interest Management consists in filtering updates in order to send them only to players who might be interested. Different types of interest management are identified in [7,12]. Some application-specific approaches may also use the fact that human attention is limited, as in [6], where a set of five interesting players is defined at any given time, in order to send frequent updates to those players, but much less to other players.

Combinations of all these techniques can be used. For example in [8], interest management is used to modify the Dead-reckoning threshold.

In the context of interest management, estimating distances between players is very useful, as a player is rarely interested in knowing the exact state of far away objects. In addition, in some application-specific cases, distance may be important, for example when implementing a spell that heals all allies within a certain range. To the best of our knowledge, no distributed algorithm has been proposed to solve the problem of estimating the distance between users of a DVE. The objective of this paper is *to provide a solution allowing players to estimate the distances between them, with a condition on the relative error, while guaranteeing that the use of bandwidth is as small as possible.* In particular, it has to be bounded against an ideal algorithm that would send a minimum number of messages, based on a perfect knowledge of the game's state.

We identify two main articles related to this objective.

In [14], two techniques are proposed. First, *local-lag* reduces short-term inconsistencies, at the cost of less responsiveness: a delay between the time an operation is issued and the time when the operation becomes effective is added. Secondly, `timewarp` is proposed, an algorithm to ensure consistency. In this algorithm, each player remembers all previous operations and the time at which they were issued. If an operation is received by a player too late, the player rewinds the state of the world, immediately recomputing the current state, using all needed operations. These operations are user initiated, thus, the number of messages is proportional to the number of players, and to the length of time.

In [11], Dead-Reckoning is used to compensate for latencies and message losses on the network. TATSI, the average spatial error on players' positions over a time interval, is estimated with no latency or loss of message. Then, under the assumption of a constant acceleration, latencies and message losses are added to the model, and it is shown that the same TATSI can be obtained by lowering the dead-reckoning threshold (thus making DVE nodes send more messages than without latency and message losses).

To summarize, solutions from the literature are very consuming in term of messages and/or target an *additive bound* on the error. By contrast, this paper focuses on bounding the *relative error* on distances and keeping the number of message exchanges low.

1.2 Contribution

In terms of optimality in number of messages, Dead-reckoning is optimal for position estimation. Indeed, when using Dead-reckoning, players know where other players see them. Thus, a player sends updates if and only if the tolerated error between his/her actual position and his/her estimated position is exceeded, making it an optimal bandwidth strategy. On the other hand, since no two players know the actual distance between them, none of them can determine the exact error over the estimated distance, making distance estimation a much harder problem.

We consider deterministic algorithms that allow each player to estimate, at any time, the distances between him/her and the other players, while having a guarantee on the errors. Initially, each player knows the exact position of every other player. The metric we use is the relative error given in Eq. 1, where, at each instant t, $d_{act}(t)$ denotes the actual distance between two players, and $d_{est}(t)$ denotes their estimated distance,

$$\text{relative error} = |d_{act}(t) - d_{est}(t)|/d_{est}(t). \tag{1}$$

We make sure this error measurement never exceeds ε, the maximum tolerated relative error for any pair of players, while minimizing the number of exchanged messages.

That is, Eq. 2 must always hold, for every pair of players,

$$(1 - \varepsilon)d_{est}(t) < d_{act}(t) < (1 + \varepsilon)d_{est}(t). \tag{2}$$

We propose an algorithm, called *local change* and denoted by $\mathcal{A}_{lc}$. It relies on the same underlying principle as Dead-reckoning, where position estimations are deterministic and each player computes his/her own position as seen by other players, using the same deterministic algorithm. In $\mathcal{A}_{lc}$, player Bob sends his actual position p_B to another player Alice as soon as the estimate $\widetilde{p_B}$ of the position of Bob as seen by Alice deviates too much from his actual position, more precisely *as soon as* Eq. 3 *is violated*, where d denotes the distance between two points. In addition, Alice will *immediately respond to Bob by also sending her actual position.*

$$d\left(p_B(t),\ \widetilde{p_B}(t)\right) < d_{est}(t) \times \varepsilon/2. \tag{3}$$

To quantify the performance of our algorithm, we compare the number of messages against an oracle with a full knowledge of the current state of the game, called *ideal algorithm* and denoted by $\mathcal{A}_{id}$. In $\mathcal{A}_{id}$, an exchange of messages happens only when, and as soon as Eq. 2 is violated.

Our results are threefold. First, without any assumption on how players move, we prove that with $\mathcal{A}_{lc}$, *when there is no latency, the maximal error is never overcome*: Eq. 2 is always satisfied (Theorem 1, Sect. 2).

Secondly, in the case where movement is limited to the random part based on players' actions, which cannot be anticipated by the deterministic prediction algorithm, we prove that, *given a fixed ε, $\mathcal{A}_{lc}$ is optimal in terms of number of message exchanges up to a constant factor*. Theorem 2 and Theorem 3, respectively in Sect. 3 and Sect. 4, use two different movement patterns, both of which consisting, at each instant $t \in \mathbb{N}$, in chosing a new position at a distance at most 1 from the last position.

Finally, this theoretical analysis is complemented by experiments in Sect. 5. We first perform experiments on synthetic traces. Then, we use actual traces from Heroes of Newerth [1], to compare $\mathcal{A}_{lc}$ with a *fixed frequency algorithm*, denoted by $\mathcal{A}_{ff}$. $\mathcal{A}_{ff}$ is commonly used in practice in online games, and sends updates periodically, by waiting w time units between updates. We show that overall, $\mathcal{A}_{lc}$ behaves better while never exceeding the maximum tolerated error.

In summary, the performance (without latency) of $\mathcal{A}_{id}$, $\mathcal{A}_{lc}$, $\mathcal{A}_{ff}$ and timewarp [14] are shown in the following table:

	Number of messages	Maximal error	Number of violations
$\mathcal{A}_{id}$	$m_{id} \leq Tn(n-1)$	$\leq \varepsilon$	0
$\mathcal{A}_{lc}$	$\mathcal{O}(m_{id})$	$\leq \varepsilon$	0
$\mathcal{A}_{ff}$	$\frac{T}{w}n(n-1)$	0 if $w=1$ unbounded otherwise	$\Theta(Tn^2)$
timewarp	$\mathcal{O}(Tn^2)$	0	0

T denotes the duration of the experiment, and n the number of participants in the DVE. We consider as a reference m_{id}, the (perfect knowledge based) number of messages sent by $\mathcal{A}_{id}$. In the worst case, $\mathcal{A}_{id}$ would make players send one message each instant (if there is no restriction on movement, players may move each turn in such a way that the distance between players increases or decreases too much with respect to Eq. 2 at each instant). Thus we have $m_{id} \leq Tn(n-1)$. Note that timewarp functions slightly differently than the others: it is intended to ensure strict consistency. The *number of violations* counts, over T time units, the number of distance pairs for which the error is above ε.

2   Model and Algorithms

2.1   Model

Let us first assume that $\varepsilon \in]0; 1[$. Indeed, $\varepsilon = 0$ means that no error is tolerated, while $\varepsilon = 1$ would accept any estimate on the distance, provided it is larger than half the actual distance, which is not very informative. Since $\mathcal{A}_{lc}$ must enforce that Eq. 3 holds true for any pair of players, we focus on two players Alice and Bob. We assume that the communication channel connecting them is without message loss nor latency, that local computations do not take time and that all players share a synchronized clock. At any instant $t \in \mathbb{N}$, let us denote the positions of both players as $p_A(t)$ and $p_B(t)$. A position is a vector whose dimension depends on the virtual world (for example, for a 3D world, a position is described by a vector in $\mathbb{N}^3$, or $\mathbb{R}^3$ in the case of continuous moves). Each player knows his/her own actual position, but may not know exactly where the other player is. These positions can change unpredictably, through the actions of users.

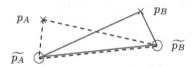

Fig. 1. Knowledge of Alice (dashed blue lines) and Bob (continuous red lines) (color figure online)

In Sects. 3 and 4, analyses are for two types of movement patterns. As these movements are random, the best possible estimation of the position of other players is to assume they remain still, so that a player will estimate that the other players are at their last known position.

Random Walk is a discrete movement taking place on a d-dimensional grid. Thus, positions can be represented as values from $\mathbb{Z}^d$. If at instant $t \in \mathbb{N}$, a player following such movement is at position $p = (p_1, p_2, \ldots, p_d)$ he/she has $2d$ neighbors: $(p_1 - 1, p_2, \ldots, p_d)$, $(p_1 + 1, p_2, \ldots, p_d)$, $(p_1, p_2 - 1, \ldots, p_d)$, etc. The movement consists, at each instant, to choose one of the neighbors, each one having probability $\frac{1}{2d}$ to be chosen.

Continuous Movement consists at each instant, to select a value smaller than one, and to add a vector of norm equal to this value, and with a direction randomly chosen. **In 1D**, a moving player adds at each instant, a random number following a uniform distribution on $[-1, 1]$ to their position. **In 2D**, at each instant t, a moving player X chooses ρ_t and θ_t following uniform distributions respectively on $[0, 1]$ and $[0, 2\pi]$, so that $p_X(t + 1) = p_X(t) + (\rho_t, \theta_t)$, where (ρ_t, θ_t) is the vector with polar coordinates ρ_t and θ_t. **In 3D**, at each instant t, a moving player chooses ρ_t, θ_t, and φ_t following uniform distributions respectively on $[0, 1]$, $[0, 2\pi]$ and $[0, \pi]$, to add as spherical coordinates.

2.2   Algorithm

As explained in Sect. 1.2, players will estimate their distance to each other. To do this, each player will compute a deterministic estimation of the other player's

---

Algorithm 1. Local change ($\mathcal{A}_{lc}$), from the point of view of Alice

---

1: $p_A \leftarrow$ Alice's initial position ▷ Actual position of Alice. This is a read-only input to the algorithm
2: $\widetilde{p_A} \leftarrow$ Alice's initial position ▷ Position of Alice, as estimated by Bob, the other player
3: $\widetilde{p_B} \leftarrow$ Bob's initial position ▷ Estimated position of Bob
4: $d_{est} \leftarrow d(\widetilde{p_A}, \widetilde{p_B})$ ▷ Estimated distance. Will always be equal to $d(\widetilde{p_A}, \widetilde{p_B})$
5: **procedure** CHECK_FOR_UPDATE ▷ to be called at each $t \in \mathbb{N}$, after movement
6:     **if** $d(p_A, \widetilde{p_A}) \geq \frac{\varepsilon}{2} d_{est}$ **then**
7:         $\widetilde{p_A} \leftarrow p_A$
8:         $d_{est} \leftarrow d(\widetilde{p_A}, \widetilde{p_B})$
9:         send message $(p_A, \text{begin\_update})$ to Bob
10:     **end if**
11: **procedure** RECEIVE_MESSAGE(position, type) from Bob ▷ to be called when receiving a message
12:     $\widetilde{p_B} \leftarrow$ position
13:     $d_{est} \leftarrow d(\widetilde{p_A}, \widetilde{p_B})$
14:     **if** type = begin_update **then** ▷ type distinction is to avoid infinite messages
15:         send message $(p_A, \text{update\_reply})$ to Bob
16:     **end if**

---

position, in order to get $d_{est}(t)$, i.e. Bob computes $\widetilde{p_A}(t)$, the estimate of the position of Alice, and Alice computes $\widetilde{p_B}(t)$. As they use the same deterministic algorithm, these computations can be replicated, and $\widetilde{p_A}(t)$ and $\widetilde{p_B}(t)$ become a shared knowledge, as seen on Fig. 1 (even without communication). Thus, we will use the distance between those two (estimated but shared) positions as distance estimate, $d_{est}(t)$. In practice, $\widetilde{p_A}(t)$ is generally based on an extrapolation of Alice's position, speed and acceleration, from the time of the last message exchanged between Alice and Bob.

In Theorem 1, we prove that $\mathcal{A}_{lc}$ satisfies Eq. 2, provided that $\mathcal{A}_{lc}$ sends an update of the actual position as soon as Eq. 3 is not satisfied, as depicted in Algorithm 1. Thus, the correctness of $\mathcal{A}_{lc}$ is established.

Theorem 1. *Using $\mathcal{A}_{lc}$, Eq. 2 holds true at any instant (regardless of movement).*

Proof. The following inequalities hold true:

$$\begin{cases} d_{act}(t) - d_{est}(t) \leq d(p_A(t), \widetilde{p_A}(t)) + d(p_B(t), \widetilde{p_B}(t)) \& \text{(triangle inequality)} \\ d_{est}(t) - d_{act}(t) \leq d(p_A(t), \widetilde{p_A}(t)) + d(p_B(t), \widetilde{p_B}(t)) \& \text{(triangle inequality)} \\ d(p_B(t), \widetilde{p_B}(t)) < \frac{\varepsilon}{2} d_{est}(t) \& \text{(by construction)} \\ d(p_A(t), \widetilde{p_A}(t)) < \frac{\varepsilon}{2} d_{est}(t) \& \text{(by construction)} \end{cases}$$

so that $|d_{act}(t) - d_{est}(t)| < \varepsilon d_{est}(t)$, which is equivalent to Eq. 2.

$\square$

3   Random Walk

The performance of $\mathcal{A}_{lc}$ is measured by M, the number of message exchanges (a message and its response counting as one) between two players using $\mathcal{A}_{lc}$, before the first message sent with $\mathcal{A}_{id}$. Our result that $\mathcal{A}_{lc}$ is optimal is formally stated in Theorem 2 by an upper bound on the expectation of M:

Theorem 2. *Let* $\Delta_r = \left\lceil \frac{\log(1+\varepsilon) - \log(1-\varepsilon)}{\log(1+\frac{\varepsilon}{2})} \right\rceil$, *with* $\varepsilon \in]0;1[$. *For any two players following a random walk on* $\mathbb{Z}^d$ *(with* $d \leq 3$*),* $\mathbb{E}[\![M]\!] \leq \Delta_r \times \left(2^{d+1}\right)^{\Delta_r}$. *Moreover, if only one of the players moves on* $\mathbb{Z}$, *with* $\Delta_l = \left\lceil \frac{\log(1-\varepsilon) - \log(1+\varepsilon)}{\log(1-\frac{\varepsilon}{2})} \right\rceil$, *then* $\mathbb{E}[\![M]\!] \leq \min \left(\Delta_l \times 2^{\Delta_l} ; \left\lceil \frac{4}{\pi}\Delta_l^2 \right\rceil \times 8 \right)$.

Due to space limitations, only the 2D-case with two players moving will be proved in this Section. 1D and 3D cases can be found in [5].

For our analysis, we will use the L^1 distance (Manhattan distance), that is, for two positions $p = (p_1, p_2)$ and $p' = (p'_1, p'_2)$, the distance is $d(p, p') = |p_1 - p'_1| + |p_2 - p'_2|$.

Let us denote by d_{est} and $\widetilde{p}$ the estimates for $\mathcal{A}_{lc}$. As seen in Sect. 1.2, Algorithm $\mathcal{A}_{id}$ generates a message exchange as soon as Eq. 2 becomes false (this is the definition of $\mathcal{A}_{id}$). Equivalently, $\mathcal{A}_{id}$ generates a message exchange as soon as d_{act} leaves $\mathcal{I}_{id}$, where $\mathcal{I}_{id}$ is defined by $\mathcal{I}_{id} =]d_0(1-\varepsilon) ; d_0(1+\varepsilon)[$, with $d_0 = d_{act}(0)$.

Let us consider t_i (with $i \geq 1$), defined as the instant at which the i-th round trip of the messages is sent with $\mathcal{A}_{lc}$. With $t_{opt} = \min\{t : d_{act}(t) \notin \mathcal{I}_{id}\}$, the instant of the first message sent by $\mathcal{A}_{id}$, we have $M = \max\{i, t_i \leq t_{opt}\}$. We may then define the auxiliary random variable $M' : \min\{i, d_{est}(t_i) \notin \mathcal{I}_{id}\}$. M' represents the index i of the first message of $\mathcal{A}_{lc}$ so that $d_{est}(t_i)$ is outside $\mathcal{I}_{id}$. As at this instant t_i, there was an exchange of messages, we have $d_{est}(t_i) = d_{act}(t_i)$, thus, by construction, $\mathcal{A}_{id}$ already sent a message, so that $M' \geq M$.

Let us call $\mathcal{B}_A(t)$ (resp. $\mathcal{B}_B(t)$) the L^1-ball of radius $\left\lceil d_{est}(t)\frac{\varepsilon}{2} \right\rceil$, and of center $\widetilde{p_A}(t)$ (resp. $\widetilde{p_B}(t)$). Thus, $\mathcal{B}_A(t)$ is the set of positions that are at a distance from $\widetilde{p_A}(t)$ less than or equal to $\left\lceil d_{est}(t)\frac{\varepsilon}{2} \right\rceil$ (this is the lower square on Fig. 2a).

Note that, as we supposed that the estimated positions do not evolve between two message exchanges, the same goes for the estimated distance, as well as for $\mathcal{B}_A$ and $\mathcal{B}_B$. That is, for all t and t' in $[\![t_i; t_{i+1}[\![, d_{est}(t) = d_{est}(t'), \mathcal{B}_A(t) = \mathcal{B}_A(t')$, and $\mathcal{B}_B(t) = \mathcal{B}_B(t')$.

Let us assume without loss of generality, that Bob is the player that triggers the $(i+1)$-th message. Additionally, as we are interested only in the positions of Alice and Bob relatively to each other, we can always put the center of the coordinates on $\widetilde{p_A}$; thus, at each instant, $\widetilde{p_A}(t) = 0$.

Remark 1. With $\mathcal{A}_{lc}$, the $(i+1)$-th message is sent when Bob is on the border of $\mathcal{B}_B(t_i)$.

Proof. With $\mathcal{A}_{lc}$, the $(i + 1)$-th message is sent when Bob gets at a position that is at a distance at least $\frac{\varepsilon}{2}d_{est}(t_i)$ from $\widetilde{p_B}(t_i)$. As movement is on integer positions, the first positions satisfying this are all on the border of $\mathcal{B}_B(t_i)$.

$\square$

Each instant t_{i+1} where Bob gets out of $\mathcal{B}_B(t_i)$, the estimated distance changes from $d_{est}(t_i)$ to $d_{est}(t_{i+1})$. Before being able to identify the effect a message has on the estimated distance (Lemma 3), we analyze how far away from Alice the new estimated position of Bob can get (Lemma 1).

The border of $\mathcal{B}_B(t_i)$ has 4 faces. As shown on Fig. 2b, we may draw cones over each of these faces, with $\widetilde{p_B}(t_i)$ as the apex: if we draw two lines intersecting on $\widetilde{p_B}(t_i)$, one horizontal and one vertical, we divide the plane in four cones. All points of the space will be in only one of the cones, except for points on the borders (on Fig. 2b, the borders of the cones are the dashed lines). In the case where $\widetilde{p_A}(t_i)$ is not on one of the borders, let us call $\mathcal{R}$ the face of the border of $\mathcal{B}_B(t_i)$ that is included in the cone opposing the cone containing $\widetilde{p_A}(t_i)$. In the case where $\widetilde{p_A}(t_i)$ is on one of the borders (this happens when $\widetilde{p_B}(t_i)$ is on one of the axes), than any of the two opposing faces can be taken as $\mathcal{R}$.

Lemma 1. *If* $\widetilde{p_B}(t_i) \neq \widetilde{p_A}(t_i)$, $\mathbb{P}\left(d\left(\widetilde{p_A}(t_i), \widetilde{p_B}(t_{i+1})\right) \geq \left\lceil d_{est}(t_i)\left(1 + \frac{\varepsilon}{2}\right)\right\rceil\right) \geq \frac{1}{4}$.

Proof. All points of $\mathcal{R}$ are at distance $\left\lceil d_{est}(t_i)\left(1 + \frac{\varepsilon}{2}\right)\right\rceil$ of $\widetilde{p_A}(t_i)$ (to see this, consider one of the endpoints of the face, like α on Fig. 2b, for which one coordinate is the same as for $\widetilde{p_B}(t_i)$, and the absolute value of the other coordinate is larger by $\left\lceil \frac{\varepsilon}{2}d_{est}(t_i)\right\rceil$).

As the random walk is symmetric, and by Remark 1, we have a probability of at least $\frac{1}{4}$ that Bob sends the $(i + 1)$-th message by going on face $\mathcal{R}$.

$\square$

Note that the case where $\widetilde{p_B}(t_i) = \widetilde{p_A}(t_i)$ has not to be treated, as it means that both players shared the same position at instant t_i. If Alice and Bob start on the same position, $M = 1$; if Alice and Bob start on different positions, it is impossible for Bob to move to Alice's position without $\mathcal{A}_{id}$ sending a message.

In Lemma 1, the movement of Alice is not taken into account. Let us call Π the line parallel to $\mathcal{R}$ and containing $\widetilde{p_A}(t_i)$ (see Fig. 2a).

Remark 2. As Π contains $\widetilde{p_A}(t_i)$, the center of $\mathcal{B}_A(t_i)$, Π divides $\mathcal{B}_A(t_i)$ into two halves of same area.

Lemma 2. *At least half of the positions* $p \in \mathcal{B}_A(t_i)$ *satisfy*

$$d\left(p, \widetilde{p_B}(t_{i+1})\right) \geq d\left(\widetilde{p_A}(t_i), \widetilde{p_B}(t_{i+1})\right).$$

Proof. By definition of the L^1-norm, and because Π is parallel to $\mathcal{R}$, if we draw, on Π, the points γ and δ that are the projections of $\widetilde{p_B}(t_{i+1})$ parallel to the two axes (see Fig. 2a), then all points on the line segment $[\![\gamma\delta]\!]$ are at the same distance to $\widetilde{p_B}(t_{i+1})$. Also, by definition of $\mathcal{R}$, $\widetilde{p_A}(t_i) \in [\![\gamma\delta]\!]$. Thus, all points of $[\![\gamma\delta]\!]$ are at a distance to $\widetilde{p_B}(t_{i+1})$ equal to $d\left(\widetilde{p_A}(t_i), \widetilde{p_B}(t_{i+1})\right)$.

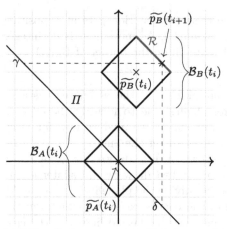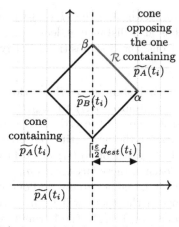

(a) When Bob gets on $\mathcal{R}$, half of the possible positions of Alice are further away.

(b) One of the face of $\mathcal{B}_B$ is always sufficiently far away from $\widetilde{p_A}(t_i)$.

Fig. 2. Random walk, two-dimensional situation

If we draw the L^1-ball of center $\widetilde{p_B}(t_{i+1})$ and of radius $d(\widetilde{p_A}(t_i), \widetilde{p_B}(t_{i+1}))$, then $[\![\gamma\delta]\!]$ is one of the faces of the ball. By Remark 2, we have that at least half of the points from $\mathcal{B}_A(t_i)$ are outside this ball, with a distance to $\widetilde{p_B}(t_{i+1})$ higher than the radius.

$\square$

This allows us to finally look at the change in estimated distance.

Lemma 3. *As long as* $\widetilde{p_B}(t_i) \neq \widetilde{p_A}(t_i)$, $\mathbb{P}\left(d_{est}(t_{i+1}) \geq \lceil d_{est}(t_i)\left(1+\frac{\varepsilon}{2}\right)\rceil\right) \geq \frac{1}{8}$.

Proof. As Alice does not get out of $\mathcal{B}_A(t_i)$, we know that $\widetilde{p_A}(t_{i+1}) \in \mathcal{B}_A(t_i)$. By Lemma 2, and by symmetry of the random walk, $d(\widetilde{p_A}(t_{i+1}), \widetilde{p_B}(t_{i+1})) \geq d(\widetilde{p_A}(t_i), \widetilde{p_B}(t_{i+1}))$ with probability $\frac{1}{2}$. Combined with Lemma 1, we get the result.

$\square$

Let $r_{rw} : x \mapsto \lceil x\left(1+\frac{\varepsilon}{2}\right)\rceil$. We can now prove Lemma 4 which states that, if there are enough successive messages so that $d_{est}(t_{i+1}) \geq r_{rw}(d_{est}(t_i))$, then Bob will get out of $\mathcal{I}_{id}$, whatever his initial position in the interval $\mathcal{I}_{id}$.

Lemma 4. *For all* $x \in \mathcal{I}_{id}$, $r_{rw}^{\Delta_r}(x) \geq d_0(1+\varepsilon)$.

Proof. $x \in \mathcal{I}_{id} \Rightarrow x \geq d_0(1-\varepsilon) \Rightarrow r_{rw}^{\Delta_r}(x) \geq r_{rw}^{\Delta_r}(d_0(1-\varepsilon))$ since r_{rw} is increasing, implying that $r_{rw}^{\Delta_r}(x) \geq d_0(1-\varepsilon)\left(1+\frac{\varepsilon}{2}\right)^{\Delta_r}$ since $\forall x, r_{rw}(x) \geq x\left(1+\frac{\varepsilon}{2}\right)$. Moreover, since, $\Delta_r \geq \frac{\log(1+\varepsilon)-\log(1-\varepsilon)}{\log(1+\frac{\varepsilon}{2})}$, then $(1-\varepsilon)\left(1+\frac{\varepsilon}{2}\right)^{\Delta_l} \geq (1+\varepsilon)$ and $x \in \mathcal{I}_{id} \Rightarrow r_{rw}^{\Delta_r}(x) \geq d_0(1+\varepsilon)$.

$\square$

Proof (Proof of Theorem 2, 2D case). Let us split the sequence of all the instants t_i into *phases* of length Δ_r and let us denote by j the index of the phase containing instants from $t_{(j-1)\Delta_r}$ to $t_{j\Delta_r-1}$. Let us consider the following possible events (i) $\mathcal{S}_j$: there is at least one $i \in [\![(j-1)\Delta_r; j\Delta_r]\!]$ such that $d_{est}(t_i) \notin \mathcal{I}_{id}$ and (ii) $\mathcal{S}'_j$: for all $i \in [\![(j-1)\Delta_r; j\Delta_r - 1]\!]$, $d_{est}(t_{i+1}) \geq r_{rw}(d_{est}(t_i))$. In turn, these events can be used to define useful random variables: (i) $X_j = 1$ if $\mathcal{S}_j$ is true, 0 otherwise (ii) $X'_j = 1$ if $\mathcal{S}'_j$ is true, 0 otherwise, (iii) $Y = j$ if $X_j = 1$ and $X_k = 0$ for every $k < j$ and (iv) $Y' = j$ if $X'_j = 1$ and $X'_k = 0$ for every $k < j$. Thus, Y denotes the index of the first phase during which $\mathcal{A}_{id}$ sends a message.

If $\mathcal{S}'_j$ is true, then $d_{est}(t_{j\Delta_r}) \geq r_{rw}{}^{\Delta_r}(d_{est}(t_{(j-1)\Delta_r}))$ (as r_{rw} is increasing). Thus, by Lemma 4, $\mathcal{S}'_j \Rightarrow \mathcal{S}_j$, so that $X'_j = 1 \Rightarrow X_j = 1$. Therefore $Y' = j \Rightarrow X'_j = 1 \Rightarrow X_j = 1 \Rightarrow Y \leq j$ and finally

$$\mathbb{E}[Y] \leq \mathbb{E}[Y'] \, . \tag{4}$$

We may then note that Y' follows a geometric distribution with parameter $\mathbb{P}(\mathcal{S}'_j)$. Moreover, as $\mathbb{P}(\mathcal{S}'_j) \geq \frac{1}{8^{\Delta_r}}$ $\Big($because by Lemma 3, there is at least a probability $\frac{1}{8}$ that $d_{est}(t_{i+1}) \geq r_{rw}\big(d_{est}(t_i)\big)\Big)$, we have $\mathbb{E}[Y'] \leq 8^{\Delta_r}$. Thus, by Eq. 4, we have $\mathbb{E}[Y] \leq 8^{\Delta_r}$. Since Y denotes the index of the first phase during which d_{act} gets out of $\mathcal{I}_{id}$, $M' \in [\![(Y-1)\Delta_r; Y\Delta_r]\!]$. In particular, $M' \leq Y\Delta_r$ and $\mathbb{E}[M'] \leq \Delta_r \times 8^{\Delta_r}$. Finally, as $M' > M$, we have $\mathbb{E}[M] \leq \Delta_r \times 8^{\Delta_r}$.

$\square$

4 Continuous Movement

As in the previous section, we present bounds on M for continuous movements (Theorem 3), but prove only the 2D-case.

Theorem 3. *With* $\Delta_l = \left\lceil \frac{\log(1-\varepsilon)-\log(1+\varepsilon)}{\log(1-\frac{\varepsilon}{2})} \right\rceil$, *and with two players following a random continuous movement in 1D, then* $\mathbb{E}[M] \leq \Delta_l \times 4^{\Delta_l}$. *Let* $\Gamma = 2 \frac{\log(1+\varepsilon)-\log(1-\varepsilon)}{\log\left(1+\frac{\varepsilon}{\sqrt{2}}+\frac{\varepsilon^2}{4}\right)}$. *If two players follow a random continuous movement in 2D, then* $\mathbb{E}[M] \leq \Gamma \times 8^{\Gamma}$. *With moves in 3D, then* $\mathbb{E}[M] \leq \Gamma \times 14^{\Gamma}$.

In this section, players follow the 2D continuous movement described in Sect. 2.1. Theorem 3 can be proved following the same general principle as with Theorem 2, but with slightly different lemmas. In particular, instead of r_{rw}, we have to use another function, $r_{cm} : x \mapsto x\sqrt{\left(1+\frac{\varepsilon^2}{4}+\frac{\varepsilon}{\sqrt{2}}\right)}$.

Once again, Bob is the player who gets out the first of his set of authorized positions with $\mathcal{A}_{lc}$, meaning that Bob is the player to initiate communication at instant t_{i+1}. In this setting, we will use the euclidean distance, thus $\mathcal{B}_B(t_i)$ takes the form of a disk of center $\widetilde{p_B}(t_i)$ and of radius $\frac{\varepsilon}{2}d_{est}$. In order to identify messages that make a sufficient increase on the estimated distance, we will look at the annulus of inner circle $\mathcal{B}_B(t_i)$, and with an outer circle of radius $\frac{\varepsilon}{2}d_{est}+1$. We will call $\mathcal{R}$ the portion of this annulus on the opposing side of $\widetilde{p_A}(t_i)$, (represented as a red hatched zone on Fig. 3a), that deviates not more than $\frac{\pi}{4}$ from the straight line between $\widetilde{p_A}(t_i)$ and $\widetilde{p_B}(t_i)$. More formally, with t the intersection between $\mathcal{B}_B$ and the line $(\widetilde{p_A}(t_i)\widetilde{p_B}(t_i))$, on the opposite side of $\widetilde{p_A}(t_i)$, and with $\angle s\widetilde{p_B}(t_i)t$ the measure of the angle formed by the points s, $\widetilde{p_B}(t_i)$, and t, then

$$\mathcal{R} = \left\{ s, \angle s\widetilde{p_B}(t_i)t \in \left[-\frac{\pi}{4}, \frac{\pi}{4}\right] \text{ and } d(s, \widetilde{p_B}(t_i)) \in \left[\frac{\varepsilon}{2}d_{est}(t_i), \frac{\varepsilon}{2}d_{est}(t_i) + 1\right] \right\}.$$

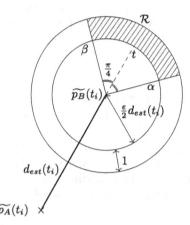

(a) Representation of the points corresponding to a growth in distance

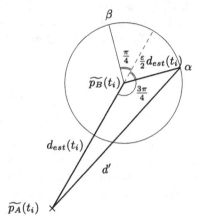

(b) Representation of the different values used to measure a growth in distance

Fig. 3. Continuous movement, two-dimensional situation

First, we get, in Lemma 5, the probability that $\widetilde{p_B}(t_{i+1})$ lands in $\mathcal{R}$.

Lemma 5. *In two dimensions,* $\mathbb{P}\big(\widetilde{p_B}(t_{i+1}) \in \mathcal{R}\big) = \frac{1}{4}$.

Proof. As Bob does not move more than one distance unit per time unit, the first instant where he is outside of $\mathcal{B}_B(t_i)$, on $\widetilde{p_B}(t_{i+1})$, he will be in the annulus. $\mathcal{R}$ represents one fourth of the total area of the annulus, and movement is symmetric with respect to the center of the annulus, thus we have probability one fourth that $\widetilde{p_B}(t_{i+1}) \in \mathcal{R}$.

$\square$

We may then see, in Lemma 6, that when $\widetilde{p_B}(t_{i+1})$ lands in $\mathcal{R}$, there is a high probability that the message $i + 1$ leads to a significant increases of d_{est} (where "significant" is represented by r_{cm}).

Lemma 6. *With two players moving,* $\mathbb{P}\big(d_{est}(t_{i+1}) \geq r_{cm}\big(d_{est}(t_i)\big) \mid \widetilde{p_B}(t_{i+1}) \in \mathcal{R}\big) \geq \frac{1}{2}$.

Proof. Let us assume $\widetilde{p_B}(t_{i+1}) \in \mathcal{R}$. The two points of $\mathcal{R}$ that are closest to $\widetilde{p_A}(t_i)$ are the rightmost and leftmost points that are both on $\mathcal{R}$ and the border of $\mathcal{B}_B(t_i)$ (α and β on Fig. 3a). Thus, if we call d' the distance between $\widetilde{p_A}(t_i)$ and α, we have $d(\widetilde{p_A}(t_i), \widetilde{p_B}(t_{i+1})) \geq d'$. As can be seen on Fig. 3b, the value of d' can be resolved by the law of cosines, relatively to the value of $d_{est}(t_i)$:

$$d' = \sqrt{d_{est}(t_i)^2 + \frac{\varepsilon^2}{4} d_{est}(t_i)^2 - d_{est}(t_i)^2 \varepsilon \cos\left(\frac{3\pi}{4}\right)} = d_{est}(t_i)\sqrt{\left(1 + \frac{\varepsilon^2}{4} + \frac{\varepsilon}{\sqrt{2}}\right)}.$$

Thus $d' = r_{cm}(d_{est}(t_i))$, so that $\mathbb{P}\Big(d(\widetilde{p_A}(t_i), \widetilde{p_B}(t_{i+1})) \geq r_{cm}(d_{est}(t_i))$ $\mid \widetilde{p_B}(t_{i+1}) \in \mathcal{R}\Big) = 1$. We may then notice that, by symmetry of Alice's movement, the probability that $\widetilde{p_A}(t_{i+1})$ is further away from $\widetilde{p_B}(t_{i+1})$ than $\widetilde{p_A}(t_i)$ is at least one half. This ends the proof.

□

Finally, we get in Lemma 7 a similar result to Lemma 3, identifying the probability that with an exchange of messages, there is a significant increase in the estimated distance.

Lemma 7. *With two players moving,* $\mathbb{P}\Big(d_{est}(t_{i+1}) \geq r_{cm}(d_{est}(t_i))\Big) \geq \frac{1}{8}$.

Proof. The result is immediate with Lemmas 5 and 6, and the law of total probability.   □

The last needed property, similarly to Lemma 4, is that successively applying r_{cm} to the estimated distance will make $\mathcal{A}_{id}$ send a message:

Lemma 8. *With* $\Gamma = \frac{\log(1+\varepsilon) - \log(1-\varepsilon)}{\log\left(\sqrt{1 + \frac{\varepsilon^2}{4} + \frac{\varepsilon}{\sqrt{2}}}\right)}$, *for all* $x \in \mathcal{I}_{id}$, $r_{cm}{}^{\Gamma}(x) \geq d_0(1+\varepsilon)$.

Proof. $x \in \mathcal{I}_{id} \Rightarrow x \geq d_0(1-\varepsilon) \Rightarrow r_{cm}{}^{\Gamma}(x) \geq r_{cm}{}^{\Gamma}(d_0(1-\varepsilon))$ since r_{cm} is increasing, so that $r_{cm}{}^{\Gamma}(x) \geq d_0(1-\varepsilon)\left(1 + \varepsilon^2/4 + \varepsilon/\sqrt{2}\right)^{\Gamma/2}$. Moreover, by definition of Γ,

$(1-\varepsilon)\left(1 + \varepsilon^2/4 + \varepsilon/\sqrt{2}\right)^{\Gamma/2} \geq (1+\varepsilon)$, so that finally $x \in \mathcal{I}_{id} \Rightarrow r_{cm}{}^{\Gamma}(x) \geq d_0(1+\varepsilon)$.

□

Proof (Proof of Theorem 3 , 2D case). It turns out the proof for the 2D case of Theorem 3 is exactly the same as the 2D case of Theorem 2, but using Lemma 7 and Lemma 8 instead of Lemma 3 and Lemma 4, and replacing Δ_r with Γ, and r_{rw} with r_{cm}.

□

5   Experiments

In order to analyze in practice the performance of $\mathcal{A}_{lc}$ with respects to $\mathcal{A}_{id}$ and $\mathcal{A}_{ff}$, we propose simulation results of two types: with synthetic and with real traces.

5.1   Synthetic Traces

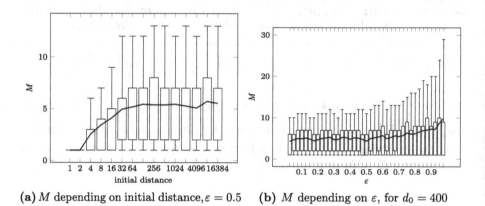

(a) M depending on initial distance, $\varepsilon = 0.5$ (b) M depending on ε, for $d_0 = 400$

Fig. 4. Two players following a random walk in 2D: values of M

The first set of simulations corresponds to random walks and continuous movements. We execute both $\mathcal{A}_{lc}$ and $\mathcal{A}_{id}$ with the same set of random movements (of one or two players) and we display M, the number of message exchanges induced by $\mathcal{A}_{lc}$ at the time the first message is induced by $\mathcal{A}_{id}$. Everywhere, we repeat the experiments 500 times to account for the stochastic nature of the movements, which are represented with boxplots (with first and ninth decile and first ans third quartile). Blue lines indicate the average value of M.

In the case of a two-dimensional random walk, with two players moving, the evolution of M with the initial distance is depicted in Fig. 4a. As expected, we observe that M remains bounded and does not depend much on the initial distance (except when the distance is very small with respect to movement amplitudes). We also plot the evolution of M with the given maximal tolerated error, ε in Fig. 4b. We observe that M increases when ε gets close to 1, which suggests that dependency on ε in our theoretical bounds is unavoidable. The same set of experiments with random walks and continuous movements in 1D, 2D, and 3D were also performed, and very similar results were obtained (see the companion technical report [5]).

5.2   Actual Traces

Comparison of $\mathcal{A}_{lc}$ with Fixed Frequency Strategies. We compare $\mathcal{A}_{lc}$ to a fixed frequency strategy, denote by $\mathcal{A}_{ff}$, that is used in practice in actual games [2]. This algorithm does not take a maximal error as parameter, but a fixed wait time w between message exchange of any pair of players. In [9], traces containing the time-stamped positions of players in 98 games of Heroes of Newerth [1] are

Table 1. Comparison of $\mathcal{A}_{lc}$ and $\mathcal{A}_{ff}$, **without Dead-reckoning** (with Dead-reckoning)

	$\mathcal{A}_{id}$	$\mathcal{A}_{lc}$		$\mathcal{A}_{ff}$		
ε	msg/time unit	messages per time unit	violations	w	msg/time unit	violations
0.1	**3.26** (2.23)	**10.44** (4.71)	0.0	**9** (19)	**10.00** (4.73)	**2.9%** (5.13%)
0.2	**1.49** (1.24)	**5.41** (3.02)	0.0	**17** (30)	**5.30** (3.00)	**2.74%** (4.66%)
0.3	**0.91** (0.84)	**3.60** (2.26)	0.0	**25** (40)	**3.60** (2.25)	**2.6%** (4.26%)
0.4	**0.63** (0.62)	**2.65** (1.81)	0.0	**34** (50)	**2.65** (1.80)	**2.53%** (3.88%)
0.5	**0.46** (0.46)	**2.07** (1.50)	0.0	**43** (60)	**2.09** (1.50)	**2.42%** (3.51%)

used.[1] There are 10 players, therefore, a wait time of w induces an average of $\frac{9*10}{w}$ messages per time unit. Even if a smaller w makes information more accurate, $\mathcal{A}_{ff}$ comes without guarantee on maximal error violations, contrarily to $\mathcal{A}_{lc}$. To evaluate the performance of $\mathcal{A}_{ff}$ in terms of accuracy in our simulations, we counted the *number of violations per time unit*, that is, the number of distance estimates among the players that violate Eq. 2. As there are ten players, and each one has an estimate for all nine others, the number of violations has a maximum of 90 for one time unit.

In order to perform a fair comparison between $\mathcal{A}_{lc}$ and $\mathcal{A}_{ff}$, we used the following protocol. First, we ran $\mathcal{A}_{lc}$ for several values of ε, and measured the resulting average number of messages per time unit. Then, we plugged the obtained value as w in $\mathcal{A}_{ff}$, so as to compare both algorithms in terms of accuracy (to estimate approximated distance) while they use the same average message frequency. The average proportion of violations is shown in bold font in Table 1, along with the optimal number of messages, that is, $\mathcal{A}_{id}$, for different values of ε. We can observe that $\mathcal{A}_{lc}$ is far better than $\mathcal{A}_{ff}$ for satisfying Eq. 2. For instance, it sends only 10.44 messages per time unit for $\varepsilon = 0.1$. With $\mathcal{A}_{ff}$, the only way to ensure Eq. 2 is by having $w = 1$. This would lead to 90 messages per time unit with $w = 1$, that is, about ten times more than $\mathcal{A}_{lc}$.

Influence of Better Prediction Strategies. As mentioned in Sect. 1.1, Dead-reckoning is a popular method for reducing the error on positions of elements of an online game. This is why we added Dead-reckoning to our simulations to assess its benefits. To do this, we rely on a speed based position prediction algorithm, where speed is calculated according to the two last known positions, and is used to extrapolate the previous known position. The results of the same experiment as above, with this prediction algorithm, are shown on Table 1, within parenthesis. We can observe that the number of message exchanged in $\mathcal{A}_{lc}$ decreases more significantly than $\mathcal{A}_{id}$. Moreover, Dead-reckoning seems more beneficial to $\mathcal{A}_{lc}$ than to $\mathcal{A}_{ff}$, as the decrease in message number is not compensated for in terms of violations by the improved prediction precision.

---

[1] The traces are available at https://doi.org/10.5281/zenodo.583600.

6 Conclusion and Future Work

In this paper, we propose a distributed algorithm $\mathcal{A}_{lc}$, for each player to estimate the distance separating them from each other player, with a relative condition on the error. This type of property is desirable in DVE such as online games. We prove that (in a restricted setting), this algorithm is optimal in terms of number of message exchanges up a to a constant factor. We also show through simulations, based on actual game traces, that $\mathcal{A}_{lc}$ performs significantly less communications than the fixed frequency algorithm which is commonly used in online game, while bounding the error.

A summary of our bounds can be found in the following table:

	Random walk	Continuous movement
1D case	$\min\left(\Delta_l \times 2^{\Delta_l}\ ;\ \left\lceil \frac{4}{\pi}\Delta_l{}^2 \right\rceil \times 8\right)$	$\Delta_l \times 4^{\Delta_l}$
2D case	$\Delta_r \times 8^{\Delta_r}$	$\Gamma \times 8^{\Gamma}$
3D case	$\Delta_r \times 16^{\Delta_r}$	$\Gamma \times 14^{\Gamma}$

This work opens several perspectives. The first one is to extend the theoretical results proved in this paper, either by improving the constants or by increasing the scope of the results and to consider more sophisticated prediction algorithms. Another longer term perspective is to extend the set of properties that can be maintained in DVEs at the price of re-computations and a (constant) increase in exchanged messages. It was known in the literature that maintaining the positions was possible with no increase in the number of messages and the present paper shows that a constant increase is enough to maintain relative distances. Extending the class of such properties is highly desirable, both in theory and practice.

References

1. Heroes of Newerth. http://www.heroesofnewerth.com/. Accessed 27 Aug 2019
2. Source Multiplayer Networking - Valve Developer Community. https://developer.valvesoftware.com/wiki/Source_Multiplayer_Networking. Accessed 27 Aug 2019
3. IEEE standard for distributed interactive simulation-application protocols. IEEE Std 1278.1-2012 (Revision of IEEE Std 1278.1-1995), pp. 1–747, December 2012. https://doi.org/10.1109/IEEESTD.2012.6387564
4. Aggarwal, S., Banavar, H., Khandelwal, A., Mukherjee, S., Rangarajan, S.: Accuracy in dead-reckoning based distributed multi-player games. In: 3rd ACM SIGCOMM Workshop on Network and System Support for Games, pp. 161–165. NetGames, ACM (2004). https://doi.org/10.1145/1016540.1016559
5. Beaumont, O., Castanet, T., Hanusse, N., Travers, C.: Approximation algorithm for estimating distances in distributed virtual environments. Research report, February 2020. https://hal.archives-ouvertes.fr/hal-02486218

6. Bharambe, A., et al.: Donnybrook: enabling large-scale, high-speed, peer-to-peer games. In: ACM SIGCOMM Conference on Applications, Technologies, Architectures, and Protocols for Computer Communications, pp. 389–400. ACM (2008). https://doi.org/10.1145/1402946.1403002

7. Boulanger, J.S., Kienzle, J., Verbrugge, C.: Comparing interest management algorithms for massively multiplayer games. In: Proceedings of 5th ACM SIGCOMM Workshop on Network and System Support for Games. NetGames 2006. ACM, New York (2006). https://doi.org/10.1145/1230040.1230069

8. Cai, W., Lee, F.B.S., Chen, L.: An auto-adaptive dead reckoning algorithm for distributed interactive simulation. In: Workshop on Parallel and Distributed Simulation (1999). https://doi.org/10.1109/PADS.1999.766164

9. Carlini, E., Lulli, A.: A spatial analysis of multiplayer online battle arena mobility traces. In: Heras, D.B., Bougé, L. (eds.) Euro-Par 2017. LNCS, vol. 10659, pp. 496–506. Springer, Cham (2018). https://doi.org/10.1007/978-3-319-75178-8_40

10. Kharitonov, V.Y.: Motion-aware adaptive dead reckoning algorithm for collaborative virtual environments. In: 11th ACM SIGGRAPH International Conference on Virtual-Reality Continuum and Its Applications in Industry, VRCAI 2012, pp. 255–261. ACM (2012). https://doi.org/10.1145/2407516.2407577

11. Li, Z., Tang, X., Cai, W., Li, X.: Compensatory dead-reckoning-based update scheduling for distributed virtual environments. Simulation **89**(10), 1272–1287 (2013). https://doi.org/10.1177/0037549712470857

12. Liu, E.S., Theodoropoulos, G.K.: Interest management for distributed virtual environments: A survey. ACM Comput. Surv. **46**(4), 51:1–51:42 (2014). https://doi.org/10.1145/2535417

13. Marshall, D., McLoone, S., Ward, T.E., Delaney, D.: Does reducing packet transmission rates help to improve consistency within distributed interactive applications? In: CGAMES06, November 2006. http://mural.maynoothuniversity.ie/1283/

14. Mauve, M., Vogel, J., Hilt, V., Effelsberg, W.: Local-lag and timewarp: providing consistency for replicated continuous applications. IEEE Trans. Multimedia **6**, 47–57 (2004). https://doi.org/10.1109/TMM.2003.819751

15. Millar, J.R., Hodson, D.D., Peterson, G.L., Ahner, D.K.: Consistency and fairness in real-time distributed virtual environments: paradigms and relationships. J. Simul. **11**(3), 295–302 (2017). https://doi.org/10.1057/s41273-016-0035-8

16. Ricci, L., Carlini, E.: Distributed virtual environments: from client server to cloud and P2P architectures. In: 2012 International Conference on High Performance Computing Simulation (HPCS), pp. 8–17 (2012). https://doi.org/10.1109/HPCSim.2012.6266885

17. Zhou, S., Cai, W., Lee, B.S., Turner, S.J.: Time-space consistency in large-scale distributed virtual environments. ACM Trans. Model. Comput. Simul. **14**(1), 31–47 (2004). https://doi.org/10.1145/974734.974736

On the Power of Randomization in Distributed Algorithms in Dynamic Networks with Adaptive Adversaries

Irvan Jahja$^{(\boxtimes)}$, Haifeng Yu, and Ruomu Hou

National University of Singapore, Singapore 119077, Singapore
{irvan,haifeng,houruomu}@comp.nus.edu.sg

Abstract. This paper investigates the power of randomization in *general* distributed algorithms in *dynamic networks* where the network's topology may evolve over time, as determined by some *adaptive adversary*. In such a context, randomization may help algorithms to better deal with i) "bad" inputs to the algorithm, and ii) evolving topologies generated by "bad" adaptive adversaries. We prove that randomness offers limited power to better deal with "bad" adaptive adversary. We define a simple notion of *prophetic adversary* for determining the evolving topologies. Such an adversary accurately predicts all randomness in the algorithm beforehand, and hence the randomness will be useless against "bad" prophetic adversaries. Given a randomized algorithm P whose time complexity satisfies some mild conditions, we prove that P can always be converted to a new algorithm Q with comparable time complexity, even when Q runs against prophetic adversaries. This implies that the benefit of P using randomness for dealing with the adaptive adversaries is limited.

Keywords: Dynamic networks · Power of randomization · Adversaries

1 Introduction

Background. Understanding the power of randomization has long been a key goal in algorithms research. Over the years, researchers have obtained many interesting results on the power of randomization, such as in centralized algorithms (e.g., [25]), in parallel algorithms (e.g., [21]), and in algorithms in static networks (e.g., [7,8,10,11,22]). This paper aims to gain deeper insights into the power of randomization in *general* distributed algorithms in *dynamic networks* with *adaptive adversaries*. Dynamic networks [4,6,19,23] model communication networks whose topologies may change over time, and has been a growing research topic in distributed computing. While randomization has been used extensively to solve various specific problems in dynamic networks (e.g., [17,19]),

---

The first two authors of this paper are alphabetically ordered. Irvan Jahja is the corresponding author.

© Springer Nature Switzerland AG 2020
M. Malawski and K. Rzadca (Eds.): Euro-Par 2020, LNCS 12247, pp. 376–391, 2020.
https://doi.org/10.1007/978-3-030-57675-2_24

prior works have not focused on the power of randomization in *general* distributed algorithms in dynamic networks (i.e., to what extent randomized algorithms can outperform deterministic ones).

Our Setting. We consider a synchronous dynamic network with a fixed set of n nodes. The network topology in each round is some arbitrary connected and undirected graph as determined by an *adaptive adversary*, and we adopt the following commonly-used model [16,18,26]: The adaptive adversary decides the round-r topology based on the algorithm's coin flip outcomes so far (i.e., up to and including round r). The adaptive adversary does not see the coin flip outcomes in round $r+1$ or later. We follow the communication model in [14,26]: In each round, a node may choose to either send an $O(\log n)$ size message (i.e., the broadcast $\mathcal{CONGEST}$ model [24]) or to receive. A message sent is received, by the end of that round, by all the receiving neighbors of the sender in that round. Each node has some *input* of arbitrary size and a unique id between 0 and $n-1$. We consider *general distributed computing problems* modeled as some arbitrary function of the n input values (as an input vector). The output of the function is also a vector of length n, and node i should output the $(i+1)$-th entry of that vector. There is no constraint on the output size. An algorithm in this paper always refers to some algorithm for solving some distributed computing problem as modeled in the above way. Note that many problems that are not typically defined as functions, such as computing a unique minimum spanning tree (of some input graph) and token dissemination [9,17], can nevertheless be modeled as a function. The *time complexity* is defined to be the number of rounds needed for all nodes to output. An algorithm P's *time complexity*, denoted as $\text{tc}_P(n,d)$, corresponds to its time complexity under the *worst-case scenario*. Here the *worst-case scenario* consists of i) the *worst-case input (vector)*, and ii) the *worst-case adaptive adversary* for generating dynamic networks with at most n nodes and at most d dynamic diameter. The dynamic diameter [18] of a dynamic network, intuitively, is the minimum number of rounds needed for a node u to causally influence another node v, when considering the worst-case u and v in the dynamic network. Section 2 gives a full description of the model.

Randomness in Dynamic Networks. For any given deterministic algorithm, informally, let us call its corresponding worst-case scenario as a "bad" scenario. A "bad" scenario for one deterministic algorithm may very well not be a "bad" scenario for other deterministic algorithms. Since a randomized algorithm is a distribution of deterministic algorithms, intuitively, randomization potentially helps to better deal with all those "bad" scenarios. For algorithms in dynamic networks, a "bad" scenario consists of a "bad" input and a "bad" adaptive adversary.

For dealing with "bad" inputs in dynamic networks, it is not hard to see that randomization can help to reduce the time complexity *exponentially*. For example, consider the two-party communication complexity (CC) problem EQUALITY [20]. Let m be the size of the input, then EQUALITY has a randomized CC of $O(\log m)$ bits, and a deterministic CC of $\Omega(m)$ bits [20]. Under our setting of dynamic networks with congestion, this exponential gap in the CC of EQUALITY directly translates to an exponential gap in the time complexity.

A Quick Conjecture? For dealing with "bad" adaptive adversaries, on the other hand, one may quickly conjecture that randomness has limited power: On the surface, since the randomness in round r is already visible to the adaptive adversary when it chooses the round-r topology, such randomness offers no help for better dealing with the round-r topology. But a deeper look shows that the randomness in round r could potentially help the algorithm to better deal with round-r' ($1 \leq r' < r$) topologies: Consider an example algorithm that uses the first $r - 1$ rounds to flood a certain token in the network, where $r - 1$ can be smaller than the network's dynamic diameter d. Let S be the set of nodes that have received the token by the end of round $r - 1$. In round r and later, the algorithm may want to estimate the size of S (e.g., to estimate whether the token has reached some constant fraction of the nodes). The adaptive adversary can influence S, by manipulating the topologies in the first $r - 1$ rounds. But by the end of round $r - 1$, the set S will be fixed—effectively, the adaptive adversary has now committed to S. The algorithm's randomness in round r and later is independent of S. Thus for the remainder of the algorithm's execution (i.e., the part starting from round r), S can be viewed as a "midway input". The randomness in the remainder of the algorithm's execution can potentially help to better deal with such "midway inputs", and hence help indirectly to better deal with the adaptive adversary's "bad" behavior in the first $r - 1$ rounds.

Given such possibility, it is unclear whether the earlier quick conjecture holds or whether it may even be wrong. Resolving this will be our goal.

Our Results for LV Algorithms. As our main novel result, we prove that the earlier conjecture does hold, subject to some mild conditions on the algorithm's time complexity. (We will fully specify these mild conditions later.) As one will see later, proving this conjecture is far from trivial. We first need to expose the power of randomization for dealing with adaptive adversaries, and in particular, to properly isolate such power from the power of randomization for dealing with inputs. It is not immediately obvious how to do this since the same randomness may be used for dealing with both inputs and adaptive adversaries. To this end, we define a simple notion of *prophetic adversary* for determining the dynamic network. A *prophetic adversary* first sees (accurately predicts) all coin flip outcomes of a randomized algorithm in all rounds, and then decides the dynamic network (i.e., topologies in each round). This enables a prophetic adversary to always choose the worst-case dynamic network for the given coin flip outcomes. Hence the randomness in the algorithm can never help to better deal with dynamic networks generated by "bad" prophetic adversaries.

Now let us consider adaptive adversaries that generate dynamic networks with at most n nodes and at most d dynamic diameter. Let P be any Las Vegas (LV) algorithm whose time complexity (under the worst-case among all such adaptive adversaries) is $\text{tc}_P(n, d) = \Theta(f(n) \cdot g(d))$, for some $f(n)$ and $g(d)$ where there exists some constant a such that $\Omega(1) \leq f(n) \leq O(n^a)$ and

$\Omega(d) \leq g(d) \leq O(d^a)$.[1,2] We prove (Theorem 1 and 2) that P can always be converted into another LV algorithm Q whose time complexity under worst-case *prophetic adversaries* is $O(\text{polylog}(n)) \cdot \text{tc}_P(n, d)$. This means that even when the adversary accurately predicts all randomness in Q, Q's time complexity is still only $O(\text{polylog}(n)) \cdot \text{tc}_P(n, d)$. In turn, the benefit of randomization (in P) for dealing with the adaptive adversaries is at most to reduce the complexity by a $O(\text{polylog}(n))$ factor. This proves the earlier conjecture affirmatively (under the previous mild conditions).

The more general version (Theorem 2) of our results actually hold for P as long as P's time complexity is upper bounded by some polynomial — namely, as long as there exists some constant a such that $\Omega(1) \leq \text{tc}_P(n, n) \leq O(n^a)$, and without any other constraints on $\text{tc}_P(n, d)$. Here for any given LV algorithm P, we can construct another LV algorithm Q whose time complexity under prophetic adversaries is $O((d \log^3 n) \times \text{tc}_P(n, a' \log n))$ for some constant a'. Hence in this more general case, our results imply that the power of randomization (in P) for dealing with adaptive adversaries is at most a $O(d \log^3 n)$ multiplicative factor when $d \geq a' \log n$.

Finally, the above shows that for dealing with adaptive adversaries, the power of randomization is inherently limited. This suggests that if an algorithm is not using randomness for better dealing with the inputs, we should be able to derandomize it efficiently. The full version [13] of this paper shows how this can be done for LV algorithms.

Our Results for MC Algorithms. We have also obtained similar results for Monte Carlo (MC) algorithms. We defer the details to the full version [13] of this paper, and provide a summary here. Consider any constant $\epsilon \in (0, 1 - \delta)$ and any δ-error Monte Carlo (MC) algorithm P such that $\text{tc}_P(n, d) = \Theta(f(n) \cdot g(d))$, where there exists some constant a such that $\Omega(n) \leq f(n) \leq O(n^a)$ and $\Omega(d) \leq g(d) \leq O(d^a)$. Then we can always construct another $(\delta + \epsilon)$-error MC algorithm Q for solving the same problem and whose time complexity under worst-case prophetic adversaries is $O(\text{polylog}(n)) \cdot \text{tc}_P(n, d)$. A more general version of this result holds for P as long as there exists some constant a such that $\Omega(1) \leq \text{tc}_P(n, n) \leq O(n^a)$, and without any other constraints on $\text{tc}_P(n, d)$. In this more general version, our algorithm Q will have a time complexity of $O((d \log^3 n) \times \text{tc}_P(n, a' \log n) + n \log^2 n)$.

Our Techniques. To obtain Q from P, we essentially need to "derandomize" the part of P's randomness used to deal with the adaptive adversaries. It turns out that such randomness is less amenable to typical derandomization methods such as pairwise independence, conditional expectation, or network decomposition. This motivated us to take a rather different route from prior derandomization efforts [5, 7, 8, 10, 11, 21, 22, 25].

---

[1] Throughout this paper, $\Omega(h_1(x)) \leq h_2(x) \leq O(h_3(x))$ means $h_2(x) = \Omega(h_1(x))$ and $h_2(x) = O(h_3(x))$.

[2] Some quick examples of $\text{tc}_P(n, d)$ satisfying such a condition include $\Theta(d \log n)$, $\Theta(dn \log d)$, and $\Theta(d^{1.1} n^{1.5})$. On the other hand, $\text{tc}_P(n, d) = \Theta(d^2 + \sqrt{n})$ does not satisfy the condition.

Specifically, we will have Q simulate the execution of P against some adaptive adversary $\alpha^{\epsilon,t}$ that we construct. (Namely, Q simulates both P and $\alpha^{\epsilon,t}$.) To work against prophetic adversaries, Q will perform the simulation by only doing simple floodings. We will carefully design $\alpha^{\epsilon,t}$ so that: i) Q can efficiently simulate the execution of P against $\alpha^{\epsilon,t}$ via simple floodings, ii) the dynamic networks generated by $\alpha^{\epsilon,t}$ will have $O(\log n)$ dynamic diameter with at least $1 - \epsilon$ probability, and iii) there are some sufficient conditions, which can be efficiently checked in a distributed fashion, for guaranteeing the $O(\log n)$ dynamic diameter. Next, a central difficulty in the simulation is that Q does not know the dynamic diameter of the dynamic network over which it runs, which will cause various problems in the floodings. While Q can naturally use the standard doubling-trick to guess the dynamic diameter, the challenge is that Q cannot easily tell whether the guess is correct. As a result, we will carefully reason about the properties of the simulation when the guess is wrong, and design Q correspondingly.

Other Types of Adversaries. The adaptive adversaries in this paper (also called *strongly adaptive adversaries* [2,9,16,18]) are not the only type of adversaries in dynamic networks. A more general notion is *z-oblivious adversaries* [1], which can see all randomness up to and including round $r - z$ when deciding the round-r topology. Prophetic adversaries and strongly adaptive adversaries correspond to z-oblivious adversaries with $z = -\infty$ and $z = 0$, respectively. Researchers have also considered 1-oblivious adversaries (also called *weakly adaptive adversaries* [9,12]) and ∞-oblivious adversaries (also called *oblivious adversaries* [2,3,12]). The results in this paper are only for 0-oblivious adversaries, but our proofs are already non-trivial. The power of the algorithm's randomization will likely increase as z increases. On the other hand, we suspect that our conjecture could potentially be extended to 1-oblivious adversaries — we leave this to future work.

Related Work. Randomization has been extensively used for solving various specific problems in dynamic networks (e.g., [17,19]). However, prior works have not focused on the power of randomization in *general* distributed algorithms in dynamic networks. On the other hand, there have been many works on the power of randomization in other settings, and we discuss the most relevant ones in the following.

In centralized setting, an *online algorithm* processes a sequence of *requests*, one by one. In this context, an *adaptive adversary* generates the i-th request after seeing the algorithm's behavior (and coin flips) on request 1 through $i - 1$. It is well-known [5] that randomized online algorithms against adaptive adversaries can always be effectively derandomized. However, the measure of goodness for online algorithms is competitive ratio, and hence the derandomized algorithm can afford to have exponential computational complexity. In our distributed setting, adopting the techniques from [5] would require us to collect all the n input values to one node, which would result in unbounded time complexity (i.e., number of rounds) since the sizes of our inputs are not constrained. Due to these fundamental differences, our results and techniques are all quite different from [5].

More recently, there have been a series of breakthrough results on derandomizing distributed algorithms in *static networks* [7,8,10,11,15,22]. These derandomization results are all for *local algorithms*, where the output (or the correctness of the output) of a node only depends on its small neighborhood instead of on the entire network. In fact, many of them consider algorithms with $O(1)$ time complexity. Such a notion of local algorithms is perhaps no longer well-defined in dynamic networks, where a node's neighborhood changes over time. In comparison to these works, this paper considers i) *general* distributed algorithms that are not necessarily local, and ii) *dynamic networks* instead of static networks. Also because of this, our results and techniques are all quite different. For example, some of the key methods used in [7,8,10,11,15,22] include network decomposition and conditional expectations, while we mainly rely on a novel simulation against a novel adaptive adversary.

2   Model

Dynamic Network and Adversary. We consider a synchronous network with a fixed set of n nodes, where the nodes proceed in lock-step rounds. Throughout this paper, we assume that n is publicly known and that $n \geq 2$. All nodes start execution, simultaneously, from round 1. The nodes have unique ids from 0 through $n - 1$. Each node has some input value, and there is no constraint on the size of each input value. We will view the n input values as an input vector of length n. We consider *general distributed computing problems* where the n nodes aim to compute a certain function of the input vector. The output of the function is a vector of length n, where node i should output the $(i + 1)$-th entry in that vector. There is no constraint on the size of each output entry. An algorithm in this paper always refers to some algorithm for solving some problem that can be modeled as the above way.

The topology among the n nodes may change from round to round. Following [16,18,26], we assume that the topology is determined by some *adaptive adversary*. An *adaptive adversary* τ is an infinite sequence of functions $\tau_r(P, I, C_{[1:r]})$ for $r \geq 1$. Here τ_r takes as parameters the randomized algorithm P, the input vector I, and P's coin flip outcomes $C_{[1:r]}$ in round 1 (inclusive) to round r (inclusive). The function τ_r then outputs some connected and undirected graph with n nodes, as the topology of the network in round r. There is no other constraint on the graph. We also call this infinite sequence of graphs (starting from round 1) as a *dynamic network*, and say that τ is an adaptive adversary with n nodes. With a slight abuse of notation, we use $\tau(P, I, C)$ to denote the dynamic network produced by τ, under algorithm P, input vector I, and P's coin flip outcomes C across all rounds. (This is a slight abuse since τ is not a function.) For any given dynamic network $G = G_1 G_2 \ldots$ where G_r is the round-r topology of G, we define the special adaptive adversary γ^G to be $\gamma_r^G(P, I, C_{[1:r]}) = G_r$ for all r, P, I, and $C_{[1:r]}$. A *prophetic adversary* ψ is a function mapping the tuple (P, I, C) to a dynamic network $H = \psi(P, I, C)$. Since ψ is a single function (instead of a sequence of functions), ψ can see all coin flip outcomes of P in all rounds (i.e., C), before deciding the topology in each round.

We follow the communication model in [14,26]: In each round, a node may choose to either send an $O(\log n)$ size message (i.e., the broadcast $\mathcal{CONGEST}$ model [24]) or to receive, as determined by the algorithm running on that node. A message sent in round r is received, by the end of round r, by all the receiving neighbors of the sender in round r.

Diameter. We adopt the standard notion of *dynamic diameter* [18] (or *diameter* in short) for dynamic networks. Formally, we define $(u, r) \to (v, r + 1)$ if either $u = v$ or v is u's neighbor in round r. Let the relation "$\rightsquigarrow$" be the transitive closure of "$\to$". The *diameter* is defined as the smallest d such that $(u, r) \rightsquigarrow (v, r + d)$ holds for all u, v, and $r \geq 1$. Trivially, the diameter of a dynamic network with n nodes is at most $n - 1$. Since the diameter is controlled by the adversary, it is not known to the algorithm beforehand. The *diameter* of an adaptive adversary τ (prophetic adversary ψ) is the smallest d where the diameter of $\tau(P, I, C)$ ($\psi(P, I, C)$) is at most d for all P, I, and C.

Time Complexity and Error. For the time complexity of an execution, we define the function $\mathrm{tc}(P, I, \tau, C)$ to be the number of rounds needed for all nodes to output in P, when algorithm P runs with input vector I, adaptive adversary τ, and coin flip outcomes C. For the error of an execution, we define the binary function $\mathrm{err}(P, I, \tau, C)$ to be 1 iff P's output is wrong (on any node), when P runs with I, τ, and C.

In the following, $\max_\tau$ will be taken over all adaptive adversaries τ with at most n nodes and at most d diameter. Unless otherwise specified, an algorithm in this paper can be either a Las Vegas (LV) algorithm or a Monte Carlo (MC) algorithm. We define a randomized algorithm P's *time complexity against adaptive adversaries* as $\mathrm{tc}_P(n, d) = \max_I \max_\tau E_C[\mathrm{tc}(P, I, \tau, C)]$ if P is an LV algorithm, or $\mathrm{tc}_P(n, d) = \max_I \max_\tau \max_C \mathrm{tc}(P, I, \tau, C)$ if P is an MC algorithm. We define an MC algorithm P's *error against adaptive adversaries* as $\mathrm{err}_P(n) = \max_I \max_d \max_\tau E_C[\mathrm{err}(P, I, \tau, C)]$.

We will need to reason about the properties of algorithm Q running against prophetic adversaries. Given Q's coin flip outcomes C in all rounds, since prophetic adversaries always see C beforehand, the worst-case prophetic adversary can always choose the worst-case dynamic network H for such C. Hence if Q is an LV algorithm, we define its *time complexity against prophetic adversaries* to be $\mathrm{tc}_Q^*(n, d) = \max_I E_C[\max_H \mathrm{tc}(Q, I, \gamma^H, C)]$. Note that here $\max_H$ is taken after C is given, and is taken over all dynamic networks with at most n nodes and at most d diameter. If Q is an MC algorithm, then its *time complexity/error against prophetic adversaries* will be $\mathrm{tc}_Q^*(n, d) = \max_I \max_C \max_H \mathrm{tc}(Q, I, \gamma^H, C)$ and $\mathrm{err}_Q^*(n) = \max_I E_C[\max_d \max_H \mathrm{err}(Q, I, \gamma^H, C)]$, respectively.

Conventions. All logarithms in this paper are base 2. We sometimes consider round 0 for convenience, where the algorithm does nothing and all nodes are receiving.

3   Adaptive Adversary Simulated by Q

As mentioned in Sect. 1, given some arbitrary randomized algorithm P, we want to construct algorithm Q that simulates the execution of P against some novel adaptive adversary $\alpha^{\epsilon,t}$. We want $\alpha^{\epsilon,t}$ to have small diameter so that P's time complexity (when running against $\alpha^{\epsilon,t}$) is small. Let H be the dynamic network over which Q runs. We further need Q to have good complexity and error guarantees, even if H is constructed by prophetic adversaries.

3.1   Intuition

Starting Point. Recall that in any given round r, an adaptive adversary knows whether each node in P will be sending or receiving in that round (since the adaptive adversary sees C_r), before the adversary decides the topology in that round. Let us consider the following trivial topology as a starting point. In this topology, all nodes that are sending in the round form a clique, and all nodes that are receiving in the round form a clique. Some of the sending nodes will be chosen as *centers* for that round. A center will be connected to all other nodes (including all other centers) directly. To simulate P for one round over such a topology, we only need to deliver the message sent by each center to each of the receiving nodes. To do so, for each center, Q will flood the message (sent by the center) in the dynamic network H. Such flooding will obviously still work even if H is generated by a prophetic adversary. It takes total $d \cdot x$ rounds to simulate one round of P, where x is the number of centers and d is the diameter of H.

   But there are several issues. Since only sending nodes can be centers and since a node may not always be sending in all rounds, we may be forced to keep switching the centers from round to round. This may then cause the (dynamic) diameter of the dynamic network to be large, despite the topology in each round having a small static diameter. One naive way to avoid this problem is to choose all sending nodes as centers. But doing so would result in too many centers, rendering the simulation inefficient. The following explains how we overcome these issues.

Choosing the Centers. Our design of $\alpha^{\epsilon,t}$ uses only a logarithmic number of centers in each round. To obtain some intuition, consider any two consecutive rounds $r - 1$ and r, where $r \geq 3$. We define $A_r^{RS} = \{u \mid u$ receives (hence the superscript "R") in round $r - 1$ and sends (hence the superscript "S") in round $r\}$. Here "sends"/"receives" refers to u sending/receiving in the execution of P against $\alpha^{\epsilon,t}$. We similarly define the remaining three sets A_r^{SS}, A_r^{SR}, and A_r^{RR}. We hope to choose the centers in such a way that for some small d (e.g., $O(\log n)$), we have $(u, r - 1) \rightsquigarrow (v, r + d - 1)$ for all u and v. We will soon see that it will be convenient to consider u's in the 4 sets seperately.

   For round r, we will first pick some (arbitrary) node $w \in A_r^{RS}$ as a center. Such a center will ensure that for all $u \in A_r^{RS}$ and all v, we have $(u, r - 1) \rightarrow (w, r) \rightarrow (v, r + 1)$. Similarly, we will pick some (arbitrary) node $w \in A_r^{SS}$ as another center, to take care of $u \in A_r^{SS}$. Next, for any $u \in A_r^{SR}$, note that u must be in either A_{r-1}^{RS} or A_{r-1}^{SS}. If we chose the centers in round $r-1$ also according to the earlier rules, then such a u has already been taken care of as well.

The Trickier Case. The case for $u \in A_r^{RR}$ is trickier. In fact, to get some intuition, consider a node u that continuously receives in round 1 through round d. We want to ensure that $(u,1) \leadsto (v, d+1)$ for all v. Let S_r be the set of nodes that are sending in round r and let W_r be the set of centers in round r, for $1 \leq r \leq d$. For all $v \in \cup_r W_r$, we clearly have $(u,1) \leadsto (v, d+1)$. For all $v \notin \cap_r S_r$, v must be receiving in some round $i \in [1,d]$, and hence we have $(u,i) \to (v, i+1)$ and we are done.

The case for $v \in (\cap_r S_r) \setminus (\cup_r W_r)$ is more complicated. Such a v has always been sending, but is never chosen as a center. Now consider such a v, and observe that if some center w in round r sends (again) in some round i where $r+1 \leq i \leq d$, then we must have $(u,1) \leadsto (w,r) \leadsto (w,i) \to (v, i+1) \leadsto (v, d+1)$. Based on this observation, we will want to choose W_r from S_r such that some node in W_r will send in some round $i \geq r+1$. But whether a node sends in future rounds may depend on future coin flip outcomes of P, as well as the incoming messages in those rounds. An adaptive adversary (for P) does not have the incoming messages in future rounds. It is not supposed to see future coin flip outcomes either.

Our next observation is that the adaptive adversary in round r, before deciding the round-r topology, can actually determine the *probability* that a node u will be sending (again) in round $r+1$, *if the node u is currently already sending in round r*. The reason is that u will not receive any incoming messages in round r, no matter what the topology is. Hence the probability is uniquely determined by u's state at the beginning of round r. Now given such probabilities for all the nodes in S_r, when choosing the centers, we will choose those nodes from S_r whose probabilities (of sending in round $r+1$) are at least 0.5, and we call such nodes as *promising nodes*. If we include logarithmic number of promising nodes in W_r, then with good probability, there will exist some $w \in W_r$ that sends in round $r+1$. Due to some technicality, the number of promising nodes in W_r will actually need to increase with r, so that we can eventually take a union bound across even infinite number of rounds.

Finally, it is possible that we never have a sufficient number (i.e., logarithmic number) of promising nodes. In such a case, we will show that $(\cap_r S_r) \setminus (\cup_r W_r)$ will be empty with good probability.

3.2   Our Novel Adaptive Adversary $\alpha^{\epsilon,t}$

We now formally define $\alpha^{\epsilon,t}$ for $0 < \epsilon < 1$ and $t \geq 1$. The adaptive adversary $\alpha^{\epsilon,t}$ always generates a clique as the topology for round r when $r > t$. If $r \leq t$, then consider the given algorithm P, input vector I, and coin flip outcomes $C_{[1:r]}$. Based on C_r and the state of P at the beginning of round r, $\alpha^{\epsilon,t}$ can infer which nodes will be sending in round r, and which nodes are promising nodes. For all pairs of nodes u and v where either they are both sending in round r or they are both receiving in round r, the adversary $\alpha^{\epsilon,t}$ adds an undirected edge between

Algorithm 1 LV-P-Converted-To-Q().

/* This algorithm Q simulates P's execution against $\alpha^{\epsilon,t}$. For clarity, the pseudo-code does not explicitly include the input to Q (which is relayed to P). Without loss of generality, P's output on a node (when viewed as a numerical value) is assumed to be always non-negative. A node outputs only once in this algorithm. A node will suppress output if it previously has already outputted. */

```
1:  ε ← 0.1; k ← 2;
2:  repeat forever
3:     forall integers d′ ≥ 1 and t ≥ 2 where i) d′ and t are both powers of 2, ii)
          d′t log t ≤ k, and iii) SimulateP() has not been previously executed for such d′ and
          t in Step 5 do
4:        C^{d′,t} ← fresh coin flips, for all rounds in P;
5:        return_v ← SimulateP(ε, d′, t, C^{d′,t});
6:        /* See Algorithm 2 for pseudo-code of SimulateP(). */
7:        if (return_v ≥ 0) then output return_v;
8:     endforall
9:     k ← 2k;
```

them. Next $\alpha^{\epsilon,t}$ chooses up to $(2\log\frac{2r}{\epsilon} + 3)$ nodes as *centers* for round r. For every center w and every node v, $\alpha^{\epsilon,t}$ adds an edge between w and v, if there is not already such an edge.

The centers are chosen in the following way. First, among all the nodes that were receiving in round $r - 1$ and are sending in round r, if there are such nodes, choose the one with the smallest id as a center. Second, among all the nodes that were sending in round $r - 1$ and are again sending in round r, if there are such nodes, choose the one with the smallest id as a center. Third, among all the nodes that were centers in round $r - 1$ and are sending in round r, if there are such nodes, choose the one with the smallest id as a center. Finally, rank all the promising nodes in round r, by their ids from smallest to largest. Choose the first $2\log\frac{2r}{\epsilon}$ nodes from this sequence as centers. If the sequence contains less than $2\log\frac{2r}{\epsilon}$ nodes, choose all of them. Since these 4 criteria are not necessarily exclusive, a node may be chosen as a center multiple times.

One can easily verify that the topology generate by $\alpha^{\epsilon,t}$ in each round is always connected. We will be able to eventually prove (see proof in the full version [13] of this paper) that with probability at least $1 - \epsilon$, the dynamic network generated by the adversary $\alpha^{\epsilon,t}$ has a diameter of at most $8\log\frac{8tn}{\epsilon}$.

4   Conversion from LV Algorithm P to LV Algorithm Q

4.1   Pseudo-code and Intuition

Overview. Given any LV algorithm P, our algorithm Q (pseudo-code in Algorithm 1) will simulate the execution of P against $\alpha^{\epsilon,t}$. (Effectively, Q will be simulating both P and the adversary $\alpha^{\epsilon,t}$.) We will ensure that Q works even against prophetic adversaries. In the following, a *simulated round* refers to one

Algorithm 2 SimulateP(ϵ, d', t, $C^{d',t}$).

/* This subroutine simulates P's execution against $\alpha^{\epsilon,t}$ for t simulated rounds, while feeding coin flip outcomes $C^{d',t}$ into P, and while using d' as the guess for the diameter of the dynamic network over which Q runs. Without loss of generality, P's output (if viewed as a numerical value) is assumed to be non-negative. A node, once flagged, will do nothing in all steps except Step 19 and 23, but the node will still spend the same number of rounds to go through each step as other nodes. When the pseudo-code says a node u "floods" something for d' rounds, it means that the flooding originates from u, and all nodes in the system will spend exactly d' rounds participating in this flooding. */

1: flagged $\leftarrow$ *false*; return_v $\leftarrow$ -1;
2: **for** $(r \leftarrow 1;\ r \leq t;\ r \leftarrow r + 1)$ **do**
3:     **if** I will send in the simulated round r of P **then**
4:         simulate P's execution in round r using $C_r^{d',t}$;
5:         msg $\leftarrow$ message sent by me in P;
6:     **else**
7:         msg $\leftarrow$ m_bad;
8:     **endif**
9:     $S \leftarrow \emptyset$; center[] $\leftarrow$ GetCenters(ϵ, r, d'); /* GetCenters() takes $\Theta(d' \log \frac{r}{\epsilon} \log n)$ rounds and returns a list of $2 \log \frac{2r}{\epsilon} + 3$ centers. See Algorithm 3 for pseudo-code. */
10:     **for** each j where $1 \leq j \leq 2 \log \frac{2r}{\epsilon} + 3$ **do**
11:         node 0 floods its center[j] for d' rounds;
12:         **if** (I do not receive anything in the flooding at Step 11) or (my center[j] is different from what I received) **then** flagged $\leftarrow$ *true*;
13:         // At this point, the value of center[j] must be the same on all non-flagged nodes.
14:         **if** (center[j] $\neq \perp$) **then** the node corresponding to center[j] floods its msg for d' rounds; **else** spend d' rounds doing nothing;
15:         **if** (center[j] $\neq \perp$) and (I receive some message in the flooding at Step 14) and (the message received is not m_bad) **then** $S \leftarrow S \cup \{\text{message received}\}$;
16:         **if** (center[j] $\neq \perp$) and (I receive either the message m_bad or no message in the flooding at Step 14) **then** flagged $\leftarrow$ *true*;
17:     **endfor**
18:     **if** I will receive in the simulated round r of P **then** simulate P's execution in round r using $C_r^{d',t}$, with S being the set of received messages;
19:     **if** (flagged) **then** send m_flag; **else** receive for 1 round;
20:     **if** m_flag received **then** flagged $\leftarrow$ *true*;
21:     **if** P has output in simulated round r **then** return_v $\leftarrow$ P's output;
22: **endfor**
23: **if** (flagged) **then** return -2; **else** return return_v;

Algorithm 3 GetCenters(ϵ, r, d').

/* This subroutine returns an array of $2\log\frac{2r}{\epsilon}+3$ centers, some of which can be $\bot$. The centers are chosen according to the construction of $\alpha^{\epsilon,t}$ in Section 3.2. The subroutine does a binary search to find out the value for each entry in the array. It uses d' as the guess for the diameter of the dynamic network, and takes total $d'(2\log\frac{2r}{\epsilon}+3)\log(n+1)$ rounds. */

1: let center$[]$ be an array of size $2\log\frac{2r}{\epsilon}+3$;
2: **if** (I was receiving in simulated round $(r-1)$ of P) and (I am sending in simulated round r of P) **then** $z \leftarrow$ my_id; **else** $z \leftarrow n$;
3: center$[1] \leftarrow$ FindMin(z, d'); /* See Algorithm 4 for pseudo-code of FindMin(). */
4: **if** (I was sending in simulated round $(r-1)$ of P) and (I am sending in simulated round r of P) **then** $z \leftarrow$ my_id; **else** $z \leftarrow n$;
5: center$[2] \leftarrow$ FindMin(z, d');
6: **if** (I was a center in simulated round $(r-1)$ of P) and (I am sending in simulated round r of P) **then** $z \leftarrow$ my_id; **else** $z \leftarrow n$;
7: center$[3] \leftarrow$ FindMin(z, d');
8: **for** ($i = 4$; $i \le 2\log\frac{2r}{\epsilon}+3$; $i \leftarrow i+1$) **do**
9:     **if** (I am a promising node in simulated round r of P) and (center$[j] \ne$ my_id for all $4 \le j \le i-1$) **then** $z \leftarrow$ my_id; **else** $z \leftarrow n$;
10:     center$[i] \leftarrow$ FindMin(z, d');
11: **endfor**
12: **for all** $1 \le i \le 2\log\frac{2r}{\epsilon}+3$ **if** center$[i] = n$ **then** center$[i] \leftarrow \bot$;
13: **return** center$[]$;

Algorithm 4 FindMin(z, d').

/* The input parameter z is an integer in $[0,n]$. This subroutine tries to use a binary search to find out the minimum input value among all nodes. It uses d' as the guess for the diameter of the dynamic network, and takes total $d'\log(n+1)$ rounds. */

1: let z's binary form be $b_1 b_2 \ldots b_{\log(n+1)}$, with b_1 being the most significant bit;
2: **for** ($s = 1$; $s \le \log(n+1)$; $s \leftarrow s+1$) **do**
3:     $x \leftarrow$ ExistValue(b_s, 0, d'); // See Algorithm 5 for pseudo-code of ExistValue().
4:     **if** (x) and ($b_s \ne 0$) **then** $b_{s'} \leftarrow 1$ for all $s' \ge s+1$ and $b_s \leftarrow 0$;
5: **endfor**
6: **return** $b_1 b_2 \ldots b_{\log(n+1)}$ as an integer;

Algorithm 5 ExistValue(z, x, d').

/* This subroutine tries to check whether any node in the dynamic network has invoked this subroutine with $z = x$. It uses d' as the guess for the diameter of the dynamic network, and takes total d' rounds. */

1: **if** ($z = x$) **then** exist $\leftarrow$ *true*; **else** exist $\leftarrow$ *false*;
2: **repeat** d' rounds
3:     **if** (exist) **then** send m_exist; **else** receive for 1 round;
4:     **if** I receive m_exist **then** exist $\leftarrow$ *true*;
5: **return** exist;

round of P in its simulated execution. Recall that in each simulated round, $\alpha^{\epsilon,t}$ chooses $O(\log \frac{r}{\epsilon})$ centers. For each center, Q will do a binary search (via logarithmic number of sequential floodings) to find the id of that center. For example, for the first center, Q will use a binary search to find the node with the smallest id, among all nodes that were receiving in the previous simulated round and are sending in the current simulated round. Next, for each center (which must be sending in P for the current simulated round), Q will determine the message it should send in P. Q will then flood this message, and then feed this message into all nodes that are receiving in P for the current simulated round.

Challenges and Our Solutions. A key difficulty in the above simulation is that Q does not know the diameter d of the dynamic network over which it runs. This means that Q does not know how long it takes for each flooding to complete. Of course, Q can naturally use the standard doubling-trick and maintains a guess d' for d. Recall that Q uses flooding i) for finding the centers via binary searches, and ii) for disseminating the messages of the centers. When $d' < d$, obviously both steps can be incorrect. We need to design Q so that it can deal with such incorrect behavior.

As a starting point, for each binary search, we have a designated node (node 0) flood for d' rounds its result of the binary search. If a node does not see such flooding from node 0, or if its binary search result is different, it knows that something is wrong and flags itself. Next for each center in this list, if it is not flagged, it will flood the message (that it should send in P) for d' rounds. Again, whoever not seeing this flooding will flag itself. In our design, once a node gets flagged, it will not participate in any of the flooding or binary search any more (for the current d' value), but will nevertheless spend the corresponding number of rounds doing nothing, so that it remains "in sync" with the non-flagged nodes.

At this point, we have three possibilities: i) $d' \geq d$ and no node gets flagged, ii) $d' < d$ and no node gets flagged, iii) $d' < d$ and some nodes get flagged. For the second case, because $d' < d$, it is not immediately clear what guarantees the simulation can offer — for example, whether the binary search still finds the smallest id. Fortunately, we will be able to prove that as long as no node gets flagged, the simulation is still "correct". Specifically, for disseminating the centers' messages, it is obvious that if no node gets flagged, then all nodes must have received those messages, regardless of whether $d' < d$. For the binary search part, we will be able to prove the following strong property: As long as the binary search returns the same value on all nodes (which is a necessary condition for no nodes being flagged), the result of the binary search must be correct, *even if* $d' < d$. Putting these together, this means that the second case still corresponds to a proper execution of P against $\alpha^{\epsilon,t}$.

The third case (i.e., $d' < d$ and some nodes get flagged) is trickier. The challenge is that the non-flagged nodes may think everything is fine and then happily generate a potentially wrong output. To deal with this, our design first lets the flagged nodes send a special message — whoever receives this message will get flagged as well. For each simulated round of P, our algorithm Q will allocate exactly one dedicated round in Q to do this.

Next, as a key technical step, we will be able to prove that with such a mechanism, somewhat interestingly, those non-flagged nodes actually still constitute *part* of a valid execution of P against some prophetic adversary ψ (but not a valid execution of P against $\alpha^{\epsilon,t}$). Our proof will explicitly construct this prophetic adversary ψ. Let G be the dynamic network generated by ψ. We will prove that G's topology is always connected in every round, while leveraging the fact that the topology of the dynamic network H (over which Q runs) is always connected. It is important to note that here we need to use a prophetic adversary (instead of an adaptive adversary) to generate G, since G depends on H, and since H is generated by some prophetic adversary.

To quickly summarize, we effectively have that i) if no node gets flagged, then Q must have properly simulated P's execution against $\alpha^{\epsilon,t}$, and ii) if some nodes get flagged, then Q (on the non-flagged nodes) must have properly simulated P's execution against some prophetic adversary ψ. Now since P is an LV algorithm, it will never have any error when running over any G, even if G is generated by a prophetic adversary. The reason is that G could also be generated by some adaptive adversary (e.g., by the adaptive adversary that always outputs G, regardless of P's inputs and P's coin flip outcomes), and P promises zero error under all adaptive adversaries. Thus the outputs of those non-flagged nodes will never be wrong, and can always be safely used. Of course, P's time complexity guarantee will no longer hold when running against ψ. But this will not cause any problem—if P takes too long to output, Q will increase d' and retry.

Using Fresh Coins. Finally, since we are using the doubling-trick to guess d already, we will use the same trick to guess the number of rounds needed for P to output. This will make our proof on Q a constructive proof, instead of an existential proof. It is worth mentioning that for each d' (the guess on d) and t (the guess on the number of simulated rounds needed for P to output), Q will simulate P using a fresh set of random coins. This is necessary because for a given set of coin flip outcomes, the adversary $\alpha^{\epsilon,t}$ may happen to have large diameter, causing P to take too many rounds to output. Finally, for each pair of d' and t values, the simulation of P takes about $d't\log t$ rounds. To make the guessing process efficient, we maintain a budget k that keeps doubling. For a given budget k, we simulate P for all (d', t) pairs where $d't\log t \leq k$ and that are constant factors apart from each other.

4.2   Final Results

Theorem 1 next states that Q's output will never be wrong. Its proof (in the full version [13] of this paper) mainly relies on the intuition in the previous section. The proof is involved, because it is not sufficient to just consider whether a node is flagged at a certain time point in each simulated round — we actually consider two separate time points in each simulated round.

Theorem 1. *For any LV algorithm P, the output of Q (Algorithm 1) will never be wrong.*

Theorem 2 next (see [13] for the proof) is our final result on Q's time complexity, when Q runs against a prophetic adversary.

Theorem 2. *Let Q be Algorithm 1, and let P be any LV algorithm where $\Omega(1) \le \text{tc}_P(n,n) \le O(n^{a_1})$ for some constant a_1.*

- *There exists constant a' (independent of n) such that for all d, we have $\text{tc}_Q^*(n,d) = \max_I E_C[\max_H \text{tc}(Q,I,\gamma^H,C)] = d \cdot O(\log^3 n \times \text{tc}_P(n,a'\log n))$, where $\max_H$ is taken over all dynamic networks H with at most n nodes and at most d diameter.*
- *If $\text{tc}_P(n,d) = \Theta(f(n) \cdot g(d))$ for some $f(n)$ and $g(d)$ where there exists some constant a_2 such that $\Omega(1) \le f(n) \le O(n^{a_2})$ and $\Omega(d) \le g(d) \le O(d^{a_2})$, then we have $\text{tc}_Q^*(n,d) = O(\text{polylog}(n)) \cdot \text{tc}_P(n,d)$.*

Acknowledgments. We thank the anonymous Euro-Par reviewers for the helpful feedbacks on this paper. This work is partly supported by the grant MOE2017-T2-2-031 from Singapore Ministry of Education.

References

1. Ahmadi, M., Ghodselahi, A., Kuhn, F., Molla, A.: The cost of global broadcast in dynamic radio networks. In: OPODIS (2015)
2. Ahmadi, M., Kuhn, F., Kutten, S., Molla, A.R., Pandurangan, G.: The communication cost of information spreading in dynamic networks. In: ICDCS (July 2019)
3. Augustine, J., Avin, C., Liaee, M., Pandurangan, G., Rajaraman, R.: Information spreading in dynamic networks under oblivious adversaries. In: Gavoille, C., Ilcinkas, D. (eds.) DISC 2016. LNCS, vol. 9888, pp. 399–413. Springer, Heidelberg (2016). https://doi.org/10.1007/978-3-662-53426-7_29
4. Avin, C., Koucký, M., Lotker, Z.: How to explore a fast-changing world (cover time of a simple random walk on evolving graphs). In: Aceto, L., Damgård, I., Goldberg, L.A., Halldórsson, M.M., Ingólfsdóttir, A., Walukiewicz, I. (eds.) ICALP 2008. LNCS, vol. 5125, pp. 121–132. Springer, Heidelberg (2008). https://doi.org/10.1007/978-3-540-70575-8_11
5. Ben-David, S., Borodin, A., Karp, R., Tardos, G., Wigderson, A.: On the power of randomization in online algorithms. Algorithmica **11**(1), 2–14 (1994)
6. Casteigts, A., Flocchini, P., Quattrociocchi, W., Santoro, M.: Time-varying graphs and dynamic networks. Int. J. Parallel Emergent Distrib. Syst. **27**(5), 384–408 (2012)
7. Censor-Hillel, K., Parter, M., Schwartzman, G.: Derandomizing local distributed algorithms under bandwidth restrictions. Distrib. Comput. **33**, 349–366 (2020). https://doi.org/10.1007/s00446-020-00376-1
8. Chang, Y., Kopelowitz, T., Pettie, S.: An exponential separation between randomized and deterministic complexity in the LOCAL model. In: FOCS (2016)
9. Dutta, C., Pandurangan, G., Rajaraman, R., Sun, Z., Viola, E.: On the complexity of information spreading in dynamic networks. In: SODA (January 2013)
10. Feuilloley, L., Fraigniaud, P.: Randomized local network computing. In: SPAA (2015)
11. Ghaffari, M., Harris, D., Kuhn, F.: On derandomizing local distributed algorithms. In: FOCS (Oct 2018)

12. Ghaffari, M., Lynch, N., Newport, C.: The cost of radio network broadcast for different models of unreliable links. In: PODC (July 2013)
13. Jahja, I., Yu, H., Hou, R.: On the power of randomization in distributed algorithms in dynamic networks with adaptive adversaries. Technical report, School of Computing, National University of Singapore (2020). https://www.comp.nus.edu.sg/%7Eyuhf/derandomize-europar20-tr.pdf
14. Jahja, I., Yu, H., Zhao, Y.: Some lower bounds in dynamic networks with oblivious adversaries. Distrib. Comput. **33**(1), 1–40 (2019). https://doi.org/10.1007/s00446-019-00360-4
15. Kawarabayashi, K., Schwartzman, G.: Adapting local sequential algorithms to the distributed setting. In: DISC (October 2018)
16. Kuhn, F., Lynch, N., Newport, C., Oshman, R., Richa, A.: Broadcasting in unreliable radio networks. In: PODC (July 2010)
17. Kuhn, F., Lynch, N., Oshman, R.: Distributed computation in dynamic networks. In: STOC (June 2010)
18. Kuhn, F., Moses, Y., Oshman, R.: Coordinated consensus in dynamic networks. In: PODC (June 2011)
19. Kuhn, F., Oshman, R.: Dynamic networks: models and algorithms. SIGACT News **42**(1), 82–96 (2011)
20. Kushilevitz, E., Nisan, N.: Communication Complexity. Cambridge University Press, Cambridge (1996)
21. Luby, M.: Removing randomness in parallel computation without a processor penalty. J. Comput. Syst. Sci. **47**(2), 250–286 (1993)
22. Naor, M., Stockmeyer, L.: What can be computed locally? SIAM J. Comput. **24**(6), 1259–1277 (1995)
23. O'Dell, R., Wattenhofer, R.: Information dissemination in highly dynamic graphs. In: Joint Workshop on Foundations of Mobile Computing (DIALM-POMC) (September 2005)
24. Peleg, D.: Distributed Computing: A Locality-Sensitive Approach. Society for Industrial and Applied Mathematics (1987)
25. Vadhan, S.: Pseudorandomness. Found. Trends Theor. Comput. Sci. **7**(1–3), 1–336 (2012)
26. Yu, H., Zhao, Y., Jahja, I.: The cost of unknown diameter in dynamic networks. J. ACM **65**(5), 311–3134 (2018)

3D Coded SUMMA:
Communication-Efficient and Robust
Parallel Matrix Multiplication

Haewon Jeong[1]([✉]), Yaoqing Yang[2], Vipul Gupta[2], Christian Engelmann[3],
Tze Meng Low[1], Viveck Cadambe[4], Kannan Ramchandran[2],
and Pulkit Grover[1]

[1] Carnegie Mellon University, Pittsburgh, USA
[2] UC Berkeley, Berkeley, USA
haewon@seas.harvard.edu
[3] Oak Ridge National Laboratory, Oak Ridge, USA
[4] Penn State University, State College, USA

Abstract. In this paper, we propose a novel fault-tolerant parallel
matrix multiplication algorithm called *3D Coded SUMMA* that achieves
higher failure-tolerance than replication-based schemes for the same
amount of redundancy. This work bridges the gap between recent developments in *coded computing* and fault-tolerance in high-performance
computing (HPC). The core idea of coded computing is the same as
algorithm-based fault-tolerance (ABFT), which is weaving redundancy in
the computation using error-correcting codes. In particular, we show that
MatDot codes, an innovative code construction for parallel matrix multiplications, can be integrated into three-dimensional SUMMA (Scalable
Universal Matrix Multiplication Algorithm [30]) in a communication-
avoiding manner. To tolerate any two node failures, the proposed 3D
Coded SUMMA requires ∼50% less redundancy than replication, while
the overhead in execution time is only about 5–10%.

Keywords: Parallel matrix multiplication · Fault-tolerant
algorithms · Algorithm-based fault tolerance · Coded computing ·
Communication-efficient algorithms · Error detection and correction

1 Introduction

Upcoming exascale computing systems are expected to bring about new challenges in building resilience against failures and faults [3,4,15,26]. To see how
the scale affects reliability, let us consider the upcoming exascale supercomputer,

This work was sponsored by the U.S. Department of Energy's Office of Advanced
Scientific Computing Research. This manuscript has been authored by UT-Battelle,
LLC under Contract No. DE-AC05-00OR22725 with the U.S. Department of Energy.
The United States Government retains and the publisher, by accepting the article for
publication, acknowledges that the United States Government retains a non-exclusive,
paid-up, irrevocable, world-wide license to publish or reproduce the published form
of this manuscript, or allow others to do so, for United States Government purposes.
The Department of Energy will provide public access to these results of federally sponsored research in accordance with the DOE Public Access Plan (http://energy.gov/
downloads/doe-public-access-plan).

© Springer Nature Switzerland AG 2020
M. Malawski and K. Rzadca (Eds.): Euro-Par 2020, LNCS 12247, pp. 392–407, 2020.
https://doi.org/10.1007/978-3-030-57675-2_25

the Fugaku system that is now being built to be available in 2021. The Fugaku system will have 150,000 physical nodes with a total of 8 million cores [22]. To build a system with mean-time-between-failure (MTBF) of 24–48 h, the MTBF of each node must be 411–822 years. This can create a huge burden on component manufacturers and the system vendor as it leaves little-to-no room for unexpected reliability issues that have been experienced in the past, such as bad solder, dirty power, unexpected early wear-out, and so on [16].

The most widely used method for fault tolerance in high-performance computing (HPC) is checkpoint-restart, which saves the state of computation at specific intervals and can recover from detected faults by rolling back to a checkpointed state. While the checkpoint-restart approach is universal, it generates a significant amount of I/O overhead and its efficiency decreases with the increasing system size. The deployment of node-local nonvolatile memory, such as solid state disks, has eased the I/O pressure for checkpoint/restart, but it will not be sufficient in the long run. Another method considered is replication, where the application is executed either in parallel or sequentially multiple times such as triple modular redundancy (TMR) [14,15,23]. Despite the high resource overhead of replication, it has been shown that process replication strategies can outperform traditional checkpoint-restart approaches for a certain range of system parameters [3].

In this paper, we study a different approach called *coded computing* [12,21, 33], more widely known as algorithm-based fault-tolerance (ABFT) [10,11] in the HPC community. This approach reduces the overhead of checkpointing or replication by sacrificing universality and designing the redundancy tailored to a specific numerical algorithm. For designing low-overhead redundancy, both ABFT and coded computing utilize error-correcting codes (in short, coding or codes), a tool extensively used in communication or storage systems. While ABFT uses off-the-shelf classical codes and adapts them to practical problems in HPC, coded computing literature studies devising a new code tailor-made for computation by assuming a simple theoretical computing model. These endeavors in coded computing have shown remarkable improvements in the failure tolerance versus memory/computation trade-off, improving over classical codes designed for communication or storage systems. However, due to the simplified models in coded computing that can be unrealistic in practical HPC systems, it is unclear if the new code constructions can be applied in the HPC context. This paper bridges this gap and demonstrates that the new advances in coded computing can be mapped to HPC systems with careful integration.

We propose a novel algorithm for robust and communication-efficient parallel matrix multiplication called *3D Coded SUMMA*. In 3D Coded SUMMA, we incorporate MatDot codes (storage-optimal matrix-multiplication codes) [12] with 3D SUMMA (communication-efficient matrix multiplication algorithm) [27]. Applying ABFT to a three-dimensional matrix multiplication algorithm was studied before [24]. Their goal was to apply ABFT within each node to detect/correct soft errors locally. On the other hand, our aim is to construct a coding strategy that can be applied across distributed nodes to recover from node failures, where we cannot recover any partial result from the failed node. We show that MatDot codes can be integrated into 3D SUMMA seamlessly with small communication overhead. The amount of redundancy required in 3D Coded SUMMA is considerably smaller than replication for cases where more than one failure, or where node corruptions (nodes affected by soft errors) are to be tolerated. For instance, to provide resilience against any two node failures, or against a single corruption, 3D Coded SUMMA requires ∼50% fewer nodes than the baseline replication strategy. To provide resilience against any two node corruptions, 3D Coded SUMMA requires ∼100% fewer nodes compared to replication. Finally, we show through theoretical and experimental analysis that 3D Coded SUMMA achieves higher failure resilience with small overhead in execution time: 5–7% more execution time compared to replication on an $8 \times 8 \times 4$ grid of nodes.

2 Background

2.1 3D SUMMA

We introduce a 3-dimensional matrix multiplication algorithm, 3D SUMMA. Three-dimensional algorithms for matrix multiplication in which nodes are placed on a 3D grid were proposed [1, 25, 27] and proved to achieve the optimal communication time in scaling sense [27] under some constraints. 3D SUMMA we present here is an adaptation of 2.5D matrix multiplication algorithm [27]: instead of using Cannon's algorithm on each layer as in [27], we use 2D SUMMA on each layer. In this work, for simplicity, we assume that nodes are placed on layers of square grids, i.e., on a $n \times n \times m$ grid where m is the number of layers and n is the layer size. The goal is to compute matrix product:

$$\mathbf{C} = \mathbf{AB}. \tag{1}$$

We assume matrices $\mathbf{A}, \mathbf{B}, \mathbf{C}$ all have dimension $N \times N$.[1] We use $P(i, j, l)$ to denote the node on the (i, j, l)-th coordinate on the 3D grid.

We summarize the algorithm of 3D SUMMA below.

1. Matrix product in (1) is split into outer-products as follows:

$$\mathbf{A} = \begin{bmatrix} \mathbf{A}_1 \cdots \mathbf{A}_m \end{bmatrix}, \mathbf{B} = \begin{bmatrix} \mathbf{B}_1 \\ \vdots \\ \mathbf{B}_m \end{bmatrix}, \mathbf{C} = \mathbf{A}_1\mathbf{B}_1 + \cdots + \mathbf{A}_m\mathbf{B}_m, \tag{2}$$

where $\mathbf{A}_i$'s and $\mathbf{B}_i$'s $(i = 1, \ldots, m)$ are $N \times N/m$ and $N/m \times N$ dimensional submatrices, respectively.

---

[1] Throughout the paper, we will assume that m and n divide N for simplicity. In practice, when N is not divisible by m, n, the matrix can be zero-padded to make N divisible by m and n. Also, the assumption that they are square matrices is only for simplicity, and the algorithm can be used for rectangular matrices as well.

2. Initially, all $\mathbf{A}_i$'s and $\mathbf{B}_i$'s are stored at the nodes on the first layer of the 3D grid. The first layer scatters $\mathbf{A}_i$ and $\mathbf{B}_i$ to the i-th layer.
3. Each layer performs 2D SUMMA[2] to compute $\mathbf{C}_i = \mathbf{A}_i\mathbf{B}_i$ in parallel.
4. All layers reduce to the first layer and the first layer obtains:

$$\mathbf{C} = \mathbf{C}_1 + \cdots + \mathbf{C}_m.$$

2.2 MatDot Codes

MatDot codes [12] are one of the latest advances in coded computing and proven to be optimal in terms of *recovery threshold*[3] for parallel matrix multiplication under certain constraints [33]. Classical error-correcting codes such as Reed-Solomon codes encode data through polynomial evaluations where the coefficients of the polynomial are the raw data. These algorithms use polynomial interpolation for decoding to recover the polynomial coefficients, *i.e.*, the raw data, when the number of evaluations that survive after failures is larger than the degree of the polynomial. The construction of MatDot codes is inspired by this approach, but the polynomials are carefully constructed so that the matrix product can be extracted from the polynomial coefficients at the end of computation. A main innovation is the construction of encoding polynomials $p_{\mathbf{A}}(x)$ and $p_{\mathbf{B}}(x)$ that exploit the sum of outer-product structure in (2):

$$p_{\mathbf{A}}(x) = \sum_{i=1}^{m} \mathbf{A}_i x^{i-1}, \quad p_{\mathbf{B}}(x) = \sum_{j=1}^{m} \mathbf{B}_j x^{m-j}. \tag{3}$$

Note that the co-efficients are placed in reverse order in $p_{\mathbf{B}}(x)$. Then, in 3D SUMMA, the i-th layer will receive encoded versions of matrices:

$$\widetilde{\mathbf{A}}_i = p_{\mathbf{A}}(\alpha_i) = \mathbf{A}_1 + \alpha_i \mathbf{A}_2 + \cdots + \alpha_i^{m-1}\mathbf{A}_m,$$
$$\widetilde{\mathbf{B}}_i = p_{\mathbf{B}}(\alpha_i) = \mathbf{B}_m + \alpha_i \mathbf{B}_{m-1} + \cdots + \alpha_i^{m-1}\mathbf{B}_1,$$

and then compute matrix multiplication on the encoded matrices:

$$\widetilde{\mathbf{C}}_i = \widetilde{\mathbf{A}}_i\widetilde{\mathbf{B}}_i = p_{\mathbf{A}}(\alpha_i)p_{\mathbf{B}}(\alpha_i) = p_{\mathbf{C}}(\alpha_i).$$

The polynomial $p_{\mathbf{C}}(x)$ has degree $2m - 2$ and has the following form:

$$p_{\mathbf{C}}(x) = \sum_{i=1}^{m}\sum_{j=1}^{m} \mathbf{A}_i\mathbf{B}_j x^{m-1+(i-j)}. \tag{4}$$

Because of our judicious choice of $p_{\mathbf{A}}(x)$ and $p_{\mathbf{B}}(x)$, the coefficient of x^{m-1} in $p_{\mathbf{C}}(x)$ is $\mathbf{C} = \sum_{i=1}^{m} A_i B_i$. Since $p_{\mathbf{C}}(x)$ is a polynomial of degree $2m - 2$, its

---

[2] For more details on 2D SUMMA, please see [30].
[3] Recovery threshold is one metric to measure the performance of a code, which is the minimum number of workers required to recover the computation output.

coefficients can be recovered as long as we have evaluations of $p_C(x)$ at any $2m-1$ distinct points. Hence the recovery threshold is $K = 2m - 1$. In the context of 3D SUMMA, we need m layers for the uncoded strategy. The recovery threshold $K = 2m - 1$ implies that when we have $M = 2m - 1 + r$ layers, it is guaranteed to tolerate any r failed layers. On the other hand, to tolerate any r failures with replication, we need $M = rm$ layers. This will be further discussed in Sect. 4.1.

Systematic MatDot Codes: A code is called *systematic* if, for the first m layers, the output of the r-th layer is the product $\mathbf{A}_r\mathbf{B}_r$. We refer to the first m layers as *systematic layers*. Systematic codes are useful because if all the systematic layers complete their computation successfully, there is no need for decoding. Systematic MatDot codes are achieved by using Lagrange polynomials for encoding. Let

$$p_\mathbf{A}(x) = \sum_{i=1}^{m} \mathbf{A}_i L_i(x), \quad p_\mathbf{B}(x) = \sum_{i=1}^{m} \mathbf{B}_i L_i(x), \tag{5}$$

where $L_i(x)$ is defined as: $L_i(x) = \displaystyle\prod_{j\in\{1,\dots,m\}\setminus\{i\}} \frac{x - x_j}{x_i - x_j}$ for $i \in \{1,\dots,m\}$. Using these polynomials, the worst-case recovery threshold remains the same as non-systematic MatDot codes [12].

2.3 Related Work in ABFT

Algorithm-based fault tolerance (ABFT) was first proposed by Huang and Abraham to detect and correct errors on circuits during linear algebra operations. Recently, Chen and Dongarra discovered that a similar technique could be used for parallel matrix algorithms for HPC systems [10]. A follow-up work [6] experimentally showed that the overhead of ABFT is less than 12% with respect to the fastest failure-free implementation of PDGEMM (Parallel General Matrix Multiplication). Numerical stability of the ABFT technique was also examined in [8] and applied to soft error detection [9]. The ABFT technique is extended to matrix factorization algorithms such as Cholesky factorization [17] and LU factorization [11,32].

Our work goes beyond existing works in ABFT for HPC as we employ the novel MatDot codes which go beyond traditional error-correcting codes. MatDot codes are designed specifically for distributed matrix multiplication where the matrix product is split into the sum of outer products.

3   3D Coded SUMMA

We propose a failure-resilient and communication-efficient parallel-matrix multiplication algorithm, 3D Coded SUMMA, by integrating MatDot codes into 3D SUMMA. Since 3D SUMMA partitions matrix multiplication into outer products across layers, we can weave MatDot codes into the third dimension (the l-axis) of the algorithm.

Recall that the recovery threshold of MatDot codes is $K = 2m-1$. This means that if we have any K successful (non-failed) nodes, we can recover the matrix product $\mathbf{C}$, and thus to tolerate one failure, we need $K + 1 = 2m$ nodes. For failure resilience, we need at least m redundant layers and use a total of $M \geq 2m$ layers. This redundancy is the same as replication for a single failure. A thorough comparison between 3D Coded SUMMA and replication for an arbitrary number of failures will be provided in the next section. In this section, we focus on the algorithm design of 3D Coded SUMMA and demonstrate a simple example of $(n = 2, m = 2, M = 4)$. The full algorithm is given in Algorithm 1.

Example 1 (3D Coded SUMMA for $(n = 4, m = 2, M = 4)$).
Initial Data Distribution: The node $P(i, j, 1)$ initially has $\mathbf{A}_{i,j}$ and $\mathbf{B}_{i,j}$ for $i, j = 1 \cdots 4$ where $\mathbf{A}_{i,j}$'S and $\mathbf{B}_{i,j}$'s are $N/m \times N/m$ sub-blocks as follows:

$$\mathbf{A} = \begin{bmatrix} \mathbf{A}_{1,1} & \cdots & \mathbf{A}_{1,4} \\ \vdots & \ddots & \vdots \\ \mathbf{A}_{4,1} & \cdots & \mathbf{A}_{4,4} \end{bmatrix}, \mathbf{B} = \begin{bmatrix} \mathbf{B}_{1,1} & \cdots & \mathbf{B}_{1,4} \\ \vdots & \ddots & \vdots \\ \mathbf{B}_{4,1} & \cdots & \mathbf{B}_{4,4} \end{bmatrix} \tag{6}$$

Encoding: To encode MatDot codes, we begin with splitting $\mathbf{A}_{i,j}$ into two equal-sized column blocks and $\mathbf{B}_{i,j}$ into two equal-sized row blocks as follows:

$$\mathbf{A}_{i,j} = \begin{bmatrix} \mathbf{A}_{i,j}^{(1)} & \mathbf{A}_{i,j}^{(2)} \end{bmatrix}, \mathbf{B}_{i,j} = \begin{bmatrix} \mathbf{B}_{i,j}^{(1)} \\ \mathbf{B}_{i,j}^{(2)} \end{bmatrix}. \tag{7}$$

Then, the node $P(i, j, 1)$ locally computes four encoded column-blocks and row-blocks as follows:

$$\widetilde{\mathbf{A}}_{i,j,1} = \mathbf{A}_{i,j}^{(1)} + \alpha_1 \mathbf{A}_{i,j}^{(2)}, \quad \widetilde{\mathbf{B}}_{i,j,1} = \alpha_1 \mathbf{B}_{i,j}^{(1)} + \mathbf{B}_{i,j}^{(2)},$$

$$\widetilde{\mathbf{A}}_{i,j,2} = \mathbf{A}_{i,j}^{(1)} + \alpha_2 \mathbf{A}_{i,j}^{(2)}, \quad \widetilde{\mathbf{B}}_{i,j,2} = \alpha_2 \mathbf{B}_{i,j}^{(1)} + \mathbf{B}_{i,j}^{(2)},$$

$$\widetilde{\mathbf{A}}_{i,j,3} = \mathbf{A}_{i,j}^{(1)} + \alpha_3 \mathbf{A}_{i,j}^{(2)}, \quad \widetilde{\mathbf{B}}_{i,j,3} = \alpha_3 \mathbf{B}_{i,j}^{(1)} + \mathbf{B}_{i,j}^{(2)},$$

$$\widetilde{\mathbf{A}}_{i,j,4} = \mathbf{A}_{i,j}^{(1)} + \alpha_4 \mathbf{A}_{i,j}^{(2)}, \quad \widetilde{\mathbf{B}}_{i,j,4} = \alpha_4 \mathbf{B}_{i,j}^{(1)} + \mathbf{B}_{i,j}^{(2)},$$

where $\alpha_1, \cdots, \alpha_4$ are four distinct real numbers.[4] Then $P(i, j, 1)$ sends $\mathbf{A}_{i,j,k}$ to $P(i, j, k)$ for $k = 2, 3, 4$ using MPI Scatter operation.

After MatDot encoding step, the node $P(i, j, k)$ will have $\mathbf{A}_{i,j,k}$ and $\mathbf{B}_{i,j,k}$ for all $i, j, k = 1, \ldots, 4$.

Computation: Perform 2D SUMMA [30] on each layer in parallel.

Decoding: Any $K = 2m - 1 = 3$ layers out of $M = 4$ layers are sufficient to decode the final output. Instead of performing MPI Reduce on the raw output, each node will scale their output with the decoding coefficients and then perform MPI Reduce. E.g., if $P(i, j, 4)$ fails, $P(i, j, 1), P(i, j, 2), P(i, j, 3)$ will send

---

[4] We can also use systematic MatDot codes where $\mathbf{A}_{i,j,1} = \mathbf{A}_{i,j}^{(1)}$ and $\mathbf{A}_{i,j,2} = \mathbf{A}_{i,j}^{(2)}$ by using the polynomials given in (5). However, for simplicity, we only discuss the non-systematic formulation.

Algorithm 1. 3D Coded SUMMA

1: **Initial Data Distribution:** $P(i,j,1)$ has $\mathbf{A}_{i,j}$ and $\mathbf{B}_{i,j}$.
2: /* Encoding $\mathbf{A}$, $\mathbf{B}$ and Scattering encoded data */
3: **for** $i = 1$ **to** n **do**
4:    **for** $j = 1$ **to** n **do**
5:       **for** $l = 1$ **to** M **do**
6:          $P(i,j,1)$ computes: /* All $P(i,j,1)$ in parallel */

$$\widetilde{\mathbf{A}}_{i,j,l} = \mathbf{A}_{i,j}^{(1)} + \alpha_l \mathbf{A}_{i,j}^{(2)} + \cdots + \alpha_l^{m-1}\mathbf{A}_{i,j}^{(m)} \tag{8}$$

$$\widetilde{\mathbf{B}}_{i,j,l} = \alpha_l^{m-1}\mathbf{B}_{i,j}^{(1)} + \alpha_l^{m-2}\mathbf{B}_{i,j}^{(2)} + \cdots + \mathbf{B}_{i,j}^{(m)} \tag{9}$$

7:       **end for**
8:       $P(i,j,1)$ scatters $\widetilde{\mathbf{A}}_{i,j,l}$ and $\widetilde{\mathbf{B}}_{i,j,l}$ to $P(i,j,l)$'s $(l = 1,\ldots,M)$
9:    **end for**
10: **end for**
11: /* 2D SUMMA Computation */
12: **for** $l = 1$ **to** m **do**
13:    All l-th layers in parallel, perform 2D SUMMA to compute: $\widetilde{\mathbf{A}}_l^{\text{col}} \cdot \widetilde{\mathbf{B}}_l^{\text{row}}$.
14: **end for**
15: /* Decoding and Reduce to recover $\mathbf{C}$ */
16: **for** $i = 1$ **to** n **do**
17:    **for** $j = 1$ **to** n **do**
18:       **for** $l = 1$ **to** M **do**
19:          /* All i,j,l in parallel */
20:          $P(i,j,l)$ knows which nodes failed among $P(i,j,k)$'s $(k = 1,\ldots,M)$.
21:          $P(i,j,l)$ computes $d_l\widetilde{\mathbf{C}}_{i,j,l}$ and reduce to $P(i,j,1)$
22:       **end for**
23:    **end for**
24: **end for**

$d_1\widetilde{\mathbf{C}}_{i,j,1}, d_2\widetilde{\mathbf{C}}_{i,j,2}$, and $d_3\widetilde{\mathbf{C}}_{i,j,3}$, then the first layer will have the final output $\mathbf{C}_{i,j} = d_1\widetilde{\mathbf{C}}_{i,j,1} + d_2\widetilde{\mathbf{C}}_{i,j,2} + d_3\widetilde{\mathbf{C}}_{i,j,3}$.[5]   ∎

Notice that the encoding of MatDot codes does not require any communication as encoding computation is performed at each local node. There is no additional communication required for MatDot decoding either as the decoding process is embedded in the final reduce step. The only communication cost increase comes from the initial MPI Scatter and the final MPI Reduce with the bigger size, *i.e.*, scatter/reduce over 4 layers instead of 2.

We want to make a remark that we can apply the ABFT technique [10,18] (rediscovered as Product codes in [21]) at each layer of 2D SUMMA for fault tolerance. Although in terms of additional nodes required, ABFT can be more efficient than MatDot codes, for higher failure tolerance, MatDot codes are a more communication-efficient solution. In the encoding of the ABFT strategy,

---

[5] The decoding coefficients, $d_1,\ldots,d_4$ are determined by the choice of $\alpha_1,\ldots,\alpha_4$. For more information on how to compute $d_1,\ldots,d_4$, see [12].

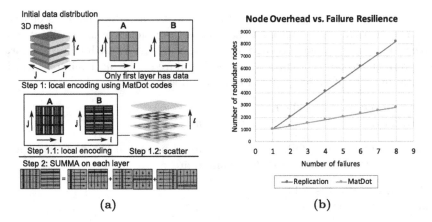

Fig. 1. (a) Summary of 3D Coded SUMMA algorithm. (b) Number of redundant nodes required to be resilient to f failures in the node/layer failure scenario for $n = 16, m = 4$.

one has to compute linear combinations of the column (row) blocks of **A** (**B**), which requires column (row) shuffling, or multiple reduce operations to parity nodes. Furthermore, for decoding, for recovering from more than one failure, nodes have to perform peeling decoding (see [21]) which can potentially require many rounds of communication. However, depending on which resource (communication delay or the number of compute nodes) is more expensive in the system, one can choose between ABFT on each layer and MatDot codes across layers as proposed in the first version of this work [20].

4 Performance Analysis

In this section, we will show how 3D Coded SUMMA can provide higher resilience for the same number of nodes compared to replication. Then, we analyze the overhead of the MatDot-coded strategy in terms of communication and computation time, and prove that the total overhead is negligible when $m = o(n)$. Finally, we demonstrate through experimental evaluations that the total execution time of 3D Coded SUMMA is only about 5–7% more compared to replication.

4.1 Node Overhead vs. Failure Resilience

To analyze the failure resilience, we will consider three different failure scenarios:

1. Node failure: This corresponds to *a fail-stop error* where a node fails and the entire data or intermediate result on the failed node is lost.
2. Layer failure: All nodes on one layer fail at once. This can be relevant when one layer is placed under the same rack and a rack failure occurs.
3. Node corruption: A node is corrupted by a soft error (a bit flip), and an arbitrary amount of data is affected beyond the capability of correction/detection at the local node. This can be due to error propagation during computation.

We say that a strategy is resilient to f failures in a certain failure scenario if we can recover the entire output $\mathbf{C}$ as long as the number of failures is at most f. We now compare replication and 3D Coded SUMMA for each failure scenario. To be resilient to any f failures in the node failure or the layer failure scenario, the total number of nodes required are the following:

- Replication: $p = (f + 1) \cdot mn^2$.
- 3D Coded SUMMA: $p = (2m - 1 + f) \cdot n^2$.

To be resilient to any s failures (*i.e.*, corrupted nodes) in the node corruption scenario, the total number of nodes required are[6]:

- Replication: $p = (2s + 1) \cdot mn^2$.
- 3D Coded SUMMA: $p = (2m - 1 + 2s) \cdot n^2$.

Let us make this more concrete by considering an example of $n = 16$ and $m = 4$. To be resilient to any single failure, both replication and 3D Coded SUMMA require 2048 nodes, which is twice more than the uncoded algorithm without any resilience. To be resilient to any two node failures (or any one node corruption), replication requires 3072 nodes while 3D Coded SUMMA requires 2304 nodes. To be resilient to any two node corruptions, replication requires 5120 nodes while 3D Coded SUMMA requires 2816 nodes. Because the recovery threshold of MatDot codes is $K = 2m - 1$, there is an upfront cost of 2x node redundancy in 3D Coded SUMMA. However, increasing resilience from one failure to more failures only requires incremental overhead compared to the replication strategy (Fig. 1b).

4.2   Execution Time Analysis

We now analyze the overhead of MatDot coding in terms of its execution time: communication + computation. For communication time, we use the simple α-β model [7]:

$$T_{\text{comm}} = C_1 \alpha + C_2 \beta, \tag{10}$$

where C_1 is the number of communication rounds and C_2 is the number of bytes communicated on the critical path. The α term is latency cost and the β term is per-byte bandwidth cost. For computation time, we count number of floating-point operations (flops). For 3D Coded SUMMA that encodes an $n \times n \times m$ grid into an $n \times n \times M$ grid using MatDot codes and computes a matrix product of dimension $N \times N$, the communication overhead of MatDot coding is summarized in the following theorem.

Theorem 1. *Suppose we use a MatDot code with a constant rate, i.e., $M = \Theta(m)$. Then, the total communication time of 3D Coded SUMMA is:*

$$T_{\text{comm}}^{total} = \left[\alpha \Theta \left(\log n \right) + \beta \Theta \left(N^2 / n^2 \right) \right] \cdot \frac{n}{m}, \tag{11}$$

---

[6] Using the recently proposed collaborative decoding [28] might further reduce the number of nodes required for 3D Coded SUMMA, but we use a conservative estimate.

and the communication time overhead of MatDot encoding and decoding is:

$$T_{comm}^{MatDot} = \alpha\Theta(\log n) + \beta\Theta(N^2/n^2). \tag{12}$$

The theorem implies that both the latency and the bandwidth of MatDot encoding/decoding is negligible if $m = o(n)$. Note that this is the same condition for the 3D SUMMA to outperform the 2D version of SUMMA [27].

Proof (Proof of Theorem 1). We will analyze the time complexity of each step.

Encoding MatDot Codes and Scattering the Encoded Matrices: The first layer has $n \times n$ nodes. Each node has a square matrix of size N^2/n^2. Each local square matrix is partitioned into m small blocks and encoded into M blocks. The M encoded blocks are scattered to M layers (across the l-axis). Both **A** and **B** need encoding and scattering.

- Local encoding cost: $C_{enc} = 2N^2/n^2 \cdot M$.
- Communication cost (scatter using recursive-halving [29]): $T_{scatter} = 2\alpha \log M + 2\beta\frac{N^2}{n^2} \cdot \frac{M}{m}$.

Matrix Multiplication with 2D SUMMA: The data on each layer is gathered into n^2/m nodes, i.e., the nodes in each row and column are partitioned into groups of size m and a local data gathering is carried out. Then, SUMMA proceeds in n/m rounds. In each round, one node in each row broadcasts data of size $\frac{N^2}{n^2m} \cdot m = \frac{N^2}{n^2}$ to the entire row, and similarly for each column. Then, local computation is carried out, which multiplies two matrices of size $N/n \times N/n$.

- Local gathering using recursive-doubling [29]: $T_{gather} = 2\alpha \log m + \frac{2N^2}{n^2}\beta$.
- Broadcast in SUMMA (scatter using recursive-halving followed by all-gather using recursive-doubling): $T_{bcast} = (4\alpha \log n + \frac{4N^2}{n^2}\beta) \cdot (n/m)$.
- Local matrix-matrix multiplication: $C_{MxM} = (N^3/n^3) \cdot (n/m) = \frac{N^3}{n^2m}$.

Decoding and Reduction: The decoding of MatDot codes only requires a reduce across layers. The data size at each node in the reduction phase is still N^2/n^2, and the number of layers required in the reduce is $2m - 1$ (for MatDot codes).

- Decoding MatDot codes (reduce using recursive-halving followed by tree-gather [29]): $T_{reduce} = 2\alpha \log(2m - 1) + (2N^2/n^2)\beta$.

Note that this communication cost analysis is the worst-case analysis because if we use *systematic* codes, we only need to reduce the first m systematic layers. Putting this altogether, we obtain the total communication time as follows:

$$
\begin{aligned}
T_{comm}^{total} &= T_{scatter} + T_{gather} + T_{bcast} + T_{reduce} \\
&= 2\alpha \log M + 2\beta\frac{N^2}{n^2} \cdot \frac{M}{m} + 2\alpha \log m + \frac{2N^2}{n^2}\beta \\
&\quad + (4\alpha \log n + \frac{4N^2}{n^2}\beta) \cdot (n/m) + 2\alpha \log(2m - 1) + (2N^2/n^2)\beta \\
&\overset{(a)}{=} \left[\alpha\Theta(\log n) + \beta\Theta(N^2/n^2)\right] \cdot \frac{n}{M},
\end{aligned}
$$

where in step (a), we use the fact that $M = \Theta(m)$, *i.e.*, the code has a constant rate. Finally, total communication overhead of using MatDot codes only come from the increased size of gather and reduce operations:

$$
\begin{aligned}
T_{\text{comm}}^{\text{MatDot}} &= T_{\text{scatter}} + T_{\text{reduce}} \\
&= 2\alpha \log m + \frac{2N^2}{n^2}\beta + 2\alpha \log(2m-1) + (2N^2/n^2)\beta \\
&= \alpha\Theta(\log M) + \beta\Theta(N^2/n^2).
\end{aligned}
$$

Computation time overhead of MatDot coding is summarized below.

Theorem 2. *Suppose we use a MatDot code with a constant rate, i.e., $M = \Theta(m)$. Then,*

$$
T_{comp}^{total} = \Theta\left(\frac{N^3}{n^2 m}\right) + \Theta\left(\frac{mN^2}{n^2}\right) + \Theta\left(m^2\right), \tag{13}
$$

$$
T_{comp}^{MatDot} = \Theta\left(\frac{mN^2}{n^2}\right) + \Theta\left(m^2\right). \tag{14}
$$

Notice that the computation time overhead of MatDot coding is negligible when $m = o(\sqrt{N})$, which is often the case since the matrix dimension N is orders of magnitude bigger than the number of layers m.

Proof (Proof of Theorem 2). The number of flops required at each local node for each step is given below:

– MatDot encoding: Each node generates M encoded blocks of dimension $N/n \times N/mn$ (or $N/mn \times N/n$), each of which is a linear combinations of m small sub-blocks of the same dimension. Hence,

$$
T_{\text{enc}} = 2M \cdot m \cdot \frac{N^2}{mn^2} = \Theta\left(\frac{mN^2}{n^2}\right).
$$

– Matrix multiplication: $T_{\text{MxM}} = \Theta\left(\frac{N^3}{n^2 m}\right)$
– MatDot decoding: Each node has to obtain decoding coefficient depending on which nodes have failed through polynomial interpolation, which has computation complexity of at most $\Theta(m^2)$. Then, it scales its output matrix by the decoding coefficient. Thus,

$$
T_{\text{dec}} = \Theta(m^2) + \Theta(N^2/n^2).
$$

$\square$

4.3   Experimental Evaluation

In this section, we evaluate the performance of 3D Coded SUMMA through experiments. In our experimental setup, we used a cluster with 40 compute nodes, each of which has two 12-Core AMD Opteron (tm) Processor 6164 HE,

64 GB DRAM, and 500 GB hard disk. Nodes are connected through Gigabit Ethernet under a single switch. We used each core as one MPI process, *i.e.,* one core was one logical node $P(i, j, l)$. To ensure that there is no MPI communication within the same compute node, we used cyclic distribution of compute nodes. We injected a layer failure by artificially ignoring the result from one layer in the reduce phase. We assumed that the information about the failed node will be made available at all surviving nodes. We recorded execution time of: memory allocation, MatDot Encoding (line 6 in Algorithm 1), MPI Scatter (line 8 in Algorithm 1), 2D SUMMA (line 12–14 in Algorithm 1), and Decoding + MPI Reduce (line 16–24 in Algorithm 1).

Table 1. Execution time comparison of $(n = 8, m = 2, M = 4)$ 3D Coded SUMMA and replication. We used systematic MatDot codes and 8 cores per node.

N	Strategy	Memory Allocation (s)	Encoding (s)	Scatter (s)	2D SUMMA (s)	Decoding + Reduce (s)	Total (s)
10000	Replication	0.1	0	1.505	19.583	0.926	22.245
	MatDot	0.105	0.124	2.25	18.621	1.384	22.486
20000	Replication	0.369	0	6.574	87.792	3.626	98.681
	MatDot	0.362	0.402	9.075	88.371	5.502	103.357
30000	Replication	0.75	0	14.993	214.798	7.859	239.035
	MatDot	0.752	0.864	19.773	224.232	12.316	257.883
40000	Replication	1.317	0	25.613	438.356	13.941	480.464
	MatDot	1.325	1.418	39.496	440.872	21.853	505.41

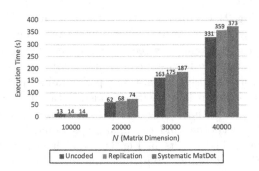

Fig. 2. Comparison of the total execution time between uncoded 3D SUMMA (no resilience), replication, and 3D Coded SUMMA for $(n = 8, m = 2, M = 2)$. We used 16 cores per node.

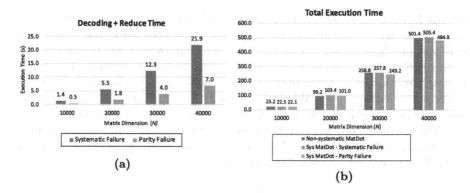

Fig. 3. (a) Comparison of decoding+reduce time using Systematic MatDot codes. When the failed node is a parity node, systematic code is ∼3x faster. (b) Comparison of total execution time for using non-systematic MatDot codes and systematic Mat-Dot codes. For systematic failures, non-systematic and systematic codes share similar performance. For parity failures, systematic codes show a clear advantage.

Since the cluster we used for experiments had total of 960 cores, the most extensive experiments were run on an $8 \times 8 \times 4$ grid with total of 256 cores.[7] We first compare our proposed MatDot-coded approach and replication. Execution time comparison of the two is summarized in Table 1. First notice that almost 90% of the total execution time is used in 2D SUMMA operations. Then, the next significant portion of the execution time is MPI Scatter and Reduce. Computation time for MatDot encoding and decoding makes up less than 1% of the total time. When we compare the total execution time, the overhead of MatDot coding is about 5–7% compared to replication. This is mainly due to the increased communication cost in the scatter and reduce communication as predicted in the previous section. We further compare the total execution time of replication and MatDot against the uncoded counterpart that does not provide any resilience (See Fig. 2). Compared to the uncoded strategy, the execution time of replication is 5–9% higher and 3D Coded SUMMA is about 10–18% higher.

Figure 3 shows the difference between using systematic and non-systematic codes. In Fig. 3a, systematic failure means a node failure in a systematic layer (the first m layers with the original data) and parity failure means a node failure in a parity layer (the last m layers with encoded data). The biggest benefit of using systematic codes is that when there is no failure in systematic nodes, there is no need for decoding, and the final steps would be no different from the uncoded strategy. The results in Fig. 3a show that this is indeed true in experiments and the last reduce step (including decoding) is about 3x times faster when we have only parity failures, and no systematic failure. Because of this effect, we can see that using systematic codes is about 3–5% faster than non-systematic codes when there is no systematic failure in Fig. 3b.

---

[7] Bigger grids with the dimensions of non-power-of-two numbers are not included as they showed worse performance.

5   Discussion and Future Work

In this paper, we examined a new fault-tolerant parallel matrix multiplication algorithm that integrates MatDot codes and 3D SUMMA. In our experiments, we assumed that failure information would be provided to every node. Although the current MPI implementation does not provide such functionality, there have been various research works to incorporate fault mitigation into MPI library [2,5] which include failure reporting and rearranging MPI communicator after the failure. Implementing 3D Coded SUMMA on these prototype fault-tolerant MPI libraries would be interesting future work.

Our work is a first step towards introducing coded computing to HPC applications and showing the feasibility through experiments. We believe that there is an abundance of possibilities in developing practical fault-tolerant algorithms by marrying new developments in coding theory and systems research (see [13] for the recent review in this direction). For instance, our work focuses only on dense matrix multiplication. Extending it to sparse matrix multiplication (e.g., sparse SUMMA) is not a straightforward question since the encoding process would reduce the sparsity of matrices. For linear system solving or eigendecomposition problems, one can consider using the substitute decoding technique for sparse matrices [31].

Acknowledgements and Data Availability Statement. This project was supported partially by NSF grant CCF 1763657 and supported by the U.S. Department of Energy, Office of Science, Office of Advanced Scientific Computing Research, program managers Robinson Pino and Lucy Nowell. This manuscript has been authored by UT-Battelle, LLC under Contract No. DE-AC05-00OR22725 with the U.S. Department of Energy.

The datasets and code generated during and/or analysed during the current study are available in the Figshare repository: https://doi.org/10.6084/m9.figshare.12560 330 [19].

References

1. Agarwal, R.C., et al.: A three-dimensional approach to parallel matrix multiplication. IBM J. Res. Dev. **39**(5), 575–582 (1995)
2. Ashraf, R.A., Hukerikar, S., Engelmann, C.: Shrink or substitute: handling process failures in HPC systems using in-situ recovery. In: 2018 26th Euromicro International Conference on Parallel, Distributed and Network-based Processing (PDP), pp. 178–185. IEEE (2018)
3. Benoit, A., Herault, T., Fèvre, V.L., Robert, Y.: Replication is more efficient than you think. In: Proceedings of the International Conference for High Performance Computing, Networking, Storage and Analysis. SC 2019, New York, USA (2019)
4. Bergman, K., et al.: Exascale computing study: technology challenges in achieving exascale systems. DARPA Technical report (2008)
5. Bland, W., Bouteiller, A., Herault, T., Bosilca, G., Dongarra, J.: Post-failure recovery of MPI communication capability: Design and rationale. Int. J. High Perform. Comput. Appl. **27**(3), 244–254 (2013)

6. Bosilca, G., et al.: Algorithmic based fault tolerance applied to high performance computing (2008)
7. Chan, E., et al.: Collective communication: Theory, practice, and experience. Concurr. Comput. Pract. Exp. **19**(13), 1749–1783 (2007)
8. Chen, Z.: Optimal real number codes for fault tolerant matrix operations. In: Proceedings of the Conference on High Performance Computing Networking, Storage and Analysis, p. 29. ACM (2009)
9. Chen, Z.: Online-ABFT: An online algorithm based fault tolerance scheme for soft error detection in iterative methods. ACM SIGPLAN Not. **48**(8), 167–176 (2013). https://doi.org/10.1145/2442516.2442533
10. Chen, Z., Dongarra, J.: Algorithm-based checkpoint-free fault tolerance for parallel matrix computations on volatile resources. In: Proceedings 20th IEEE International Parallel & Distributed Processing Symposium (2006)
11. Davies, T., Karlsson, C., Liu, H., Ding, C., Chen, Z.: High performance linpack benchmark: A fault tolerant implementation without checkpointing. In: Proceedings of the International Conference on Supercomputing, pp. 162–171 (2011). https://doi.org/10.1145/1995896.1995923
12. Dutta, S., et al.: On the optimal recovery threshold of coded matrix multiplication. IEEE Trans. Inf. Theory **66**(1), 278–301 (2019)
13. Dutta, S., et al.: Addressing unreliability in emerging devices and Non-Von Neumann architectures using coded computing. Proc. IEEE (2020)
14. Engelmann, C., Ong, H.H., Scott, S.L.: The case for modular redundancy in large-scale high performance computing systems. In: Proceedings of the 8th IASTED International Conference on Parallel and Distributed Computing and Networks (2009)
15. Ferreira, K., et al.: Evaluating the viability of process replication reliability for exascale systems. In: Proceedings of 2011 International Conference for High Performance Computing, Networking, Storage and Analysis (2011)
16. Geist, A.: How to kill a supercomputer: Dirty power, cosmic rays, and bad solder. IEEE Spectr. **10**, 2–3 (2016)
17. Hakkarinen, D., Chen, Z.: Algorithmic Cholesky factorization fault recovery. In: 2010 IEEE International Symposium on Parallel & Distributed Processing (IPDPS), pp. 1–10. IEEE (2010)
18. Huang, K.H., Abraham, J.A.: Algorithm-based fault tolerance for matrix operations. IEEE Trans. Comput. **33**(6), 518–528 (1984)
19. Jeong, H., et al.: Artifact instructions to generate experimental results for Euro-Par 2020 paper: 3D Coded SUMMA: Communication-Efficient and Robust Parallel Matrix Multiplication, July 2020. https://doi.org/10.6084/m9.figshare.12560330, https://springernature.figshare.com/articles/software/Artifact_instructions_to_gen erate_experimental_results_for_Euro-Par_2020_paper_3D_Coded_SUMMA_Commu nication-Efficient_and_Robust_Parallel_Matrix_Multiplication/12560330/0
20. Jeong, H., et al.: Coded SUMMA: Fully-decentralized coded matrix multiplication for high performance computing (2019). http://www.andrew.cmu.edu/user/ haewonj/documents/codml19_full_summa.pdf
21. Lee, K., et al.: Speeding up distributed machine learning using codes. IEEE Trans. Inf. Theory **64**(3), 1514–1529 (2017)
22. Limited, F.: Fujitsu begins shipping supercomputer Fugaku (2019, Press release)
23. Lyons, R.E., Vanderkulk, W.: The use of triple-modular redundancy to improve computer reliability. IBM J. Res. Dev. **6**(2), 200–209 (1962)

24. Moldaschl, M., Prikopa, K.E., Gansterer, M.N.: Fault tolerant communication-optimal 2.5D matrix multiplication. J. Parallel Distrib. Comput. **104**, 179–190 (2017)
25. Schatz, M.D., Van de Geijn, R.A., Poulson, J.: Parallel matrix multiplication: A systematic journey. SIAM J. Sci. Comput. **38**(6), 748–781 (2016)
26. Shalf, J., Dosanjh, S., Morrison, J.: Exascale computing technology challenges. In: Palma, J.M.L.M., Daydé, M., Marques, O., Lopes, J.C. (eds.) VECPAR 2010. LNCS, vol. 6449, pp. 1–25. Springer, Heidelberg (2011). https://doi.org/10.1007/978-3-642-19328-6_1
27. Solomonik, E., Demmel, J.: Communication-optimal parallel 2.5D matrix multiplication and LU factorization algorithms. In: Jeannot, E., Namyst, R., Roman, J. (eds.) Euro-Par 2011. LNCS, vol. 6853, pp. 90–109. Springer, Heidelberg (2011). https://doi.org/10.1007/978-3-642-23397-5_10
28. Subramaniam, A.M., Heiderzadeh, A., Narayanan, K.R.: Collaborative decoding of polynomial codes for distributed computation. In: 2019 IEEE Information Theory Workshop (ITW), pp. 1–5 (2019)
29. Thakur, R., Rabenseifner, R., Gropp, W.: Optimization of collective communication operations in MPICH. Int. J. High Perform. Comput. Appl. **19**(1), 49–66 (2005)
30. Van De Geijn, R.A., Watts, J.: Summa: Scalable universal matrix multiplication algorithm. Concurr. Pract. Exp. **9**(4), 255–274 (1997)
31. Yang, Y., Grover, P., Kar, S.: Coding for a single sparse inverse problem. In: 2018 IEEE International Symposium on Information Theory (ISIT), pp. 1575–1579 (2018)
32. Yao, E., Zhang, J., Chen, M., Tan, G., Sun, N.: Detection of soft errors in LU decomposition with partial pivoting using algorithm-based fault tolerance. Int. J. High Perform. Comput. Appl. **29**(4), 422–436 (2015). https://doi.org/10.1177/1094342015578487
33. Yu, Q., Maddah-Ali, M.A., Avestimehr, A.S.: Straggler mitigation in distributed matrix multiplication: Fundamental limits and optimal coding. In: IEEE International Symposium on Information Theory (ISIT), pp. 2022–2026 (2018)

Parallel and Distributed Programming, Interfaces, and Languages

Managing Failures in Task-Based Parallel Workflows in Distributed Computing Environments

Jorge Ejarque$^{(\boxtimes)}$ ⓘ, Marta Bertran ⓘ, Javier Álvarez Cid-Fuentes ⓘ,
Javier Conejero ⓘ, and Rosa M. Badia ⓘ

Barcelona Supercomputing Center, Barcelona, Spain
{jorge.ejarque,javier.alvarez,francisco.conejero,
rosa.m.badia}@bsc.es

Abstract. Current scientific workflows are large and complex. They normally perform thousands of simulations whose results combined with searching and data analytics algorithms, in order to infer new knowledge, generate a very large amount of data. To this end, workflows comprise many tasks and some of them may fail. Most of the work done about failure management in workflow managers and runtimes focuses on recovering from failures caused by resources (retrying or resubmitting the failed computation in other resources, etc.) However, some of these failures can be caused by the application itself (corrupted data, algorithms which are not converging for certain conditions, etc.), and these fault tolerance mechanisms are not sufficient to perform a successful workflow execution. In these cases, developers have to add some code in their applications to prevent and manage the possible failures. In this paper, we propose a simple interface and a set of transparent runtime mechanisms to simplify how scientists deal with application-based failures in task-based parallel workflows. We have validated our proposal with use-cases from e-science and machine learning to show the benefits of the proposed interface and mechanisms in terms of programming productivity and performance.

Keywords: Failure management · Scientific workflows · Parallel programming · Distributed computing

1 Introduction

E-science has evolved very fast during last few decades. At the beginning, small computations were performed in a single machine, while nowadays, large complex scientific workflows are executed in large distributed computing platforms. These workflows combine the execution of thousands of simulations with searching and data analytic algorithms to infer new knowledge from a large amount of data. Due to the nature of the infrastructure and the algorithms used on the workflow, some components of the computation can fail or become blocked. This can be

© Springer Nature Switzerland AG 2020
M. Malawski and K. Rzadca (Eds.): Euro-Par 2020, LNCS 12247, pp. 411–425, 2020.
https://doi.org/10.1007/978-3-030-57675-2_26

due to resource failures, data corruption, or just because the initial conditions of a simulation do not converge into a valid solution. These failures can make the whole workflow execution fail or hang without generating the expected results.

Most workflow managers, such as Galaxy [1] or Pegasus [5], have some fault tolerance mechanisms, but they are mainly focused on resource failures, and they do not deal with application failures or exceptions. In these cases, the responsible to deal with failures is the developer, who has to include some code in the application in order to implement custom mechanisms to make the whole workflow reliable. In a sequential application, this customized management inside the code requires additional software development efforts which can be managed with traditional error handling mechanisms provided by the programming languages, such as managing exceptions or inspecting the return values to decide how to adapt the code in case of failure. However, tasks in parallel and distributed workflows are asynchronously executed in remote resources, so implementing similar defensive codes for these workflows are more complex and can produce performance losses due to the unnecessary synchronizations and transfers to inspect task results.

This paper proposes a simple user interface to allow developers to easily indicate how to manage application failures. This interface extends the task definition in order to allow developers to provide hints about how the runtime has to react in case of a failure occurs during the task execution. Based on this developer hint, the runtime transparently implements a set of mechanisms to efficiently handle these failures, reducing the development efforts because developers do not need to add defensive code as explained above, and without affecting application performance, because the failure management is concurrently performed with the application execution.

A prototype of this proposal has been implemented in COMPSs [3], a task-based parallel programming model to easily implement parallel workflows for distributed computing environments, and it has been validated through two real applications from e-Science and Machine Learning areas. We have evaluated the productivity and performance of this solution compared to a user-developed alternative. The results of this evaluation demonstrate that the proposed solution reduces the code complexity and achieves better performance than a user-managed approach.

The rest of the paper is organized as follows: Sect. 2 presents the related work; Sect. 3 introduces the proposed mechanisms and Sect. 4 describes how they have been implemented in COMPSs. Then, Sect. 5 presents the evaluation; Finally, Sect. 6 draws the conclusions.

2   Related Work

Failures in the execution of workflows are frequent, especially when executed in distributed computing platforms. For this reason, several workflow management systems provide some way of tolerating failures and its management.

For example, Galaxy [1] provides automatic job re-submission (e.g., on job failure due to a temporary cluster error). Also, in order to make Galaxy more robust in a production environment, technologies to enhance Galaxy's portability, security, reliability, and scalability have been adopted. Galaxy utilizes uWSGI[1] as its default web application server. It has several advantages, including improved fault tolerance, and the possibility of restarting Galaxy uninterruptedly. The mechanisms supported by Taverna [15] are similar, with retries at service and workflow level. Several retry types are supported, such as exponential back-off of retry times.

Kepler [12] proposes three complementary mechanisms for fault tolerance: a) a forward recovery mechanism that offers retries and alternative versions at the workflow level; b) a checkpointing mechanism, also at the workflow layer, that resumes the execution in case of a failure at the last saved good state; and c) an error-state and failure handling mechanism to address issues that occur outside the scope of the workflow layer.

Cylc [13] is a workflow management system proposed by the Earth Science community. It provides checkpointing, which keeps a list of completed tasks, and if the scheduler does not respond properly, the user can restart the experiment, from the last checkpoint. Users can also define retries for the different experiment jobs.

Pegasus [5] provides some failure management features as well. In case of transient infrastructure failures, such as a node being temporarily down in a cluster, Pegasus will automatically retry jobs. After a given number of retries (usually once), a hard failure occurs, because of which the workflow will eventually fail. In most of the cases, these errors are correctable (either the resource comes back online or application errors are fixed). Once the errors are fixed, the Pegasus workflow can be restarted from the point of failure. While executing a workflow, Pegasus creates the rescue workflow, which contains the description of the work that remains to be done.

Nextflow [6] provides several failure management mechanisms. First, it provides continuous checkpointing: all the intermediate results produced during the pipeline execution are automatically tracked. This allows to resume the execution from the last successfully executed step. Nextflow also provides a mechanism that allows tasks to be automatically re-executed when a command terminates with an error exit status. In Nextflow, it is also possible to define the *errorStrategy* directive in a dynamic manner for a given task. This is useful to re-execute failed jobs only if a certain condition is verified.

What is presented in this paper differs from previous approaches since what we propose is an individual and tailored management policy for each task type. The last approach described above (Nextflow) is the one closer to what it is presented in this paper, but it differs since it does not support all the possible policies for task failure management proposed in this paper. The proposed errorStrategy does not allow to indicate what to do with the non generated data or what to do with tasks which depend on the failed tasks. Moreover, Nextflow provides their own scripting language, and they do not offer the possibility of managing task exceptions as well as managing tasks which enter a hang state.

---

[1] http://projects.unbit.it/uwsgi.

3   Application Failure Management

As raised in the introduction, developers are responsible to make applications reliable, predicting what could be the possible failures in each part of the application and implementing a code to recover the execution from these failures. In sequential programming, developers use return values, which are inspected in the main code to decide what to do in case the function returns a problem. However, in distributed parallel workflows, this management is not efficient because workflow tasks are executed in an asynchronous remote way, so waiting for a result to decide what to do next, requires unnecessary synchronization points and data movements to transfer results back and inspect them. The next subsections present common workflow task failures, their implications and the mechanisms that we propose to easily and efficiently manage them.

3.1   Common Workflow Task Failures and Implications

Workflow failures can be classified in the types enumerated below. Each of these types has different implications, which are described in the next paragraphs.

- **Tasks which stop their execution before completion.** They can be produced by an invalid input or errors returned by simulators. The main consequence of these failures is that task results are not completely generated and all the successor tasks could also fail or their results be invalid.
- **Task execution blocked or lasting more than expected.** These failures can be produced by tasks which are running algorithms that, depending on the input, can enter in a deadlock or never converge.
- **Tasks throwing exceptions.** These failures are similar to the first type but they can affect not only the dependent tasks but also others which are in the group or block.

3.2   Failure Management Mechanisms

To allow workflow developers to easily manage the different type of failures, we propose to extend the task definition and the runtime mechanism to implement the following features:

- **Failure reaction policy**: It allows developers to indicate to the runtime what to do when a task fails. This policy is described in the task definition interface and it is applied by the runtime to decide what to do with the successor tasks and what to do with the expected task results.
- **Automatic cancellation after timeout**: This feature is also activated by including the *timeout* property in the tasks definition. It allows users to define a maximum duration per task to avoid tasks running forever. Tasks cancelled because of exceeding the timeout are considered failures. Therefore, this feature can be combined with the failure reaction policy to decide what to do with the rest of the workflow.

- **Parallel distributed exception**: It allows developers to create "try/catch" blocks in task-based parallel workflows for distributed environments. With this functionality, the developer can implement a try code block using the programming model syntax, where tasks invoked inside this block will belong to the same task group. If one of these remote tasks throws an exception the runtime will catch it and the current and pending tasks of this group will be cancelled as it is done in try/catch blocks provided by some programming languages.

4   Implementation

This section provides more details about how the proposed mechanisms are implemented in COMPSs, by extending the COMPSs syntax to allow developers to specify a failure reaction policy, a timeout per task type and to define a try/catch block in parallel workflows, and by implementing the management of these extensions in the COMPSs runtime.

4.1   COMPSs Overview

COMP Superscalar (COMPSs) is a task-based parallel programming for distributed computing. Based on sequential programming, application developers, by means of code annotations, select a set of methods whose invocations are considered tasks and indicate the direction of their parameters.

COMPSs runtime [10] orchestrates the execution of applications and its tasks on the underlying infrastructure. For this purpose, for each invocation to a task it analyses the data dependencies with previous ones according to the parameter annotations. With this information, COMPSs runtime builds a Directed Acyclic Graph (DAG) where nodes represent tasks and edges represent data dependencies between them. COMPSs runtime is able to infer the task-level parallelism from this graph, and schedules and submits tasks for execution. The runtime also takes care of all required data transfers. If a partial failure raises during a task execution, the master node handles it with job resubmission and rescheduling techniques. However, after a maximum number of retries, the whole workflow is considered as failed and the whole execution is stopped.

COMPSs provides Java as native programming language and it also provides bindings for Python (PyCOMPSs [2]) and C/C++ [8]. Figure 1 shows an example of a task annotation and COMPSs main program. The first line contains the task annotation in the form of a Python decorator, while the rest of the code is a regular Python method. The parameter `f_res` is of type INOUT (the data is read and written by the method), and the parameter `p_res` is set to the default type IN (the data is only read by the method). These directionality clauses are used at execution time to derive the data dependencies between tasks and are applied at object level, taking into account its references to identify when two tasks access the same object, and can also be applied at file level when parameters are files. A tiny synchronisation API completes the PyCOMPSs syntax. For

```
1   @task()
2   def word_count(block):
3       ...
4       return res
5
6   @task(f_res=INOUT)
7   def merge_count(f_res, p_res):
8       ...
```

```
1   for block in data:
2       p_result = word_count(block)
3       reduce_count(result, p_result)
4   result = compss_wait_on(result)
```

(a) Task annotation example   (b) Main code example

Fig. 1. PyCOMPSs application example.

instance, as shown in Listing 1.b, the `compss_wait_on` waits until all the tasks modifying the `result`'s value have finished and brings the value to the node which executes the main program (line 4). Once the value is retrieved, the execution of the main program code is resumed. Given that PyCOMPSs is mostly used in distributed environments, synchronising may imply a data transfer from remote storage or memory space to the node executing the main program.

4.2   Failure Reaction Policy

As introduced above, the failure reaction action policy provides a hint to the runtime about what to do if a task fails. This hint is provided in the task definition as indicated in Fig. 2 and it will apply to all the instances of this type of task. It consists of adding the *on_failure* property to the task decorator, and the *default_value* property to the task parameter description. For the first case, the user can choose one of the following options:

- **FAIL**: If a task with this option fails, the whole application is stopped recovering the computed data until the moment of the failure.
- **RETRY** (Default): If a task with this option fails, the runtime re-executes it in the same node and, if the failure persists, resubmits it to a different one. If the task after these retries still fails, it applies the *FAIL* procedure.
- **IGNORE**: If a task with this option fails, the failure is ignored, the data not generated (return or with direction OUT) is set as indicated in the *default_value* property, and successor tasks are executed using these values.
- **CANCEL_SUCCESSORS**: If a task with this option fails, the runtime ignores the failure, recursively cancels its successors, and deletes all the data and versions which are not going to be generated by the failed task and its successors in order to keep the data coherence of the rest of the workflow.
- **IGNORE_AFTER_RETRY**: If a task with this option fails, the runtime first applies the *RETRY* procedure to try to recover from temporary resource failures. If the failure persists, it applies the *IGNORE* procedure.
- **CANCEL_SUCCESSORS_AFTER_RETRY**: As in the previous option, if a task with this option fails, the runtime applies the *RETRY* procedure and, if the failure persists, it applies the *CANCEL_SUCCESSORS* procedure.

```
1  @task(output_file={type:FILE, direction=OUT, default_value="EMPTY"}, on_failure="IGNORE")
2  def task_example(output_file):
3      ...
```

Fig. 2. Task definition with failure reaction policy and default value.

As we have seen before, an important issue when ignoring a failure is the value of data that has not been generated by the failed task. This value can be indicated by setting one of the following options in the *default_value* property:

- **EMPTY** (Default): The runtime will create an empty file or an empty object (an object created with the default constructor) depending on the parameter type.
- **NONE**: It will set the object or the file path as None (null in Java).
- **[Path/to/file]**: The parameter will be set as the content of a file indicated by a path (it can also be a serialized object).

The diagram depicted in Fig. 3, summarises how the COMPSs runtime manages task failures. First, it captures task failures at worker processes. These failures are notified to the master, which applies the procedures defined in the policies, resubmitting or cancelling tasks, as well as doing the proper data management (e.g.setting default values, version rollback, data deletion) to keep the application execution consistency.

4.3 Timeout Task Cancellation

Sometimes, the execution of a task may freeze due to a resource failure or it may never end (e.g., an optimization algorithm not converging to a solution). In these situations, workflow engines require a mechanism to avoid that the whole application gets blocked due to a single task. In our case, we propose to use a timeout mechanism combined with the failure reaction policies described above. As in the previous case, this mechanism will be also indicated in the task

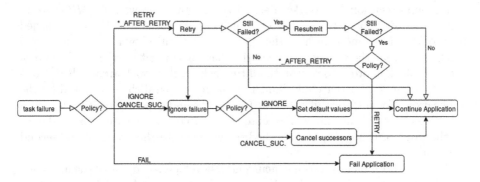

Fig. 3. Task failure management at runtime.

definition with the *time_out* property as shown in Fig. 4. The *time_out* property indicates the maximum duration (in seconds) for a task before being considered failed.

The defined timeout for a task is passed to the runtime worker when it is submitted. The worker sets up a timer according to the specified timeout duration which will send a signal when the timeout is reached. To manage the timeout, a custom signal handler is defined which will throw an exception interrupting the task execution and producing a failure in the task execution. The failure is managed according to the failure reaction policy as indicated above.

```
1  @task(time_out=50, on_failure="CANCEL_SUCCESSORS")
2  def task_timeout_example():
3      ...
```

Fig. 4. Task definition with timeout.

4.4   Exceptions in Parallel Distributed Workflows

Another mechanism to treat application failures is the exception. This is supported by most modern programming languages, however supporting this mechanism on parallel workflows executed in distributed environments is not trivial. In the next paragraphs, we will describe how the exception mechanism is implemented in COMPSs. Typically, exceptions are used in the following way: a user defines a *try* code block where some of the statements in the block can throw an exception; if an exception is thrown, the rest of the block execution is cancelled; and if a *catch* or *except* block (depending on the language) is defined, it is executed after catching the exception.

We propose to apply the same concept in parallel distributed workflows as shown in Fig. 5a. In this case, we create a task group block (line 9) where some of the tasks invoked in this block can throw a *COMPSsException* during its remote asynchronous execution; this special exception type is defined to differentiate from other exceptions which just produce a task failure. At runtime, during the task group execution, the worker detects when a task throws a *COMPSsException* and sends it back to the master, which cancels the rest of the non-finished tasks of the group and continues the application execution by running the *except* block. Note that the task group definition has an implicit barrier at the end of the code block in order to wait until all the tasks of this block are finished. However, this implicit barrier could limit the maximum parallelism achieved by the application. For instance, if we want to run two independent task groups in a loop, the COMPSs runtime will execute the group of the first iteration and once all the tasks of this group are finished, it will execute the group of the second iteration.

To allow both blocks to run concurrently, developers can follow the approach described in Fig. 5b. The implicit barrier can be disabled when defining the task group block (line 8), and an explicit barrier can be set by adding a call of the

```
1  @task()
2  def task_exception():
3      ...
4      raise COMPSsException()
5  ...
6  if __name__ == '__main__':
7      ...
8      try:
9          with TaskGroup("group_name"):
10             task_A()
11             task_exception()
12             task_B()
13         except COMPSsException:
14             task_C()
15     ...
```

(a) Exception management with implicit synchronization

```
1  @task()
2  def task_exception():
3      ...
4      raise COMPSsException()
5  ...
6  if __name__ == '__main__':
7      ...
8      with TaskGroup("group_name", false):
9          task_A()
10         task_exception()
11         task_B()
12     ...
13     try:
14         compss_barrier_group("group_name")
15     except COMPSsException:
16         task_C()
17     ...
```

(b) Exception management with explicit synchronization

Fig. 5. Code examples for remote exception management in parallel workflows.

compss_barrier_group (line 14). In both cases, tasks of the group will be canceled once the exception is thrown. However, the code area where the exception is thrown to the main code differs depending on the case. For the implicit synchronization case, the try/except block is set after the task group block, while in the explicit case, the exception is thrown in the *compss_barrier_group*, so the try/except block must be set at this point of the code.

5 Evaluation

To validate our proposal, we have applied the failure management mechanism in the following use cases where we have performed several experiments to evaluate the benefits of our approach in terms of productivity and performance.

5.1 BioExcel Biobb: Model Protein Mutants Workflow

BioExcel[2] is the European Centre of Excellence for provisioning support to academic and industrial researchers in the use of high-performance computing (HPC) and high-throughput computing (HTC) in biomolecular research. The BioExcel was established to provide the necessary solutions for long-term support of the biomolecular research communities: fast and scalable software, user-friendly automation workflows and a support base of expert core developers. In the framework of this project, BSC is developing together with the Institute for Research in Biomedicine (IRB) the *biobb*. The *biobb* is a library of Python wrappers offering a layer of compatibility and interoperability over the BioExcel computational biomolecular tools, such as GROMACS [14]. The *biobb* is enabled by PyCOMPSs for its executions in large scale systems. The Model

---

[2] https://bioexcel.eu.

Protein Mutants workflow has been developed on top of the *biobb* (and runs on top of PyCOMPSs). This workflow can be described as an automated protocol to generate structures for protein variants detected from genomics data. The workflow combines multiple data transformations with invocations to GROMACS.

```
1   @task(structure=FILE_OUT)
2   def fix_side_chain(structure):
3     # task code
4   if __name__ == '__main__':
5     fix_side_chain("init_struct.pdb")
6     for n in range(num_mut):
7       mutate(n, "init_struct.pdb", "mutate.pdb")
8       pdb2gmx(n, "mutate.pdb", "pdb2gmx.gro", "pdb2gmx.zip")
9       editconf(n, "pdb2gmx.gro", "editconf.gro")
10      solvate(n, "editconf.gro","pdb2gmx.zip", "solvate.gro",
           ↪ "solvate.zip")
11      grompp(n, "solvate.gro", "solvate.zip", "gppion.tpr")
12      genion(n, "gppion.tpr", "pdb2gmx.zip", "genion.gro", "genion.zip")
13      grompp(n, "genion.gro", "genion.zip", "gppmin.tpr")
14      mdrun(n, "gppmin.tpr", "min.gro")
15      grompp(n, "min.gro", "genion_top.zip", "gppnvt.tpr")
16      mdrun_cpt(n, "gppnvt.tpr", "nvt.gro", "nvt.cpt")
17      grompp_cpt(n, "nvt.gro", "nvt.cpt", "genion.zip", "gppnpt.tpr")
18      mdrun_cpt(n, "gppnpt.tpr", "npt.gro", "npt.cpt")
19      grompp_cpt(n, "npt.gro", "npt.cpt", "genion.zip", "gppmd.tpr")
20      mdrun_cpt(n, "gppmd.tpr", "md"+str(n)+".gro", "md"+str(n)+".cpt")
```

Fig. 6. Protein Mutants workflow code and generated DAG for 2 mutations

The first experiment to validate our failure management approach consists of making the protein mutants workflow reliable to application failures. In this experiment, we evaluate the productivity comparing the implementation using our proposed approach with the alternative of coding this feature directly in the application code. Figure 6 shows the main code of the protein mutants workflow and the task dependency graph generated when executing it with two mutations. As we can see, this application is composed of different independent chains of tasks. Therefore, a failure in one of the tasks of the chain invalidates the results of the whole chain. So, the most suitable mechanism for this application pattern is setting the *on_failure* property to *CANCEL_SUCCESSORS* in all tasks. In contrast to this, if we want to observe the same behaviour in this application when it is not supported by COMPSs, developers should modify the application in the way shown in Fig. 7, where we have to capture the failure in the task code, and return this as well as modify the main workflow to continue the workflow execution depending on its result. This implementation required to add 87 lines of code and the cyclomatic complexity [11] of the code increased from 2 to 41 (measured with Radon[3]) due to the split of the main loop and the different *if* paths.

---

[3] https://pypi.org/project/radon/.

```
1   #task code
2   @task(input_file=FILE_IN, output_file=FILE_OUT)
3   def mutate_pc(input_file, out_file):
4       try:
5           # original task_code where a failure generated an exception
6           return 0
7       except :
8           return 1
9   #main workflow
10  if __name__ == '__main__':
11      ...
12      for n in range(num_mut):
13          result[n] = mutate_pc(n, "init_struct.pdb", "mutate.pdb")
14      #The folowing pattern is repeated for invoking next tasks
15      for n in range(num_mut):
16          result[n] = compss_wait_on(result[n])
17          if (result[n] == 0 ):
18              result[n] == pdb2gmx_pc(n, "mutate.pdb", "pdb2gmx.gro")
19      ...
```

Fig. 7. Cancel successor code alternative.

Apart from the failure reaction policy, some of the GROMACS calls implement optimization algorithms which, depending on the input, might not converge. So, we have set the *time_out* property in *mdrun* and *mdrun_cpt* task definitions. Implementing the same feature in the task codes can be done as shown in Fig. 8b and required adding 18 lines of code.

```
1   @task
2   def task_example(out_file):
3       try:
4           #original task_code
5       except :
6           import os
7           if not os.path.exists(out_file):
8               with open('/tmp/test', 'w'):
9                   pass
```

(a) Failure Ignore code alternative

```
1   #Timeout exception
2   class TimeOutError(BaseException):
3       pass
4   #SIGALRM handler
5   def task_timed_out(signum, frame):
6       raise TimeOutError
7   #task implementation
8   @task(...)
9   def task_example(..., time_out):
10      import signal
11      signal.signal(signal.SIGALRM,
            ↪ task_timed_out)
12      signal.alarm(time_out)
13      try:
14          #original_code
15          signal.alarm(0)
16      except TimeOutError :
17          ...
```

(b) Time out code alternative

Fig. 8. Failure detection code alternatives.

Another variant of this workflow is done by adding a final task which merges the results in a single graph. In this variant, the *CANCEL_SUCCESSORS* policy is not suitable since a failure will also cancel the merge task. To avoid this, we can change the *on_failure* policy to *IGNORE*, which by default will generate an empty file per failed result which can be ignored by the merge task. In case the developers have to code this feature in the application, they have to add the code of the figure for each output parameter. In the case of study, it required adding 108 lines of code.

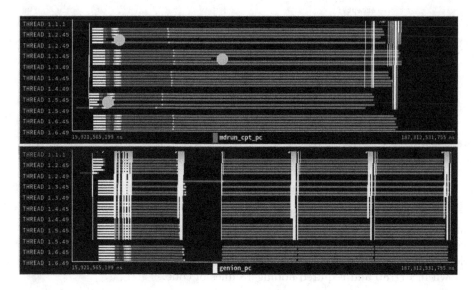

Fig. 9. Mutations workflow execution trace comparison. Each trace shows a timeline of task executions in the different computing resources. Horizontal color lines indicate the different tasks executions (Colors are the same as in Fig. 6b). Vertical yellow lines indicate transfers between computing nodes.

Besides the productivity aspects, the proposed contribution also has a performance impact. Figure 9 shows the execution traces of the protein mutants workflow evaluating 30 mutations, where three of them produce failures. One failure is due to an incorrect mutation, another is due to an incorrect GROMACS configuration, and the last one produces a long execution time in the simulation. The upper trace shows the execution with the proposed failure management implemented in COMPSs and the lower traces show the execution with the coding alternative as explained above. The light blue dots show the points in time where the failures have occurred and we can observe that the successors of these tasks have not been executed. Yellow lines in the traces show data transfers. We can see that the execution with the new approach performs better since it does not require synchronizations and requires less data transfers.

5.2   Machine Learning Algorithms

Another area of application of the new features presented in this paper has been the dislib library[4] [4], a distributed computing machine learning library

---

[4] https://dislib.bsc.es.

parallelized with PyCOMPSs. Some machine learning algorithms are iterative, where convergence is checked at every iteration step to decide whether the next iteration is necessary. Examples of this iterative behaviour are the K-means and Gaussian Mixture clustering algorithms, and Cascade Support Vector Machines (C-SVM) classification algorithm [9].

When implementing these algorithms in PyCOMPSs, it required a data synchronization in the main code to evaluate its convergence criterion and decide if a new iteration is required. Adding this data synchronization in the main loop implies a task barrier, where the main code waits for all tasks to finish. When running a single algorithm individually, this is not that critical, but when running several at the same time, this synchronization serializes all the executions. Cases where we would like to run multiple algorithms at a time occur in hyperparameter optimization algorithms, like Grid Search or Randomized Search.

In this paper, we have modified dislib's Cascade Support Vector Machine algorithm (C-SVM) in such a way that the evaluation of the convergence criterion is performed in a task. This task raises a *COMPSsException* whenever the convergence criterion is met. This has been combined with the Grid Search algorithm, that fits multiple models with multiple parameters. The objective is to be able to run the multiple models in parallel, which before was not possible due to the synchronization required to check the convergence criterion. Grid Search has been also modified to cancel non executed tasks when a *COMPSsException* is raised during the fitting process of one of the models.

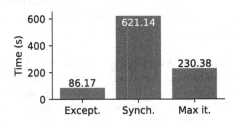

Fig. 10. Execution time of Grid Search with C-SVM using the exceptions mechanism (Except.), without the exceptions mechanism (Synch.), and without checking the convergence (Max it.).

Figure 10 shows the execution time of Grid Search in three scenarios. The first scenario (*Except.*) corresponds to using the exception mechanism presented in this paper to avoid synchronizations in the fitting of C-SVM. The second scenario (*Synch.*) corresponds to not using exceptions and synchronizing after every iteration. The third scenario (*Max it.*) corresponds to running C-SVM for a fixed number of iterations (10) instead of checking the convergence criteria. In all cases, the Grid Search algorithm fits 10 models in total.

We see that although the number of fitted models is low, Grid Search greatly benefits from avoiding convergence checks. Using the exception mechanism achieves 7x speedup over the scenario with synchronizations, and 2.7x speedup over running the models for a fixed number of iterations. In the first case, the improvement is because Grid Search can overlap the fitting of the different models. In the second case, the improvement is due to some models converging in less than 10 iterations. We expect this improvement in execution time to increase further if more than 10 models are trained simultaneously.

6   Conclusion

This paper presents a set of mechanisms to easily manage common application failures in task-based parallel workflows executed in distributed computing environments. We have proposed an extension to the task definition to enable developers to define how the runtime should react if a task of this type is failing or lasting a certain duration (timeout). We have also proposed different policies that are suitable for different types of failures and application patterns. Finally, we have also proposed mechanisms to support the exceptions management in parallel workflows where tasks are asynchronously executed in remote resources.

The proposed mechanisms have been validated with a bioinformatic workflow and a machine learning application where we have seen how the different policies are applied to real workflows and we have compared them with the alternative of coding these features inside the application code. We have observed that these features allow users to add failure management mechanisms without requiring to increase the amount of lines and complexity of the application codes. Moreover, as these mechanisms are automatically managed at runtime concurrently with the application execution, they avoid unnecessary synchronizations and transfers with their corresponding gain in performance.

Acknowledgments and Data Availability Statement. This work has been supported by the Spanish Government (contracts SEV2015-0493 and TIN2015-65316-P), by the Generalitat de Catalunya (contract 2014-SGR-1051), and by the European Commission's Horizon 2020 Framework program through BioExcel Center of Excellence (contracts 823830, and 675728). The research leading to these results has received funding from the collaboration between Fujitsu and BSC (Script Language Platform).

The datasets and code generated during and/or analysed during the current study are available in the Figshare repository: https://doi.org/10.6084/m9.figshare. 12556445 [7].

References

1. Afgan, E., et al.: The galaxy platform for accessible, reproducible and collaborative biomedical analyses: 2018 update. Nucleic Acids Res. **46**(1), 537–544 (2018). https://doi.org/10.1093/nar/gky379
2. Amela, R., Ramon-Cortes, C., Ejarque, J., Conejero, J., Badia, R.M.: Enabling Python to Execute Efficiently in Heterogeneous Distributed Infrastructures with PyCOMPSs. In: Proceedings of the 7th Workshop on Python for High-Performance and Scientific Computing, pp. 1–10. ACM, New York, NY, USA (2017). https://doi.org/10.1145/3149869.3149870

3. Badia, R.M., et al.: COMP superscalar, an interoperable programming framework. SoftwareX **3**, 32–36 (2015). https://doi.org/10.1016/j.softx.2015.10.004
4. Álvarez Cid-Fuentes, J., SolàÂ, S., Álvarez, P., Castro-Ginard, A., Badia, R.M.: dislib: Large scale high performance machine learning in python. In: Proceedings of the 15th International Conference on eScience, pp. 96–105 (2019). https://doi.org/10.1109/eScience.2019.00018
5. Deelman, E., et al.: Pegasus, a workflow management system for science automation. Fut. Gener. Comput. Syst. **46**, 17–35 (2015). https://doi.org/10.1016/j.future.2014.10.008
6. Di Tommaso, P., Chatzou, M., Floden, E.W., Barja, P.P., Palumbo, E., Notredame, C.: Nextflow enables reproducible computational workflows. Nat. Biotechnol. **35**(4), 316–319 (2017). https://doi.org/10.1038/nbt.3820
7. Ejarque, J., Bertran, M., Conejero, J., Badia, R.M., Alvarez Cid-Fuentes, J.: Artifact to reproduce the experiments of Europar 2020 Paper: Managing Failures in Task-based Parallel Workflows in Distributed Computing Environments (2020). https://doi.org/10.6084/m9.figshare.12556445, https://springernature.figshare.com/articles/software/Artifact_to_reproduce_the_experiments_of_Europar_2020_Paper_Managing_Failures_in_Task-based_Parallel_Workflows_in_Distributed_Computing_Environments_/12556445/1
8. Ejarque, J., Domínguez, M., Badia, R.M.: A hierarchic task-based programming model for distributed heterogeneous computing. Int. J. High Perform. Comput. Appl. **33**(5), 987–997 (2019). https://doi.org/10.1177/1094342019845438
9. Graf, H.P., Cosatto, E., Bottou, L., Durdanovic, I., Vapnik, V.: Parallel support vector machines: The cascade SVM. In: Proceedings of the 17th International Conference on Neural Information Processing Systems, pp. 521–528 (2004)
10. Lordan, F., et al.: ServiceSs: An interoperable programming framework for the cloud. J. Grid Comput. **12**(1), 67–91 (2013). https://doi.org/10.1007/s10723-013-9272-5
11. McCabe, T.J.: A complexity measure. IEEE Trans. Software Eng. **2**(4), 308–320 (1976). https://doi.org/10.1109/TSE.1976.233837
12. Mouallem, P., Crawl, D., Altintas, I., Vouk, M., Yildiz, U.: A fault-tolerance architecture for Kepler-based distributed scientific workflows. In: Gertz, M., Ludäscher, B. (eds.) SSDBM 2010. LNCS, vol. 6187, pp. 452–460. Springer, Heidelberg (2010). https://doi.org/10.1007/978-3-642-13818-8_31
13. Oliver, H.J.: Cylc (the cylc suite engine). Technical report (2016), http://cylc.github.io/cylc/
14. Pronk, S., et al.: Gromacs 4.5: A high-throughput and highly parallel open source molecular simulation toolkit. Bioinformatics **29**(7), 845–854 (2013). https://doi.org/10.1093/bioinformatics/btt055
15. Wolstencroft, K., et al.: The taverna workflow suite: Designing and executing workflows of web services on the desktop, web or in the cloud. Nucleic Acids Res. **41**(W1), W557–W561 (2013). https://doi.org/10.1093/nar/gkt328

Accelerating Nested Data Parallelism: Preserving Regularity

Lars B. van den Haak[1,2]([✉]) , Trevor L. McDonell[2] , Gabriele K. Keller[2] , and Ivo Gabe de Wolff[2]

[1] Eindhoven University of Technology, Eindhoven,
The Netherlands
l.b.v.d.haak@tue.nl
[2] Utrecht University, Utrecht, The Netherlands
{t.l.mcdonell,g.k.keller,i.g.dewolff}@uu.nl

Abstract. Irregular nested data-parallelism is a powerful programming model which enables the expression of a large class of parallel algorithms. However, it is notoriously difficult to compile such programs to efficient code for modern parallel architectures. Regular data-parallelism, on the other hand, is much easier to compile to efficient code, but too restricted to express some problems conveniently or in a manner to exploit the full parallelism. We extend the regular data-parallel programming model to allow for the parallel execution of array-level conditionals and iterations over irregular nested structures, and present two novel static analyses to optimise the code generated for these programs which reduces the costs of this more powerful irregular model. We present benchmarks to support our claim that these extensions are effective as well as feasible, as they enable to exploit the full parallelism of an important class of algorithms, and together with our optimisations lead to an improvement in absolute performance over an implementation limited to exploiting only regular parallelism.

Keywords: Arrays · GPGPU · Nested data parallelism · Parallel functional programming

1 Introduction

The collection-oriented approach to data-parallel programming, where computations are expressed in terms of higher-order functions—such as maps, folds, and scans—over (multi-dimensional) arrays provides a powerful and convenient programming model. By allowing programmers to identify the parallelism of an algorithm explicitly, yet in an abstract, architecture-independent way, languages such as Futhark [7,12–14], Manticore [9], Lift [23], and Accelerate [3,6,17,18] have demonstrated that it is possible to achieve performance comparable to hand-optimised, low-level code on a range of concrete hardware architectures, such as GPUs and multi-core CPUs.

© Springer Nature Switzerland AG 2020
M. Malawski and K. Rzadca (Eds.): Euro-Par 2020, LNCS 12247, pp. 426–442, 2020.
https://doi.org/10.1007/978-3-030-57675-2_27

These languages are typically restricted to *regular* data-parallelism: they support executing nested loops in parallel only if the inner loop bounds are independent of the indices of the outer loops, thereby limiting the kinds of parallel algorithms which can be conveniently expressed. While it is possible to transform any *irregular* data-parallel computation into one containing only regular data-parallelism [2], doing so efficiently in practice has still, in general, not been achieved. Instead, techniques to add limited support for irregular computations to regular data-parallel languages—without compromising performance—are used [6,7]. This work is a further step in this direction. We discuss our approach in the context of the language Accelerate [3], but it applies to any similarly structured language. The main contributions of the paper are:

1. An extension of the regular data-parallel programming model to allow for the parallel execution of array-level conditionals and iterations over irregular nested structures, enabling a larger class of problems using irregular nested parallelism to be executed efficiently (Sect. 3)
2. A shape analysis to detect at compile time when shapes of nested arrays are equal (Sect. 4)
3. A program analysis to identify the regular subcomputations of an irregular program (Sect. 4)
4. Benchmarks demonstrating the effect of the optimisations enabled by the shape equality and regularity detection analyses (Sect. 5)

We defer the discussion of related work to Sect. 6.

2 Background

In this section, we give an overview of Accelerate as a representative of the collection-oriented programming model. We discuss the difference between regular and irregular data parallelism, and why the expressiveness of the latter significantly complicates the mapping of the high-level operations to efficient code.

2.1 Accelerate's Programming Model

The collective operations with which we express parallel computations in Accelerate are based on the scan-vector model [4, 22], and consist of multi-dimensional array variants of familiar Haskell list operations such as map and fold, as well as array-specific operations such as index permutations. In this paper we use a slightly simplified syntax for Accelerate programs for the sake of readability: Accelerate is deeply embedded in Haskell, so the types of expressions are wrapped in a type constructor, which we omit here, as we do with class constraints. For example, to compute the dot product of two arrays, we write:

```
dotp :: Array DIM_{n+1} Float → Array DIM_{n+1} Float → Array DIM_n Float
dotp xs ys = fold (+) 0 (zipWith (*) xs ys)
```

Accelerate is rank-polymorphic, meaning that operations work on arrays of arbitrary rank, or dimensionality. The rank of an array is encoded in the type, denoted by a subscript in our example code. The function dotp consumes two multidimensional arrays of rank $n+1$ and produces an array of rank n as output, by folding along the innermost dimension. The type of fold is:

$$\text{fold} :: (a \rightarrow a \rightarrow a) \rightarrow a \rightarrow \text{Array DIM}_{n+1}\ a \rightarrow \text{Array DIM}_n\ a$$

There are two sources of parallelism here: the actual reduction can be done in parallel in $\log n$ steps using a tree fold, and for arrays of rank two and higher, we can do all the tree folds in parallel. In Accelerate, both sources of parallelism are exploited. This is a limited form of nested parallelism—regular nested parallelism—where the size of the inner parallel loop is the same for all iterations.

The generate operation is a parallel loop construct which takes as input a shape descriptor of type DIM_n specifying the extent of the resulting array, and a function that will be applied to each index of that shape to compute the value at that index. In the regular data-parallel model, the operation passed to generate is restricted to a sequential function returning a single scalar value:

$$\text{generate} :: \text{DIM}_n \rightarrow (\text{DIM}_n \rightarrow a) \rightarrow \text{Array DIM}_n\ a$$

All parallel operations so far have the property that the extent of the output array is independent of the values of the array elements. Unfortunately, there are useful operations for which this is not the case. For example, consider the function filter, which removes elements of an array which do not satisfy a given predicate. A rank-polymorphic filter, where the output array has the same nesting depth as the input array, requires that the shape of the innermost nesting level is ragged. We use the type IArray DIM_n DIM_m a for an array of nesting depth n+m, where the outermost n dimensions are guaranteed to be regular, and the inner m are potentially irregular. The type of the filter operation becomes:

$$\text{filter} :: (e \rightarrow \text{Bool}) \rightarrow \text{Array DIM}_{n+1}\ e \rightarrow \text{IArray DIM}_n\ \text{DIM}_1\ e$$

We also have segmented versions of parallel operations, which take irregular arrays as input. For example, the segmented fold calculates the sum of each of the innermost segments of an irregular array in parallel, and has the type:

$$\text{foldSeg} :: (a \rightarrow a \rightarrow a) \rightarrow a \rightarrow \text{IArray DIM}_n\ \text{DIM}_{m+1}\ a \rightarrow \text{IArray DIM}_n\ \text{DIM}_m\ a$$

Apart from collection-oriented operations, we have an array-level conditional operator cond c es_1 es_2, and an iteration construct while p_f b_f es, which iteratively applies the function b_f to initial array es as long p_f applied to the current iteration value is True. For example, assume bubble is a (potentially) parallel implementation of the inner loop of Bubblesort, and `notSorted` a function which check whether an array is sorted, then we can write:

```
bubbleSort :: Array DIM₁ Float → Array DIM₁ Float
bubbleSort xs = while notSorted bubble xs
```

In this example, the size of the resulting array is the same as the size of the input array, independent of the number of iterations, as `bubble` should not change the size of its input. In general, however, this is not the case. Similarly, the two branches of a conditional do not need to evaluate to arrays of the same shape.

We extend the regular data-parallel programming model by allowing both `cond` and `while` to occur inside of regular nested parallel loops. This generalisation introduces the possibility for this previously regular operation to introduce irregular nested parallelism, but affords the programmer more flexibility to express a larger range of applications. The techniques we present in this paper are aimed at minimising the costs of irregular parallelism arising from these constructs.

Continuing our previous example, if we want to apply the parallel bubble sort program in parallel to a collection of arrays, we can now write:

```
bubbleSortAll :: IArray DIMₙ DIM₁ Float → IArray DIMₙ DIM₁ Float
bubbleSortAll xss = generate (extent xss) (λi → bubbleSort (xss ! i))
```

where `extent` returns the outer regular shape of an array, which in this example is the number of inner arrays n. Since we know that `bubbleSort` leaves the size of its input unchanged, we also know that `bubbleSortAll` will return an array with the same shape as its input. In particular, if the input array happens to be regular, then the output array will also be regular. The aim of our shape analysis (Sect. 4.2) is exactly to check whether shapes stay the same. Our regularity detection (Sect. 4.3) can then use this information to find regular subcomputations.

3   Preserving Regularity

Flat arrays of primitive type are, for the majority of parallel architectures, the most efficient representations, and in case of GPUs, actually the only structure which is supported. Therefore, we need to represent the nested arrays of our source language by flat data arrays with the shape information stored separately.

For regular nested arrays of rank n, that is not a problem as they can be represented efficiently by storing the elements in a flat data vector in row-major order, and we can store the size of each dimension as an array of integer values of length n. For example, consider the two arrays `xss` and `yss` in Fig. 1. The former is regular, and the shape can be represented compactly, whereas we have to store the size of each segment for the latter, which can incur a significant memory overhead, especially if there are many small or even empty segments. Operations like indexing into the array are also more expensive for irregular representations. To index into the third subarray in Fig. 1, we have to calculate the sum of the sizes of all the preceding subarrays in the irregular case, whereas for the regular, calculating the offset is just a simple multiplication.

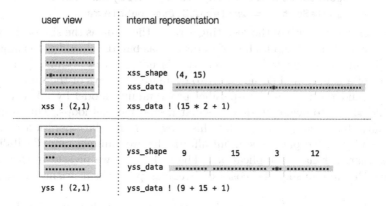

Fig. 1. Representation and indexing for regular and irregular arrays

Programs manipulating irregular arrays are therefore more expensive, both in terms of the additional memory required to store the size of each segment on every level, as well as the extra processing required to maintain and manipulate the segment descriptor. This is exactly why we want to use the regular array representation whenever possible.

3.1 Statically Determining Regularity

Clifton-Everest [6] added irregular arrays to Accelerate with support for a single level of nested parallelism. In that formulation, the regularity of an expression is evident from the type of the operators used; for example, the map operation preserves the regularity of its input and fold removes the innermost dimension while preserving the regularity of the outer $n - 1$ dimensions.

We extend that work by adding support for regularity preservation in the presence of nested *control-flow* operators, cond and while.

Let us go back to our bubbleSortAll example (see Fig. 2), and replace the function bubble with the function double, which returns an array twice the size of the input array. If we don't know how many iterations the while-loop performs on each subarray, we can't ensure that the resulting nested array is regular. However, if we know that the number of iterations depends only on the size of the input array, then we again know that regularity is preserved as the termination condition function returns the same value for each row of a regular array, even if we do not statically know its exact shape.

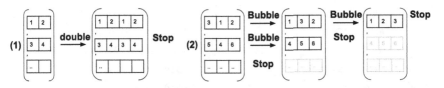

Fig. 2. The parallel `while` function preserves regularity if (1) the iteration is applied the same number of times to all subarrays or (2) the iteration function does not alter the shape of its input.

The parallel application of the `cond` operation preserves regularity, for example when either all conditionals take the same branch, or the subarrays of the true and false branch have the same shape. In the first case we will end up with one of the two regular branches, thus will stay regular. In the second case, subcomputations may take different branches, but the output shape has the same shape as the two branches and therefore remains regular.

Both parallel `while`-loops and conditionals occur in many applications, so it is worthwhile to detect the cases where their use preserves the regularity of their inputs, and use regular code and array representations in these cases. The next section formalises the analyses we use to detect patterns such as those mentioned above, where regularity is preserved.

4   Program Analyses

The goal of our two program analyses is to identify, at compile time, the regular (sub-)computations of the program, so that the more efficient regular dataparallel operations and array representation can be used for those computations. Our analysis consists of two parts: *regularity detection* generalises vectorisation avoidance [16] and identifies sub-expressions that are independent of their surrounding parallel context, using information from our *shape analysis* that determines equivalence of array shapes. We discuss these analyses in the following section in the context of a small nested data-parallel core language.

4.1   Core Language

Listing 1 gives the grammar of the core language which we use to describe our analyses. This language is a generalisation of the core language of Clifton-Everest [6], allowing for arbitrary nesting depth and with the addition of control flow constructs `cond` and `while`.

$$t ::= \text{Int} \mid \text{Bool} \mid (t, \dots, t)$$
$$\mid \text{Array DIM}_l \; t$$
$$l ::= 0 \mid 1 \mid \dots$$
$$b ::= \text{True} \mid \text{False}$$
$$c ::= l \mid b \mid [c, \dots]_{(l,\dots,l)}$$
$$p ::= (+) \mid (*) \mid (-) \mid \dots$$

$$e ::= v \mid c \mid e \, ! \, e \mid p \, e \, e \mid (e, \dots, e) \mid \pi_l(e)$$
$$\mid \text{let } v = e \text{ in } e \mid \text{extent } e$$
$$\mid \text{generate } e \; (\lambda v \to e)$$
$$\mid \text{fold } (\lambda v \; v \to e) \; e \; e$$
$$\mid \text{cond } e \; e \; e$$
$$\mid \text{while } (\lambda v \to e) \; (\lambda v \to e) \; e$$

Listing 1. Grammar of the nested data-parallel core language.

Expressions e consist of variables v; scalar and array constants c (subscript $(l,\dots,l)$ indicates the exact dimensions); array indexing !; application of primitive operators p; let-expressions; as well as tuples and projections from tuples π_l, where l is the index of an element in the tuple. The operator **extent** returns the outer regular shape of an array; **generate** constructs an array of the given regular shape by applying the function to every index of that shape in data-parallel; **fold** performs a parallel tree-reduction over the inner-most dimension of an array using the supplied binary function and initial element; **cond** and **while** are conditional and iteration constructs as described in Sect. 2.1. Irregular nested arrays are introduced as array constants, or constructed via **generate**, which—in contrast to Accelerate—does not limit the result type of the generator function to scalar values.

4.2 Shape Analysis

Before we formalise our shape analysis, first consider the following example, which illustrates a common pattern we wish to detect:

```
yss = generate (extent xss)
        (λsh → generate (extent (xss ! sh))
        (λsh' → (xss ! sh) ! sh'+1))
```

This term uses nested applications of **generate** to add one to every element of the array xss :: Array DIM$_N$ (Array DIM$_M$ Int). The goal of the analysis is to determine that the shape of xss and yss are, in fact, identical.

We use the shape analysis in Sect. 4.3 to identify regular subcomputations, but it can be used to enable other optimisations, such as preventing redundant recomputation of segment descriptors, array recycling, and identifying opportunities to use destructive updates.

Formalisation. Our shape analysis proceeds by first building an abstract shape descriptor for every array in the program, and then simplifying these descriptors so that they can be compared for equivalence. We write $ns_1 = ns_2$ to denote

$$\frac{v : (ns, i) \in \Sigma_j}{\Sigma_j \vdash v :_S ns} \ [\text{VAR}] \qquad \frac{\Sigma_j \vdash e :_S ns}{\Sigma_j \vdash e \,!\, e_{ix} :_S Inner \ ns \ \langle \Sigma; e_{ix} \rangle} \ [\text{INDEX}]$$

$$\frac{e \text{ has a scalar type}}{\Sigma_j \vdash e :_S \mathbb{S}} \ [\text{SCALAR}] \qquad \frac{\Sigma_j \vdash \overline{e} :_S \overline{ns}}{\Sigma_j \vdash (\,\overline{e}\,) :_S (\overline{ns})} \ [\text{TUPLE}]$$

$$\frac{\Sigma_j \vdash \overline{c} :_S ns}{\Sigma_j \vdash [\,\overline{c}\,]_{\overline{l}} :_S \langle \Sigma_j; (\,\overline{l}\,) \rangle \,\triangleright\, ns} \ [\text{CONST-SHAPE}] \qquad \frac{\Sigma_j \vdash e :_S ns}{\Sigma_j \vdash \pi_l(e) :_S \pi_l(ns)} \ [\text{PROJECT}]$$

$$\frac{\Sigma_j \vdash e_1 :_S ns_1 \quad \Sigma_j, v : (ns_1, \emptyset) \vdash e_2 :_S ns_2}{\Sigma_j \vdash \texttt{let } v = e_1 \texttt{ in } e_2 :_S ns_2} \ [\text{LET}]$$

$$\frac{\Sigma_{j+1}, v : (\mathbb{S}, j) \vdash e_2 :_S ns}{\Sigma_j \vdash \texttt{generate } e_1 \ (\lambda v \to e_2) :_S \langle \Sigma_j; e_1 \rangle \,\triangleright\, ns} \ [\text{GENERATE}]$$

$$\frac{\Sigma_j \vdash e_3 :_S ns \quad ns' = Folded \ (Outer \ ns) \,\triangleright\, \mathbb{S}}{\Sigma_j \vdash \texttt{fold } (\lambda \ v_0 \ v_1 \to e_1) \ e_2 \ e_3 :_S ns'} \ [\text{FOLD}]$$

$$\frac{\Sigma_j \vdash e_2 :_S ns_2 \quad \Sigma_j \vdash e_3 :_S ns_3 \quad ns_2 = ns_3}{\Sigma_j \vdash \texttt{cond } e_1 \ e_2 \ e_3 :_S ns_2} \ [\text{COND-SHAPE}]$$

$$\frac{\Sigma_j \vdash e_3 :_S ns_3 \quad \Sigma_j, v : (ns_3, \emptyset) \vdash e_2 :_S ns_2 \quad ns_2 = ns_3}{\Sigma_j \vdash \texttt{while } (\lambda \ v. \ e_1) \ (\lambda \ v. \ e_2) \ e_3 :_S ns_3} \ [\text{WHILE-SHAPE}]$$

$$\frac{l \text{ is a fresh label}}{\Sigma_j \vdash e :_S u_l} \ [\text{FALLBACK}]$$

Listing 2. Inference rules of shape analysis.

the shape equivalence. Note that this comparison is not exact; since we do not have all information available to us at compile time, the equivalence test is necessarily conservative: if two shape descriptors are found to be equal, their associated arrays will definitely have the same shape at runtime, but the reverse is not necessarily true.

Our shape descriptors are constructed using the following grammar:

$$s ::= \langle \Sigma_j; e \rangle \mid Folded \ s \mid Outer \ ns$$
$$ns ::= \mathbb{S} \mid s \triangleright ns \mid (ns, \dots, ns) \mid \pi_l(ns) \mid Inner \ ns \ \langle \Sigma_j; e \rangle \mid u_l$$

A shape s is either an expression e of type $\texttt{DIM}_N$, which may contain free variables bound in environment Σ_j; $Folded \ s$, which drops the innermost dimension of s; or $Outer \ ns$, the outermost shape of the nested shape ns. Nested shapes ns are $\mathbb{S}$-terminated lists of s; tuples of nested shapes; the result of projections; or the result of indexing into a shape list with an expression e of type $\texttt{Int}$, thus taking the $Inner$ shape. Complex (irregular) shapes or shapes for which we don't have any static information are represented by a unique label u_l.

The judgement $\Sigma_j \vdash e :_S ns$ denotes the derivation of shape descriptor ns for the expression e under environment Σ_j according to the rules in Listing 2. The environment maps every variable v to its shape descriptor (ns) and nesting level (i) of the `generate` whose function bound v. Variables not introduced via a `generate` function—that is, are not a potential source of nested parallelism—have nesting level $\emptyset$. The environment is annotated with an index j, denoting the number of `generate` calls we entered. This index is used as the nesting level of the variable introduced by the next `generate` combinator and we thus increment the index when entering its body.

Returning to our initial example, assuming environment $\Sigma = [\text{xss} : (u_0, \emptyset)]$ containing only the array `xss`, about which we have no static information, we can then deduce:

$$\Sigma_0 \vdash \text{xss} :_S u_0$$
$$\Sigma_0 \vdash \text{yss} :_S (\langle \Sigma_0; \text{extent xss}\rangle \triangleright \langle \Sigma_1, sh : (\mathbb{S}, 0); \text{extent (xss!sh)}\rangle) \triangleright \mathbb{S}$$

where we apply the [GENERATE] rule twice and subsequently the [SCALAR] rule.

Although the two shape descriptors for `xss` and `yss` are equivalent, they are not syntactically equal. We thus introduce shape equivalence, denoted by $ns_1 \asymp ns_2$, which compares shape descriptors after partially evaluating the shape descriptors, for example by applying projections to tuples. Furthermore we simplify certain patterns which we found to occur frequently. Note that other domain-specific simplification rules may also be possible. The following steps can always be applied to a single shape descriptor:

S1. $\langle \Sigma_j; \text{extent e}\rangle$: we apply shape analysis on e, $\Sigma_j \vdash e :_S ns$, and take the outer shape as a result, $Outer\ ns$. This is exactly the semantics of `extent`.
S2. $Outer\ ns \triangleright \mathbb{S}$: if ns is not nested, which can be determined from type information, it simplifies to ns.
S3. $Outer\ (s \triangleright ns)$ simplifies to s.
S4. $Outer\ ns_1 \triangleright Inner\ ns_2\ \langle \Sigma_j; v\rangle$: this pattern arises from nested `generate`s, e.g. `generate (extent xss) (`λ`v` $\rightarrow$ `generate (xss ! v) e)`. If $ns_1 \asymp ns_2$ and v's nesting level matches the nesting depth of the shape, the shape descriptor simplifies to ns_1. The nesting depth of the shape denotes how many $\triangleright$ are in front of the shape in the $\triangleright$-separated list. For instance, in $s' \triangleright s \triangleright ns$, the whole shape has a nesting depth of 0, $s \triangleright ns$ has depth 1, and ns has 2.

After the simplification, when two shapes are compared, we check on syntactical equivalence. However, when comparing shape expressions we have a few more equivalence rules:

E1. $\langle \Sigma; e\rangle$: any variables inside `e` that were introduced by a `generate` only have to match by their nesting level. This is stored in the shape environment Σ_j.
E2. $\langle \Sigma_j; e\rangle$: when we encounter `extent` e_1 (as a subexpression) in `e`, we apply shape analysis on e_1.

Using these simplification rules, the shape descriptor `yss` can be rewritten to be equal to the shape descriptor of `xss` in the following steps:

$$= Outer\ u_0 \triangleright Outer\ (Inner\ u_0\ \langle \Sigma, sh : (\mathbb{S}, 0); sh\rangle) \triangleright \mathbb{S} \qquad \text{(S1, S1)}$$
$$= Outer\ u_0 \triangleright Inner\ u_0\ \langle \Sigma, sh : (\mathbb{S}, 0); sh\rangle \qquad \text{(S2)}$$
$$= u_0 \qquad \text{(S4)}$$

The shape analysis can be parameterised by which simplification rules to apply; it depends on the application context of the shape analysis which rules are worthwhile. One additional rule which we do use is inlining of all let-bound variables in expressions, for which we have another environment containing the definitions for all variables which are in scope.

4.3   Regularity Detection

Regularity detection identifies (sub-)expressions which are either constant or produce regular parallelism with respect to the surrounding parallel context. For example, if we map the function $\lambda x \rightarrow x+(6*7)$ over an array in parallel, then the value of x depends on the parallel context, but the expression $6*7$ is constant with respect to that context.

Keller [16] provide an algorithm to identify these subexpressions in the presence of arbitrarily nested contexts, however that work does not take regularity information into account, and therefore misses important optimisation opportunities. Take for example the term $\lambda sh \rightarrow$ extent (xss ! sh); if xss is a regular nested structure this function returns the same result for all values sh, so the term as a whole is constant even though it depends on the parallel context. In the remainder of the section we formalise our generalisation of the vectorisation avoidance [16] algorithm to take this information into account.

Formalisation. Listing 3a presents the grammar for the analysis, where regularity information is stored as a triple d, with i denoting whether the full term is totally independent ($\top$) or not ($\bot$); n records for each nesting level whether it is regular (R) or irregular (Ir); and k tracks the nesting level of the variables introduced by generate (only generate can introduce nested computations which are dependent on the parallel context). Merging of regularity information is done via the operator $\wedge$ given in Listing 3c. The analysis uses the results of shape analysis and thus passes around a shape environment Σ_j besides the regularity environment Γ, mapping variables to their regularity. The judgement $\Gamma; \Sigma_j \vdash e :_R d$ denotes that expression e has regularity d under environments Σ_j and Γ. We present the rules of regularity detection in Listings 4 and 5, where we use $\Gamma; \Sigma_j \vdash e : (d, ns)$ to denote the results of both analyses:

$$\frac{\Gamma; \Sigma_j \vdash e :_R d \quad \Sigma_j \vdash e :_S ns}{\Gamma; \Sigma_j \vdash e : (d, ns)} \tag{1}$$

The rules for cond and while must check whether the shapes are respectively fixed (rules [...-SHAPE]), independent ([...-INDEP]), or whether we must assume that they may be irregular ([...-IRR]). Rule [EXTENT-REGULAR] checks whether the argument array is regular, in which case it always returns the same extent and is therefore independent. We have three rules for generate, rule [GENERATE-1] checks whether the nesting level k of the function is greater than or equal to the current level; if so the function is independent of any outer generate operations. Rule [GENERATE-2] checks whether the outer shape of the generate is

$$T \wedge T \qquad = T$$
$$\_ \wedge \_ \qquad = \bot$$
$$r_1 \rhd n_1 \wedge r_2 \rhd n_2 \qquad = r_1 \wedge r_2 \rhd n_1 \wedge n_2$$
$$\mathbb{S} \wedge n \qquad = n$$
$$n \wedge \mathbb{S} \qquad = n$$
$$R \wedge R \qquad = R$$

$d ::= \langle n, i, k \rangle \mid (d, \ldots, d)$

$n ::= \mathbb{S} \mid r \rhd n$

$r ::= R \mid Ir$

$i ::= T \mid \bot$

$k ::= \infty \mid l$

(a) Grammar

$$\_ \wedge \_ \qquad = Ir$$
$$\langle n_1, i_1, l_1 \rangle \wedge \langle n_2, i_2, l_2 \rangle = \langle n_1 \wedge n_2, i_1 \wedge i_2,$$
$$\min(l_1, l_2) \rangle$$

$ir(\langle n, i, l \rangle) = \langle ir_n(n), i, k \rangle$

$ir(d_1, \ldots, d_n) = (ir(d_1), \ldots, ir(d_n))$ $(d_1, \ldots, d_n) \wedge (d'_1, \ldots, d'_n) = (d_1 \wedge d'_1, \ldots, d_n \wedge d'_n)$

$ir_n(\_ \rhd n) = Ir \rhd ir_n(n)$ $(d_1, \ldots, d_n) \wedge d \qquad = (d_1 \wedge d, \ldots, d_n \wedge d)$

$ir_n(\mathbb{S}) = \mathbb{S}$ $d \wedge (d_1, \ldots, d_n) \qquad = (d_1 \wedge d, \ldots, d_n \wedge d)$

(b) The ir helper function   **(c)** Lattice definitions

Listing 3. The annotation used for regularity detection.

independent, meaning the operation as a whole is regular, and [GENERATE-3] is the fallback case.

We want to conclude with a more interesting example, we modified our previous example from Sect. 4.2 to contain a conditional.

```
yss = generate (extent xss)
        (λsh → let c = ((xss ! sh) ! 0)>10 in
          let t = xss ! sh in
          let e = generate (extent (xss ! sh))
                     (λsh' → (xss ! sh) ! sh'+1)
          in cond c t e)
```

The shape analysis can detect that yss has the same shape as xss, but it will also show that t and e have the same shape. Suppose we know that xss is a regular nested array. We show that the regularity detection detects that the sub-computations stay regular. Formally, we now have the environment $\Gamma; \Sigma = [\text{xss} : \langle R \rhd R \rhd \mathbb{S}, T, \infty \rangle, \text{sh} : \langle \mathbb{S}, \bot, 0 \rangle]; [\text{xss} : (u_0, \emptyset), \text{sh} : (\mathbb{S}, 0)]$, where we added the variable sh introduced by the outer generate. Let us inspect the result of c, t and e, which we need for cond c t e.

$$\Gamma; \Sigma_1 \vdash c :_R \langle \mathbb{S}, \bot, 0 \rangle$$
$$\Gamma, c : \ldots; \Sigma_1, c : \ldots \vdash t :_R \langle R \rhd \mathbb{S}, \bot, 0 \rangle$$
$$\Gamma, c : \ldots, t : \ldots; \Sigma_1, c : \ldots, t : \ldots \vdash e :_R \langle R \rhd \mathbb{S}, \bot, 0 \rangle$$

$$\frac{}{\Gamma; \Sigma_j \vdash l :_R \langle \mathbb{S}, \top, \infty \rangle} \text{ [LITERAL]}$$

$$\frac{\Gamma; \Sigma_j \vdash e :_R (d_1, \ldots, d_l, \ldots, d_n)}{\Gamma; \Sigma_j \vdash \pi_l(e) :_R d_l} \text{ [PROJECT]}$$

$$\frac{}{\Gamma; \Sigma_j \vdash b :_R \langle \mathbb{S}, \top, \infty \rangle} \text{ [BOOL]}$$

$$\frac{}{\Gamma; \Sigma_j \vdash e :_R \langle \_ \triangleright n, i, k \rangle}$$

$$\frac{\Gamma; \Sigma_j \vdash \overline{e} :_R \overline{d}}{\Gamma; \Sigma_j \vdash (\,\overline{e}\,) :_R (\,\overline{d}\,)} \text{ [TUPLE]}$$

$$\frac{\Gamma; \Sigma_j \vdash e_{ix} :_R d}{\Gamma; \Sigma_j \vdash e \,!\, e_{ix} :_R \langle n, i, k \rangle \wedge d} \text{ [INDEX]}$$

$$\frac{\Gamma; \Sigma_j \vdash e_1 : (d_1, ns_1) \qquad \Gamma, v : d_1; \Sigma_j, v : (ns_1, \emptyset) \vdash e_2 :_R d_2}{\Gamma; \Sigma_j \vdash \text{let } v = e_1 \text{ in } e_2 :_R d_2} \text{ [LET]}$$

$$\frac{\Gamma; \Sigma_j \vdash e_1 :_R d_1 \quad \Gamma; \Sigma_j \vdash e_2 :_R d_2}{\Gamma; \Sigma_j \vdash p \, e_1 \, e_2 :_R d_1 \wedge d_2} \text{ [OP]}$$

$$\frac{v : d \in \Gamma}{\Gamma; \Sigma_j \vdash v :_R d} \text{ [VAR]}$$

$$\frac{\Gamma; \Sigma_j \vdash \overline{c} : (\langle n, \top, \infty \rangle, ns)}{\Gamma; \Sigma_j \vdash [\,\overline{c}\,]_{\overline{l}} :_R \langle R \triangleright n, \top, \infty \rangle} \text{ [CONST-REGULAR]}$$

$$\frac{\Gamma; \Sigma_j \vdash \overline{c} :_R \overline{d} \quad \langle n, \top, \infty \rangle = \bigwedge \overline{d}}{\Gamma; \Sigma_j \vdash [\,\overline{c}\,]_{\overline{l}} :_R \langle R \triangleright ir(n), \top, \infty \rangle} \text{ [CONST-IRR]}$$

$$\frac{\Gamma; \Sigma_j \vdash e :_R \langle R \triangleright \_, \_, \_ \rangle}{\Gamma; \Sigma_j \vdash \text{extent } e :_R \langle \mathbb{S}, \top, \infty \rangle} \text{ [EXTENT-REGULAR]}$$

$$\frac{\Gamma; \Sigma_j \vdash e :_R \langle Ir \triangleright \_, i, k \rangle}{\Gamma; \Sigma_j \vdash \text{extent } e :_R \langle \mathbb{S}, i, k \rangle} \text{ [EXTENT-IRR]}$$

$$\frac{\Gamma; \Sigma_j \vdash e_1 :_R d_1 \quad \Gamma; \Sigma_j \vdash e_2 : (d_2, ns_2)}{ns_2 = ns_3 \qquad \Gamma; \Sigma_j \vdash e_3 : (d_3, ns_3)}{\Gamma; \Sigma_j \vdash \text{cond } e_1 \, e_2 \, e_3 :_R d_1 \wedge d_2 \wedge d_3} \text{ [COND-SHAPE]}$$

$$\frac{\Gamma; \Sigma_j \vdash e_1 :_R \langle \mathbb{S}, \top, k \rangle \quad \Gamma; \Sigma_j \vdash e_2 :_R d_2}{d = d_2 \wedge d_3 \qquad \Gamma; \Sigma_j \vdash e_3 :_R d_3}{\Gamma; \Sigma_j \vdash \text{cond } e_1 \, e_2 \, e_3 :_R \langle \mathbb{S}, \top, k \rangle \wedge d} \text{ [COND-INDEP]}$$

$$\frac{\Gamma; \Sigma_j \vdash e_1 :_R d_1}{\Gamma; \Sigma_j \vdash e_2 :_R d_2 \quad \Gamma; \Sigma_j \vdash e_3 :_R d_3}{\Gamma; \Sigma_j \vdash \text{cond } e_1 \, e_2 \, e_3 :_R d_1 \wedge ir(d_2 \wedge d_3)} \text{ [COND-IRR]}$$

$$\frac{\Gamma; \Sigma_j \vdash e_3 : (d_3, ns_3) \quad \Gamma, v : d_3; \Sigma_j, v : (ns_3, \emptyset) \vdash e_2 : (d_2, ns_2)}{ns_2 = ns_3 \qquad \Gamma, v : (d_2 \wedge d_3); \Sigma_j, v : (ns_3, \emptyset) \vdash e_1 :_R d_1}{\Gamma; \Sigma_j \vdash \text{while } (\lambda \, v. \, e_1) \, (\lambda \, v. \, e_2) \, e_3 :_R d_1 \wedge d_2 \wedge d_3} \text{ [WHILE-SHAPE]}$$

$$\frac{\Gamma, v : d_3; \Sigma_j, v : (ns_3, \emptyset) \vdash e_2 : (d_2, ns_2) \qquad \Gamma; \Sigma_j \vdash e_3 : (d_3, ns_3)}{\Gamma, v : (d_2 \wedge d_3); \Sigma_j, v : (ns_2, \emptyset) \vdash e_1 :_R \langle \mathbb{S}, \top, k \rangle}{\Gamma; \Sigma_j \vdash \text{while } (\lambda \, v. \, e_1) \, (\lambda \, v. \, e_2) \, e_3 :_R \langle \mathbb{S}, \top, k \rangle \wedge d_2 \wedge d_3} \text{ [WHILE-INDEP]}$$

$$\frac{\Gamma, v : d_3; \Sigma_j, v : (ns_3, \emptyset) \vdash e_2 : (d_2, ns_2) \qquad \Gamma; \Sigma_j \vdash e_3 : (d_3, ns_3)}{\Gamma, v : (d_2 \wedge d_3); \Sigma_j, v : (ns_3, \emptyset) \vdash e_1 :_R d_1}{\Gamma; \Sigma_j \vdash \text{while } (\lambda \, v. \, e_1) \, (\lambda \, v. \, e_2) \, e_3 :_R d_1 \wedge ir(d_2 \wedge d_3)} \text{ [WHILE-IRR]}$$

Listing 4. First set of inference rules for regularity detection. (1/2)

The results of c and t are a simple application of a combination of the [INDEX], [OP], [VAR] and [LITERAL] rules and you can view them as a scalar and a regular array respectively. Both are also dependent ($\bot$) on the outer generate (0). The

$$\Gamma; \Sigma_j \vdash e_1 :_R \langle \_, \top, k_1 \rangle$$

$$\frac{\Gamma, v : \langle \mathbb{S}, \perp, j \rangle; \Sigma_{j+1}, v : (\mathbb{S}, j) \vdash e_2 :_R \langle n, \_, k_2 \rangle \quad k_2 \geqslant j}{\Gamma; \Sigma_j \vdash \text{generate } e_1 \ (\lambda v \to e_2) :_R \langle R \rhd n, \top, \min(k_1, k_2) \rangle} \ [\text{Generate-1}]$$

$$\frac{\Gamma; \Sigma_j \vdash e_1 :_R \langle \_, \top, k_1 \rangle \quad \Gamma, v : \langle \mathbb{S}, \perp, j \rangle; \Sigma_{j+1}, v : (\mathbb{S}, j) \vdash e_2 :_R \langle n, i, k_2 \rangle}{\Gamma; \Sigma_j \vdash \text{generate } e_1 \ (\lambda v \to e_2) :_R \langle R \rhd n, i, \min(k_1, k_2) \rangle} \ [\text{Generate-2}]$$

$$\frac{\Gamma; \Sigma_j \vdash e_1 :_R \langle \_, \perp, k_1 \rangle \quad \Gamma, v : \langle \mathbb{S}, \perp, j \rangle; \Sigma_{j+1}, v : (\mathbb{S}, j) \vdash e_2 :_R \langle n, \_, k_2 \rangle}{\Gamma; \Sigma_j \vdash \text{generate } e_1 \ (\lambda v \to e_2) :_R \langle Ir \rhd n, \perp, \min(k_1, k_2) \rangle} \ [\text{Generate-3}]$$

$$\Gamma; \Sigma_j \vdash e_2 :_R d_2 \quad \Gamma; \Sigma_j \vdash e_3 :_R d_3$$

$$\frac{d = d_2 \wedge d_3 \quad \Gamma, v_0 : d, v_1 : d; \Sigma_j, v_0 : (\mathbb{S}, \emptyset), v_1 : (\mathbb{S}, \emptyset) \vdash e_1 :_R d_1}{\Gamma; \Sigma_j \vdash \text{fold } (\lambda \ v_0 \ v_1 \to e_1) \ e_2 \ e_3 :_R d_1 \wedge d_3} \ [\text{Fold}]$$

Listing 5. Second set of inference rules for regularity detection. (2/2)

result of e is the same as t, but the [Extent-Regular] [Generate-2] rules are used.

With the above results and the fact that t and e have the same shape, we use the [Cond-Shape] rule to get:

$$\Gamma, ...; \Sigma_1, ... \vdash \text{cond c t e} :_R \langle R \rhd \mathbb{S}, \perp, 0 \rangle$$

Thus the body of the generate has sub-computations that are dependent, but regular. Finally, using [Generate-1] on the outer generate, gets us that yss is a nested regular array that is independent of any other parallel context.

5   Evaluation

The objective of this work is to extend the data-parallel programming model to efficiently execute array-level conditionals and iterations over irregularly nested structures. In this section we evaluate the effectiveness of our work through a number of benchmarks. Our benchmarks are conducted using a GeForce RTX 2080 Ti (compute capability 7.0, 68 multiprocessors = 4352 cores at 1.65 GHz, 11 GB GDDR6) backed by a 16-core Threadripper 2950X (1.9 GHz, 64 GB RAM, hyperthreading is enabled) running GNU/Linux (Ubuntu 19.10). We used GHC-8.6.3, LLVM-9, and CUDA-10.1.

Our implementation in the deeply embedded language Accelerate means that the analyses presented here, as well as all other compiler stages such as optimisation and code generation, occur during the runtime of the host language program. In order to focus on the effectiveness of the optimisations presented in this paper, which are generally applicable and not related to our specific implementation, we report total kernel execution time on the GPU including memory transfer overhead rather than overall application runtime.

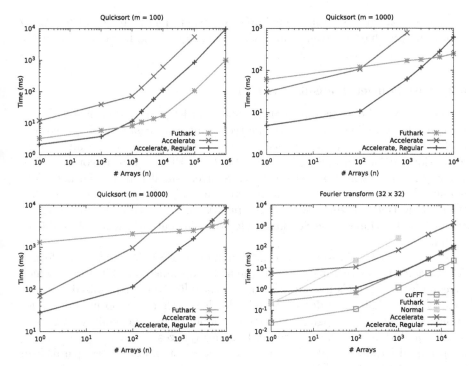

Fig. 3. Weak scaling of benchmark programs. The results of this work are shown in purple (Accelerate, Regular), compared to unoptimised Accelerate programs in green (Accelerate). (Color figure online)

5.1 Quicksort

To evaluate the overhead of irregularity we use a loop-based implementation of the Quicksort [15] algorithm,[1] which is representative of irregular divide-and-conquer algorithms that require both the intra- and inter-routine parallelism to achieve optimal parallel work complexity. This benchmark is chosen because it has minimal computation: the runtime of the algorithm is entirely dominated by data movement, so the cost of managing segment descriptors for irregular arrays cannot be hidden.

The benchmark sorts each row of an $n \times m$ matrix in parallel, so each row of the matrix iterates a different number of times over its subarray. Our analysis detects that the iteration leaves the shapes of the subarrays unchanged so can be optimised as regular nested parallelism. The results are shown in Fig. 3, showing that our optimised version is 6 to 13 times faster than the unoptimised Accelerate program.

Futhark uses a different method to support nested parallelism [14]. For small arrays the GPU is not fully utilised, but for larger arrays their approach has

---

[1] https://github.com/AccelerateHS/accelerate-examples/tree/master/examples/quicksort.

lower overhead and overtakes our implementation. The incremental flattening approach of Futhark is orthogonal to this work, so it would be possible to utilise both approaches simultaneously.

5.2 Fast Fourier Transform (FFT)

We benchmark three versions of the Split-Radix FFT algorithm in Accelerate: *normal*, where we do not exploit the nested parallelism; *regular* with nested parallelism and optimisations switched on; and *irregular*, a nested parallel implementation without optimisation. The Split-Radix FFT algorithm consists of an outer while loop which operates over successively smaller arrays. Futhark does not support irregular nested parallelism and their algorithm can not detect that the computation is regular, so their compiler is unable to compile this program. We instead benchmark the Stockham algorithm in Futhark, which it is able to compile.

Figure 3 shows the results of execution a number of 32×32 Fourier transforms. As a baseline we also compare against the highly optimised cuFFT library, which we call via Accelerate's foreign function interface [5]. The unoptimised *irregular* code is more than an order of magnitude slower than our optimised *regular* implementation. The program *normal* is unable to execute multiple FFTs in parallel and thus performs poorly at large array sizes—even compared to the unoptimised *irregular* implementation—as it does not expose enough parallelism to properly utilise the GPU.

6 Related Work

Languages like NESL [2] and Data Parallel Haskell [19] support fully irregular nested data parallelism, but they struggle to achieve good performance. Nessie [21] is ongoing work on a NESL compiler which targets GPUs. Manticore [9] also supports irregular nested data parallel computations on CPU multicores by flattening the data structures [1], but not the parallel computations.

To control excessive parallelism due to regular nested parallelism, *incremental flattening* [14] executes the inner parallelism sequentially of a nested computation in some circumstances, which allows for better use of shared memory in GPUs. More recently Futhark added more support for a certain kind of irregular nested parallelism [7], but this has not been integrated into the backend yet [8]. Futhark also performs shape analysis [12] to symbolically determine the exact shape of arrays if possible but switches to dynamic handling if necessary. Our analysis aims to compare shapes, not determine them exactly, so it can be done completely statically. We can capture some irregular structures of arrays, whereas Futhark only works with regular structures.

Other data parallel languages, like Halide [20], Obsidian [24], Lift [23] and SaC [10] all aim at producing high performing code for CPUs and/or GPUs. We believe they could benefit from the work presented here, in the implementation of irregular nested data parallelism or to allow more programs which expose regular subcomputations.

7 Conclusion

We presented two analyses for irregular nested parallel array languages, and demonstrated how this analyses can be used to identify and specialise code for regular sub-computations within nested irregular computations. We extended the Accelerate language with two constructs to enable expressing a limited form of irregular nested parallelism, together with our regularity optimisations, and provide benchmarks demonstrating the effect of these optimisations. Our work is open source and available at https://github.com/sakehl/accelerate/tree/feature/sequences.

Acknowledgements and Data Availability Statement. We would like to thank the reviewers for their detailed feedback and suggestions also with respect to possible future work directions, and Manuel Chakravarty for his comments on an earlier version of this paper.

The datasets and code generated during and/or analysed during the current study are available in the Figshare repository: https://doi.org/10.6084/m9.figshare.12555 275 [11].

References

1. Bergstrom, L., Fluet, M., Rainey, M., Reppy, J., Rosen, S., Shaw, A.: Data-only flattening for nested data parallelism. In: Principles and Practice of Parallel Programming (2013)
2. Blelloch, G.E., Sabot, G.W.: Compiling collection-oriented languages onto massively parallel computers. Parallel Distrib. Comput. **8**(2), 119–134 (1990)
3. Chakravarty, M.M.T., Keller, G., Lee, S., McDonell, T.L., Grover, V.: Accelerating haskell array codes with multicore GPUs. In: Declarative Aspects of Multicore Programming (2011)
4. Chatterjee, S., Blelloch, G.E., Zagha, M.: Scan primitives for vector computers. In: Supercomputing (1990)
5. Clifton-Everest, R., McDonell, T.L., Chakravarty, M.M.T., Keller, G.: Embedding foreign code. In: Practical Aspects of Declarative Languages (2014)
6. Clifton-Everest, R., McDonell, T.L., Chakravarty, M.M.T., Keller, G.: Streaming irregular arrays. In: Haskell (2017)
7. Elsman, M., Henriksen, T., Serup, N.G.W.: Data-parallel flattening by expansion. In: Libraries, Languages and Compilers for Array Programming (2019)
8. Elsman, M., Larsen, K.F.: Efficient translation of certain irregular data-parallel array comprehensions. In: Trends in Functional Programming (2020)
9. Fluet, M., Rainey, M., Reppy, J., Shaw, A., Xiao, Y.: Manticore: a heterogeneous parallel language. In: Declarative Aspects of Multicore Programming (2007)
10. Grelck, C.: Single assignment C (SAC): high productivity meets high performance. In: Central European Functional Programming School (2012)
11. van den Haak, L., McDonell, T., Keller, G., de Wolff, I.G.: Artifact for Euro-Par 2020 paper Accelerating Nested Data Parallelism: Preserving Regularity (July 2020). https://doi.org/10.6084/m9.figshare.12555275. https://springernature.figsh are.com/articles/software/Artifact_for_Euro-Par_2020_paper_Accelerating_Nested_Data_Parallelism_Preserving_Regularity/12555275/1

12. Henriksen, T., Elsman, M., Oancea, C.E.: Size slicing: a hybrid approach to size inference in futhark. In: Functional High-Performance Computing (2014)
13. Henriksen, T., Serup, N.G.W., Elsman, M., Henglein, F., Oancea, C.E.: Futhark: purely functional GPU-programming with nested parallelism and in-place array updates. In: Programming Language Design and Implementation (2017)
14. Henriksen, T., Thorøe, F., Elsman, M., Oancea, C.: Incremental flattening for nested data parallelism. In: Principles and Practice of Parallel Programming (2019)
15. Hoare, C.A.: Quicksort. Comput. J. **5**(1), 10–16 (1962)
16. Keller, G., Chakravarty, M.M.T., Leshchinskiy, R., Lippmeier, B., Peyton Jones, S.: Vectorisation avoidance. In: Haskell (2012)
17. McDonell, T.L., Chakravarty, M.M.T., Grover, V., Newton, R.R.: Type-safe runtime code generation: accelerate to LLVM. In: Haskell (2015)
18. McDonell, T.L., Chakravarty, M.M.T., Keller, G., Lippmeier, B.: Optimising purely functional GPU programs. In: International Conference on Functional Programming (2013)
19. Peyton Jones, S., Leshchinskiy, R., Keller, G., Chakravarty, M.M.T.: Harnessing the multicores: nested data parallelism in Haskell. In: Foundations of Software Technology and Theoretical Computer Science (2008)
20. Ragan-Kelley, J., Barnes, C., Adams, A., Paris, S., Durand, F., Amarasinghe, S.: Halide: a language and compiler for optizing parallelism, locality, and recomputation in image processing pipelines. In: Programming Language Design and Implementation (2013)
21. Reppy, J., Sandler, N.: Nessie: a NESL to CUDA compiler. In: Compilers for Parallel Computing (2015)
22. Sengupta, S., Harris, M., Zhang, Y., Owens, J.D.: Scan primitives for GPU computing. In: Graphics Hardware (2007)
23. Steuwer, M., Remmelg, T., Dubach, C.: Lift: a functional data-parallel IR for high-performance GPU code generation. In: Code Generation and Optimization (2017)
24. Svensson, B.J., Sheeran, M., Claessen, K.: Obsidian: a domain specific embedded language for parallel programming of graphics processors. In: Implementation and Application of Functional Languages, pp. 156–173 (January 2008)

Using Dynamic Broadcasts to Improve Task-Based Runtime Performances

Alexandre Denis[1,2], Emmanuel Jeannot[1,2], Philippe Swartvagher[1,2(✉)],
and Samuel Thibault[1,2]

[1] Inria Bordeaux – Sud-Ouest, 33405 Talence, France
{alexandre.denis,emmanuel.jeannot,philippe.swartvagher}@inria.fr
[2] Labri, University of Bordeaux, 33405 Talence, France
samuel.thibault@labri.fr

Abstract. Task-based runtimes have emerged in the HPC world to take benefit from the computation power of heterogeneous supercomputers and to achieve scalability. One of the main bottlenecks for scalability is the communication layer. Some task-based algorithms need to send the same data to multiple nodes. To optimize this communication pattern, libraries propose dedicated routines, such as MPI_Bcast. However, MPI_Bcast requirements do not fit well with the constraints of task-based runtime systems: it must be performed simultaneously by all involved nodes, and these must know each other, which is not possible when each node runs a task scheduler not synchronized with others. In this paper, we propose a new approach, called dynamic broadcasts to overcome these constraints. The broadcast communication pattern required by the task-based algorithm is detected automatically, then the broadcasting algorithm relies on active messages and source routing, so that participating nodes do not need to know each other and do not need to synchronize. Receiver receives data the same way as it receives point-to-point communication, without having to know it arrives through a broadcast. We have implemented the algorithm in the STARPU runtime system using the NEWMADELEINE communication library. We performed benchmarks using the CHOLESKY factorization that is known to use broadcasts and observed up to 30% improvement of its total execution time.

Keywords: Task-based runtime systems · Communications · Collective · Broadcast

1 Introduction

Scalability of applications over clusters is limited, among other things, by synchronizations, an extreme example being *Bulk Synchronized Parallelism* (BSP). To increase performance, task-based runtime systems try to avoid any synchronization through asynchronicity in the way they schedule tasks on nodes. To follow this scheduling model in order to ensure scalability, communications have also to support asynchronicity.

© Springer Nature Switzerland AG 2020
M. Malawski and K. Rzadca (Eds.): Euro-Par 2020, LNCS 12247, pp. 443–457, 2020.
https://doi.org/10.1007/978-3-030-57675-2_28

For communications, task-based runtime systems often rely on MPI. However, MPI libraries and the MPI interface are not designed with such use in mind. A problem arises when a piece of data produced by one task is a dependency for several other tasks on several nodes. A natural way to send the same data to multiple nodes would be to use the MPI_Bcast or MPI_Ibcast primitives. However, this approach assumes all nodes know in advance that this data will arrive through a broadcast instead of a point-to-point operation, and that they know each other. This assumption is not met in the case of a dynamic task-based runtime system, where nodes ignore the state of the task scheduler on other nodes, and thus they typically use a naive broadcast algorithm with linear complexity.

In this paper, we propose an algorithm for a dynamic broadcast, where only the root knows the list of all recipients, and recipients do not have to know in advance whether data will arrive through a broadcast or a point-to-point operation, while still being able to leverage optimized tree-based broadcast algorithms.

In short, this paper makes the following contributions: we propose a dynamic broadcast algorithm, suitable for use by task-based runtime systems; we implemented the mechanism in our NEWMADELEINE [5] communication library, and modified STARPU [4] to take benefit from it; we performed benchmarks to show the performance improvement.

The rest of this paper is organized as follows. Section 2 details why broadcasts using MPI_Bcast are not suitable for task-based runtime systems. Section 3 introduces our algorithm for dynamic broadcasts. Section 4 presents its implementation in NEWMADELEINE and STARPU. In Sect. 5, we evaluate our solution using micro-benchmarks and a CHOLESKY factorization kernel. In Sect. 6 we present related works, and Sect. 7 concludes.

2   Broadcasts in Dynamic Task-Based Runtime Systems

With task-based runtime systems, the application programmer writes applications decomposed into several tasks with dependencies. Each task is a subpart of the main algorithm. All tasks with their dependencies form a DAG (Direct Acyclic Graph); tasks are vertices, and edges represent a data dependency between two tasks: the child task needs data produced by its predecessor(s). In order to get task-based runtime systems to work on distributed systems, tasks are distributed among available nodes. When dependent tasks are not located on the same node, an edge spans across two different nodes and the runtime system automatically handles the data transfer.

A given piece of data may be a dependency for multiple tasks (a vertex with several outgoing edges). If the receiving tasks are located on different nodes, the same data will have to be sent to multiple nodes. This communication pattern is generally known as a *multicast*, or a *broadcast* in MPI speaking, which is a kind of *collective* communication.

The naive way to perform a broadcast is to send data from the root to each node using independent point-to-point transfers. With such an implementation, the duration of a broadcast is *linear* with the number of nodes. MPI libraries usually implement much better algorithms [12,13,15] for MPI_Bcast, such as binary trees, binomial trees, pipelined trees, or 2-trees, which exhibit a *logarithmic* complexity with the number of nodes. It is thus strongly advised to use MPI_Bcast to broadcast data when possible.

However, for task-based runtime systems that dynamically build the DAG (such as STARPU [3] or QUARK [9]), nodes do not have a global view of data location and do not synchronize their scheduling. This makes the use of MPI_Bcast or MPI_Ibcast difficult and inefficient, for several reasons:

detection – all the information the runtime system knows about data transfers is the DAG. A broadcast appears as a task whose result is needed by multiple other tasks. However, in general the whole DAG is not known statically but generated while the application is running. Therefore, the runtime system cannot know whether the list of recipient is complete or if another recipient will be added later.

explicit – function MPI_Bcast has to be called explicitly by the sender and the receivers. Therefore, each receiver node have to know in advance whether a given piece of data will arrive through an MPI_Bcast or a point-to-point MPI_Recv. Application programmer cannot give any hint, since communications are driven by the DAG, and thus depends on where tasks are mapped during the execution.

communicator – function MPI_Bcast works on a *communicator*, a structure containing all nodes taking part in the broadcast (sender node and recipients). The construction of a communicator is also a collective operation: to build it, each node participating in a communicator must know the list of all nodes in the communicator. Thus, if we build a communicator containing a specific list of nodes for a given broadcast operation, all nodes have to know the list of all nodes participating in the broadcast.

Yet, the runtime system on a node only has a local view of the task graph: receiver nodes know which node will send them the data, but they do not know all other nodes which will also receive the same data. Hence, building an MPI communicator is impossible without first sending the list of nodes to all nodes, but that would mean we need a broadcast before being able to do a broadcast!

synchronization – even if we use a non-blocking MPI_Ibcast instead of a blocking MPI_Bcast, it works on a communicator. The creation of a communicator with the precise set of nodes is a blocking operation and has to be performed by all nodes at the same time. This constraint is somewhat alleviated by the non-blocking flavor of communicator creation in the future MPI 4.0 version. Nonetheless, a single communicator creation may take place at the same time. This means broadcasts, and their associated communicator creation, must nonetheless be executed in the same order by all nodes, which implies some kind of synchronization to agree on broadcast scheduling, thus hindering one of the most important feature of distributed task-based runtime system: its ability to scale by avoiding unnecessary synchronization.

As a consequence, the mechanisms needed to actually use an MPI_Bcast to broadcast data in a task-based runtime system are likely to cost more than the benefit brought by the use of an optimized broadcast. The general problem is being able to use desynchronized and optimized broadcasting algorithms, without all nodes of the broadcast know each other. We present in this paper the solution we developed to achieve this goal.

3   Our Solution: Dynamic Broadcasts

3.1   Detection of Collectives

As explained in Sect. 2, the detection of broadcast patterns is not straightforward since the DAG is dynamic.

From the dependency graph view, a broadcast is a set of outgoing edges from the same vertex and going to tasks executed on different nodes. During task graph submission, the runtime system creates a send request for each of these edges, even before the data to send is available. When the data becomes available, the requests are actually submitted to the communication library.

The detection of broadcast consists in noticing on creating a send request that one already exists for the same data, and aggregating them into a single request with a list of recipients. When the data becomes available, if the list contains more than one recipient, a broadcast is submitted to the communication library.

This method may miss some send requests if they are posted after the data became ready, *i.e.* if a task is submitted after the completion of the task that produces the data it depends on. This happens if the task graph submission takes longer than the task graph execution (which is not supposed to happen in general), or if the application delays submission of parts of the task graph for its own reasons, in which case the runtime system did not need to send this data sooner anyway. Code instrumentation showed that 98 % of broadcasts were detected with the correct number of recipients for the CHOLESKY decomposition described in Sect. 5. These missed broadcasts correspond only to communications performed during the very beginning of the algorithm, when the application has only started submitting the task graph, and thus task execution has indeed caught up quickly and made some data available before the application could submit all inter-node edges for them. Quickly enough, tasks submission proceeds largely ahead of tasks execution, and all broadcasts are detected.

To avoid redundant transfers of the same data between two nodes, a cache mechanism is used [3]. If two tasks scheduled on the same node need a piece of data from another node, only one communication will be executed. Hence, the recipient list does not contain duplicates.

3.2   Dynamic Broadcast Algorithm

We propose here a broadcast algorithm, that we call *dynamic broadcast*, that fulfills the requirements to be used by task-based runtime systems, namely: use optimized broadcast algorithms; all recipients of the broadcast do not have to know each other; have a seamless integration for the receiver who is expecting a point-to-point communication.

Optimized Broadcast Algorithm. Several optimized algorithms for broadcast exist [16]. The main idea of all these optimized algorithms is that after a node received data, it sends this data to other recipients, so that the root node has less communications to execute, which shortens the global execution time. For most algorithms, routing is organized as a tree: the source node sends to a set of nodes, each of these nodes then sends to a set of other nodes, and then recursively until all recipients get the data. Tree-based algorithms have usually a logarithmic complexity in the number of nodes. The choice of a broadcast algorithm depends mainly on the number of recipients and the size of data to transmit.

We choose to implement binomial trees because this broadcast algorithm is the best trade-off for a single all-purpose algorithm to get good performance on a wide range of data sizes and numbers of nodes. Other optimized algorithms [12, 13, 15] could be used in our dynamic broadcast, following the same approach.

In the binomial tree algorithm, each node receiving data contributes to the diffusion by sending data to next nodes, and keep sending data to other recipients until all nodes received the data. The Fig. 1 illustrates a broadcast to 6 recipients: node 0 starts by sending to node 4, then 0 sends to 2 and at the same time 4 sends to 6 and finally while 0 is sending to 1, 2 is sending to 3 and 4 is sending to 5. The binomial tree has a logarithmic complexity in the number of nodes.

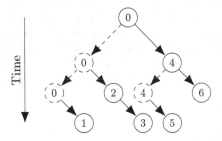

Fig. 1. Example of binomial tree with six recipients. Levels in the tree are steps in the algorithm.

Self-contained Messages. Since nodes do not know in advance whether they will be participating in a broadcast, our algorithm is based on self-contained messages. They are active messages, processed outside of the application flow, without requiring the application to call specific primitives in the communication library. The message contains all the information needed to unroll the collective algorithm.

Only the root of the broadcast knows the complete list of recipients. Recipients themselves only need to know to which nodes they will need to forward the data, *i.e.* the sub-tree below them. We send this list of nodes together with data, in the header of the active message. When a node forwards data to other nodes, it trims the list of nodes so as to include only the nodes contained in the relevant sub-tree.

In the case depicted in Fig. 1, the list of nodes sent by node 0 to 4 is $\{5, 6\}$, the list sent to 2 is $\{3\}$ and the list sent to 1 is empty.

The runtime system sets a *priority* level for each communication request, depending on task priorities, defined by the application (during the submission of tasks, the user can define the priority of each task, by specifying an integer). This information may be used by a communication library that is able to schedule packets by priority like NEWMADELEINE. We reorder the list of nodes of broadcasts so that higher-priority requests are closer to the root of the tree, for them to get data earlier. Moreover, in addition to the list of nodes, we transmit the list of priorities. This way, when inner nodes of the tree have to forward messages, they get inserted in their local packet flow with the right priority.

The general idea behind this mechanism is that routing information are transmitted with the data itself, and are not assumed to be prior knowledge, as MPI_Bcast would otherwise require.

Transparent Receive. When a request which is part of a broadcast is received, the data is forwarded to nodes contained in the list, following the binomial tree algorithm, and data is delivered locally. Since nodes cannot predict whether data will arrive through point-to-point communication or through a broadcast, on the receiver side our algorithm injects data received by a broadcast in the path of point-to-point receive. The runtime system posts a regular point-to-point receive request, and when data arrives through a dynamic broadcast, it is actually received by this point-to-point request for a seamless integration.

We called our algorithm *dynamic broadcast* because nodes realize they take part in a broadcast in a dynamic fashion, on the fly at the same time when data arrives.

4   Implementation

Our implementation was made within the STARPU task-based runtime and the NEWMADELEINE communication library. This Section introduces both libraries and presents implementation details of our dynamic broadcast algorithm.

4.1   StarPU

STARPU [4] is a task-based parallel and distributed runtime system. In its single-node form, STARPU lets HPC applications submit a sequential flow of tasks, it infers data dependencies between tasks from that flow, and it schedules tasks concurrently while enforcing these dependency constraints. The distributed version of STARPU [3] extends the Sequential Task Flow model. The application gives an initial distribution of data on the participating nodes, and every node submits the same flow of tasks to its local STARPU instance. Each STARPU instance then infers whether to execute a task or not from the piece of data the task writes to. The instance that owns the piece of data written to, executes the task. Moreover, each STARPU instance infers locally when to generate send and receive communications to serve inter-instance data dependencies. This distributed execution model does not involve any master node or synchronization. Instead, all instances are implicitly coordinated by running the same state machine from the sequential task flow.

Two back-ends are implemented in the distributed version of STARPU. One relies on MPI standard and has to be used with an MPI implementation (such as OPENMPI). The other one uses NEWMADELEINE routines to take benefit from its specific features beyond the MPI interface.

4.2   NewMadeleine

NEWMADELEINE [5] is a communication library which exhibits its own native interface in addition to a thin MPI layer called MadMPI. The work described in this paper is located in the NEWMADELEINE native interface. The originality of NEWMADELEINE compared to other communication libraries and MPI implementations is that it decouples the network activity from the calls to the API by the user. In the interface presented to the end-user, primitives send and receive *messages*. NEWMADELEINE applies an optimizing strategy so as to form *packets* ready to be sent to the network. A *packet* may contain multiple *messages* (aggregation), a *message* may be split across multiple *packets* (multi-rail), and *messages* may be actually sent on the wire out-of-order depending on packet scheduler decision and priorities. NEWMADELEINE core activity is triggered by the network. When the network is busy, *messages* to be sent are simply enqueued; when the network becomes ready, an optimization strategy is called to form a new *packet* from the pending *messages*. A receive is always posted to the driver, and all the activity is made of up-calls (event notifiers) triggered from the lowest layer when the receive is completed, which make active messages a natural paradigm for NEWMADELEINE.

4.3   Dynamic Collectives Implementation

Dynamic broadcasts were implemented as a new interface of NEWMADELEINE, and the NEWMADELEINE backend of STARPU was adapted to exploit this new interface.

The detection of broadcasts is implemented in STARPU. When the application submits a task B which depends on data produced by a task A mapped on a different node, an inter-node communication request is issued. If a previous request or collective was already detected for this data, the new request is merged in to get a bigger collective. Most often, task submission proceeds quickly, and thus the submission front is largely ahead of the execution front. As a consequence, when task B is submitted, task A will probably not have been executed yet, and similarly for all tasks which depend on A. This is why our approach catches most potential for broadcasts. Once task A is completed and thus the data available for sending, the whole collective request is handed to NEWMADELEINE.

The dynamic broadcast itself is implemented in NEWMADELEINE, using its non-blocking `rpc` interface for active messages. They use a dedicated communication channel that is separate from the channel used for point-to-point communications. Thus, the library distinguishes broadcasts, which needs special processing, from regular point-to-point messages. The library is always listening for `rpc` requests and is thus able to always process dynamic broadcasts for all tags and from all nodes.

To manage seamless receive of a broadcast by a point-to-point request, point-to-point requests are registered by the dynamic broadcast subsystem. Conversely, if the data for a receive comes by the point-to-point way, the request is removed from the table in the dynamic broadcast subsystem.

When a broadcast is received, the matching point-to-point receive is searched and data is received in-place in the buffer of the point-to-point request, forwarded to nodes in sub-trees, and the point-to-point request is notified completion. If the matching point-to-point receive was not posted yet, the broadcast request is locally postponed until the matching point-to-point receive is posted. To be able to match a message arriving through a broadcast with a point-to-point request, the original source node (root of the broadcast) is also sent together with data, the list of nodes, and their associated priority.

5   Evaluation

In this section, we present the performance results we obtain for mechanisms presented in this paper. We executed micro-benchmarks to ensure the broadcast performances are as expected and then we evaluated the impact on a real computing kernel, the CHOLESKY factorization.

The benchmarks were carried out on two different clusters: `inti` from CEA and `plafrim`. `inti` nodes are dual Xeon E5-2680 at 2.7 GHz, with 16 cores and 64 GB RAM, and equipped with Connect-IB *InfiniBand* QDR (MT27600). Default MPI on the machine is OpenMPI 2.0; since this version is ancient, we compiled the latest OpenMPI 4.0. `plafrim` nodes are dual Xeon Gold 6240 at 2.6 GHz with 36 cores and 192 GB RAM, and equipped with Intel *Omni-Path* 100 series network. Default MPI on `plafrim` are OpenMPI 3.0 and OpenMPI 4.0.

5.1   Micro-benchmarks

To be sure our algorithm and its implementation have the expected performances, we conducted micro-benchmarks of the dynamic broadcast and compared its performance against `MPI_Bcast` and `MPI_Ibcast` of MadMPI, and a

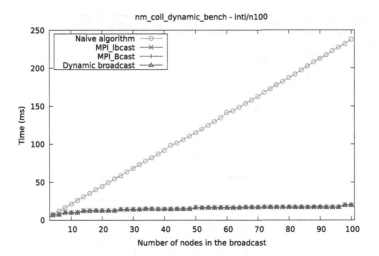

Fig. 2. NEWMADELEINE micro-benchmark on cluster `inti` on 100 nodes (1600 cores), comparing broadcast algorithms

naive broadcast (a loop of point-to-point requests to the recipient nodes). The duration of the broadcast is defined as the time difference between the start on the root node and the last received data on the last node.

The result of this micro-benchmark on 100 nodes of the `inti` cluster is depicted in Fig. 2 for 8 MB of data. As expected, naive broadcast exhibits a linear complexity with the number of recipients and both dynamic and regular broadcasts have a logarithmic complexity. The performance difference between dynamic broadcast and regular MPI broadcast is insignificant, which shows that the additional routing data and the treatment when receiving data is negligible.

5.2 Cholesky Factorization

To evaluate the gain brought by dynamic broadcast, we have evaluated its performance on a CHOLESKY factorization.

Description. In Algorithm 1, we depict the tiled version of the CHOLESKY Factorization algorithm. For a given symmetric positive definite matrix A, the CHOLESKY algorithm computes a lower triangular matrix L such that $A = LL^T$. In the tiled version used here, the matrix is decomposed in $T \times T$ square tiles where $A[i][j]$ is the tile of row i and column j. At each step k it performs a CHOLESKY factorization of the tile on the diagonal of panel k (POTRF kernel) then it updates the remaining of the tiles of the panel using triangular solve (TRSM kernel). The trailing sub-matrix is updated using the SYRK kernel for tiles on the diagonal and matrix multiply (GEMM kernel) for the remaining tiles.

Algorithm 1: Tiled version of the CHOLESKY factorization.

```
1 for k = 0...T − 1 do
2 |   A[k][k] ← POTRF(A[k][k])
3 |   for m = k + 1...T − 1 do
4 |   |   A[m][k] ← TRSM(A[k][k], A[m][k])
5 |   for n = k + 1...T − 1 do
6 |   |   A[n][n] ← SYRK(A[n][k], A[n][n])
7 |   |   for m = n + 1...T − 1 do
8 |   |   |   A[m][n] ← GEMM(A[m][k], A[n][k], A[m][n])
```

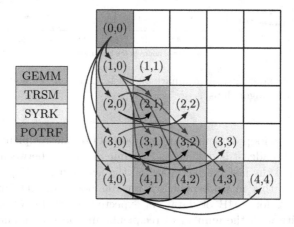

Fig. 3. The 2 different types of broadcasts for the CHOLESKY factorization for $T = 5$ and $k = 0$. Blue arrows : from 1 POTRF to $T - k - 1 = 4$ TRSM. Green and black arrows from 1 TRSM to $T - k - 2 = 3$ GEMM and red arrows to 1 SYRK. (Color figure online)

This algorithm is a good use-case for the dynamic broadcast problem. Indeed, as shown in Fig. 3, the $A[k][k]$ tile computed by the POTRF kernel is broadcasted to the $T - k - 1$ TRSM kernels of the same panel (blue arrows). Moreover, each $A[m][k]$ ($m > k$) tile generated by the TRSM kernels (line 4), is used by one SYRK kernel (to update the tile $A[m][m]$, red arrows) and $T - k - 2$ GEMM kernels (to update the tiles $A[m][n]$ ($k < n < m$), black arrows ; and the tiles $A[m][n]$ ($m < n < T$), green arrows. As seen in Sect. 3, in STARPU, all the communication and especially the collective communication are inferred at runtime by the system based on the dependencies that are described in the task graph generated from the program. Furthermore, since for both cases, the same tile is broadcasted to all the kernels and several kernels are executed by a same node, the runtime system is able to factorize the communication by giving the list of compute nodes that require the considered tile. In practice, as nodes are layout using squared 2D Block-cyclic distribution, the maximum number of nodes involved in a broadcast is $\mathcal{O}(\sqrt{P})$ where P is the total number of nodes.

We used the CHOLESKY factorization from the CHAMELEON library [2], which can use STARPU as task-based runtime system.

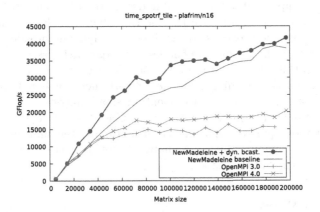

Fig. 4. CHAMELEON CHOLESKY factorization performance on cluster `plafrim` on 16 nodes (512 cores)

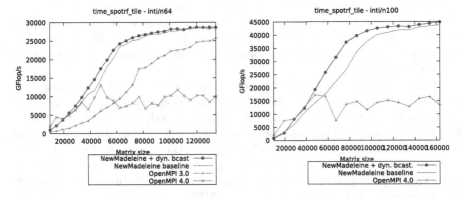

Fig. 5. CHAMELEON CHOLESKY factorization performance on cluster `inti`: on left, on 64 nodes (1024 cores); on right, on 100 nodes (1600 cores)

Results. Results of the CHOLESKY benchmark on cluster `plafrim` on 16 nodes is depicted in Fig. 4. Results for machine `inti` on 64 and 100 nodes is shown in Fig. 5. There is one MPI process per node and each point on graphs is the average of two runs. We compare the *baseline* NEWMADELEINE version without dynamic broadcast against NEWMADELEINE with dynamic broadcast. Additionally we represent the performance we obtain with MPI as a reference. The performance difference between NEWMADELEINE and MPI is explained [8] by other mechanisms beyond the scope of this paper.

On all 3 cases, dynamic broadcasts improve performances[1] of the CHOLESKY factorization, mainly on small matrices. On `plafrim` on 16 nodes (Fig. 4), the best performance improvement is 25 %. On `inti` (see Fig. 5) on 64 nodes the improvements is up to 20 % and on 100 nodes up to 30 %. Since the number of nodes in broadcasts increases with the total number of nodes, the more nodes are used, the more the broadcast takes time, thus dynamic broadcasts improve overall scalability with the number of nodes. For larger matrices, communications have less impact since there are always enough ready tasks to execute before having to wait for data coming from the network, hence it is not surprising to observe the best performance improvement for small matrices.

The impact of using *dynamic broadcasts* in CHOLESKY execution needs to be more studied and requires a deep analysis of runtime system and communication library internal behaviours. Since this analysis is not straightforward, we consider it as out of the scope of this paper.

6   Related Works

Broadcasting algorithms have already been discussed a lot [12,13,15,16], but are an orthogonal problem to work described in this paper which can rely on any tree-based algorithm.

The idea to optimize collective communications by sending only one message per receiving node when multiple tasks with the same input share the same node has been proposed in early task-based runtime systems [10]. However, in this work, no optimization was performed in the way the data was broadcasted to the different nodes.

PARSEC [7] is a task-based runtime system, based on a *Parameterized Task Graph* (PTG), an algebraic representation of the dependency graph. Such kind of graph can be entirely stored in the memory of each node since the memory used for its representation is linear in the number of task types, and not in the number of tasks. Since all nodes know the full task graph, they can easily know all nodes involved in a broadcast and the entire graph being known at the beginning of the execution, explicit call to broadcast routines can be made. In practice, PARSEC uses binomial or chained trees, on the top of MPI point-to-point requests. Broadcasts are identified directly from the algebraic representation of the task graph, which the application programmer thus has to provide, while our approach can be introduced in most task-based runtime systems, which use a dynamic task submission API.

CLUSTERSS [14] is a task-based runtime system built with a master-slave model: only a master node knows the whole task graph and distributes tasks to slave nodes. Thus the master node can easily detect broadcasts and tells to slave nodes how to handle them. However, no information is published about the optimization of broadcasts.

---

[1] It is important to note that the improvement is measured on the total performance and not on the communication part only.

CHARM++ [1] is a parallel programming model relying on tasks called *chares*. It comes with the TRAM subsystem for collective communications, but it is supposed to be used explicitly by the application, which makes its constraints different from our use case.

LEGION [6] is a task-based runtime system focused on data locality. Its default scheduling policy is work-stealing, even to another node. No detail is given about a potential communication optimization, but with work-stealing there is not synchronization between different nodes that request the same data.

HPX [11] is a runtime system which executes task on remote nodes *via* active messages. Its API contains routines to explicitly invoke a broadcast involving several nodes.

All in all, other task-based runtime systems either do not optimize broadcasts, or have an API or a DAG representation that allows for explicit use of broadcasts, which are different constraints than dynamic task submission.

7 Conclusion and Future Works

Task-based runtime systems are used to program heterogeneous supercomputers in a scalable fashion. In their DAG, a situation may appear where a given piece of data needs to be sent to multiple nodes. The use of an optimized broadcast algorithm is desirable for scalability. However, the constraints of relaxed synchronization and asynchronous schedulers on nodes make it difficult to use MPI_Bcast.

In this paper, we have introduced a *dynamic broadcast* mechanism which makes it possible to use an optimized tree-based broadcast algorithm without needing all the participating nodes know all the other nodes, and without even needing them know they are involved in a broadcast at all. The integration is seamless and nodes receive data with a regular point-to-point receive API. We have implemented the algorithm in NEWMADELEINE, used it in STARPU, and evaluated its performance on a CHOLESKY factorization. Results show that our dynamic broadcast may improve overall performance up to 30 % and that it improves scalability.

In the future, we will work on integrating different broadcast algorithms (binary trees, pipelined trees) to get the best performance for all message sizes. We study the implementation of similar algorithm using a generic MPI library, by emulating active messages with a communication thread. Finally, the biggest remaining challenge consists in analyzing finely the global performance of STARPU with regard to networking.

Acknowledgements. This work is supported by the Agence Nationale de la Recherche, under grant ANR-19-CE46-0009.

This work is supported by the Région Nouvelle-Aquitaine, under grant 2018-1R50119 *HPC scalable ecosystem*.

Experiments presented in this paper were carried out using the PlaFRIM experimental testbed, supported by Inria, CNRS (LABRI and IMB), Université de Bordeaux, Bordeaux INP and Conseil Régional d'Aquitaine (see https://www.plafrim.fr/).

This work was granted access to the HPC resources of CINES under the allocation 2019- A0060601567 attributed by GENCI (Grand Equipement National de Calcul Intensif).

The authors furthermore thank Olivier AUMAGE and Nathalie FURMENTO for their help and advice regarding to this work.

References

1. Acun, B., et al.: Parallel programming with migratable objects: Charm++ in practice. In: Proceedings of the International Conference for High Performance Computing, Networking, Storage and Analysis, SC'14, pp. 647–658. IEEE (2014)
2. Agullo, E., et al.: Faster, cheaper, better - a hybridization methodology to develop linear algebra software for GPUs. In: Hwu, W.W. (ed.) GPU Computing Gems, vol. 2. Morgan Kaufmann (September 2010). https://hal.inria.fr/inria-00547847
3. Agullo, E., et al.: Achieving high performance on supercomputers with a sequential task-based programming model. IEEE Trans. Parallel Distrib. Syst. (2017). https://hal.inria.fr/hal-01618526
4. Augonnet, C., Thibault, S., Namyst, R., Wacrenier, P.-A.: STARPU: a unified platform for task scheduling on heterogeneous multicore architectures. In: Sips, H., Epema, D., Lin, H.-X. (eds.) Euro-Par 2009. LNCS, vol. 5704, pp. 863–874. Springer, Heidelberg (2009). https://doi.org/10.1007/978-3-642-03869-3_80
5. Aumage, O., Brunet, E., Furmento, N., Namyst, R.: NewMadeleine: a fast communication scheduling engine for high performance networks. In: Workshop on Communication Architecture for Clusters, CAC 2007, Long Beach, California, United States (March 2007). https://hal.inria.fr/inria-00127356
6. Bauer, M., Treichler, S., Slaughter, E., Aiken, A.: Legion: expressing locality and independence with logical regions. In: Proceedings of the International Conference on High Performance Computing, Networking, Storage and Analysis, SC '12, pp. 1–11 (November 2012). https://doi.org/10.1109/SC.2012.71
7. Bosilca, G., Bouteiller, A., Danalis, A., Herault, T., Luszczek, P., Dongarra, J.: Dense linear algebra on distributed heterogeneous hardware with a symbolic dag approach. Scalable Comput. Commun. Theor. Pract., 699–735 (2013)
8. Denis, A.: Scalability of the NewMadeleine communication library for large numbers of MPI point-to-point requests. In: 19th Annual IEEE/ACM International Symposium in Cluster, Cloud, and Grid Computing, CCGrid 2019, Larnaca, Cyprus (May 2019) https://hal.inria.fr/hal-02103700
9. Dongarra, J.: Architecture-Aware Algorithms for Scalable Performance and Resilience on Heterogeneous Architectures (2013). https://doi.org/10.2172/1096392
10. Jeannot, E.: Automatic multithreaded parallel program generation for message passing multiprocessors using parameterized task graphs. In: International Conference on Parallel Computing 2001, ParCo2001, Naples, Italy (September 2001)
11. Kaiser, H., Brodowicz, M., Sterling, T.: Parallex an advanced parallel execution model for scaling-impaired applications. In: 2009 International Conference on Parallel Processing Workshops, pp. 394–401 (September 2009). https://doi.org/10.1109/ICPPW.2009.14
12. Pješivac-Grbović, J., Angskun, T., Bosilca, G., Fagg, G.E., Gabriel, E., Dongarra, J.J.: Performance analysis of MPI collective operations. Clust. Comput. 10(2), 127–143 (2007)

13. Sanders, P., Speck, J., Träff, J.L.: Two-tree algorithms for full bandwidth broadcast, reduction and scan. Parallel Comput. **35**(12), 581–594 (2009). Selected papers from the 14th European PVM/MPI Users Group Meeting. https://doi.org/10.1016/j.parco.2009.09.001

14. Tejedor, E., Farreras, M., Grove, D., Badia, R.M., Almasi, G., Labarta, J.: A high-productivity task-based programming model for clusters. Concurrency Comput. Pract. Exp. **24**(18), 2421–2448 (2012). https://doi.org/10.1002/cpe.2831

15. Träff, J.L., Ripke, A.: Optimal broadcast for fully connected processor-node networks. J. Parallel Distrib. Comput. **68**(7), 887–901 (2008). https://doi.org/10.1016/j.jpdc.2007.12.001

16. Wickramasinghe, U., Lumsdaine, A.: A survey of methods for collective communication optimization and tuning. CoRR abs/1611.06334 (2016). http://arxiv.org/abs/1611.06334

A Compression-Based Design for Higher Throughput in a Lock-Free Hash Map

Pedro Moreno🆔, Miguel Areias$^{(\boxtimes)}$🆔, and Ricardo Rocha🆔

CRACS & INESCTEC, Faculty of Sciences,
University of Porto, Rua do Campo Alegre, 1021/1055,
4169-007 Porto, Portugal
{pmoreno,miguel-areias,ricroc}@dcc.fc.up.pt

Abstract. Lock-free implementation techniques are known to improve the overall throughput of concurrent data structures. A hash map is an important data structure used to organize information that must be accessed frequently. A key role of a hash map is the ability to balance workloads by dynamically adjusting its internal data structures in order to provide the fastest possible access to the information. This work extends a previous lock-free hash map design to also support *lock-free compression*. The main goal is to significantly reduce the depth of the internal hash levels within the hash map, in order to minimize cache misses and increase the overall throughput. To materialize our design, we redesigned the existent search, insert, remove and expand operations in order to maintain the lock-freedom property of the whole design. Experimental results show that lock-free compression effectively improves the search operation and, in doing so, it outperforms the previous design, which was already quite competitive when compared against the concurrent hash map design supported by Intel.

Keywords: Hash maps · Lock-freedom · Concurrency · Performance

1 Introduction

Hash maps are a very common and efficient data structure used to map keys to values, where the mapping between the unique key K and the associated value V is given by a *hash function*. Hash tries (or hash array mapped tries) are a trie-based data structure with nearly ideal characteristics for the implementation of hash maps [3]. An essential property of the trie data structure is that common prefixes are stored only once [6], which in the context of hash maps allows us to efficiently solve the problems of setting the size of the initial hash table and of dynamically resizing it in order to deal with hash collisions.

This work is funded by National Funds through the Portuguese funding agency, FCT – Fundação para a Ciência e a Tecnologia, within project UIDB/50014/2020. Pedro Moreno and Miguel Areias are funded by the FCT grants SFRH/BD/143261/2019 and SFRH/BPD/108018/2015, respectively.

M. Malawski and K. Rzadca (Eds.): Euro-Par 2020, LNCS 12247, pp. 458–473, 2020.
https://doi.org/10.1007/978-3-030-57675-2_29

However, trie-based hash maps are prone to generate higher cache misses than traditional hash maps, thus they tend to perform worse as the depth of the trie increases. Fortunately, tries are widely used in different domains and literature shows a significant amount of effort in studying their properties and implementations [9] and, in particular, for cache-based architectures, in studying how to mitigate cache effects to achieve better performance [1]. Recently, Li *et al.* studied the throughput of several kinds of hash map designs and presented a high-throughput and memory-efficient concurrent cuckoo-based hashing technique that supports multiple readers and writers [10].

Lock-freedom is an important concurrency technique that is known to improve the overall throughput of concurrent data structures. Lock-freedom allows individual threads to starve but guarantees system-wide throughput. In particular, lock-free trie-based hash maps offer a viable alternative to memory-efficient hash-mapping [2,15]. However, the cache misses problem was also observed by Prokopec *et al.* when they compared the CTries data structure [14], a lock-free trie-based hash map, against other state-of-the-art hash map designs.

Arguably, a well-know workaround to improve the performance of a trie-based data structure is to apply some sort of *compression technique* [7,11] as a way to reduce the average depth of the trie data structure. Compression can be done at shallow or deeper trie levels, but a key advantage is that it can be done concurrently with the other operations. Two good examples are: (i) the B*-tree proposal [17], which supports a compression procedure that runs concurrently with regular operations, such as searches, insertions and removals, to merge nodes that are underfull; and (ii) the relaxed B-slack trees proposal [4] that supports a similar concurrent absorb operation that reduces the number of levels in the data structure.

In this work, we focus on extending a sophisticated implementation of a lock-free trie-based hash map, named *Lock-Free Hash Map (LFHT)* [12], to support *lock-free compression*. The original LFHT implements a hierarchy of hash levels whose branching factor is given by a fixed (and pre-defined) number of bucket entries per hash level. Traversing the hash levels in the LFHT data structure is $\mathcal{O}(\log_B K)$, where B represents the fixed number of bucket entries in a hash level and K is the overall number of keys inserted in the hash map. Our compress operation will be working on adjusting B to significantly reduce the average depth of the internal hash levels within the hash map, i.e., instead of a fixed number of bucket entries per hash level, we now support hash levels of different sizes. Compression is done incrementally, affecting well-defined clusters of hash levels, in order to meet varying (local) workloads. Since the number of levels to be traversed is expected to be lower, this reduces cache misses and increases the overall throughput. Experimental results show that lock-free compression effectively improves the search operation and, in doing so, it outperforms the previous design [12], which was already quite competitive, when compared against the concurrent hash map design in Intel's TBB library [16]. To materialize our design, we redesigned the existent search, insert, remove and expand operations in order to maintain the lock-freedom property of the whole design.

The remainder of the paper is organized as follows. First, we introduce some background regarding the LFHT design. Next, we discuss the main aspects of our design by example. Then, we describe implementation details and present the key algorithms required to easily reproduce our implementation by others. Finally, we show experimental results and end by outlining conclusions and further work.

2   Lock-Free Hash Tries

The LFHT data structure has two kinds of nodes: *hash nodes* and *leaf nodes*. The leaf nodes store key/value pairs and the hash nodes implement a hierarchy of hash levels of fixed size 2^w. To map a key/value pair *(k,v)* into this hierarchy, we compute the hash value h for k and then use chunks of w bits from h to index the appropriate hash node, i.e., for each hash level H_i, we use the ith group of w bits of h to index the entry in the appropriate bucket array of H_i. To deal with collisions, the leaf nodes form a linked list in the respective bucket entry until a threshold is met and, in such case, an expansion operation updates the nodes in the linked list to a new hash level H_{i+1}, i.e., instead of growing a single monolithic hash table, the hash trie settles for a hierarchy of small hash tables of fixed size 2^w. Figure 1 shows how the insertion of nodes is done in a hash level.

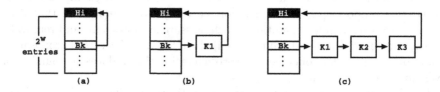

Fig. 1. Insertion of nodes in a hash level

Fig. 1(a) shows the initial configuration of a hash level H_i. A hash level is formed by: (i) a hash node, which includes a header where control information is stored and a bucket array of 2^w entries; and by (ii) the corresponding chain of leaf nodes per bucket entry. Initially, all bucket entries are empty. In Fig. 1, B_k represents a particular bucket entry of H_i. A bucket entry stores either a reference to a hash node (initially the current hash node) or a reference to a separate chain of leaf nodes, corresponding to the hash collisions for that entry. Figure 1(b) shows the configuration after the insertion of node K_1 on B_k and Fig. 1(c) shows the configuration after the insertion of nodes K_2 and K_3. The insertion of nodes is done at the end of the chain and a new inserted node closes the chain by referencing back the current hash level. A leaf node holds both a reference to a next-on-chain node and a flag with the condition of the node, which can be *valid* (*V*) or *invalid* (*I*). The initial condition of a node is valid and turns invalid when the node is marked for removal.

When the number of valid nodes in a chain reaches a given threshold, the next insertion causes the corresponding bucket entry to be expanded to a new hash level (in what follows, we consider a threshold value of three). Figure 2 shows how nodes are remapped in the new level. The expansion operation starts by inserting a new hash node H_{i+1} at the end of the chain with all its bucket entries referencing H_{i+1} (as shown in Fig. 2(a)). From this point on, new insertions will be done on the new level H_{i+1} and the chain of leaf nodes on B_k will be moved, one at a time, to H_{i+1}. Figure 2(b) and Fig. 2(c) show how node K_3 is first remapped in H_{i+1} (bucket B_n) and then moved from H_i (bucket B_k). When the last node is moved, the bucket entry B_k in H_i is made to refer to the new hash node H_{i+1} (Fig. 2(d)).

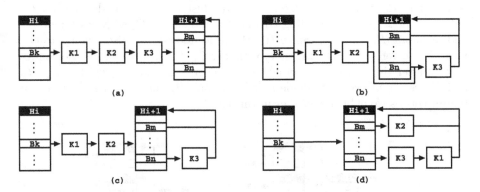

Fig. 2. Expansion of nodes in a hash level

In what follows, we base our work on the LFHT implementation [12] which supports the search, insert, remove and expand operations concurrently in a lock-free fashion and where threads collaborate to finish the undergoing expansions in a path before inserting new nodes. This implementation also supports a memory reclamation design, named *HHL (Hazard Hash and Level)*, that uses hazard pairs to define well-defined regions of memory to be protected from reclamation, which explores the characteristics of the LFHT data structure in order to achieve efficient memory reclamation with low and well-defined memory bounds.

3   Our Design by Example

In this section, we present our design by example. Our design takes advantage of the fine-grained and fully synchronized atomic CAS operation, which is at the heart of many lock-free data structures [8].

In a nutshell, the key idea of our design is to apply lock-free compression to clusters of hash nodes in order to reduce the average depth of hash levels needed to be traversed within the hash map. To activate compression on a cluster, the condition is to have a hash node (called the *head node* of the cluster of hash nodes) with all its bucket entries referring other hash nodes. A second condition is that the head node does not belong to a second cluster where another compression is undergoing. If two or more compressions intersect, then priority is given to the compression whose head node has the lowest depth (i.e., near to the root of the hash map). Non-priority compressions are postponed (or aborted) until the top priority one completes. At the end of a compression, the cluster of hash nodes is replaced by a single hash node representing the cluster and the depth of any path traversing the cluster is reduced in one level.

Figure 3 shows an example of applying *lock-free compression* to a cluster of hash levels. For the sake of simplicity of illustration, we consider that hash nodes are initially allocated with two bucket entries and that R_1 to R_6 represent references to arbitrary hash or leaf nodes. Figure 3(a) shows the initial configuration where one can observe the existence of two clusters of hash nodes: cluster C_1 with head node H_i and including H_k and H_l; and cluster C_2 with head node H_k and including H_m and H_n. Since H_k, the head node of C_2, also belongs to C_1, priority is given to the compression of cluster C_1. Figure 3(b) shows the configuration after the compression of cluster C_1 where one can observe that H_i, H_k and H_l were replaced by a single new hash node H_x that has twice the size of bucket entries (four bucket entries in this case).

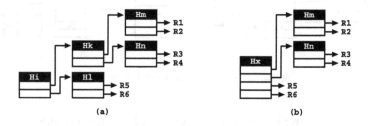

Fig. 3. Compression of a cluster of hash levels

Consider a thread traversing the configuration in Fig. 3 looking for reference R_3. Without compression (Fig. 3(a)), the thread begins by visiting H_i, then follows the reference in the first bucket to access H_k, next the reference in the second bucket to access H_n, and finally the reference in the first bucket to reach R_3. In the worst case, if the header and the corresponding bucket entry for each hash node do not fit inside the same cache line, reaching R_3 will require six memory accesses (two times the number of hash levels). After compression (Fig. 3(b)), the thread begins by visiting H_x and reaching R_3 requires one less hash level, corresponding to four memory accesses, in the worst case.

Let us consider now that lock-free compression is first triggered and successfully applied to C_2 and only then H_l is concurrently added to the hash map data structure to form cluster C_1. Figure 4(a) shows the resulting configuration, where one can observe that H_k, H_m and H_n were replaced by a single new hash node H_z with four bucket entries. As before, the access to references R_1, R_2, R_3 and R_4 were all reduced by one level, but the access to R_5 and R_6 remains unchanged and still requires traversing two hash levels. This illustrates one of the advantages of prioritizing the compressions near the root of the hash map. A second advantage is that the application of compressions following the priority order of being near the root of the hash map converges to a *canonical structure*, while any other order of application can lead to different configurations at the end. A key motivation of lock-free compression is that regardless of which cluster is compressed first, the hash hierarchy will converge to a canonical structure. We next discuss how this is done in our design.

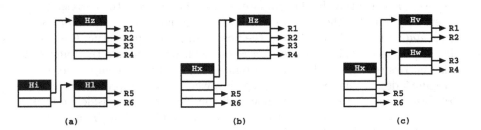

Fig. 4. Splitting of previously compressed hash levels

Starting from the configuration in Fig. 4(a), we now have a cluster C_1 formed by the head node H_i and including H_z and H_l. The problem is that, due to the fact that H_z already represents two hash levels as a result of a previous compression, H_z and H_l have a different number of bucket entries (4 and 2 entries, respectively) and, therefore, we cannot replace cluster C_1 by a single new hash node, as done previously. Figure 4(b) and Fig. 4(c) show two alternative approaches for compressing C_1 in this case.

The approach illustrated in Fig. 4(b) tries to preserve previous compressions. A new hash node H_x is introduced to represent C_1 (thus replacing H_i and H_l) but H_z is maintained. As intended, this approach succeeds in reducing the access to R_5 and R_6 in one level. However, since H_z represents two hash levels, the first two bucket entries of H_x are made to refer to H_z. This violates an invariant of the LFHT design, which requires not having more than one bucket entry referencing the same hash node, and makes it impossible to swap references to hash nodes with just a single word CAS operation.

The approach illustrated in Fig. 4(c) tries to preserve the canonical structure. Since H_z represents a less priority compression, it proceeds by undoing the previous compression and, for that, it splits H_z in two hash levels (H_v and H_w in Fig. 4(c)), each with half the bucket entries. Then, a new hash node H_x is still introduced to represent C_1, thus replacing H_i, H_l and part of H_z. As before, this approach succeeds in reducing the access to all references in one level, but now each bucket entry in H_x holds a reference to different hash nodes. One can observe that this configuration is similar to the one presented in Fig. 3(b), which represents the canonical form. This example shows that, regardless of the order of cluster compression, the hash hierarchy will converge to a canonical structure although, as in this situation, the compress operation would require extra steps.

4 Implementation Details

Starting from the high-level description of the previous section, we now discuss in more detail how lock-free compression is implemented on top of the LFHT data structure. Such detail is important since we want to show that lock-free compression is implemented by following a well-defined sequence of CAS operations. To implement lock-free compression, the following extensions were made to the LFHT data structure: (i) bucket entries now include a *freeze flag* that, when set, indicates that further updates cannot be made to the corresponding bucket entry; and (ii) the header of the hash nodes now includes a *compression representative* field, which refers to the new hash node representing the cluster being compressed, and a *compression count* field, which counts the number of bucket entries referring to hash nodes (and is used to trigger compression).

Figure 5 details the sequence of steps involved in the compression of a *standard* cluster of hash nodes, i.e., without splitting. For that, it considers a bucket entry B_k referring to a cluster with head node H_i and including H_k and H_l. As before, R_1, R_2, R_3 and R_4 represent references to arbitrary hash or leaf nodes.

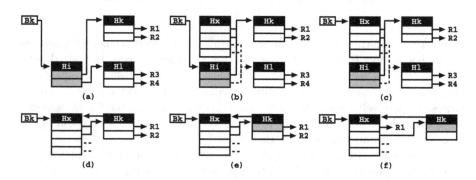

Fig. 5. A step by step compression operation without splitting

Figure 5(a) shows the first step of the compression procedure, where CAS operations are used to set the freeze flag of each bucket entry in the head node H_i (in what follows, frozen entries are marked gray). Remember that a frozen entry remains unchanged for the remaining lifetime. This freezing process is important because it implements the strategy where priority is given to the compression whose head node has the lowest depth. For example, if a less priority compression is being done on cluster with head node H_k, it will be aborted because it cannot update the corresponding first (frozen) bucket entry of H_i.

Next, Fig. 5(b) shows the second step of the compression procedure, where a new hash node H_x is first allocated and then initialized by copying the references from the bucket entries in H_i. In this case, since H_k and H_l are default sized (non-compressed) hash nodes, the size of H_x corresponds to doubling the size of H_i, and each pair of bucket entries in H_x is initialized to match the corresponding H_i's entry. For example, the first two bucket entries of H_x are set to H_k, which is the reference in H_i's first entry, whereas the second two bucket entries of H_x are set to H_l, which is the reference in H_i's second entry. After this initialization, H_x is ready to be inserted in the LFHT data structure and, for that, a CAS operation is applied to B_k trying to replace H_i with H_x. Figure 5(c) shows the resulting configuration. It is important to notice that lock-freedom requires that, at any moment of the compression procedure, no thread can be blocked from traversing and accessing the available hash and leaf nodes. Figure 5(c) show us that, even in a scenario where a thread T is preempted in H_i, T is still able to traverse forward to the deeper levels H_k and H_l.

At this point, it is also important to notice that the configuration in Fig. 5(c) violates the invariant of not having more than one bucket entry referencing the same hash node. However, here, this is not a problem because the bucket entries in H_x are not yet the synchronization points for further updates on the cluster, since they are still referring to H_k and H_l. Thus, the next steps involve copying R_1 to R_4 from the bucket entries of H_k and H_l to the bucket entries of H_x. Figure 5(d) to Fig. 5(f) show how this is done for reference R_1. The same process applies to the remaining references (not shown here to simplify the illustration).

The next step is to set the new compression representative (header) fields of H_k and H_l to refer to H_x. Figure 5(d) shows the configuration after setting the compression representative field of H_k. The same process applies to H_l (not shown here to simplify the illustration). Note that copying the references R_1 and R_2 to H_x, will turn H_k invalid. The compression representative field implements a kind of reconnection path for invalid hash nodes. For example, in a scenario where a thread T is preempted in H_k and H_k turns invalid, the compression representative field allows T to recover to H_x.

The final steps involve freezing the first bucket entry of H_k, meaning that no further updates can be done there, and applying a CAS to the corresponding bucket entry in H_x in order to update it to R_1. Figure 5(e) shows the configuration after the freezing and Fig. 5(f) shows the configuration after the updating of R_1 in H_x. The same process is applied afterwards to the remaining bucket entries in H_x, adjusting R_2, R_3 and R_4, to finish the compression procedure. Note that these final steps do not violate the lock-freedom property of a search, insert, remove or expand operation being done concurrently, since the synchronization point in H_k is being moved to the corresponding bucket entry in H_x. In other words, an operation that would require updating the frozen bucket entry in H_k, will now follow the compression representative field to reach H_x and change the corresponding bucket entry there.

We conclude this section by describing a second compression situation, but now for a scenario leading to the splitting of previously compressed hash levels, as illustrated in Fig. 4. Figure 6 details the sequence of steps involved in the compression of a cluster with head node H_i and including H_z and H_l, where H_z is already the result of a previous compression.

As before, Fig. 6(a) shows the first step of the compression procedure, where CAS operations are used to set the freeze flag of each bucket entry in the head node H_i. Then, Fig. 6(b) shows the second step of the compression procedure,

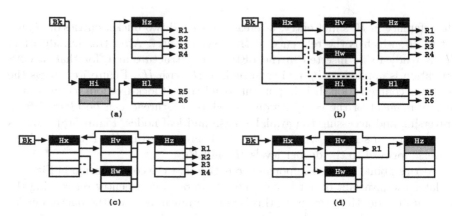

Fig. 6. A step by step compression operation with splitting

where new hash nodes H_x, H_v and H_w are first allocated (H_v and H_w representing the splitting of H_z in two hash levels, each with half the bucket entries) and then initialized by copying the references from the bucket entries in H_i. Next, Fig. 6(c) shows the configuration after updating the compression representative field of H_z to refer to H_x. The same process applies to H_l (not shown here to simplify the illustration). Note that H_v and H_w are not set as representative as, in general, this would require not a single representative field but an array of representatives (equal to the number of bucket entries per hash node). Finally, Fig. 6(d) shows the configuration after freezing the first bucket entry of H_z and after applying a CAS to the corresponding bucket entry in H_v in order to update it to R_1. The same process is then applied to the remaining bucket entries in H_v and H_w, adjusting references R_2 to R_6, to finish the compression procedure.

5 Algorithms

This section presents the key algorithms required to easily reproduce our implementation.[1] We begin with Algorithm 1 to show the pseudo-code for the lock-free compression procedure for a given head node H_i.

Algorithm 1. *Compression(hash node H_i)*

1: *FreezeBucketEntries*(H_i)
2: $H_x \leftarrow CompressionInit(H_i)$
3: **if** *CompressionCommit*(H_i, H_x) **then**
4:     *CompressionReps*(H_x)
5:     *CompressionRefs*(H_x)

FreezeBucketEntries() starts by implementing the first step of the compression procedure, as shown in Fig. 5(a) and Fig. 6(a). Then, *CompressionInit*()

---
[1] Available from https://gitlab.com/pedromoreno/lfht-hhl/.

implements the second step, as shown in Fig. 5(b) and Fig. 6(b). Next, the conditional call to *CompressionCommit*() implements the step where H_i is replaced by H_x, as shown in Fig. 5(c). If it fails, meaning that there is an overlapping high priority compression being done, then H_x is simply deallocated. Otherwise, *CompressionReps*() sets the compression representative fields, as shown in Fig. 5(d) and Fig. 6(c), and *CompressionRefs*() updates the references in the bucket entries of the new hash nodes, as shown in Fig. 5(e–f) and Fig. 6(d). Pseudo-code for *CompressionInit*(), *CompressionReps*() and *CompressionRefs*() is presented in more detail in Algorithms 2, 3 and 4, respectively.

Algorithm 2. *CompressionInit(hash node H_i)*

1: $H_x \leftarrow AllocHashNode(HashSize(H_i) \times HS)$
2: **for** $i \leftarrow 0$ **to** $HashSize(H_i)$ **do**
3:     $H_j \leftarrow H_i.bucket[i]$
4:     **if** $HashSize(H_j) = HS$ **then**
5:         **for** $j \leftarrow 0$ **to** HS **do**
6:             $H_x.bucket[i \times HS + j] \leftarrow H_j$
7:     **else** {splitting case}
8:         **for** $j \leftarrow 0$ **to** HS **do**
9:             $H_v \leftarrow AllocHashNode(HashSize(H_j) \div HS)$
10:            $H_x.bucket[i \times HS + j] \leftarrow H_v$
11:            **for** $v \leftarrow 0$ **to** $HashSize(H_v)$ **do**
12:                $H_v.bucket[v] \leftarrow H_j$
13: **return** H_x

Algorithm 3. *CompressionReps(hash node H_x)*

1: $i \leftarrow 0$
2: **while** $i < HashSize(H_x)$ **do**
3:     $H_k \leftarrow H_x.bucket[i]$
4:     **if** $HashLevel(H_k) \neq HashLevel(H_x)$ **then** {splitting case}
5:         $H_k \leftarrow H_k.bucket[0]$
6:     $H_k.compr\_representative \leftarrow H_x$
7:     $i \leftarrow i + HS$

In these algorithms, HS is the default number of bucket entries for a standard hash node, $HashSize$() returns the number of bucket entries in a hash node, and $HashLevel$() returns the initial depth of a hash node. In Algorithm 4, the $compr\_count$ field counts the number of bucket entries in a hash node referring to deeper hash nodes and is used to trigger lock-free compression when all bucket entries are referring to deeper hash nodes (lines 18–21 in Algorithm 4).

Algorithm 4. $CompressionRefs(hash\ node\ H_x)$

1: $xCount \leftarrow 0$
2: **for** $x \leftarrow 0$ **to** $HashSize(H_x)$ **do**
3:    $H_k \leftarrow H_x.bucket[x]$
4:    **if** $GetLevel(H_k) = GetLevel(H_x)$ **then**
5:       $R \leftarrow FreezeBucketEntry(\&(H_k.bucket[x \bmod HS]))$
6:       $CAS(\&(H_x.bucket[x]), H_k, R)$
7:       **if** $IsHash(R)$ **then**
8:          $xCount \leftarrow xCount + 1$
9:    **else**
10:       $xCount \leftarrow xCount + 1$
11:       $kCount \leftarrow 0$
12:       **for** $k \leftarrow 0$ **to** $HashSize(H_k)$ **do**
13:          $H_z \leftarrow H_k.bucket[k]$
14:          $R \leftarrow FreezeBucketEntry(\&(H_z.bucket[(x \bmod HS) \times HashSize(H_k) + k]))$
15:          $CAS(\&(H_k.bucket[k]), H_z, R)$
16:          **if** $IsHash(R)$ **then**
17:             $kCount \leftarrow kCount + 1$
18:       **if** $AtomicAdd(H_k.compr\_count, kCount = HashSize(H_k)$ **then**
19:          $Compression(H_k)$
20: **if** $AtomicAdd(H_x.compr\_count, xCount) = HashSize(H_x)$ **then**
21:    $Compression(H_x)$

---

6   Performance Analysis

The environment for our experiments was a SMP system based in a NUMA architecture with two Intel Xeon X5650, each having 6 cores (12 hyperthreads) at 2.66 GHz, 12 MB Intel Smart Cache, 96 GB of main memory, and running the Linux kernel 4.15.0-72. To measure execution time, all programs were compiled with GCC 9.2.0 with -O3 and using the jemalloc memory allocator 5.0 [5]. We ran each benchmark 5 times and took the mean of those runs.

6.1   Compression Benefits

Compression benefits heavily rely on the memory environment where we are running our benchmarks. Factors like cache sizes, placement policies, prefetching optimizations can have a significant impact on the overall performance of the LFHT design. To put our results in perspective, first we ran a specific benchmark designed to address the potential gains that one would expect to have when using compression. For that, we used a static version of the LFHT design that implements fixed predefined configurations of hash levels, with a different number of bucket entries on each hash node, and we measured the execution time for one thread performing only search operations on those configurations.

Starting from a maximal configuration of 24 uncompressed hash levels, all with the same minimal size of 2^1 bucket entries, we studied the effect of applying two different types of compression operations: (i) by reducing the number of hash levels from the root hash node to the leaf hash nodes; and (ii) by reducing the number of hash levels from the leafs to the root. Figure 7 shows the execution time, in seconds, for executing 2^{24} search operations with one thread when reducing the number of hash levels in both directions (Fig. 7(a) for the root to leafs compression and Fig. 7(b) for the leafs to root compression) until reaching the configuration with just a single hash node with 2^{24} bucket entries. The x-axis represents the number of hash levels compressed in a configuration. In both figures, the x-axis value of 1 represents the maximal configuration of 24 uncompressed hash levels and the x-axis value of 24 represents the single fully compressed hash node with 2^{24} bucket entries. The other x-axis values represent intermediate configurations. For example, the x-axis value of 10, in Fig. 7(a) represents the configuration whose first hash node includes 2^{10} bucket entries followed by 14 uncompressed hash levels, and in Fig. 7(b) represents the configuration with 14 initial uncompressed hash levels followed by a final hash node with 2^{10} bucket entries.

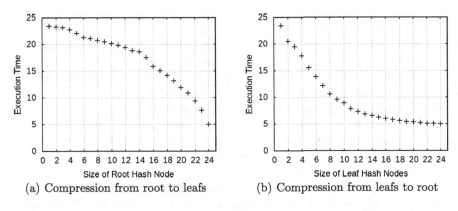

(a) Compression from root to leafs   (b) Compression from leafs to root

Fig. 7. LFHT's compression effects for 2^{24} search operations with one thread

In Fig. 7(a), one can observe that, for root hash nodes with less than 2^{14} bucket entries, the benefits are small, but then, for higher compression ratios, the results show a significant impact on reducing the execution time. This happens because most of the execution time is spent on waiting for swaps between the different levels of memory and because the hash nodes closest to the root tend to remain in cache. Consequently, compressing the first 14 levels only reduces the amount of cache accesses, which results in a poor impact on the total executing time. On the other hand, further compression is able to reduce effectively the number of memory accesses and memory swaps.

In Fig. 7(b), one can observe that compressions up to a size of about 2^{10} are quite effective in reducing the execution time, whereas after that size they are not as much. This can be explained by the fact that, after a certain size, the benefits of compression are absorbed by the caching effects.

As a result of this study, in what follows, we have chosen to set the root hash node of the LFHT design with 2^{16} bucket entries, thus ensuring that compressions would have an impact in the execution time. This will create a memory overhead, which can be considered negligible, since it amounts to just 512 KB. All the other hash nodes, allocated during execution, begin with 2^4 bucket entries, which is the minimum size allowed by the original LFHT design.

6.2 Performance Results

In this subsection, we analyze the performance of our compression design in three different scenarios: (i) *Search Only*, where threads search for N keys in a hash map with the N keys inserted; (ii) *Insert Only*, where threads insert N keys in an empty hash map; and (iii) *Remove Only*, where threads remove N keys in a hash map with N random keys.[2] On each scenario, we used two sets of N random keys, namely 10^8 and 10^9 keys. To support concurrent randomicity on each thread, we used glibc PRNG (Pseudo Random Number Generator), such that, for insertions we just insert random keys by giving each thread a different seed, and for search and remove, we reuse the seeds used for insertion, ensuring that we search or remove each key only once. Although these scenarios are not real-world applications, they do provide a strong insight about the expected behavior of the design. Note that, since hash-maps use hash functions to disperse keys among the internal data structures, we argue that real-world applications should provide similar results to the ones that we present next.

Figure 8 shows throughput results (higher is better) comparing our compressed design (LFHT-Compress) against the original design (LFHT-Original), and the Concurrent Hash Map design (CHM) of Intel-TBB library [16], when running a number of threads from 1 to 24 with 10^8 and 10^9 keys in the three previously mentioned scenarios.

Figure 8(a) and Fig. 8(b) show throughput results for the *Search Only* scenario. Comparing the two LFHT designs, one can observe that LFHT-Compress obtains improvements against LFHT-Original of around 50% with 10^8 keys and around 100% with 10^9 keys. When comparing against CHM, LFHT-Compress has almost always the best results, with CHM very close. This can be explained by the fact that the final configuration of both designs is quite similar, since CHM also uses only a root hash level to do the initial scatter of keys.

Figure 8(c) and Fig. 8(d) show throughput results for the *Insert Only* scenario. Comparing the two LFHT designs, one can observe that both achieve similar results for 10^8 keys but LFHT-Compress is clearly better for 10^9 keys. Even though LFHT-Compress is doing more work by compressing hash levels, it is able to improve the overall throughput. This happens because the cost of doing extra work on compression is compensated by the shorter paths leading to the insertion points. When comparing with CHM, LFHT-Compress has almost always the best results, however in this scenario the difference is more significant as we increase the number of threads. One reason that can explain this

---

[2] We have also tested other scenarios that mix the search, remove and insert operations, but have not obtained relevant results. This can be explained by the fact that the interference between different types of operations is rare enough to not impact performance.

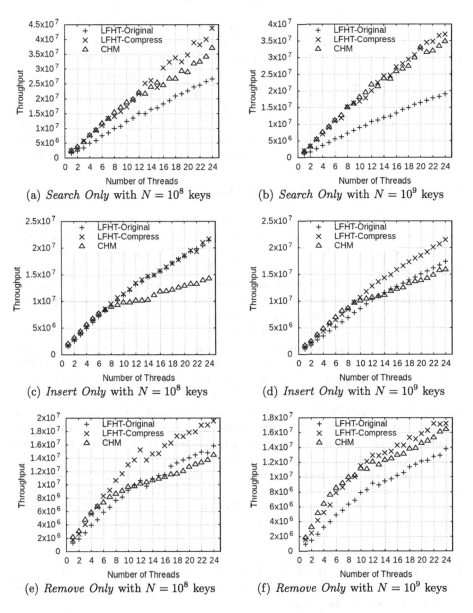

Fig. 8. Throughput for the *Search Only, Insert Only* and *Remove Only* scenarios

difference is the fact that, since CHM is lock-based, it seems unable to scatter the concurrency spots as we increase the number of threads, since each lock is being used to block a large portion of paths within the hash map. On the other hand, since LFHT-Compress is lock-free, it is able to control the concurrency spots with the fine grain given by the CAS operation.

Finally, Fig. 8(e) and Fig. 8(f) show throughput results for the *Remove Only* scenario. Comparing the two LFHT designs, one can observe that LFHT-Compress is again better than LFHT-Original and that the difference increases as we increase the number of threads. This can be explained by the gains observed for LFHT-Compress on the search operation. When comparing with CHM, LFHT-Compress is again better by far than CHM in the 10^8 scenario, with the difference increasing as the number of threads increases, whereas in the 10^9 scenario the difference is almost constant. This can be explained by the same reasons mentioned before for the *Insert Only* scenario (lock-based vs lock-free).

7   Conclusions and Further Work

We have presented a novel lock-free compression design for a lock-free trie-based hash map, named LFHT, that is able to significantly reduce the depth of the internal hash levels within the hash map structure. By doing so, our design is able to minimize cache misses and increase the overall throughput of the default search, insert and remove operations. To materialize our design, we redesigned the LFHT data structure in order to maintain the lock-freedom property of the existent search, insert, remove and expand operations.

Experimental results show that lock-free compression effectively improves the default operations and, in doing so, it outperforms the previous design, which was already quite competitive when compared against the concurrent hash map design in Intel's TBB library. We argue that our experimental results are very interesting and show the potential of our design since it was able to achieve better throughput ratios than CHM, in almost all scenarios, and, for some thread launches, the difference between the two is very significant. This is quite an accomplishment if we consider that both the CHM design and the hardware architecture are implemented by Intel.

As further work, we plan to extend our design to implement a scheme that allows lock-free compression to be split into several subtasks that can be executed concurrently by different threads, instead of just a single thread as it is now, and compare its performance in different hardware architectures using real-world applications.

Data Availability Statement. The datasets and code generated during and/or analysed during the current study are available in the Figshare repository: https://doi.org/10.6084/m9.figshare.12560228 [13].

References

1. Acharya, A., Zhu, H., Shen, K.: Adaptive algorithms for cache-efficient trie search. In: Goodrich, M.T., McGeoch, C.C. (eds.) ALENEX 1999. LNCS, vol. 1619, pp. 300–315. Springer, Heidelberg (1999). https://doi.org/10.1007/3-540-48518-X_18
2. Areias, M., Rocha, R.: Towards a lock-free, fixed size and persistent hash map design. In: International Symposium on Computer Architecture and High Performance Computing, pp. 145–152. IEEE (2017)

3. Bagwell, P.: Ideal hash trees. Es Grands Champs **1195** (2001)
4. Brown, T.: Techniques for Constructing Efficient Lock-free Data Structures. Ph.D. thesis, University of Toronto (2017)
5. Evans, J.: Tick tock, malloc needs a clock. In: Applicative 2015. ACM, New York, NY, USA (2015)
6. Fredkin, E.: Trie memory. Commun. ACM **3**, 490–499 (1962)
7. Grossi, R., Ottaviano, G.: Fast compressed tries through path decompositions. J. Exp. Algorithmics **19** (2015)
8. Herlihy, M., Wing, J.M.: Axioms for concurrent objects. In: ACM Symposium on Principles of Programming Languages, pp. 13–26. ACM (1987)
9. Knuth, D.E.: The Art of Computer Programming: Volume 3: Sorting and Searching, 2nd edn. Addison-Wesley, Upper Saddle River (1998)
10. Li, X., Andersen, D.G., Kaminsky, M., Freedman, M.J.: Algorithmic improvements for fast concurrent cuckoo hashing. In: Proceedings of the Ninth European Conference on Computer Systems, EuroSys '14. ACM (2014)
11. Mehta, D.P., Sahni, S.: Handbook of Data Structures and Applications. Chapman & Hall, London (2004)
12. Moreno, P., Areias, M., Rocha, R.: Memory reclamation methods for lock-free hash tries. In: International Symposium on Computer Architecture and High Performance Computing, pp. 188–195. IEEE (2019)
13. Moreno, P., Areias, M., Rocha, R.: Artifact and instructions to generate experimental results for conference proceeding 2020 paper: a compression-based design for higher throughput in a lock-free hash map (July 2020). https://doi.org/10.6084/m9.figshare.12560228. https://springernature.figshare.com/articles/software/Artifactandinstructionstogenerateexperimentalresultsforconferenceproceeding2020paperACompression-BasedDesignforHigherThroughputinaLock-FreeHashMap/12560228/1
14. Prokopec, A.: Cache-tries: concurrent lock-free hash tries with constant-time operations. In: ACM SIGPLAN Symposium on Principles and Practice of Parallel Programming, pp. 137–151. ACM (2018)
15. Prokopec, A., Bronson, N.G., Bagwell, P., Odersky, M.: Concurrent tries with efficient non-blocking snapshots. In: ACM Symposium on Principles and Practice of Parallel Programming, pp. 151–160. ACM (2012)
16. Reinders, J.: Intel Threading Building Blocks: Outfitting C++ for Multi-core Processor Parallelism. O'Reilly, Sebastopol (2007)
17. Sagiv, Y.: Concurrent operations on B*-trees with overtaking. J. Comput. Syst. Sci. **33**(2), 275–296 (1986)

Multicore and Manycore Parallelism

NV-PhTM: An Efficient Phase-Based Transactional System for Non-volatile Memory

Alexandro Baldassin[1](✉), Rafael Murari[1], João P. L. de Carvalho[2],
Guido Araujo[2], Daniel Castro[3], João Barreto[3], and Paolo Romano[3]

[1] UNESP – Univ Estadual Paulista, São Paulo, Brazil
{alexandro.baldassin,rafael.murari}@unesp.br
[2] UNICAMP – Institute of Computing, São Paulo, Brazil
{joao.carvalho,guido}@ic.unicamp.br
[3] INESC-ID & Instituto Superior Técnico, University of Lisbon, Lisbon, Portugal
daniel.castro@ist.utl.pt, joao.barreto@tecnico.ulisboa.pt,
romano@inesc-id.pt

Abstract. Non-Volatile Memory (NVM) is an emerging memory technology aimed to eliminate the gap between main memory and stable storage. Nevertheless, today's programs will not readily benefit from NVM because crash failures may render the program in an unrecoverable and inconsistent state. In this context, *durable transactions* have been proposed as a mechanism to ease the adoption of NVM by simplifying the task of programming NVM systems. Existing systems employ either hardware (HW) or software (SW) transactions with different performance trade-offs. Although SW transactions are flexible and unbounded, they may significantly hurt the performance of short-lived transactions. On the other hand, HW transactional memories provide low-overhead but are resource-constrained. In this paper we present NV-PhTM, a transactional system for NVM that delivers the best out of both HW and SW transactions by dynamically selecting the best execution mode according to the application's characteristics. NV-PhTM is comprised of a set of heuristics to guide online phase transition while retaining persistency in case of crashes during migration. To the best of our knowledge, NV-PhTM is the first phase-based system to provide durable transactions. Experimental results with the STAMP benchmark show that the proposed heuristics are efficient in guiding phase transitions with low overhead.

Keywords: Transactions · Transactional memory · Persistent memory

1 Introduction

Recent Non-Volatile Memory (NVM) technologies can provide persistency, fast access time and a byte-addressable interface. As NVM's access latency is approaching those of current DRAM technology, its content can be directly read

© Springer Nature Switzerland AG 2020
M. Malawski and K. Rzadca (Eds.): Euro-Par 2020, LNCS 12247, pp. 477–492, 2020.
https://doi.org/10.1007/978-3-030-57675-2_30

or written by the CPU, thus avoiding the overhead involved in block-oriented systems. However, it is challenging to write code for NVM because a system crash may render the program in an unrecoverable state. Durable transactions have been suggested as an appropriate way of programming these systems given their consolidated strong semantics and ease-of-use idiom [4,15].

Most of early works focused on providing durable transactions by carefully extending software transactional memory (STM) libraries with logging and recovery mechanisms [9,21,24,25]. Nevertheless, although flexible and unbounded, software approaches may display a considerable overhead for applications with short-lived transactions. With the availability of microprocessors with hardware transaction extensions (HTM) [16,18], researchers have proposed using this mechanism as a way of speeding up the performance of applications running on durable transactional systems. The key idea of recent HTM-enabled solutions [8,14,20] is to separate the execution of a durable transaction into two parts. In the first one, transactions are executed using the hardware support and construct a volatile redo log. The second stage consists of a transaction persisting its log and ensuring that the order is consistent with some serial execution. One important drawback of hardware-based solutions, however, is that most microprocessors only provide best-effort transactions, meaning that transactions are not guaranteed to always commit in hardware.

Although each approach (HW or SW) has distinct virtues, the decision about which one to use is usually left to programmers. However, making the right choice requires an intricate understanding of workload and system-specific characteristics, and is often dynamic (i.e., the optimal approach changes throughout an application's execution). This work is motivated by the observation that this decision is a fundamental gap that affects the effectiveness of the current state of the art on (SW and HW) durable transactions. In order to fill that gap, we propose NV-PhTM: a Non-Volatile Phased Transactional Memory system that delivers the best out of both HW and SW transactions by dynamically selecting the best execution mode according to the application's characteristics. A key decision in designing NV-PhTM concerns how to handle the concurrent execution of HW/SW transactions.

Before the emergence of NVM, the goal of combining SW and HW transactions had already received plenty of attention in the context of non-durable transactional memory [15]. Historically, the first approaches allowed both HW and SW transactions to concurrently execute in the same application, which is commonly designated as Hybrid Transactional Memory (HyTM). More recently, different studies have shown that HyTM has inherent scalability issues [1,7]. In parallel, the alternative approach of Phase-based Transactional Memory (PTM) was proposed as a pragmatic way of avoiding the fundamental pitfalls of HyTM [6,19] through a simplistic design where SW and HW transactions no longer run concurrently; instead, the execution is split into all-SW and all-HW phases. PTM systems have to deal with challenges such as when to transition the execution to different phases, accomplished through heuristics, and how to efficiently perform the transition.

To the best of our knowledge, NV-PhTM is the first system to apply the principles of PTM in the context of durable transactions. As we discuss later on, directly applying existing non-durable PTM systems to this new context is sub-optimal as it neglects new phenomena and trade-offs that durability brings about. NV-PhTM provides insights regarding the construction of new heuristics and phase transition in a NVM context. In particular, this paper makes the following contributions:

– It proposes NV-PhTM and new heuristics with the aim of allowing phase-based execution of durable transactions (see Sects. 3.1 and 3.2);
– It devises a new strategy to allow the migration between HW and SW transactions while maintaining consistency and persistency (see Sect. 3.3);
– It provides experimental results, based on the STAMP benchmark [22], showing that NV-PhTM is efficient and can provide the best of both HW and SW transactions (see Sect. 4).

The rest of the paper is organized as follows. Section 2 presents the main concepts used in this work. Section 3 gives a detailed description of the NV-PhTM design, whereas Sect. 4 presents its evaluation, comparing it against other state-of-the-art approaches. Section 5 provides an overview of related works and, finally, Sect. 6 concludes the work.

2 Background

This section briefly describes two representative HW and SW systems which provide durable transactions, namely NV-HTM and PSTM. These systems serve as the base in which NV-PhTM is built upon.

NV-HTM [8] is one of the first systems to provide durable transactions over commodity transaction-enabled hardware. Its commit stage is split into *non-durable* and *durable* stages. When a hardware transaction executes, it also stores its updates into a redo log (a per-thread structure). Upon a commit, the hardware makes the updates visible to other concurrent threads but does not necessarily persist them. This is the so-called *non-durable commit*. After that, the transaction's redo log is persisted via software (it might have to wait for the logs of transactions it depends on to be persisted as well), completing the *durable commit* stage. NV-HTM requires instrumenting the procedures to start/commit a transaction and the write operation (to construct the redo log), but read operations can proceed without any instrumentation overhead. A timestamp mechanism is used to enforce consistency: when a transaction is durably committed, all transactions serialized before it by the HTM system are already durably committed. A concurrent checkpointing process is used to persist the snapshot in NVM of all durably committed transactions, as well as pruning the redo logs. In case transactions cannot proceed in hardware, NV-HTM acquires a single global lock and serializes the execution (software transactions are not provided).

The acronym PSTM (Persistent Software Transactional Memory) usually refers to a class of implementations based on the mechanism that Mnemosyne [25] originally introduced to support durable memory transactions. It is composed of a transaction system and a transaction log. The original proposal described by Mnemosyne is based on TinySTM [13], providing lazy versioning with redo logging and eager conflict detection with encounter-time locking. With lazy versioning, data written by a transaction is stored locally in a buffer (volatile memory) and also added to a log (along with the corresponding addresses). During commit, the log is flushed to NVM and the data is persisted. Notice that lazy versioning requires, for each read operation, checking whether the required data is already present in the local buffer, in which case it contains the most recent value. In order to avoid that, some PSTM systems prefer to adopt undo logs and in-place updates instead [3,8]. Upon each write, the corresponding log entry is flushed to NVM before the data is modified in-place. During commit, the changes are flushed to NVM and a commit marker is added to the log. The cost of durable transactions is two writes to NVM with every update: one for the log entry and another for the data itself.

3   NV-PhTM Design

NV-PhTM allows the execution of HW/SW transactions in phases. It provides the following features in the context of NVM: i) new heuristics to guide transitions among hardware (HW), software (SW) and serialized (GLOCK) phases; ii) a consolidation strategy to enforce system consistency and persistency when transitioning between different phases. This section discusses NV-PhTM general system architecture, transition heuristics and state consolidation strategies.

3.1   System Architecture

The two main building blocks of NV-PhTM are NV-HTM (for HW transactions) and PSTM (for SW transactions), described previously. A general overview of the architecture is presented in Fig. 1. The first step performed by the system is to map the memory region (e.g., by using *mmap*) to the application address space, creating a Working Snapshot (WS)①. As soon as the transaction performs the first access to a page mapped on the PS, the operating system automatically uses copy-on-write (CoW) to create a volatile copy in DRAM. Hence, during execution, the load and store instructions emitted by transactions operate on DRAM-mapped pages of the WS②. When a hardware transaction completes, two actions take place. First, the HTM system non-durably commits the transaction data (volatile memory). Second, the system flushes the redo log to NVM③, in which case the transaction is durably committed. A Checkpoint Process (CP) is responsible for applying the updates stored in the logs④ into a consistent Persistent Snapshot (PS)⑤, as well as pruning the redo logs so that they do not grow beyond a given threshold. The application can also invoke the CP⑥ to perform *memory consolidation*, an operation that drains all the durable logs to the PS and discards every page that has been cloned in DRAM. It is used to consolidate the updates to the PS before migrating to SW mode.

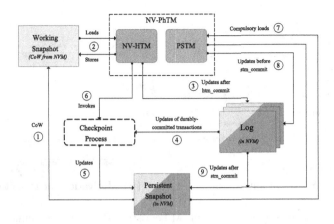

Fig. 1. NV-PhTM system architecture.

For the software part (PSTM), NV-PhTM extends the NOrec transactional system [10] with non-volatile semantics. Differently from the HW component, each transaction here is responsible for persisting its log as well as flushing the updates to PS. During transaction processing, values are initially accessed from the PS ⑦ and stored locally (DRAM) in the transaction's write set. For each memory update performed during the execution of a transaction, its corresponding log entry is flushed to NVM⑧; when a transaction finally commits, it appends a commit marker to the log and persist all updates to PS ⑨. The sequence lock of NOrec is used to order the commit events in the log. Notice that the CP component is not used while in SW mode, since the transactions themselves are responsible for consolidating the updates to PS. Another design option would be to use the idea of splitting the commit operation into stages and let the CP module perform consolidation, similarly to what is done in DudeTM [20]. However, in this initial investigation on phase-based durable transactions we opted for a more traditional design, leaving commit splitting for future work.

3.2   Transition Heuristics

Transition heuristics specify *in what conditions* and *to which phase* the system should migrate. NV-PhTM behavior is better understood by its transition automaton, showed in Fig. 2a. The system initially starts in HW mode. A HW→SW transition is triggered when two consecutive aborts occur due to capacity issues and the abort rate is above a given threshold Ⓐ. These conditions represent situations where transactions are very unlikely to make the most out of current HW transactions, thus execution falls back to SW mode. However, when the length of transactions (measured in cycles) is relatively small, the system may return to HW mode since short-running transactions tend to cause high overhead in SW mode. The SW→HW transition only completes once all deferred transactions (those that caused the HW→SW migration) are com-

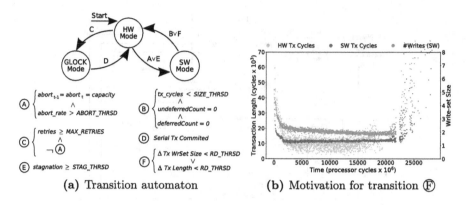

(a) Transition automaton

(b) Motivation for transition Ⓕ

Fig. 2. Design of the NV-PhTM heuristics. (Color figure online)

mitted and no other transaction is active. Internally, this is identified by the two variables, `deferredCount` and `undeferredCount`, being equal to zero Ⓑ. The variable `deferredCount` keeps track of how many transactions invoked the HW→SW transition. These are the transactions that should complete in SW before the system considers returning to HW. As for `undeferredCount`, it counts the transactions that are actively running in SW, but are only doing so because other transaction(s) invoked the switch.

The execution is serialized Ⓒ if: i) most of the aborts are not caused by capacity issues (therefore they are very likely caused by conflicts among transactions), ii) the abort rate is not high enough, and iii) the number of retries reached a given threshold, In this situation it is pointless to migrate to SW mode and thus serializing the execution may be more beneficial – as entering and leaving the GLOCK mode is much faster compared to the SW mode. When the serialized transaction is completed, the system returns to HW mode Ⓓ.

So far, the described heuristics take care of avoiding capacity and contention issues, but they do not address problems caused by NVM. For instance, a particular source of efficiency loss when running in HW mode is the persistent log structure that is used to store the updates of the transactions. Recall that the CP is responsible for pruning this log and consolidating the changes into the PS (steps ④ and ⑤ in Fig. 1). If the number of writes to the log is high, the log will probably fill up before the CP is able to free some space, stalling the execution. We named this scenario as *log-induced stagnation*, since transactions are unable to proceed until there is enough space in the log. Therefore, a new heuristic was added to NV-PhTM in order to force a HW→SW transition when stagnation is problematic (above an empirically determined threshold) Ⓔ. Recall that PSTM does not use the CP and, as a consequence, the log-induced scenario cannot happen while in SW mode.

We observed that, for some applications running solely in HW mode, the stagnation issue tends to dissipate over time. If that happens, then running in HW mode might yield better performance. But if the system migrated to SW due to heuristic Ⓔ, it has no direct way of knowing if the stagnation level would be low and whether returning to HW is a good idea. In order to have an insight into the new SW→HW heuristic that addresses this point, please refer to Fig. 2b. It shows the average transaction length (left Y axis), for both HW (red) and SW (blue) transactions, as well as the average write-set size (right Y axis, green dots), as time goes on (X axis). The plot is for the Intruder application from the STAMP benchmark running with 12 threads (see Sect. 4 for details on the experimental settings). The key point here is to notice that there is a relationship between the reduction in the write-set size (green dots) and SW transaction length (blue dots) with the stagnation level, as it is possible to observe that HW transactions become faster (red dots) when that happens (around 2 million cycles in the figure). The new SW→HW heuristic developed for NV-PhTM uses this reduction in the write-set size and length of SW transactions to force a transition when the threshold RD_THRSD is met Ⓕ.

3.3   Consolidation Strategies

If a crash occurs while executing in either HW or SW mode it is possible to recover the state by replaying the logs. However, inconsistencies might occur due to the transitions between modes. Phase transitions are handled by a shared `modeIndicator` variable, which is always read by HW transactions when they start. When the condition for HW→SW is met, the transaction that triggers the transition atomically changes `modeIndicator` to SW, which aborts all running hardware transitions. Upon restart, these transactions will notice the mode change and will run in SW mode. Notice that this behavior would allow SW transactions to start executing (and change the logs) while the CP might still be executing. Therefore, NV-PhTM requires a *barrier* when switching modes. An extra bit of `modeIndicator` is used to act as a permission flag. When the mode is changed, the flag is atomically set (using a CAS operation); the transactions that detect the HW→SW transition wait for the permission flag before entering SW mode. Meanwhile, the transaction that triggered the migration invokes and waits for the CP to perform a system consolidation procedure before resetting the permission flag. At this point all transactions will start in SW mode and the PS will be correctly updated. Handling SW→HW transition is similar, but does not require waiting for the CP since it is not used in SW mode.

4   Experimental Evaluation

This section presents a thorough quantitative evaluation of NV-PhTM by showing the effectiveness of the new heuristics and speedup numbers against state-of-the-art systems.

4.1   Setup

The experimental evaluation considers the following systems:

NV-HTM: an implementation of the work in Castro et al. [8] using a threshold of 9 consecutive retries for serialization, 10000 log entries per thread, and a log occupancy threshold of 50% (used to activate log pruning);

PSTM: based on NOrec STM [10] with redo log and lazy versioning similar to Mnemosyne [25]. As in NV-HTM, a log of 10000 entries is also used for each thread;

PhTM*: an implementation of NV-PhTM without heuristics Ⓔ and Ⓕ. It is considered here so that the effectiveness of the new NVM-aware heuristics can be assessed;

NV-PhTM: the newly proposed phase-based transactional system with durable transactions described in this paper. It uses the same core parameters of PSTM and NV-HTM, an abort threshold ($ABORT\_THRSD$) of 75%, transaction length threshold ($SIZE\_THRSD$) of 30000 cycles, and stagnation threshold ($STAG\_THRSD$) of 45%. The implementation is very lightweight and based on the rdtscp instruction for collecting timing information. The time spent by transactions waiting for the log (stagnation time) and total time are measured and the ratio is computed. The SW→HW transition is triggered when a 15% reduction (RD_THRSD) over time of the write-set size and transaction length is detected. Measurements are collected every 1000 committed transactions. See Sect. 4.4 for a brief discussion on how these parameters were selected.

The systems are evaluated using the STAMP (Stanford Transactional Applications for Multi-Processing) benchmark suite [22]. Speedup is calculated by using a NVM-aware sequential version of the applications without any concurrency control as the baseline. The experiments are performed on an 18-core Intel Xeon Gold 5220 machine (with TSX support) clocked at 2.20 GHz, 192 GB physical DRAM, and x86-64 Linux kernel 3.10. The applications were compiled using GCC 7.3.1. The reported results represent the average of 30 runs; a 95% confidence interval bar is also shown. In order to avoid some performance issues induced by the memory allocator [5,11], the TCMalloc allocator with the changes suggested by Nakaike et al. [23] is used. Finally, like previous works [8,9,20], NVM is emulated using DRAM. In particular, slow writes to NVM are modeled by adding a delay of 500ns.

4.2   SSCA2 and Intruder

This section provides a detailed discussion for two of the most representative applications of STAMP: SSCA2 and Intruder. The speedup (Y axis) as the number of threads increases (X axis) is shown in Fig. 3. In order to better understand the behavior of the systems, Table 1 presents the percentage of time spent in the different modes for NV-HTM, PhTM*, and NV-PhTM: HW for hardware, SW for software, and GL for GLOCK (their sum should add to 100% of the total execution time). Table 1 also shows the average percentage of the total time consumed by log-induced stagnation (LIS), that is, the fraction of the total time that threads need to wait for enough log space.

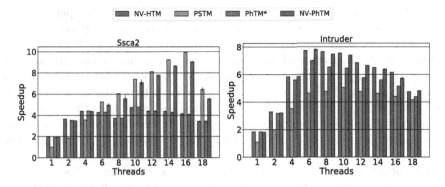

Fig. 3. Speedup numbers evaluating the effectiveness of the proposed heuristics.

Table 1. Fraction of time (%) spent in each mode (HW, SW, GL) and Log-Induced Stagnation (LIS).

App	#t	NV-HTM			PhTM*				NV-PhTM			
		HW	GL	LIS	HW	SW	GL	LIS	HW	SW	GL	LIS
	1	100.00	0.00	0.00	100.00	0.00	0.00	0.00	100.00	0.00	0.00	0.00
	2	99.99	0.01	0.26	99.99	0.00	0.01	0.21	99.99	0.00	0.01	0.20
	4	99.99	0.01	19.80	99.99	0.00	0.01	19.78	96.71	3.28	0.01	18.76
	6	99.99	0.01	31.30	99.99	0.00	0.01	30.98	22.83	77.17	0.00	7.83
SSCA2	8	99.99	0.01	36.68	99.99	0.00	0.01	36.99	14.76	85.23	0.00	6.79
	10	99.98	0.02	37.09	99.99	0.00	0.01	36.97	8.62	91.37	0.00	3.38
	12	99.98	0.02	39.66	99.98	0.00	0.01	39.64	7.65	92.35	0.00	2.55
	14	99.98	0.02	41.60	99.99	0.00	0.01	41.66	9.39	90.61	0.01	3.37
	16	99.99	0.01	43.25	99.98	0.00	0.02	43.45	11.34	88.66	0.01	4.36
	18	99.99	0.01	46.03	99.97	0.01	0.01	46.02	23.67	76.33	0.00	10.59
	1	99.81	0.19	0.02	99.77	0.02	0.21	0.02	99.80	0.00	0.20	0.02
	2	99.02	0.98	0.44	96.62	2.56	0.81	0.30	99.04	0.02	0.94	0.35
	4	96.17	3.83	2.19	89.15	8.61	2.24	2.20	96.37	0.16	3.47	2.11
	6	92.74	7.26	4.77	81.06	16.07	2.87	4.88	93.46	0.77	5.77	4.67
Intruder	8	97.39	2.61	14.79	77.10	19.43	3.47	10.85	90.91	1.12	7.96	11.82
	10	97.31	2.69	21.88	75.37	21.11	3.51	16.10	88.33	2.62	9.05	17.89
	12	95.22	4.78	26.98	71.94	23.05	5.02	19.23	83.10	4.98	11.93	20.89
	14	87.26	12.74	26.99	71.24	23.09	5.68	21.87	77.76	9.48	12.76	22.60
	16	96.70	3.30	35.26	75.22	23.91	0.86	27.75	75.83	18.51	5.66	27.64
	18	83.47	16.53	35.07	61.25	35.14	3.61	25.64	67.62	20.29	12.09	27.47

For SSCA2, it is possible to see that NV-HTM performs well up to 4 threads, but PSTM then starts to display a better performance. This is mostly due to the stagnation problem occurring in NV-HTM as showed by the column LIS in Table 1. Since PhTM* does not have the new heuristic that takes into account the stagnation time Ⓔ, it does not transition to SW and therefore performs similarly to NV-HTM, spending most of its time in HW mode. On the other hand,

NV-PhTM is able to switch to the SW mode and follows PSTM's performance closely after 4 threads. Notice also that the LIS column (highlighted) confirms the reduction of stagnation time due to the migration to SW mode. This result highlights the main feature of phase-based systems: its ability to automatically identify the best performing system (NV-HTM up until 4 threads, and PSTM after that). Because PhTM* is not aware of the stagnation issue, it continues following NV-HTM and therefore does not perform well with more than 4 threads.

Intruder is a case in which HW performs better throughout all thread configurations and therefore NV-HTM exhibits the best performance numbers. For this application, stagnation is not as severe as with SSCA2 (LIS column). Contrary to other applications, the stagnation levels in Intruder varies during its execution, with peaks at the beginning and end, when the number of writes is more accentuated (see Fig. 2b). Although PhTM* performs better than PSTM, its performance numbers are not as good as NV-PhTM from 6 threads onwards. PhTM* is still able to transition to SW because of the high overall abort rate. However, as Table 1 reveals (highlighted), it spends more time in SW than necessary because it does not have the new SW→HW heuristic based on the reduction of number of writes and transaction length Ⓕ. Overall, the results obtained with NV-PhTM show the effectiveness of the new heuristics for HW→SW (SSCA2) and SW→HW (Intruder) transitions.

4.3   Remaining STAMP Applications

The performance results for the remaining STAMP applications are shown in Fig. 4. Due to space reasons we only consider a subset of the threads. For Genome, Labyrinth and Vacation there are small performance differences between PhTM* and NV-PhTM, implying that the new heuristics do not play a major role with these applications. Stagnation is not a major issue in Genome and, for Vacation, there is a large number of capacity aborts that force HW→SW transitions. Indeed, 99% of the total execution time is spent in SW mode in Vacation starting from 8 threads. On the other hand, Genome spends about 90% of the total execution time in HW mode. Labyrinth has very long transactions, forcing HW transactions to abort almost all time. In fact, 99% of the time is serialized with NV-HTM because it employs a global lock as the fallback mechanism in case of high contention. Both PhTM* and NV-PhTM can detect the serialization issue very early and switch to SW mode.

Kmeans is an application with a high variability in execution time. Even then, it is possible to see that NV-PhTM follows the best system, NV-HTM, more closely than PhTM* up to 4 cores (the maximum speedup achieved with this application). After that, NV-HTM tends to get worse because stagnation time starts to become an issue and, eventually, at 10 threads, PSTM takes over. At this point NV-PhTM starts following PSTM whereas PhTM* does not, as seen in the configuration with 16 threads. There is a small inaccuracy with NV-PhTM

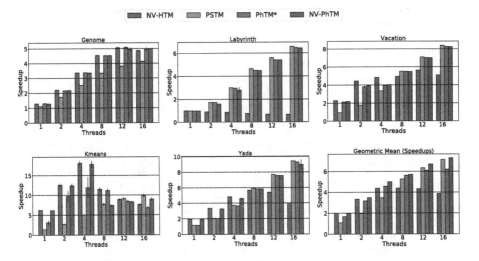

Fig. 4. Speedups for the STAMP applications.

at 8 threads as the stagnation threshold is reached and the system migrates to SW mode. Yada is an application in which stagnation is not a major concern. Capacity and conflict aborts are the major cause of its inefficiency, particularly after 4 threads, when the majority of the execution time of NV-HTM is serialized. Here, NV-PhTM correctly starts following NV-HTM but switches to PSTM as serialization starts to dominate the execution time of the HW mode. PhTM* is always using the SW mode because its heuristics force a HW→SW very early given the capacity aborts. It also cannot return to HW because the length of the transactions is way above the minimum threshold. NV-PhTM, on the other hand, can perform a SW→HW transition since Yada has a behavior similar to Intruder, in which the transaction length decreases rapidly.

The last plot in Fig. 4 shows the geometric mean of the speedups for all the applications considered. It is clear from this plot that NV-HTM tends to be faster than PSTM up until 4 threads when stagnation is still not a serious issue, but after that PSTM starts to dominate. Since the phased systems are very likely to follow the best performing system, they also display good overall results. In particular, the improved heuristics provided by NV-PhTM in the context of NVM makes it a superior option when compared to PhTM*. The reason is clear: when stagnation is not a problem, it performs similarly to PhTM*; but PhTM* heuristics cannot deal with log-induced stagnation and therefore NV-PhTM performs better overall.

Table 2. Percentage of total time spent during phase migrations and the average number of transitions (ANoT).

Application	Transition	Threads									
		1	2	4	6	8	10	12	14	16	18
Genome	HW→SW	0.00	0.01	0.03	0.03	0.03	0.04	0.05	0.06	0.11	0.10
	SW→HW	0.00	0.00	0.00	0.00	0.00	0.00	0.00	0.00	0.01	0.01
	ANoT	1.80	2.07	1.70	2.03	1.27	1.47	3.73	5.70	17.20	13.97
Intruder	HW→SW	0.00	0.00	0.00	0.01	0.07	0.22	0.56	0.56	0.06	1.02
	SW→HW	0.00	0.00	0.00	0.01	0.01	0.03	0.06	0.06	0.02	0.07
	ANoT	0.67	6.07	7.37	63.33	106.40	198.00	465.57	475.93	125.40	658.70
Kmeans	HW→SW	0.00	0.00	0.01	0.01	0.01	0.01	0.01	0.02	0.02	0.02
	SW→HW	0.00	0.00	0.01	0.00	0.00	0.00	0.00	0.01	0.01	0.01
	ANoT	1.13	1.83	43.17	39.67	48.00	47.27	48.77	47.60	49.17	65.77
Labyrinth	HW→SW	0.00	0.01	0.17	0.24	0.23	0.09	0.21	0.01	0.40	0.13
	SW→HW	0.00	0.21	0.02	0.01	0.01	0.02	0.25	0.26	0.34	0.70
	ANoT	1.00	1.50	1.03	1.00	1.00	1.00	1.00	1.00	1.07	1.00
SSCA2	HW→SW	0.00	0.00	0.00	0.01	0.01	0.01	0.02	0.02	0.02	0.06
	SW→HW	0.00	0.00	0.00	0.00	0.00	0.00	0.00	0.00	0.01	0.01
	ANoT	0.47	0.23	1.47	3.80	8.77	8.60	16.40	21.27	25.33	119.07
Vacation	HW→SW	0.00	0.01	0.04	0.16	0.03	0.03	0.03	0.03	0.03	0.03
	SW→HW	0.00	0.00	0.00	0.02	0.00	0.00	0.00	0.00	0.00	0.00
	ANoT	2.57	3.27	31.33	167.10	5.17	5.13	5.30	5.03	5.57	6.07
Yada	HW→SW	0.00	0.01	0.01	0.02	0.03	0.03	0.03	0.03	0.03	0.03
	SW→HW	0.00	0.00	0.01	0.01	0.02	0.03	0.03	0.04	0.03	0.04
	ANoT	2.13	3.40	5.10	12.40	15.87	15.20	16.47	13.13	12.40	12.07

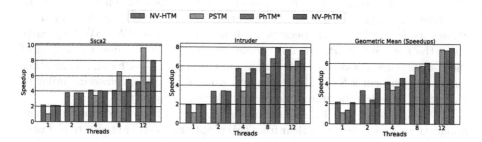

Fig. 5. Results with a Xeon E5-2648L @1.80 GHz using the same thresholds.

4.4   Discussion

The results show that NV-PhTM is able to follow the best performing mode, either HW or SW, but usually does not outperform the best of the two modes for a given configuration. The reason for this, as discussed in details by Carvalho et al. [7], is due to the lack of phases in the STAMP applications. However, the ability of dynamically adapting its behavior to exploit the best execution mode makes it a valuable option. A criticism of phased systems is that transition between modes can take a large fraction of the time because of the possible barriers. In case of NV-PhTM, this has to be analyzed since it does require a barrier when transitioning from HW to SW because of the NVM consistency requirements. In order to show that this is not a problem, Table 2 shows the percentage of the total time (averaged over 30 runs) consumed by transitions (both HW→SW and SW→HW) and The Average Number of Transitions (ANoT) for each application. As can be noticed, the largest overhead happens with Intruder (18 threads) and it only consumes about 1% of the total execution time. The reason for such low overhead is that the heuristics cause very few transitions, as can also be observed in the table.

Finally, the heuristics require some thresholds to be tuned in order to get a good performance. These values were set after a performance analysis with the STAMP benchmark, similarly to previous work [7]. To show that the results presented here are consistent, we repeated the experiments in another machine, a 14-core Intel Xeon E5-2648L running at 1.80 GHz and 32GB of RAM, without changing any of the thresholds. Notice that this machine is slightly slower and has smaller L2 and L3 caches. The main results are shown in Fig. 5 for the SSCA2, Intruder and the overall geometric mean. As can be seen, the main conclusions carried over.

5 Related Work

The works of Avni et al. with PHTM [3] (Persistent Hardware Transactional Memory) and Wang et al. with PTM [26] (Persistent Transactional Memory) were the first to explore HTM in the context of durable transactions. In both cases, the proposed solutions require changes to existing HTM designs which, in practice, limit their usage. DHTM [17] (Durable Hardware Transactional Memory) is a more recent hardware approach that also requires minor changes to the coherence protocol. HTM-enabled systems that use current microprocessors were developed recently [8,14,20]. These systems use the same idea of splitting the execution of a transaction into two parts: one that operates on volatile memory (using HTM support) and a decoupled phase responsible for persisting the changes into NVM. They differ on how this is achieved. In particular, the approach taken by Castro et al. with NV-HTM [8] avoids the use of a shared logical clock to serialize hardware transactions as in DudeTM [20]. Also, NV-HTM does not require instrumenting load operations as proposed in the work developed by Gilles et al. [14].

The closest work to ours is PHyTM [2] (Persistent Hybrid Transactional Memory), which allows the concurrent execution of both hardware and software transactions. However, PHyTM is based on PHTM [3] and, as such, cannot use current hardware support. NV-PhTM, on the other hand, does not have that limitation since it uses the decoupled HW mechanism of recent works. Moreover, recent studies have showed that hybrid systems have an inherent scalability limitation [1,7]. There are works on phase-based systems [6,7,19] but they target architectures with volatile memory. ProteusTM [12] automatically identifies the best TM implementation based on a multi-dimensional online optimization mechanism but, as with previous phase-based systems, it was design for volatile memory. Using phase-based systems with NVM, though, raises new problems concerning both the switching policies (which need to take into account specific performance issues, e.g., log stagnation, affecting NVM-related solutions) and the logic used to regulate the switching between the various execution phases (e.g., ensuring that logs are consolidated prior to switching to SW). In Section 4 we have compared the effectiveness of the switching policies used in prior phase-based systems [7] that considered volatile memory and demonstrated experimentally their inadequacy in the context of NVM.

6 Conclusion

In this paper we presented NV-PhTM: an efficient phase-based transactional system for persistent memory. NV-PhTM solves the performance issues of both hardware-only and software-only approaches by dynamically selecting the best operation mode. The key novel contributions of NV-PhTM consist of: i) new lightweight policies that allow for automatically identifying the best performing execution mode (STM or HTM) for arbitrary workloads in a NVM context, and ii) defining an architecture and phase transitioning mechanisms that allow for the safe alternation between the phased execution modes. Experimental results show that NV-PhTM can efficiently select the best execution mode and has low transition overhead.

Acknowledgments. The authors would like to thank the anonymous reviewers for their insightful comments. This work was supported by FAPESP (grants 2013/08293-7, 2016/15337-9, 2018/15519-5, and 2019/10471-7), Center for Computational Engineering and Sciences (CCES), and Fundação para a Ciência e a Tecnologia (under project UIDB/50021/2020).

References

1. Alistarh, D., Kopinsky, J., Kuznetsov, P., Ravi, S., Shavit, N.: Inherent limitations of hybrid transactional memory. Distrib. Comput. **31**(3), 167–185 (2017). https://doi.org/10.1007/s00446-017-0305-3
2. Avni, H., Brown, T.: Persistent hybrid transactional memory for databases. Proc. VLDB Endow. **10**(4), 409–420 (2016)
3. Avni, H., Levy, E., Mendelson, A.: Hardware transactions in nonvolatile memory. In: Moses, Y. (ed.) DISC 2015. LNCS, vol. 9363, pp. 617–630. Springer, Heidelberg (2015). https://doi.org/10.1007/978-3-662-48653-5_41
4. Badam, A.: How persistent memory will change software systems. Computer **46**(8), 45–51 (2013)
5. Baldassin, A., Borin, E., Araujo, G.: Performance implications of dynamic memory allocators on transactional memory systems. In: Proceedings of the 20th ACM SIGPLAN Symposium on Principles and Practice of Parallel Programming, pp. 87–96 (2015)
6. Carvalho, J.P.D., Araujo, G., Baldassin, A.: Revisiting phased transactional memory. In: Proceedings of the International Conference on Supercomputing, pp. 25:1–25:10 (2017)

7. Carvalho, J.P.D., Araujo, G., Baldassin, A.: The case for phase-based transactional memory. IEEE Trans. Parallel Distrib. Syst. **30**(2), 459–472 (2019)
8. Castro, D., Romano, P., Barreto, J.: Hardware transactional memory meets memory persistency. In: 2018 IEEE International Parallel and Distributed Processing Symposium (IPDPS), pp. 368–377, May 2018
9. Coburn, J., et al.: NV-heaps: making persistent objects fast and safe with next-generation, non-volatile memories. In: Proceedings of the Sixteenth International Conference on Architectural Support for Programming Languages and Operating Systems, pp. 105–118 (2011)
10. Dalessandro, L., Spear, M.F., Scott, M.L.: NOrec: streamlining stm by abolishing ownership records. In: Proceedings of the 15th ACM SIGPLAN Symposium on Principles and Practice of Parallel Programming, pp. 67–78 (2010)
11. Dice, D., Harris, T., Kogan, A., Lev, Y.: The influence of malloc placement on TSX hardware transactional memory. CoRR abs/1504.04640 (2015)
12. Didona, D., Diegues, N., Kermarrec, A.M., Guerraoui, R., Neves, R., Romano, P.: ProteusTM: abstraction meets performance in transactional memory. In: Proceedings of the Twenty-First International Conference on Architectural Support for Programming Languages and Operating Systems, pp. 757–771 (2016)
13. Felber, P., Fetzer, C., Riegel, T.: Dynamic performance tuning of word-based software transactional memory. In: Proceedings of the 13th ACM SIGPLAN Symposium on Principles and Practice of Parallel Programming, PPoPP 2008, pp. 237–246 (2008)
14. Giles, E., Doshi, K., Varman, P.: Continuous checkpointing of HTM transactions in NVM. In: Proceedings of the 2017 ACM SIGPLAN International Symposium on Memory Management, pp. 70–81 (2017)
15. Harris, T., Larus, J., Rajwar, R.: Transactional Memory, 2nd edn. Morgan & Claypool Publishers, San Rafael (2010)
16. Intel Corporation: Intel® Architecture Instruction Set Extensions Programming Reference (February 2012)
17. Joshi, A., Nagarajan, V., Cintra, M., Viglas, S.: DHTM: durable hardware transactional memory. In: 2018 ACM/IEEE 45th Annual International Symposium on Computer Architecture (ISCA), pp. 452–465, June 2018
18. Le, H., et al.: Transactional memory support in the IBM POWER8 processor. IBM J. Res. Dev. **59**(1), 8-1 (2015)
19. Lev, Y., Moir, M., Nussbaum, D.: PhTM: phased transactional memory. In: Workshop on Transactional Computing (Transact) (2007)
20. Liu, M., et al.: DudeTM: Building durable transactions with decoupling for persistent memory. In: Proceedings of the Twenty-Second International Conference on Architectural Support for Programming Languages and Operating Systems, pp. 329–343 (2017)
21. Memaripour, A., et al.: Atomic in-place updates for non-volatile main memories with Kamino-Tx. In: Proceedings of the Twelfth European Conference on Computer Systems, pp. 499–512 (2017)
22. Minh, C.C., Chung, J., Kozyrakis, C., Olukotun, K.: Stamp: stanford transactional applications for multi-processing. In: 2008 IEEE International Symposium on Workload Characterization, pp. 35–46, September 2008
23. Nakaike, T., Odaira, R., Gaudet, M., Michael, M.M., Tomari, H.: Quantitative comparison of hardware transactional memory for blue Gene/Q, zEnterprise EC12, intel core, and POWER8. In: Proceedings of the 42nd Annual International Symposium on Computer Architecture, pp. 144–157 (2015)

24. Team, T.N.L.: PMEM.IO: persistent memory programming. http://pmem.io/. Accessed 19 Sept 2019
25. Volos, H., Tack, A.J., Swift, M.M.: Mnemosyne: lightweight persistent memory. In: Proceedings of the Sixteenth International Conference on Architectural Support for Programming Languages and Operating Systems, pp. 91–104 (2011)
26. Wang, Z., Yi, H., Liu, R., Dong, M., Chen, H.: Persistent transactional memory. IEEE Comput. Architect. Lett. **14**(1), 58–61 (2015)

Enhancing Resource Management
Through Prediction-Based Policies

Antoni Navarro[1]([✉]) [iD], Arthur F. Lorenzon[2] [iD], Eduard Ayguadé[1] [iD],
and Vicenç Beltran[1] [iD]

[1] Barcelona Supercomputing Center, Barcelona, Spain
{antoni.navarro,eduard.ayguade,vbeltran}@bsc.es
[2] Federal University of Pampa, Alegrete, RS, Brazil
aflorenzon@unipampa.edu.br

Abstract. Task-based programming models are emerging as a promising alternative to make the most of multi-/many-core systems. These programming models rely on runtime systems, and their goal is to improve application performance by properly scheduling application tasks to cores. Additionally, these runtime systems offer policies to cope with application phases that lack in parallelism to fill all cores. However, these policies are usually static and favor either performance or energy efficiency. In this paper, we have extended a task-based runtime system with a lightweight monitoring and prediction infrastructure that dynamically predicts the optimal number of cores required for each application phase, thus improving both performance and energy efficiency. Through the execution of several benchmarks in multi-/many-core systems, we show that our prediction-based policies have competitive performance while improving energy efficiency when compared to state of the art policies.

Keywords: Energy efficiency · Resource management · Resource sharing · OmpSs-2 · Predictions · Monitoring · Cost

1 Introduction

High-performance computing (HPC) systems are widely used to execute applications from many domains, such as financial computing, medical applications, and video and image processing. These systems are usually based on many-/multi-core architectures with heterogeneous memory and computing devices. Often, this implies the existence of complex memory hierarchies and technologies that evolve each year. Hence, application developers need productive and efficient tools to keep pace with the growing power of HPC systems. Task-based programming models have emerged as a promising alternative to develop complex applications on those systems. These models provide high-level abstractions to increase the productivity of application developers, and they rely on runtime systems to cope with system complexity. The main goal of a runtime system

© Springer Nature Switzerland AG 2020
M. Malawski and K. Rzadca (Eds.): Euro-Par 2020, LNCS 12247, pp. 493–509, 2020.
https://doi.org/10.1007/978-3-030-57675-2_31

is to dynamically schedule application tasks to cores to optimize performance. However, these runtime systems must also cope with application phases with low parallelism that leave some of the cores without any task to execute. In this scenario, runtimes implement resource management policies to handle idle cores.

Commonly, resource managing policies focus on either improving performance or energy efficiency. Policies aiming to improve application performance adopt greedy strategies that always use all the available computational resources. A clear example would be OpenMP's [17] active policy, in which idle threads are actively checking for new work, consuming processor cycles and energy. On the other hand, techniques such as the ones in OpenMP's passive policy are used when the goal is to improve energy efficiency. In this case, idle threads immediately yield the processor to avoid contention inside the runtime and minimize the energy consumed. However, neither of these policies is adaptive enough to optimize both energy consumption and performance.

In order to tackle this challenge, two different hybrid approaches have been explored in the past [4,24]. The first one tries to improve performance-driven policies by adopting a greedy strategy for some time and, if no work is found in this period, yielding the processor to minimize energy consumption. Although it has positive effects on energy efficiency, the explored proposals struggle to find an optimal frequency to switch between policies. The second approach is based on policies that favor energy efficiency, in which idle resources are woken up at a specific frequency to check if new work is available. Similarly for both, finding a frequency that suffices all cases is a hassle.

In this work, we propose a novel resource management policy that can simultaneously optimize performance and energy efficiency. Our policy relies on the information provided by our monitoring and prediction framework to dynamically predict the number of cores that are required for each application phase. The main contributions of this work are: (i) the creation of the monitoring and prediction infrastructure, which is capable of making precise workload predictions for task-based programming models; (ii) the design of prediction-based resource managing policies; and (iii) the enhancing of existent resource-sharing policies through predictions. Through the execution of distinct well-known benchmarks across different many-core/multi-core architectures, we show that:

- We equal – and sometimes beat – the performance of state of the art policies that prioritize performance.
- Our policies also equal and, in some scenarios, beat the energy efficiency of state of the art policies that prioritize energy efficiency.
- Enhancing resource-sharing techniques through predictions simultaneously improves performance and energy efficiency.

The remainder of this paper is structured as follows. In Sect. 2, we discuss state of the art resource managing strategies in different parallel programming models. Next, in Sect. 3, we give insight into our monitoring and prediction infrastructure and improved prediction-based policies. In Sect. 5, we present the evaluation of our proposals across different systems and various benchmarks.

In Sect. 6 we go over related work and state of the art policies. Finally, in Sect. 7 we give concluding remarks and comment on future work.

2   Background

In this paper, we study the enhancement of performance and energy efficiency through resource management policies for one of the most widespread parallelism strategies: tasking. In tasking, parallelism is specified through tasks, – i.e., the basic unit work – which are blocks of code that can be executed concurrently. The data flow of an application is specified through dependencies between tasks, which are annotated by users. OpenMP and OmpSs-2 are some programming models that can be used to exploit task-level parallelism. In OpenMP, users define parallelism through regions of code in which two or more threads may execute simultaneously. On the other hand, in OmpSs-2, there is an implicit parallel region that covers the whole application. This allows resource management to be more malleable since, at any point in the execution, the runtime system can idle or resume threads.

Regardless of the programming model, threads that are not doing useful computation at a given time – e.g., while they are in a barrier – must wait for a new workload. While waiting, threads behave differently depending on the underlying resource managing policies. Next, we describe conventional policies in the literature, along with their advantages and flaws.

Active or Busy Policies: In these, waiting threads are kept busy-waiting until work is available. Depending on the underlying runtime, this policy allows for an instant reaction to the creation of work. Nevertheless, it is a static policy that cannot adapt to workload changes. This exposes two main drawbacks in most OpenMP implementations. The first one is dealing with the contention caused by threads constantly polling shared data structures. In OmpSs-2, this problem is resolved through subscription locking techniques. However, energy efficiency – the second drawback – is ignored in the policies of both models, as threads consume processor cycles while busy-waiting.

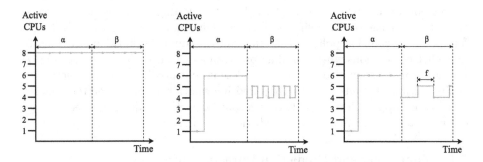

Fig. 1. Behavior of busy (left), idle (middle), and prediction policies (right)

Figure 1 exemplifies the number of active CPUs over time for a parallel region which has two different workload phases. The first phase (α) has enough work for six CPUs, while the second one (β) has enough work, on average, for four and a half CPUs. In this scenario, in busy policies – left part of the figure – at all times there are eight threads actively polling for work.

Passive or Idle Policies: In these, waiting threads do not consume processor cycles. These policies are usually not reactive, as they are implemented by idling threads for a constant amount of time. This causes benefits for energy efficiency but may be adverse for performance. In OmpSs-2, as tasks are created, threads are resumed so they may poll once again. This allows for an instantaneous reaction to the addition of work, which makes it more reactive than OpenMP. Taking into account the previous example, the middle part of Fig. 1 shows that, in these policies, threads are regularly being resumed and idled onto CPUs as the workload varies. Often, in fine-grained or irregular applications, this causes substantial amounts of overhead.

Hybrid Policies: To solve all the previously listed issues, OpenMP users can tune the rate at which waiting threads are idled and resumed. This enables users to find a balance between energy efficiency and performance. However, the chosen rate is a static value that cannot be changed at run-time. Therefore, this method cannot cope with variability in irregular applications, as these may need different rates throughout their executions.

Resource Sharing: OmpSs-2 offers an execution mode that integrates Dynamic Load Balancing (DLB). DLB [9] is a tool that is transparent to users and enables runtimes or applications to share processing elements between each other. This sharing is implemented through the Lend When Idle (LeWI) mechanism. It showcases similarities when compared to the idle policy. When threads poll for tasks and receive none, the CPU onto which they are executing is shared – instead of being idle. For this reason, depending on the application, this policy is excessively reactive and makes adverse decisions when lending/acquiring CPUs.

3 Improving Resource Managing Policies

As previously discussed, policies that do not look ahead are too naive to cope with the challenge of enhancing both energy efficiency and performance. Therefore, we advocate for policies that take into account workload predictions to make better decisions when handling processing elements. Next, we describe (i) the necessary elements to create a monitoring and prediction infrastructure to equip runtime systems with the required information to create better policies, and (ii) our approach towards finding a solution to the trade-off between energy efficiency and performance with prediction-based resource managing policies.

3.1 Monitoring and Prediction Infrastructure

In order to tackle the drawbacks of current policies and the challenges exposed in Sect. 2, we used a lightweight infrastructure capable of providing

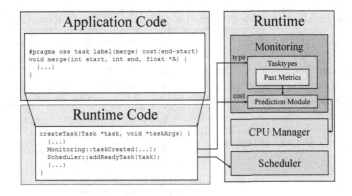

Fig. 2. A glimpse of the monitoring and prediction infrastructure

precise predictions with negligible overhead. Our infrastructure pinpoints critical changes in tasks, threads, or CPUs. Whenever possible, these changes are tracked outside the critical path of the runtime (i.e., synchronization points) so that the module is as lightweight as possible. Furthermore, to produce negligible overhead in fine-grained task scenarios, we combine the usage of atomic structures and the aggregation of metrics in a per-thread and per-task type basis.

Another critical attribute is the precision of predictions. Averaging task execution times is not precise enough due to the variability discussed in previous sections. On top of that, two tasks of the same type may behave unexpectedly depending on their input size. For instance, one of the inputs may be too large to fit within the same cache hierarchy level. Thus, to solve this, we use the cost clause, already proposed in previous works [15]. This clause specifies, in a rough way, the computational weight of a task. Such information allows normalizing metrics in order to extrapolate predictions for any task of the same type. Furthermore, this clause is user-friendly and requires little effort, as its filler value should be well-known to application developers. Figure 2 generally exposes all the elements involved in the computation of predictions. Upon a task is created and placed in the scheduler, the monitoring module predicts its metrics using past information from similar tasks. Predictions are then accumulated and passed onto the prediction module, which aids the resource manager by predicting the number of resources to use for the current workload.

Algorithm 1 shows a pseudo-code that describes how resource utilization predictions are computed. As previously mentioned, timing metrics are aggregated on a per-task type basis. This allows at any given time to have a precise prediction of the available workload (W_{i_j}) for every runtime status (i) and every task type (j). With these and normalized information from the execution of past tasks of every task type (α_j), we can precisely approximate the elapsed execution time of the available workload (β). Once a prediction rate is chosen (f), we can compute the optimal number of CPUs to utilize over that period (Δ), which takes into account the number of available tasks as well as their expected execution time. This information is then passed to the resource manager so that

---

Algorithm 1. Algorithm to predict the optimal CPU utilization (Δ)

T_i: Execution time of task i	1: **function** GETCPUPREDICTION(...)
C_i: Cost of task i	2: $\gamma \leftarrow 0$
f: Prediction frequency	3: $j \leftarrow 0$
N_{CPUs}: Maximum number of CPUs	4: **while** ($\gamma < N_{CPUs}$) **do**
W_{i_j}: Workload for runtime status i	5: $\beta \leftarrow \frac{(W_{ready_j} + W_{execution_j}) * \alpha_j}{f}$
and tasktype j	
α_j: Normalized cost for tasktype j	6: $\gamma \leftarrow \gamma + \beta$
M_j: Number of tasks of type j	7: $j \leftarrow j + 1$
Ensure: $0 < \Delta \leq N_{CPUs}$	8: **if** $i > N_{runtime\_status}$ **then**
	9: **break**
	10: **end if**
	11: **end while**
	12: $\Delta \leftarrow min(\gamma, \sum_{j=0}^{tasktype_n} M_j)$
	13: **end function**

---

the current number of CPUs can progressively be trimmed or increased to meet the prediction. Finally, to adapt to variability with haste, the normalized metrics are computed using a rolling window, which weights past metrics by their occurrence. The more recent these previous metrics are, the more weight they have towards the computation of their respective α.

3.2   Adaptive Prediction-Based Policies

Throughout Sect. 2, we describe the main flaws of current resource managing policies. To enhance these policies, we propose predicting the optimal number of CPUs at every point in time and at run-time. In other words, at a point in time T_i, we decide the number of CPUs to be used until $T_i + f$, where f is the time interval until the next prediction is made.

As shown in Sect. 3.1, our resource managing predictions are based on task timing predictions. To compute the latter, we normalize task timing metrics using their cost values in order to obtain normalized or *unitary costs* per task type. These unitary costs roughly represent the amount of time spent in the execution for each unit of cost of the task [15]. Then, we aggregate task costs per task type and runtime status separately. With these two metrics, at run-time, we compute the product of the accumulation of cost of all the task instances of a specific type by the respective unitary cost metric. Since these unitary values may vary over time, computing the product at run-time makes it susceptible to changes, which is precisely our goal. Furthermore, we average these unitary metrics using exponential moving averages. This allows them to be susceptible to variability and update as executions progress.

To compute the current amount of available workload in the system, we take into account ready and executing tasks. However, tasks in the executing status cannot account for their entire predicted time, as they may already be deep into their execution. To solve this, we aggregate task execution times through

Algorithm 2. Pseudo-code of the behavior of threads within the CPU manager

Δ: An atomic variable that holds the predicted optimal number of CPUs
δ: The current number of active CPUs
a: The action that triggered the call (polling or adding tasks)

```
1: function EXECUTEPOLICY(thread, a)                    ▷ δ is updated in a thread-safe manner
2:    if a == POLL then
3:       if queue == ∅ then
4:          if δ > Δ then
5:             δ ← δ − 1
6:             idle(thread)
7:             cpu ← getCPU(thread)
8:             releaseCPU(cpu)
9:          end if
10:      end if
11:   else [a == ADD]
12:      if δ < Δ then
13:         idleThread ← getIdleThread()
14:         idleCPU ← acquireCPU()
15:         if idleCPU ≠ ∅ then
16:            δ ← δ + 1
17:            resume(idleCPU, idleThread)
18:         end if
19:      end if
20:   end if
21: end function
```

the parent-child link between tasks. When a task finishes, its execution time is subtracted from the parent's task predicted time, if it is available.

In Algorithm 2, we show a pseudo-code of how our CPU manager uses these predictions. Rather than forcing the runtime to comply with the predicted number of CPUs (Δ), we save this value in an atomic variable. Then, when threads poll for tasks and none exist, if this value marks that the current number of active CPUs must be decreased, the thread idles until further notice, so that it does not consume CPU cycles. Reversely, when tasks are added into the scheduler and this value marks that more CPUs are required, idle threads are resumed to execute these newly created tasks.

The main benefits of our policy are twofold. If we compare our prediction policy to the idle or passive policies, a common feature is that they are both highly reactive to changes in the available workload. However, predictions occur at a specific rate. This allows our policy to avoid the overhead of continuously waking and idling threads in fine-grained or irregular applications. This benefit can also be seen as a middle ground between idle and busy policies. Taking into account the example introduced in Sect. 2, Fig. 1 shows the behavior of our prediction policy (right part). The rate at which predictions are inferred avoids multiple idling and resuming operations which, in the long run, adds up to avoid substantial overhead.

Another primary benefit of our policy is the adaptiveness to the granularity of tasks. Managing resources by only considering the number of ready tasks is enough in some scenarios. Nonetheless, for applications with fine-grained tasks, it would end up utilizing an excessive amount of CPUs for their workload. With the prediction policy this is resolved, as it takes into account the predicted granularity of tasks.

3.3   Prediction-Based Sharing of Resources

Section 2 briefly introduces the DLB integration of OmpSs-2. This mode of execution, as previously mentioned, resembles the idle policy. As it is as reactive, it may produce huge amounts of calls to the DLB library when lending or acquiring CPUs. Such calls do not come for free; they introduce non-negligible overhead.

To fix this flaw, we propose to modify the mechanism within OmpSs-2 to avoid making eager decisions. Our idea follows the same concept as the one adopted in the prediction policy. Instead of letting threads decide when CPUs are lent or acquired, we offload such decisions to an external prediction heuristic. Similarly, this heuristic predicts the amount of workload currently available in the system. Nonetheless, it is slightly modified to allow a superior number of CPUs, as DLB may provide more CPUs than the ones currently available to the runtime. When a thread polls for tasks and receives none, it will use the heuristic to decide whether its CPU must be lent. Simultaneously, as soon as predictions are inferred, the heuristic makes a single call to DLB in order to acquire as many CPUs as required. Therefore, threads do not require to do it progressively.

4   Experimental Setup

The experiments we performed were run on Intel Xeon and KNL multi-core systems, as shown in Table 1. In the same table, we also show the compilers used in each system. We present all results as the arithmetic mean of five runs for all metrics. To measure the energy efficiency, we consider the energy-delay product (EDP), which correlates both performance and energy consumption in only one value. To retrieve energy consumption metrics, we used the Intel Running Average Power Limit library [7]. The evaluation is partitioned into two phases. The first phase targets the measuring of overhead of our strategies and a comparison between the policies in two versions of OmpSs-2 and different OpenMP implementations. The second targets the evaluation of our prediction-based strategy for resource sharing using DLB.

In our experiments, we used the *Cholesky Factorization* benchmark and the *High Performance Computing Conjugate Gradients*[1] (HPCCG) mini-application. The former decomposes a matrix into the product of a lower triangular matrix and its conjugate transpose. The latter is based on the CG benchmark for a 3D chimney domain. They are both highly scalable benchmarks that present varying compute-intensive workloads. Furthermore, to test irregularity in applications, we used two versions of Cholesky; one that produces coarse-grained tasks, and another that creates an excessive amount of fine-grained tasks. Similarly, we also covered both granularity scenarios for the *MultiSAXPY* benchmark, which performs the SAXPY level one operation from the Basic Linear Algebra Subprograms package [12]. Finally, to test our policies

---

[1] HPCCG is implemented using multidependences, available in OpenMP 5.0 [17]. As the Intel 2020.0 compiler does not support them, HPCCG-*IOMP* results are missing.

Table 1. Architectures used in our experimental setup

Name	MN4	KNL
Processor	Intel Xeon Platinum 8160	Intel Xeon Phi CPU 7230
Architecture	Skylake	Knights Landing
Frequency	2.10 GHz	1.30 GHz
# of Sockets	2	1
# of Cores	48 (24 × 2)	64
Memory	96 GB	96 GB
OS	SUSE 12 SP2	SUSE 12 SP2
Intel Compiler	19.1.0.166	19.1.0.166
GNU Compiler	9.2.0	9.2.0

in memory-bound benchmarks, we used *Gauss-Seidel* and *STREAM*. The former is a solver that simulates the distribution of heat over time, and the latter is a benchmark that measures memory transfer rates in MB/s. While Gauss-Seidel could be highly parallel, to have a fair comparison against OpenMP, in the OmpSs-2 implementation we include a barrier after each time step. This produces load imbalance but, simultaneously, makes it an ideal candidate to be combined with STREAM, which is highly parallel and balanced.

5 Evaluation

Even though assessing the accuracy of our predictions was done in previous works, in Table 2 we include results of the accuracy of task timing predictions for all benchmarks and machines. In this table, we showcase the number of task instances used to compute the accuracy results and the average accuracy of all predictions. These predictions are then used towards calculating the optimal number of CPUs to use, as shown in Algorithm 1. The (**F**) and (**C**) shown next to benchmark names indicate whether the results are for the fine-grained scenario or the coarse-grained scenario, respectively. Due to the low number of task instances in coarse-grained Cholesky, CPU utilization predictions are based only on the number of available tasks, which is the go-to approach when task timing predictions are not available. Throughout the whole evaluation we used the same prediction rate – f in Algorithm 1 – of 50 μs.

To measure the overhead of our monitoring infrastructure, we ran all the previously mentioned benchmarks with varying task granularities. We compared OmpSs-2's current busy policy against a modified version of the busy policy that monitors metrics and infers predictions, but uses neither. We observed that for extreme situations with millions of fine-grained tasks, our infrastructure adds, in the worst case, a maximum overhead of **3%** to the execution time. We believe these overheads are negligible in comparison to the benefits we obtain.

Our evaluation comprises four different implementations: GCC OpenMP [16] (**gomp**), Intel OpenMP [11] (**iomp**), OmpSs-2 using its linear regions dependency system (**oss2L**), and OmpSs-2 using its improved discrete dependency system (**oss2D**). For the OpenMP implementations, we evaluate all their available thread-waiting policies: **active**, **passive**, and a **hybrid** between both. For the OmpSs-2 counterparts, we evaluate their current resource managing policies, **busy** and **idle**, and our **prediction** policy. Due to the similarities in their concepts, we group the comparison as follows: Active/Busy, Passive/Idle, and Hybrid/Prediction. In all figures, from left to right, we show the results of gomp, iomp, oss2L, and oss2D.

Figure 3 showcases the normalized performance of all benchmarks, architectures, and between all policies. For Cholesky's coarse-grained scenario, Gauss-Seidel, and HPCCG, the performance obtained using the prediction policy in both OmpSs-2 versions either equals or surpasses the performance of all other policies in MN4. In fine-grained Multisaxpy, comparing all the OmpSs-2 policies, our policy yields either similar performance (in KNL) or surpasses other policies (in MN4). Nonetheless, in the coarse-grained scenario in KNL, busy yields better

Table 2. Average prediction accuracy of each benchmark and architecture

	MN4					
Benchmark	Cholesky (F)	Cholesky (C)	HPCCG	Gauss-Seidel	Multisaxpy (F)	Multisaxpy (C)
# of Instances	$3*10^6$	600	15000	25600	$1*10^5$	20000
AVG Accuracy	88.25%	NA	78.45%	99.91%	70.63%	79.49%
	KNL					
# of Instances	$3*10^6$	600	15000	25600	$1*10^5$	20000
AVG Accuracy	92.65%	NA	75.32%	99.81%	76.83%	86.12%

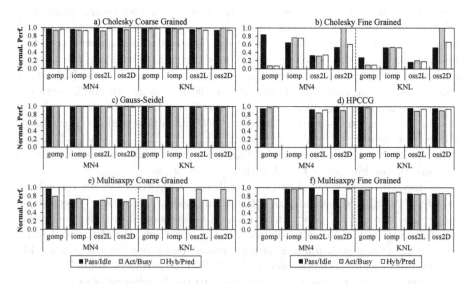

Fig. 3. Normalized performance w.r.t. the best scenario on each application

performance than prediction. We attribute this to the precision in predictions, as shown in Table 2. This accuracy could be enhanced by taking into account other metrics – as it is a memory-bound benchmark. Last but not least, in the fine-grained Cholesky scenario, the prediction policy yields similar performance when compared to OmpSs-2's linear version. However, in the discrete version, its performance remains between the busy and idle policies, being busy the most performant. This difference between versions led us to find out that the monitoring infrastructure adds slightly more overhead in OmpSs-2's discrete version, as contention is minimal and the overhead shifts to other runtime modules.

Figure 4 shows the comparison of EDP between all policies and architectures. Thus, in these plots, lower values are better. For coarse-grained Cholesky, prediction policies obtain better results than any other policies in MN4. In KNL, the only configuration that beats the prediction policy of OmpSs-2 discrete is OmpSs-2 linear's idle policy. As for the fine-grained scenario, OmpSs-2 discrete's prediction policy yields less EDP than any other policy for both architectures except when compared to GOMP's passive policy in KNL, as their results are similar. In both Gauss-Seidel and HPCCG, prediction policies beat any other policy in any implementation and architecture. Finally, for the coarse-grained Multisaxpy scenario, EDP results in KNL are very similar across policies and implementations. However, in MN4, prediction policies achieve considerably lower EDP than any other policy except when compared to GOMP's hybrid policy, which obtains similar results. Both fine-grained and coarse-grained scenarios present similarities. However, as predictions benefit from fine-grained and irregular applications, in MN4 prediction policies beat any other policy in EDP.

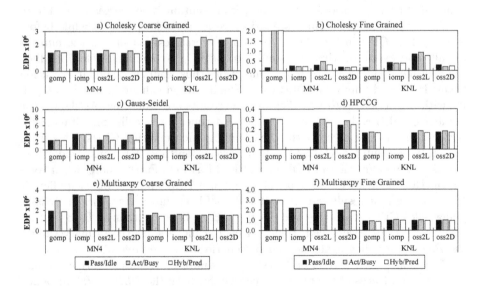

Fig. 4. EDP results (raw data) for each application and policy

To further evaluate our predictions, we created a prediction-based policy for the DLB execution mode of OmpSs-2. We chose to run the Gauss-Seidel simulation along with the STREAM benchmark in MN4, as they vary in features and, thus, combine perfectly when executed concurrently. For the former, we used an input size that generates slightly coarse-grained tasks, while in the latter, we chose an input size that generates fine-grained tasks. Thus, STREAM benefits from the lack of workload of Gauss-Seidel after each time-step. In Table 3, we show the average results of several executions with multiple configurations. We executed both applications concurrently, each in a single NUMA node (half the number of processors of the whole node) for the *Concurrent* configuration. To take into account any possible noise between shared resources – e.g., cache pollution or bandwidth thresholds – we also executed each application in a single NUMA node on its own, which is shown as the *Single* configuration. Then, we executed using DLB to share cores between applications in three configurations: *Concurrent + DLB LeWI* is the default policy. *Concurrent + DLB Hybrid* is a modified version of the DLB integration that only shares CPUs after several failed attempts of polling tasks from the scheduler – hence the similar name to OpenMP's hybrid policy. For our experiments we chose 100 as the number of attempts before a CPU is shared. Finally, *Concurrent + DLB Prediction* shows the results of the DLB execution mode enhanced with our predictions.

In the *LeWI* policy, STREAM can benefit from the lack of workload of Gauss-Seidel, thus reducing its execution time. Nevertheless, as this policy is extremely reactive, the combination of the number of calls to DLB is around 4 million in executions of 100 and 75 s, respectively. These calls add non-negligible overhead. On top of that, since Gauss-Seidel lends CPUs for short amounts of time in which neither applications can benefit, its execution time increases. To try to tackle this flaw in fine-grained scenarios, we let threads spin for a while before lending their CPU in the *Hybrid* version. Nevertheless, as shown, the number of calls and execution time are similar to *LeWi's*. By spinning before lending, the runtime is stressed with more contention, thus leading to similar execution times, EDP, and number of DLB calls. Finally, when enhancing the *LeWI* policy with predictions (*DLB Prediction*), the results are promising. As shown, the number of DLB calls is greatly reduced – **4 times fewer calls**. Simultaneously, better decisions are taken both when lending and acquiring CPUs. This leads to a **1.4x** speedup for STREAM, similar execution times for Gauss-Seidel, and a considerable reduction in EDP in STREAM as well. Furthermore, when comparing EDP metrics between policies that use DLB and the *Single* policy, it is noticeable that results are worse for the DLB counterparts. Since the *Single* policy idles CPUs when they are not used, EDP is better than in DLB policies where CPUs are never idled. Hence, if energy metrics are the primary target, the *Prediction* policy in the non-DLB scenario would be preferable.

To visualize how prediction-based policies improve resource sharing, we add the execution traces of the previous scenario for both the *DLB + Hybrid* policy (left) and the *DLB + Prediction* policy (right) in Fig. 5. To shorten execution traces, the execution of these benchmarks was slightly different in granularity of

Table 3. Comparison of metrics between OmpSs-2 + DLB policies

Config.	Time (s)		EDP		# DLB calls	
	Gauss-Seidel	Stream	Gauss-Seidel	Stream	Gauss-Seidel	Stream
Single	87.4	78.3	1097330	1223111	–	–
Concurrent	87.4	78.3	1705625	1434911	–	–
Concurrent + DLB LeWI	100.9	73.3	2318388	1427072	768078	3392692
Concurrent + DLB Hyb.	101.5	74.3	2318244	1471916	890924	3169858
Concurrent + DLB Pred.	89.6	55.8	1849275	870269	69504	842634

tasks when compared to the results shown in Table 3, hence the slight difference in execution time. The red series corresponds to the execution of Gauss-Seidel, while the light-orange series corresponds to STREAM. In the prediction policy, as shown, the granularity of sharing in resources is coarser. CPUs are not lent unless they will not be used for a certain amount of time, and they will not be acquired unless they truly are required. Reversely, in the hybrid policy, there are still flawed decisions when lending or acquiring CPUs. As shown, there is much sharing that could be removed to avoid both the delays in Gauss-Seidel and the overhead of lending and immediately after re-acquiring CPUs.

6 Related Work

Resource Management: Techniques aiming to improve performance through resource management have been thoroughly studied. Barekas et al. [2] and Callisto [10] advocate for inter-process sharing of resources in their proposals. The former presents a resource manager and a runtime system which, respectively, distribute hardware resources to OpenMP applications and adapt their degree of parallelism. Although it is capable of providing better performance than commercial implementations of OpenMP, their approach offers no policies to improve performance between parallel regions. Callisto is a resource management layer for parallel runtime systems that coordinates the execution of parallel applications. It consists of (i) a dynamic scheduler that defines which jobs can execute in parallel; and (ii) a low-level API to manage synchronization points. However, it assumes that parallel sections of jobs are CPU-bound and that runtime systems need to be adapted to use Callisto. Eichenberger et al. [8] propose a model to control thread affinity for OpenMP applications. However, their work does not present any advances regarding the optimization of resource management policies.

Other proposals [4,24] have focused on our primary target, optimizing resource policies to improve performance or maintain it while improving energy efficiency. In this line, Boguslavsky et al. [4] investigate different strategies to determine for how long processes should spin before blocking. Even though their results are promising, such static values cannot cope with irregular applications that may need different blocking rates throughout their executions. To deal with oversubscription in OpenMP applications, Yan et al. [24] define five policies: spin_busy, spin_pause, spin_yield, suspend, and terminate. However, in

OpenMP, such policies cannot change within parallel regions. Thus, this approach flaws similarly. On the other hand, our approach is capable of dealing with such situations, as our policies can adapt at any point in the execution.

Thread Malleability within Parallel Regions: A number of studies, such as Thread Reinforcer (TR) [19], Feedback-Driven Threading (FDT) [23], and ACTOR [6], investigate on optimizing either performance or energy by tuning the number of threads in parallel regions. TR [19] is a framework in which applications are executed multiple times with varying numbers of threads. FDT [23] adapts the number of threads by considering contention in locks and memory bandwidth. ACTOR [6] is a system that aims to improve the energy efficiency of parallel applications. In it, artificial neural networks are used to predict the number of threads to execute each parallel region. These previous approaches require either warm-up executions or techniques that may introduce substantial amounts of overhead when done at runtime. Several other studies target solutions at run-time. LIMO [5] is a system that monitors applications and adapts the execution accordingly. Parcae [20] is a framework that creates multiple parallel transforms of sequential programs and, at run-time, determines the degree of TLP exploitation. Similarly, ParallelismDial [22] is a model that automatically regulates the number of threads per region. Nonetheless, some of these approaches tune applications specifically for input sets and architectures. Others require OS support to intercept blocked threads to change their policies.

Energy Efficiency: Improving energy efficiency through resource management policies has been investigated as well, in studies such as OpenMPE [1], Benedict et al. [3], and LAANT [14]. In the former, an OpenMP extension designed to improve energy management is proposed. In [3], the authors propose an energy prediction mechanism for OpenMP applications using a Random Forest Modeling approach. LAANT [14] is a library that aims at optimizing the EDP metric. The study conducted in Porterfield et al. [18] similarly proposes a system to automatically adjust the number of threads based on on-line measurements of system resource usage. These works are based on adjusting the number of threads of OpenMP applications in parallel-regions or the whole application. Thus, similarly to our previous explanation, they lack adaptiveness when it comes to irregu-

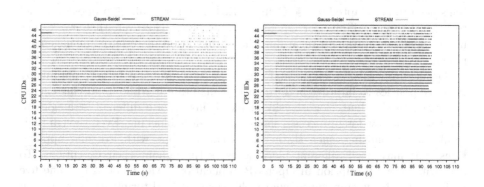

Fig. 5. Execution traces of hybrid (left) and prediction (right) DLB policies

lar applications. Li et al. [13] propose a library to reduce energy consumption for hybrid MPI/OpenMP applications. Even though their aim is out of our scope, they use prediction models to enhance energy efficiency with negligible or no loss of performance. Finally, Shafik et al. [21] propose an adaptive energy minimization model for OpenMP programs using annotations. These annotations require execution time estimations, which leads us to believe warm-up executions are needed to provide the library with such metrics.

7   Concluding Remarks and Future Work

In this paper, we presented resource management policies based on predictions that simultaneously optimize performance and energy efficiency. More specifically, we showcase (i) a prediction-based CPU managing policy that maintains performance while improving energy efficiency, and (ii) a prediction-based resource sharing mechanism which enhances both performance and energy efficiency when compared to its predecessor. We exemplify our proposal in OmpSs-2, although our approach can be applied to other parallel programming models based on tasks or fork-join.

While our prediction-based policies are capable of making better decisions than well-known policies from state of the art, we left a few aspects out of the scope which we will target in future work. Firstly, our policies could benefit from taking prediction error into account. Thus, when detecting anomalies, our infrastructure would be able to swap between CPU managing policies at runtime. We also believe that the rate at which predictions are inferred may be improved with a combined approach that triggers our mechanism when a certain number of events happen – e.g., the creation or finalization of a number of tasks. Finally, we also plan to enable an on-line task characterization so that both our policies and predictions take more than one metric into account.

Acknowledgments. This project is supported by the European Union's Horizon 2021 research and innovation programme under the grant agreement No 754304 (DEEP-EST), the Ministry of Economy of Spain through the Severo Ochoa Center of Excellence Program (SEV-2015-0493), by the Spanish Ministry of Science and Innovation (contract TIN2015-65316-P) and by the Generalitat de Catalunya (2017-SGR-1481). This work was also supported by Project HPC-EUROPA3 (INFRAIA-2016-1-730897), with the support of the EC Research Innovation Action under the H2020 Programme.

References

1. Alessi, F., Thoman, P., Georgakoudis, G., Fahringer, T., Nikolopoulos, D.S.: Application-level energy awareness for OpenMP. In: Terboven, C., de Supinski, B.R., Reble, P., Chapman, B.M., Müller, M.S. (eds.) IWOMP 2015. LNCS, vol. 9342, pp. 219–232. Springer, Cham (2015). https://doi.org/10.1007/978-3-319-24595-9_16
2. Barekas, V.K., Hadjidoukas, P.E., Polychronopoulos, E.D., Papatheodorou, T.S.: A multiprogramming aware OpenMP implementation. Sci. Program. **11**(2), 133–141 (2003)

3. Benedict, S., Rejitha, R.S., Gschwandtner, P., Prodan, R., Fahringer, T.: Energy prediction of OpenMP applications using random forest modeling approach. In: IEEE IPDPSW, pp. 1251–1260, May 2015
4. Boguslavsky, L., Harzallah, K., Kreinen, A., Sevcik, K., Vainshtein, A.: Optimal strategies for spinning and blocking. JPDC **21**(2), 246–254 (1994)
5. Chadha, G., Mahlke, S., Narayanasamy, S.: When less is more (limo):controlled parallelism for improved efficiency. In: CASES, pp. 141–150. ACM, New York (2012)
6. Curtis-Maury, M., Blagojevic, F., Antonopoulos, C.D., Nikolopoulos, D.S.: Prediction-based power-performance adaptation of multithreaded scientific codes. IEEE Trans. Parallel Distrib. Syst. **19**(10), 1396–1410 (2008)
7. David, H., Gorbatov, E., Hanebutte, U.R., Khanna, R., Le, C.: Rapl: Memory power estimation and capping. In: ISLPED, p. 189–194. ACM, New York (2010)
8. Eichenberger, A.E., Terboven, C., Wong, M., an Mey, D.: The design of OpenMP thread affinity. In: Chapman, B.M., Massaioli, F., Müller, M.S., Rorro, M. (eds.) IWOMP 2012. LNCS, vol. 7312, pp. 15–28. Springer, Heidelberg (2012). https://doi.org/10.1007/978-3-642-30961-8_2
9. Garcia, M., Corbalan, J., Labarta, J.: Lewi: a runtime balancing algorithm for nested parallelism. In: ICPP 2009, pp. 526–533, September 2009
10. Harris, T., Maas, M., Marathe, V.J.: Callisto: co-scheduling parallel runtime systems. In: European Conference on Computer Systems, pp. 1–14 (2014)
11. Intel: Intel OpenMP Runtime Library Website. https://www.openmprtl.org/download. Accessed 21 Feb 2020
12. Lawson, C.L., Hanson, R.J., Kincaid, D.R., Krogh, F.T.: Basic linear algebra subprograms for fortran usage. ACM Trans. Math. Softw. **5**(3), 308–323 (1979)
13. Li, D., de Supinski, B.R., Schulz, M., Cameron, K., Nikolopoulos, D.S.: Hybrid MPI/OpenMP power-aware computing. In: IEEE IPDPS, pp. 1–12, April 2010
14. Lorenzon, A.F., Souza, J.D., Beck, A.C.S.: Laant: A library to automatically optimize EDP for OpenMP applications. In: DATE, pp. 1229–1232, March 2017
15. Navarro, A., Mateo, S., Perez, J.M., Beltran, V., Ayguadé, E.: Adaptive and architecture-independent task granularity for recursive applications. In: de Supinski, B.R., Olivier, S.L., Terboven, C., Chapman, B.M., Müller, M.S. (eds.) IWOMP 2017. LNCS, vol. 10468, pp. 169–182. Springer, Cham (2017). https://doi.org/10.1007/978-3-319-65578-9_12
16. Novillo, D.: OpenMP and automatic parallelization in GCC. In: In the Proceedings of the GCC Developers (2006)
17. OpenMP Architecture Review Board: OpenMP API. Version 5.0, November 2018. https://www.openmp.org/. Accessed 10 Feb 2020
18. Porterfield, A.K., Olivier, S.L., Bhalachandra, S., Prins, J.F.: Power measurement and concurrency throttling for energy reduction in OpenMP programs. In: IEEE IPDPS, pp. 884–891 (2013)
19. Pusukuri, K.K., Gupta, R., Bhuyan, L.N.: Thread reinforcer: dynamically determining number of threads via os level monitoring. In: IEEE International Symposium on Workload Characterization, pp. 116–125. IEEE Computer Society, DC (2011)
20. Raman, A., Zaks, A., Lee, J.W., August, D.I.: Parcae: a system for flexible parallel execution. In: ACM SIGPLAN PLDI, pp. 133–144. ACM, New York (2012)
21. Shafik, R.A., Das, A., Yang, S., Merrett, G., Al-Hashimi, B.M.: Adaptive energy minimization of OpenMP parallel applications on many-core systems. In: Workshop on Parallel Programming and Run-Time Management Techniques for Manycore Architectures, pp. 19–24. ACM, New York (2015)

22. Sridharan, S., Gupta, G., Sohi, G.S.: Holistic run-time parallelism management for time and energy efficiency. In: International Conference on Supercomputing, pp. 337–348. ACM, New York (2013)
23. Suleman, M.A., Qureshi, M.K., Patt, Y.N.: Feedback-driven threading: power-efficient and high-performance execution of multi-threaded workloads on CMPs. SIGARCH Comput. Archit. News **36**(1), 277–286 (2008)
24. Yan, Y., Hammond, J.R., Liao, C., Eichenberger, A.E.: A proposal to OpenMP for addressing the CPU oversubscription challenge. In: Maruyama, N., de Supinski, B.R., Wahib, M. (eds.) IWOMP 2016. LNCS, vol. 9903, pp. 187–202. Springer, Cham (2016). https://doi.org/10.1007/978-3-319-45550-1_14

Accelerating Overlapping Community Detection: Performance Tuning a Stochastic Gradient Markov Chain Monte Carlo Algorithm

Ismail El-Helw[✉], Rutger Hofman, and Henri E. Bal

Vrije Universiteit Amsterdam, Amsterdam, The Netherlands
ielhelw@gmail.com, {rutger,bal}@cs.vu.nl

Abstract. Building efficient algorithms for data-intensive problems requires deep analysis of data access patterns. Random data access patterns exacerbate this process. In this paper, we discuss accelerating a randomized data-intensive machine learning algorithm using multi-core CPUs and several types of GPUs. A thorough analysis of the algorithm's data dependencies enabled a 75% reduction in its memory footprint. We created custom compute kernels via code generation to identify the optimal set of data placement and computational optimizations per compute device. An empirical evaluation shows up to 245x speedup compared to an optimized sequential version. Another result from this evaluation is that achieving peak performance does not always match intuition: e.g., depending on the GPU architecture, vectorization may increase or hamper performance.

Keywords: Algorithms for accelerators and heterogeneous systems · Performance analysis · Combinatorial and data intensive application

1 Introduction

The past decade has witnessed a tremendous increase in the applicability and usefulness of artificial intelligence in our daily lives. Much of this activity was fueled by the mainstream adoption of machine learning approaches as they provide tools to solve inherently difficult problems. However, many of these techniques require a massive amount of computation which severely limits the scale of problems that can be tackled.

In this paper, we present the methodology followed in designing and implementing a high-performance version of an existing Stochastic Gradient Markov Chain Monte Carlo (SG-MCMC) machine learning algorithm that detects overlapping communities in graphs. The algorithm analyzes pair-wise interactions between entities in order to discover hidden attributes. For instance, consider a social network represented as an undirected graph where the vertices represent individuals and edges represent relations between them. Given the relation

© Springer Nature Switzerland AG 2020
M. Malawski and K. Rzadca (Eds.): Euro-Par 2020, LNCS 12247, pp. 510–526, 2020.
https://doi.org/10.1007/978-3-030-57675-2_32

information, the algorithm can identify latent groups of individuals that represent shared interests. This problem structure differs from graph partitioning or clustering as there is a many-to-many relationship between individuals and interests. For example, each individual can have multiple interests. Simultaneously, each interest group can span multiple individuals. Formally, this problem domain is known as Mixed-Membership Stochastic Blockmodels (MMSB). The theory behind the algorithm is discussed in more detail in [10].

The focus of this work is on the computational efficiency and parallel performance of the SG-MCMC algorithm. More specifically, we discuss the process of accelerating the algorithm by developing aggressive optimizations targeting multi-core CPUs and GPUs. The parallel algorithm achieves speedup factors up to 245, compared to a well-tuned sequential C++ program which itself is a factor 1000–1500 faster than the Python/Numpy program developed by the algorithm's original authors. From a computational point of view, this algorithm differs from widespread machine learning algorithms in several ways. First, it is highly data-intensive which makes GPU acceleration particularly challenging. Second, owing to the algorithm's stochastic nature, the majority of its memory access patterns and data dependencies are non-deterministic. As a result, straightforward optimization attempts of the memory access patterns either fail or lead to non-intuitive results.

Through careful analysis of the computation and data structures we show that the algorithm's full state can be reduced by roughly 75%. Compressing the state significantly reduces the data intensity and allows for tackling larger problems while maintaining all state in memory. Further, by cataloguing and accounting for the various load and store operations, we identified the highest priority locations of data reuse. In order to navigate the unclear optimization landscape, we developed an effective kernel code generation mechanism that explores all permutations of the available optimization opportunities. These optimizations include caching in shared memory, caching in the register file, loop unrolling and explicit vectorization.

In summary, the contributions of this work are:

- decrease the algorithm's data intensity by eliminating 75% of its memory footprint;
- tune the algorithm's performance by maximizing data reuse and identify the fastest combination of optimizations through dynamic kernel code generation;
- perform a comparative performance analysis of the accelerated algorithm versions on a multi-core CPU and a number of GPUs, highlighting the particular optimization combinations that were successful per device;
- achieve speedup factors of 21 and 245 over an optimized sequential program using a multi-core CPU and a GPU respectively.

The remainder of this paper is organized as follows. A description of the sequential version of the algorithm and its data structures is provided in Sect. 2. Sect. 3 discusses the design of the parallel algorithm. Section 4 provides an empirical evaluation of the contributions of this work. Sect. 5 presents an overview of related works. Finally, Sect. 6 concludes.

2 SG-MCMC Algorithm Overview

In this section we describe the computational aspects of the SG-MCMC MMSB algorithm. Moreover, we will introduce the data structures and notation that will be used throughout this paper. A detailed explanation of the algorithm is provided in [4,10].

The network graph G consists of the undirected edges $\mathcal{E}$ and has N vertices. The algorithm starts by partitioning G into the *training set*, the *validation set* $\mathcal{E}_h$ and the test set (the latter is not used in our implementations). $\mathcal{E}_h$ and the test set are much smaller than G, typically between 1% and 10% of the edges in G. The number of communities K is specified as a model parameter to the algorithm.

The algorithm progresses by iteratively improving the global state of the learning problem, using the training set. There are two pairs of data structures that hold the global state. θ, a $K \times 2$ matrix, is used for calculating the community strength β, i.e. the probability that two members in a community share an edge. β is a vector of length K; it is the normalized version of $\theta_{k,2}$. The matrix π of dimensions $N \times K$ represents the probability for each vertex in G to be a member of each community. It is the normalized equivalent of the matrix ϕ of dimensions $N \times K$, on which the calculations occur. The definitions of β and π are:

$$\beta_k = \frac{\theta_{k,2}}{\theta_k^{sum}} \text{ where } \theta_k^{sum} = \sum_{j=1}^{2} \theta_{k,j} \tag{1}$$

$$\pi_{i,k} = \frac{\phi_{i,k}}{\phi_i^{sum}} \text{ where } \phi_i^{sum} = \sum_{j=1}^{K} \phi_{i,j} \tag{2}$$

The symbols used throughout this paper are given in Table 1.

Table 1. Definition of most important symbols

Symbol	Type	Size	Description
G			Graph
$\mathcal{K}$		K	Set of communities
$\mathcal{V}$	{vertex}	N	Vertices in G
$\mathcal{E}$	{edge}		Linked edges in G
E	{edge}		$\mathcal{V} \times \mathcal{V}$: linked and nonlinked edges
$\mathcal{E}_h$	{edge}		Held-out subset of the graph
$\mathcal{E}_n$	{edge}		Sampled mini-batch of edges in E
m			Number of vertices in $\mathcal{E}_n$
$\mathcal{V}_n$	{vertex}		Sampled neighbor set for a vertex in $\mathcal{E}_n$
θ	float vector 2-D	$K \times 2$	Reparameterization of β. $\beta_k = \theta_{k,2}/\sum_j \theta_{k,j}$
β	float vector	K	Community strength
ϕ	float vector 2-D	$N \times K$	Reparameterization of π. $\pi_{i,k} = \phi_{i,k}/\sum_j \phi_{i,j}$
π	float vector 2-D	$N \times K$	$\pi_{i,k}$ is probability that vertex i is in community k

Algorithm 1. Sequential version of SG-MCMC for a-MMSB

1: **while** sampling **do**
2:     sample a mini-batch $\mathcal{E}_n$
3:     // $\mathcal{E}_n$ may be a subset of G, or disjoint with G
4:     **for** each vertex i in $\mathcal{E}_n$ **do**
5:         sample n random 'neighbors' (not from G)
6:         **for** each edge $(i,$ neighbor$)$ **do**
7:             calculate its contribution to the gradient in ϕ
8:         update ϕ_i using stepsize s
9:     **for** each vertex i in $\mathcal{E}_n$ **do**
10:        update π_i according to changed ϕ_i
11:    **for** the edges in $\mathcal{E}_n$ **do**
12:        calculate gradients in θ and update θ
13:    **for** the edges in $\mathcal{E}_n$ **do**
14:        update β accordingly
15:    every so many iterations: // metric is perplexity
16:        verify the quality of π and β against the validation set

Pseudo-code for the algorithm is presented in Algorithm 1 which is based on the description in [4,10].

An iteration in the algorithm consists of 6 compute stages. We will highlight the data accessed in the stages as this determines the opportunities for parallelism.

The first stage (line 2 in the Algorithm) randomly draws a mini-batch $\mathcal{E}_n$, using the "stratified random node" strategy [10]. In this strategy, a coin toss is used to decide between two sample types. The first sample type chooses one random vertex i and selects all of its edges to constitute the mini-batch $\mathcal{E}_n$. This sample type is referred to as *link edges*. The second sample type randomly draws a vertex i and generates random edges of the form (i, j) such that the edges are not in G. This sample type is referred to as *nonlink edges*. The set of vertices that constitute the edges of the mini-batch $\mathcal{E}_n$ is denoted m.

In the second stage (line 5), for each vertex i in m, a neighbor set $\mathcal{V}_n$ of size n is randomly sampled with edges of the form (i, j).

Stage 3, *update_phi* (line 6–10), calculates a gradient vector $\nabla\phi_i$ for each vertex i in the mini-batch, by iterating over the edges (i, j) in i's neighbor set; the data that is used is π_i, π_j, and β. The gradient $\nabla\phi_i$ is used to update ϕ_i. Stage 4 (line 9–10), *update_pi*, updates π_i so it remains the normalized version of ϕ_i.

Stage 5, *update_theta* (line 11–12), uses β and π_a, π_b for the edges (a, b) in the minibatch $\mathcal{E}_n$ to calculate a gradient vector $\nabla\theta$. θ is updated using $\nabla\theta$. Stage 6, *update_beta* (line 13–14), recalculates β as the normalized version of $\theta_{k,2}$.

At regular intervals, the algorithm's global state is assessed by evaluating the perplexity over the edges in the validation set $\mathcal{E}_h$. Perplexity is a metric that represents the quality of the algorithm solution at a given point in time. It is used to detect the algorithm's convergence. The perplexity, as elaborated in [4,10], is the exponential of the average over time of the negative log-likelihood of meeting a link edge. In this *calculate_perplexity* stage (lines 15–16), β is used, as are π_a and π_b for each edge (a, b) in $\mathcal{E}_h$.

The graph G is queried for membership in the stages *update_phi*, *update_beta*, and *calculate_perplexity*. The validation set $\mathcal{E}_h$ is traversed in the *calculate_perplexity* stage.

3   System Design and Implementation

The process of designing an accelerated version of the SG-MCMC MMSB algorithm involved multiple transformations. First, we describe how an efficient C++ baseline was created. Further, changes to the algorithm and the data structures were carried out, for both efficient resource utilization and parallelization. This section provides an overview of the system's evolution in incremental phases, identifying the key contributions and differences between consecutive states.

3.1   An Efficient Sequential Baseline Version

The original implementation was done in Python, as is common in the machine-learning community. It relied on Numpy [16] to perform numerical computations efficiently. However, the algorithm made heavy use of Python sets and dictionaries which have no Numpy equivalent. We ported the Python code to C++, maintaining the same program structure. This transformation yielded a speedup factor of 171.

The next step was to remove a number of inefficiencies. E.g., one recurring idiom in the Python implementation was a choice expression of the form $a^y b^{1-y}$ where y is either 0 or 1. We transformed such expressions into conditional expressions which compute either a or b, and avoid floating-point exponentiation. Other optimizations were loop strength reduction and common subexpression lifting. These optimizations yielded another speedup factor of 6.

Finally, we investigated the performance effect of reducing the floating-point precision from 64-bit to 32-bit. This reduces both the computation and data intensity leading to a lower memory footprint which frees registers and enables more effective data reuse. It has been previously shown that stochastic learning algorithms do not require high precision in the presence of statistical approximations and the addition of random noise [7]. This reduction increased the speedup by a factor of 1.5.

In conclusion, porting from Python to efficient 64-bit C++ gave a speedup factor of ~ 1000, and reducing the precision to 32-bit increased that to a factor of ~ 1500. We use the resulting sequential C++ version as baseline for our performance comparisons.

3.2   Restructuring for Parallelism

The design of an accelerated version of the algorithm necessitated several crucial modifications to allow for efficient parallelization. We chose OpenCL [17] as it provides a common abstraction for a variety of compute devices which fulfilled our requirements of employing CPUs or GPUs. However, Nvidia's OpenCL SDK limits the total memory allocations within a context to 4GB which severely limits the problem sizes that can be tackled on GPUs. Therefore, we migrated the system to use the abstraction layer CLCudaAPI [15] to support both OpenCL and CUDA [14] as back-ends. We considered using OpenMP for the CPU implementation but decided against it. OpenCL offers a common platform for CPU and GPU, and hence makes performance comparison straightforward, and OpenCL allows control of the multicore vector units.

This section discusses the key contributions to attain two optimized parallel versions, catering for multi-core CPUs and GPUs. First, we present structural changes that provide compute device specific optimizations. Next, we provide an in-depth description of the optimized CPU and GPU versions respectively.

Fast Lookup of Graph Edges
The algorithm relies on a set data structure to store the edges of the graph. This set is queried frequently with randomly generated edges to check for their membership. To improve the performance of such lookups, we developed a custom set implementation that restricts its features based on its usage patterns. For example, the set is used as a container for the graph edges which are known in advance. Therefore, the set can be made immutable and does not require thread-safety.

We designed the edge set as a variant of a cuckoo hash [18]. The hash is indexed by a tuple of two 32-bit vertices that represent an edge. It uses two hash functions to address two corresponding storage spaces. Additionally, it stores 4 different 64-bit edge values per bucket as shown in Fig. 1. This set implementation allowed us to obtain a loading factor upwards of 90% which reduces the space overhead significantly.

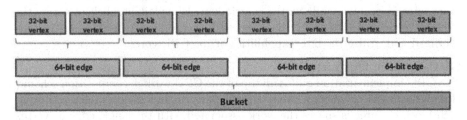

Fig. 1. Structure of a single cuckoo hash bucket containing 4 edges.

Parallelization and Data Dependencies
The original algorithm was structurally reorganized into 4 main sections with one or more kernels in each depending on data dependencies and synchronization requirements. First, the sampling of a mini-batch of edges is done on the host as it is a cheap operation. The mini-batch sampling is followed by the neighbor sampling kernel which generates uniformly random neighbors for each vertex in

the mini-batch. Second, the predominant kernel, *update_phi* is invoked to calculate the gradients for each vertex i in the mini-batch $\mathcal{E}_n$ and updates the value of $\phi_i \mid i \in \mathcal{E}_n$. Third, the *update_pi* kernel is invoked to normalize the individual ϕ_i and store the result in the corresponding π_i. Fourth, the kernels *update_theta* and *update_beta* are invoked to modify the global parameters. Finally, a dedicated kernel calculates perplexity.

Memory Footprint Reduction

A key structural change applied to the algorithm is the lossless compression of its state. This enabled the algorithm to process larger data sets while maintaining all state in memory. Moreover, as the algorithm is data-intensive, a reduction of the state is accompanied by a decrease in its data-intensity. The data structures that occupy most memory are the matrices π and ϕ of dimensions $N \times K$. However, the storage of both matrices is redundant as π is a row-normalized copy of ϕ, see Sect. 2. The storage for ϕ is discarded; ϕ_{ik} values are recalculated each time as π_{ik}/ϕ_i^{sum}, which requires maintenance of a vector ϕ^{sum} of size N. Moreover, the calculation for ϕ_{ik} can be cached. The matrix ϕ is required in two kernels only, namely, *update_phi* and *update_pi*. Both kernels access ϕ_i only for vertices i in the mini-batch $\mathcal{E}_n$, so for each iteration, the calculated values for ϕ are cached in a smaller temporary matrix of size $|\mathcal{E}_n| \times K$. This transformation trades memory storage and bandwidth for a minimal computation overhead.

Thus, the memory requirement for ϕ is reduced from $N \times K$ to a vector ϕ_{sum} of length N and a much smaller $|\mathcal{E}_n| \times K$ matrix. For sufficiently large K, this transformation roughly halves the memory footprint of the algorithm.

CPU-Specific Optimization

The multi-core CPU version of the algorithm uses OpenCL to perform its computations. The work decomposition of the CPU kernels ensures that each thread performs independent computation to avoid expensive synchronization. Edge-centric kernels that operate over mini-batch edges perform computations over every edge in parallel while vertex-centric kernels exploit parallelism across the selected vertices. Additionally, the kernels were vectorized to decrease instruction overhead and utilize the SSE capabilities of the CPU cores.

GPU-Specific Optimization

The GPU implementation builds on top of the CPU work decomposition scheme. However, instead of having every thread perform independent computations, each block of threads shares the work associated with the single edge or vertex for edge-centric and vertex-centric kernels.

Similar to the CPU optimization, we investigated the use of vector data types to decrease the instruction overhead and increase memory bandwidth for all strategies.

Since all kernels are data-bound, we investigated several memory organization strategies to exploit the GPU's memory hierarchy. As a case study, a discussion of the *update_phi* kernel is provided as it is the predominant component of the algorithm.

The *update_phi* kernel operates over every vertex i in the mini-batch and requires two temporary vectors of length K to perform its computation. For each vertex, it iterates over the randomly generated neighbors and computes a vector of probabilities $Probs_i$ of length K. The individual $Probs_i$ vectors of each (i, neighbor) tuple are used to update the gradients vector $Grads_i$ for each vertex i. Finally, the ϕ_i row is updated to reflect the changes that were accumulated in $Grads_i$ for each vertex i in the mini-batch $\mathcal{E}_n$.

A deeper analysis of the memory access patterns of the *update_phi* kernel revealed the frequency and modality of access to the data structures. The read-only accesses of π_j of the randomly generated neighbors are unique with a high probability. More precisely, each $vertex_i$ in the mini-batch randomly samples a neighbor set from the uniform distribution. Given that the total number of sampled neighbors is much smaller than N, there is a low likelihood of duplicate samples, so there is only limited potential for data reuse. Therefore, these accesses provide limited opportunities for optimization without interfering with the algorithm's entropy. The data structure usage patterns that are deterministic and most frequently accessed in read/write mode are $Probs$ and $Grads$. Similarly, π_i for each vertex in the mini-batch is read repeatedly for the calculation of $Probs$ per neighbor and again to update $Grads$.

The following strategies present alternative methods of handling the deterministic memory usage patterns of $Probs_i$, $Grads_i$ and π_i.

The naive strategy simply allocates temporary vectors in thread local memory for $Probs$ and $Grads$ which physically resides in device memory. Memory accesses are coalesced to achieve the highest possible device memory bandwidth.

The shared memory strategy allocates the temporary vectors $Probs_i$ and $Grads_i$ in shared memory. Furthermore, it copies the π_i of the selected mini-batch vertex to shared memory to avoid repeated reads of device memory.

The code generation strategy dynamically generates the code of the kernel to custom tailor its properties. It controls whether a vector is placed or cached in shared memory. Additionally, it controls which vectors explicitly reside in registers by allocating space on the stack frame, unrolling all inner loops of the kernel and substituting all vector addressing with static values. The code generation strategy allows this flexibility for the vectors of concern, namely, $Probs_i$, $Grads_i$ and π_i. Hence, this strategy allows for 8 possible configurations denoted by three letters each of which is a choice between *Register* (R) or *Shared* (S). For example, SSR denotes that $Probs_i$, $Grads_i$ and π_i were placed in *Shared*, *Shared* and *Register* respectively.

3.3 Kernel Code Generation

To support our various configuration needs, we implemented a code generator as part of the host program. It receives the model and performance tuning parameters, and produces compute kernels honoring the supplied constraints. The generated code is then compiled on the fly using the CLCudaAPI before driving the different phases of the algorithm's execution.

The code generator uses a template that defines the static structure of the kernels. Further, it employs custom syntax of placeholders that determine where dynamic content will be inserted. The code generator supports 2 forms of template substitution: type definitions and loop unrolling.

Type definitions are used to control SIMD vector widths for both CPU and GPU kernels. For example, 'Floatn' can be replaced with 'float4' when using 4-wide CUDA SIMD. Further, macros and inline functions override the standard arithmetic operations for each vector width. For example, 'ADDn(x, y)' will be replaced with 'ADD4(x, y)'. It is important to note that this substitution method influences loop lengths. For example, using a 4-wide vector instead of simple instructions reduces loop iterations by a factor of 4.

In the case of GPU kernels, type definitions also specify whether a buffer is allocated in shared or global memory.

Loop unrolling is used to force variables to be stored in registers. The kernel's static template contains placeholders that specify the type of a statement to be performed. The code generator looks for these placeholders and replaces them with one or more statements in an independent activation record.

4   Evaluation

This section discusses the performance evaluation of the various optimizations for resource utilization and parallelization from Sect. 3. First, we explore the performance benefits of parallelizing the computations on a multi-core CPU using OpenCL. Then we assess the trade-offs associated with the GPU optimization strategies and their performance effects on different types of GPUs, spanning four chip architecture generations.

All experiments were conducted on the VU Amsterdam DAS5 cluster [1]. The cluster consists of 68 compute nodes each equipped with a dual 8-core Intel Xeon E5-2630v3 CPU clocked at 2.40 GHz, 64 GB of memory and 8 TB of storage. Additionally, the cluster is fitted with a number of Nvidia GPUs including RTX 2080 Ti, GTX TitanX, GTX980, K40c and K20m; see Table 3 for an overview of their properties. The network graph used for evaluation of the algorithm's performance is *com-DBLP* from the SNAP collection [9]. It has 317 K vertices and a million edges. The focus of our paper is the effect of parallelizing the algorithm; our findings are representative for any dataset since the behavior of the calculation kernels does not depend on the dataset.

4.1   Analysis of CPU Parallelism

This section discusses the use of the multi-core CPU available on the DAS5 cluster. The parallel OpenCL version divides the work across the cores and performs independent calculations concurrently. As shown in Table 2, the dominant kernel in the computation is *update_phi*, which accounts for 66.5% of the computation time. Without exploiting the dual 8-core processor's vectorization capabilities, the speedup relative to the baseline sequential C++ version is 9.8. The model parameters for these experiments: $K = 1024$, $m = 4096$, $|\mathcal{V}_n| = 32$.

In addition to applying computations in parallel, we investigated the use of the SIMD instructions to maximize resource utilization. Figure 2 presents the performance of vectorizing the kernels with varying vector widths. A key aspect in this figure is the diminishing performance benefit for higher vector widths. As the computational performance increases, the memory throughput becomes the leading performance bottleneck. Moreover, using 16-wide SIMD gave a slight performance penalty compared to 8-wide SIMD. The 8-wide vector version improves the speedup relative to the baseline version from 9.8 to 20.9.

Table 2. Multi-core CPU performance breakdown without vectorization.

Kernel	Time (seconds)
PPX CALC	0.0364737
PPX ACCUM	0.083
SAMPLING	0.535599
UPDATE_PHI	25.6598
UPDATE_PI	0.645875
THETA SUM	0.0483902
GRADS PAR	1.92919
GRADS SUM	9.31122
UPDATE THETA	0.0548013
NORM THETA	0.001
TOTAL	38.5858

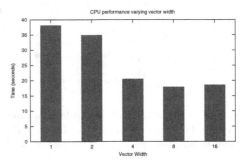

Fig. 2. Performance of CPU for varying vector widths.

4.2 Analysis of GPU Parallelism

As discussed in Sect. 3.2, we employed multiple memory organization strategies: NAIVE, SHARED and 8 variations of code generation. This section investigates the effectiveness of each on the available GPUs.

Comparison of Memory Management Strategies. Figure 3(a) presents the performance of the RTX2080 Ti GPU with an explicit vector width of 4 across the strategies. The x-axis represents *update_phi* thread block sizes while the y-axis presents the total execution time of 1000 *update_phi* invocations. The naive and shared strategies are labeled NAIVE and SHARED respectively. Further, each code generation strategy is labeled by GEN followed by the 3 choices that identify it. A zoomed-in version of Fig. 3(a) is provided as the bottom row to focus on the optimal range.

As would be expected, the naive strategy exhibits the worst performance over all thread block sizes, as it does not explicitly cache repeated device read operations.

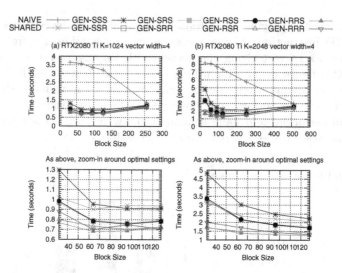

Fig. 3. Execution time of 1K *update_phi* invocations ($\mathcal{E}_n = 4096, |\mathcal{V}_n| = 32$) on the RTX2080 Ti across a sweep of *update_phi* thread block sizes. The lower figures are a zoom-in into the optimal block range of the figures above.

The SHARED and *GEN-SSS* strategies come next in terms of performance. Both strategies cache $Grads_i$, $Probs_i$ and π_i in shared memory but differ in one aspect: *GEN-SSS* explicitly unrolls the internal loops of the kernel. However, loop unrolling incurred additional overhead and made *GEN-SSS* slower than the simple SHARED strategy.

The other flavors of the code generation strategy attain higher performance as they unroll internal loops as well as cache data in registers. The RTX2080 Ti in Fig. 3(a) obtains the best performance with the *GEN-RRS* strategy. The optimal thread block size is 64 and vector width is 4. The results for other vector widths are omitted as they obtain lower performance.

A key model parameter that affects the behavior of the optimization strategies is the number of communities K. Figure 3(b) presents the same model configuration as in Fig. 3(a) but $K = 2048$ instead of $K = 1024$. The most important difference in performance between the two figures is the optimal thread block size, which grows from 64 to 128 when K is doubled. An increase in K comes with a proportional increase in the size of shared memory required by each thread block for the strategies that employ it explicitly. Similarly, GEN strategies that use the register file will require additional space. Therefore, the number of concurrent thread blocks that can execute on a single streaming multiprocessor will decrease, minimizing the GPU's occupancy and utilization. This limitation can be counteracted by selecting a larger thread block size which in turn increases the computation concurrency and occupancy. However, increasing the block sizes has diminishing returns and eventually leads to worse performance that matches the NAIVE strategy.

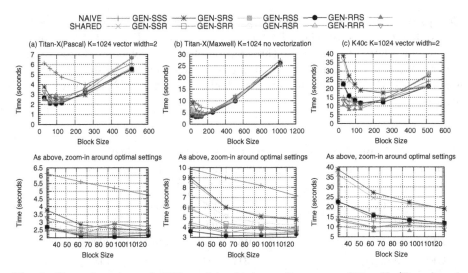

Fig. 4. Execution time of 1000 *update_phi* invocations on a Titan-X (Pascal and Maxwell) and a K40 across a sweep of *update_phi* thread block sizes. The lower figures are a zoom-in into the optimal block range of the upper figures. Other relevant model parameters: $\mathcal{E}_n = 4096$, $|\mathcal{V}_n| = 32$.

In contrast to the other GPUs, the Titan-X Pascal shows good performance with the SHARED strategy as shown in Fig. 4(a). This can be explained by its high bandwidth to computational power ratio compared to the other devices. The Pascal performs best with the *GEN-RSR* strategy, a block size of 96 and a vector width of 2. On the other hand, Fig. 4(b) shows the Titan-X Maxwell performed best with a thread block size of 64 and no vectorization.

Figure 4(c) presents the performance of the K40c GPU for the same experimental configuration as before, with a vector width of 2. The results for the versions with vector width 4 and no vectorization are omitted as they exhibit lower performance. Surprisingly, Fig. 4(c) shows that the NAIVE strategy outperforms SHARED and some of the GEN strategies. This can be explained by the unique properties of the Kepler Super Computing line of products to which the K40c belongs. These GPUs include enhanced L2 caching mechanisms that accelerate repeated and sparse memory accesses. This is especially advantageous as it caches repeated reads across streaming multiprocessors. However, the highest performance is attained by *GEN-RRS* which explicitly employs registers for both $Probs_i$ and $Grads_i$.

These performance results for a range of GPUs reinforce the importance of customizing compute kernels to each GPU's specific architecture and capabilities. For instance, each GPU achieved its highest performance by employing a different strategy. Moreover, each GPU displayed different strategy-performance orderings.

Comparison of Compute Devices. Figure 5 compares the highest speedup achieved by the RTX2080 Ti, GTX Titan-X Maxwell and Pascal, GTX980, K40c and K20m relative to the single-threaded baseline C++ version. These results are consistent with the relative capabilities of each device as listed in Table 3. For instance, the RTX2080 achieves the highest speedup of 245 relative to the baseline.

Table 3. Properties of the GPUs used in the evaluation

Device	RTX 2080 Ti	GTX Titan-X		GTX 980	K40c	K20m
Architecture	Turing	Pascal	Maxwell	Maxwell	Kepler	Kepler
Number of Cores	4352	3584	3072	2048	2880	2496
Clock (MHz)	1350	1417	1000	1126	745	706
GFlops (single)	13450	10157	6144	4612	4290	3520
GFlops (double)	420	317	192	144	1430	1170
Memory (GB)	11	12	12	4	12	5
Bandwidth (GB/s)	616	480	336.5	224	288	208

Figure 6 presents the execution time of the best-performing strategy for each GPU. In this figure, the performance is normalized over the non-vectorized kernel version for each GPU. Conforming to intuition, execution time of the RTX2080 improves with vector width. In contrast, it is notable that the Maxwell Titan-X and GTX980 achieve their highest performance with non-vectorized kernels, and the Pascal Titan-X and Kepler GPUs obtain the best performance with a vector width of 2. At one extreme, the Maxwell Titan-X exhibits an overhead factor of nearly 1.8 when using a vector width of 4. On the other hand, the RTX2080 Ti improves its performance by roughly 35% when it uses a vector width of 4 compared to the non-vectorized kernel. Therefore, explicit vectorization of the kernels can be either useful or harmful depending on the GPU architecture and the specific problem it is applied to.

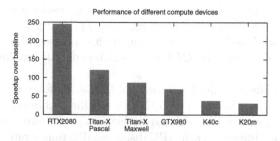

Fig. 5. Speedup comparison of best-performing parallel configurations of each compute device normalized over baseline C++ version. Relevant model parameters: $K = 1024$, $\mathcal{E}_n = 4096$, $|\mathcal{V}_n| = 32$.

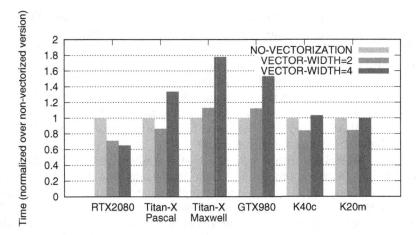

Fig. 6. Performance of the best-performing strategy per GPU, varying the vector width, normalized over the non-vectorized kernel. Relevant model parameters: $K = 1024$, $\mathcal{E}_n = 4096$, $|\mathcal{V}_n| = 32$.

5 Related Work

Several studies looked into the problem of tuning compute kernels [11,19]. Kernel Tuner [19] is a tool that facilicates the exploration of the available tuning parameters by appling multiple strategies to arrive at optimized configurations. The main focus of this work was overcoming discontinuous search spaces of established optimization techniques such as tiling and loop unrolling. On the other hand, Lim et al. [11] leveraged static code analysis to suggest tuning parameters without the need for experimentation. In contrast, our study focuses on application-specific data structures, memory and caching optimizations that required fundamental data representation changes. For example, we deduplicated matrices and re-encoded a graph as a cuckoo hash.

Recent work focused on the applicability of graph algorithms on GPUs. The common pattern is representing vertices and edges such that GPU memory hierarchies can be effectively utilized. WolfGraph [22] tackles graph processing in an edge-centric manner which prevents load imbalances associated with vertex-centric traversals. We incorporated a similar technique to avoid nondeterministic edge indirections when processing mini-batches. XBFS [5] laid out a methodology to perform breadth-first search on GPUs.

Mei et al. [13] provided a micro-benchmark that assessed the memory hierarchies of different GPU models. Similar to our evaluation results, they show how the seemingly similar memory hierarchies of different GPU models can produce non-intuitive performance outcomes.

Whereas acceleration of *deep learning* algorithms on GPUs is an ongoing success story, approximative Baysian algorithms (where our MCMC algorithm belongs) are not natural candidates for acceleration. Nevertheless, a number of projects explore this terrain. Medlar et al. [12] use GPUs with their MCMC approach to analyze parental linkage patterns in a biology context and White and Porter [20] do the same to model terrorist activity. Latent Dirichlet Allocation, another variety of Bayesian Approximation, is used on GPUs by Yan et al. [21]. There is also related work on MCMC algorithms that use the gradient to speed up convergence. Langevin and Hamiltonian dynamics are representatives of these varieties [6]. Our algorithm uses Riemann Manifold Langevin dynamics. Beam et al. [2] use GPUs to perform Hamiltonian descent using Python interfaces to access the cuBLAS library [3]. They limit GPU optimizations to reducing data transfers between host and device memory.

Another MMSB algorithm with stochastic gradient descent on the GPU is the Online Tensor approach [8]. Their implementation uses the cuBLAS library. Unlike our work, there is no attempt to hand-optimize the GPU kernels. Since they target GPUs only, the datasets they can handle are limited by the device memory of the GPU. Our implementation can also be used, with reduced speedup, on a multicore CPU which allows much larger datasets.

6   Conclusion

Identifying optimization strategies of parallel data-intensive algorithms is a complex task. The SG-MCMC algorithm discussed in this paper posed additional challenges due to its unique stochastic nature and nondeterministic memory access patterns. We presented a methodology of improving performance by fundamentally restructuring the algorithm to cater for concurrency.

A deep analysis showed the algorithm's state can be reduced by 75%. We navigated the complex optimization landscape by dynamically generating compute kernels and testing different combinations of optimizations. This effort culminated in significant speedup factors of 21 and 245 using a multi-core CPU and a GPU respectively, compared to an optimized sequential program. Finally, we contrasted the performance of several GPUs highlighting the difference between their optimal configurations.

The outcome of this work reinforces the significance of avoiding premature optimization as it can lead to unexpected results. In particular, the success of common GPU optimizations depends on the particular device in use and the problem it is applied to. Although GPU architectures and their memory hierarchies can be leveraged to obtain significant speedups, they introduce significant complexity which hinders our ability to predict their benefits.

References

1. Bal, H., et al.: A medium-scale distributed system for computer science research: infrastructure for the long term. Computer **49**(05), 54–63 (2016). https://doi.org/10.1109/MC.2016.127

2. Beam, A.L., Ghosh, S.K., Doyle, J.: Fast hamiltonian monte carlo using GPU computing. arXiv preprint (2014). https://doi.org/10.1080/10618600.2015.1035724. http://arxiv.org/abs/1402.4089
3. cuBlas Home Page. http://docs.nvidia.com/cuda/cublas
4. El-Helw, I., Hofman, R., Li, W., Ahn, S., Welling, M., Bal, H.E.: Scalable overlapping community detection. In: IPDPS Workshops 2016, Chicago, IL, USA, 23–27 May 2016, pp. 1463–1472 (2016). https://doi.org/10.1109/IPDPSW.2016.165
5. Gaihre, A., Wu, Z., Yao, F., Liu, H.: XBFS: exploring runtime optimizations for breadth-first search on GPUs. In: Proceedings of the 28th International Symposium on High-Performance Parallel and Distributed Computing HPDC 2019, pp. 121–131. ACM, New York (2019). https://doi.org/10.1145/3307681.3326606
6. Girolami, M., Calderhead, B., Chin, S.A.: Riemann manifold langevin and hamiltonian monte carlo methods. J. Roy. Stat. Soc. Ser. B (Methodological) (2012). https://doi.org/10.1111/j.1467-9868.2010.00765.x
7. Gupta, S., Agrawal, A., Gopalakrishnan, K., Narayanan, P.: Deep learning with limited numerical precision. CoRR (2015). http://arxiv.org/abs/1502.02551
8. Huang, F., Niranjan, U.N., Hakeem, M.U., Verma, P., Anandkumar, A.: Fast detection of overlapping communities via online tensor methods on GPUs. CoRR (2013). http://arxiv.org/abs/1309.0787
9. Leskovec, J., Krevl, A.: SNAP datasets: stanford large network dataset collection, June 2014. http://snap.stanford.edu/data
10. Li, W., Ahn, S., Welling, M.: Scalable MCMC for mixed membership stochastic blockmodels. CoRR (2015). http://arxiv.org/abs/1510.04815
11. Lim, R., Norris, B., Malony, A.: Autotuning GPU kernels via static and predictive analysis. In: 2017 46th International Conference on Parallel Processing (ICPP), pp. 523–532, August 2017. https://doi.org/10.1109/ICPP.2017.61
12. Medlar, A., Glowacka, D., Stanescu, H., Bryson, K., Kleta, R.: SwiftLink: parallel MCMC linkage analysis using multicore CPU and GPU. Bioinformatics 29(4), 413–419 (2013). https://doi.org/10.1093/bioinformatics/bts704
13. Mei, X., Chu, X.: Dissecting GPU memory hierarchy through microbenchmarking. IEEE Trans. Parallel Distrib. Syst. 28(1), 72–86 (2017). https://doi.org/10.1109/TPDS.2016.2549523
14. Nickolls, J., Buck, I., Garland, M., Skadron, K.: Scalable parallel programming with CUDA. Queue 6(2), 40–53 (2008). https://doi.org/10.1145/1365490.1365500
15. Nugteren, C.: CLCudaAPI: a portable high-level API with CUDA or OpenCL back-end. https://github.com/CNugteren/CLCudaAPI
16. NumPy Home Page. http://www.numpy.org
17. OpenCL - The Open Standard for Parallel Programming of Heterogeneous Systems. http://www.khronos.org/opencl/
18. Pagh, R., Rodler, F.F.: Cuckoo hashing. J. Algorithms 51(2), 122–144 (2004). https://doi.org/10.1016/j.jalgor.2003.12.002
19. van Werkhoven, B.: Kernel tuner: a search-optimizing GPU code auto-tuner. Future Gener. Comput. Syst. 90, 347–358 (2019). https://doi.org/10.1016/j.future.2018.08.004
20. White, G., Porter, M.D.: GPU accelerated MCMC for modeling terrorist activity. Comput. Stat. Data Anal. 71, 643–651 (2014). https://doi.org/10.1016/j.csda.2013.03.027

21. Yan, F., Xu, N., Qi, Y.: Parallel inference for latent dirichlet allocation on graphics processing units. In: 23rd Annual Conference on Neural Information Processing Systems. Vancouver, Canada, pp. 2134–2142 (2009). http://papers.nips.cc/paper/3788-parallel-inference-for-latent-dirichlet-allocation-on-graphics-processing-units

22. Zhu, H., He, L., Leeke, M., Mao, R.: WolfGraph: the edge-centric graph processing on GPU. Future Generation Computer Systems (2019). https://doi.org/10.1016/j.future.2019.09.052. http://www.sciencedirect.com/science/article/pii/S0167739X18325251

Parallel Numerical Methods
and Applications

A Prediction Framework for Fast Sparse Triangular Solves

Najeeb Ahmad$^{(\boxtimes)}$ ⓘ, Buse Yilmaz ⓘ, and Didem Unat ⓘ

Department of Computer Science and Engineering,
Koç University, Rumelifeneri Yolu,
34450 Sariyer, Istanbul, Turkey
{nahmad16,byilmaz,dunat}@ku.edu.tr

Abstract. Sparse triangular solve (SpTRSV) is an important linear algebra kernel, finding extensive uses in numerical and scientific computing.
The parallel implementation of SpTRSV is a challenging task due to the
sequential nature of the steps involved. This makes it, in many cases, one of
the most time-consuming operations in an application. Many approaches
for efficient SpTRSV on CPU and GPU systems have been proposed in
the literature. However, no single implementation or platform (CPU or
GPU) gives the fastest solution for all input sparse matrices. In this work,
we propose a machine learning-based framework to predict the SpTRSV
implementation giving the fastest execution time for a given sparse matrix
based on its structural features. The framework is tested with six SpTRSV
implementations on a state-of-the-art CPU-GPU machine (Intel Xeon
Gold CPU, NVIDIA V100 GPU). Experimental results, with 998 matrices
taken from the SuiteSparse Matrix Collection, show the classifier prediction accuracy of 87% for the fastest SpTRSV algorithm for a given input
matrix. Predicted SpTRSV implementations achieve average speedups
(harmonic mean) in the range of 1.4–2.7× against the six SpTRSV implementations used in the evaluation.

Keywords: Performance prediction · Sparse triangular solve ·
Heterogeneous systems · Performance autotuning

1 Introduction

The sparse triangular solve (SpTRSV) is one of the important kernels used
in direct and iterative methods for sparse linear systems and least square
problems [25]. Efficient implementation of SpTRSV on CPU and GPU has
been extensively studied and many SpTRSV implementations are available
[16,20,21,23,25,29,31,37]. However, there is no single execution platform or
algorithm that gives the best SpTRSV performance for all input matrices. This is
because, given a sparse matrix, the SpTRSV performance depends upon characteristics of the available parallelism in the matrix and implementation details of

ⓒ Springer Nature Switzerland AG 2020
M. Malawski and K. Rzadca (Eds.): Euro-Par 2020, LNCS 12247, pp. 529–545, 2020.
https://doi.org/10.1007/978-3-030-57675-2_33

the algorithm (e.g. data structures, the sequence of operations etc.) [38]. Therefore, CPU has been observed to give better SpTRSV performance for some matrices than GPU and vice versa [21,29]. Also, different SpTRSV implementations on the same platform have been observed to achieve higher performance than others for different matrices [20,29]. By selecting appropriate SpTRSV implementation for a given matrix, one can achieve higher SpTRSV performance. This can result in considerable performance gains for applications requiring multiple SpTRSV iterations, e.g., iterative solvers [34]. Given that many SpTRSV implementations are available for each platform, this selection can be a complex task. An obvious approach to select the fastest SpTRSV implementation is to run different implementations one-by-one and collect the empirical results. This, however, is a time-consuming and non-trivial process as each SpTRSV implementation has its own data structures, API, and matrix analysis requirements [25,29].

In this paper, we propose a machine learning-based framework for predicting the fastest SpTRSV algorithm for a given matrix on CPU-GPU heterogeneous systems. The framework works by extracting matrix features, collecting algorithm performance data, and training a prediction model with 998 real matrices from the SuiteSparse Matrix Collection [10]. Once trained on a given machine, the model can predict the fastest SpTRSV implementation for a given matrix by paying a one-time matrix feature extraction cost. The framework is also capable of taking into account CPU-GPU communication overheads, which might be incurred in an iterative solver. We test our prediction framework for two CPU and four GPU algorithms on a modern Intel Xeon Gold CPU and NVIDIA Tesla V100 GPU systems. The model achieves an average prediction accuracy of 87% on our selected platform. Experimental results show predicted implementation achieving an average speedup (harmonic mean) in the range 1.4×–2.7× over a lazy choice of one of the six SpTRSV implementations used in this study.

The contributions of this work are summarized below:

- We provide comparative performance results of six SpTRSV implementations on a CPU-GPU platform.
- We identify an important set of features of a sparse matrix and develop a tool for efficiently extracting these features.
- We devise a framework to automatically extract matrix features, collect SpTRSV performance data, train machine learning model, and predict the fastest SpTRSV algorithm.
- We evaluate the performance, accuracy, and overhead of the framework on a modern CPU-GPU heterogeneous system.

2   Background and Motivation

The triangular solve refers to the solution of a linear system of the form $Ly = b$ or $Ux = y$, where L and U are lower and upper triangular matrices and x, y, and b are dense vectors. Due to the presence of dependencies among unknowns, triangular solve is an inherently sequential operation not easily lending itself to

$$
\begin{array}{c}
① \\ ② \\ ③ \\ ④ \\ ⑤ \\ ⑥ \\ ⑦ \\ ⑧
\end{array}
\begin{bmatrix}
1 & 0 & 0 & 0 & 0 & 0 & 0 & 0 \\
0 & 1 & 0 & 0 & 0 & 0 & 0 & 0 \\
0 & l_{32} & 1 & 0 & 0 & 0 & 0 & 0 \\
0 & l_{42} & 0 & 1 & 0 & 0 & 0 & 0 \\
l_{51} & 0 & l_{53} & 0 & 1 & 0 & 0 & 0 \\
0 & l_{62} & l_{63} & 0 & 0 & 1 & 0 & 0 \\
l_{71} & l_{72} & l_{73} & l_{74} & 0 & 0 & 1 & 0 \\
0 & 0 & 0 & 0 & l_{85} & 0 & 0 & 1
\end{bmatrix}
\begin{bmatrix}
y_1 \\ y_2 \\ y_3 \\ y_4 \\ y_5 \\ y_6 \\ y_7 \\ y_8
\end{bmatrix}
=
\begin{bmatrix}
b_1 \\ b_2 \\ b_3 \\ b_4 \\ b_5 \\ b_6 \\ b_7 \\ b_8
\end{bmatrix}
$$

Fig. 1. A lower triangular system $Ly = b$ (left) and its dependency graph (right) [31]

efficient parallelization [23]. When L and U are sparse, some of the dependencies may be missing thus offering an opportunity to calculate some unknowns in parallel. Figure 1 shows a lower triangular system and its dependency graph. The nodes of the graph represent row numbers thus unknowns and edges represent dependencies of unknowns. The horizontal dashed lines separate the set of nodes into levels where nodes in each level can potentially be calculated in parallel [34]. The levels are numbered sequentially in the order in which computations on them can begin. As the number of levels, the number of unknowns in a level, and dependencies among unknowns is a function of matrix sparsity pattern, it is hard to devise an efficient SpTRSV algorithm for all possible input matrices.

The parallel SpTRSV algorithms proposed in the literature can be broadly categorized into (i) Level-scheduling [3] (ii) Synchronization-free [15,19,23,25] (iii) Graph coloring [20,30] (iv) Partitioned inverse [2], and (v) Iterative algorithms [5]. Most of these algorithms are comprised of two phases, an *analysis phase* in which parallelism in the matrix is discovered, and a *solve phase* in which the solver solves the linear system in parallel [20]. In level-scheduling algorithms, the analysis phase constitutes discovering the levels and unknowns within each level. In the solve phase, the algorithm proceeds level-by-level, synchronizing before starting computations on a new level. In synchronization-free methods, the number of dependencies per unknown [25] and in certain variations, the levels and unknowns within each level [20] are calculated in the analysis phase. Unlike level-scheduling approach, computations on an unknown can start as soon as its dependencies are met. The rest of the methods provide an approximate solution of the triangular system and are not the focus of this study.

For CPUs and GPUs, many implementations for the exact solution of SpTRSV are available. For CPUs, Intel MKL library [16] provides parallel *(MKL(par))* and sequential *(MKL(seq))* SpTRSV implementations. An implementation based on dependency graph sparsification has been developed by Park et al. [31] for multicore CPUs. For NVIDIA GPUs, the cuSPARSE library provides SpTRSV based on the level-scheduling approach with their legacy API *(cuSPARSE(v1))* [29]. The newer cuSPARSE SpTRSV *(cuSPARSE(v2))* works with or without level information, depending upon the user's choice [8]. Weifeng et al. [23–25] developed a synchronization-free SpTRSV algorithm *(Sync-Free)* with multiple right-hand sides for GPUs. In [20,22], the author proposes variations of SpTRSV based on synchronization-free algorithms for GPUs.

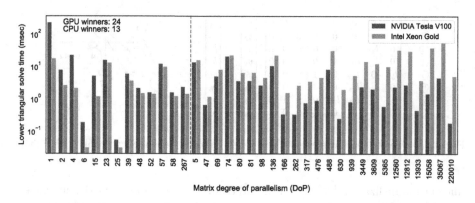

Fig. 2. SpTRSV performance on Intel Xeon Gold (6148) CPU and an NVIDIA V100 GPU (32 GB, PCIe).

Table 1 shows the breakdown of winning algorithms among six SpTRSV implementations (2 CPU, 4 GPU implementations) for a set of 37 matrices from the SuiteSparse matrix collection. Figure 2 shows the comparison for CPU and GPU winners for each of these matrices. The dashed vertical line separates the matrices into two groups; matrices attaining the best performance on CPU are on the left and on GPU, on the right. The x-axis shows the matrix degree of parallelism (DoP), which equals the average number of rows per level. Results show that no single algorithm or platform performs best for all matrices.

Table 1. SpTRSV winning algorithm breakdown for 37 matrices in Figs. 2

Arch.	SpTRSV implementation	Winner for # of matrices	Percentage
CPU	MKL(seq)	11	29.73%
	MKL(par)	2	5.41%
GPU	cuSPARSE(v1)	7	18.92%
	cuSPARSE(v2)(level-sch.)	7	18.92%
	cuSPARSE(v2)(no level-sch.)	2	5.41%
	Sync-Free	8	21.62%

To find the best SpTRSV implementation for a given matrix, one option is to test each algorithm individually and select the best performing one. This requires the programmer to learn new APIs, manage data structures, and perform data format conversions for each implementation, which is tedious and error-prone. Moreover, some algorithms require non-trivial analysis time and necessitate multiple iterations to get stable performance numbers. To aid the programmer, this work proposes a framework that hides all the mentioned complexities and reports the predicted fastest algorithm by analyzing the matrix features. This can substantially improve the programmer's productivity and solver performance.

3   Related Work

The general problem of algorithm selection [33] has been previously studied using statistical [14,36], empirical [39] and machine learning techniques. OSKI [37] is an autotuning library based on statistical techniques for sparse linear algebra kernels on CPU platforms, particularly the sparse matrix-vector multiplication (SpMV) and SpTRSV. The library can transparently tune kernels at runtime using the machine and input matrix characteristics. PetaBricks [4] is a language and compiler that allows multiple implementations of multiple algorithms for the same problem and automatically selects the best algorithm by building and using the so-called choice dependency graph. Sequoia [13] autotunes an application based on the memory hierarchy of the underlying machine. While PetaBricks and Sequoia do not take input data characteristics except the data set size, Nitro [28] framework allows programmers to guide the algorithm selection process by letting them specify characteristics of the input data they want to be considered for algorithm selection. These frameworks require programmers to learn new APIs and procedures to guide the algorithm selection process. A previous work dealing with SpTRSV execution choice between CPU and GPU is presented in [17] for the MAPS reservoir simulation system. The approach is, however, specific to reservoir simulation systems. A recent work by Dufrechou et al. [12] uses supervised machine learning to automatically select a sparse triangular solver on the GPUs. They tested their model for selection among cuSPARSE library-based SpTRSV and three variants of a CSR-based self-scheduling algorithm [11]. Their model managed to achieve an accuracy of close to 81%.

A number of works exist dealing with the selection of solvers and preconditioner-solver pairs for numerical software. Lighthouse [27] allows users to select the right solver and generate corresponding code for PETSc applications. It uses machine learning to analyze the matrix features and select the solver accordingly. Motter et al. [26] utilize machine learning techniques for selecting solver-preconditioner pairs for the PETSc framework [6] taking into account machine characteristics.

Unlike many of the previous works[12,26,27,37], our prediction framework targets heterogeneous CPU-GPU systems. Compared with other frameworks targeting heterogeneous systems [4,28], it does not require programmer guidance or target a specific application area [17]. In comparison to the similar work on the GPUs [12], our framework achieved higher accuracy (87% versus 81%) using a larger set of features for a wider (6 versus 4) and diverse set of SpTRSV algorithms. In addition, our framework is extensible allowing the inclusion of new SpTRSV algorithms as they become available [22].

4   Design and Implementation

The prediction framework is designed to automate the SpTRSV algorithm selection process for a given machine and matrix. It is composed of five main components (Fig. 3); (1) An automatically downloadable set of matrices from the

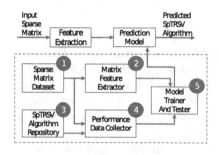

Fig. 3. The prediction framework

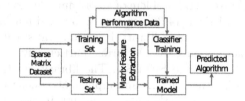

Fig. 4. Prediction model design flow

SuiteSparse Matrix Collection, (2) A matrix feature extractor, (3) An SpTRSV algorithm repository, (4) An SpTRSV performance data collector, which works by automatically downloading matrices, running each SpTRSV algorithm in the repository for each matrix, and logging the SpTRSV execution time. (5) A trainer and tester for the machine learning algorithm prediction model, which uses matrix features from the feature extractor as the input data and ID of the winning algorithm from performance data collector as the target for the model training and testing. Once the model is trained and tested, it can predict the fastest SpTRSV algorithm for a given matrix based on its features.

Figure 4 shows the design flow for our prediction model. For training the model, feature and algorithm performance data for the matrix data set is split into training and testing sets. Once trained with the training set, the model is tested with the matrices in the test set. Next, we discuss the important parts of the framework: (1) feature set selection, (2) feature extraction, and (3) machine learning model for prediction.

4.1   Feature Set Selection

SpTRSV performance is mainly affected by the sparsity pattern (i.e. the distribution of nonzero (nnz) elements in the matrix) [38]. The sparsity pattern is described by matrix structural data such as the number of rows, columns, nnzs, row and column lengths etc. We initially started with a set of around 50 structural features. After feature correlation analysis and feature score comparison, 30 structural features are finalized. We choose not to reduce the number of features further because reducing the number of features from 30 to, say, 10 negligibly improves the overhead of the feature extraction process but results in up to 10% drop in prediction accuracy. This is because many of the top-scoring features require per-level information, which in turn requires level calculation, which is generally the most time-consuming part of the matrix analysis phase [29]. The majority of the other features can be cheaply collected as a part of the level calculation process. Table 2 lists the final feature set used by the framework. The last column in the table also shows the score rank for each feature, where the lower score rank means a higher impact on performance.

Table 2. Selected feature set for the prediction framework

No.	Features	Description	Score rank
1	*nnzs*	Number of nonzeros	1
2–4	<*max, mean, std*>_nnz_pl_rw	<maximum, mean, std dev> nonzeros per level row-wise	2, 4, 5
5	*max_nnz_pl_cw*	maximum nonzeros per level column-wise	3
6	*m*	Number of rows/columns	6
7–10	<*max, mean, median, std*>_rpl	<maximum, mean, median, std dev> rows per level	7, 12, 13, 16
11–12	<*min, max*>_cl_cnt	<minimum, maximum> column length count	8, 10
13–14	<*max, min*>_rl_cnt	<maximum, minimum> row length count	9, 11
15–17	<*max,std,median*>_cl	<maximum, std dev, median> column length	14, 22, 29
18	*lvls*	Number of levels	15
19–21	*mean_*<*max, mean, std*>_cl_pl	mean <maximum, mean, std dev> columns per level	17, 18, 20
22–25	<*max,mean,median,std*>_rl	<maximum, mean, median, std dev> row length	19, 27, 28, 30
26–30	*mean_*<*max,std,mean, median,min*>_rl_pl	mean <maximum, std dev, mean, median, minimum> row length per level	21, 23, 24, 25, 26

4.2 Feature Extraction

Feature extraction is an overhead for the SpTRSV algorithm prediction and its execution time should be kept minimum. To achieve this, we employ both CPU and GPU in our feature extraction tool. This process completes in three steps. In the first step, row dependencies (row lengths) for lower/upper triangular matrices are calculated on GPU. Then, we use a slightly modified CUDA implementation of Kahn's algorithm [9] presented in [20] to construct levels in a triangular matrix. The algorithm calculates levels and rows in a level by performing topological sorting on the dependency graph. It recursively finds rows with zero dependencies, saves the row IDs of the current level into a queue, and then removes these rows and their outgoing edges from the graph until no more rows to process. In addition to level calculation, we also collect some statistics such as the number of rows per level, row and column lengths per level, and the nnzs per level. Finally, the remaining features listed in Table 2 are calculated using the NVIDIA Thrust library [7]. For this purpose, while CPU iterates over levels, GPU is used to calculate features for that level.

4.3   Machine Learning Model and Training

For training the model, we use the Scikit-learn machine learning library in Python [32]. As the matrix data set, we choose 998 real square matrices with 1000 or more rows (up to 16M rows) from the SuiteSparse Matrix Collection. We train the model with two CPU SpTRSV algorithms, namely *MKL(seq)* and *MKL(par)*, and four GPU algorithms, namely *cuSPARSE(v1)*, *cuSPARSE(v2)* with and *without level-scheduling* and synchronization-free algorithm (*Sync-Free*) [25].

We assign a unique integer ID to each of these algorithms and collect features and SpTRSV performance data for each matrix in our data set in an automated fashion using the libufget library [18] and our feature extraction tool. The matrix features and the ID of the fastest SpTRSV implementation then serve as input and target, respectively, for training the machine learning model.

For selecting appropriate classifier for the prediction model, we evaluated a number of supervised machine learning-based classifiers provided by the Scikit-learn library including Decision Trees, Random Forest, Support Vector Machines (with grid-search), K-Nearest Neighbors, and Multi-Layer Perceptron Classifier using the Scikit-learn `model_selection` class. Based on the cross-validation scores, we choose Random Forest classifier for prediction. The feature scores are calculated using `feature_selection` class (`SelectKBest` function) with chi-squared used as the score function. Although Deep Neural Networks are suitable for classification tasks and feature selection is done by the model itself, they take considerable amount of time to train and a large training set is required. Hence, we preferred classical supervised machine learning techniques mentioned above and obtained good prediction accuracy.

To evaluate the performance of the prediction model, we utilize cross-validation functionality provided by the Scikit-learn `model_selection` class. For this purpose, features in the input data set are first scaled using Standard Scaler and the data set is then split into test and training data with `train_test_split` function that randomly splits the data set into 75% training data and 25% test data by default. We keep the default split ratios for our evaluation. Next, we use k-fold cross-validation with k set to 10. In k-fold cross-validation, training data set is divided into k smaller sets. For each of k sets, *k-1* sets are used as training data while the remaining set is used for validating the model. The performance of the k-fold cross-validation is then the average of these results.

4.4   Effects of CPU-GPU Data Transfers

In a CPU-GPU system, executing the fastest SpTRSV algorithm may require data transfers between CPU and GPU. For instance, GMRES solver with ILU-preconditioning performs sparse matrix-vector multiplication and vector products in addition to SpTRSV in each iteration [35]. With data transfer overheads, the fastest SpTRSV algorithm may no longer be the fastest as another implementation may require no data transfer.

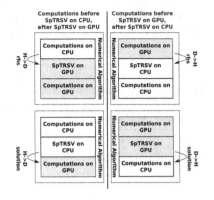

Fig. 5. CPU-GPU data exchange when computations just before and after SpTRSV execute on different platforms

Fig. 6. CPU-GPU data exchange when computations just before and after SpTRSV execute on the same platforms

Table 3. SpTRSV winning algorithm breakdown for the 998 matrices from SuiteSparse

Arch.	SpTRSV implementation	Winner for # of matrices	Percentage
CPU	MKL(seq)	411	41.18%
	MKL(par)	11	1.10%
GPU	cuSPARSE(v1)	111	11.12%
	cuSPARSE(v2)(level-sch.)	61	6.12%
	cuSPARSE(v2)(no level-sch.)	15	1.50%
	Sync-Free	389	38.98%

To elaborate on this, consider a lower triangular system $Ly = b$ to be solved with SpTRSV (see Sect. 2). For iterative methods, matrix L is generally fixed while b and y are updated every iteration. Consider the scenarios shown in Fig. 5, where computations just before and after SpTRSV, execute on different platforms. In Fig. 5, H->D and D->H represent host-to-device and device-to-host data transfers, respectively. As shown in the figure, the data transfer for either the right-hand side or solution vector is inevitable. Therefore, it is always beneficial to choose the fastest SpTRSV algorithm irrespective of whether it runs on the CPU or on the GPU. For the scenarios where computations, just before and after SpTRSV, execute on the same platform and SpTRSV executes on a different platform (Fig. 6), two data transfers are incurred; (the right-hand side and the solution vector). Consequently, this data transfer overhead may change the algorithmic choice. To cater for such scenarios, our framework allows users to specify whether the rest of the numerical solvers executes on a CPU (CPU-centric) or a GPU (GPU-centric). For the CPU-centric scenario, the data transfer time (for the right-hand side and solution vector) is added to each of the GPU algorithms during the training phase. Similarly, for the GPU-centric scenario, the data transfer time is added to each of the CPU algorithms before training the model. Thus, the prediction framework can identify the fastest SpTRSV in presence of data communication overheads.

Table 4. Number of rows and nonzero statistics for the 998 matrices from SuiteSparse

	Minimum	Median	Maximum
Number of rows	1K	12.5K	16.24M
Number of nonzeros	1.074K	105.927K	232.232M

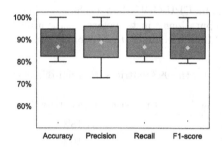

Fig. 7. Model cross validation scores with 30 features in the feature set

Fig. 8. Model cross validation scores with 10 features in the feature set

5 Evaluation

This section evaluates the performance of different SpTRSV algorithms, our framework's prediction accuracy, its performance, and its overhead compared to the analysis phase of SpTRSV algorithms. The performance results were collected on a CPU-GPU machine with an Intel Xeon Gold (6148) CPU and NVIDIA Tesla V100 GPU. CPU has 2 sockets with 20 cores in each and comes with a 512 GB of memory. GPU has 32 GB of memory. The Intel MKL implementations are compiled with `icpc` compiler from Intel Parallel Studio 2019 with -O3 optimization. For *MKL(par)*, all available CPU cores are used without hyperthreading. The cuSPARSE and Sync-Free implementations are compiled using nvcc compiler from CUDA version 10.1 with options `-gencode arch=compute _70,code=sm_70`. Statistics for the number of rows and nonzeros for the matrix data set are given in Table 4.

5.1 Performance of SpTRSV Algorithms

This section presents the experimental results for the six SpTRSV algorithms. For this purpose, each of the six SpTRSV implementations is run 100 times for each matrix in the data set and mean execution time is reported. The results presented here are for the solution of the lower triangular system. Table 3 shows the breakdown of the winning implementations for the entire matrix data set. As regards the number of times an SpTRSV implementation was the fastest for the data set, we observe that, in general, there is no clear GPU advantage over CPU. Intel *MKL(seq)* is the fastest for a high percentage of the matrices than any other implementation. This is possibly due to the fact that some matrices exhibit very low parallelism that can be exploited or variable degrees of parallelism. In general, Intel *MKL(par)* shows poor performance. The *cuS-PARSE(v1)* surprisingly performs better than two variants of *cuSPARSE(v2)* combined. Moreover, on GPU, the *Sync-Free* implementation is dominant over cuSPARSE implementations.

5.2   Accuracy of the Framework

The performance of the machine learning model is measured using typical metrics of accuracy, precision, recall, and f1-score. Figure 7 shows the 10-fold cross-validation results for the Random Forest classifier with 300 forests and feature set with 30 features presented in Table 2. The yellow diamond shows the mean value for each parameter. The classifier achieves an average weighted score of 87% for accuracy, recall, f1-score, and 89% for precision. It means that our SpTRSV framework correctly predicts the best algorithm for 87% of the data set.

To evaluate the effect of reducing the number of features on the prediction model performance, we keep the top 10 features in the feature data set based on their feature scores (score rank in Table 2) and perform 10-fold cross-validation of the resultant model. As shown in Fig. 8, there is a 7–10% drop in performance metrics with the reduced set of features. In addition, there is a wider spread of performance. Considering the possibility of inclusion of new algorithms into the framework in the future, we keep the 30 features listed in Table 2.

Possible reasons for incorrect predictions by the framework include (1) limited diversity in matrix data set (2) comparable algorithm performance for a matrix so that incorrect prediction does not really matter (3) limited feature set. We will further investigate these reasons in the future.

5.3   Speedup Gained by the Framework

To evaluate the performance benefits of our framework, we compare the speedup over the *lazy* choice made by the user for an SpTRSV implementation. Unlike an *aggressive* programmer, who may test all the algorithms to find the best performing algorithm, the lazy programmer always uses the same SpTRSV algorithm regardless of the input matrix. The speedup is defined as $s = T_l/T_p$, where T_l is the execution time of the algorithm that the programmer lazily uses, and T_p is the predicted algorithm by the framework, which may or may not be the fastest algorithm. The speedup is calculated based on the SpTRSV running times and does not include the analysis phase for the algorithms for T_l or T_p.

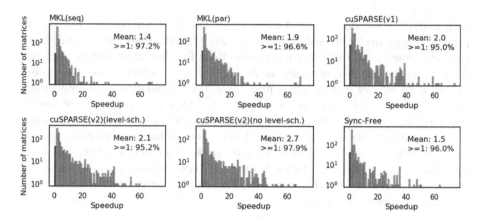

Fig. 9. Speedup gained by predicted over lazy choice algorithm. >= 1 indicates speedup of greater or equal to 1. (Harmonic) mean refers to average speedup achieved by the framework over the lazy choice. Each bin covers a speedup range e.g. first bin covers speedups between 0-0.99, second one covers speedups between 1–1.99 and so on.

Figure 9 shows the histogram for the speedups achieved by the prediction framework over each of the six implementations for the entire data set. The figure also shows the percentage when the predicted algorithm achieves equal or better performance than the lazy choice. The results show that the predicted fastest SpTRSV algorithm achieves the same or better performance for greater or equal to 95% of the matrices. Note that for the aggressive programmer, our prediction is 87%, which is presented in Sect. 5.2. We also observe that the speedup obtained by the prediction framework can reach tens of times for some SpTRSV implementations. Thus, using the framework is highly attractive than an arbitrary algorithmic choice for the SpTRSV execution.

To evaluate performance loss incurred by incorrect predictions, we compared the actual fastest SpTRSV against the incorrectly predicted implementation by our model. The results show that for roughly $3/4^{th}$ of the incorrect predictions, the predicted implementation is less than 2 times slower. Considering the prediction accuracy, speedups achieved with correct predictions, and programming benefits of the framework, we believe this performance loss is reasonable.

5.4   Framework Prediction Overhead

In this section, we evaluate the overhead associated with our algorithm prediction framework. This overhead includes the time spent in feature extraction and for the model to predict the fastest implementation. The feature extraction time depends on matrix sparsity pattern and its size while prediction time is constant for all matrices. Feature extraction includes computing dependencies in triangular matrices, calculating levels, collecting matrix statistics (e.g. row per level etc.), and calculating the final feature set from these statistics. This phase is very similar to the analysis phase of the SpTRSV algorithms based on the level-set method such as *cuSPARSE(v1)* and *(v2)* with levels.

We compare the framework overhead with empirical execution overhead. For the empirical overhead, there are two different types of users: a *lazy* user, who conservatively uses the same algorithm and an *aggressive* user who tests all six algorithms and chooses the best performing SpTRSV implementation. The empirical overhead for an aggressive user for N algorithms is calculated using the equation:

$$Empirical\ Overhead = \sum_{i=1}^{N}(A_i + 10 * (TS)_i) \tag{1}$$

where A_i and $(TS)_i$ are the matrix analysis phase and single SpTRSV iteration times for algorithm i, respectively. The factor 10 in Eq. 1 refers to the approximate number of SpTRSV executions required to get a stable time estimate of a single SpTRSV iteration. For the lazy user, there is only a matrix analysis phase as the lazy user does not question the suitability of the algorithm.

For overhead analysis, we divide the matrices into three groups based on their sizes (1K-100K, 100K-1000K, >1000K). For each group, we compare the mean time spent by the framework, by the aggressive user to select the fastest algorithm, and by the lazy user to run the analysis phase of their chosen algorithm. We assume, without loss of generality, that each SpTRSV implementation runs its own ILU factorization phase except *cuSPARSE(v2)(no level-sch.)* that can use ILU factorization from *cuSPARSE(v2)(level-sch.)*. In some cases, it might be possible for some implementations to use ILU factorization from another implementation. However, it will generally require extra effort from the programmer and might add its own processing overhead (e.g. converting ILU factors from one data structure to another). For the sake of fairness, we provide an overhead comparison with ILU factorization time included (*w ILU*) and excluded (*w/o ILU*) ILU from A_i as well as framework overhead. For *Sync-Free* implementation, extraction of upper and lower triangular parts of the input matrix as ILU factorization time as it does not perform actual ILU factorization [24].

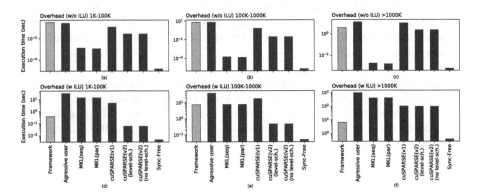

Fig. 10. Mean overhead of framework versus mean empirical execution time for aggressive and lazy users. 1K-100K, 100K-1000K and >1000K refer to matrix size ranges.

Figure 10(a), (b), (c) compare overhead for the three groups of matrices with ILU factorization time excluded. For matrix sizes less than 1000K, the average framework overhead is comparable with the time spent by the aggressive user. For matrix sizes >1000K, the framework overhead is on average 4 times less than the overhead of the aggressive user. Figure 10(d), (e), (f) compare overhead for the three groups of matrices with ILU factorization time included. For all matrix sizes, the average overhead of the framework is observed to be considerably less than aggressive user time by factors ranging between 5 (for 100K-1000K range) and 161 (for >1000K range). Overall, considerable time savings can be obtained by using our framework, especially for large matrices.

We also compute the number of SpTRSV iterations of the predicted algorithm required to amortize the cost of the framework overhead. For all matrix sizes, the mean number of iterations required to amortize the framework overhead is within the range of hundreds. For instance, for the largest group of matrices (>1000K), a mean number of 127 SpTRSV iterations of the predicted algorithm are required to compensate for the framework overhead. Considering that an iterative solver generally requires several hundreds of iterations for convergence, we claim that the overhead of the framework is acceptable. For aggressive users, we provide an option to aggressively test each implementation and bypass the prediction, thus saving time and effort of manual implementation of each algorithm.

6   Conclusions

SpTRSV is an important and often most time consuming computational kernel with no single SpTRSV implementation shown to give the best performance for all matrices. In this work, we propose a machine learning-based framework for predicting the fastest implementation for SpTRSV for a given input matrix on heterogeneous systems. We train the prediction model with 30 features for each of the 998 square, real matrices selected from SuitSparse collection, and six SpTRSV algorithms. The experimental results, on an Intel Gold CPU with NVIDIA V100 GPU, show our framework achieving an average prediction accuracy of 87% and an average speedup (harmonic mean) in the range 1.4–2.7× over the *lazy* programmer scenario whereby the programmer always chooses the same alogrithm. The framework is extensible with new algorithms as they become available.

Acknowledgements and Data Availability Statement. Authors would like to thank Aramco Overseas Company and SaudiAramco for funding this research.

The datasets and code generated during and/or analysed during the current study are available in the Figshare repository: https://doi.org/10.6084/m9.figshare. 12622523 [1].

References

1. Ahmad, N., Yilmaz, B., Unat, D.: Prediction Framework for Fast Sparse Triangular Solves (2020). https://doi.org/10.6084/m9.figshare.12622523, https://springernature.figshare.com/articles/software/Prediction_Framework_for_Fast_Sparse_Triangular_Solves/12622523/0
2. Alvarado, F.L., Schreiber, R.: Optimal parallel solution of sparse triangular systems. SIAM J. Sci. Comput. **14**(2), 446–460 (1993). https://doi.org/10.1137/0914027
3. Anderson, E., Saad, Y.: Solving sparse triangular linear systems on parallel computers. Int. J. High Speed Comput. **1**(01), 73–95 (1989). https://doi.org/10.1142/S0129053389000056
4. Ansel, J., et al.: Petabricks: a language and compiler for algorithmic choice. SIGPLAN Not. **44**(6), 38–49 (2009). https://doi.org/10.1145/1543135.1542481
5. Anzt, H., Chow, E., Dongarra, J.: Iterative sparse triangular solves for preconditioning. In: Träff, J.L., Hunold, S., Versaci, F. (eds.) Euro-Par 2015. LNCS, vol. 9233, pp. 650–661. Springer, Heidelberg (2015). https://doi.org/10.1007/978-3-662-48096-0_50
6. Balay, S., et al.: PETSc users manual. Technical report ANL-95/11 - Revision 3.11, Argonne National Laboratory (2019). https://www.mcs.anl.gov/petsc
7. Bell, N., Hoberock, J.: Thrust: a productivity-oriented library for CUDA. In: GPU Computing Gems Jade Edition, pp. 359–371. Morgan Kaufmann, Boston (2012). https://doi.org/10.1016/B978-0-12-385963-1.00026-5
8. N Coporation: Cusparse library, user's guide, November 2019
9. Cormen, T., Leiserson, C., Rivest, R.L., Stein, C.: Introduction To Algorithms. MIT Press, Cambridge (2001)
10. Davis, T.A., Hu, Y.: The university of Florida sparse matrix collection. ACM Trans. Math. Softw. **38**(1), 1:1–1:25 (2011). https://doi.org/10.1145/2049662.2049663
11. Dufrechou, E., Ezzatti, P.: Solving sparse triangular linear systems in modern GPUs: a synchronization-free algorithm. In: 2018 26th Euromicro International Conference on Parallel, Distributed and Network-based Processing (PDP), pp. 196–203 (2018). https://doi.org/10.1109/PDP2018.2018.00034
12. Dufrechou, E., Ezzatti, P., Quintana-Orti, E.S.: Automatic selection of sparse triangular linear system solvers on GPUs through machine learning techniques. In: 2019 31st International Symposium on Computer Architecture and High Performance Computing (SBAC-PAD), pp. 41–47 (2019). https://doi.org/10.1109/SBAC-PAD.2019.00020
13. Fatahalian, K., et al.: Sequoia: programming the memory hierarchy. In: Proceedings of the 2006 ACM/IEEE Conference on Supercomputing, p. 4, November 2006. https://doi.org/10.1109/SC.2006.55
14. Guo, H.: A Bayesian approach for automatic algorithm selection. In: Proceedings of the International Conference on Artificial Intelligence, Mexico, pp. 1–5 (2003)
15. Heath, M., Romine, C.: Parallel solution of triangular systems on distributed-memory multiprocessors. SIAM J. Sci. Stat. Comput. **9**(3), 558–588 (1988). https://doi.org/10.1137/0909037
16. Intel Incorporated: Intel MKL—Intel Software (2019). https://software.intel.com/en-us/mkl/documentation/view-all
17. Klie, H., et al.: Exploiting capabilities of many core platforms in reservoir simulation. In: SPE Reservoir Simulation Symposium 2011, pp. 264–275 (6 2011). https://doi.org/10.2118/141265-MS

18. Köhler, M.: libUFget - the UF sparse collection C interface, September 2017. https://doi.org/10.5281/zenodo.897632
19. Li, G., Coleman, T.F.: A parallel triangular solver for a distributed-memory multiprocessor. SIAM J. Sci. Stat. Comput. **9**(3), 485–502 (1988). https://doi.org/10.1137/0909032
20. Li, R.: On parallel solution of sparse triangular linear systems in CUDA. ArXiv abs/1710.04985 (2017)
21. Li, R., Saad, Y.: GPU-accelerated preconditioned iterative linear solvers. J. Supercomput. **63**(2), 443–466 (2013). https://doi.org/10.1007/s11227-012-0825-3
22. Li, R., Zhang, C.: Efficient parallel implementations of sparse triangular solves for GPU architectures. In: Proceedings of the 2020 SIAM Conference on Parallel Processing for Scientific Computing, pp. 106–117 (2020). https://doi.org/10.1137/1.9781611976137.10
23. Liu, W., Li, A., Hogg, J., Duff, I.S., Vinter, B.: A synchronization-free algorithm for parallel sparse triangular solves. In: Dutot, P.-F., Trystram, D. (eds.) Euro-Par 2016. LNCS, vol. 9833, pp. 617–630. Springer, Cham (2016). https://doi.org/10.1007/978-3-319-43659-3_45
24. Liu, W., et al.: Benchmark SpTRSM using CSC, September 2017. https://github.com/bhSPARSE/Benchmark_SpTRSM_using_CSC
25. Liu, W., et al.: Fast synchronization-free algorithms for parallel sparse triangular solves with multiple right-hand sides. Concurr. Comput.: Pract. Exp. **29**(21) (2017). https://doi.org/10.1002/cpe.4244
26. Motter, P.: Hardware awareness for the selection of optimal iterative linear solvers. Ph.D. thesis, University of Colorado at Boulder (2017)
27. Motter, P., Sood, K., Jessup, E., Boyana, N.: Lighthouse: an automated solver selection tool. In: Proceedings of the 3rd International Workshop on Software Engineering for High Performance Computing in Computational Science and Engineering, pp. 16–24 (2015). https://doi.org/10.1145/2830168.2830169
28. Muralidharan, S., Shantharam, M., Hall, M., Garland, M., Catanzaro, B.: Nitro: a framework for adaptive code variant tuning. In: IEEE 28th IPDPS 2014, pp. 501–512. IEEE (2014). https://doi.org/10.1109/IPDPS.2014.59
29. Naumov, M.: Parallel solution of sparse triangular linear systems in the preconditioned iterative methods on the GPU. NVIDIA Technical report NVR-2011-001 (2011)
30. Naumov, M., Castonguay, P., Cohen, J.: Parallel graph coloring with applications to the incomplete-LU factorization on the GPU. NVIDIA Technical report NVR-2015-001 (2015)
31. Park, J., Smelyanskiy, M., Sundaram, N., Dubey, P.: Sparsifying synchronization for high-performance shared-memory sparse triangular solver. In: Kunkel, J.M., Ludwig, T., Meuer, H.W. (eds.) ISC 2014. LNCS, vol. 8488, pp. 124–140. Springer, Cham (2014). https://doi.org/10.1007/978-3-319-07518-1_8
32. Pedregosa, F., et al.: Scikit-learn: machine learning in Python. J. Mach. Learn. Res. **12**, 2825–2830 (2011)
33. Rice, J.R.: The algorithm selection problem. In: Advance in Computer, vol. 15, pp. 65–118. Elsevier (1976). https://doi.org/10.1016/S0065-2458(08)60520-3
34. Saad, Y.: Iterative Methods for Sparse Linear Systems, 2nd edn. Society for Industrial and Applied Mathematics, Philadelphia (2003). https://doi.org/10.1137/1.9780898718003
35. Saad, Y., Schultz, M.H.: GMRES: a generalized minimal residual algorithm for solving nonsymmetric linear systems. SIAM J. Sci. Stat. Comput. **7**(3), 856–869 (1986). https://doi.org/10.1137/0907058

36. Vuduc, R., Demmel, J.W., Bilmes, J.A.: Statistical models for empirical search-based performance tuning. Int. J. High Perform. Comput. Appl. **18**(1), 65–94 (2004). https://doi.org/10.1177/1094342004041293
37. Vuduc, R., Demmel, J.W., Yelick, K.A.: OSKI: a library of automatically tuned sparse matrix kernels. J. Phys: Conf. Ser. **16**, 521–530 (2005). https://doi.org/10.1088/1742-6596/16/1/071
38. Vuduc, R.W.: Automatic performance tuning of sparse matrix kernels. Ph.D. thesis, University of California, Berkeley (2003)
39. Whaley, R.C., Dongarra, J.J.: Automatically tuned linear algebra software. In: Proceedings of the IEEE Conference on Supercomputing. SC 1998, pp. 1–27 (1998). https://doi.org/10.1109/SC.1998.10004

Multiprecision Block-Jacobi for Iterative Triangular Solves

Fritz Goebel[1]($^{(\boxtimes)}$), Hartwig Anzt[1,2], Terry Cojean[1], Goran Flegar[3], and Enrique S. Quintana-Ortí[4]

[1] Steinbuch Centre for Computing, Karlsruhe Institute
of Technology, Karlsruhe, Germany
fritz.goebel@kit.edu
[2] Innovative Computing Lab (ICL),
University of Tennessee, Knoxville, USA
[3] Dept. de Ingeniería y Ciencia de Computadores,
Universidad Jaume I, Castellón, Spain
[4] Dept. de Informática de Sistemas y Computadores,
Universitat Politècnica de València, Valencia, Spain

Abstract. Recent research efforts have shown that Jacobi and block-Jacobi relaxation methods can be used as an effective and highly parallel approach for the solution of sparse triangular linear systems arising in the application of ILU-type preconditioners. Simultaneously, a few independent works have focused on designing efficient high performance adaptive-precision block-Jacobi preconditioning (block-diagonal scaling), in the context of the iterative solution of sparse linear systems, on many-core architectures. In this paper, we bridge the gap between relaxation methods based on regular splittings and preconditioners by demonstrating that iterative refinement can be leveraged to construct a relaxation method from the preconditioner. In addition, we exploit this insight to construct a highly-efficient sparse triangular system solver for graphics processors that combines iterative refinement with the block-Jacobi preconditioner available in the Ginkgo library.

Keywords: Sparse linear algebra · Incomplete factorization preconditioning · Graphics processing units (GPUs) · Multiprecision · Block-Jacobi

1 Introduction

A significant number of today's leader high performance computing systems integrate hardware accelerators, such as graphics processing units (GPUs), with hundreds to thousands of arithmetic units. In consequence, there is a strong urge to extract as much parallelism as possible from this type of platforms when implementing numerical algorithms to satisfy the ever-increasing computational demands of complex simulations. Furthermore, as memory traffic is much more

© Springer Nature Switzerland AG 2020
M. Malawski and K. Rzadca (Eds.): Euro-Par 2020, LNCS 12247, pp. 546–560, 2020.
https://doi.org/10.1007/978-3-030-57675-2_34

expensive than computation in current systems, minimizing the overhead due to memory accesses is crucial in order to implement well performing algorithms.

Keeping these aspects in mind, in this paper we aim to combine efforts in both directions –exploit hardware parallelism efficiently while tackling the memory bandwidth bottleneck– to construct highly efficient iterative solvers for sparse triangular (linear) systems.

Previous research has shown that block-Jacobi relaxation provides a favourable means to exploit parallelism for the solution of sparse triangular systems arising in incomplete factorization preconditioning [4] when approximate solutions are acceptable. Independently, it has also been found that, for certain type of problems, using adaptive-precision in block-Jacobi preconditioning [3] can drastically reduce memory traffic and, therefore, runtime.

In this paper, we make the following contributions by combining the insights gained from in [4] and [3]:

- We propose an alternative approach to derive relaxation methods based on regular matrix splittings. This enables us to establish an explicit relation between iterative refinement, preconditioners, and relaxation methods (Sect. 2).
- Furthermore, we exploit this link in practice, by leveraging the highly optimized adaptive-precision block-Jacobi preconditioner and the iterative refinement components from the Ginkgo[1] open source library in order to assemble an adaptive-precision block-Jacobi relaxation method (Sect. 3).
- In addition, we employ this relaxation method as triangular solver for the Incomplete Cholesky (IC) preconditioner in a Conjugate Gradient (ICCG, Sect. 3).
- Finally, we evaluate the efficiency and effectiveness of the presented methods by testing them on a selection of matrices from the SuiteSparse Matrix Collection [1] (Sect. 4). Concretely, we compare the performance of our adaptive-precision block-Jacobi implementation against a fixed precision block-Jacobi relaxation method as well as Ginkgo's direct triangular solvers.

The main goal of this paper is to demonstrate the benefits of our adaptive-precision block-Jacobi approach versus a fixed-precision block-Jacobi relaxation. For this reason, we choose test problems for which an iterative solver is a valid choice for the triangular solves appearing in incomplete factorization preconditioning. We recognize that the applicability of our approach remains problem dependent [4], and there are cases where it will not provide an efficient alternative, particularly because the iterative triangular system solvers do not converge quickly.

2 Background

Consider the linear system $Ax = b$, where A is an $n \times n$ input matrix, b is the input right-hand side vector, comprising n components, and x is the sought-after

---

[1] https://ginkgo-project.github.io.

solution, also with n components. The iterative refinement method (IR) for this linear system is then defined as the recurrence [7]:

$$r_k := b - Ax_k, \tag{1}$$

$$q_k := \text{Solve}(A, r_k), \tag{2}$$

$$x_{k+1} := x_k + q_k, \tag{3}$$

where x_k is the current approximation to the solution x; r_k is the current residual; $\text{Solve}(A, b)$ denotes a "coarse" solver that provides an approximated solution to $Ax = b$; and q_k corresponds to the approximation of the error $x - x_k$ obtained using the coarse solver. This method can be also expressed as a single equation:

$$x_{k+1} := x_k + \text{Solve}(A, b - Ax_k), \tag{4}$$

which is the formulation that will be used in the remainder of this work.

Preconditioning refers to replacing the system $Ax = b$ with an equivalent counterpart $M^{-1}Ax = M^{-1}b$ (a variant known as left preconditioning) in the hope of improving the numerical properties of the transformed system matrix $(M^{-1}A)$, which in turn accelerates the convergence of the iterative method used to tackle the transformed system. Applying preconditioning to IR, by replacing every occurrence of A with $M^{-1}A$ and those of b with $M^{-1}b$, yields the preconditioned iterative refinement method (PIR):

$$x_{k+1} := x_k + \text{Solve}(M^{-1}A, M^{-1}b - M^{-1}Ax_k) \tag{5}$$

$$= x_k + \text{Solve}(M^{-1}A, M^{-1}(b - Ax_k)). \tag{6}$$

Equation (6) can be viewed as a variant of IR where the coarse method Solve is replaced with its preconditioned variant Solve_M, which tackles the system $Ax = b$ by applying Solve to the transformed (preconditioned) system $M^{-1}Ax = M^{-1}b$:

$$x_{k+1} := x_k + \text{Solve}_M(A, b - Ax_k). \tag{7}$$

The convergence rate of IR (or PIR) is directly tied to the accuracy of Solve (or Solve_M). In particular, if the relative accuracy of Solve is given by a parameter δ, (i.e., $\|\hat{q}_k - q_k\| \leq \delta\|\hat{q}_k\|$, where $\hat{q}_k$ denotes the true solution of the system $A\hat{q}_k = r_k$,) then the errors of two consecutive approximations to the solution x satisfy:

$$\|x - x_{k+1}\| \leq \delta\|x - x_k\|. \tag{8}$$

This is a direct consequence of the following two equalities:

$$\hat{q}_k = A^{-1}(b - Ax_k) = x - x_k; \text{ and} \tag{9}$$

$$\hat{q}_k - q_k = x - x_k - q_k = x - x_{k+1}. \tag{10}$$

A simple method to approximate the solution of the system consists in using $\text{Solve}(A, b) := b$; that is, the solution is approximated by the right-hand side vector of the system b. The preconditioned version of this method is therefore obtained by applying the same reasoning to the system $M^{-1}Ax = M^{-1}b$, which results in $\text{Solve}_M(A,b) := M^{-1}b$. That is, the solution is obtained from the preconditioner application to the right-hand side vector. Since the preconditioner application is one of the most crucial kernels involving preconditioners, an added bonus for this approach is that sparse linear algebra libraries usually include highly optimized kernels for its computation.

Using the definition of $\text{Solve}_M(A,b) := M^{-1}b$ in PIR from Eq. (7) results in the method:

$$
\begin{aligned}
x_{k+1} &:= x_k + \text{Solve}_M(A, b - Ax_k) \\
&= x_k + M^{-1}(b - Ax_k) \\
&= M^{-1}Mx_k + M^{-1}b - M^{-1}Ax_k \\
&= M^{-1}(M - A)x_k + M^{-1}b \\
&= M^{-1}Nx_k + M^{-1}b,
\end{aligned}
\tag{11}
$$

where the matrix $N := M - A$ satisfies that $A = M - N$.

A number of relevant observations follow from the previous elaboration:

- Eq. (11) is exactly the definition of a relaxation method induced by the regular splitting $A = M - N$ [9]. Thus, every such method can be expressed as an IR whose inner solver is $\text{Solve}(A,b) := b$ preconditioned with the matrix M from the regular splitting.
- Additionally, a PIR method preconditioned with $M = A - R$, where R is the preconditioner's residual matrix, induces a relaxation method $x_{k+1} := M^{-1}Rx_k + M^{-1}b$.
- Finally, Eq. (8) demonstrates that the convergence rate of such methods is given by the parameter δ of the preconditioner M:

$$
\delta := \max_{y \in \mathbb{R}^n} \frac{\|M^{-1}y - A^{-1}y\|}{\|A^{-1}y\|}, \quad y \neq 0.
\tag{12}
$$

3   Assemblinag the Algorithm with Ginkgo's Components

The open-source Ginkgo linear algebra library provides high-performance implementations of popular Krylov methods and preconditioners. Ginkgo also includes efficient realizations of IR, particularly for manycore accelerators such as GPUs. While there is (yet) no direct support for the block-Jacobi relaxation method in Ginkgo, the library is equipped with a highly optimized implementation of the block-Jacobi preconditioner. This implementation also integrates an adaptive-precision storage scheme [5], which reduces the total volume of data fetched from memory at each iteration, while preserving the quality of the preconditioner measured by δ.

The previous section showed that a relaxation method can be easily constructed by combining IR with a preconditioner. Concretely, the adaptive-precision block-Jacobi preconditioner from Ginkgo yields an adaptive-precision version of the block-Jacobi relaxation method. While the full-precision block-Jacobi relaxation method proved effectiveness in providing an approximate solution for sparse triangular systems arising from incomplete LU (ILU)-type preconditioners [4], in this work we focus on the method automatically constructed from the preconditioner in Ginkgo, which allows seamless enhancements via the adaptive-precision storage scheme. The code used to construct this method is illustrated in Listing 1.1.

Listing 1.1. Realization of the adaptive block-Jacobi relaxation method using the open-source Ginkgo linear algebra library.

```
1   #include <ginkgo/ginkgo.hpp>
2   #include <iostream>
3
4   int main() {
5     auto gpu = gko::CudaExecutor::create(0,
          gko::OmpExecutor::create());
6     auto A = gko::read<gko::matrix::Csr<>>(std::cin,
          gpu);
7     auto b = gko::read<gko::matrix::Dense<>>(std::cin,
          gpu);
8     auto x = gko::read<gko::matrix::Dense<>>(std::cin,
          gpu);
9     auto solver =
10      gko::solver::Ir<>::build()
11        .with_solver(
12          gko::preconditioner::Jacobi<>::build()
13            .with_storage_optimization(
14              gko::precision_reduction::autodetect())
15            .on(gpu))
16        .with_criteria(
17          gko::stop::Iteration::build()
18            .with_max_iters(1000u).on(gpu),
19          gko::stop::ResidualNormReduction<>::build()
20            .with_reduction_factor(1e-15)
21            .on(gpu))
22        .on(gpu);
23    solver->generate(give(A))->apply(lend(b), lend(x));
24    write(std::cout, lend(x));
25  }
```

Note that, with the new approach, we have to perform a matrix-vector multiplication with M^{-1} and a second matrix-vector product with A (per iteration), whereas the classical block-Jacobi method involves one matrix-vector multiplication with N and second with M^{-1} (per iteration). Since in the block-Jacobi method M is a block-diagonal submatrix of A, $N = M - A$ will generally have less nonzero elements than A. This means that the IR-induced formulation can be expected to perform more floating-point operations per iteration than the classical block-Jacobi method. However, the IR approach can leverage Ginkgo's highly optimized block-Jacobi kernels, including their adaptive-precision storage realization. Furthermore, as presented in Listing 1.1, the development effort is minimal.

Ginkgo also offers a direct means to generate an ILU-type preconditioner, with IR as inner solver, and integrate the generated preconditioner into a Krylov solver in order to obtain a general sparse linear system solver. Listing 1.2 shows the complete code needed to tackle a sparse symmetric positive definite (s.p.d.) system with a CG solver preconditioned with an ILU/incomplete Cholesky (IC) decomposition using the presented adaptive-precision IR approach for solving the triangular systems occurring at each iteration when applying the preconditioner.

In the next section, we compare the efficiency of the new IR-induced adaptive-precision block-Jacobi solver for solving triangular systems against using direct triangular solves as well as the IR-induced block-Jacobi method operating in fixed (double) precision.

Listing 1.2. Realization of the adaptive block-Jacobi relaxation method using the open-source Ginkgo linear algebra library.

```
1   #include <ginkgo/ginkgo.hpp>
2   #include <iostream>
3
4   int main() {
5     auto gpu = gko::CudaExecutor::create(0,
          gko::OmpExecutor::create());
6     auto A = gko::read<gko::matrix::Csr<>>(std::cin,
          gpu);
7     auto b = gko::read<gko::matrix::Dense<>>(std::cin,
          gpu);
8     auto x = gko::read<gko::matrix::Dense<>>(std::cin,
          gpu);
9
10    unsigned int block_size = 16u;
11
12    auto ilu_factory =
13      gko::factorization::ParIlu<>::build()
14        .with_skip_sorting(false).on(gpu);
15    auto ilu_decomposition =
        ilu_factory->generate(gko::share(A));
16
17    auto triangular_solver_factory =
18      gko::solver::Ir<>::build()
19        .with_solver(
20          gko::preconditioner::Jacobi<>::build()
21            .with_max_block_size(block_size)
22            .with_storage_optimization(
23              gko::precision_reduction::autodetect())
24            .on(gpu))
25        .with_criteria(
26          gko::stop::Iteration::build()
27            .with_max_iters(5u).on(gpu))
```

```
28              .on(gpu);
29
30     auto ilu_preconditioner_factory =
31        gko::preconditioner::Ilu<gko::solver::Ir<>,
32                gko::solver::Ir<>>::build()
33           .with_l_solver_factory(
34              gko::clone(triangular_solver_factory))
35           .with_u_solver_factory(
36              gko::clone(triangular_solver_factory))
37           .on(gpu);
38
39     auto ilu_preconditioner =
40        ilu_preconditioner_factory->generate(
41           gko::share(ilu_decomposition));
42
43     auto solver =
44        gko::solver::Cg<>::build()
45           .with_criteria(
46              gko::stop::Iteration::build()
47                 .with_max_iters(1500u).on(gpu),
48              gko::stop::ResidualNormReduction<>::build()
49                 .with_reduction_factor(1e-15).on(gpu))
50           .with_generated_preconditioner(
51              gko::share(ilu_preconditioner))
52           .on(gpu);
53
54     solver->generate(give(A))->apply(
55        gko::lend(b), gko::lend(x));
56     write(std::cout, gko::lend(x));
57  }
```

4 Experimental Evaluation

4.1 Test Problems

This section collects results for 24 s.p.d. matrices from the SuiteSparse Matrix Collection [1] arising in real applications or artificial academic problems. The test matrices are listed in Table 1. For the block-Jacobi preconditioner, we use supervariable amalgamation [4] for identifying strongly connected components with a maximum block size of 16.

4.2 Hardware Setup

All results were collected on an NVIDIA Volta V100 GPU placed in the Summit supercomputer. This GPU contains 16 GB of DDR4 memory and 80 streaming multiprocessors with 32 double precision units each. The hardware specifications show that peak performance for double precision operations is 7.8 TFLOP/s (i.e.,

$7.8 \cdot 10^{12}$ floating-point operations per second) and the bandwidth to access the main memory is 900 GB/s [8].
All results were gathered using the CUDA Toolkit 10.1.243 and Ginkgo 1.1.1. In particular, when we compare against exact triangular solves, Ginkgo interfaces to the cuBLAS routine `csrsm2`.
As our complete codes run on the GPU, the features of the platform (CPU, main memory, PCI bus bandwidth, etc.) where the GPU resides are not relevant for the following analysis.

Table 1. Test matrices along with key characteristics. The stated condition number are an estimate to the 1-norm condition number obtained with Matlab's condest function.

Name	Problem kind	#rows	#nonzeros	Cond. number
apache1	Structural problem	80,800	542,184	3.99e+06
bodyy4	Structural	17,546	121,550	1.02e+03
bundle1	Computer graphics	10,581	770,811	1.33e+04
crystm01	Materials	4,875	105,339	421.17
crystm02	Materials	13,965	322,905	448.91
crystm03	Materials	24,696	583,770	467.76
Dubcova1	2D/3D	16,129	253,009	2.62e+03
Dubcova3	2D/3D	146,689	3,636,643	1.15e+04
finan512	Economic	74,752	596,992	98.39
jnlbrng1	Optimization	40,000	199,200	187.16
Muu	Structural	7,102	170,134	155.06
qa8fm	Acoustics	66,127	1,660,579	109.6
t2dah_e	Model reduction	11,445	176,117	1.37e+09
s1rmt3m1	Structural	5,489	217,651	5.35e+06
s2rmt3m1	Structural	5,489	217,681	4.84e+08
shallow_water1	Comp. fluid dynamics	81,920	327,680	3.63
shallow_water2	Comp. fluid dynamics	81,920	327,680	11.28
ted_B	Thermal	10,605	144,579	3.02e+07
ted_B_unscaled	Thermal	10,605	144,579	2.04e+11
thermal1	Thermal	82,654	574,458	4.96e+05
thermomech_dM	Thermal	204,316	1,423,116	120.74
thermomech_TC	Thermal	102,158	711,558	119.82
torsion1	Duplicate optimization	40,000	197,608	41.00
Trefethen_20000	Combinatorial	20,000	554,466	2.01e+05

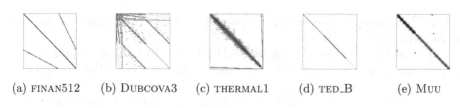

(a) FINAN512   (b) DUBCOVA3   (c) THERMAL1   (d) TED_B   (e) MUU

Fig. 1. Sparsity patterns of selected test matrices.

4.3 Numerical Experiments on HPC GPU

Initially, we want to investigate whether an iterative triangular solver based on block-Jacobi can be faster than a conventional direct triangular solver. For that purpose, we consider five sparse problems, FINAN512, DUBCOVA3, THERMAL1, TED_B and MUU, coming from different application scenarios; see Table 1 for the matrix characteristics and Fig. 1 for the sparsity patterns.

The results for this first experiment are shown in in Fig. 2. The left-hand side column of plots in that figure displays the number of iterations a Conjugate Gradient method preconditioned with Incomplete Cholesky (ICCG) needs to converge depending on how the triangular systems are solved: either using exact triangular solves or, alternatively, block-Jacobi inside an IR method. Here, the ICCG method is considered to have converged when the norm of the relative residual

$$r_{\text{rel}} = \frac{b - Ax}{\|b - Ax_0\|}$$

is less than $1e - 16 \cdot$ cond, where cond is the estimated condition number of A found in Table 1. As we can observe, when the number of sweeps of block-Jacobi IR per triangular solve is low, there is a significant increase in terms of ICCG iterations. When using more than 5 block-Jacobi IR sweeps though, the increase of ICCG iterations shrinks to a moderate level. A large number of block-Jacobi sweeps fully compensates the approximate characteristics, and retains the ICCG iteration count observed for the variant using exact triangular solves. We note that, in terms of convergence of the ICCG solver, there is no relevant difference between the realizations that integrate the adaptive-precision block-Jacobi and the fixed-precision block-Jacobi.

The center column of plots in Fig. 2 displays the number of block-Jacobi sweeps to the ICCG runtime. Here, the performance advantage of a block-Jacobi IR iteration over an exact triangular solver becomes visible: Although the number of ICCG iterations is much higher when using only a few IR iterations, the total runtime can be much shorter than leveraging a direct triangular solve. For the FINAN512, THERMAL1 and DUBCOVA3 problems, the ICCG using block-Jacobi IR is faster than ICCG using exact triangular solves. For the large problems FINAN512, THERMAL1 and DUBCOVA3, we can appreciate significant runtime benefits when using the adaptive-precision block-Jacobi. For the much smaller TED_B problem, the block-Jacobi IR is faster if we perform more than 2 IR sweeps. Only for MUU, which is both small and well conditioned, the approach

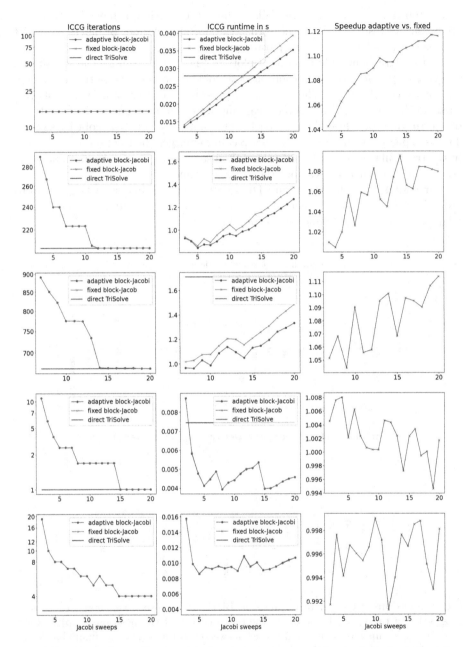

Fig. 2. Relating the effect of the block-Jacobi sweep count in the iterative triangular solution in incomplete factorization preconditioning for the matrix problems FINAN512, DUBCOVA3, THERMAL1, TED_B and MUU (from top to bottom): PCG iteration count (left), time-to-solution, and speedup of using adaptive-precision block-Jacobi over fixed-precision block-Jacobi (right).

using iterative triangular solves fails to beat the runtime achieved with direct triangular solves. Overall, we note that the optimal number of block-Jacobi IR sweeps is a problem-dependent parameter.

In the right-hand side column of plots in Fig. 2, we visualize the speedup of ICCG with the adaptive-precision block-Jacobi IR over its fixed-precision block-Jacobi IR counterpart. Where the adaptive-precision technique yields shorter runtime than the fixed-precision technique we observe a general positive trend of the runtime benefits when increasing the number of block-Jacobi IR sweeps. This is expected as increasing the sweep count enlarges the fraction of time spent in the triangular solves, which is where the use of adaptive precision reduces the volume of memory accesses and, therefore, runtime.

For FINAN512, THERMAL1 and DUBCOVA3, the runtime savings grow up to around 10%. This is in accordance with a previous experimental analysis of adaptive-precision block-Jacobi preconditioning [3].

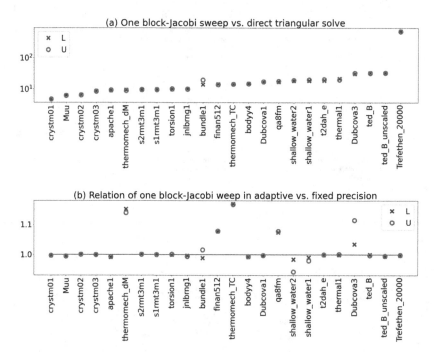

Fig. 3. Speed-up of one adaptive-precision Block-Jacobi sweep versus a direct triangular solve of the L and U factors of the regarded ILU decompositions (top) and the according speedup versus one fixed-precision sweep (bottom). The maximum block size is 16. The time of one iteration is taken as the average over the first 100 iterations.

For the following experiment, we select a set of 24 test matrices where block-Jacobi IR is a viable option for the triangular solver. This selection recognizes that iterative triangular solves can fail to propagate the accuracy needed by

ICCG to solve the problem. Furthermore, it also acknowledges that, depending on the matrix sparsity structure and the implied dependency tree, iterative triangular solves are not necessarily always faster than exact triangular solves [2]. For these problems (all those listed in Table 1), on the left-hand side plot in Fig. 3 we visualize the speedup of one adaptive-precision block-Jacobi sweep over the level-based direct triangular solve. In the right-hand side plot of the same figure, we display the speedup of the adaptive-precision over the fixed-precision block-Jacobi sweeps. While there are three problems where we suffer small slowdowns, for most of the selected matrices we obtain a speedup, and for some problems we save around 20% computing time.

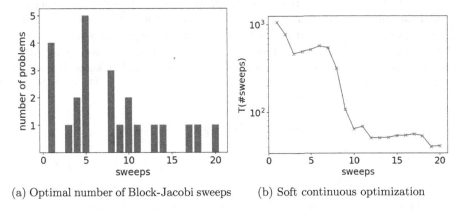

(a) Optimal number of Block-Jacobi sweeps   (b) Soft continuous optimization

Fig. 4. Optimal number of adaptive-precision Block-Jacobi sweeps to minimize PCG runtime (left) and soft continuous optimization (right).

Next, in Fig. 4 we use the test set of 24 matrices to identify the optimal number of sweeps. Looking at the results in the left-hand side in Fig. 4, we observe that there is no overall optimal sweep count. In order to choose a reasonable number of sweeps count, we give each of our test matrices an index i and define $\mathrm{ICCG}(n_{\mathrm{sweeps}}, i)$ as the ICCG runtime for matrix i using n_{sweeps} block-Jacobi sweeps in the triangular solves. With this, we define the normalized ICCG runtime for matrix i with n_{sweeps} block-Jacobi sweeps in the triangular solves,

$$t_i(n_{\mathrm{sweeps}}) = \frac{\mathrm{ICCG}(n_{\mathrm{sweeps}}, i)}{min_{j=1}^{20}\mathrm{ICCG}(j, i)},$$

as the relation between the actual and minimal ICCG runtime. We then look at the soft optimization function

$$T(n_{\mathrm{sweeps}}) = \sum_{i=1}^{24} t_i(n_{\mathrm{sweeps}}).$$

The right-hand side of Fig. 4 shows that for this problem test suite, T is small for about 19 block-Jacobi sweeps per ICCG iteration.

Finally, we compare the optimal number of block-Jacobi IR sweeps for each matrix and the default setting of 19 sweeps to quantify the benefits of using adaptive-precision in the block-Jacobi IR over using fixed-precision block-Jacobi IR. In Fig. 5, we report the speedup of ICCG equipped with adaptive-precision block-Jacobi IR for the triangular solves over ICCG using fixed-precision block-Jacobi IR for the triangular solves. We first focus on the problem-specific optimization of the block-Jacobi IR sweep count. For this setting (minimizing the ICCG overall runtime), we observe that, for about two thirds of the problems, the use of adaptive precision has only a negligible impact or none at all. For roughly one third of the problems, we have single-digit speedups over the fixed-precision usage.

If we fix the number of block-Jacobi IR sweeps to 19 (not considering the problem-specific optimization reducing the ICCG runtime), the benefits of using adaptive-precision over fixed-precision are generally larger. This implies that, when using a default setting – which is realistic for practical use– adopting a adaptive-precision block-Jacobi instead of a fixed-precision block-Jacobi renders significant benefits.

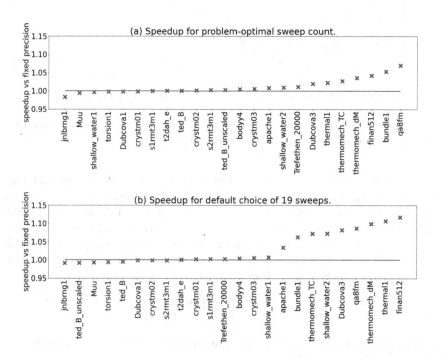

Fig. 5. Speedup of ICCG with adaptive-precision block-Jacobi vs. fixed-precision block-Jacobi for the optimal number of sweeps for each matrix (top) and 19 sweeps per iteration as resulting from evaluating the soft continuous optimization function T (bottom).

5 Summary

In this work, we have investigated the benefits of using adaptive precision block-Jacobi for iteratively solving the triangular systems arising in incomplete factorization preconditioning. This was accomplished by linking relaxation methods to iterative refinement and preconditioners. Using the Ginkgo open source library for numerical linear algebra, we set up a Conjugate Gradient (CG) solver using an incomplete Cholesky decomposition preconditioner which replaces exact triangular solves with iterative triangular solves based on block-Jacobi iterative refinement.

Comparing the performance on high-end GPUs, we revealed that using adaptive precision block-Jacobi iterations is generally faster than using fixed precision block-Jacobi iterations.

In accordance with [4], we emphasize that using iterative triangular solves based on (adaptive) precision block-Jacobi is not always the fastest option. But we emphasize that if using block-Jacobi iterations for solving triangular systems in incomplete factorization preconditioning is a valid option, it is likely that the performance can be improved by replacing fixed precision block-Jacobi with our adaptive precision block-Jacobi method.

Acknowledgments and Data Availability Statement. Hartwig Anzt, Fritz Göbel, and Terry Cojean were supported by the "Impuls und Vernetzungsfond" of the Helmholtz Association under grant VH-NG-1241. G. Flegar and E. S. Quintana-Ortí were supported by project TIN2017-82972-R of the MINECO and FEDER and the H2020 EU FETHPC Project 732631 "OPRECOMP".

The datasets and code generated during and/or analysed during the current study are available in the Figshare repository: https://doi.org/10.6084/m9.figshare.12562154 [6].

References

1. Suitesparse Matrix Collection. https://sparse.tamu.edu (2020). Accessed Jan 2020
2. Anzt, H., Chow, E., Dongarra, J.: Iterative sparse triangular solves for preconditioning. In: Träff, J.L., Hunold, S., Versaci, F. (eds.) Euro-Par 2015. LNCS, vol. 9233, pp. 650–661. Springer, Heidelberg (2015). https://doi.org/10.1007/978-3-662-48096-0_50
3. Anzt, H., Dongarra, J., Flegar, G., Higham, N.J., Quintana-Ortí, E.S.: Adaptive precision in block-Jacobi preconditioning for iterative sparse linear system solvers. Concurrency Comput. Pract. Experience **31**(6), e4460 (2019)
4. Chow, E., Anzt, H., Scott, J., Dongarra, J.: Using Jacobi iterations and blocking for solving sparse triangular systems in incomplete factorization preconditioning. J. Parallel Distrib. Comput. **119**, 219–230 (2018)
5. Flegar, G., Anzt, H., Cojean, T., Quintana-Ortí, E.S.: Customized-precision Block-Jacobi preconditioning for Krylov iterative solvers on data-parallel manycore processors. ACM Trans. Math. Softw. (2020), under review. Available from the authors

6. Goebel, F., Anzt, H., Quintana-Ortí, E.S., Cojean, T., Flegar, G.: Instructions to generate experimental results for conference proceedings 2020 paper: multi-precision block-Jacobi for Iterative Triangular Solves, July 2020. https://doi.org/10.6084/m9.figshare.12562154, https://springernature.figshare.com/articles/data setInstructions_to_generate_experimental_results_for_conference_proceedings_2020_p aper_Multiprecision_block-Jacobi_for_Iterative_Triangular_Solves/12562154/1
7. Higham, N.J.: Accuracy and Stability of Numerical Algorithms, 2nd edn. SIAM, Philadelphia (2002)
8. NVIDIA Corporation: Whitepaper: NVIDIA TESLA V100 GPU ARCHITECTURE (2017)
9. Saad, Y.: Iterative Methods for Sparse Linear Systems, 2nd edn. SIAM, Philadelphia (2003)

Efficient Ephemeris Models for Spacecraft Trajectory Simulations on GPUs

Fabian Schrammel[1,2,3], Florian Renk[2], Arya Mazaheri[1(✉)], and Felix Wolf[1]

[1] Technische Universität Darmstadt, Darmstadt, Germany
fabian.schrammel@gmv.com
[2] European Space Agency (ESA), Darmstadt, Germany
florian.renk@esa.int
[3] GMV Gmbh, Darmstadt, Germany
{mazaheri,wolf}@cs.tu-darmstadt.de

Abstract. When a spacecraft is released into space, its initial condition and future trajectory in terms of position and speed cannot be precisely predicted. To ensure that the object does not violate space debris mitigation or planetary protection standards, such that it causes potential damage or contamination of celestial bodies, spacecraft-mission designers conduct a multitude of simulations to verify the validity of the set of all probable trajectories. Such simulations are usually independent from each other, making them a perfect match for parallelization. The European Space Agency (ESA) developed a GPU-based simulator for this purpose and achieved reasonable speedups in comparison with the established multi-threaded CPU version. However, we noticed that the performance starts to degrade as the spacecraft trajectories diverge in time. Our empirical analysis using GPU profilers showed that the application suffers from poor data locality and high memory traffic. In this paper, we propose an alternative data layout, which increases data locality within thread blocks. Furthermore, we introduce alternative model configurations that lower both algorithmic effort and the number of memory requests without violating accuracy requirements. Our experiments show that our method is able to accelerate the computations up to a factor of 2.6.

Keywords: GPU · Simulation · Profiling · Astrodynamics

1 Introduction

In space mission design astrodynamics simulations are instrumental in determining the probabilities of spacecraft and space debris trajectories. At the point of release or in-orbit failure, the position and speed of the object as well as the properties (e.g. surface reflectivity) are only known to the mission architects only with a certain precision. Hence, Monte-Carlo simulations containing thousands of object samples are conducted in during the mission preparation phase. Based on the results, the team will choose a nominal separation state or trajectory

© Springer Nature Switzerland AG 2020
M. Malawski and K. Rzadca (Eds.): Euro-Par 2020, LNCS 12247, pp. 561–577, 2020.
https://doi.org/10.1007/978-3-030-57675-2_35

that satisfies the rules of the current planetary protection and space-debris mitigation guidelines. For instance, during the *BepiColombo* mission [3], currently being flown to Mercury by the European Space Agency (ESA), the upper stage of the Ariane 5 launcher places the mission spacecraft into the desired transfer orbit before release. After the required passivation of the upper stage to prevent further break-up, this object becomes space debris and it is not allowed to impact e.g. Mars or return to near-earth space by a certain probability.

To verify cases like this, the European Space Agency (ESA) has recently designed a tool called *cudajectory* to run such simulations on CUDA-capable devices and achieved a speedup ranging from 1.9× to 10.5× in comparison with established multi-threaded solutions on CPUs [6]. However, we found out that the GPU implementation can benefit from further improvements.

To accelerate such highly parallelizable simulations, we analyze the state of the art and suggest alternative methods to gain performance without violating accuracy requirements. The simulations are typically performed using numerical integration methods, such as the Runge-Kutta-Fehlberg 78 scheme [4]. The use of variable step integration methods is extremely efficient for spacecraft trajectories, since the step size can vary from days in interplanetary space to only seconds, when the object moves very close to a celestial body. In such numerical integration methods, the equations of motions are implemented, and force or acceleration models are used. One of these models is the ephemeris model, which we will focus on in this paper since its performance is often bound by memory. The ephemeris model provides the position of the celestial bodies at a given epoch/time and allows us to derive the gravity field affecting the spacecraft trajectory. For the trajectory of a single object being calculated, the simulation will sequentially go through the ephemeris calculations as the simulated time progresses. However, when different spacecraft or object samples are simulated in parallel, this is no longer the case. Even if the samples have the same initial time, which is not the case in all problems, the integration steps can have different lengths. Thus, each simulated object requires the positions of the celestial objects at a different epochs. In a different problem to be investigated a spacecraft failure shall be simulated along the nominal flight path and thus already the initial epochs of all samples are different. Such initial difference or divergence during the integration process leads to different sets of data requested by the ephemeris routines, overloading the on-chip memory, which indeed results in register-spilling. Therefore, memory bandwidth becomes a bottleneck and decreases the overall performance tremendously.

In this paper, we propose an alternative data layout for the ephemeris data. This new data layout improves data locality. The ephemeris data is restructured from a memory layout optimized for sequential processing to a layout more suitable for parallel processing. We increase the likelihood that the required ephemeris data is available in the caches for several threads running on the GPU, thus preventing threads from stalling. Additionally, we were able to shrink the ephemeris model while maintaining the required accuracy. First of all, some celestial bodies may exert forces small enough to be disregarded. Then, planetary systems can be handled as a single body adding a small error. Lastly, a different type of function can be used to approximate the movement of these bodies. Originally, Chebyshev polynomials [5,12] with a degree between 6 to 14 were being used in ephemeris models. However, previous experiments [7,15] already demonstrated that cubic splines are more memory efficient and straightforward while providing reasonable accuracy. Such optimizations reduce the algorithmic effort and the number of data requests, thus improving data locality. In essence, this paper makes the following major contributions:

- A novel data-locality aware data structure to hold ephemeris model data
- A method for balancing the trade-off between simulation accuracy and speed

In the remainder of the paper, we first provide background on the spacecraft trajectory simulation using GPUs. Then, in Sect. 3, the effect of alternative model configurations is analyzed to identify further case-dependent optimizations, followed by an evaluation in Sect. 4. A concise review of related work is presented in Sect. 5. Finally, we conclude the paper in Sect. 6.

2 Background on Astrodynamic Simulations

When objects in space are passivated, the point in time, position, and speed are only known with a certain precision. For in-orbit failures, however, the problem is more random as they can occur at any point during the mission. In addition other uncertainties can occur, e.g. the surface reflectivity of an object and thus the solar radiation pressure acting on will depend on the future attitude of the S/C and the properties can also be determined only with a specific accuracy prior to launch. Tiny deviations of the state parameters can lead to a significant difference in the trajectory after years and decades of space travel. Therefore, the Monte-Carlo method [8] is applied beforehand to generate a set of sample states and propagated forward in time to generate their trajectory path. Depending on the case, these samples may be located around an initial guess, as presented in the first picture of Fig. 1, or along a specifically planned and controlled trajectory. Once a sufficient amount of such samples (often up to hundreds of thousands) is simulated for an appropriate period, we can produce a meaningful probabilistic result from the predicted trajectories, such as impact probability to a specific celestial body.

2.1 *cudajectory*: ESA Tool for Trajectory Simulations on GPUs

A spacecraft trajectory can be simulated step by step using numerical integration methods. Within each step, the change in position and velocity of the spacecraft is calculated by applying a physics model. ESA developed an in-house tool called *cudajectory* [6], solely designed to simulate the trajectories of a set of initial spacecraft states, a.k.a samples. The tool parallelizes the trajectory simulations by starting one GPU thread per sample, as described in Fig. 1. They are numerically integrated until every simulation of a sample reaches the end

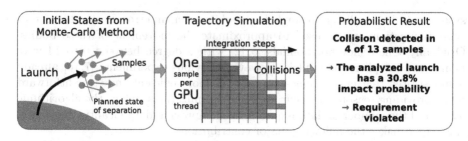

Fig. 1. Example of the main aspects of a collision analysis of space debris after separation. In a first step samples are generated, which need to be propagated in time in a second step and the results need to be analyzed in a third step. The second part of this process is implemented by cudajectory.

of a fixed simulation period or collides with a celestial body. The Runge-Kutta method [9] of seventh order is used for step-wise integration, and the eighth order is added via the Fehlberg method [4] to apply dynamic step-size control. Here, each step contains 13 evaluations of the ordinary differential equation (ODE) on eleven different points in time. Each ODE evaluation applies the physics model, which includes routines to calculate gravitational forces, solar radiation pressure, and collision detection regarding the nearby celestial bodies. All of these calculations require the position of one or more celestial bodies at the current time, retrieved from an ephemeris model.

An ephemeris is a collection of models and values that can describe the position and velocity of astronomical objects over specific periods. Releases from the Jet Propulsion Laboratory (JPL) are known to be the most accurate models nowadays, and the applied data format (*Type 2*) is widely used in the industry [2,11]. These models contain functions of time returning the three-dimensional cartesian position of a body. Chebyshev polynomials are the method of choice for high-precision orbit approximation (See Fig. 5) as they are best suited in terms of accuracy, interpolation error, and applicability [12]. For each body, a series of polynomials of fixed interval length and polynomial degree is provided to approximate its orbit over the simulated period. Only the coefficients of each polynomial will be stored in program memory, which are applied during position calculations.

DE432 is the latest release by JPL [5] and serves as a baseline during our research. It covers eleven major celestial bodies and planetary systems of the solar system, where the center of mass (barycenter) is used to include moons.

2.2   State-of-the-Art Performance

Experiments show that the current implementation of cudajectory can be about 10× faster than established multi-threaded CPU solutions on different types of input samples and physics models. However, we noticed that one major performance bottleneck of cudajectory happens for samples at very different points

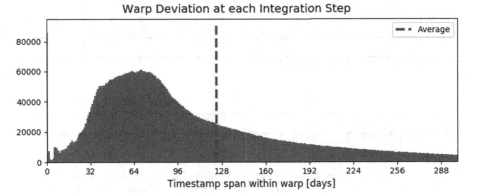

Fig. 2. Distribution of the time difference between the simulation epoch at each integration step within warps of the BepiColombo case example. The maximum range observed difference was 2352 days within a warp. A difference of 0 days indicates that all threads can use the same ephemeris data block.

of simulation time [6]. The step sizes applied during the samples for the Bepi-Colombo case range from several seconds to almost nine days. In the main implementation, GPU threads are divided into fixed groups called warps in CUDA terms, each executing in parallel. When the range of the timestamps within a warp increases due to different start times or dynamic step size control, the threads require different sets of ephemeris polynomials to calculate the position of a specific celestial body. These differences in time can be significant as depicted in Fig. 2. If not all data can be made available the whole warp stalls until all of these polynomials have their coefficients data ready. Therefore, when this situation occurs the memory traffic is immensely increased and leads to significant performance degradation.

3   Efficient Ephemeris Formats and Configurations

We analyze the original record-based ephemeris data format on GPUs and propose an alternative data format to improve performance. This format stores the polynomial data in a different order and offers the opportunity to apply cubic splines instead of the current Chebyshev polynomials. Finally, we present additional ways to reduce algorithmic effort, as well as data requirements.

We profiled the performance of the BepiColombo case, running 420,000 threads packed in 13,125 warps on a Tesla V100 using the Nvidia Visual Profiler [14]. The results showed that 95.7% of the memory traffic is linked to local-memory instructions. This is a strong hint to the existence of excessive register spilling, as this memory space can not be utilized manually. Instead, the program automatically includes such instructions to spill and reload the register data. We also identified a high execution efficiency of over 98%, indicating almost no processor idle time. However, such a large fraction of executed instructions is likely

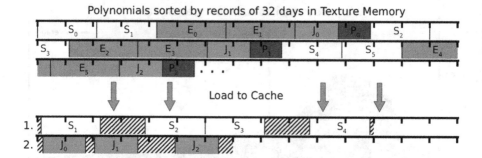

Fig. 3. Two caching examples for DE432 data stored in record-based format, where e.g. the first record spans from S_0 to P_0. We depict data of polynomials for the Sun (S_i), the Earth (E_i), Jupiter (J_i) and Pluto (P_i). Multiple polynomials of the same body are loaded in the cache lines of 128 bytes (between two black ticks) [13]. The loaded but unneeded data in the cache is displayed by diagonal grey stripes.

linked to register spilling, which reduces the overall efficiency. To alleviate the register spilling, the overall memory traffic must be reduced. Therefore, we apply a different data alignment and memory access pattern, which helps us to improve data locality.

The data format of DE432 is designed to improve the data locality of single-thread execution. All data required for the position calculations of a specific point in time is collected in one record, which covers 32 days. This method increases the spatial locality, as some coefficients of the latter bodies in the list are pre-cached by requests to earlier bodies. Since the move to the subsequent point in time rarely exceeds 7.0 days, the ephemeris data valid for the previous timestamp will often be reused, which provides temporal locality. Figure 3 describes DE432 data stored in the GPU texture memory. As the data size for each polynomial is often not a multiple of the cache line size, they will not be stored at the start of a cache line. When a warp requests the polynomial coefficients for one specific body covering a specific period, the relevant cache lines are loaded into the on-chip cache. The first request targets four Sun polynomials of 1056 bytes, for which twelve cache lines are loaded, although they would fit into nine. This results in 1536 bytes loaded, which is roughly 45% more than requested. In the second example shown in Fig. 3 regarding Jupiter polynomials, 40% more cache lines containing 56% more data than needed are loaded. When all polynomials within the records are applied at some point during the calculations, a fraction of the unneeded data may be used for a different body or point in time. If cached until this point, the data is then immediately available. However, getting a warp instruction ready for execution will generally involve more memory traffic than theoretically necessary. Additionally, a cache overload will replace former cached polynomials, alleviating both spatial and temporal locality effects.

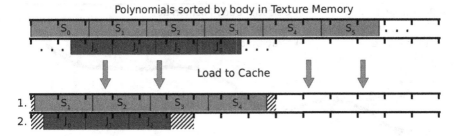

Fig. 4. Same ephemeris model data and example requests as in Fig. 3 but with the polynomials sorted first by body and then by time.

3.1 CUBE: CUdajectory Binary Ephemeris Format

An efficient ephemeris data format for massively parallelized cudajectory requires a different view of data locality. Instead of looking at the locality within a single thread, we need to focus on the data that is requested at once by the threads of one warp. By fitting the data's alignment to the access pattern, we can reduce the memory traffic and register spilling.

The threads within a warp will all perform the position calculation for the same body by design of the software. In case they evaluate the same polynomial, they will also need the same data. For higher timestamp ranges, however, this ranges over multiple polynomials. Therefore, storing the list of polynomials sorted first by the body and then by timestamp will result in a more efficient format than the original record-based approach. This is the exact idea behind the proposed CUBE format.

Figure 4 describes the same data requests as in Fig. 3, but now the polynomials are stored in the CUBE format. For the Sun polynomials, we load the minimum necessary number of cache lines, where only 9% more data than needed is included. In the case of Jupiter, still, one more cache line than theoretically necessary is loaded, which is caused by the alignment of the polynomials to the cache lines in texture memory. However, we still perform much better compared to the record-based format because only 20% more cache lines and 33% more data than needed are loaded. Overall, we achieve a 21% reduction of loaded cache lines (From 19 down to 15) by merely changing the alignment of the data, promising a notable performance gain.

Furthermore, we identified a difference in the storage structure of coefficients within each polynomial and the order of accesses by the cudajectory implementation. Thus, there is a chance for additional performance improvement when either the algorithm is adjusted, or the CUBE format is further improved.

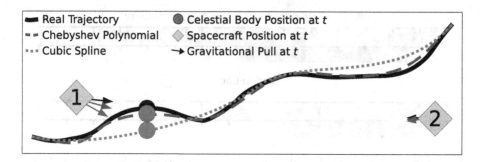

Fig. 5. Exaggerated illustration of an arbitrary body's position obtained from trajectory approximations of different accuracy. The gravitational pull on a spacecraft, calculated from this position, is affected by the position deviation introduced by the approximation, especially when close as shown for spacecraft 1.

3.2   Alternative Models and Configurations

Using Cubic Splines; Popular types of ephemeris models apply Chebyshev polynomials [2,12] to approximate the position and velocity of celestial bodies. However, Korvenoja et al. [7] showed that ephemeris models for satellite orbits could be computed using cubic splines, achieving high accuracy with significantly lower effort. Moreover, Russell and Arora [15] demonstrated that this technique could also be applied to ephemeris models of celestial bodies. When an alternative model is applied, the deviation in the calculated body positions affects the direction and magnitude of the gravitational pull exerted on the simulated spacecraft as depicted in Fig. 5. However, if this effect is small enough (e.g. for spacecraft 2 in the figure), this model may be applied without consequences.

Cubic splines are polynomials of degree three, interpolating between a sequence of knots. When generating an alternative ephemeris model for a specific celestial body, the positions at equally-spaced points in time retrieved from the original DE432 model can be used as knots. By applying a model containing such cubic splines instead of the DE432 Chebyshev polynomials, we are able to improve the efficiency of specific position calculations. Chebyshev polynomials are evaluated by a recursive algorithm, including six to fourteen three-dimensional coefficients (Table 1). On the other hand, a cubic spline is simpler to evaluate and reduces the number of coefficients to four and 96 bytes per polynomial. Additionally, the CUBE format lets us choose the spline interval size for each body independently, as we are not bound to the record's interval anymore. Here, longer intervals increase data reuse both within each specific sample simulation and between different GPU threads.

Furthermore, an ephemeris model using cubic splines turns out to have a very stable deviation compared to the positions retrieved from the original model. The maximum deviation of such a cubic spline model against the original can be calculated statically and later used as accuracy metric to support model selection. Increasing the polynomial interval increases the maximum deviation and decreases the approximation accuracy of the model. However, we improve

Table 1. Statistics on type 2 polynomials from DE432 with $N + 1$ three-dimensional coefficients of double precision floating point type [2,11].

Celestial body or	Interval	Polynomial	Per polynomial		Per 32 days record	
Barycentre (BC)	[days]	Degree N	Values	Bytes	Values	Bytes
Sun	16	10	33	264	66	528
Mercury	8	13	42	336	168	1 344
Venus	16	9	30	240	60	480
Earth BC	16	12	39	312	78	624
Moon	4	12	39	312	312	2 496
Mars BC	32	10	33	264	33	264
Jupiter BC	32	7	24	192	24	192
Saturn BC	32	6	21	168	21	168
Uranus BC	32	5	18	144	18	144
Neptune BC	32	5	18	144	18	144
Pluto BC	32	5	18	144	18	144

the reuse of data as fewer different polynomials need to be loaded to cover the same timestamp range. For bodies in the outer solar system, cubic splines seem to be an efficient alternative. While using intervals much longer than set by DE432, we still provide very high accuracy. For bodies closer to the Sun, however, cubic splines are not able to provide more efficient intervals while achieving overall acceptable accuracy levels. This is because of more extreme direction changes in their movement caused by the surrounding close and massive bodies like the Sun and Jupiter. Especially the trajectory of Mercury is heavily perturbed making it very hard to apply cubic splines in an efficient way.

Celestial Bodies Exclusion; Another method to increase the performance is to exclude a subset of bodies from simulations. An entire celestial body may be excluded from the physics model if its full gravitational effect on the spacecraft state is small enough. This skips the related position calculation and ephemeris data loads within each step and thread, providing a significant performance boost. Although such model modifications are not specific to GPU applications, they are the extreme case of the deviation analysis and, therefore, included in the upcoming experiments.

Planetary Systems Abstraction; The last optimization method is to abstract planetary systems. In case a planet and its moons are treated as individual bodies by the physics model, they may be abstracted using a fictional body of combined mass at their barycentre, instead. For our applications, this method can be applied for the Earth-Moon system, when the introduced error is small enough to be accepted. We call this method *EMB abstraction* in the rest of this paper.

4 Experimental Results

To assess the impact of the proposed method on the simulation runtime, we execute the disposal analysis for the BepiColombo mission and two additional artificial test cases with different ephemeris models. Here, only the runtime spent on the selected CUDA device is measured. The baseline applies the original DE432 model, and on top of that, the speedup is calculated for runs using alternative ephemeris models. The experiments are executed on Tesla K80, K20XM, and K40M devices as well as on a Tesla V100 in selected cases. The latter is primarily used for detailed investigations of the performance via the Nvidia Visual Profiler because it provides additional insight into the utilization of the device compared to older GPU generations.

4.1 Accuracy Levels of Test Cases

To accelerate position calculations, we pick case-specific ephemeris models without violating accuracy requirements. For this purpose, the accuracy level of the conducted analysis is defined before we select a model for each celestial body. We always opt for simpler models, provided that they guarantee the required accuracy. This way, both the algorithmic complexity as well as the required data size can be reduced.

Regarding the disposal analysis of the BepiColombo upper stage, the model selection will be based on the astrodynamical analysis presented in Fig. 6. It requires only a rough guess of the simulated trajectory range and leads to no significant increase in runtime.

The ephemeris model configurations for a range of accuracy levels are presented in Table 2. For each celestial body, either the original polynomials, cubic splines of a specific maximum deviation, or exclusion is selected. The determined collection of polynomials is then stored in the CUBE format supported by cudajectory.

For high accuracy applications at, e.g., 10^{-20} km/s^2, all listed celestial bodies are included as their gravitational effect is of relevant magnitude (see the left plot of Fig. 6). Since small position offsets of most bodies already have a worst-case effect larger than 10^{-20} km/s^2, we inherit the original polynomials for these. Only for Uranus, Neptune, and Pluto, cubic splines of lower accuracy are selected. These bodies are always very far away from the spacecraft. Thus, a position deviation of 10 or 10^5 km, respectively, is accepted (see the right plot of Fig. 6).

For lower accuracy levels, less accurate cubic splines can be selected for most of the bodies, and some may be excluded entirely when their overall gravitational acceleration is determined to be lower than the level at all times. For instance, Pluto and its moons can safely be excluded when an accuracy level of 10^{-16} or higher is applied, as shown in Fig. 6. The model for the lowest level in the table (10^{-10}) includes only six of the eleven bodies. Four of them still require the original accuracy as the spacecraft might have a close encounter, and for the other two, the Sun and Jupiter, cubic splines of quite a high deviation can be selected.

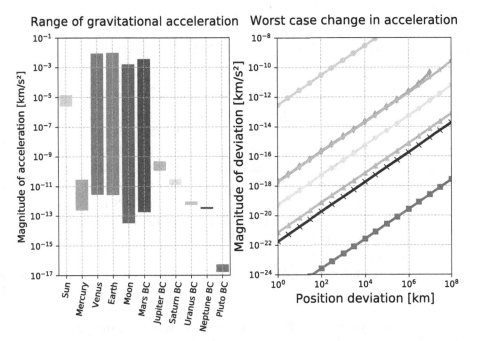

Fig. 6. The analysis of the overall range of gravitational acceleration (left) and worst-case change of acceleration on given position offset (right) per celestial body on a spacecraft between 9.8×10^7 and 2.3×10^8 km from the center of the solar system (Potential distances for the BepiColombo upper stage around the Sun). As Venus, the Earth, the Moon, and Mars orbit within this range, their potential gravitational pull [km/s^2] can be much higher (on close encounter) than for the rest and position deviations would be more critical. For this, these bodies are not included on the right.

The models for all of the given accuracy levels produce results that can be used to get the first idea of this specific problem, while 10^{-20} and 10^{-15} can also be applied for the final analysis.

Two artificial sample sets on static circular orbits between Earth and Mars are also included to test alternative models not covered by the BepiColombo case. Additionally, we configured their timestamp ranges to stay at zero and 64 days to investigate its effect on the performance. We define an accuracy level at 10^{-11} km/s^2, where cubic spline models at 100 km (Sun), 10^6 km (Venus, Mars, and Jupiter) and 10^8 km (Beyond Jupiter) maximum deviation are applied. Mercury, Uranus, Neptune, and Pluto are excluded from the model if the body exclusion feature is enabled. EMB abstraction can safely be applied at every step, as its maximum error is two magnitudes below the selected accuracy level.

When the original model is applied by one of the cases, the total of all position calculations for one point in time requires 2520 bytes of polynomial coefficients. Using the alternative models for the BepiColombo case without EMB abstraction, this data size is reduced by 6% at level 10^{-20} to 48% at

Table 2. Ephemeris configurations for accuracy levels in km/s^2 regarding the Bepi-Colombo analysis. For each body either the original polynomials (DE432), cubic splines of given maximum deviation in kilometers or exclusion (empty) is selected.

Accuracy level	10^{-20}	10^{-15}	10^{-12}	10^{-10}
Sun	DE432	DE432	CS 1	CS 10^2
Mercury	DE432	DE432	DE432	
Venus	DE432	DE432	DE432	DE432
Earth BC	DE432	DE432	DE432	DE432
Moon	DE432	DE432	DE432	DE432
Mars BC	DE432	DE432	DE432	DE432
Jupiter BC	DE432	CS 10^2	CS 10^5	CS 10^7
Saturn BC	DE432	CS 10^4	CS 10^7	
Uranus BC	CS 10	CS 10^6		
Neptune BC	CS 10	CS 10^6		
Pluto BC	CS 10^5			

level 10^{-10}. However, when EMB abstraction is activated, a reduction of up to 60% can be achieved. The described model for the artificial case can improve this further to 69% reduced memory consumption, while 45% of the position calculations per point in time are skipped entirely.

4.2   Speedup Gained from Ephemeris Model Changes

The BepiColombo analysis applies step size control, which causes an average of 120 days range of timestamps within warps. To identify the performance impact of this timestamp range, we execute the artificial cases without step size control. One case contains samples starting at the same time, and thus the timestamp range will always be zero. Within the second case, however, the samples' start times are equally distributed so that two days are in between every pair of subsequent samples. This results in a static timestamp range of 64 days within every warp of 32 threads.

The speedup displayed in Fig. 7 is observed for the mentioned cases when applying different ephemeris model configurations. All configuration features individually, as well as the fully adapted models, are able to achieve a significant runtime speedup of up to 2.6×, where roughly 62% of execution time is saved. When the data is structured using the CUBE format, a speedup of 1.3× to 1.37× is observed for the BepiColombo case on the tested GPUs. For cases of smaller timestamp ranges, even higher speedup is achieved with over 1.4× and 1.5×, respectively.

The impact of the individual configuration features was tested on artificial cases. Here, the performance gain is similar for both timestamp ranges. However, all features combined are able to speed up the case of 64 days range more than the

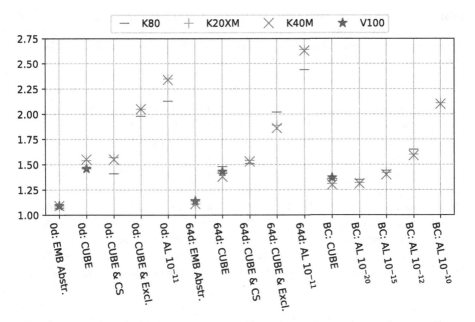

Fig. 7. The speedup of efficient ephemeris models used by the listed cases and configurations. The cases are BepiColombo (BC), zero days (0d), 64 days (64d) timestamp range. The model features include CUBE format, EMB abstraction, cubic splines (CS), and the full exclusion of bodies, which are all included for the accuracy level (AL) configurations.

case of zero-days range. The higher range causes a runtime increase by a factor of 1.13× in the first place, which is reversed by applying the optimizations.

The high accuracy model used for the BepiColombo case already gains a decent performance boost, which is, however, mostly caused by the format change. The included cubic splines do not make a big difference. The less accurate models drive the runtime down to a speedup of 2.1× at the accuracy level of 10^{-10}, which is mainly due to the exclusion of specific bodies.

4.3   Performance Profiles of Ephemeris Model Changes

We profiled the cudajectory using the baseline data format and all the proposed methods. The details are presented in Table 3. The CUBE format reduces the overall runtime by 29.3%, where especially the heavy ephemeris routines are accelerated. Further optimization methods are less affected but still faster by at least 15%. The number of ephemeris data requests is unchanged, but we see a significant reduction of total loads from device memory by over 26%. The only change between the first two runs is the data structure of the texture memory. We can determine that the improved load efficiency results in an increased L2 cache hit rate and fewer reloads of data in both global and local memory. Especially the 12 billion requests saved in local memory have a very beneficial impact

Table 3. Performance profiles of one CUDA kernel call till the first clustering break of the BepiColombo case on a Tesla V100 for DE432 model (baseline) and CUBE format. The third case uses cubic splines on top, while the fourth case excludes Mercury, Saturn, Uranus, Neptune and Pluto on top of the CUBE format.

	DE432	CUBE		Cub. Splines		Exclusion	
Full kernel runtime	10.81 s	7.64 s	−29.3%	7.56 s	−1%	5.99 s	−22%
for integration	0.46 s	0.39 s	−15.2%	0.42 s	+8%	0.42 s	+8%
for physics model	2.22 s	1.74 s	−21.6%	1.85 s	+6%	1.45 s	−17%
for ephemeris model	7.45 s	4.82 s	−35.3%	4.52 s	−6%	3.41 s	−29%
for positions copy	0.52 s	0.43 s	−17.3%	0.46 s	+7%	0.48 s	+12%
Local memory overhead	95.7%	94.7%	−1.0%	95.9%	+1%	94.9%	0
L2 Cache hit rate	38.0%	47.0%	+9.0%	53.0%	+6%	42.0%	−5%
Device memory loads (TiB)	2.508	1.847	−26.4%	1.738	−6%	1.612	−13%
Global memory requests	4.5 G	3.3 G	−26.7%	3.9 G	+18%	2.1 G	−36%
Texture memory requests	90.2 G	90.2 G	0	61.9 G	−31%	56.7 G	−37%
Local memory requests	56.0 G	44.6 G	−20.4%	49.8 G	+12%	31.9 G	−28%

on the runtime. Although the local memory overhead was only reduced by 1%, we can state that register spilling is reduced significantly by applying the CUBE format.

When the cubic splines are now applied on top, we observe a further reduction of the ephemeris model runtime. However, the other program sections experience an increase, which results in only a small speedup. This is in line with the observations from Fig. 7, where only a small to no speedup is identified for cubic splines on top of the CUBE format. The load requests to texture memory were reduced by 31% as cubic splines are polynomials of lower degree involving fewer coefficients. As the covered intervals are increased as well, we also observe an increase in the L2 cache hit rate. However, the little extra logic in cudajectory to support different types of polynomials introduces additional overhead and thus increases register spilling. This is most likely why we encounter higher rates of local and global memory requests and almost no additional speed.

When specific bodies are excluded entirely from the simulation, a large fraction of the algorithmic effort and data requests are skipped. Thus, the runtime decreases significantly, which makes case-specific model configurations very beneficial. This can be seen in the observed speedup and the presented performance profile for body exclusion. Compared to the CUBE format, 22% of the kernel runtime is saved when 45% of the bodies are excluded. Most of the skipped bodies' orbits are approximated by Chebyshev polynomials of sixth or seventh degree, where, in comparison, fewer coefficients and algorithmic effort are involved. However, with Mercury involving polynomials of degree 14, the most expensive position calculation is also excluded. In total, we perform 37% fewer ephemeris data requests and reduce the device memory traffic by 13%, which subsequently reduces the need for register spilling (28% less local memory requests). As mostly polynomials of shorter intervals are computed, the data reuse and thus the L2 cache hit rate decreases as well.

Although the analyzed configuration features have different impacts on the performance, they were not able to reduce the overall local memory overhead. This states that the pressure on the memory bus due to register spilling is still very high, and a significant amount of time is spent on moving register data back and forth. Additionally, when executing a merged configuration of those cubic splines and exclusions, we get a total runtime per kernel of 5.82 s, which is a reduction of 1.73 s or 24% against the CUBE format and slightly more than the sum of both individual changes. This draws the conclusion that the changes boost each other and explains the much higher speedups achieved by the lower accuracy level configurations compared to those in the profiles.

5   Related Work

Various astrodynamic simulations utilize the power of GPUs to accelerate their computations. However, we noticed that achieving an efficiency level close to the hardware peak performance necessitates modifications to both the algorithm and data structure. Thus, each problem requires tailor-made optimizations, different from other domains. In the following, we mention similar works in this field.

Russell et al. [16] parallelized the computation of a Mascon model, a high-precision description of the mass distribution of a celestial body for one trajectory simulation. In another work by the same authors [1], they use GPUs to simulate trajectories generated by Lambert's algorithm as an alternative to the Monte-Carlo method. Massari et al. [10], on the other hand, present numerical methods to improve the performance of Monte-Carlo simulations on GPUs, which in theory could also be used in cudajectory. Russell [15] and Korvenja [7] demonstrated that cubic splines and cubic Hermite polynomials produce acceptable ephemeris accuracy while reducing both memory requirements and computation time significantly. Thus, we implemented this concept to reduce the data size of the ephemeris model in cudajectory. To the best of our knowledge, an efficient GPU-specialized ephemeris model for a parallel set of trajectory simulations is not introduced so far.

6   Conclusion and Outlook

Trajectory simulations can benefit significantly from massive parallelization on GPUs. However, with the increase of simulation timestamps within one warp, different ephemeris data need to be loaded into memory, thus causing considerable memory traffic and register spilling. In this paper, we introduced a new data format, called CUBE, which restructures the data to improve data locality. Our experiments showed that by just using the CUBE data format, we could obtain higher speedups of at least 1.3×. Additionally, we noticed that by excluding specific celestial bodies from simulations while losing negligible accuracy, we could reduce the algorithmic complexity and data accesses within the ephemeris model computations and achieve significant speedup. Another approach that yields higher performance with the cost of losing accuracy level is to use cubic splines as an alternative polynomial type. This method decreases the accuracy of the orbit approximation but also simplifies the calculation and reduces the size of the required data. Additionally, adjusting the polynomial intervals affects the data locality within warps of higher timestamp ranges. While the use of cubic splines further improves caching, it also increases the need for register spilling and thus results in only a small runtime improvement on top of the CUBE format. However, in combination with body exclusion, the model changes can boost each other. Thus, cubic splines are a valuable ephemeris model setting. All the proposed optimization methods enabled us to accelerate the trajectory simulations on a real-world scenario between 1.31×–2.11×, depending on the desired accuracy level.

Acknowledgments. This research has been supported by the European Space Agency, Hessian LOEWE initiative within the Software-Factory 4.0 project, and the German Research Foundation (DFG) through the Program Performance Engineering for Scientific Software. The calculations for this research were conducted on the Lichtenberg high performance computer of the Technical University of Darmstadt and European Space Agency.

References

1. Arora, N., Russell, R.P.: A GPU accelerated multiple revolution lambert solver for fast mission design. AAS/AIAA Space Flight Mech. Meet. **136**, 10–198 (2010)
2. Bachman, N.J.: SPK Required Reading of NAIF SPICE Toolkit Hypertext Documentation (2017). http://naif.jpl.nasa.gov/pub/naif/toolkit_docs
3. ESA and JAXA: BepiColombo: The Europe's first mission to Mercury (2019). https://sci.esa.int/bepicolombo
4. Fehlberg, E.: Classical Fifth-, Sixth-, seventh-, and Eight-Order Runge-Kutta Formulas with Stepsize Control. National Aeronautics and Space Administration (1968)
5. Folkner, W.M., Williams, J.G., Boggs, D.H., Park, R.S., Kuchynka, P.: The planetary and lunar ephemerides DE430 and DE431. Interplanetary Netw. Prog. Rep. **196**, 1–81 (2014)
6. Geda, M.: Massive Parallelization of Trajectory Propagations Using GPUs. Master's thesis, Delft University of Technology (2019)
7. Korvenoja, P., Piché, R.: Efficient satellite orbit approximation. In: Proceedings of 13th International Technical Meeting of the Institute of Navigation Satellite Division, pp. 1930–1937 (2000)
8. Kroese, D.P., Brereton, T., Taimre, T., Botev, Z.I.: Why the Monte Carlo method is so important today. Wiley Interdisc. Rev.: Comput. Stat. **6**(6), 386–392 (2014)
9. Kutta, W.: Beitrag zur näherungweisen Integration totaler Differentialgleichungen. Z. Math. Phys. **46**, 435–453 (1901)
10. Massari, M., Di Lizia, P., Rasotto, M.: Nonlinear uncertainty propagation in astrodynamics using differential algebra and graphics processing units. J. Aerospace Inf. Syst. **14**, 493–503 (2017)

11. NAIF: SPICE Ephemeris Toolkit (2017). https://naif.jpl.nasa.gov/naif/toolkit.html
12. Newhall, X.: Numerical representation of planetary ephemerides. In: Applications of Computer Technology to Dynamical Astronomy, vol. 45, pp. 305–310. Cambridge University Press (1989)
13. Nvidia: Cuda toolkit documentation (2020). https://docs.nvidia.com/cuda
14. Nvidia: Visual profiler (2020). https://developer.nvidia.com/nvidia-visual-profiler
15. Russell, R., Arora, N.: FIRE: a fast, accurate, and smooth planetary body ephemeris interpolation system. Celest. Mech. Dyn. Astron. **108**(2), 107–124 (2010)
16. Russell, R.P., Arora, N.: Global point mascon models for simple, accurate, and parallel gepotential computation. J. Guidance Control Dyn. **35**(5), 1568–1581 (2012)

Parallel Finite Cell Method
with Adaptive Geometric Multigrid

S. Saberi[1($\boxtimes$)], A. Vogel[1], and G. Meschke[2]

[1] High-Performance Computing in the Engineering Sciences,
Ruhr University Bochum, Universitätsstr. 150, 44801 Bochum, Germany
seyed.saberi@rub.de
[2] Institute for Structural Mechanics, Ruhr University Bochum,
Universitätsstr. 150, 44801 Bochum, Germany

Abstract. Generation of appropriate computational meshes in the context of numerical methods for partial differential equations is technical and laborious and has motivated a class of advanced discretization methods commonly referred to as unfitted finite element methods. To this end, the finite cell method (FCM) combines high-order FEM, adaptive quadrature integration and weak imposition of boundary conditions to embed a physical domain into a structured background mesh. While unfortunate cut configurations in unfitted finite element methods lead to severely ill-conditioned system matrices that pose challenges to iterative solvers, such methods permit the use of optimized algorithms and data patterns in order to obtain a scalable implementation. In this work, we employ linear octrees for handling the finite cell discretization that allow for parallel scalability, adaptive refinement and efficient computation on the commonly regular background grid. We present a parallel adaptive geometric multigrid with Schwarz smoothers for the solution of the resultant system of the Laplace operator. We focus on exploiting the hierarchical nature of space tree data structures for the generation of the required multigrid spaces and discuss the scalable and robust extension of the methods across process interfaces. We present both the weak and strong scaling of our implementation up to more than a billion degrees of freedom on distributed-memory clusters.

Keywords: Unfitted finite element · Finite cell · Geometric multigrid · Massively parallel · High-performance computing

1 Introduction

In the context of numerical approximation of partial differential equations (PDE) for scientific and engineering applications alike, the generation of appropriate

Supported by the German Research Foundation (*Deutsche Forschungsgemeinschaft, DFG*) in the collaborative research center SFB 837 *Interaction Modeling in Mechanized Tunneling.*

M. Malawski and K. Rzadca (Eds.): Euro-Par 2020, LNCS 12247, pp. 578–593, 2020.
https://doi.org/10.1007/978-3-030-57675-2_36

computational meshes is still one of the narrowest bottlenecks. This has given rise to isogeometric analysis (IGA) [18] on the one hand and unfitted finite element and meshfree methods [2] on the other. Although unfitted finite element methods encompass several classes, including the extended finite element method (XFEM) [3], cutFEM [5] and finite cell method (FCM) [10, 22], their common goal is to try to find the solution to the PDE without the need for a boundary-conforming discretization. As an unfitted finite element method, the finite cell method combines adaptive quadrature integration and high-order FEM together with the weak imposition of boundary conditions.

Although mesh generation is essentially circumvented, unfitted finite element methods face several challenges, the most conspicuous of which is ill-conditioning of the system matrix and imposition of essential boundary conditions [27]. The former issue limits the usability of many iterative solvers, which has led the majority of studies to focus on direct solvers. While direct solvers based on LU factorization have proven to be robust, their scalability suffers greatly due to poor complexity and concurrency [25]. Recently, a geometric multigrid preconditioner with a penalty formulation has been studied for the finite cell method [23] to formulate an efficient iterative solver.

On the other hand, unfitted FEM possesses characteristics that can be exploited to its advantage, especially for parallel computing. For instance, the computational mesh in unfitted FEM can normally be regular and Cartesian that in turn permits efficient computation and precomputation of finite element values. A parallel implementation of multi-level h-p-adaptive finite element with a shared mesh was recently applied to the finite cell method, employing a CG solver with an additive Schwarz preconditioner in [19] and AMG preconditioning in [20].

The main contributions of the present work can be summarized as follows:

- We employ a fully distributed, space-tree-based discretization of the computation domain with low memory foot print to allow the storage and manipulation of large problems and adaptive mesh refinement (AMR)
- We present the parallelization of the finite cell method with adaptive refinement, focusing on the scalability of different aspects of the computation via exploiting space-tree data structures and the regularity of the discretization
- We formulate a scalable hybrid Schwarz-type smoother for the treatment of cut cells to use in our geometric multigrid solver
- We employ parallel adaptive geometric multigrid to solve large-scale finite cell systems and focus on the process-local generation of the required spaces and favorable communication patterns
- We present the strong and weak scalability of different computational components of our methods

In Sect. 2, the FCM formulation of a model problem is set up. The geometric multigrid solver is formulated in Sect. 3. The developed methods are applied to a number of numerical experiments in Sect. 4. Finally, conclusions are drawn in Sect. 5.

2   Finite Cell Method

In the context of unfitted finite element methods, a given physical domain Ω with essential and natural boundaries Γ_D and Γ_N, respectively, is commonly placed in an embedding domain Ω_e with favorable characteristics, such as axis alignment as shown in Fig. 1. Consequently, appropriate techniques are required for integration over Ω and imposition of boundary conditions on Γ_D and Γ_N. In this work, we used the Poisson equation as model problem given by

$$
\begin{aligned}
-\Delta u &= f && \text{in } \Omega, \\
u &= g && \text{on } \Gamma_D, \\
\nabla u \cdot \boldsymbol{n} &= t && \text{on } \Gamma_N,
\end{aligned}
\tag{1}
$$

where Ω is the domain, $\Gamma = \Gamma_D \cup \Gamma_N$ is the boundary, $\boldsymbol{n}$ is the normal vector to the boundary and u is the unknown solution.

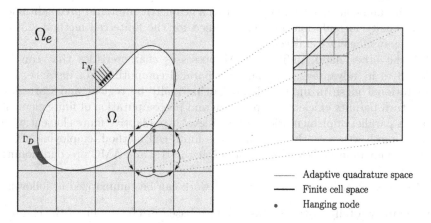

Fig. 1. Illustration of a typical unfitted finite element setting, where the physical domain Ω is embedded in an embedding domain Ω_e. Γ_D and Γ_N are essential and natural boundaries, respectively. Adaptive refinement in both FCM and integration spaces is demonstrated for a cut cell

2.1   Boundary Conditions

Natural Boundary Conditions. In the context of standard finite element method, natural boundary conditions are commonly integrated over the surface of those elements that coincide with the natural part of the physical boundary Γ_N; however, in the general case, the physical domain does not coincide with cell boundaries in the context of the finite cell method. Therefore, a separate description of the boundary is necessary for integration of natural boundary conditions. Except for an appropriate Jacobi transformation from the surface space to volume space, integration of natural boundary conditions does not require special treatment.

Essential Boundary Conditions. The imposition of essential boundary conditions is a challenging task in unfitted finite element methods. Penalty methods [1, 4, 30], Lagrange multipliers [6, 12–14] and Nitsche's method [7, 9, 11, 17, 21] are commonly used for this purpose. We use a stabilized symmetric Nitsche's method with a local estimate for the stabilization parameter that has the advantage of retaining the symmetry of the system, not introducing additional unknowns and being variationally consistent. The weak form is therefore given by

$$
\int_{\Omega} \nabla v \cdot \nabla u \, dx - \int_{\Gamma_D} v (\nabla u \cdot n) \, ds
$$
$$
- \int_{\Gamma_D} (u - g)(\nabla v \cdot n) \, ds + \int_{\Gamma_D} \lambda v(u - g) \, ds \qquad (2)
$$
$$
= \int_{\Omega} v f \, dx + \int_{\Gamma_N} v t \, ds,
$$

where λ is the stabilization parameter. The computation of λ is further explained in Sect. 2.3.

2.2 Spatial Discretization

Unfitted finite element methods normally permit the use of a structured grid as the embedding domain. We employ distributed linear space trees [8] for the discretization of the finite cell space. Space tree data structures not only require minimal work for setup and manipulation, they also allow for distributed storage, efficient load balancing and adaptive refinement and have a small memory footprint. We make use of Morton ordering as illustrated in Fig. 2.

An attractive aspect of computation on structured spaces is the optimization opportunities it provides, which is exactly where unfitted methods can seek to benefit compared to their boundary-conforming counterparts. For example, we compute element size, coordinates and Jacobian transformation efficiently on the fly without caching during integration.

A natural repercussion of adaptive refinement on space tree data structures is the existence of hanging nodes in the discretized space as shown in Fig. 1. To ensure the continuity of the solution, we treat hanging nodes by distributing their contribution to their associated non-hanging nodes and removing them from the global system. The influence of hanging nodes is thereby effectively local and no additional constraint conditions or unknowns appear in the solution space.

2.3 Volume Integration

The physical domain is free to intersect the embedding domain. During volume integration, the portion of the embedding domain that lies outside of the physical domain, $\Omega_e \setminus \Omega$, is penalized by a factor $\alpha \ll 1$. This stage is essentially where the physical geometry is recovered from the structured embedding mesh. Therefore, cells that are cut by the physical boundary must be sufficiently integrated in

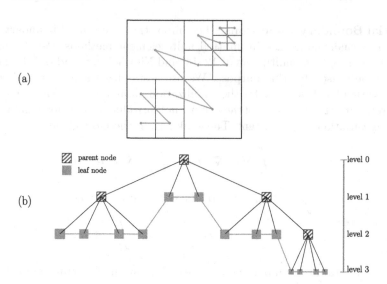

(a)

parent node
leaf node

level 0

(b)

level 1

level 2

level 3

Fig. 2. (a) The z-curve (Morton) ordering on a 2D example with one level of refinement and (b) the tree representation of the domain in (a)

order to accurately resolve the geometry. On the other hand, the accuracy of standard Gaussian quadrature is decidedly deteriorated by discontinuities in the integrand. Thus, methods such as Gaussian quadrature with modified weights and points [24] and uniform [22] and adaptive [10] refinement, also known as composed Gaussian quadrature, have been proposed for numerical integration in the face of discontinuities in the integrand.

We use adaptive quadrature for volume integration within the finite cell discretization. A number of adaptive integration layers are thereby added on top of the function space of Ω_e for cut cells as shown in Fig. 1. The concept of space tree data structures is congenial for adaptive quadrature integration as the integration space can readily be generated by refinement towards the boundary intersection. Furthermore, the integration space retains the regularity of the parent discretization. This scheme is especially suitable to our parallel implementation, where a given cell is owned by a unique process; therefore, the adaptive quadrature integration procedure is entirely performed process locally, and duplicate computations on the ghost layer are avoided.

Introducing a finite-dimensional function space $V_h \subset H^1(\Omega_e)$, the finite cell formulation of the model problem can be written as

$$\text{Find } u_h \in V_h \subset H^1(\Omega_e) \text{ such that for all } v_h \in V_h$$
$$a_h(u_h, v_h) = b_h(v_h) \tag{3}$$

with

$$a_h(u_h, v_h) := \int_{\Omega_e} \alpha \nabla v_h \cdot \nabla u_h \, dx - \int_{\Gamma_D} v_h (\nabla u_h \cdot n) \, ds$$

$$- \int_{\Gamma_D} u_h (\nabla v_h \cdot n) \, ds + \int_{\Gamma_D} \lambda v_h u_h \, ds, \tag{4}$$

$$b_h(v_h) := \int_{\Omega_e} \alpha v_h f \, dx + \int_{\Gamma_N} v_h t \, ds$$

$$- \int_{\Gamma_D} g(\nabla v_h \cdot n) \, ds + \int_{\Gamma_D} \lambda v_h g \, ds, \tag{5}$$

where

$$\begin{cases} \alpha = 1, & \text{in } \Omega, \\ \alpha \ll 1, & \text{in } \Omega_e \backslash \Omega. \end{cases} \tag{6}$$

The stabilization parameter drastically affects the solution behavior, and its proper identification is vital to achieving both convergence in the solver and the correct imposition of the boundary conditions. There are several methods, including local and global estimates, for the determination of the stabilization parameter [9,15]. We employ a local estimate based on the coercivity condition of the bilinear form that can be formulated as a generalized eigenvalue problem of the form

$$AX = BX\Lambda, \tag{7}$$

where the columns of X are the eigenvectors, Λ is the diagonal matrix of the eigenvalues, and A and B are formulated as

$$\begin{cases} A_{ij} := \int_{\Gamma_D^c} (\nabla \phi_j \cdot n)(\nabla \phi_i \cdot n) \, ds, \\ \\ B_{ij} := \int_{\Omega^c} \alpha \nabla \phi_j \cdot \nabla \phi_i \, dx, \end{cases} \tag{8}$$

where Γ_D^c and Ω^c are the portion of the essential boundary that intersects a given cell and the cell domain, respectively. The stabilization parameter can be chosen as $\lambda > \max(\Lambda)$. This formulation leads to a series of relatively small generalized eigenvalue problems. On the other hand, global estimates assemble a single, large generalized eigenvalue problem by integration over the entire domain. The local estimate is more desirable in the context of parallel computing since it allows for the process-local assembly and solution of each problem. Moreover, most generalized eigensolver algorithms have non-optimal complexities, and a smaller system is nevertheless preferred.

3   Geometric Multigrid

We employ a geometric multigrid solver [16] for the resultant system of the finite cell formulation. Unfitted finite element methods in general and finite cell in particular usually lead to the ill-conditioning of the system matrix due to

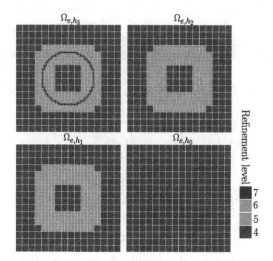

Fig. 3. A sample four-level grid hierarchy generated using Algorithm 1

the existence of cut elements, where the embedding domain is intersected by the physical domain [27]. Small cut fractions exacerbate this problem. Therefore, an efficient multigrid formulation requires special treatment of this issue. Nevertheless, the main components of geometric multigrid remain unaltered.

3.1   Grid Hierarchy

The hierarchical nature of space tree data structures allows for the efficient generation of the hierarchical grids required by geometric multigrid methods [26,29]. We generate the grid hierarchy top-down from the finest grid. In order to keep the coarsening algorithm process local, sibling cells (cells that belong to the same parent) are kept on the same process for all grids. While the coarsening rules are trivial in the case of uniform grids, adaptively refined grids require elaboration. Starting from a fine grid Ω_{e,h_l}, we generate the coarse grid $\Omega_{e,h_{l-1}}$ according to Algorithm 1. Aside from keeping cell families on the same process, the only other major constraint is 2:1 balancing, which means that no two neighbor cells can be more than one level of refinement apart. In practice, load balancing and the application of the mentioned constraints are carried out in a single step. Figure 3 shows a sample four-level grid hierarchy with the finest grid adaptively refined towards a circle in the middle of the square domain.

3.2   Transfer Operators

Transfer operators provide mobility through the grid hierarchy, i.e., restriction from level l to $l-1$ and prolongation from level $l-1$ to l. In order to minimize communication and avoid costly cell lookup queries, we perform these operations in two steps. Restriction starts by transferring entities from the distributed fine

```
input  : Ω_{e,h_l}
output: Ω^i_{e,h_{l-1}} and Ω_{e,h_{l-1}}

Ω^i_{e,h_{l-1}} ← Ω_{e,h_l};
// r_c is the refinement level of cell c
r^{max} ← max(r_c ∈ Ω^i_{e,h_{l-1}});

for c ∈ Ω^i_{e,h_{l-1}} do // process-local part of the domain

    if r_c == r^{max} then
        // This replaces c and all its siblings with their parent
        coarsen c ;
    end
end

Ω_{e,h_{l-1}} ← Ω^i_{e,h_{l-1}};
Apply 2:1 balance on Ω_{e,h_{l-1}} ;
Adjust process interfaces of Ω_{e,h_{l-1}};
Load balance Ω_{e,h_{l-1}};
```

Algorithm 1: Generation of process-local and distributed coarse grids $\Omega^i_{e,h_{l-1}}$ and $\Omega_{e,h_{l-1}}$, respectively, from fine grid Ω_{e,h_l}

grid Ω_{e,h_l} to an intermediate coarse grid $\Omega^i_{e,h_{l-1}}$ followed by a transfer to the distributed coarse grid $\Omega_{e,h_{l-1}}$. Conversely, prolongation starts by transferring entities from the distributed coarse grid $\Omega_{e,h_{l-1}}$ to the intermediate coarse grid $\Omega^i_{e,h_{l-1}}$ followed by a transfer to the distributed fine grid Ω_{e,h_l}. The intermediate grids are generated and accessed entirely process locally and only store minimal information regarding the Morton ordering of the local part of the domain. A similar approach is taken in [29]. The restriction and prolongation operations of a vector v can be summarized as

$$v_{l-1} = T_l R_l v_l \tag{9}$$

$$v_l = P_{l-1} T_{l-1}^{-1} v_{l-1} \tag{10}$$

where $R_l = P_l^T$. T represents the transfer operator between intermediate and distributed grids.

This scheme allows R and P to be resolved in parallel, process locally and without the need for cell lookup queries. Additionally, flexible load balancing is achieved which is especially important for adaptively refined grids. The only additional component to establish effective communication between grids is the transfer operator T, which concludes the majority of the required communication.

3.3   Parallelized Hybrid Schwarz Smoother

Special treatment of cut cells is crucial to the convergence of the solver for finite cell systems. This special treatment mainly manifests itself in the smoother operator S in the context of geometric multigrid solvers. We employ a Schwarz-type

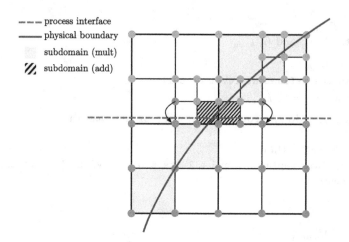

Fig. 4. Subdomain designation for cut cells and parallel application of the hybrid Schwarz smoother on a sample domain. Every node that does not appear in any of the designated cut cell subdomains composes a subdomain with the functions supported only on that node. All nodal subdomains are applied multiplicatively. Nodes are colored based on their owner process

smoother (e.g. [28], cf. also [19,23]), where subdomains are primarily determined based on cut configurations: A subdomain is designated for every cut cell that includes all the functions supported on that cell. The remaining nodes, which do not appear in any cut cells, each compose a subdomain with only the functions supported on that node. The selection of subdomains is illustrated in Fig. 4. The Schwarz-type smoother can be applied in two manners: additively and multiplicatively as given by

$$u^{k+1} = u^k + \mathcal{S}(f - Au^k) \tag{11}$$

with

$$\mathcal{S}^{add} = \left[(R_{s,n}^T A_n R_{s,n}) + \cdots + (R_{s,1}^T A_1 R_{s,1}) \right] \tag{12}$$

$$\mathcal{S}^{mult} = \left[(R_{s,n}^T A_n R_{s,n}) \ldots (R_{s,1}^T A_1 R_{s,1}) \right] \tag{13}$$

where $R_{s,i}$ are the Schwarz restriction operators, $A_i = R_{s,i} A R_{s,i}^T$ are the subdomain matrices and n is the number of subdomains. The Schwarz restriction operator $R_{s,i}$ essentially extracts the rows corresponding to the functions of subdomain i, and its transpose, the Schwarz prolongation operator, takes a vector from the subdomain space to the global space by padding it with zeros.

Parallelization in the first approach is a relatively straightforward task. Each process can simultaneously apply the correction from the subdomains that occur on it, and within each process, subdomain corrections can be applied concurrently. Since any given cell is owned by a unique process, no communication is required during this stage. The only communication takes place when the correction is synchronized over process interfaces at the end.

Parallel realization of the latter approach however is a challenging task. Strict implementation of the multiplicative Schwarz method requires substantial communication not only for exchanging updated residual values but also for synchronizing the application of subdomain corrections, which is clearly not a desirable behavior for the parallel scalability of the algorithm; therefore, we employ a more compromised approach that adheres to the multiplicative application of the smoother as much as possible while minimizing the required communication. To this end, subdomains, whose support lies completely within their owner process are applied multiplicatively, while at process interfaces, the additive approach is taken. This application approach is demonstrated in Fig. 4.

4 Numerical Studies

We perform a number of numerical studies to investigate the performance of the methods outlined in the previous sections. We use the finite cell formulation developed in Sect. 2 and employ geometric multigrid from Sect. 3 as a solver. We consider both uniform and adaptive grids and present the weak and strong scaling of different components of the computation. The computations are performed on a distributed-memory cluster with dual-socket Intel Xeon Skylake Gold 6148 CPUs with 20 cores per socket at 2.4 GHz per core, 192 GB DDR4 main memory per node and a 100 GBit/s Intel Omni-Path network interconnect via PCIe x16 Gen 3. All nodes run Red Hat Enterprise Linux (RHEL) 7, and GCC 7.3 with the O2 optimization flag is used to compile the project. All computations are performed employing MPI parallelization without additional shared-memory parallelization and utilizing up to 40 MPI processes per node which equals the number of cores per node.

The physical domain considered in this benchmark example is a circle that is embedded in a unit square embedding domain throughout this section (see Fig. 3). The finite cell formulation of the Poisson equation is imposed on the embedding domain. An inhomogeneous Dirichlet boundary condition is imposed on an arch to the left of the circle and a homogeneous Neumann boundary condition is imposed on the remaining part. This example is chosen to act as a reproducible benchmark. The conditioning of finite cell matrices directly depends on the configuration of cells cut by the physical domain. The circular domain covers a wide variety of cut configurations on each grid level due to its curvature. Therefore, the resultant matrices include the ill-conditioning associated with the finite cell method and can represent more general geometries. Furthermore, other computational aspects, e.g., volume integration are virtually independent of the geometry and mainly vary with problem size.

The geometric multigrid solver is set up with three steps of pre- and post-smoothing each, employing a combination of the hybrid multiplicative Schwarz smoother as in Sect. 3.3 and a damped Jacobi smoother. The Schwarz smoother is applied only to the three finest grids in each problem, and the damped Jacobi smoother is applied to the remaining grids. A tolerance of 10^{-9} for the residual is used as the convergence criterion.

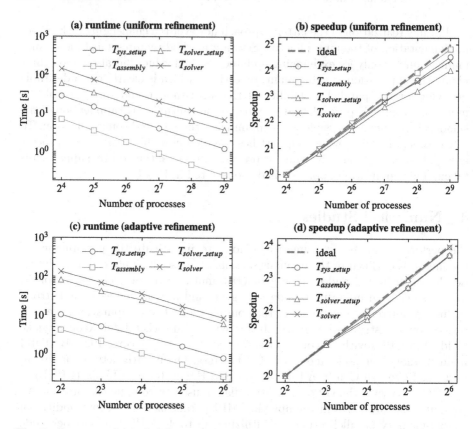

Fig. 5. Strong scaling of different components of the computation on a uniformly refined grid with 268,468,225 degrees of freedom (a and b) and an adaptively refined grid with 16,859,129 degrees of freedom (c and d)

The scaling studies report the runtime of different components of the computation. System setup T_{sys_setup} includes setup and refinement of the main discretization, load balancing, setup of the finite cell space and resolution of the physical boundary. Assembly $T_{assembly}$ is the time required for the assembly of the global system, i.e., integration and distribution of all components of the weak form. Solver setup T_{solver_setup} concerns the generation and setup of the hierarchical spaces for geometric multigrid and includes the grid hierarchy, transfer operators and smoothers. Finally, T_{solver} and $T_{iteration}$ refer to the total runtime and the runtime of a single iteration of the geometric multigrid solver, respectively.

A model with roughly 268 million degrees of freedom with uniform refinement and another model with roughly 16.8 million degrees of freedom with adaptive refinement towards the boundary are chosen to investigate the strong scalability of the computation as shown in Fig. 5. In both cases, the speedup of all components are compared to the ideal parallel performance. Ideal or perfect speedup is

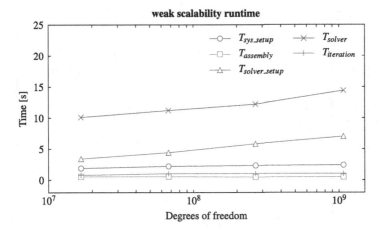

Fig. 6. Weak scaling of different components of the computation using grids that range in size from roughly 16.7 million degrees of freedom to 1.1 billion degrees of freedom

driven by Amdahl's law and is defined as a speedup that is linearly proportional to the number of processing units, normalized to the smallest configuration that can accommodate the memory demand, i.e., 16 processes for the uniform grid and 4 processes for the adaptively refined grid. Except $T_{assembly}$ that virtually coincides with ideal speedup, other components show slightly smaller speedups; however, these minor variations are practically inevitable in most scientific applications due to communication overhead and load imbalances. The strong scalability of all components can be considered excellent as there are no breakdowns or plateaus and the differences from ideal speedup remain small.

On the other hand, weak scalability is investigated for a number of uniformly refined grids, ranging in size from approximately 16.7 million to 1.07 billion degrees of freedom as shown in Fig. 6. In addition to keeping roughly constant the number of degrees of freedom per core, in order to study the scalability of the geometric multigrid solver, the size of the coarse problem is kept constant on all grids; therefore, a deeper hierarchy is employed for larger problems as detailed in Table 1. The convergence behavior of the multigrid solver is shown in Fig. 7. Within the weak scaling study, each problem encounters many different cut cell configurations on each level of the grid hierarchy. The observed boundedness of the iteration count is therefore a testament to the robustness of the approach. All components exhibit good weak scalability throughout the entire range. While T_{sys_setup} and $T_{assembly}$ are virtually constant for all grid sizes, T_{solver_setup} and T_{solver} slightly increase on larger problems. The difference in T_{solver_setup} can be imputed to the difference in the number of grid levels for each problem, i.e., larger problems with deeper multigrid hierarchies have heavier workloads in this step. On the other hand, T_{solver} has to be considered in conjunction with the iteration count. Although the multigrid solver is overall scalable in terms of the iteration count, there are still minor differences in the necessary number of

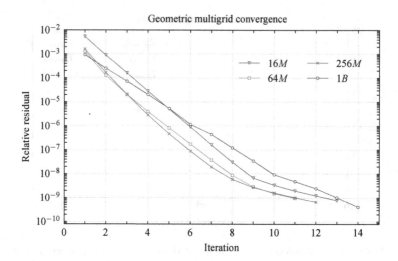

Fig. 7. The convergence behavior of the geometric multigrid solver for the grids in the weak scaling study

iterations between different problems (see Fig. 7). $T_{iteration}$ can be considered a normalized metric in this regard, which remains virtually constant. Nevertheless, the differences in runtime remain small for all components and are negligible in practical settings.

Although a direct comparison is not possible due to differences in formulation, problem type and setup, hardware, etc., we try to give a high-level discussion on some aspects of the methods with respect to closely related works. In [23], a multigrid preconditioner with Schwarz smoothers was presented, showing bounded iteration counts. However, a parallelization strategy was not reported. In [20], a PCG solver with an AMG preconditioner was used. Similarly, a PCG solver with a Schwarz preconditioner was used in [19]. In both studies, a shared base mesh was employed. The size of the examples in [20] and [19] were smaller in comparison to the ones considered here, which further hinders a direct comparison; nevertheless, the multigrid solver presented in this work shows promising results both in terms of parallel scalability and absolute runtime for similarly sized problems. The multigrid solver is furthermore robust with respect to broad variations in problem size, whereas the iteration count of the PCG solver in [19] significantly increased for larger problems, which was directly reflected in the runtime. Geometric multigrid is used as a solver in this work. It is expected that even more robustness and performance can be gained if it is used in conjunction with a Krylov subspace accelerator, such as the conjugate gradient (CG) method.

Table 1. Problem and solver configuration for the weak scaling study. n_{proc} is the number of processes, n_{DoF} is the number of degrees of freedom, $n_{hierarchy}^{gmg}$ is the depth of the geometric multigrid hierarchy, $n_{iteration}^{gmg}$ is the number of required iterations and n_{DoF}^{coarse} is the number of degrees of freedom on the coarsest grid

n_{proc}	n_{DoF}	$n_{hierarchy}^{gmg}$	$n_{iteration}^{gmg}$	n_{DoF}^{coarse}
16	16,785,409	6	13	16,641
64	67,125,249	7	11	16,641
256	268,468,225	8	12	16,641
1,024	1,073,807,361	9	14	16,641

5   Conclusions

A parallel adaptive finite cell formulation along with an adaptive geometric multigrid solver is presented in this work. Numerical benchmarks indicate that the core computational components of FCM as well as the GMG solver scale favorably in both weak and strong senses. The use of distributed space-tree-based meshes allows not only the scalable storage and manipulation of extremely large problems, but also effective load balancing, which is above all manifest in the perfect scalability of the integration of the weak form. Furthermore, the suitability of the space-tree-based algorithms to parallel environments for the generation of multigrid spaces is demonstrated by the scalability of the solver setup. The geometric multigrid solver with the Schwarz-type smoother exhibits robustness and scalability both in terms of the required iteration count for different problem sizes and parallelization. We strive to minimize communication in the parallelization of the multigrid components, especially for the application of the Schwarz smoother; nevertheless, iteration counts do not suffer from parallel execution, and the solver shows good weak and strong scalability. The ability to solve problems with more than a billion degrees of freedom and the scalability of the computations are promising results for the application of the finite cell method with geometric multigrid to large-scale problems on parallel machines. Nevertheless, further examples and problem types are necessary to extend the applicability of the presented methods. Moreover, the main algorithms and underlying data structures that are used in the presented methods are suitable to hardware accelerators such as GPUs and FPGAs, and we expect that a scalable implementation should be achievable for such architectures given optimized data paths and communication patterns. In particular, the semi-structuredness of the adaptive octree approach is conducive to a hardware-oriented implementation compared to unstructured meshing approaches. We intend to explore these opportunities as a future work.

Acknowledgments. Financial support was provided by the German Research Foundation (*Deutsche Forschungsgemeinschaft, DFG*) in the framework of subproject C4 of the collaborative research center SFB 837 *Interaction Modeling in Mechanized Tunneling*. This support is gratefully acknowledged. We also gratefully acknowledge the computing time on the computing cluster of the SFB837 and the Department of Civil and Environmental Engineering at Ruhr University Bochum, which has been employed for the presented studies.

References

1. Babuška, I.: The finite element method with penalty. Math. Comput. **27**(122), 221–228 (1973)
2. Belytschko, T., Chen, J.: Meshfree and Particle Methods. Wiley, Chichester (2009)
3. Belytschko, T., Moës, N., Usui, S., Parimi, C.: Arbitrary discontinuities in finite elements. Int. J. Numer. Meth. Eng. **50**(4), 993–1013 (2001)
4. Burman, E.: Ghost penalty. C. R. Math. **348**(21), 1217–1220 (2010)
5. Burman, E., Claus, S., Hansbo, P., Larson, M.G., Massing, A.: CutFEM: discretizing geometry and partial differential equations. Int. J. Numer. Meth. Eng. **104**(7), 472–501 (2015)
6. Burman, E., Hansbo, P.: Fictitious domain finite element methods using cut elements: I. A stabilized Lagrange multiplier method. Comput. Methods Appl. Mech. Eng. **199**(41–44), 2680–2686 (2010)
7. Burman, E., Hansbo, P.: Fictitious domain finite element methods using cut elements: II. A stabilized Nitsche method. Appl. Numer. Math. **62**(4), 328–341 (2012)
8. Burstedde, C., Wilcox, L.C., Ghattas, O.: p4est: scalable algorithms for parallel adaptive mesh refinement on forests of octrees. SIAM J. Sci. Comput. **33**(3), 1103–1133 (2011)
9. Dolbow, J., Harari, I.: An efficient finite element method for embedded interface problems. Int. J. Numer. Meth. Eng. **78**(2), 229–252 (2009)
10. Düster, A., Parvizian, J., Yang, Z., Rank, E.: The finite cell method for three-dimensional problems of solid mechanics. Comput. Methods Appl. Mech. Eng. **197**(45–48), 3768–3782 (2008)
11. Embar, A., Dolbow, J., Harari, I.: Imposing Dirichlet boundary conditions with Nitsche's method and spline-based finite elements. Int. J. Numer. Meth. Eng. **83**(7), 877–898 (2010)
12. Fernández-Méndez, S., Huerta, A.: Imposing essential boundary conditions in mesh-free methods. Comput. Methods Appl. Mech. Eng. **193**(12–14), 1257–1275 (2004)
13. Flemisch, B., Wohlmuth, B.I.: Stable Lagrange multipliers for quadrilateral meshes of curved interfaces in 3D. Comput. Methods Appl. Mech. Eng. **196**(8), 1589–1602 (2007)
14. Glowinski, R., Kuznetsov, Y.: Distributed Lagrange multipliers based on fictitious domain method for second order elliptic problems. Comput. Methods Appl. Mech. Eng. **196**(8), 1498–1506 (2007)
15. Griebel, M., Schweitzer, M.A.: A particle-partition of unity method part V: boundary conditions. In: Hildebrandt, S., Karcher, H. (eds.) Geometric Analysis and Nonlinear Partial Differential Equations, pp. 519–542. Springer, Heidelberg (2003). https://doi.org/10.1007/978-3-642-55627-2_27
16. Hackbusch, W.: Multi-Grid Methods and Applications, vol. 4. Springer, Heidelberg (2013). https://doi.org/10.1007/978-3-662-02427-0
17. Hansbo, A., Hansbo, P.: An unfitted finite element method, based on Nitsche's method, for elliptic interface problems. Comput. Methods Appl. Mech. Eng. **191**(47–48), 5537–5552 (2002)

18. Hughes, T.J., Cottrell, J.A., Bazilevs, Y.: Isogeometric analysis: CAD, finite elements, NURBS, exact geometry and mesh refinement. Comput. Methods Appl. Mech. Eng. **194**(39–41), 4135–4195 (2005)

19. Jomo, J.N., et al.: Robust and parallel scalable iterative solutions for large-scale finite cell analyses. Finite Elem. Anal. Des. **163**, 14–30 (2019)

20. Jomo, J.N., et al.: Parallelization of the multi-level HP-adaptive finite cell method. Comput. Math. Appl. **74**(1), 126–142 (2017)

21. Nitsche, J.: Über ein variationsprinzip zur lösung von dirichlet-problemen bei verwendung von teilräumen, die keinen randbedingungen unterworfen sind. Abh. Math. Semi. Univ. Hamburg **36**, 9–15 (1971). https://doi.org/10.1007/BF02995904

22. Parvizian, J., Düster, A., Rank, E.: Finite cell method. Comput. Mech. **41**(1), 121–133 (2007). https://doi.org/10.1007/s00466-007-0173-y

23. de Prenter, F., et al.: Multigrid solvers for immersed finite element methods and immersed isogeometric analysis. Comput. Mech. **65**(3), 807–838 (2019). https://doi.org/10.1007/s00466-019-01796-y

24. Rabczuk, T., Areias, P., Belytschko, T.: A meshfree thin shell method for nonlinear dynamic fracture. Int. J. Numer. Meth. Eng. **72**(5), 524–548 (2007)

25. Saad, Y.: Iterative Methods for Sparse Linear Systems, vol. 82. SIAM, Philadelphia (2003)

26. Sampath, R.S., Biros, G.: A parallel geometric multigrid method for finite elements on octree meshes. SIAM J. Sci. Comput. **32**(3), 1361–1392 (2010)

27. Schillinger, D., Ruess, M.: The finite cell method: a review in the context of higher-order structural analysis of cad and image-based geometric models. Arch. Comput. Methods Eng. **22**(3), 391–455 (2015). https://doi.org/10.1007/s11831-014-9115-y

28. Smith, B., Bjorstad, P., Gropp, W.: Domain Decomposition: Parallel Multilevel Methods for Elliptic Partial Differential Equations. Cambridge University Press, Cambridge (1996)

29. Sundar, H., Biros, G., Burstedde, C., Rudi, J., Ghattas, O., Stadler, G.: Parallel geometric-algebraic multigrid on unstructured forests of octrees. In: Proceedings of the International Conference on High Performance Computing, Networking, Storage and Analysis, p. 43. IEEE Computer Society Press (2012)

30. Zhu, T., Atluri, S.: A modified collocation method and a penalty formulation for enforcing the essential boundary conditions in the element free Galerkin method. Comput. Mech. **21**(3), 211–222 (1998). https://doi.org/10.1007/s004660050296

Accelerator Computing

cuDTW++: Ultra-Fast Dynamic Time Warping on CUDA-Enabled GPUs

Bertil Schmidt[1(✉)] and Christian Hundt[2]

[1] Institut für Informatik, JGU Mainz, Mainz, Germany
bertil.schmidt@uni-mainz.de
[2] NVIDIA AI Technology Center, Luxembourg City, Luxembourg
chundt@nvidia.com

Abstract. Dynamic Time Warping (DTW) is a widely used distance measure in the field of time series data mining. However, calculation of DTW scores is compute-intensive since the complexity is quadratic in terms of time series lengths. This renders important data mining tasks computationally expensive even for moderate query lengths and database sizes. Previous solutions to accelerate DTW on GPUs are not able to fully exploit their compute performance due to inefficient memory access schemes. In this paper, we introduce a novel parallelization strategy to drastically speed-up DTW on CUDA-enabled GPUs based on using low latency warp intrinsics for fast inter-thread communication. We show that our CUDA parallelization (cuDTW++) is able to achieve over 90% of the theoretical peak performance of modern Volta-based GPUs, thereby clearly outperforming the previously fastest CUDA implementation (cudaDTW) by over one order-of-magnitude. Furthermore, cuDTW++ achieves two-to-three orders-of-magnitude speedup over the state-of-the-art CPU program UCR-Suite for subsequence search of ECG signals.

Keywords: Data mining · Dynamic Time Warping · GPUs · CUDA

1 Introduction

The rapid growth of recorded data through automated monitoring results in vast quantities of time series with prominent examples including electrocardiograms (ECGs), stock prices, gene activities, and audio signals. Thus, the comparison of time series is an important data mining task with a variety of applications such as database search, clustering, classification, or anomaly detection. When comparing (or aligning) two time series elastic measures such as *Dynamic Time Warping* (DTW) are often preferred to lock-step measures such as Euclidean distance. As a consequence, DTW schemes have been proposed for a variety of tasks [7, 11, 16, 22–24, 27].

© Springer Nature Switzerland AG 2020
M. Malawski and K. Rzadca (Eds.): Euro-Par 2020, LNCS 12247, pp. 597–612, 2020.
https://doi.org/10.1007/978-3-030-57675-2_37

However, the complexity of computing the DTW distance between a pair of time series is proportional to the product of their length. This can result in high execution times for database scans or subsequence searches. Corresponding runtime requirements are expected to become even more severe due to the growing amount of recorded data. As a consequence, parallelization of DTW has been proposed on a variety of architectures including GPUs [4,25], FPGAs [20], Xeon Phis [8], big data clusters [28], and even customized fabrics [26].

However, existing GPU implementations are limited by inefficient memory access schemes and thus cannot fully exploit the performance of modern GPUs. The main contributions of this paper are the design of a novel fine-grained parallelization strategy based on warp intrinsics for DTW targeting massively parallel architectures and their implementation on CUDA-enabled accelerators. We demonstrate that our implementation (cuDTW++) can achieve up to 92% of the available peak performance on Volta-based GPUs in practice. For subsequence search of ECG signals, cuDTW++ achieves over two orders-of-magnitude speedup for short queries and over three orders-of-magnitude speedup for long queries compared to the state-of-the-art CPU code (UCR-Suite [17]). Furthermore, for database scans, cuDTW++ achieves over one order-of-magnitude speedup compared to the previously fastest GPU code (cudaDTW [4]) on the same hardware. Consequently, we are able to reduce corresponding data analysis runtimes drastically enabling researchers to perform exploratory time series analysis in an interactive manner, which makes our approach particular useful for integration in modern accelerated data science frameworks such as RAPIDS [14]. cuDTW++ is publicly available at https://github.com/asbschmidt/cuDTW.

The rest of the paper is organized as follows. Section 2 provides some background about DTW, GPUs, and reviews related work. Section 3 describes our fine-grained parallelization scheme for CUDA-enabled GPUs. Performance is evaluated in Sect. 4. Section 5 concludes the paper.

2   Background

2.1   Dynamic Time Warping

Consider two real-valued time series $Q = (q_0, \ldots, q_i, \ldots, q_{m-1})$ (query) and $S = (s_0, \ldots, s_j, \ldots, s_{n-1})$ (subject) of length m and n, respectively. DTW is a method to measure the similarity of Q and S by means of an elastic assignment of their indices. An example of a DTW alignment of two voice recordings is shown in Fig. 1.

Consider the Cartesian product $\mathcal{I} \times \mathcal{J}$ of the index domains of Q and S; i.e., $\mathcal{I} = \{0, \ldots, m-1\}$ and $\mathcal{J} = \{0, \ldots, n-1\}$. DTW compares Q and S by computing a sequence of index pairs $\gamma := ((i_l, j_l) \in \mathcal{I} \times \mathcal{J})_l$, called a *warping path*. Any considered warping path γ has to fulfill the following conditions:

- The first/last entries of Q and S are matched resulting in a global alignment; i.e. $(i_0, j_0) = (0, 0)$ and $(j_{|\gamma|-1}, j'_{|\gamma|-1}) = (|Q| - 1, |S| - 1)$.

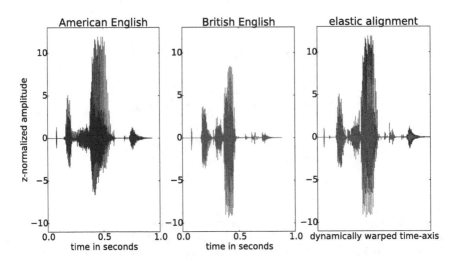

Fig. 1. Example of two voice recordings of the word *exact* in American (left) and British (middle) English. Their optimal DTW alignment is displayed on the right.

- Any two subsequent index pairs have to increment either i, or j, or both indices by 1; i.e. $\min(i_{l+1} - i_l, j_{l+1} - j_l) \geq 0$ and $\max(i_{l+1} - i_l, j_{l+1} - j_l) = 1, \forall l \in \{0, ..., |\gamma| - 2\}$. This means that at each step we either increment the index of the query, the index of the subject, or both.

Furthermore, we define a weight function $w(i, j)$ for each index pair (i, j) by the squared distance of the two corresponding time series values q_i and s_j:

$$w : \mathcal{I} \times \mathcal{J} \to \mathbb{R}_0^+, w(i, j) = (q_i - s_j)^2.$$

The objective of DTW is to find an (the) optimal warping path (score) $\hat{\gamma}$ ($\hat{d}$) out of the set of all valid paths Γ that minimizes the associated accumulated weights; i.e.

$$\hat{\gamma} := \operatorname*{argmin}_{\gamma \in \Gamma} \sum_{(i,j) \in \gamma} w(i, j), \quad \text{and} \quad \hat{d} := \min_{\gamma \in \Gamma} \sum_{(j,j') \in \gamma} w(j, j').$$

In this paper we focus on computing $\hat{d}$ for a large number of DTWs computed in database scans or subsequence search tasks.

This problem can be described in terms of a *directed acyclic graph* (DAG) $G = (V, E)$ with the set of nodes $V = \mathcal{I} \times \mathcal{J}$ and a directed edge between any two nodes (i, j) and (k, l) with $\min(k - i, l - j) \geq 0$ and $\max(k - l, l - j) = 1$. The set of valid warping paths is then equivalent to the set of paths from node $(0, 0)$ to $(m - 1, n - 1)$ in G (see Fig. 2). By associating the weight $w(i, j)$ to each incoming edge of a node (i, j) in G, the problem of finding an optimal warping path can be solved by applying the *single-source shortest path* (SSSP) problem on G with source $(0, 0)$.

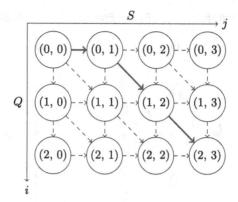

Fig. 2. DAG representation for comparing two time series of length three and four. Nodes are connected by horizontal, vertical, and diagonal edges. Any warping path (e.g. the bold red path) starts in the upper left cell and ends in the lower right cell. (Color figure online)

In practice, computation is achieved by filling a **dynamic programming** (DP) matrix M of size $(m+1) \times (n+1)$ with the relaxation scheme:

$$M[i,j] = w(i-1, j-1) + \min \begin{cases} M[i-1, j] \\ M[i, j-1] \\ M[i-1, j-1] \end{cases} \tag{1}$$

using the initial conditions $M[0,0] = 0$, $M[0,j] = M[i,0] = \infty, 1 \leq i \leq m, 1 \leq j \leq n$. The score of an optimal warping path is then stored in $M[m,n]$ which can be computed in time $\mathcal{O}(m \times n)$. Furthermore, an associated optimal warping path can be determined by a traceback procedure.

2.2 GPU Computing

We briefly review a number of relevant features for GPU computing with the CUDA programming model. CUDA kernels are executed using a number of independent thread blocks. Each thread block is mapped onto exactly one streaming multiprocessor (SM) and consists of a number of warps. All 32 threads within a warp are executed in lock-step fashion (SIMD). CUDA-enabled GPUs contain several types of memory: large but high latency global memory and fast but small on-chip shared and constant memory. Nevertheless, the fastest way to access data is through usage of the thread-local register file. Modern GPUs provide instructions for warp-level collectives [2] in order to efficiently support communication of data stored in registers between threads within a warp without the need for accessing global or shared memory.

A crucial feature of our approach is the usage of warp shuffles for low latency communication and minimization of memory traffic. In particular, we take advantage of the warp-level collectives __shfl_down_sync()

and `__shfl_up_sync()`; e.g. the intra-warp communication operation `R1 = __shfl_up_sync(0xFFFFFFFF, R0, 1, 32);` moves the contents of register `R0` in thread i within each warp to register `R1` in thread $i + 1$ for $0 \leq i < 32$.

2.3 Related Work

The UCR-Suite [17] is the state-of-the-art CPU program for subsequence search that makes excessive use of lower bounds before performing actual DTW calculations. Sart et al. [20] were the first to propose GPU and FPGA parallelizations of DTW. Their approach computes one independent DTW score per CUDA thread for subsequence search tasks. However, their approach is inefficient due to excessive global memory accesses. CS-DTW [15] is based on the same approach but is uses more efficient texture memory by means of shader programming. It reports a speedup of around 30 on a GTX1070 compared to the sequential UCR-suite.

Hundt et al. [4] use a more efficient wavefront parallelization scheme for DTW (called cudaDTW) in order to accelerate the UCR-Suite on GPUs, thereby outperfoming Sart et al. [20] by over one order-of-magnitude. In their approach each CUDA thread block computes one DTW score whereby threads compute cells along a minor diagonal of the DP matrix M in parallel. Data between neighboring diagonals is communicated via shared memory. There are also other algorithms featuring similar data-dependency relationships such as the Smith-Waterman algorithm for pairwise sequence alignment. Previous work in porting this algorithm to GPUs based on wavefront patterns include CUDAlign [19] and CUDASW++ [10]. However, even the state-of-the-art bioinformatics libraries such as NVBIO [13] and AnySeq [12] can only achieve a sequence alignment performance of up to 241 GCUPS (billion cell updates per second) on a Titan V GPU [12].

Our approach is also based on a wavefront pattern but eliminates the need of storing intermediate diagonals in shared memory. We compute one DTW score per (sub)warp (or cooperative group) thereby allowing for fast communication between thread-local registers by means of warp shuffles. We will show in Sect. 4 that we can clearly outperform both cudaDTW and UCR-Suite and can achieve a performance of up to 4.36 TCUPS on two GV100 GPUs.

An alternative approach to parallelize wavefront algorithms has been proposed based on parallel prefix computations [3,25]. However, Xiao et al. [25] are only able to achive a performance of up to 4 GCUPS for DTW on a GTX480 GPU.

3   Parallelization Strategy

We base our approach on computing a DTW score per (**sub**)**warp** – a group of sychnronized CUDA threads executed in lock-step fashion that can also communicate by means of warp-level collectives. Threads in a (sub)warp cooperate to compute all values of a DP matrix M. Note that according to Eq. 1 each cell in M depends on its left, upper, and upper-left neighbour, which means that (parallel) computation of DP cells has to follow this topological order. In order to unlock the full potential of modern GPUs for DTW, we apply the following techniques:

- Full in-register computation of the recurrence relation in Eq. 1.
- Low latency communication of neighbouring DP cells between threads through warp shuffles.
- Replacing frequent loading of time series values from memory by means of a communication scheme based on warp shuffles.
- DP matrix partitioning scheme for large time series sizes
- Integrating a novel early-exit strategy for subsequence search through warp-level collectives and atomic variables.

3.1   Mapping DP Matrix and Time Series to Threads

We compute a DTW score between two time series Q (query) and $S^{(i)}$ (the ith subject sequence) per (sub)warp; i.e., a group of p threads with $p \in \{4, 8, 16, 32\}$ executed in lock step. Different (sub)warps within a CUDA kernel compare the same query to different subject sequences. This is a common requirement in DTW-based data mining tasks such as database classification, anomaly detection, or subsequence search in data streams.

Assume Q of length m and $S^{(i)}$ of length $n = k \cdot p - 1$ are compared by a (sub)warp consisting of p threads $T_0, \ldots, T_{p-1}$. We assign k columns of the DP matrix to be calculated to each thread (see Fig. 3). Computation proceeds along a **wavefront** in $m + p$ iterations: in Iteration i, Thread T_t, calculates k cells of the DP matrix row $i - t$. Virtual cells located outside the DP matrix are initialized with ∞. At the end of the procedure, the final DTW score is stored in the lower right cell of thread T_{p-1}.

Each DP matrix cell depends on its left, upper, and upper-left neighbor (cf. Eq. 1). All cells of the current and previous iteration are stored in thread-local registers. The required access of Thread T_t to the rightmost value of Thread T_{t-1} computed in the previous iteration (see Fig. 3) is accomplished by using the low-latency warp shuffle instruction __shfl_up_sync().

Initially, k values of the subject time series $S_j^{(i)}, t \cdot k - 1 \leq j < t \cdot k + k - 1$, are loaded from global memory by each thread $T_t, 0 \leq t < p$, and stored in registers. While subject values remain constant for each column throughout DP matrix computation, the required values of Q vary. We avoid their expensive reads from memory in each iteration step by using two registers Reg_Q0 and Reg_Q1 as follows. Only in iteration steps $i, 0 \leq i < m + p$ with $i \mod p = 0$ a new value Q_{i+t} is loaded from memory by each Thread t and stored in Reg_Q1. The value of Q actually used for computation by each thread (Q_{i-t-1}) is stored in Reg_Q0. At the beginning of every iteration, both Reg_Q0 and Reg_Q1 are updated by values from neighboring threads, whereby the required communication can be accomplished by the low-latency warp shuffle instruction __shfl_up_sync() for Reg_Q0 and __shfl_down_sync() for Reg_Q1 (see green values in Fig. 3). Before shuffling, the value stored in Reg_Q1 needs to be copied to Reg_Q0 in Thread 0.

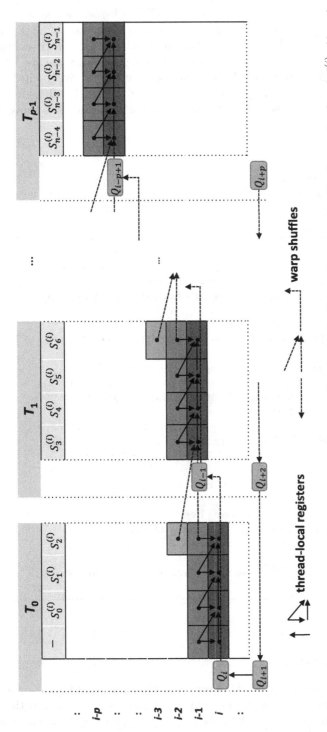

Fig. 3. Example of mapping of a DTW score computation to p threads of a (sub)warp for comparing the time series Q and $S^{(i)}$ of length $n = k \cdot p - 1$ using $k = 4$. Within each iteration 4 cells per thread within a row (red) are calculated using values from the first antecedent row (blue) and an additional value from the second antecedent row (gray). Values in the right column and the required values of Q (green) are communicated between threads by using warp shuffles. Furthermore, one value of $S^{(i)}$ is stored in a thread-local register for each column (yellow). (Color figure online)

The following listing shows pseudocode of a CUDA kernel for the described algorithm where each CUDA thread block consists of a single warp of 32 threads. Template parameters k and p are used define the number of DP matrix columns assigned to each thread and the (sub)warp thread group size. Before kernel execution, we transfer Q to read-only constant memory (cQ[]). Every p iteration steps, we load one query value per thread to register Reg_Q1. By changing the definitions of p and k kernels for the different problem sizes discussed above can be generated.

```
// k = number of DP matrix columns per thread
// p = thread group size (calculate one DIW score per group)
template<int k, int p>
__global__ void DIW(float *subjects, float *scores, int m) {
    float S[k]; // k registers storing subject data
    float M[k]; // k registers storing DP matrix cells
    float M_left, M_diag; // 2 reg. for data from left neighbor
    float Reg_Q0, Reg_Q1; // 2 registers storing query data

    init_DP_matrix(M, M_left, M_diag, k, p);
    load_subject(S, subjects, threadIdx.x, blockIdx.x, k, p);
    // load one query value per thread
    Reg_Q1 = cQ[threadIdx.x%p];
    if (threadIdx.x%p == 0) Reg_Q0=Reg_Q1; else Reg_Q0=INFTY;

    for (int i=1; i<=m+p; i++) { // wavefront loop
        // compute k DP cells per thread using registers only
        update_DP_matrix(M, M_left, M_diag, S, Reg_Q0, k);
        M_diag = M_left;
        // copy rightmost DP cell to neighboring thread
        M_left = __shfl_up_sync(M[k], 1);
        if (threadIdx.x % p == 0) M_left = INFTY;
        // load new query data to register every p iterations
        if (i%p == 0) Reg_Q1 = cQ[i+threadIdx.x%p];
        // shuffle query registers
        Reg_Q0 = __shfl_up_sync(Reg_Q0, 1);
        if (threadIdx.x % p == 0) Reg_Q0=Reg_Q1;
        Reg_Q1 = __shfl_down_sync(Reg_Q1, 1);
    }
    output_DTW_score(M[k], scores, threadIdx.x, blockIdx.x, k, p);
}
```

3.2 Partitioning Scheme

The amount of registers per thread is limited to 256 on modern CUDA-enabled GPUs. This restricts the maximum number of columns assigned to each thread in our parallelization scheme to $k = 64$ in practice, which in turn limits the supported subject time series length to $64 \cdot 32 - 1 = 2047$. Even though this is sufficient for a number of applications, we now present a partitioning scheme for time series of larger size.

Consider a (sub)warp of p threads $(T_0, \ldots, T_{p-1})$ where k DP matrix columns are assigned to each thread and the two time series Q and $S^{(i)}$ to be compared are of length m and $n = l \cdot p \cdot k - 1$ with $l \geq 1$, respectively. We partition the DP matrix into l non-overlapping submatrices of size $(m + 1) \times \frac{(n+1)}{k \cdot p}$ each. Computation proceeds in l stages from left-to-right, where in each stage one submatrix is calculated. In every iteration within each stage the calculated DP cells in the right column of Thread T_{p-1} needs to be saved and loaded by Thread T_0 in the subsequent stage (see Fig. 4). We thus need to store m cells per (sub)warp (which can be re-used for each stage) in memory.

We use shared memory if the amount of required memory for 4 warps does not exceed 64 KB. Otherwise, we use global memory. In case of fast shared memory, we output the calculated right DP cell in T_{p-1} in every iteration step. For high latency global memory, we distribute the DP cells of the right column across threads using warp shuffles and then perform one coalesced write using p threads every p iteration steps. Reading of intermediate values from memory is done in similar fashion.

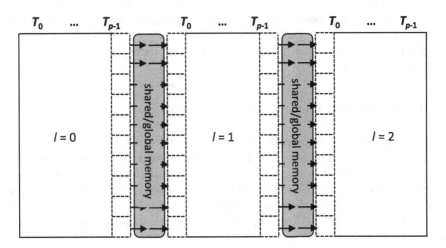

Fig. 4. Example of our partitioning scheme for a subject time series processed in $l = 3$ stages from left-to-right by p threads. Each stage compares the full query to one third of the subject.

3.3 Early Exit Strategy for Subsequence Search

Consider a query Q of length m and a data stream S of length $n \gg m$. Each (sub)warp extracts one of the $n - m + 1$ subsequences of length m –

say $S^{(i)} = (S_i, \ldots, S_{i+m-1})$ – from the stream and initially performs a local z-normalization before calculating the DTW measure between Q and $S^{(i)}$. *Subsequence search* is interested in subsequences with a very low DTW score, which is important for stream monitoring [18] and anomaly detection [6]. Lower bounding techniques are often utilized to prune unpromising candidates. For example, in the UCR-Suite [17] the sum of the optimal alignments of the first and last k entries (e.g. using $k = 3$) of Q and $S^{(i)}$ is included as the first lower bound. If this value exceeds a certain threshold (e.g. the best DTW score computed so far) we can prune the subsequence candidate before computing a full DTW. However, existing pruning methods tend to become ineffective for longer query sizes.

We have incorporated a new early exit strategy within our parallelization scheme presented in Sect. 3.1 for $p = 32$ threads. In iteration steps $i, 0 \leq i < m+p$ with $i \mod p = 0$ we calculate the minimum value of the newly computed DP cells (the red cells in Fig. 3) as a lower bound. If this value exceeds a certain threshold, the DP matrix computation can prematurely terminate (by means of an early exit of the respective warp) since the full DTW score can only be larger than this value. Calculation can be achieved efficiently by determining the minimum within each thread and then using the warp collective `__any_sync()` to check in parallel if any of the local minima is still smaller than the threshold.

The threshold value itself is dynamically updated by the various warps during a subsequence search task. Thus, we have defined it as a system-wide atomic variable (called `bsf` (best-so-far)). Whenever a newly computed DTW score is smaller than `bsf`, the best-so-far value can be updated by using the atomic function `atomicMin`.

4   Performance Evaluation

We have implemented our method (cuDTW++) using CUDA C++ v10.2. The configuration of the workstation with two Volta-based GV100 GPUs used for benchmarking is listed in Table 1. We evaluate the performance of cuDTW++ for database scanning in Sect. 4.1 and for subsequence search of ECG signals in Sect. 4.2 based on single precision floating point data. We evenly distribute the workload between both GPUs by splitting the input database or the input ECG signal into two equal-sized parts.

4.1   Database Scan Performance

For our experiments we generate several instances (databases) of the popular *Cylinder-Bell-Funnel* (CBF) dataset. Each database consists of $N = 2^{19+\frac{2048}{n+1}}$ time series (subjects) of length n each for $n \in \{127, 255, 511, 1023, 2047\}$. CBF is a synthetically created set of time series consisting of three characteristic classes (cylinder, bell, and funnel) using corresponding randomized generator functions [5]. We scan each database using queries of the same length; i.e. a

Table 1. Configuration of the workstation used for benchmarking.

Host System	CPU	Dual Intel Xeon Gold 6238 2.1 GHz, 2 × 22 cores, HT
	RAM	192 GB DDR4
	OS	Ubuntu 18.04.2
CUDA Device	Device	Dual NVIDIA Quadro GV100 (Volta)
	GPU Cores	2 × 5120 SPs @ 1.85 GHz
	DRAM	2 × 32 GB HBM2
Compilers	Host	g++ 7.4.0
	Device	nvcc 10.2.89

query of length n is compared to every subject of length n by computing their pairwise DTW scores.

We evaluate the performance of GPU-based DTW implementations in terms of **Trillion Cell Updates Per Second** (TCUPS). Based on the TCUPS measure, we model the *theoretical peak performance* (TPP) of the utilized GPU hardware as:

$$\text{TPP} = \frac{\#\text{GPUs} \times \#\text{Cores} \times \text{Clock}}{\text{Cycles\_one\_cell\_update}} = \frac{2 \times 5120 \times 1.85 \text{ GHz}}{4} = 4.7 \text{ TCUPS} \quad (2)$$

Cycles_one_cell_update in Eq. 2 models the maximum attainable performance constrained by the algorithm structure. In our case it refers to the minimal number of clock cycles needed by an individual core of the utilized hardware to calculate one DP matrix cell according to Eq. 1. This is determined as 4 on Volta GPUs based on the following SASS assembly instructions: two minimum instructions (`FMNMX`), one subtraction (`FADD`), and one fused multiply-add instruction (`FFMA`).

We first evaluate the impact of varying the value of k (the number of columns assigned to each thread) for a constant number of threads. Measured kernel runtimes are converted into actually achieved TCUPS performance. Efficiency is then determined dividing the achieved performance by TPP. The results are shown in Fig. 5 for $k \in \{1, 2, 4, 8, 16, 32\}$, $p = 32$ threads, and $n \in \{127, 255, 511, 1023\}$. In cases where $k \cdot p < n$, our partitioning scheme presented in Sect. 3.2 is used to calculate the DP matrix in several stages using shared memory for storing intermediate results. The results show that performance constantly improves when increasing k for a constant n. This can be explained by an improved compute-to-communication ratio, i.e., when doubling k the amount of computation per thread also doubles but the overhead for warp shuffling, reading Q-values, and intermediate value I/O for partitioning (cf. Figs. 3 and 4) remains constant. The highest efficiency of 96% is thus achieved for $k = 32$ and $n = 1023$. Further increasing the number of columns assigned to each thread to 64 is still possible but lowers performance; e.g., efficiency drops to 70% for $k = 64, p = 32, n = 2047$ (see Table 2, right column). This can be explained by increased register pressure; i.e., for $k = 64$ there are not enough registers available for storing two rows of the DP matrix (cf. red and blue cells in Fig. 3). Thus, registers need to be re-used by overwriting the DP cells of the previous row, which in turn requires an additional instruction to save values in a temporary register, which decreases efficiency.

Second, we analyze the slowdown caused by our partitioning scheme. From Fig. 5 we can see that efficiency decreases by 16.1% on average when comparing performance of using the same value of k with and without partitioning; i.e. $k = 4 : n = 127$ compared to $n \geq 255$ (grey bars), $k = 8 : n = 255$ compared to $n \geq 511$ (yellow bars), and $k = 16 : n = 511$ compared to $n = 1023$ (dark blue bars).

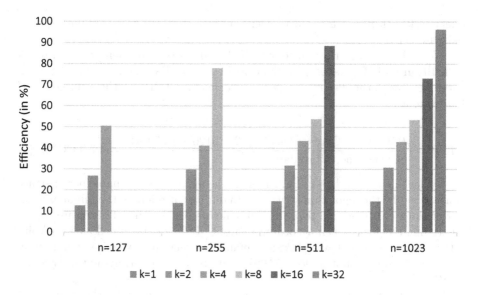

Fig. 5. Efficiency of cuDTW++ kernels for various values of k using a constant number of $p = 32$ threads for different time series lengths n. (Color figure online)

Note that the results shown in Fig. 5 only consider kernel execution times but not data transfers between host and devices. In order to overlap required data transfers over the PCIe bus and CUDA kernel execution, we have implemented a framework using CUDA streams. We have observed that for time series of length $n \geq 1023$ kernel execution times dominate when scanning a database with a single query. However, for smaller lengths ($n \leq 511$) data transfer times become significant. Thus, for these cases we increase the computational load by scanning the same database with a set of 16 different queries.

Furthermore, our parallelization scheme allows for varying the number of threads used per DTW score computation. Thus, we can employ the identified optimal value of $k = 32$ for various time series sizes $n \in \{127, 255, 511, 1023\}$, by setting the number of utilized threads correspondingly to $p = \frac{n+1}{32}$. Table 2 reports the performance and efficiency in comparison to cudaDTW ([4] and §7

Table 2. Performance (in terms of TCUPS) and efficiency of cuDTW++ and cudaDTW for different time series sizes n with corresponding speedups (including data transfers over the PCIe bus).

	Query size	127	255	511	1023	2047
TCUPS (Effic.)	cuDTW++	3.97 (84%)	4.10 (87%)	4.12 (87%)	4.36 (92%)	3.32 (70%)
	cudaDTW	0.25 (5%)	0.282 (6%)	0.285 (6%)	0.282 (5%)	0.272 (6%)
	Speedup	15.9	14.4	14.4	15.5	12.2

Table 3. Runtimes (in seconds) of subsequence search of an ECG signal with $\approx$20 million data points for early-exit cuDTW++, full cuDTW++, and UCR-DTW for different query lengths (averaged over 8 queries). Corresponding speedups of early-exit cuDTW++ compared to full cuDTW++ and UCR-DTW are also reported.

	Query size	127	255	511	1023	2047
Runtime	Early-exit cuDTW++	0.027 s	0.053 s	0.17 s	0.8 s	5.4 s
	Full cuDTW++	0.09 s	0.34 s	1.22 s	4.78 s	25.1 s
	UCR-DTW	3.69 s	23.3 s	455 s	3247 s	30629 s
Speedup	Early-exit to full cuDTW++	3.3	6.4	7.2	6.0	4.6
	Early-exit cuDTW++ to UCR-DTW	137	440	2676	4059	5672

in [21]) executed on the same hardware (also using both GPUs). The average (maximum) speedup achieved by cuDTW++ over cudaDTW is 14.5 (15.9).

4.2 Subsequence Search Performance

For our experiments we search an ECG dataset consisting of approximately 22 hours streamed electrocardiograms ($\approx$20 million data points) using different queries of length $n \in \{127, 255, 511, 1023, 2047\}$. cudaDTW++ is compared to the banded DTW portion of the UCR-Suite (UCR-DTW) running on the CPU (using a band of size 20% of the query length). The comparison is fair because our implementation uses an unbanded (full) version of nearest neighbor DTW search with an effective band width of 100% and thus has a significant lower pruning efficiency than UCR Suite's lower bound cascade. A banded GPU version might perform even better. Note that UCR-DTW is only single-threaded but features a cascade of three early-exit strategies for pruning of unpromising candidates including the reordering of query indices and using warping envelopes. However, we have found that many of these techniques cannot be easily mapped onto a GPU and can also be ineffective for longer queries. As a result, we developed the GPU-friendly early-exit strategy presented in Sect. 3.3.

Table 3 reports the measured execution times (averaged over 8 different queries), which include data transfers over the PCIe bus. We can see that early-exit cuDTW++ is on average 5.5 times faster than the full cuDTW++ version. Furthermore, the average (maximal) speedup achieved by early-exit cuDTW++ compared to UCR-DTW is 2597 (5672). Note that the speedup is constantly increasing with the query size. This shows that the cuDTW++ early-exit strategy is more effective than the lower-bound cascade used by UCR-DTW for longer queries.

5   Conclusion

In this paper we have introduced a fine-grained parallelization strategy for DTW which can achieve close-to-peak performance on modern GPUs. Our approach employs thread-local register files as a cache thereby removing the bottleneck of (global or shared) memory accesses. To communicate data between threads, our scheme relies on low-latency warp-level collectives. Furthermore, we have proposed a corresponding DP matrix partitioning schemes and a suitable early-exit strategy. Our cuDTW++ implementation outperforms state-of-the-art algorithms, namely cudaDTW and the UCR-Suite, by over one order-of-magnitude and over two-to-three orders-of-magnitude, respectively. Thus, our approach allows for fast and interactive processing of exceedingly bigger streams or sets of time series data.

Our parallelization scheme is in general not limited to DTW but is applicable to a wider range of DP-based algorithms. Examples include the Smith-Waterman algorithm for pairwise biological sequence alignment and the Viterbi algorithm for finding (the score of) a most likely sequence of hidden states in a hidden Markov model. It would be interesting to evaluate the performance of our approach when applied to these algorithms. Corresponding codes could also be automatically generated by using DSL tools such as AnyDSL [9] or SSAM [1].

cuDTW++ is publicly available at https://github.com/asbschmidt/cuDTW.

Acknowledgments. We acknowledge support by the BMBF project MetaDL.

References

1. Chen, P., Wahib, M., Takizawa, S., Takano, R., Matsuoka, S.: A versatile software systolic execution model for GPU memory-bound kernels. In: Proceedings of the International Conference for High Performance Computing, Networking, Storage and Analysis, pp. 1–81 (2019)
2. Harris, M., Perelygin, K.: Cooperative groups: flexible CUDA thread programming (2017). https://devblogs.nvidia.com/cooperative-groups/
3. Hou, K., Wang, H., Feng, W.C., Vetter, J.S., Lee, S.: Highly efficient compensation-based parallelism for wavefront loops on GPUs. In: 2018 IEEE International Parallel and Distributed Processing Symposium (IPDPS), pp. 276–285. IEEE (2018)
4. Hundt, C., Schmidt, B., Schömer, E.: CUDA-accelerated alignment of subsequences in streamed time series data. In: 2014 43rd International Conference on Parallel Processing, pp. 10–19. IEEE (2014)
5. Kadous, M.W.: Learning comprehensible descriptions of multivariate time series. In: Bratko, I., Dzeroski, S. (eds.) Proceedings of the 16th International Conference of Machine Learning (ICML-1999), pp. 454–463. Morgan Kaufmann, San Francisco (1999)

6. Keogh, E., Lin, J., Fu, A.: Hot sax: efficiently finding the most unusual time series subsequence. In: Fifth IEEE International Conference on Data Mining (ICDM 2005), p. 8. IEEE (2005)

7. Keogh, E., Ratanamahatana, C.A.: Exact indexing of dynamic time warping. Knowl. Inf. Syst. **7**(3), 358–386 (2004). https://doi.org/10.1007/s10115-004-0154-9

8. Kraeva, Y., Zymbler, M.: Scalable algorithm for subsequence similarity search in very large time series data on cluster of Phi KNL. In: Manolopoulos, Y., Stupnikov, S. (eds.) DAMDID/RCDL 2018. CCIS, vol. 1003, pp. 149–164. Springer, Cham (2019). https://doi.org/10.1007/978-3-030-23584-0_9

9. Leißa, R., et al.: AnyDSL: a partial evaluation framework for programming high-performance libraries. Proc. ACM Program. Lang. **2**(OOPSLA), 1–30 (2018)

10. Liu, Y., Wirawan, A., Schmidt, B.: CUDASW++ 3.0: accelerating Smith-Waterman protein database search by coupling CPU and GPU SIMD instructions. BMC Bioinformatics **14**(1), 117 (2013). https://doi.org/10.1186/1471-2105-14-117

11. Maršík, L., Rusek, M., Slaninová, K., Martinovič, J., Pokorný, J.: Evaluation of chord and chroma features and dynamic time warping scores on cover song identification task. In: Saeed, K., Homenda, W., Chaki, R. (eds.) CISIM 2017. LNCS, vol. 10244, pp. 205–217. Springer, Cham (2017). https://doi.org/10.1007/978-3-319-59105-6_18

12. Müller, A., et al.: AnySeq: a high performance sequence alignment library based on partial evaluation. arXiv preprint arXiv:2002.04561 (2020)

13. Pantaleoni, J., Subtil, N.: NVBIO (2015). https://nvlabs.github.io/nvbio

14. Patterson, J.: Rapids - the platform inside and out (2019). https://docs.rapids.ai/overview/latest.pdf

15. Pietroszek, K., Pham, P., Eckhardt, C.: CS-DTW: real-time matching of multivariate spatial input against thousands of templates using compute shader DTW. In: Proceedings of the 5th Symposium on Spatial User Interaction, pp. 159–159 (2017)

16. Pouw, W., Dixon, J.A.: Gesture networks: introducing dynamic time warping and network analysis for the kinematic study of gesture ensembles. Discourse Process. **57**(4), 301–319 (2019)

17. Rakthanmanon, T., et al.: Searching and mining trillions of time series subsequences under dynamic time warping. In: Proceedings of the 18th ACM SIGKDD International Conference on Knowledge Discovery and Data Mining, pp. 262–270 (2012)

18. Sakurai, Y., Faloutsos, C., Yamamuro, M.: Stream monitoring under the time warping distance. In: 2007 IEEE 23rd International Conference on Data Engineering, pp. 1046–1055. IEEE (2007)

19. Sandes, E.F.O., de Melo, A.C.M.: CUDAlign: using GPU to accelerate the comparison of megabase genomic sequences. In: Proceedings of the 15th ACM SIGPLAN Symposium on Principles and Practice of Parallel Programming, pp. 137–146 (2010)

20. Sart, D., Mueen, A., Najjar, W., Keogh, E., Niennattrakul, V.: Accelerating dynamic time warping subsequence search with GPUs and FPGAs. In: 2010 IEEE International Conference on Data Mining, pp. 1001–1006. IEEE (2010)

21. Schmidt, B., Gonzalez-Dominguez, J., Hundt, C., Schlarb, M.: Parallel Programming: Concepts and Practice. Morgan Kaufmann, Cambridge (2017)

22. Spooner, M., Kulahci, M.: Monitoring batch processes with dynamic time warping and k-nearest neighbours. Chemometr. Intell. Lab. Syst. **183**, 102–112 (2018)

23. Wang, Z., et al.: DTWscore: differential expression and cell clustering analysis for time-series single-cell RNA-seq data. BMC Bioinformatics 18(1), 270 (2017). https://doi.org/10.1186/s12859-017-1647-3

24. Williams, A.H., et al.: Discovering precise temporal patterns in large-scale neural recordings through robust and interpretable time warping. Neuron 105(2), 246–259 (2020)

25. Xiao, L., Zheng, Y., Tang, W., Yao, G., Ruan, L.: Parallelizing dynamic time warping algorithm using prefix computations on GPU. In: 2013 IEEE 10th International Conference on High Performance Computing and Communications & 2013 IEEE International Conference on Embedded and Ubiquitous Computing, pp. 294–299. IEEE (2013)

26. Xu, X., et al.: Accelerating dynamic time warping with memristor-based customized fabrics. IEEE Trans. Comput. Aided Des. Integr. Circuits Syst. 37(4), 729–741 (2017)

27. Zheng, Z., Wei, X., Hildebrandt, A., Schmidt, B.: A computational method for studying the relation between alternative splicing and DNA methylation. Nucleic Acids Res. 44(2), e19–e19 (2016)

28. Ziehn, A., Charfuelan, M., Hemsen, H., Markl, V.: Time series similarity search for streaming data in distributed systems. In: EDBT/ICDT Workshops (2019)

Heterogeneous CPU+iGPU Processing for Efficient Epistasis Detection

Rafael Campos$^{(\boxtimes)}$, Diogo Marques, Sergio Santander-Jiménez, Leonel Sousa, and Aleksandar Ilic

INESC -ID, Instituto Superior Técnico, Universidade de Lisboa, Lisbon, Portugal
{rafael.campos,diogo.marques,sergio.jimenez,las,ilic}@inesc-id.pt

Abstract. Epistasis detection represents a fundamental problem in biomedicine to understand the reasons for occurrence of complex phenotypic traits (diseases) across a population of individuals. Exhaustively examining all possible interactions of multiple Single-Nucleotide Polymorphisms provides the most reliable way to identify accurate solutions, but it is both computationally and memory intensive task. To tackle this challenge, this work proposes a modular and self-adaptive framework for high-performance and energy-efficient epistasis analysis on modern tightly-coupled heterogeneous platforms composed of multicore CPUs and integrated GPUs. To fully exploit the capabilities of these systems, the proposed framework incorporates both task- and data-parallel approaches specifically tailored to enhance single and multiobjective epistasis detection on each device architecture, along with allowing efficient collaborative execution across all devices. The experimental results show the ability of the proposed framework to handle the heterogeneity of an Intel CPU+iGPU system, achieving performance and energy-efficiency gains of up to 5× and 6× in different parallel execution scenarios.

Keywords: Epistasis detection · Heterogeneous computing · Integrated GPU+CPU platforms

1 Introduction

In the last decade, the increasing research focus on Genome-Wide Association Studies (GWAS) resulted in considerable developments in the understanding of human genomics [15]. These studies provide insight into the biological importance of Single-Nucleotide Polymorphisms (SNPs) and their k-order interactions,

This work was supported by Intel Corporation, the FCT (Fundação para a Ciência e a Tecnologia, Portugal) and the ERDF (European Regional Development Fund, EU) through the projects UIDB/50021/2020 and LISBOA-01-0145-FEDER-031901 (PTDC/CCI-COM/31901/2017, HiPErBio). Sergio Santander-Jiménez and Diogo Marques are supported by FCT fellowships under Grants SFRH/BPD/119220/2016 and SFRH/BD/136053/2018.

M. Malawski and K. Rzadca (Eds.): Euro-Par 2020, LNCS 12247, pp. 613–628, 2020.
https://doi.org/10.1007/978-3-030-57675-2_38

known as epistasis. As the variation of interacting SNPs is highly coupled with trait changes in the phenotype of each individual, epistasis analysis represents a fundamental tool to identify the relationship between particular genotypes and the risk of development of complex diseases. While some diseases are correlated to pairwise combinations of SNPs ($k = 2$) [2], other illnesses, such as Alzheimer's and type-2-diabetes, depend on higher-order epistasis ($k > 2$) [14,19]. Since the computational complexity increases exponentially with the interaction order k, due to the higher number of SNP combinations, achieving an efficient execution of this analysis is a challenging task. This is even more demanding when considering multi-objective optimization, which is increasingly being used in state-of-the-art works to improve the accuracy of epistasis detection [4,5,8].

To tackle this issue, the algorithms for epistasis detection can be deployed and optimized in modern processors, with powerful out-of-order cores [5]. On the other hand, the high computational complexity of high-order epistasis and the characteristics of modern processors may lead to a decreased energy-efficiency. An alternative is the utilization of low power devices, such as the integrated Graphics Processing Unit (iGPU) contained in the chip package of modern desktop processors [7]. However, the lower power consumption in these devices comes at the cost of reduced performance. To address this challenge, heterogeneous architectures constituted by multi-core Central Processing Units (CPUs) and an iGPU can be used to balance performance and energy-efficiency. However, it is not trivial to fully exploit the capabilities of these systems. CPUs and iGPU share part of the memory hierarchy, thus, the execution of one device may affect the performance of the other [7]. Furthermore, each device has distinct capabilities and, in order to achieve accurate load balancing and maximize the exploitation of parallelism, the data needs to be carefully partitioned across each device.

State-of-the-art works on epistasis are strongly focused on the performance boosting of optimization algorithms in several devices, such as CPUs [13,16,18], discrete GPUs [6,9], FPGAs [10] and co-processors [17]. Other works propose methods based on machine-learning and evolutionary algorithms [1,4]. Although these stochastic approaches allow high-order epistasis detection, they provide sub-optimal solutions to the problem. On the other hand, exhaustive methods have a deterministic nature that guarantees optimal solutions, at the expense of higher computational restrictions difficult to handle for higher-order epistasis. For these reasons, the work herein proposed focuses on addressing the challenges of exhaustive epistasis detection, in order to attain an efficient execution when targeting SNP interactions of order $k \geq 2$ on single and multi-objective search scenarios. To the best of our knowledge, there are no state-of-the-art works that explore heterogeneous computing at this level of integration (CPU+iGPU) to enhance the performance and energy-efficiency of epistasis detection.

To close this gap, this work proposes a modular and robust framework for single and multi-objective exhaustive epistasis analysis, targeting heterogeneous systems-on-chip with multi-core CPU and iGPU. Moreover, the efficiency of the proposed framework is experimentally assessed in an Intel CPU+iGPU platform, for a range of parallel and single-device execution scenarios, several data-sets with diverse characteristics and for different optimization goals, *i.e.*, performance, power consumption or energy-efficiency. In particular, this work includes the following contributions:

- Parallel algorithms for exhaustive epistasis detection on two different architectures, namely a modern multi-core CPU and a low-power iGPU;
- Configurable execution framework for collaborative single-objective and multi-objective epistasis detection on heterogeneous computing platforms;
- Insights into the performance, energy-efficiency and power consumption trade-offs when performing epistasis detection on modern CPU+iGPU systems.

This paper is structured as follows: Sect. 2 introduces the epistasis detection and its optimization challenges, while Sect. 3 provides algorithm and CPU+iGPU architecture overview. Section 4 describes the proposed framework and device-targeted optimizations, while Sect. 5 presents the experimental results. Section 6 concludes the paper and suggests future research directions.

2   Problem Formulation

The likelihood of certain phenotypic traits, e.g. diseases, is often governed by the joint interaction of different SNPs in the genome of a particular individual. The epistasis detection is targeted at identifying such interactions by processing genotypic information from a case-control data set D of size $N \times (M + 1)$, where N is the number of individual samples and M the number of SNPs under study. Each entry $D[i, j], i \in \{1, ..., N\}, j \in \{1, ..., M\}$ displays the genotypic value observed at the j-th SNP from the i-th sample, represented as 0 (homozygous major allele), 1 (heterozygous allele), or 2 (homozygous minor allele). The disease status y for the i-th sample is stored in the last entry $(D[i, M + 1])$, where $y = 0$ for control samples and $y = 1$ for case samples.

Epistasis procedures often implement optimization engines to identify the combination of k SNPs $x = [x_1, x_2, ..., x_k]$ best supported by some biological criteria, where $x_i \in \{1, ..., M\}$. The number k of SNPs in the combination is designated as 'interaction order' and represents a key element from a computational perspective. When looking for higher-order epistatic interactions ($k > 2$, as in the case of complex diseases), the search space of all possible solutions increases exponentially according to the expression $\frac{M!}{k!(M-k)!}$ [12], thus impacting the times required to conduct accurate experimental campaigns in real-world scenarios.

The approach presented in this paper is aimed at dealing with such complexity issues by exploiting the heterogeneous computing capabilities of CPU+iGPU architectures. Several biological criteria, implemented as objective functions, can be adopted in our proposal. In the present work, two widely-used objective functions have been examined: Bayesian K2 score [11] and Mutual Entropy [3]. Built upon Bayesian network principles, the K2 score can be expressed as:

$$K2 = \sum_{i=1}^{I} \left(\sum_{b=1}^{r_i+1} \log(b) - \sum_{j=1}^{J} \sum_{d=1}^{r_{ij}} \log(d) \right), \tag{1}$$

where I is the number of possible genotypic combinations among k SNPs ($I = 3^k$), J the number of phenotypic states ($J = 2$ in case-control scenarios), r_i the frequency of a certain genotypic combination i at the evaluated SNPs $x = [x_1, x_2, ..., x_k]$, and r_{ij} the number of samples that satisfy the occurrence of the phenotypic state j with the genotypic combination i at the evaluated SNPs. Lower K2 score denote better solution quality.

The second objective function employs information theory concepts to quantify the quality of the evaluated SNP interaction. More specifically, the mutual entropy ME is the reciprocal of the mutual information $I(x, y)$:

$$I(x,y) = \sum_{i=1}^{I} \sum_{j=1}^{J} p(x[i], y[j]) log \frac{p(x[i], y[j])}{p(x[i])p(y[j])}, \qquad (2)$$

where $p(x[i])$ is the probability of observing the genotypic combination i at x, $p(y[j])$ the probability of the phenotypic state j, and $p(x[i], y[j])$ the probability of j under the genotypic combination i. Similarly to the K2 function, candidate solutions with lower ME scores are preferred from a quality perspective.

The proposed heterogeneous strategies are aimed at allowing efficient epistasis detection supporting single-objective and multi-objective searches. While single-objective approaches seek a single optimal solution (attending to the chosen objective function, K2 or ME), a multi-objective search looks for a comprehensive set of non-dominated[1], Pareto-optimal solutions that represent the best trade-offs across the considered objectives (K2 and ME simultaneously).

3   Algorithm – Architecture Overview

This section is devoted to the description of the epistasis search workflow, design strategies, and characterization of the targeted CPU+iGPU architecture. In order to identify the SNPs interactions that best explain the traits in the input data set, a number of well-defined steps must be followed (Fig. 1(a)):

1. Generation of the combination of k interactive SNPs $x = [x_1, x_2, ..., x_k]$ subject to evaluation, given by an integer array for solution encoding purposes.
2. Identification of genotype frequencies across case-control samples in the data set, at the SNPs $x_1, x_2, ..., x_k$.
3. Scoring of the evaluated combination according to the considered objective function (single-objective search) or functions (multi-objective search).
4. Evaluation of the candidate solution:
   (a) Single-objective optimization: the currently evaluated interaction is retained in memory in case it improves the objective score of the best solution identified in previous iterations of the search.

---

[1] Given two solutions s_1 and s_2 and n objective functions $\boldsymbol{f}(s) = [f_1(s), ..., f_n(s)]$, s_1 dominates s_2 iff 1) $\forall\ i \in [1, 2, ..., n]$, $f_i(s_1)$ is not worse than $f_i(s_2)$ and 2) $\exists\ i \in [1, 2, ..., n]$ such that $f_i(s_1)$ is better than $f_i(s_2)$. Those solutions that are not dominated by any other candidate compose the Pareto-optimal set. The representation of this set in the objective space is commonly designated as Pareto front.

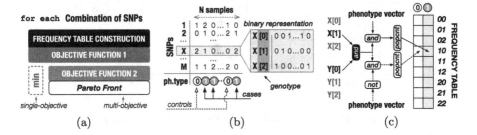

Fig. 1. General overview of epistasis detection: a) exhaustive search steps; b) binarized data set representation; c) frequency table construction.

(b) Multi-objective optimization: the currently evaluated interaction is stored in the Pareto set (front) in case it is not dominated by any other previous solution kept in the set. All the solutions in the set that are dominated by the new interaction are consequently removed.

These steps are performed for each possible combination of k sorted, non-repeated SNPs. In a single-objective search, the combination with minimal objective score represents the most supported solution. On the other hand, a multi-objective search returns the combinations that compose the Pareto-optimal set.

According to these steps, the representation and efficient processing of the input case-control data set represents a major concern to boost the performance of epistasis detection. The input data matrix can contain thousands of SNPs and samples, potentially resulting in high memory requirements. This can lead to an increased contention in shared memory resources of modern processors, thus reducing application performance. Since the range of genotypic values that a SNP can take is limited to three (0, 1 or 2), this issue can be mitigated by compressing the data. This is attained by binarizing the data matrix, *i.e.*, each element is codified in individual bits of a larger data element, *i.e.*, a 32-bit integer, as illustrated in Fig. 1(b). By using the binary encoding, each SNP is represented with three binary vectors (with indexes 0, 1 and 2), one for each genotypic value. Each bit in the vector reflects the presence (1) or absence (0) of a genotypic value the processed sample exhibits at the considered SNP. The disease status array is also binarized.

In the proposed work, the computations performed to calculate objective scores use a frequency table as support, where the instances of all possible genotypic combinations for the evaluated SNP interaction are accounted. This frequency table has 3^k rows, where k is the interaction order, and two columns, one per disease state, as presented in Fig. 1(c). To construct this table, the bitwise operations AND, NOT and POPCOUNT (POPCNT) are used to extract from the binary data the information required by each objective function. As shown in Fig. 1(c) for $k = 2$ and two SNPs X and Y, a bitwise AND is performed between the binarized data elements X[1] and Y[0] to calculate the observations of the genotypic combination '10' across samples. After this step, AND and

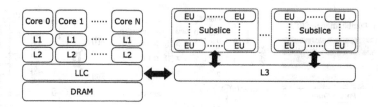

Fig. 2. General heterogeneous CPU+iGPU architecture.

AND+NOT operations are performed between this intermediate result and the disease status, resulting in two arrays that identify which observations belong to cases and which ones to controls. Finally, the POPCNT is performed over the two arrays and the frequency table is updated in the position corresponding to the considered genotype combination. Once the frequency table is filled, the objective scores can be computed by using the expressions in Eqs. 1 and 2.

In order to enhance epistasis searches through parallelism (namely targeting the parallel processing of independent SNP combinations and the data parallelism exhibited by frequency calculations), this work explores heterogeneous CPU+iGPU systems. Since each device has distinct hardware specifics, it is necessary to analyze their micro-architectures to understand the implementation scenarios that benefit the most from CPU and iGPU capabilities.

As shown in Fig. 2, modern processors are complex systems-on-chip containing several CPU cores and iGPU. In particular, CPU cores are equipped with powerful out-of-order engines that support diverse instruction types, including vector instructions to handle multiple computations per instruction, leading to higher performance. The vector length varies according to the micro-architecture, e.g., Intel processors may support 128-bit, 256-bit or even 512-bit AVX instructions. The CPU memory hierarchy usually encapsulates two private caches (L1 and L2), and shared memory levels: LLC and DRAM. Data sharing between cores is performed through the ring interconnect, which also provides a communication interface between the CPU LLC and the iGPU L3 cache, allowing data transfer between them.

The iGPU micro-architecture is organized in several slices, each formed by subslices, as illustrated in Fig. 2. The subslices consist on a set of Execution Units (EUs) containing the Arithmetic Logic Units (ALUs) and FP units that also perform vector instructions. These EUs handle several threads simultaneously, in order to exploit data-level parallelism. The subslices have access to the shared L3 cache, and also contain private L1 and L2 caches (reserved for sampling tasks, thus not used for general-purpose computing). The presence of an iGPU in the processor package and its sharing of the memory subsystem differentiates it from discrete GPUs. While discrete GPUs have its own dedicated memory, iGPUs share the memory subsystem with the CPU, which reduces the impact of data transfers between the two devices. When executing memory-intensive tasks, such as epistasis detection, this allows to fully extract the potential of the

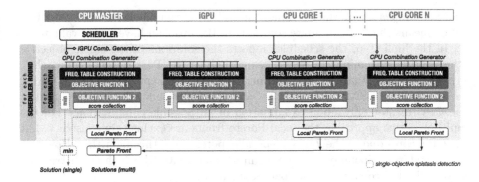

Fig. 3. Framework for heterogeneous exhaustive epistasis detection.

heterogeneous architecture. The application performance can be further improved by reducing its memory footprint (*e.g.* by binarizing the data set).

Due to the micro-architectural differences between CPU and iGPU, the heterogeneous implementation of epistasis detection algorithms should rely on different programming models that allow to fully exploit the properties of each device type, including their memory and compute resources. In the scope of this work, OpenMP is used for the CPU to efficiently distribute work across the multi-core processor, achieving task-level parallelism. For the iGPU, OpenCL was chosen, an often employed and highly optimized programming model that explores the compute abilities of these highly parallel devices. This can be explored to offload the iGPU kernels and exploit data-level parallelism in this application.

4   Heterogeneous Framework for Epistasis Detection

To achieve an efficient and collaborative search for optimal epistasis solutions in tightly-coupled multi-core CPU+iGPU systems, this work proposes a heterogeneous framework, presented in Fig. 3, that uses task and data-level parallelism as a mean to exploit the full potential of CPUs and iGPU, not only for performance, but also for power consumption and energy-efficiency.

In the proposed framework, the CPU master thread, *i.e.*, the scheduler, is responsible for assuring the load balancing by distributing different amount of combinations to be processed at the iGPU and all CPUs cores (including the scheduler). Besides the total number of combinations, each CPU core also receives the initial SNP combination number, which is used by the CPU combination generators to locally determine the next combination to be processed. At the CPU master, the iGPU kernel is enqueued and the iGPU combination generator creates a buffer containing the SNP combinations to be offloaded for the iGPU processing. While the iGPU performs these combinations, the scheduler enqueues the next iGPU kernel and refills the combination buffer with the next combinations to be processed. Some SNP combinations are also attributed to the scheduler, in order to maximize the utilization of the CPU cores. This process is repeated by the scheduler until all SNP combinations are exhausted, which means that all candidate solutions to the problem have been evaluated.

In the final step, the scheduler reports the solutions of the single-objective (the solution with minimum score) or multi-objective (Pareto front) approaches. It is worth to note that the local optimum solutions are kept at each device during the processing of SNP combinations, and the final solution(s) are produced at the CPU master only upon examination of all possible combinations. For the multi-objective approach, the local Pareto fronts are exclusively constructed at the CPU cores due to the low data-parallel potential of this algorithm. However, these local fronts include the scores computed at the iGPU, which are distributed across all CPU cores to ensure load balancing.

Due to its modular design, the proposed framework can be divided in distinct modules, each representing a processing element of the heterogeneous implementation of the algorithm presented in Sect. 3.

4.1 Multi-core CPU Parallelization and Vectorization

To exploit the task-level parallelism of multi-core CPUs, OpenMP is used to allow for the SNP combinations evaluation among the available threads. As shown in Fig. 3, after receiving the number of combinations and the initial SNP combination from the scheduler, each CPU core proceeds with the frequency table construction. To fully exercise the data-level parallel processing capabilities offered by modern CPUs, vectorization techniques are applied at this processing stage, which is accomplished by using the SIMD instructions supported by the CPU micro-architecture. For example, Intel 8th generation CPUs have AVX instructions, which can be employed to perform bitwise operations required by the algorithm, *i.e.*, AND and AND+NOT operations presented in Fig. 1(c) (see Sect. 3), using up to 256-bit wide vectors. In this case, the AND operation is performed with the _mm256_and_si256 intrinsic, while AND+NOT operation is also implemented by a single intrinsic instruction, *i.e.*, _mm256_andnot_si256, allowing to compute AND+NOT for 256-bit wide data in a single clock cycle. As the POPCOUNT operation is not available as an intrinsic Intel 256-bit AVX instruction, it is implemented using the _popcnt64 instruction on 64-bit data.

After the frequency table construction, the scores of the *Objective Function 1* (and *Objective Function 2* for the multi-objective algorithm) are calculated, as illustrated in Fig. 3. For the considered objective functions, *i.e.*, K2 score and Mutual Entropy, it is necessary to perform calculations based on the natural and base-2 logarithms, respectively. Since logarithm operations are computationally intensive, their repeated utilization may potentially lead to significant performance degradation (especially due to a high probability of recalculating the same logarithm value when evaluating a large set of SNP combinations). To overcome this issue, in the proposed work, look-up tables were employed to store and reuse the values for the logarithms. To reduce the memory impact of the look-up tables, their size is kept small, thus it is only needed to compute the values that surpass the maximum table size. Moreover, to increase the performance of the K2 score, the $\log(n!)$ function is replaced by a gamma function, a less computationally demanding alternative that removes the need to compute factorials. To limit the size of the look-up table while maintaining accuracy in the solutions, the gamma function is only used for higher values of n. For low n values, the look-up table is accessed to obtain $\log(n!)$.

After the score calculation, the best local solution or the partially composed Pareto set are stored locally in each thread, to minimize the communication costs between threads. This process is repeated until each CPU core has finished evaluating all the attributed SNP combinations. When all threads have finished this stage, the globally optimal solutions, i.e., a solution with the minimum score for the single-objective or Pareto-optimal set for the multi-objective approach, are constructed by the scheduler thread.

4.2 iGPU Implementation

The iGPU implementation explores the capabilities of the OpenCL programming model to offload work to the accelerator. The kernel function is defined to contain all operations related to the evaluation of a SNP combination through the building of the frequency table and calculation of objective function(s). The combinations to be evaluated by different work-items are provided in a buffer, which is created in the *iGPU Combinations Generator* module at the CPU master thread, as shown in Fig. 3. Each work-item in the iGPU independently processes the assigned SNP combinations, in parallel with the remaining work-items, in order to explore the data-parallel potential of this architecture.

Similarly to the CPU implementation, frequency table construction is implemented with vectorized instructions and specific OpenCL vector data types, thus employing the vector functional units contained in the iGPU EUs to maximize the overall performance. For example, each EU in Intel Gen9.5 iGPU supports 128-bit wide instructions [7], thus uint4 data type is used, which corresponds to four 32-bit unsigned integers. By using these data types, the AND and NOT operators are vectorized, along with the POPCOUNT operation used in the proposed algorithm. After filling the frequency table, the scores of the objective functions are calculated by using the look-up tables and gamma function, similar to the procedure elaborated in the CPU implementation. The look-up tables are built by the CPU master and transferred to the iGPU before kernel execution.

For single-objective optimization, the minimum solutions are kept locally (in the iGPU L3 cache) on a per work-item basis, and communicated back to the CPU master only when all SNP combinations of the data-set are examined. This process is described in pseudo-code in Fig. 4. The combination (comb) to be processed by the specific work-item (identified by id) is obtained from the combs array and its score is computed with the get_score() function. This value is compared to the local best score and solution, which is updated if necessary. To compute the score, the kernel iterates through the patients (n_patients in total), filling the frequency table ft (with 3^k rows and 2 columns), using logical operations (AND, NOT and POPCOUNT) with the SNP and disease state (state). Following this, the final score for the combination is obtained by applying the objective function (represented by obj_function()).

```
kernel(combs, scores, solutions)        get_score(comb)
{                                       {
    id = work_item_id()                     for(j = 0:n_patients)
    comb = combs[id]                        for(i = 0:3^k){
    score = get_score(comb)                     for(x = 0:k)
    if(score < scores[id])                          res &= SNP[comb[x]][j]
    {                                           ft[i][0] += popc(res & ~state[j])
        scores[id] = score                      ft[i][1] += popc(res & state[j])
        solutions[id] = comb                }
    }                                       return obj_function(ft)
}                                       }
```

Fig. 4. Pseudo-code for the iGPU kernel computing the score for a given combination of SNPs.

In the case of multi-objective optimization, the two scores are computed in the iGPU within each work-item and distributed to the CPU cores for the local Pareto front construction, as previously referred. It is worth emphasizing that the involvement of CPU cores for generating combinations, Pareto fronts and look-up table is crucial for attaining the high performance execution on iGPU, due to the low potential for data-level parallelization of these routines that involve a high amount of complex control statements, as it will be shown in Sect. 5.

4.3 Execution Orchestration for Multi-core CPU+iGPU Processing

As previously referred (see Fig. 3), the scheduler in the CPU master is responsible for distributing workload among the processing entities, *i.e.*, iGPU and CPU cores. Additionally, the scheduler also participates in the evaluation of SNP combinations, in order to fully exploit the multi-core CPU capabilities.

To attain an efficient data distribution across the devices, dynamic load balancing is applied with the goal of minimizing potential idle times at the CPU and iGPU sides. While the SNP combinations handled by the iGPU are performed in several rounds with the fixed amount of work-items per kernel invocation, the combinations evaluated in the CPU threads (in each scheduling round) is defined as $N_{CPU} = \frac{N_{iGPU}}{P_{iGPU}} \times P_{CPU}$, where N_{iGPU} is the number of SNP combinations assigned to the iGPU, while P_{iGPU} and P_{CPU} denote the measured performance of the iGPU and CPU, respectively (both assessed during the algorithm run-time to ensure self-adaptive nature of the proposed framework).

In the case of single-objective evaluation, the CPU master is responsible for performing the final reduction stage on the local optimum solutions encountered at each processing entity, thus determining the final optimal epistasis solution. For multi-objective optimization, this reduction stage consists on building the final Pareto front from the partial fronts built by the remaining CPU cores.

5 Experimental Results

In order to evaluate the benefits and drawbacks of the proposed heterogeneous framework for single and multi-objective epistasis detection on CPU+iGPU, its performance, energy-efficiency and power consumption needs to be compared and evaluated against different implementations and configurations. With this aim, four main comparative execution scenarios are considered, *i.e.*: the baseline CPU algorithm presented in Sect. 3 (Popcnt), its vectorized CPU implementation (Popcnt_Vec), execution of the search in the iGPU alone (iGPU), and execution in the iGPU with the CPU running only the scheduler thread (Sched).

The iGPU execution scenario was included to characterize the iGPU when working as a single device, which implied placing the operations necessary to iterate through combinations in an iterating kernel executing in the iGPU. Additionally, single-objective optimization is performed for the considered two objective functions, *i.e.*, K2 score and Mutual Entropy, separately.

5.1   Experimental Setup

The experimental platform involves an Intel i7-8700K processor and the Gen9.5 iGPU, following the architecture described in Sect. 3. This system has 32 GB of DRAM and runs Linux-based CentOS 7.5, with OpenCL 2.1 NEO drivers, version 19.34.13959. The CPU was kept at its base frequency of 3.7 GHz, and the number of OpenMP threads defined for execution was equal to the number of cores (6), and each thread was bound to a single core. The applications were compiled using ICC, version 19.0.5.281, with O3 optimization enabled. For the iGPU, the number of OpenCL work-items chosen was the same across all configurations of the framework, while the work-group dimension was defined as the maximum allowed in this iGPU, *i.e.*, 256 work-items. As work-items in the same group reside in the same subslice, the total number of work-items was defined as a multiple of $3 \times 256 = 768$. The value chosen was 76800 work-items, as this amount was experimentally determined to lead to better performance across the different test cases, *i.e.*, varying number of samples, SNPs and epistasis orders.

To perform an experimental evaluation for diverse amounts of SNPs and individual samples, three data sets from [5] are considered in this work, namely: small data set, with 23 SNPs and 10000 samples; medium data set, with 1000 SNPs and 4000 samples; large data set, with 31339 SNPs and 146 samples. Five individual tests were performed for each application implementation, for the epistasis orders $k = 2$ and $k = 3$.

Performance is reported as the amount of operations executed per second (OPS/s), while the energy-efficiency corresponds to the amount of operations per joule (OPS/J). For all the test cases considered in this work, the number of operations, OPS, is defined as $OPS = nCr(M, k) \times N$, where M is the number of SNPs, k the interaction order, N the number of individual samples, and $nCr(n, k)$ the number of k-combinations in a set of n items. The power consumption (W) and consumed energy are obtained through the RAPL interface, which allows the measurement of the energy consumption in the package (CPU and iGPU), iGPU and CPU cores. For all versions the package power was considered, except for the iGPU version, where the iGPU power is evaluated instead.

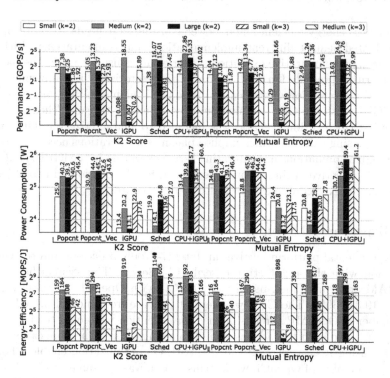

Fig. 5. Performance, power consumption and energy-efficiency results for single-objective configurations.

5.2   Single-Objective Evaluation

As a first step, the results obtained for the single-objective configurations are analyzed, aiming at determining the characteristics of each implementation depending on the execution scenario and input data set. Figure 5 contains the results for single-objective optimization. The performance and energy-efficiency units presented in the plots (OPS/s and OPS/J) were chosen to facilitate comparisons across different tests, as the time and energy results vary greatly, with the small data set having very short execution times and reduced energy consumption, and the larger tests executing in minutes, with large energy consumption. This is mainly due to the epistasis order, since the number of SNP combinations to be processed vastly increases with it, making the tests increase in complexity. For example, the number of SNP combinations for the medium data set increases from 4.99×10^5 with $k = 2$ to 1.66×10^8 with $k = 3$, which results in greatly increased average execution times (from 145 ms to 168 s) and average energy consumption (from 5 J to 6801 J). For the large data set (resulting in a total of 4.91×10^8 SNP combinations for $k = 2$), the average execution time was of 312 s, and the average consumed energy was 4295 J. The tests with the small data set have average execution time of 17 ms and average consumed energy of 383 mJ.

As can be observed, except for the simplest data set and epistasis order of $k = 2$, *i.e.*, small ($k = 2$), the CPU+iGPU architecture corresponds to the highest performance for the remaining test cases. For the small ($k = 2$) test, the amount of combinations to process is very small, which does not allow to fully exploit the data-level parallelism provided by the iGPU. For this test, Popcnt_Vec achieves the maximum performance for both objective functions across all execution scenarios. Moreover, by comparing Popcnt and Popcnt_Vec across all tests, it is possible to conclude that the use of vectorization leads to performance increases of up to 79%, in the case of the medium data set ($k = 2$).

On the other hand, executing solely on the iGPU leads to worse performance in all tests except for the medium data set. For this test, the iGPU scenario registered higher performance than Popcnt_Vec for $k = 2$ and $k = 3$. This behavior mainly occurs due to the execution time of the iterating kernel of the iGPU. According to the GPU Hotspots analysis in Intel VTune Amplifier, for $k = 2$, it takes 0.1 ms for the small data set (1 execution), 7 ms for the medium data set (7 executions), and 240 ms for the large data set (6395 executions). This indicates that the architecture of the iGPU is not suited for performing nested conditional statements and loops such as the ones necessary to iterate through combinations of SNPs, as the execution time grows exponentially with the number of SNPs. The number of iterating kernel executions also indicates that the medium data set makes full use of the iGPU data parallelism, while the small data set is not able to use all available work-items, as it only needs 1 execution to complete its work, resulting in lower performance.

Regarding the power consumption results, it can be observed that Popcnt_Vec has higher power consumption than Popcnt, due to the use of 256-bit vector execution units. The iGPU scenario reports the lowest power consumption values. This result is expected given the fact that this device operates in more strict power requirements than the CPU cores. Following it, the Sched scenario presents lower power consumption values than the remaining, which is explained by it only utilizing one CPU core with the scheduler thread and the iGPU. This same reason explains the highest power consumption registered for the CPU+iGPU fully operating simultaneously.

When comparing energy efficiency results, the Popcnt_Vec and Popcnt scenarios present higher efficiency than the iGPU operating by itself in all tests except for the medium data set, which is the same trend followed in the performance results, where the iGPU showed greater performance in these tests. This indicates that although the strategies operating in the CPU require more power, they compensate for it when it comes to energy efficiency, due to lower execution times. This correlation between high performance and high energy-efficiency is also observed when comparing just Popcnt_Vec and Popcnt, with the former having up to 60% higher energy-efficiency (medium data set, $k = 2$), despite the higher power-consumption values. Regardless, the energy-efficiency is highest for the Sched scenario, due to its high performance and especially low power consumption, whereas CPU+iGPU has lower energy-efficiency due to its high power values.

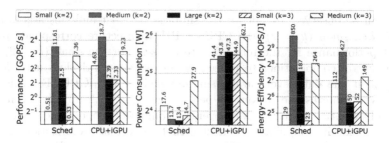

Fig. 6. Performance, Power consumption and energy-efficiency results for multiobjective heterogeneous configurations.

All performance, power or energy results are consistent through the two different objective functions, demonstrating that the differences between methods used to compute the K2 and ME scores are negligible for performance or energy.

5.3   Multi-objective Evaluation

The results obtained for the multi-objective configurations are presented in Fig. 6, focusing the comparisons with the Sched execution scenario. The average execution times for the medium data set are of 133 ms and 79 s, for $k = 2$ and $k = 3$ respectively. The same tests have energy consumption of 3 and 3280 J. For the large data set $(k = 2)$, the average execution time is 18 s, and the average consumed energy is 374 J. Both tests with the small data have low execution times and energy consumption, in average 16 ms and 276 mJ, respectively.

Performance-wise, the CPU+iGPU proposal presents better results in all tests, similarly to the single-objective configurations. The Sched approach presents lower performance values, with the largest difference in performance being observed for the test with the large data set. This difference is due to the fact that the build of the Pareto front with the results from the iGPU is done only in the master thread in the Sched scenario, while in CPU+iGPU this task is divided across the processing threads, minimizing the workload and leaving the master thread available to send work for the iGPU as soon as it is available. The power and energy results herein shown are similar to the results for the heterogeneous single-objective versions, with the added CPU cores used for processing in the CPU+iGPU proposal increasing power consumption and decreasing energy-efficiency.

In summary, the attained results demonstrate the benefits in performance and energy efficiency when using heterogeneous strategies for exhaustive epistasis analysis. While the CPU or iGPU only provide advantage in specific tests, as is the case of the medium data set for the iGPU, the heterogeneous configurations, especially CPU+iGPU, show consistently better parallel performance in overall terms. The power consumption and energy-efficiency results are generally better for the Sched approach, as CPU+iGPU uses all CPU cores and the iGPU, while the Sched scenario uses only the iGPU and a single CPU thread, which in most cases leads to an energy efficiency advantage. These results are consistent when using a multi-objective method with the K2 and ME scores.

6 Conclusions

Epistasis detection is a fundamental GWAS research topic aimed at identifying interactive SNPs responsible for complex traits, with significant applications in biology and human health. In this context, exhaustive search methods are adopted to provide accurate solutions to the problem, at the cost of higher complexity, especially for high interaction orders. To tackle this issue, this work proposed a heterogeneous framework for efficient exhaustive epistasis detection in multi-core CPU+iGPU systems. The proposed framework considers both single and multi-objective optimization, based on the K2 score and Mutual Entropy objective functions. To fully exploit the potential of each device, OpenMP and OpenCL programming models were used and the adaptive scheduling was employed to attain efficient collaborative execution across several CPU cores and iGPU. The experimental evaluation shows that the proposed framework allows attaining performance and energy-efficiency gains of 5× and 6×, respectively, for different data sets and execution scenarios. Future directions involve the extension of the framework for other hybrid architectures, e.g., CPU+FPGA and/or different CPU+iGPU systems, as well as the evaluation of performance and energy-efficiency benefits when applying dynamic voltage and frequency scaling.

References

1. Che, K., et al.: Epistasis detection using a permutation-based gradient boosting machine. In: 2016 IEEE International Conference on Bioinformatics and Biomedicine (BIBM), pp. 1247–1252. IEEE (2016)
2. Dinu, I., et al.: SNP-SNP interactions discovered by logic regression explain Crohn's disease genetics. PloS One **7**(10), e43035 (2012)
3. Fan, R., et al.: Entropy-based information gain approaches to detect and to characterize gene-gene and gene-environment interactions/correlations of complex diseases. Genet. Epidemiol. **35**(7), 706–721 (2011)
4. Gallego-Sánchez, D., et al.: Parallel multi-objective optimization for high-order epistasis detection. In: Ibrahim, S., Choo, K.K.R., Yan, Z., Pedrycz, W. (eds.) ICA3PP 2017. LNCS, vol. 10393, pp. 523–532. Springer, Cham (2017). https://doi.org/10.1007/978-3-319-65482-9_38
5. Gonçalves, F., et al.: Parallel evolutionary computation for multiobjective gene interaction analysis. J. Comput. Sci. **40**(101068), 1–15 (2020)
6. González-Domínguez, J., Schmidt, B.: GPU-accelerated exhaustive search for third-order epistatic interactions in case-control studies. J. Comput. Sci. **8**, 93–100 (2015)
7. Intel Corporation: The Compute Architecture of Intel® Processor Graphics Gen9 (2015)
8. Jing, P.J., Shen, H.B.: MACOED: a multi-objective ant colony optimization algorithm for SNP epistasis detection in genome-wide association studies. Bioinformatics **31**(5), 634–641 (2015)

9. Joubert, W., et al.: Attacking the opioid epidemic: determining the epistatic and pleiotropic genetic architectures for chronic pain and opioid addiction. In: SC18: International Conference for High Performance Computing, Networking, Storage and Analysis, pp. 1–57. IEEE (2018)

10. Kässens, J.C., et al.: High-speed exhaustive 3-locus interaction epistasis analysis on FPGAs. J. Comput. Sci. **9**, 131–136 (2015)

11. Li, X., et al.: Nature-inspired multiobjective epistasis elucidation from genome-wide association studies. IEEE/ACM T. Comput. Biol. (2018). https://doi.org/10.1109/TCBB.2018.2849759

12. Ritchie, M.D.: Finding the epistasis needles in the genome-wide haystack. In: Moore, Jason H., Williams, Scott M. (eds.) Epistasis. MMB, vol. 1253, pp. 19–33. Springer, New York (2015). https://doi.org/10.1007/978-1-4939-2155-3_2

13. Schüpbach, T., et al.: FastEpistasis: a high performance computing solution for quantitative trait epistasis. Bioinformatics **26**(11), 1468–1469 (2010)

14. Sun, J., et al.: Hidden risk genes with high-order intragenic epistasis in alzheimer's disease. J. Alzheimer's Dis. **41**(4), 1039–1056 (2014)

15. Visscher, P.M., et al.: 10 years of GWAS discovery: biology, function, and translation. Am. J. Hum. Genet. **101**(1), 5–22 (2017)

16. Wan, X., et al.: Boost: a fast approach to detecting gene-gene interactions in genome-wide case-control studies. Am. J. Hum. Genet. **87**(3), 325–340 (2010)

17. Weeks, N.T., et al.: High-performance epistasis detection in quantitative trait gwas. Int. J. High Perform. Comput. Appl. **32**(3), 321–336 (2018)

18. Yang, C., et al.: SNPHarvester: a filtering-based approach for detecting epistatic interactions in genome-wide association studies. Bioinformatics **25**(4), 504–511 (2009)

19. Yang, J.K., et al.: Interactions among related genes of renin-angiotensin system associated with type 2 diabetes. Diab. Care **33**(10), 2271–2273 (2010)

SYCL-Bench: A Versatile Cross-Platform Benchmark Suite for Heterogeneous Computing

Sohan Lal[1](✉), Aksel Alpay[2], Philip Salzmann[3], Biagio Cosenza[4],
Alexander Hirsch[3], Nicolai Stawinoga[1], Peter Thoman[3], Thomas Fahringer[3],
and Vincent Heuveline[2]

[1] Technical University of Berlin, Berlin, Germany
sohan.lal@tu-berlin.de
[2] Heidelberg University, Heidelberg, Germany
[3] University of Innsbruck, Innsbruck, Austria
[4] University of Salerno, Fisciano, Italy

Abstract. The SYCL standard promises to enable high productivity in heterogeneous programming of a broad range of parallel devices, including multicore CPUs, GPUs, and FPGAs. Its modern and expressive C++ API design, as well as flexible task graph execution model give rise to ample optimization opportunities at run-time, such as the overlapping of data transfers and kernel execution. However, it is not clear which of the existing SYCL implementations perform such scheduling optimizations, and to what extent. Furthermore, SYCL's high level of abstraction may raise concerns about sacrificing performance for ease of use. Benchmarks are required to accurately assess the performance behavior of high-level programming models such as SYCL. To this end, we present SYCL-Bench, a versatile benchmark suite for device characterization and run-time benchmarking, written in SYCL. We experimentally demonstrate the effectiveness of SYCL-Bench by performing device characterization of the NVIDIA TITAN X GPU, and by evaluating the efficiency of the hipSYCL and ComputeCpp SYCL implementations.

Keywords: SYCL benchmarks · Heterogeneous computing · SYCL runtime · Cross platform

1 Introduction

The pursuit of high performance and energy efficiency led to the emergence of heterogeneous computing, where different parts of an application benefit from specialized hardware better suited for the problem. Hardware accelerators such as GPUs, FPGAs, and many-core CPUs are used as co-processors resulting in heterogeneous architectures. To achieve optimal performance, such hardware typically also requires dedicated code paths. However, existing programming models either lack industry support, are specific to certain vendors (such as NVIDIA's CUDA), or too low level and cumbersome to use (e.g. OpenCL) to

© Springer Nature Switzerland AG 2020
M. Malawski and K. Rzadca (Eds.): Euro-Par 2020, LNCS 12247, pp. 629–644, 2020.
https://doi.org/10.1007/978-3-030-57675-2_39

find universal adoption. SYCL [12] is a recent, royalty-free open standard published by the Khronos Group intended for programming a wide range of heterogeneous architectures. Its high-level single-source programming model combines the portability of OpenCL with modern C++ constructs and idioms. Mundane tasks such as scheduling, data management, and synchronization are handled implicitly by the SYCL runtime, increasing programmer productivity. While the SYCL runtime may automatically perform optimizations such as overlapping data transfers and kernel executions, it is not apparent whether any particular implementation actually employs such optimizations for a given code pattern. As SYCL is a recent standard, to the best of our knowledge only individual benchmarks exist to evaluate the different implementations, whereas a cross-platform benchmark suite has not yet been proposed. We present *SYCL-Bench*[1], a versatile benchmark suite written in SYCL. The main goal of SYCL-Bench is to evaluate the performance of both devices and different SYCL implementations. To this end, SYCL-Bench not only contains benchmarks to characterize hardware, but also SYCL-specific benchmarks that present optimization opportunities to the SYCL runtime and test how well a particular implementation capitalizes on those opportunities. In summary, we make the following main contributions:

- We present the first benchmark suite designed specifically for SYCL: SYCL-Bench includes 62 codes suited for hardware characterization and 9 codes to evaluate SYCL-specific runtime features.
- The benchmark suite models various use cases and enables detailed evaluation of different SYCL implementations and their optimization strategies, thereby facilitating adoption and further development of SYCL.
- We experimentally demonstrate the effectiveness of SYCL-Bench by performing device characterization on an NVIDIA GTX TITAN X and by evaluating two different implementations, hipSYCL and ComputeCpp.

2   The SYCL Programming Model

SYCL is a programming model for heterogeneous computing that builds on pure C++. This means that SYCL does not extend the C++ language itself in any way. As a SYCL program is always a valid C++ program, a SYCL implementation for CPUs can be implemented without requiring a dedicated compiler. This property can, for example, be used to debug heterogeneous applications written in SYCL with regular CPU debugging tools. When accelerators are targeted, a SYCL implementation requires a dedicated SYCL compiler that identifies kernels, extracts them, and compiles them either into an intermediate representation (such as SPIR or PTX) or machine code for the accelerator. The resulting device binary is then typically embedded by the SYCL implementation within the host binary for execution. Unlike OpenCL, where kernel code is usually either loaded at runtime from a source file or stored in an application as a string, kernel code and host code in SYCL are stored in the same source file, similarly to e.g. CUDA.

---

[1] https://github.com/bcosenza/sycl-bench.

SYCL is, therefore, a *single-source* programming model, enabling modern C++ design approaches such as templates to work seamlessly and in a type-safe manner across boundaries of host and device code.

In SYCL, the execution of data parallel kernels is organized by a task graph. This task graph is implicitly constructed by the SYCL runtime based on data access specifications that a programmer associates with a kernel by constructing *accessor* objects. If two kernels request conflicting accesses to the same data (e.g. both require read-write access), the SYCL runtime introduces a dependency between the two kernels based on the order in which they were submitted. Note that this only guarantees correctness with respect to the execution order of multiple kernels, race conditions within kernels (e.g., on the level of individual instructions) are not covered.

SYCL follows the execution and memory model of OpenCL: *work items* constitute a unit of work that is processed in parallel. They are grouped in *work groups*. Within a work group, the execution of work items can be synchronized. There is a host memory, a global memory on the accelerator, local memory that is shared between the work items of a group and per-work-item private memory.

SYCL kernels can be submitted in four different ways:

- A single, non-parallel task is submitted using `single_task()` functionality.
- A basic `parallel_for` mechanism that, from the programmer's point of view, does not group parallel work items together in work groups.
- An hierarchical parallel for, where a first level of parallelism for the work groups is initiated using `parallel_for_work_group()`. Inside the invocation `parallel_for_work_group()`, another level of parallelism can be created using `parallel_for_work_item()`. With hierarchical parallel for kernels, the programmer can optionally control the work group size that will be used to execute the kernel on the hardware. Additionally, local memory can be used in these types of kernels.
- `ndrange parallel_for` provides a method for invoking kernels that grants explicit control over work group sizes, allowing the usage of local memory and explicit barriers in SYCL code. In principle, it is not more powerful than hierarchical parallel for, but rather provides a programming model that is more familiar to programmers who have a background in OpenCL or CUDA.

While SYCL is still a relatively new programming model with the first implementation reaching official specification conformance in August 2018 [13], there is a growing SYCL ecosystem including projects such as the SYCL parallel STL, a Tensorflow port to SYCL as well as four major SYCL implementations: Codeplay's commercial ComputeCpp [6], the open-source LLVM-based SYCL [10] led by Intel, hipSYCL [2], an open-source implementation led by Heidelberg University, as well as triSYCL [21], an open-source project mainly funded by Xilinx. Together, these four implementations allow a SYCL program to target any CPU[2], GPUs from at least four vendors, and FPGAs from two vendors. Table 1 summarizes different implementations and supported platforms.

---

[2] Given that a suitable C++ compiler exists for the hardware.

Table 1. A summary of different SYCL implementations, backends, supported platforms, and specification conformance.

Implementation	Backends	Supported hardware	Conformance
ComputeCpp	OpenCL SPIR/SPIR-V OpenCL PTX (Experimental)	Intel CPUs, Intel GPUs, ARM Mali NVIDIA GPUs	SYCL 1.2.1
hipSYCL	CPU (OpenMP) CUDA ROCm	any CPU NVIDIA GPUs AMD GPUs	Pre-conformance
LLVM SYCL	OpenCL SPIR-V CUDA (Experimental)	Intel CPUs Intel GPUs, Intel FPGAs NVIDIA GPUs	Pre-conformance
triSYCL	CPU (OpenMP, TBB) OpenCL SPIR (Experimental)	any CPU Xilinx FPGAs	Pre-conformance

3 Benchmarks Design Methodology

SYCL-Bench has been designed to accomplish multiple goals. First, like traditional benchmark suites, it contains benchmarks designed to characterize the performance of existing and future hardware that can be programmed using SYCL. The range of potential target architectures is very broad: it includes all OpenCL-conformant devices, addressed with the approach defined by SYCL 1.2.1 of interpreting SYCL as a higher-level model for OpenCL[3]; alternatively, SYCL implementations may support additional ways to target specific hardware without using OpenCL (e.g., hipSYCL targets NVIDIA and AMD devices by extending Clang's CUDA frontend with support for SYCL constructs). For device characterization, particular attention is given to GPU architectures, addressed with a specific set of microbenchmarks. This set of architectural microbenchmarks is complemented by a set of applications and single kernels.

The SYCL programming model and its peculiar aspects are also central to the design of the benchmarks. For example, the benchmark codes are written in modern C++, using template types to broaden the evaluation set.

Additionally, SYCL-Bench includes a number of codes that explicitly create complex inter-task dependencies, thus implicitly stressing the efficiency of the SYCL runtime implementations. Since SYCL implementations may implement the various mechanisms to submit SYCL kernels (see Sect. 2) differently and with varying performance characteristics, many benchmarks include variants for several of those mechanisms. Lastly, we also present a set of synthetic patterns

---

[3] This approach assumes the existence of one or more OpenCL implementations available on the host machine. If no OpenCL implementation is available, then the SYCL implementation provides only the SYCL host device to run kernels on [12].

to benchmark the SYCL runtime overhead and task throughput. To summarize, SYCL-Bench contains three categories of benchmarks:

Microbenchmarks. A set of architectural microbenchmarks with different patterns stressing different hardware subsystems, e.g. arithmetic or the memory subsystem. They have been designed to emphasize performance characterization on GPU devices.

Applications/Kernels. These are real-world applications and kernels from different domains such as linear algebra, image processing, molecular dynamics. The main goal of this category is to test the performance of different devices and SYCL implementations for real-world code patterns.

SYCL Runtime Benchmarks. These benchmarks are designed to stress the SYCL runtime. This category includes multiple-kernels that can generate different task graphs and stress different aspects of the SYCL runtime. Examples include the benchmarks to measure the scheduling latency and the capabilities of the SYCL implementation to automatically overlap compute operations and data transfers.

3.1 Microbenchmarks

We present five distinct microbenchmarks designed to quantitatively evaluate various device performance characteristics through the lens of SYCL. The first, DRAM, measures the achievable device memory bandwidth by copying single and double precision floating-point values between two buffers. As an added twist, it can also measure the performance for two and three-dimensional buffers, thus indirectly quantifying how efficient a given SYCL implementation's mapping of higher-dimensional indices to the underlying hardware is. The local_mem benchmark is similar in spirit, measuring the attainable local memory bandwidth by repeatedly swapping single and double precision floating-point values inside a work group's local memory allocation.

The arith and sf benchmarks exercise the device's main arithmetic units and special function units, respectively. Both execute a tight loop, the former doing repeated multiply-add operations, and the latter applying three trigonometric functions (sin, cos, tan) in series. Finally, host_device_bandwidth measures the transfer bandwidth between the host and device memory, by copying large, contiguous and strided chunks of one, two, and three-dimensional buffers.

3.2 Applications/Kernels

To ensure the diversity of the benchmark suite, it is essential to include applications/kernels from different domains. Even applications from the same domain may exhibit different features. Therefore, we include applications/kernels from a wide range of domains such as image processing, linear algebra, data mining, data analytics. There are mainly two sources of applications and kernels. We ported 15 CUDA applications/kernels from PolyBench suite [9] to SYCL and developed 9 additional SYCL applications/kernels to cover image processing, data analytics, and physics simulation domains. In addition, applications and kernels are also equipped with a functional validation framework that further validates SYCL implementations on a wide range of benchmarks. Table 2 shows the list of applications and kernels along with their domain.

3.3   SYCL Runtime Benchmarking

DAG Task Throughput for Sequential Tasks. In this benchmark, for a given problem size N, N kernels are launched that request read-write access to the same buffer, and the time from submission to the completion of all N kernels is measured. Because more than one kernel accesses the same memory object, a read-write conflict arises that forces the SYCL runtime to process the kernels sequentially. These memory accesses, therefore, represent an edge in the resulting DAG (directed acyclic graph). In order to verify that each kernel has completed successfully, the buffer holds a counter which is incremented by one by each kernel. Since the kernel itself is trivial, this benchmark is dominated by the scheduling latency of the SYCL implementation and the latency of the backend used by the SYCL implementation (e.g. OpenCL for ComputeCpp or HIP for hipSYCL). Because SYCL implementations may have different scheduling code paths or different amounts of execution overhead for different types of kernel invocations, this benchmark comes in variants that utilize the various mechanisms in SYCL to submit kernels (`single_task`, basic `parallel_for`, ndrange `parallel_for` and hierarchical `parallel_for`).

DAG Task Throughput for Independent Tasks. The DAG task throughput benchmark for independent tasks is very similar to the benchmark described in Sect. 3.3. However, here given a problem size N, N independent tasks are spawned. The independence is guaranteed by creating one buffer per kernel so that each kernel only accesses its own buffer and no conflicts arise. To verify that each kernel has been executed successfully, each kernel simply sets the content of the buffer to a unique number that is different for each kernel submission. The runtime to submit and complete all kernels is measured. While this benchmark is also sensitive to the scheduling latencies and overheads in the SYCL implementation, it additionally allows the SYCL implementation to exploit hardware concurrency, such as running multiple kernels concurrently on a device to improve the overall throughput. Note that, while more complex dependencies between tasks compared to our two throughput benchmarks may be interesting to increase the load on the SYCL task synchronization mechanisms and the task dependency analysis, the throughput benchmarks provide a way of testing two easy-to-understand extreme cases: The case where no tasks can be run concurrently (sequential throughput benchmark) and the case where everything can run concurrently (independent throughput benchmark). They can therefore be used to estimate the overhead that can be expected from a SYCL implementation in ideal, well-defined scenarios.

Block Transform. The blocked transform benchmark divides an input array into chunks of configurable size, and submits a kernel for each chunk that requests read/write access only to its chunk. Each kernel then performs a tunable number of Mandelbrot iterations on the input data. This only serves as a dummy workload to extend the kernel runtime. The actual focus of the benchmark is to test whether the SYCL implementation is able to automatically overlap the data transfers needed to copy the chunk data to the device and the kernels operating on each chunk. Because the kernels are independent, a SYCL implementation might even be able to execute multiple kernels concurrently, if this is supported by the hardware. Additionally, the benchmark is also sensitive to whether the SYCL implementation is capable of transferring data at sub-buffer granularity at all (i.e., individual data transfers per chunk). When running on CPU, a SYCL implementation might also be able to remove the data transfers entirely as the kernel and host would be running in the same memory space. This can also be investigated with this benchmark. The resulting DAG is illustrated in Fig. 1.

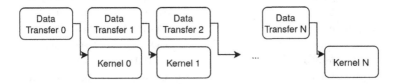

Fig. 1. The DAG for blocked transform. The arrows represent dependencies.

Table 2 shows the full list of benchmarks in the SYCL-Bench suite. The three categories **Micro**, **Application/Kernel**, and **Runtime** contain five, twenty four, and three benchmarks, respectively. We also leverage SYCL's support for C++ templates to instantiate benchmarks with different data types. As a result, the SYCL-Bench consists of 26 microbenchmarks codes, 36 applications/kernels codes (total 62 codes for hardware characterization) and 9 codes to evaluate the efficiency of the SYCL-runtime.

4   Experimental Evaluation

We present results obtained on a machine equipped with both a high-end NVIDIA GPU and Intel CPU, representing two important target architectures for SYCL. However, given the selective support of different hardware platforms in current SYCL implementations as shown in Table 1, the set of implementations to compare was limited. It was, therefore, necessary to restrict the evaluated SYCL implementations to a common denominator that supports both our CPU and GPU, namely hipSYCL and ComputeCpp. Table 3 shows details of our experimental setup.

Table 2. The detailed list of benchmarks included in the SYCL-Bench suite.

Category	Benchmark Name	Short	Domain
Micro	arith, DRAM, local_mem, sf	-	Microbench
	host_device_bandwidth	-	Microbench
App/Kernel	lin_reg_coeff	LRC	Data Analytics
	lin_reg_error	LRE	Data Analytics
	median	MEDIAN	Image Processing
	mol_dyn	MD	Physics Simulation
	scalar_prod	SP	Linear Algebra
	sobel3/5/7	SOBEL3/5/7	Image Processing
	vec_add	VA	Linear Algebra
	2DConvolution[a]	2DCON	Image Processing
	2mm[a]	2MM	Linear Algebra
	3DConvolution[a]	3DCON	Image Processing
	3mm[a]	3MM	Linear Algebra
	atax[a]	ATAX	Linear Algebra
	bicg[a]	BICG	Linear Algebra
	correlation[a]	CORR	Data Mining
	covariance [a]	COV	Data Mining
	fdtd2d[a]	FTD2D	Stencils
	gemm[a]	GEMM	Linear Algebra
	gesummv[a]	GESUM	Linear Algebra
	gramschmidt[a]	GRAMS	Linear Algebra
	mvt[a]	MVT	Linear Algebra
	syr2k[a]	SYR2K	Linear Algebra
	syrk[a]	SYRK	Linear Algebra
Runtime	blocked_transform	BT	Microbench
	dag_task_throughput_independent	DTI	Microbench
	dag_task_throughput_sequential	DTS	Microbench

[a]Ported from PolyBench suite [9].

4.1   ComputeCpp PTX Performance

In order to target NVIDIA GPUs with ComputeCpp 1.3, it is necessary to use the experimental[4] ComputeCpp PTX backend. This is because the NVIDIA OpenCL implementation does not support ingesting kernels in the SPIR format, which is normally used by ComputeCpp. Because of the experimental quality of this backend, we expect to see an overall lower performance in microbenchmarks and applications/kernels when compared to hipSYCL.

However, we found that even very short running kernels (of the order of microseconds, when executed using hipSYCL) could sometimes run for tens of *milliseconds*. In fact, with very high probability ($> 90\%$) the third consecutive

---

[4] https://developer.codeplay.com/products/computecpp/ce/guides/platform-support/targeting-nvidia-ptx?version=1.3.0.

Table 3. Hardware and software used for our experiments.

Hardware	Intel Xeon CPU E5-2699 v3	2.30 GHz 32 GiB	DDR4
	NVIDIA GTX TITAN X (Maxwell)	1.0 GHz/1.215 GHz	(boost)
Software	Ubuntu 16.04	Linux 4.15	Clang 9.0.1
	NVIDIA OpenCL 1.2	Intel OpenCL 2.0	CUDA 10.1
	hipSYCL 0.8.1-master(12406c8c)	ComputeCpp 1.3	

run of a very short running kernel would inexplicably require approximately 100 ms to complete. As a workaround for this performance anomaly, we determined that by using SYCL's built-in event profiling capabilities, we were able to obtain timings that were in line with our expectations. As these timings reflect the actual kernel execution time in hardware, relying solely on them would give ComputeCpp an unfair advantage over hipSYCL's host-side timings. We, therefore, decided to proceed as follows: For all measurements taken on NVIDIA hardware using ComputeCpp, we will provide two values. Results marked as **ComputeCpp PTX** include the full execution time as observed by the user, including the inexplicable overhead. A second value, **Kernel only**, shows the execution time that is close to what could ideally be expected without the overhead. Crucially however, unlike for hipSYCL, these results include no runtime, driver, and kernel launch overhead. Note that we cannot rely on event profiling in general, as this functionality is currently not available in some SYCL implementations, including hipSYCL.

4.2 Microbenchmarking

This section describes the results we obtained by running the benchmarks described in Sect. 3.1 on an NVIDIA GTX TITAN X. Figure 2 shows the microbenchmarking results. All microbenchmarks were executed 20 times, and we present the best result obtained out of these runs. Missing bars indicate failed verification of benchmark results. For the DRAM benchmark 3.375 GiB of memory were copied between two buffers. As can be seen in Fig. 2a, ComputeCpp's real-world performance is limited considerably by the aforementioned performance bug. Considering ComputeCpp's kernel time only, both implementations achieve about 78% of the Titan X's 336.6 GiB/s theoretical maximum for one and two-dimensional single and double-precision floating-point copies. For three-dimensional copies, hipSYCL exhibits a significant drop in throughput. On first sight, this might indicate a choice of work group size that does not allow for full memory coalescing. However, closer investigation reveals that the computation of linear buffer offsets becomes too expensive in three dimensions to be completely hidden by DRAM access latencies. More specifically, the device code generated by hipSYCL performs the same linear offset computation twice, once for the reading buffer access, and another time for the write access. Explicitly computing the linear offset once within the kernel, and using raw pointer

accesses for reading and writing, alleviates this inefficiency and allows hipSYCL
to achieve full throughput again. Figure 2b indicates that host ↔ device copy
bandwidth is relatively unaffected by the type of transfer performed, with only
three-dimensional contiguous and strided device-to-host copies dipping slightly
for hipSYCL. ComputeCpp's performance is somewhat worse for host-to-device
copies and considerably worse for device-to-host copies. Furthermore, many of
the variants could not correctly be verified for ComputeCpp, which we again
attribute to the experimental nature of the PTX backend. Figure 2c shows similar
local memory performance for both implementations, achieving approximately
3300 GiB/s for single and double precision copies. This is in line with results for
the GTX TITAN X published by Lopes et al. [17], when adjusting for the higher
boost clock used in our testing setup.

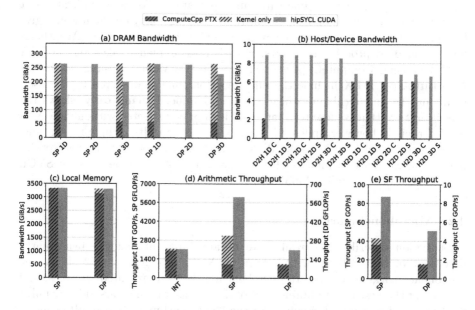

Fig. 2. Microbenchmarking results on NVIDIA GTX TITAN X.

Moving on to arithmetic throughput in Fig. 2d, we see that integer performance is considerably lower than single-precision performance for both implementations. This is to be expected, as the IMAD instructions used in `arith` are
emulated on Maxwell [11]. Curiously, with 3134 single-precision GFLOP/s, even
for the idealized kernel-only measurement, ComputeCpp achieves little more
than half of hipSYCL's 6016 GFLOP/s. This indicates that the device compiler
might not map the benchmark kernel's multiply-add operations to corresponding FMA instructions. Examination of the PTX device code generated by ComputeCpp confirms that this is indeed the case. Both implementations approximately achieve the expected ⅓₂-th in double-precision performance compared to
single precision. Finally, for the `sf` benchmark's result, shown in Fig. 2e, we again

see ComputeCpp achieving only about half of hipSYCL's single-precision performance, and a third in double precision. However, even hipSYCL's performance is much lower than the theoretical maximum (which, with Maxwell's 32 SFUs per SM should be approximately 1000 GOP/s, depending on clock speed). Examination of the PTX device code reveals that both implementations emulate the trigonometric functions rather than mapping to the corresponding SFU intrinsics (e.g. CUDA's __cosf). At the time of writing, it is therefore not possible to benchmark SFU throughput on NVIDIA using either SYCL implementation.

4.3 Applications / Kernels

Figure 3 and Fig. 4 show the execution time of benchmarks using hipSYCL and ComputeCpp implementations running on NVIDIA GTX TITAN X and Intel Xeon CPU, respectively. For measuring the execution time, we run each benchmark 10 times and pick the median of the samples. In this work, we focus on 32-bit data types.

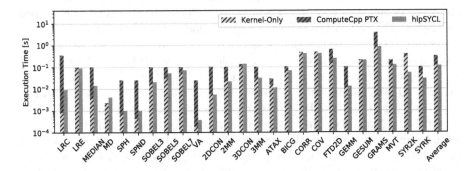

Fig. 3. hipSYCL and ComputeCpp runtime on NVIDIA TITAN X.

Figure 3 shows that hipSYCL outperforms the ComputeCpp implementation across most of the benchmarks. On average, hipSYCL is 2.7× faster than ComputeCpp on NVIDIA TITAN X. As mentioned earlier, this is primarily due to the experimental PTX backend support for NVIDIA GPUs which has limitations such as no support for OpenCL builtins. The suffixes ND and H are used to differentiate between ndrange parallel_for and hierarchical parallel_for implementations. The scalar_prod (SP) benchmark provides both variants.

Figure 4 shows the execution time of benchmarks using hipSYCL and ComputeCpp implementations running on Intel Xeon CPU. Figure 4 shows that the setup consisting of ComputeCpp with Intel's OpenCL implementation outperforms hipSYCL with the LLVM OpenMP implementation across most of the benchmarks except SOBEL3, SOBEL5, SOBEL7, and 2DCON benchmarks. On average, ComputeCpp is 25.2× faster than hipSYCL on CPU. The main reason for the higher execution time for hipSYCL is that some benchmarks use ndrange

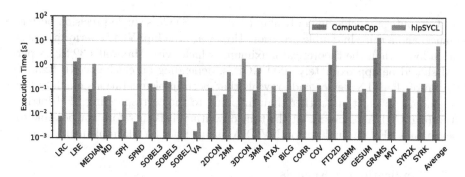

Fig. 4. Comparison of hipSYCL and ComputeCpp runtime on Intel Xeon CPU.

parallel_for. ndrange parallel_for cannot be implemented efficiently by library-based SYCL implementations without dedicated compiler support (such as the CPU backends in hipSYCL and triSYCL) because it allows for explicit barriers. To implement correct barrier semantics, a SYCL implementation is forced to launch one thread per SYCL work item. For the usual fine-grained parallelism exposed in typical SYCL applications at the work item level, this forces the SYCL implementation to spawn a very large number of threads (often much more than numbers of cores available in typical CPUs), each of which is only assigned a small amount of work. This parallelization scheme is not a good fit for CPU architectures. If we take out benchmarks which implement ndrange parallel_for (LRC, SPND), ComputeCpp is 4.5× faster than hipSYCL.

Of the evaluated benchmarks in this category, for instance, SPND and LRC use ndrange parallel_for. The execution time of LRC and SPND are 94.07 (s) and 51.33 (s) using hipSYCL compared to 0.008 (s) and 0.005 (s) using ComputeCpp, respectively. Therefore, for applications that are expected to show performance portability, it is highly recommended to prefer hierarchical parallel for over ndrange parallel_for. The figure shows that the hierarchical parallel_for implementation (SPH) is significantly faster for scalar_prod. It will be interesting for future work to test other C++ compilers and OpenMP implementations with hipSYCL (e.g., Intel C++ Compiler with Intel OpenMP implementation).

4.4   SYCL Runtime

We measured the runtime of hipSYCL and ComputeCpp implementations using dag_task_throughput_sequential and dag_task_throughput_independent benchmarks on NVIDIA TITAN X. We varied the problem size that corresponds to the number of submitted kernels. For the dag_task_throughput_sequential, we observed that not only is the SYCL runtime overhead almost the same for hipSYCL and ComputeCpp, but also for the four different kernel invocations. This is likely because for sequential GPU tasks, runtimes are dominated by latencies below the level of the SYCL implementation (driver, PCIe, GPU).

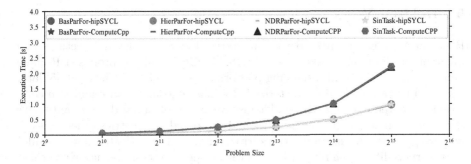

Fig. 5. SYCL runtime overhead of hipSYCL and ComputeCpp implementations on NVIDIA GTX TITAN X. The DAG consists of independent tasks.

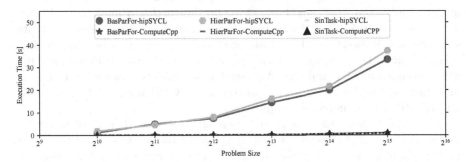

Fig. 6. SYCL runtime overhead of hipSYCL and ComputeCpp implementations on Intel Xeon CPU. The DAG consists of independent tasks.

Figure 5 shows the SYCL runtime overhead of hipSYCL and ComputeCpp implementations when executing `dag_task_throughput_independent` on NVIDIA TITAN X. In contrast to the sequential tasks, we see that the ComputeCpp stack exhibits a higher runtime overhead compared to the hipSYCL implementation. Moreover, the gap is proportional to the number of submitted tasks, which means that ComputeCpp has a higher average latency per submitted kernel. There are two possible explanations for this behavior. An implementation could be faster for this test because it executes the kernels concurrently on the hardware, or because it has a lower scheduling overhead. Since hipSYCL does not launch kernels concurrently for this benchmark, the performance performance gap can be explained by a lower scheduling overhead in hipSYCL.

Figure 6 shows the execution time of the `dag_task_throughput_independent` benchmark on Intel Xeon CPU. As shown in the figure, submitting independent kernels is significantly slower for hipSYCL basic parallel for and hierarchical parallel for kernels compared to hipSYCL single task kernels and ComputeCpp. Since basic and hierarchical parallel for kernel invocations in hipSYCL require spawning OpenMP threads, OpenMP overheads are likely an explanation for this behavior.

5   Related Work

Benchmarking has been used to characterize heterogeneous architectures and different programming models [1,3–5,7,8,14]. Che et al. [4] proposed Rodinia benchmark suite to study emerging platforms such as GPUs. Che et al. [5] later extended their work and characterized Rodinia benchmark suite and also compared to contemporary CMP workloads. Burtscher et al. [3] did a quantitative study of irregular programs on GPUs and presented two metrics called control-flow irregularity and memory-access irregularity and investigated how irregular GPU kernels differ from regular kernels with respect to these metrics. Kulkarni et al. [14] presented a benchmark suite called Lonestar that is targeted for graph-based irregular programs and characterized the first five programs from this suite. The results show that even irregular applications can be accelerated using modern multi-core machines. Fang et al. [8] designed and implemented Mars, a runtime system for distributed data processing. They also ported six representative applications on Mars. Danalis et al. [7] designed a benchmark suite called Scalable HeterOgeneous Computing benchmark suite (SHOC) and used it to compare OpenCL and CUDA programming models. Grauer-Gray et al. [9] implemented PolyBench codes for processing on GPU using CUDA, OpenCL, and HMPP, a pragma-based compiler.

Some researchers have used microbenchmarks as well as benchmarks to understand the performance as well as power characteristics of GPUs [15,18, 22,24]. Thoman et al. [22] proposed microbenchmarks suite called uCLbench to characterize and compare OpenCL performance of existing and future devices. Zhang et al. [24] designed a set of microbenchmarks to study the power consumption of different functional units of a GPU. Mei and Chu [18] studied the characteristics of the memory hierarchy using microbenchmarks. Specifically, they investigated GPU cache systems and investigated the throughput/latency of GPU global and shared memory. Lal et al. [15] studied bottlenecks that cause low performance and low energy efficiency in GPU workloads.

There are a few works on SYCL benchmarking as it a relatively new programming model [19,20]. Potter and Keir [19] described a methodology for creating efficient domain specific embedded languages on top of the SYCL for the OpenCL standard. There are also some works which compare different programming models. For example, Silva et al. [20] analyzed the performance and characteristics of SYCL, OpenMP, and OpenCL using two benchmarks. The results indicated that benchmarks that rely on SYCL runtimes are not on par with OpenMP and OpenCL. However, the gap is shrinking compared to previous studies. Thoman et al. [23] developed the Celerity programming environment based on SYCL, enabling developers to scale C++ applications to distributed memory clusters with relative ease, and included some benchmark results comparing against an MPI+OpenCL software stack. While these works provide some limited insight into SYCL performance compared to other programming models, we present the first SYCL benchmark suite that contains a complete and diverse set of benchmarks to characterize both hardware devices and runtime performance aspects of different SYCL implementations.

6   Conclusions

We presented SYCL-Bench, the first benchmark suite specifically written in and for SYCL, featuring three categories of benchmarks and a total of 71 code patterns. We experimentally demonstrated the effectiveness of SYCL-Bench by performing device characterization of the NVIDIA TITAN X GPU, showing that near-peak performance can be achieved for metrics such as arithmetic throughput and DRAM bandwidth. We also evaluated the efficiency of two SYCL implementations: hipSYCL outperformed ComputeCpp on average by 2.7× in real-world performance on TITAN X, and ComputeCpp was 4.5× faster than hipSYCL on Intel Xeon without ndrange benchmarks. While ComputeCpp's performance on TITAN X is primarily hampered by the experimental PTX backend, hipSYCL's CPU performance is much lower because of API constructs that cannot be implemented efficiently without a dedicated compiler. In the future work, we plan to evaluate other SYCL implementations such as triSYCL and Intel SYCL. SYCL-Bench is publicly available along with the testing framework.

Acknowledgements and Data Availability Statement. This research has been partially funded by the FWF (I 3388) and DFG (CO 1544/1-1, project number 360291326) as part of the DACH project CELERITY.

The datasets and code generated during and/or analysed during the current study are available in the Figshare repository: https://doi.org/10.6084/m9.figshare.12562670 [16].

References

1. Parboil Benchmarks Suite (2007). http://impact.crhc.illinois.edu/parboil.php
2. Alpay, A.: hipSYCL. https://github.com/illuhad/hipSYCL
3. Burtscher, M., Nasre, R., Pingali, K.: A quantitative study of irregular programs on GPUs. In: Proceedings of IEEE, IISWC (2012)
4. Che, S., et al.: Rodinia: a benchmark suite for heterogeneous computing. In: Proceedings of the IEEE International Symposium on Workload Characterization, IISWC (2009)
5. Che, S., Sheaffer, J.W., Boyer, M., Szafaryn, L.G., Wang, L., Skadron, K.: A characterization of the Rodinia benchmark suite with comparison to contemporary CMP workloads. In: Proceedings of the IEEE International Symposium on Workload Characterization, IISWC (2010)
6. Codeplay Software: ComputeCpp. https://codeplay.com/products/computesuite/computecpp
7. Danalis, A., et al.: The scalable heterogeneous computing (SHOC) benchmark suite. In: Proceedings of the 3rd Workshop on GPGPU (2010)
8. Fang, W., He, B., Luo, Q., Govindaraju, N.K.: Mars: accelerating MapReduce with graphics processors. IEEE Trans. Parallel Distrib. Syst. **22**, 608–620 (2011)
9. Grauer-Gray, S., Xu, L., Searles, R., Ayalasomayajula, S., Cavazos, J.: Auto-tuning a high-level language targeted to GPU codes. In: Proceedings InPar (2012)
10. Intel: SYCL Compiler. https://github.com/intel/llvm
11. Jia, Z., Maggioni, M., Smith, J., Scarpazza, D.P.: Dissecting the NVidia Turing T4 GPU via microbenchmarking. arXiv preprint arXiv:1903.07486 (2019)

12. Khronos: SYCL 1.2.1. Technical report, Khronos Group, Inc. (2020). https://www.khronos.org/registry/SYCL/specs/sycl-1.2.1.pdf
13. Khronos Group: Codeplay announces world's first fully-conformant sycl 1.2.1 solution (2018). https://www.khronos.org/news/permalink/codeplay-announces-worlds-first-fully-conformant-sycl-1.2.1-solution
14. Kulkarni, M., Burtscher, M., Cascaval, C., Pingali, K.: Lonestar: a suite of parallel irregular programs. In: IEEE International Symposium on Performance Analysis of Systems and Software, ISPASS (2009)
15. Lal, S., Lucas, J., Andersch, M., Alvarez-Mesa, M., Elhossini, A., Juurlink, B.: GPGPU workload characteristics and performance analysis. In: International Conference on Embedded Computer Systems: Architectures, Modeling, and Simulation, SAMOS (2014)
16. Lal, S., et al.: Artifact and Instructions to Generate Main Experimental Results for Conference Proceeding 2020 Paper: SYCL-Bench: A Versatile Cross-Platform Benchmark Suite for Heterogeneous Computing (2020). https://doi.org/10.6084/m9.figshare.12562670, https://springernature.figshare.com/articles/dataset/Artifact_and_Instructions_to_Generate_Main_Experimental_Results_for_Conference_Proceeding_2020_Paper_SYCL-Bench_A_Versatile_Cross-Platform_Benchmark_Suite_for_Heterogeneous_Computing/12562670/1
17. Lopes, A., Pratas, F., Sousa, L., Ilic, A.: Exploring GPU performance, power and energy-efficiency bounds with cache-aware roofline modeling. In: IEEE International Symposium on Performance Analysis of Systems and Software, ISPASS, pp. 259–268 (2017)
18. Mei, X., Chu, X.: Dissecting GPU memory hierarchy through microbenchmarking. IEEE Trans. Parallel Distrib. Syst. **28**, 72–86 (2017)
19. Potter, R., Keir, P., Bradford, R.J., Murray, A.: Kernel composition in SYCL. In: Proceedings of the 3rd Workshop on OpenCL, IWOCL (2015)
20. Silva, H.C.D., Pisani, F., Borin, E.: A Comparative Study of SYCL, OpenCL, and OpenMP. In: Proceedings of SBAC-PADW (2016)
21. The triSYCL Project: triSYCL. https://github.com/trisycl/trisycl
22. Thoman, P., Kofler, K., Studt, H., Thomson, J., Fahringer, T.: Automatic OpenCL device characterization: guiding optimized kernel design. In: Jeannot, E., Namyst, R., Roman, J. (eds.) Euro-Par 2011. LNCS, vol. 6853, pp. 438–452. Springer, Heidelberg (2011). https://doi.org/10.1007/978-3-642-23397-5_43
23. Thoman, P., Salzmann, P., Cosenza, B., Fahringer, T.: Celerity: high-level C++ for accelerator clusters. In: Yahyapour, R. (ed.) Euro-Par 2019: Parallel Processing. LNCS, vol. 11725, pp. 291–303. Springer, Heidelberg (2019). https://doi.org/10.1007/978-3-030-29400-7_21
24. Zhang, Y., Hu, Y., Li, B., Peng, L.: Performance and power analysis of ATI GPU: a statistical approach. In: Proceedings of 6th NAS (2011)

Author Index